TOURS

There's a business school for everyone. Meet yours.

The world's top business schools are coming to a free GMAC Tours event in a city near you. Connect in-person with admissions decision-makers or through virtual 1:1 meetings. Meeting representatives is crucial to your application, don't miss out!

Find an event near you

mba.com/gmactours

GMAT™

Your best GMAT score is still ahead!

Think your score can't improve? Think again.

Data shows retaking the GMAT™ exam can increase your score by **20-30 points**. Don't settle for your first attempt and give yourself the best chance at business school success – the second time's a charm!

Xavier Lorenzo/Getty Images

Take the GMAT again
mba.com/gmat

BUSINESS FUNDAMENTALS
POWERED BY KAPLAN

Learn the skills you need to succeed in your program!

GMAC Business Fundamentals is designed to give you the confidence and fundamental quantitative knowledge you need to start business school.

Learn at Your Own Pace
Access a variety of resources including videos, quizzes, and practical exercises.

Master Core Concepts
Gain a solid foundation in Statistics, Accounting, and Finance, ensuring you're ready to excel from day one.

Showcase Your Learning
Earn digital badges that highlight your skills and achievements.

> "I am very grateful that I took the Business Fundamentals courses. My classmates who didn't are struggling in classes where I feel confident."
> — MBA Candidate, Portland State University

> "The courses provided exactly what I was looking for. The instructors were great, the content was well delivered, and I now feel back to school ready."
> — MBA Candidate, Emory University

Start business school off right
mba.com/businessfundamentals

GMAT™

Power up your prep with Official Practice Exams

Research shows that first-time GMAT test takers can **increase their scores by up to 75 points** after taking all Official Practice Exams!

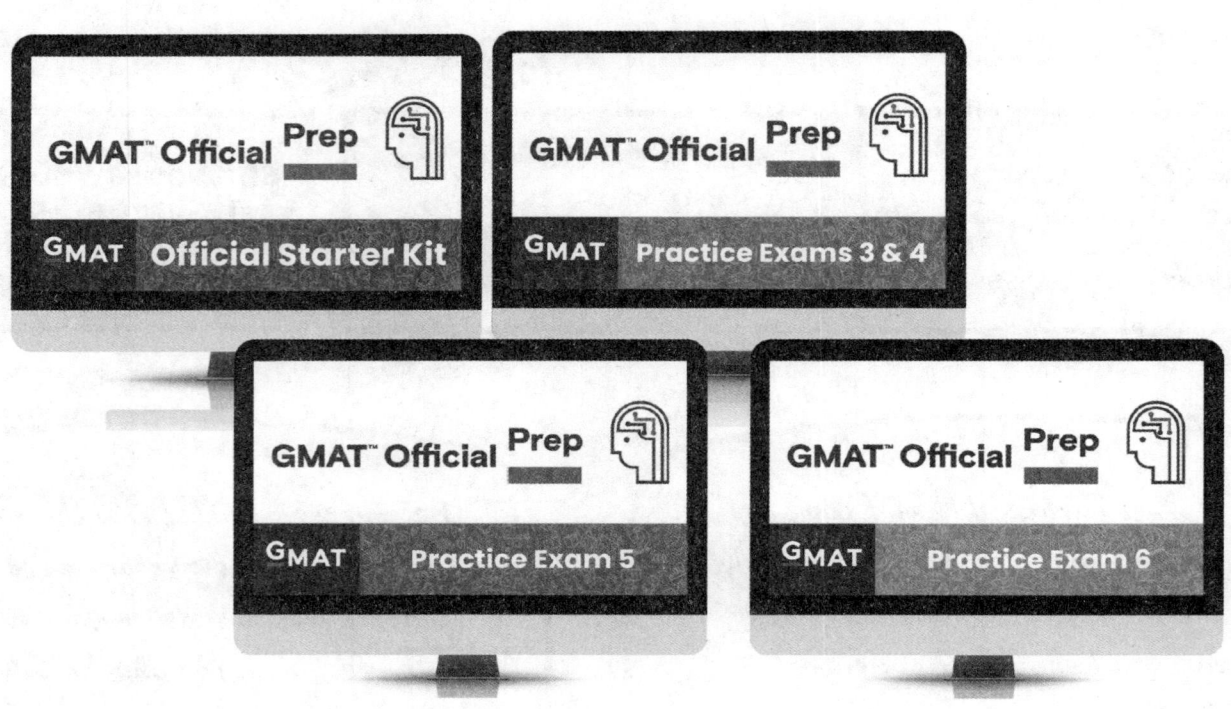

 Full-length, adaptive GMAT practice exams that simulate the real test-taking experience

 Scaled section scores and a total score that aligns to the actual test

 Detailed score performance report, including time management

Get started with GMAT Official Practice Exams

mba.com/gmatprep

©2025 Graduate Management Admission Council (GMAC). All rights reserved. GMAT™ and Graduate Management Admission Council™ are trademarks of GMAC in the United States and other countries. Apple, the Apple logo, iPhone, and iPad are trademarks of Apple Inc., registered in the U.S. and other regions. App Store is a service mark of Apple Inc. Google Play and the Google Play logo are trademarks of Google LLC.

GradSelect

Want to get noticed by top business schools?

GradSelect is your connection to more than 500 global business and management programs that are looking for the best candidate – YOU.

Why connect with schools through GradSelect?

 GradSelect is part of the Graduate Management Admission Council (GMAC), a global mission-driven organization of top business schools.

 Through GradSelect, you can receive exclusive information on school programs, financial aid, and scholarships.

 You can quickly connect with the world's leading schools and discover new opportunities you may not have been familiar with.

 It's free to use!

Join GradSelect

 mba.com/gradselect

GMAT™

GMAT™ Official Guide Verbal Review 2025–2026

From the makers of the GMAT™ exam

 Only study guide that features **real exam questions**

 275+ practice questions with detailed answer explanations

 Digital flashcards, games, a **customizable question bank**, and more

 Exclusive **tips and tricks** for exam success from the exam creators

GMAT™ Official Guide Verbal Review 2025–2026

Copyright © 2025 by the Graduate Management Admission Council®. All rights reserved.

Published by John Wiley & Sons, Inc., Hoboken, New Jersey.

No part of this publication may be reproduced, stored in a retrieval system or transmitted in any form or by any means, electronic, mechanical, photocopying, recording, scanning or otherwise, except as permitted under Sections 107 or 108 of the 1976 United States Copyright Act, without either the prior written permission of the Publisher, or authorization through payment of the appropriate per-copy fee to the Copyright Clearance Center, 222 Rosewood Drive, Danvers, MA 01923, (978) 750-8400, fax (978) 646-8600, or on the Web at www.copyright.com. Requests to the Publisher for permission should be addressed to the Permissions Department, John Wiley & Sons, Inc., 111 River Street, Hoboken, NJ 07030, (201) 748-6011, fax (201) 748-6008, or online at http://www.wiley.com/go/permissions.

The publisher and the author make no representations or warranties with respect to the accuracy or completeness of the contents of this work and specifically disclaim all warranties, including without limitation warranties of fitness for a particular purpose. No warranty may be created or extended by sales or promotional materials. The advice and strategies contained herein may not be suitable for every situation. This work is sold with the understanding that the publisher is not engaged in rendering legal, accounting, or other professional services. If professional assistance is required, the services of a competent professional person should be sought. Neither the publisher nor the author shall be liable for damages arising here from. The fact that an organization or Web site is referred to in this work as a citation and/or a potential source of further information does not mean that the author or the publisher endorses the information the organization or Web site may provide or recommendations it may make. Further, readers should be aware that Internet Web sites listed in this work may have changed or disappeared between when this work was written and when it is read.

Trademarks: Wiley, the Wiley Publishing logo, and related trademarks are trademarks or registered trademarks of John Wiley & Sons, Inc. and/or its affiliates. The GMAT logo, GMAC™, GMASS™, GMAT™, Graduate Management Admission Council™, and Graduate Management Admission Test™ are trademarks of GMAC in the United States and other countries. All other trademarks are the property of their respective owners. Wiley Publishing, Inc. is not associated with any product or vendor mentioned in this book.

For general information on our other products and services or to obtain technical support please contact our Customer Care Department within the U.S. at (877) 762-2974, outside the U.S. at (317) 572-3993 or fax (317) 572-4002.

Wiley also publishes its books in a variety of electronic formats. Some content that appears in print may not be available in electronic books. For more information about Wiley products, please visit our Web site at www.wiley.com.

ISBN 978-1-394-33388-2 (pbk); ISBN 978-1-394-33505-3 (ePub)

Printed in the United States of America

SKY10100319_041025

Table of Contents

		Letter from the President and CEO, GMAC™	xi
1.0		**What Is the GMAT™ Exam?**	**2**
	1.1	What Is the GMAT™ Exam?	3
	1.2	Why Take the GMAT™ Exam?	3
	1.3	GMAT™ Exam Format	4
	1.4	What Is the Testing Experience Like?	6
	1.5	What Is the Exam Content Like?	6
	1.6	Verbal Reasoning Section	6
	1.7	How Are Scores Calculated?	7
2.0		**How to Prepare**	**10**
	2.1	How Should I Prepare for the GMAT™ Exam?	11
	2.2	Getting Ready for Exam Day	12
	2.3	How to Use the *GMAT™ Official Guide Verbal Review 2025–2026*	12
	2.4	How to Use Other GMAT™ Official Prep Products	14
	2.5	Tips for Taking the Exam	14
	2.6	Verbal Reasoning Section Strategies	16
3.0		**Verbal Review**	**18**
	3.0	Verbal Review	19
	3.1	Analyzing Passages	19
	3.2	Inductive Reasoning	26
	3.3	Deductive Reasoning	32
4.0		**Verbal Reasoning**	**42**
	4.0	Verbal Reasoning	43
	4.1	What Is Measured	43
	4.2	Question Types	44
	4.3	Tips for Answering Verbal Reasoning Questions	50
	4.4	Practice Questions: Reading Comprehension	52
	4.5	Answer Key: Reading Comprehension	109
	4.6	Answer Explanations: Reading Comprehension	110
	4.7	Practice Questions: Critical Reasoning	196
	4.8	Answer Key: Critical Reasoning	262
	4.9	Answer Explanations: Critical Reasoning	263
5.0		**GMAT™ Official Guide Verbal Review Question Index**	**416**
	5.0	GMAT™ Official Guide Verbal Review Question Index	417
Appendix A		**Answer Sheets**	**428**
		Reading Comprehension Answer Sheet	429
		Critical Reasoning Answer Sheet	430

Dear GMAT™ Test Taker,

Thank you for taking this important step toward your graduate management education. The GMAT exam stands as the global standard in business school admissions, used by more than 7,700 graduate programs worldwide to identify excellence in candidates for MBA, business master's, and other graduate-level management degrees. Seven out of ten business school applicants choose to differentiate themselves with a GMAT exam score.*

By choosing the GMAT™ Official Guide, you're preparing with the most authoritative resource available—the only guide featuring real GMAT questions published by the Graduate Management Admission Council (GMAC™), the makers of the GMAT exam. Combined with our prep tools at www.mba.com, this guide will build your confidence and help you achieve your personal best on exam day.

For more than 70 years, the GMAT exam has empowered candidates like you to demonstrate their readiness for academic success and signal their commitment to business education. Schools use and trust the GMAT because it consistently predicts classroom performance and indicates your potential to excel in your chosen program.

At GMAC, our purpose is to ensure no talent goes undiscovered. We're committed to providing the tools and insights you need throughout your business school journey, continuously enhancing the GMAT exam, and helping you connect with programs that match your aspirations. We applaud your commitment to advancing your education and wish you every success in your future educational and professional endeavors.

Sincerely,

signature

Joy J. Jones
CEO, Graduate Management Admission Council

---

* Top 100 *Financial Times* full-time MBA programs

GMAT™ Official Guide
Verbal Review 2025–2026

1.0 What Is the GMAT™ Exam?

1.1 What Is the GMAT™ Exam?

The Graduate Management Admission Test™ (GMAT™) is used in admissions decisions by more than 7,700 graduate management programs at over 2,400 business schools worldwide. Unlike undergraduate grades and courses, whose meanings vary across regions and institutions, your GMAT scores are a standardized, statistically valid, and reliable measure for both you and these schools to predict your future performance and success in core courses of graduate-level management programs.

Hundreds of studies across hundreds of schools have demonstrated the validity of GMAT scores as being an accurate indicator of business school success. Together, these studies have shown that performance on the GMAT predicts success in business school even better than undergraduate grades.

The exam tests you on skills expected by management faculty and admission professionals for incoming graduate students. These skills include problem-solving, data analysis, and critical thinking, which all require complex judgments and are tested in the three sections of the GMAT exam: Quantitative Reasoning, Data Insights, and Verbal Reasoning. These three sections feature content relevant to today's business challenges and opportunities, ensuring you are prepared for graduate business school and beyond.

Your GMAT Official Score is meant to be an objective, numeric measure of your ability and potential for success. Business schools will use it as part of their holistic admissions processes, which may also consider recommendation letters, essays, interviews, work experiences, and other signs of social and emotional intelligence, as well as leadership. Even if your program does not require a GMAT score, you can stand out from the crowd by doing well on the exam to show you are serious about business school and have the skills to succeed.

The exam is always delivered in English on a computer, either online (such as at home) or at a test center. The exam tests your ability to apply foundational knowledge in the following areas: algebra and arithmetic, analyzing and interpreting data, reading and comprehending written material, and reasoning and evaluating arguments.

> *Myth* -vs- **FACT**
>
> *M* – **My GMAT score does not predict my success in business school.**
>
> F – **The GMAT exam measures your critical thinking skills, which you will need in business school and your career.**

1.2 Why Take the GMAT™ Exam?

Taking the exam helps you stand out as an applicant and shows you're ready for and committed to a graduate management education. Schools use GMAT scores in choosing the most qualified applicants. They know an applicant who has taken the exam is serious about earning a graduate business degree, and they know the exam scores reliably predict how well applicants can do in graduate business programs.

No matter how you do on the exam, you should contact schools that interest you to learn more about them, and to ask how they use GMAT scores and other criteria in admissions decisions. School admissions offices, websites, and publications are key sources of information when you are researching business schools. Note that schools' published GMAT scores are *averages* of the scores of their admitted students, not minimum scores needed for admission.

While you might aim to get a high or perfect score, such a score is not required to get into top business school programs around the world. You should try your best to achieve a competitive score that aligns with the ranges provided by the schools of your choice. Admissions officers will use GMAT scores as one factor in admissions decisions along with undergraduate records, application essays, interviews, letters of recommendation, and other information.

To learn more about the exam, test preparation materials, registration, and how to use your GMAT Official Score in applying to business schools, please visit **www.mba.com/gmat.**

> *Myth* -vs- **FACT**
>
> M – If I don't get a high GMAT score, I won't get into my top-choice schools.
>
> F – Schools use your GMAT score as a part of their holistic evaluation process.

1.3 GMAT™ Exam Format

The GMAT exam has three separately timed sections (see the table on the following page). The Quantitative Reasoning section and the Verbal Reasoning section consist of only multiple-choice questions. The Data Insights section includes multiple-choice questions along with other kinds of graphical and data analysis questions. Before you start the exam, you can choose any order in which you will take the three sections. For example, you can choose to start with Verbal Reasoning, then do Quantitative Reasoning, and end with Data Insights. Or you can choose to do Data Insights first, followed by Verbal Reasoning, and then Quantitative Reasoning. You can take one optional ten-minute break after either the first or second section.

All three GMAT sections are computer adaptive. This means the test chooses from a large bank of questions to adjust itself to your ability level, so you will not get many questions that are too hard or too easy for you. The first question will be of medium difficulty. As you answer each question, the computer uses your answer, along with your responses to earlier questions, to choose the next question with the right level of difficulty. Because the computer uses your answers to choose your next question, you cannot skip questions.

Computer adaptive tests get harder as you answer more questions correctly. But getting a question that seems easier than the last one doesn't always mean your last answer was wrong. At the end of each section, you can review any question(s) and edit up to three answers within the allotted section time.

Though each test taker gets different questions, the mix of question types is always consistent. Your score depends on the difficulty and statistical traits of the questions you answer, as well as on which of your answers are correct. If you don't know how to answer a question, try to rule out as many wrong answer choices as possible. Then pick the answer choice you think is best. By adapting to each test taker, the exam can accurately and efficiently gauge a full range of skill levels, from very high to very low. Many factors may make the questions easier or harder, so don't waste time worrying if some questions seem easy.

To make sure every test taker gets equivalent content, the test gives specific numbers of questions of each type. While the test covers the same kinds of questions for everyone, some questions may seem harder or easier for you because you may be stronger in some questions than in others.

At the end of the exam, you will see your unofficial score displayed on the screen. A few days after your exam, you will receive your Official Score Report, which includes detailed performance insights. Once you receive your report, you can select to send your Official Score to schools of your choice.

Format of the GMAT™ Exam

	Questions	Timing
Quantitative Reasoning Problem-Solving	21	45 min.
Data Insights Data Sufficiency Multi-Source Reasoning Table Analysis Graphics Interpretation Two-Part Analysis	20	45 min.
Verbal Reasoning Reading Comprehension Critical Reasoning	23	45 min.
	Total Time	135 min.

A ten-minute optional break can be taken after the first or the second section.

Each section of the GMAT exam contains the following features:

- **Bookmarking:** Mark any questions you are unsure about so you can easily get back to them after you complete the section. Bookmarking can make the Question Review & Edit process more efficient.

- **Question Review & Edit:** Review as many questions as you would like (whether or not they're bookmarked) and change or edit up to three answers per section, within the section's allotted time.

> **Myth -vs- FACT**
>
> *M* – Getting an easier question means I answered the previous one wrong.
>
> F – Many factors may make the questions easier or harder, so don't waste time worrying if some questions seem easy.

1.4 What Is the Testing Experience Like?

You can take the exam either online (such as at home) or at a test center—whichever you prefer. You may feel more comfortable at home with the online delivery format. Or you may prefer the uninterrupted, structured environment of a test center. It is your choice. Both options have the same content, structure, features, optional ten-minute break, scores, and score scales.

At the Test Center: Over 700 test centers worldwide administer the GMAT exam under standardized conditions. Each test center has proctored testing rooms with individual computer workstations that allow you to take the exam in a peaceful, quiet setting, with some privacy. To learn more about exam day, visit **www.mba.com/gmat**.

Online: In available regions, the GMAT exam is delivered online and is proctored remotely, so you can take it in the comfort of your home or office. You will need a quiet workspace with a desktop or laptop computer that meets minimum system requirements, a webcam, microphone, and a reliable internet connection. For more information about taking the exam online, visit **www.mba.com/gmat**.

Whether you're taking the GMAT exam online or at a test center, there are several accommodations available. To learn more about available accommodations for the exam, visit **www.mba.com/accommodations**.

1.5 What Is the Exam Content Like?

The GMAT exam measures several types of analytical reasoning skills. The Quantitative Reasoning section gives you basic arithmetic and algebra problems. The questions present you with a mix of word or pure math problems. The Data Insights section asks you to use diverse reasoning skills to solve real-world problems involving data. It also asks you to interpret and combine data from different sources and in different formats to reach conclusions. The Verbal Reasoning section tests your ability to read and comprehend written material and to reason through and evaluate arguments.

The test questions are contextualized in various subject areas, but each question provides you everything you need to know to answer it correctly. In other words, you do not need detailed outside knowledge of the subject areas.

1.6 Verbal Reasoning Section

The GMAT Verbal Reasoning section measures how well you reason, understand what you read, and evaluate arguments. The Verbal Reasoning section includes passages about many topics. Verbal Reasoning questions do not assume you have any background knowledge on the topic. Therefore, all of the information you need to answer the questions correctly is contained in the passages.

The Verbal Reasoning section has two types of questions:

- **Reading Comprehension:** These questions measure your ability to read and understand written statements, understand logical relationships between significant points, and draw inferences and conclusions. More specifically, you'll be asked to identify main and supporting ideas, draw inferences from information presented in the passage, apply knowledge learned from the passage to unrelated contexts, and recognize the logical structures and style of the passage.
- **Critical Reasoning:** These questions measure your ability to make valid arguments, evaluate different lines of reasoning, and formulate or assess a plan of action. Critical Reasoning questions are based on a short reading passage, usually fewer than 100 words. Typically, the short text is followed by a question that asks you which of the five answer options strengthens or weakens the argument, tells why the argument is flawed, or strongly supports or damages the argument. You will not need specialized knowledge of the subject matter to answer the questions.

Chapter 3 of this book, "Verbal Review," reviews the basic verbal analysis and reasoning skills you need for the Verbal Reasoning section. Chapter 4, "Verbal Reasoning," explains the Verbal Reasoning question subtypes. It also provides test-taking tips for each subtype, as well as practice questions and answer explanations both in this book and in the Online Question Bank.

1.7 How Are Scores Calculated?

The Quantitative Reasoning, Data Insights, and Verbal Reasoning sections are each scored on a scale from 60 to 90, in 1-point increments. You will get four scores: a Section Score each for Quantitative Reasoning, Data Insights, and Verbal Reasoning, along with a Total Score based on your three section scores. The Total Score ranges from 205 to 805. Your scores depend on:

- Which questions you answered correctly.
- How many questions you answered.
- Each question's difficulty and other statistical characteristics.

There is a penalty for not completing each section of the exam. If you do not finish in the allotted time, your score will be penalized, reflecting the number of unanswered questions. Your GMAT exam score will be the best reflection of your performance when all questions are answered within the time limit.

Immediately after completing the exam, your unofficial scores and percentile for the Quantitative Reasoning, Data Insights, and Verbal Reasoning, as well as your Total Score, are displayed on-screen. You are **not** allowed to record, save, screenshot, or print your unofficial score. You will receive an email notification when your Official Score Report is available in your **www.mba.com** account.

The following table summarizes the different types of scores and their scale properties.

Score Type	Scale	Increment
Quantitative Reasoning	60–90	1
Data Insights	60–90	1
Verbal Reasoning	60–90	1
Total	205–805	10

Your GMAT Official Scores are valid for five years from your exam date. Your Total GMAT Score includes a percentile ranking, which shows the percentage of tests taken with scores lower than your score.

In addition to reviewing your Total and Section Scores, it's important to pay attention to your percentile ranking. Percentile rankings indicate what percentage of test takers you performed better than. For example, a percentile ranking of 75% means that you performed better than 75% of other test takers, and 25% of test takers performed better than you. Percentile ranks are calculated using scores from the most recent five years. Visit **www.mba.com/scores** to view the most recent predicted percentile rankings tables.

To better understand the exam experience and view score reports before exam day, we recommend taking at least one GMAT official practice exam to simulate the test-taking experience and gauge your potential score. The more practice exams you take, the better prepared you will be on your actual testing day. Visit **www.mba.com/examprep** to learn more about the practice exams offered by GMAC.

To register for the GMAT™ exam, go to www.mba.com/register

2.0 How to Prepare

2.1 How Should I Prepare for the GMAT™ Exam?

The GMAT™ exam has several unique question formats. We recommend that you familiarize yourself with the test format and the different question types before you take the test. The key to prepping for any exam is setting a pace that works for you and your lifestyle. That might be easier said than done, but the **GMAT™ Official 6-Week Study Planner** does the planning for you! Our step-by-step planner will help you stick to a schedule, inform your activities, and track your progress. Go to **www.mba.com/examprep** to download the planner.

Here are our recommended steps to starting your prep journey with your best foot forward.

1. **Study the structure.** Use the study plan in our **free GMAT™ Official Starter Kit** to become familiar with the exam format and structure. The study plan will guide you through each question type and give you sample questions. This will boost your confidence come test day when you know what to expect.

2. **Understand the question types.** Beyond knowing how to answer questions correctly, learn what each type of question is asking of you. GMAT questions rely on logic and analytical skills, not underlying subject matter mastery, as detailed in the **GMAT™ Official Guide 2025–2026 and Online Question Bank**.

3. **Establish your baseline.** Take the **GMAT™ Official Practice Exam 1 (FREE)** to establish your baseline. It uses the same format and scoring algorithm as the real test, so you can use the Official Score Report to accurately assess your strengths and growth areas.

4. **Study the answer explanations.** Take advantage of each question you get wrong by studying the correct answers, so you know how to get it right the next time. **GMAT™ Official Practice Questions** provide detailed answer explanations for hundreds of real GMAT questions. This will help you understand why you got a question right or wrong.

5. **Simulate the test-taking experience.** Take the **GMAT™ Official Practice Exams**. All GMAT™ Official Practice Exams use the same algorithm, scoring, and timing as the real exam, so take them with test-day-like conditions (e.g., quiet space, use the tools allowed on test day) for the truest prep experience.

Remember, the exam is timed, so learning to pace yourself and understanding the question formats and the skills you need can be a stepping stone to achieving your desired score. The timed practice in the **Online Question Bank** can help you prepare for this. The time management performance chart provided in practice exam score reports can also help you practice your pacing.

Because the exam assesses reasoning rather than knowledge, memorizing facts probably won't help you. You don't need to study advanced math, but you should know basic arithmetic and algebra. Likewise, you don't need to study advanced vocabulary words, but you should know English well enough to understand writing at an undergraduate level.

> "In Reading Comprehension and Critical Reasoning, carefully review the question and pay attention to its specific perspective."
>
> —A test instructor from New Oriental Educational and Technological Group

2.2 Getting Ready for Exam Day

Whether you take the exam online or in a test center, knowing what to expect will help you feel confident and succeed. To understand which exam delivery is right for you, visit **www.mba.com/plan-for-exam-day**.

Our Top Exam Day Strategies:

1. Get a good night's sleep the night before.
2. Pacing is key. Consult your on-screen timer periodically to avoid having to rush through sections.
3. Read each question carefully to fully understand what is being asked.
4. Don't waste time trying to solve a problem you recognize as too difficult or time-consuming. Instead, eliminate answers you know are wrong and select the best from the remaining choices.
5. Leverage the bookmarking tool to make your question review and edit process more efficient.

> "During the test, you should avoid making mistakes on relatively simple questions. Do not waste too much time on questions that you do not know how to answer. Your mastery of assumptions determines your success in critical reasoning. Grasping the types of information in articles that are often used for exam questions can improve your reading efficiency."
>
> —A test instructor from Merica Group

> "Don't take a 'brute force' approach to GMAT questions—think strategically instead."
>
> —A test instructor from GMAT Genius

> "Compile summarized notes that can be reviewed on the morning of the test. Awareness of the key points and types of mistakes will boost your scores."
>
> —A test instructor from LEADERSMBA

2.3 How to Use the *GMAT™ Official Guide Verbal Review 2025–2026*

The GMAT™ Official Guide series is the largest official source of actual GMAT questions. You can use this series of books and the included Online Question Bank to practice answering the different types of questions. The *GMAT™ Official Guide Verbal Review* is designed for those who have completed the Verbal Reasoning questions in the *GMAT™ Official Guide 2025–2026* and are looking for additional practice questions, as well as those who are interested in practicing only Verbal Reasoning questions. Questions of each type are organized by difficulty level of easy, medium, and hard. Your rate of accuracy in each level might differ from what you expect. You might be able to answer the "hard" questions easily, while the "easy" ones are challenging. This is common and is not an indicator of exam performance. The questions in this book are not adaptive based on your performance but are meant to serve as exposure to the range of question types and formats you might encounter on the exam. Also, the proportions of questions about different content areas in this book don't reflect the proportions in the actual exam. To find questions of a specific type and difficulty level (for example, easy reading comprehension questions), use the index of questions in Chapter 5.

We recommend the steps below for how to best use this book:

1. Start with the review chapter to gain an overview of the required concepts.

> "Building a strong foundation is crucial to achieve a high score. If you struggle with fundamental questions, your progress on more advanced questions will be hindered."
>
> —A test instructor from XY Education

2. Go through the practice questions in this book. Once you've familiarized yourself with the concepts and question types, use the Online Question Bank to further customize your practice by choosing your preferred level of difficulty, category of concepts, or question types.

> "The Official Guide offers in-depth answer explanations. After completing a question, reviewing it alongside the explanation helps you gain a deeper understanding of the question's key concepts and solution strategies. On the result interface of the online question bank, it serves a dual purpose: on one hand, it encourages us to review incorrect answers; on the other hand, it provides detailed insights into the time spent on each question, aiding in optimizing our pace during exercises."
>
> —A test instructor from Jiangjiang GMAT

3. Use the **Online Question Bank** to continue practicing based on your progress. To better customize and enhance your practice, use the Online Question Bank to:

    a. Review and retry practice questions to improve performance by using the untimed or timed features along with a study mode or an exam mode.

    b. Analyze key performance metrics to help assess focus area and track improvement.

    c. Use flashcards to master key concepts.

> "The biggest mistake students make is completing too many new problems. Completing problems doesn't move your score! Learning from problems does. Keep a list of questions you want to go back to and redo. Redo at least three of these questions every time you study. This book is one of the most important resources you can use to create the future you want. Make sure you understand every question you complete extremely well. You should be able to explain every problem you complete to someone who is new to the exam. Don't focus on simply 'getting through' the book. That mindset will work against you and your dreams."
>
> —A test instructor from The GMAT Strategy

 TIP

Since the exam is given on a computer, we suggest you practice the questions in this book using the **Online Question Bank** accessed via **www.mba.com/my-account**. It includes all the questions in this book, and it lets you create practice sets—both timed and untimed—and track your progress more easily. The Online Question Bank is also available on your mobile device through the GMAT™ Official Practice mobile app. To access the Online Question Bank on your mobile device, first create an account at **www.mba.com**, and then sign into your account on the mobile app.

2.4 How to Use Other GMAT™ Official Prep Products

We recommend using our other GMAT™ Official Prep products along with this guidebook.

- **For a realistic simulation of the exam:** GMAT™ Official Practice Exams 1–6 are the only practice exams that use real exam questions along with the scoring algorithm and user interface from the actual exam. The first two practice exams are free to all test takers at **www.mba.com/gmatprep**.

- **For more practice questions:** *GMAT™ Official Guide Data Insights Review 2025–2026* and *GMAT™ Official Guide Quantitative Review 2025–2026* offer over 400 additional practice questions not included in this book.

- **For focused practice:** GMAT™ Official Practice Questions for Quantitative, Data Insights, and Verbal products offer 100+ questions that are not included in the Official Guide series.

> "Build teaching-level depth; don't just finish content mindlessly. Even if you solve thousands of questions on a shaky foundation, you will remain stuck on a really low accuracy."
>
> —A test instructor from Top One Percent

2.5 Tips for Taking the Exam

Tips for answering questions of the different types are given later in this book. Here are some general tips to help you do your best on the test.

1. **Before the actual exam, decide in what order to take the sections.**
   The exam lets you choose in which order you'll take the sections. Use the GMAT™ Official Practice Exams to practice and find your preferred order. No order is "wrong." Some test takers prefer to complete the section that challenges them the most first, while others prefer to ease into the exam by starting with a section that they're stronger in. Practice each order and see which one works best for you.

2. **Try the practice questions and practice exams.**
   Timing yourself as you answer the practice questions and taking the practice exams can give you a sense of how long you will have for each question on the actual test, and whether you are answering them fast enough to finish in time.

 TIP

After you've learned about all the question types, use the practice questions in this book and practice them online at **www.mba.com/my-account** to prepare for the actual test.

3. **Review all test directions ahead of time.**
   The directions explain exactly what you need to do to answer questions of each type. You can review the directions in the GMAT™ Official Practice Exams ahead of time so that you don't miss anything you need to know to answer properly. To review directions during the test, you can click on the Help icon. But note that your time spent reviewing directions counts against your available time for that section of the test.

4. **Study each question carefully.**
   Before you answer a question, understand exactly what it is asking, then pick the best answer choice. Never skim a question. Skimming may make you miss important details or nuances.

5. **Use your time wisely.**
   Although the exam stresses accuracy over speed, you should use your time wisely. On average, you have just about 2 minutes and 9 seconds per Quantitative Reasoning question; 2 minutes and 15 seconds per Data Insights question; and under 2 minutes per Verbal Reasoning question. Once you start the test, an on-screen clock shows how much time you have left. You can hide this display if you want, but by checking the clock periodically, you can make sure to finish in time.

6. **Do not spend too much time on any one question.**
   If finding the right answer is taking too long, try to rule out answer choices you know are wrong. Then pick the best of the remaining choices and move on to the next question.

   Not finishing sections or randomly guessing answers can lower your score significantly. As long as you've worked on each section, you will get a score even if you didn't finish one or more sections in time. You don't earn points for questions you never get to see.

   Pacing is important. If a question stumps you, pick the answer choice that seems best and move on. If you guess wrong, the computer will likely give you an easier question, which you're more likely to answer correctly. Soon the computer will return to giving you questions matched to your ability. You can bookmark questions you get stuck on, then return to change up to three of your answers if you still have time left at the end of the section. But if you don't finish the section, your score will be reduced.

7. **Confirm your answers ONLY when you are ready to move on.**
   In the Quantitative Reasoning, Data Insights, and Verbal Reasoning sections, once you choose your answer to a question, you are asked to confirm it. As soon as you confirm your response, the next question appears. You can't skip questions. In the Data Insights and Verbal Reasoning sections, several questions based on the same prompt may appear at once. When more than one question is on a single screen, you can change your answers to any questions on that screen before moving on to the next screen. But until you've reached the end of the section, you can't navigate back to a previous screen to change any answers.

Myth -vs- FACT

M – Avoiding wrong answers is more important than finishing the test.

F – Not finishing can lower your score a lot.

Myth -vs- FACT

M – The first ten questions are critical, so you should spend the most time on them.

F – All questions impact your score.

2.6 Verbal Reasoning Section Strategies

Utilize the strategies below to better prepare for the exam. Creating a solid study plan and selecting the right prep materials are two key elements of getting accepted into your top business schools. But knowing how to strategically approach the exam is another crucial factor that can increase your confidence going into test day and help you perform your best.

> **"Don't just read explanations. Review your notes and learn from your mistakes."**
> —**A test instructor from Admit Master**

Reading Comprehension Questions

- Do not expect to be completely familiar with the material presented in passages. Your understanding of the subject matter is not required to answer the question.
- Read and analyze the passage carefully before reading the questions.
- Focus on key words and phrases to maintain an overall sense about the context of the passage.
- Select the answer that fits based on the information given in the passage.
- Don't rush through the passages. This section is about comprehension, not speed.

Critical Reasoning Questions

- Determine exactly what the question is asking. For this section, read the question first and then the material on which it is based.
- Keep the following in mind as you read through the passage:
  - What is put forward as factual information?
  - What is not said but necessarily follows from what is said?
  - What is claimed to follow from facts that have been put forward?
  - How well are those claims substantiated?
- When reading arguments, determine how sound the reasoning is. It is not necessary to pass judgment on the actual truth of anything put forward as fact.
- If a question is based on an argument, identify what part of the argument is its conclusion.

3.0 Verbal Review

3.0 Verbal Review

To prepare for the GMAT™ exam's Verbal Reasoning section and Data Insights section, and to succeed in graduate business programs, you need basic skills in analyzing and evaluating texts and the ideas they express. This chapter explains concepts to help you develop these skills. This is only a brief overview. So, if you find unfamiliar terms or concepts, consult outside resources to learn more.

The sections below can help you develop skills you need for the Verbal Reasoning and Data Insights sections of the GMAT exam.

Section 3.1, "Analyzing Passages," includes:

1. Arguments
2. Explanations and Plans
3. Narratives and Descriptions

Section 3.2, "Inductive Reasoning," includes:

1. Inductive Arguments
2. Generalizations and Predictions
3. Causal Reasoning
4. Analogies

Section 3.3, "Deductive Reasoning," includes:

1. Deductive Arguments
2. Logical Operators
3. Reasoning with Logical Operators
4. Necessity, Probability, and Possibility
5. Quantifiers
6. Reasoning with Quantifiers

3.1 Analyzing Passages

1. Arguments

A. An *argument* gives one or more ideas as reasons to accept one or more other ideas. Often some of these ideas are implied but not stated.

> *Example:*
>
> The sidewalk is dry, so it must not have rained last night.
>
> This argument gives the observation that the sidewalk is dry as a reason to accept that it didn't rain last night. The argument implies but doesn't say that rain typically leaves sidewalks wet.

B. A *premise* is an idea that an argument gives as a reason to accept another idea. An argument can have any number of premises.

The words and phrases below often mark premises:

after all	*for one thing*	*moreover*
because	*furthermore*	*seeing that*
for	*given that*	*since*
for the reason that	*in light of the fact that*	*whereas*

> *Example:*
>
> Our mayor shouldn't support the proposal to expand the freeway **because** the expansion's benefits wouldn't justify the costs. **Furthermore**, most voters oppose the expansion.
>
> This is an argument with two stated premises. The word *because* marks the first premise, that the expansion's benefits wouldn't justify the costs. The word *furthermore* marks the second premise, that most voters oppose the expansion. These premises are given as reasons the mayor shouldn't support the proposal.

C. A *conclusion* is an idea an argument supports with one or more premises. An *intermediate conclusion* is a conclusion the argument uses to support another conclusion. A *main conclusion* is a conclusion the argument doesn't use to support any other conclusion.

The words and phrases below often mark conclusions:

clearly	it follows that	suggests that
entails that	proves	surely
hence	shows that	therefore
implies that	so	thus

> *Example:*
>
> Julia just hiked fifteen kilometers, **so** she must have burned a lot of calories. **Surely**, she's hungry now.
>
> This argument has a premise, an intermediate conclusion, and a main conclusion. The word *so* marks the intermediate conclusion: that Julia must have burned a lot of calories. The word *surely* marks the main conclusion: that Julia is hungry now. The premise that Julia just hiked fifteen kilometers supports the intermediate conclusion, which in turn supports the main conclusion.

Conclusions may be stated before, between, or after premises. Sometimes no marker words show which statements are premises and which are conclusions. To find premises and conclusions without marker words, consider which statements the author gives as reasons to accept which other statements. The reasons given are the premises. The ideas the author tries to persuade readers to accept are the conclusions.

> *Example:*
>
> For healthy eating, Healthful Brand Donuts are the best donuts you can buy. Unlike any other donuts on the market, Healthful Brand Donuts have plenty of fiber and natural ingredients.
>
> In this argument, the author tries to persuade the reader that Healthful Brand Donuts are the best donuts to buy for healthy eating. So, the first sentence is the conclusion. The statement about Healthful Brand Donuts' ingredients is a premise because it's given as a reason to accept the conclusion. Since the author's intent is clear, no marker words are needed.

D. A *valid* argument is one whose conclusions follow from its premises. A valid argument can have false premises and conclusions. In a valid argument with false premises, the conclusion **would** follow if the premises **were** true.

A *sound* argument is a valid argument with true premises. Since a sound argument's premises are true, and its conclusions follow from those premises, its conclusions must also be true.

> *Examples:*
>
> (i) Everyone who tries fried eggplant is guaranteed to love the taste. So, if you try it, you'll love the taste too.
>
> In example (i), the premise is false: not everyone who tries fried eggplant is guaranteed to love the taste. So, example (i) is not a sound argument. But it is a valid argument because if everyone who tried fried eggplant **were** guaranteed to love the taste, it would follow that you, too, would love the taste if **you** tried it.
>
> (ii) Some people who try fried eggplant dislike the taste. So, if you try it, you'll probably dislike the taste too.
>
> In example (ii), the premise is true: some people who try fried eggplant do dislike the taste. However, example (ii) is an invalid argument, so it's not sound. **Some** people dislike the taste of fried eggplant, but that does not mean **you personally** will **probably** dislike the taste.

E. An *assumption* is an idea taken for granted. An assumption may be a premise in an argument, a claim about a cause or effect in a causal explanation, a condition a plan relies on, or any other type of idea taken for granted. A conclusion is never an assumption—an argument doesn't take a conclusion for granted, but rather gives reasons to accept it.

A passage may also have *implicit assumptions* the author considers too obvious to state. These unstated ideas fill logical gaps between the passage's statements.

An argument, plan, or explanation with implausible assumptions is weak and vulnerable to criticism.

F. A *necessary assumption* of an argument is an idea that must be true for the argument's stated premises to be good enough reasons to accept its conclusions. That is, a necessary assumption is one the argument needs in order to work.

> *Example:*
>
> Mario has booked a flight scheduled to arrive at 5:00 p.m.—which should let him get here by around 6:30 p.m. So, by 7:00 p.m. we'll be going out to dinner with Mario.
>
> In this argument, one necessary assumption is that the flight Mario booked will arrive not much later than scheduled. A second necessary assumption is that Mario caught his flight. Unless these and all the argument's other necessary assumptions are true, the argument's stated premises aren't good enough reasons to accept the conclusion.

G. A *sufficient assumption* of an argument is an idea whose truth would make the argument's main conclusion follow from the stated premises. That is, adding a sufficient assumption to an argument makes the argument valid.

> *Example:*
>
> The study of poetry is entirely without value since poetry has no practical use.
>
> In this argument, one sufficient assumption is that studying anything with no practical use is entirely without value. This assumption, together with the argument's stated premise, is enough to make the conclusion follow. If both the premise and the assumption are true, the conclusion must also be true. But this sufficient assumption is not a necessary assumption.

H. Arguments are often classified based on what kinds of conclusions they have.

    i. A *prescriptive* argument has a conclusion about what should or shouldn't be done. Prescriptive arguments may advocate for or against policies, procedures, strategies, goals, laws, or ethical norms.

> *Example:*
>
> Our company's staff is too small to handle our upcoming project. So, to make sure the project succeeds, the company **should** hire more employees.
>
> Another example of a prescriptive argument is shown above in Section 3.1.1.B. That argument is prescriptive because it concludes that the mayor ***should not*** support the proposed freeway expansion.

    ii. An *evaluative* argument concludes that something is good or bad, desirable or undesirable, without advocating any particular policy or actions.

> *Example:*
>
> This early novel is clearly one of the greatest of all time. Not only did it pioneer brilliantly innovative narrative techniques, but it did so with exceptional grace, subtlety, and sophistication.

    iii. An *interpretive* argument has a conclusion about something's underlying significance. An interpretive argument may be about the meaning, importance, or implications of observations, a theory, an artistic or literary work, or a historical event.

> *Example:*
>
> Many famous authors have commented emphatically on this early novel, either praising or condemning it. This suggests the novel has had an enormous influence on later fiction.

iv. A *causal* argument concludes that one or more factors did or did not contribute to one or more effects. A causal argument may be about the causes, reasons, or motivations for an event, condition, decision, or outcome. For example, a causal argument may support or oppose an account of the influences behind a literary or artistic style or movement.

Example:

Our houseplant started to thrive only when we moved it to a sunny window. So, probably the reason it was sickly before then was that it wasn't getting enough sunlight.

Another causal argument can be found in the example in Section 3.1.1.C above, which concludes that Julia must be hungry now.

v. A basic *factual* argument has a factual conclusion that doesn't fit in any other category explained above.

Example:

All dogs are mammals. Rover is a dog. Therefore, Rover is a mammal.

2. Explanations and Plans

A. A *causal explanation* claims that one or more factors contribute to one or more effects. A causal explanation might not be an argument. It might have no premises or conclusions. But a causal explanation can be a premise or conclusion in an argument.

The words and phrases below often mark a causal explanation:

as a result	*due to*	*results in*
because	*leads to*	*that's why*
causes	*produces*	*thereby*
contributes to	*responsible for*	*thus*

Some of these words can also mark premises or conclusions in arguments. To tell what the words mark, you may have to judge whether the author is giving reasons to accept a conclusion or only saying what causes an effect. If the author is only saying what causes an effect, without trying to persuade the reader that the effect is real, then the passage is a causal explanation but not an argument.

Just as an argument may have premises, intermediate conclusions, and main conclusions, a causal explanation may claim that one or more factors cause one or more intermediate effects that, in turn, cause further effects.

> *Example:*
>
> Julia just hiked fifteen kilometers, **thereby** burning a lot of calories. **That's why** she's hungry now.
>
> This is a causal explanation claiming that a factor (Julia's fifteen-kilometer hike) caused an intermediate effect (Julia burning a lot of calories) that, in turn, caused another effect (Julia being hungry now). The word *thereby* marks the intermediate effect, and the phrase *that's why* marks the final effect. This explanation doesn't try to convince the reader that Julia's hungry. It just explains what made her hungry. So, it's not an argument.

B. An *observation* is a claim that something was observed or is otherwise directly known. In the example of a causal explanation above, the claims that Julia just hiked fifteen kilometers and that she's hungry are observations. But if her burning of calories was not directly known or observed, the claim that she burned a lot of calories is not an observation.

C. A *hypothesis* is a tentative idea neither known nor assumed to be true. A hypothesis can be an argument's conclusion. Causal explanations are often hypotheses. A passage may discuss **alternative hypotheses**, such as competing explanations for the same observation. Sometimes a passage gives pros and cons of alternative hypotheses without arguing for any particular hypothesis as a conclusion.

> *Example:*
>
> A bush in our yard just died. The invasive insects we've seen around the yard lately might be the cause. Or the bush might not have gotten enough water. It's been a dry summer.
>
> This example presents two alternative hypotheses. The first hypothesis gives the observation that invasive insects have been in the yard as a possible causal explanation for the bush's observed death. This hypothesis assumes the insects can hurt bushes like the one in the yard. The second hypothesis provides the observation that it's been a dry summer as an alternative causal explanation for the bush's observed death. This hypothesis assumes dry weather can result in bushes getting too little water. The passage presents observations to tentatively support each hypothesis. But it doesn't argue for either hypothesis as a conclusion.

D. A *plan* describes an imagined set of actions meant to work together to achieve one or more goals. A plan is not itself an argument. Its actions aren't proposed as reasons to accept a goal, but rather as ways to reach the goal. However, a prescriptive argument may recommend or oppose a plan. A plan may also be among an argument's premises.

Just as an argument may have premises, intermediate conclusions, and main conclusions, a plan may suggest actions to reach intermediate goals that, in turn, are meant to help achieve main goals. And like an argument, a plan may have assumptions, including necessary and sufficient assumptions. A necessary assumption of a plan is one that must be true for the plan to achieve its goals. And a sufficient assumption of a plan is one whose truth guarantees the plan would achieve its goals if followed.

A plan is not a causal explanation. The actions a plan suggests haven't been done yet, so they can't have caused anything. However, any plan does assume possible future causal links between its proposed actions and its goals.

Example:

To repaint our house, we'll need to buy gallons of paint. To do that, we could go to the hardware store.

In this plan, going to the hardware store is an action imagined to help reach the intermediate goal of getting gallons of paint. The intermediate goal is imagined to help reach the main goal of repainting the house. This plan isn't itself an argument. But, combined with the premise that we ***should*** repaint the house, the plan could be part of a prescriptive argument that we ***should*** go to the hardware store.

3. Narratives and Descriptions

A. A ***narrative*** describes a sequence of related events. A narrative is not an argument, an explanation, or a plan. But it may contain one or more arguments, causal explanations, or plans—or be contained in them.

The words and phrases below often show narrative sequence:

after	*earlier*	*then*
afterwards	*later*	*thereafter*
before	*previously*	*until*
beforehand	*since*	*while*
during	*subsequently*	*when*

Example:

While Julia was hiking fifteen kilometers, she burned a lot of calories. **Afterwards**, she felt hungry.

This narrative describes a sequence of three events. The word ***while*** shows that Julia's hike and her burning of calories happened at the same time. The word ***afterwards*** shows that her hunger arose soon after the first two events. Although you can reasonably assume these events were causally linked, the narrative doesn't say they were. So, it's not an explicit causal explanation. And since the narrative doesn't report the events as reasons to accept a particular conclusion, it's not an argument either.

B. Not all passages are arguments, causal explanations, plans, or narratives. Some passages report on views, findings, innovations, places, societies, artistic works, devices, organisms, etc., without arguing for a conclusion, explaining what caused what, suggesting actions to reach a goal, or narrating what happened.

C. Likewise, not all statements in passages are premises, conclusions, observations to be explained, hypotheses, or reports of events. Statements in passages can also:

- Give background information to help the reader understand the rest of the passage
- Describe details of something that the passage is discussing
- Express the author's attitude toward material in the passage
- Provide examples to illustrate general statements
- Summarize ideas that the passage is arguing against

3.2 Inductive Reasoning

1. **Inductive Arguments**

    A. In an *inductive argument*, the premises are meant to support a conclusion but not to fully prove it. For example, the premises may just be meant to give evidence that the conclusion is **probably** true, leaving a chance that the conclusion is false despite that evidence.

    B. An inductive argument may be *strengthened* by adding reasons that directly support the conclusion or that help the argument's premises better support the conclusion. Conversely, an inductive argument may be *weakened* by adding reasons that directly cast doubt on the argument's conclusion, or that make the argument's premises less effective at supporting the conclusion. Below, we discuss how various types of inductive arguments are evaluated, strengthened, and weakened.

2. **Generalizations and Predictions**

    A. An argument by *generalization* often uses premises about a sample of a population to support a conclusion about the whole population.

    > *Example:*
    >
    > Six of the eight apartments available for lease in this building are studio apartments. So, probably about $\frac{3}{4}$ of all the apartments in the building are studio apartments.
    >
    > In this example, the whole set of apartments in the building is a population. The apartments available for lease are a *sample* of that population. Since six of the eight apartments available for lease are studio apartments, $\frac{3}{4}$ of the apartments in the sample are studio apartments. The argument generalizes from this by assuming the whole population is probably like the sample. It concludes that as in the sample, probably about $\frac{3}{4}$ of the apartments in the population are studio apartments.

    B. A similar type of argument by generalization uses premises about a whole population to support a conclusion about part of that population.

    > *Example:*
    >
    > About $\frac{3}{4}$ of all the apartments in the building are studio apartments. So, probably about $\frac{3}{4}$ of the apartments on the building's second floor are studio apartments.
    >
    > This example uses a premise about the proportion of studio apartments in the population of all the apartments in the building to support the conclusion that there's a similar proportion of studio apartments in just a part of the population—the apartments on the second floor.

    C. A *predictive* argument by generalization uses a premise about the sample observed so far in a population to support a conclusion about another part of the population.

> *Example:*
>
> Of the eight apartments I've visited in this building so far, six have been studio apartments. So, probably about six out of the next eight apartments I visit in the building will also be studio apartments.
>
> In this example, the apartments the author has visited so far are a sample of the total population of apartments in the building. The observation about the proportion of studio apartments in the sample supports a prediction that roughly the same proportion of studio apartments will be found in another part of the population—the next eight apartments the author will visit in the building.

D. The strength of an argument by generalization partly depends on how similar the sample is to the overall population, or to the unobserved part of the population a prediction is about. A sample chosen in a way likely to make it relevantly different than the population is a ***biased sample***. An argument using a biased sample is flawed.

> *Example:*
>
> In a telephone survey of our city's residents, about four out of every five respondents said they usually answer the phone when it rings. So, about four out of every five residents of our city usually answer the phone when it rings.
>
> In this example, the sample is the respondents to the telephone survey. People who usually answer the phone when it rings are more likely than other people to respond to telephone surveys. Because the sample was selected through a telephone survey, probably a greater proportion of the sample than of all city residents usually answer the phone when it rings. So, the argument is flawed because the sample is biased.

E. The strength of an argument generalizing from a sample also partly depends on the sample's size. The smaller the sample, the weaker the argument. This is because a smaller sample is statistically likely to differ more from the population in its average traits. An argument by generalization that uses too small a sample to justify its conclusion is flawed by ***hasty generalization***.

> *Example:*
>
> A coin came up heads five of the eight times Beth flipped it. This suggests the coin she flipped is weighted to make it come up heads more often than tails.
>
> In this argument, the sample is the eight flips of the coin, and the population is all the potential flips of the same coin. The sample is probably not biased because Beth's flips of the coin are probably no more likely than anyone else's flips of the same coin to come up heads or tails. However, the sample is too small to justify the conclusion that the coin is weighted to favor heads. A fair, unweighted coin flipped eight times usually comes up heads more or fewer than exactly four times—just by chance. So, this argument is flawed by hasty generalization. If Beth and other people flipped the coin thousands or millions of times, and still saw it come up heads in five out of every eight flips, that would strengthen the argument. But no matter how many times the coin was flipped to confirm this pattern, a tiny chance would be left that the coin was not weighted to favor heads and that the results had been purely random.

F. An argument by generalization is weaker when its conclusion is more precise, and stronger when its conclusion is vaguer, given the same premises. That's because a sample usually doesn't precisely match the population it's extracted from. A less precise conclusion allows a larger range of potential mismatches between sample and population. So, it's more likely to be true, given the same evidence. An argument whose conclusion is too precise for its premises to justify is flawed by the ***fallacy of specificity***.

Example:

Biologists carefully caught, weighed, and released fifty frogs out of the hundreds in a local lake. These fifty frogs weighed an average of 32.86 grams apiece. So, the frogs in the lake must also weigh an average of 32.86 grams apiece.

In this example, the sample might be biased because frogs of certain types might have been easier for the biologists to catch. But even if the biologists avoided any sampling bias, the average weight of the fifty sampled frogs probably wouldn't exactly match the average weight of the hundreds of frogs in the lake. The conclusion is too precise, so the argument suffers from the fallacy of specificity. A stronger argument might use the same evidence to conclude less precisely that the frogs in the lake weigh on average between 25 and 40 grams apiece. This less precise conclusion would still be true even if the average weight of the sampled frogs didn't exactly match the average weight of all the frogs in the lake. Since the less precise conclusion is more likely to be true given the same evidence, that evidence justifies it better. That means the argument for the less precise conclusion is stronger.

3. Causal Reasoning

A. Causal arguments use premises about correlations or causal links to support conclusions about causes and effects. Causal reasoning is hard because causal links can't be directly observed. And there's no scientific or philosophical consensus about what causality is. But saying that one type of situation causally contributes to another usually implies that after a situation of the first type, situations of the second type are more likely. It also implies that situations of the first type help to explain situations of the second type.

Example:

Bushes of the species in our yard tend to die after several weeks without water. So, they must need water at least every few weeks to survive.

In this example, the premise is that after situations of one type (bushes of a certain species getting no water for several weeks), situations of another type become more likely (the bushes dying). The conclusion implies that the first type of situation causes the second: getting no water for several weeks causes bushes of that species to die.

B. A causal argument may use a general correlation to support the conclusion that a situation of one type caused a situation of another type.

Example:

A bush in our yard just died. There's been no rain this summer, and no one has been watering the yard. Bushes of the species in our yard tend to die after several weeks without water. So, probably, the bush died because it didn't get enough water.

In this example, the first premises say that a ***specific*** situation of one type (a bush of a specific species dying) followed a specific situation of another type (the bush going without water for weeks). The final premise says that ***in general***, situations of the first type (bushes of that species dying) follow situations of the second type (bushes of that species getting no water for weeks). These premises together support the conclusion that the lack of water caused the bush to die.

C. Causal arguments can be weakened by observations that suggest alternative causal explanations. A way to check which of two competing explanations is stronger is to look at situations with the possible cause from one explanation but not the possible cause from the other.

Example:

Explanation 1: Bushes of this species tend to die after several weeks without water. Maybe the lack of water kills the bushes.

Explanation 2: Bushes of this species grow only in a region where long dry spells are always very hot. Maybe the heat alone kills these bushes during weeks without water.

To check which of these two hypothetical explanations is stronger, we can run two experiments. Each experiment creates a situation with one of the two proposed causes but not the other.

Experiment 1: Water some of the bushes often during weeks of extreme heat and see how well they survive.

Experiment 2: Keep some of the bushes dry in cooler weather and see how well they survive.

Finding that the bushes survive well in Experiment 1 but not in Experiment 2 would support Explanation 1 and cast doubt on Explanation 2.

Finding that the bushes survive well in Experiment 2 but not in Experiment 1 would support Explanation 2 and cast doubt on Explanation 1.

Finding that the bushes always die in both experiments would support both explanations, suggesting either heat or drought alone can kill the bushes.

Finding that the bushes survive well in both experiments would cast doubt on both explanations. It would suggest that something other than drought or heat is killing the bushes—or that drought and heat must occur together to kill the bushes.

D. Experiments to test causal hypotheses shouldn't add or remove possible causal factors other than those tested for.

> *Examples:*
>
> (i) To run Experiment 1 above, a scientist planted some of the bushes in a tropical rainforest where very hot days are usually rainy.
>
> (ii) To run Experiment 2 above, a scientist planted some of the bushes under an awning where rain couldn't reach them in cooler weather.
>
> These versions of the two experiments are problematic because they add other possible causal factors. In example (i), the rainforest's soil type, insects, or humidity might make it harder or easier for the bushes to survive, regardless of the heat and rainfall. In example (ii), putting the bushes under an awning would likely help keep them shaded. That, too, might make it easier or harder for the bushes to survive, regardless of the heat and rainfall. These experimental design flaws cast doubt on any argument that cites these versions of the experiments as evidence to support Explanation 1 or Explanation 2.

Testing a hypothesis through experiments usually means reasoning by generalization: a conclusion about a whole population is reached by observing a sample in the experiment. Causal arguments based on experiments can have the flaws discussed above in Section 3.2.2, "Generalizations and Predictions." A causal argument is weak if it generalizes from a sample that's too small or chosen in a biased way. In small or biased samples, correlations between factors that aren't causally linked often appear just by chance or because of outside factors.

E. Even when two factors clearly are causally linked, it can be hard to tell which causes which, or whether a third, underlying factor causes them both.

> *Example:*
>
> One type of earthworm is far more often found in soil under healthy bushes of a certain species than in soil under sickly bushes of that same species.
>
> Even if the earthworms' presence is causally linked to the bushes' health, the causal link could be that:
>
> (i) the earthworms improve the bushes' health, or
>
> (ii) healthier bushes attract the earthworms, or
>
> (iii) certain soil conditions both improve the bushes' health and attract the earthworms.
>
> More than one of these causal links, and others, may hold at once. A way to untangle the causal links is to find out:
>
> (i) how healthy the bushes are in the same soil conditions without earthworms,
>
> (ii) how attracted the earthworms are to those soil conditions without the bushes, and
>
> (iii) whether the earthworms tend to appear around healthier bushes even in different soil conditions.

F. Even reliable correlations sometimes arise just by chance. One way to check whether a correlation between two types of situations is just a coincidence is to test whether stopping situations of the first type also stops situations of the other type. Even when no test is possible, you can consider whether there's any plausible way either type of situation could cause the other.

> *Example:*
>
> For years, Juan has arrived at work at a hair salon every weekday at exactly 8:00 a.m. Five hundred miles to the north, over the same years, Ashley has arrived at work at a car dealership every weekday at exactly 8:01 a.m. So, Juan's daily arrival at his work must make Ashley arrive at her work a minute later.
>
> In this example, even though for years Ashley has always arrived at work a minute after Juan has, the argument is absurdly weak. That's because Juan's arrival at his work has no apparent way to affect when Ashley arrives at her work. But we could still test the hypothesis in the argument's conclusion. For example, we could persuade Juan to vary his arrival times, then see whether Ashley's arrival times change to match. With no plausible link between the two workers' arrival times, we'd need a lot of evidence like this to reasonably overcome the suspicion that the correlation is pure coincidence. However, finding out that Juan and Ashley know each other and have reasons to coordinate their work schedules could give us a plausible causal link between their arrival times. That would greatly strengthen the argument that their arrival times are indeed causally linked.

4. Analogies

A. An argument by *analogy* starts by saying two or more things are alike in certain ways. The argument then gives a claim about one of those two things as a reason to accept a similar claim about the other.

> *Example:*
>
> Laotian cuisine and Thai cuisine use many of the same ingredients and cooking techniques. Ahmed enjoys Thai cuisine. So, if he tried Laotian cuisine, he'd probably enjoy it.
>
> This example starts by saying how Laotian cuisine and Thai cuisine are alike: they use similar ingredients and cooking techniques. The argument then makes a claim about Thai cuisine: that Ahmed enjoys it. By analogy, these premises support a similar claim about Laotian cuisine: Ahmed would enjoy it if he tried it.

B. For an argument by analogy to work well, the noted similarities must be **relevant** to whether the two things are also similar in the way the conclusion claims. The argument in the example above meets this standard. A cuisine's ingredients and cooking techniques usually affect how much a specific person would enjoy it. Noting that Laotian cuisine and Thai cuisine have similar ingredients and cooking techniques is relevant to whether Ahmed is likely to similarly enjoy the two cuisines.

An argument by analogy is weaker if its premises only note similarities that are less relevant to its conclusion.

> *Example:*
>
> Laotian cuisine and Latvian cuisine both come from nations whose English names start with the letter *L*. Ahmed enjoys Latvian cuisine. So, if he tried Laotian cuisine, he'd probably enjoy it too.
>
> This example notes that Laotian cuisine and Latvian cuisine are similar with respect to the English names of the nations they're from. Since the spelling of a nation's name almost never affects how much anyone enjoys that nation's cuisine, this similarity is irrelevant to whether Ahmed would similarly enjoy the two cuisines. The analogy is absurd, so the argument is flawed. To save the argument, we'd need a good reason why the noted similarity is relevant after all—for example, evidence that Ahmed is an unusual person whose enjoyment of different cuisines depends on English spellings.

C. A reasonable argument by analogy can be strengthened by noting other relevant similarities between the things compared, or weakened by noting relevant dissimilarities.

> *Example:*
>
> Beth and Alan are children living on the same block in the Hazelfern School District. Beth attends Tubman Primary School. Therefore, Alan probably does as well.
>
> Noting that Beth and Alan are both in the same grade would strengthen this moderately reasonable argument, because that similarity increases the odds that they attend the same school. However, noting that Beth is eight years older than Alan would weaken the argument, because that dissimilarity suggests Alan may be too young to attend the school Beth attends.

3.3 Deductive Reasoning

1. Deductive Arguments

A. The premises of a *deductive argument* are given to fully prove its conclusion. A valid deductive argument with only true premises **must** have a true conclusion. An argument presented as deductive is flawed if its premises can all be true while its conclusion is false. However, a flawed deductive argument might still work well as an inductive argument if the author doesn't wrongly present the premises as **proving** the conclusion. Deductive arguments often use *logical operators* or *quantifiers* or both, as explained below.

2. Logical Operators

A. A *logical operator* shows how the truth or falsehood of one or more statements affects the truth or falsehood of a larger statement made from those statements and the operator. The basic logical operators are **negations**, **logical conjunctions**, **disjunctions**, and **implications**.

B. A statement's **negation** is true just when the statement is false. Words and phrases like *not*, *it is false that*, and *it is not the case that* often mark negation.

Statements are often vague, ambiguous, context-sensitive, or subjective. They may be true in one sense and false in another, they may be only partly true, or their truth may be indefinite. If a statement is true only in one way or to a limited degree, its negation is false in the same way and to the same degree.

> *Example:*
>
> "The cat is on the mat" can have the negation "The cat is not on the mat." Either of these statements is true if the other is false—but only when both are about the same cat and the same mat, in the same sense and the same context. If you make the first statement while the cat is sleeping on the mat, but then the cat wakes up and leaves before you make the second statement, the context has changed. Then your second statement isn't the negation of your first. If the cat is only partly on the mat when both statements are made, then the second statement is *partly* false just as much as the first is partly true, and in just the same way.

C. A *logical conjunction* of two statements is true just when both are true. The words and phrases below can mark a logical conjunction of statements *A* and *B*:

A and B	*A even though B*	*not only A but also B*
Although A, B	*A. Furthermore, B.*	*A, whereas B*
A but B	*A, however, B*	

The conjunction markers **and**, **furthermore**, and **not only ... but also** usually imply that *A* and *B* are relevant to each other or mentioned for similar reasons—for example, that both are premises supporting the same conclusion. On the other hand, the conjunction markers **although**, **but**, **even though**, **however**, and **whereas** suggest tension between *A* and *B*—for example, that it's surprising *A* and *B* are both true, or that *A* and *B* support conflicting conclusions, or that *A* and *B* differ in some other unexpected way.

> *Examples:*
>
> (i) Raul has worked for this company a long time, **and** he's searching for another job.
>
> (ii) **Although** Raul has worked for this company a long time, he's searching for another job.
>
> Both these examples say that Raul has worked for the company a long time, and that he's searching for another job. But in example (ii), *although* suggests Raul's search for another job is **surprising**, given that he's worked for the company a long time. In contrast, the *and* in example (i) suggests Raul's search for another job is **unsurprising** now that he's worked for the company a long time.

D. A *disjunction* of two statements is true only when one of them is true. The words and phrases *A or B*, *either A or B*, and *A unless B* often mark a disjunction of *A* and *B*.

There are two kinds of disjunction. An *inclusive disjunction* of two statements is true when **at least** one of them is true, and **also** when both are. An *exclusive disjunction* of two statements is true just when **exactly** one of them is true—**not** when both are. English disjunctions often aren't clearly inclusive or clearly exclusive. But *A or B or both* clearly means inclusive disjunction. And *A or B but not both* clearly means exclusive disjunction.

Examples:

(i) It will **either** rain **or** snow tomorrow.

(ii) It will rain tomorrow **unless** it snows.

These examples both say that at least one of the statements "It will rain tomorrow" and "It will snow tomorrow" is true. But neither example clearly says whether or not it might *both* rain *and* snow tomorrow. To clarify, we can say:

(iii) Tomorrow, it will rain or snow—or both. (*inclusive disjunction*)

or

(iv) Tomorrow, it will either rain or snow, but not both. (*exclusive disjunction*)

E. A *conditional* says that for one statement to be true, another must be true. In other words, a conditional means the first statement entails the second. The words and phrases below all mark the same conditional link between statements *A* and *B*:

A would mean that B	*B if A*	*A only if B*
If A, then B	*Not A unless B*	*B provided that A*

Conditionals of these forms do not mean that *A* is true, nor that *B* is. They do not give *A* as a reason to accept *B*. So, in a conditional, *A* isn't a premise and *B* isn't a conclusion. That is, a conditional is not an argument. However, the conditional *if A, then B* does mean that correctly assuming *A* as a premise lets you correctly reach *B* as a conclusion.

Examples:

(i) It will snow tonight **only if** the temperature falls below 5 degrees Celsius.

(ii) It **won't** snow tonight **unless** the temperature falls below 5 degrees Celsius.

(iii) **If** it snows tonight, it'll mean the temperature has fallen below 5 degrees Celsius.

These three conditionals all mean the same thing. Each says that snow tonight would require a temperature below 5 degrees Celsius. They do not say that it **will** snow tonight, nor that the temperature **will** be below 5 degrees Celsius. But they do suggest, for example, that seeing it snow tonight would tell you the temperature must be below 5 degrees Celsius.

Although conditionals often make or suggest causal claims, their meaning isn't always causal. The examples above do not mean that snow tonight would **cause** the temperature to fall below 5 degrees Celsius, nor vice versa.

None of these examples imply that it **must** snow if the temperature falls below 5 degrees Celsius tonight. A conditional *if A, then B* does not imply that *if B, then A*.

F. Two *logically equivalent* statements *A and B* are always both true or both false under the same conditions. Each implies the other. That is, *if A, then B*, and *if B, then A*. These two conditionals can be combined as *A if and only if B*.

3. Reasoning with Logical Operators

A. Here's a list of some types of logically equivalent statements made with logical operators. In this list, *not* means negation, *and* means logical conjunction, *or* means inclusive disjunction, and *if . . . then* means conditional implication.

Logical Equivalences with Logical Operators		
A and B	is logically equivalent to	*B and A*
not (A and B)	is logically equivalent to	*not-A or not-B*
A or B	is logically equivalent to	*B or A*
not (A or B)	is logically equivalent to	*not-A and not-B* (in other words, *neither A nor B*)
if A, then B	is logically equivalent to	*if not-B, then not-A*
if A, then (B and C)	is logically equivalent to	*(if A, then B) and (if A, then C)*
if A, then (B or C)	is logically equivalent to	*(if A, then B) or (if A, then C)*
if (A or B), then C	is logically equivalent to	*(if A, then C) and (if B, then C)*

B. Of any two logically equivalent statements, either can be a premise supporting the other as a conclusion in a valid deductive argument. For any line in the list above, a valid deductive argument has a premise of the form on one side and a logically equivalent conclusion of the form on the other side.

Examples:

The second line in the list above says that for any statements *A* and *B*, the statement *not (A and B)* is logically equivalent to *not-A or not-B*. This gives us two valid deductive arguments:

(i) *not (A and B), therefore not-A or not-B*

and

(ii) *not-A or not-B, therefore not (A and B)*

For example, the statement *Ashley and Tim don't both live in this neighborhood* is logically equivalent to *Either Ashley doesn't live in this neighborhood or Tim doesn't*. This lets us make two valid deductive arguments:

(iii) Ashley and Tim don't both live in this neighborhood. Therefore, either Ashley doesn't live in this neighborhood or Tim doesn't.

and

(iv) Either Ashley doesn't live in this neighborhood or Tim doesn't. Therefore, Ashley and Tim don't both live in this neighborhood.

C. Here's a list of some other valid deductive argument forms with logical operators, and of invalid forms often confused with them.

Valid and Invalid Inferences with Logical Operators	
Valid: *A and B, therefore A*	**Invalid:** *A, therefore A and B*
Valid: *A, therefore A or B*	**Invalid:** *A or B, therefore A*
Valid: *not-A and not-B, therefore not (A and B)*	**Invalid:** *not (A and B), therefore not-A and not-B*
Valid: *not (A or B), therefore not-A or not-B*	**Invalid:** *not-A or not-B, therefore not (A or B)*
Valid: *if A, then B; and A; therefore B*	**Invalid:** *if A, then B; and B; therefore A*
Valid: *if A, then B; and not-B; therefore not-A*	**Invalid:** *if A, then B; and not-A; therefore not-B*

Examples:

The third line in the table above says that ***not-A and not-B, therefore not (A and B)*** is valid, but ***not (A and B), therefore not-A and not-B*** is invalid. A simple example of a **valid** argument is:

(i) Ashley doesn't live in this neighborhood, and Tim doesn't either. Therefore, Ashley and Tim don't both live in this neighborhood.

But swapping argument (i)'s premise with its conclusion makes this **invalid** argument:

(ii) Ashley and Tim don't both live in this neighborhood. Therefore, Ashley doesn't live in this neighborhood and Tim doesn't either.

As another example, the table's fifth line says that ***if A, then B; and A; therefore B*** is valid, but ***if A, then B; and B; therefore A*** is invalid. So, another **valid** argument is:

(iii) If Ashley lives in this neighborhood, so does Tim. Ashley does live in this neighborhood. Therefore, Tim also lives in this neighborhood.

However, swapping argument (iii)'s second premise with its conclusion makes this **invalid** argument:

(iv) If Ashley lives in this neighborhood, so does Tim. Tim does live in this neighborhood. Therefore, Ashley lives in this neighborhood.

4. Necessity, Probability, and Possibility

A. Some words and phrases mark how likely a statement is to be true. For example, they may mean that:

- The statement is *necessarily* true; that is, there's a 100 percent chance the statement is true; or
- The statement is *probably* true; that is, there's a good chance the statement is true;
- The statement is *possibly* true; that is, the odds are greater than 0 percent that the statement is true.

Saying a claim is possibly true or probably true usually implies it's not necessarily true.

B. The table below shows three categories of words and phrases that can stand for degrees of probability:

Words Standing for Necessity, Probability, and Possibility		
Necessity	**Probability**	**Possibility**
certainly	*probably*	*can*
clearly	*likely*	*could*
definitely	*more likely than not*	*may*
must		*maybe*
necessarily		*might*
surely		*perhaps*
		possibly

The words ***probably*** and ***likely*** sometimes mean high probability, like a 95 percent chance. Other times they mean a medium chance, even one below 50 percent. Don't give these terms any exact meanings when you find them on the GMAT exam.

C. The table below lists some valid deductive argument forms with necessity, probability, and possibility, as well as invalid forms often confused with them.

Valid and Invalid Inferences with Necessity, Probability, and Possibility	
Valid: *Probably A, therefore possibly A*	**Invalid:** *Possibly A, therefore probably A*
Valid: *Possibly (A and B), therefore possibly A and possibly B*	**Invalid:** *Possibly A and possibly B, therefore possibly (A and B)*
Valid: *Probably (A and B), therefore probably A and probably B*	**Invalid:** *Probably A and probably B, therefore probably (A and B)*
Valid: *Probably A or probably B, therefore probably (A or B)*	**Invalid:** *Probably (A or B), therefore probably A or probably B*
Valid: *Necessarily A or necessarily B, therefore necessarily (A or B)*	**Invalid:** *Necessarily (A or B), therefore necessarily A or necessarily B*

Examples:

The table's second line says that ***possibly (A and B), therefore possibly A and possibly B*** is valid, while ***possibly A and possibly B, therefore possibly (A and B)*** is invalid. A simple **valid** argument is:

(i) Possibly Tim and Ashley both live in this house. So, possibly Tim lives in this house, and possibly Ashley does.

Swapping argument (i)'s premise with its conclusion gives us this **invalid** argument:

(ii) Possibly Tim lives in this house, and possibly Ashley does. So, possibly both Tim and Ashley live in this house.

To see that argument (ii) is invalid, suppose you know only one person lives in the house, but you don't know whether that person is Tim, Ashley, or someone else. Then argument (ii)'s premise would be true, but its conclusion would be false.

5. Quantifiers

A. A *quantifier* is a word or phrase for a proportion, number, or amount. Some basic quantifiers are *all*, *most*, *some*, and *none*.

   i. A quantifier like *all* means 100 percent of the individuals in a category, or the whole of an amount.

   ii. A quantifier like *most* usually means more than half the individuals in a category, or more than half of a whole. *Most* usually implies *not all*, but not always. Writing *most but not all*, or else *most or all*, can clarify the meaning.

   iii. A quantifier like *some* often means one or more individuals in a category, or part of a whole. *Some* usually but not always implies *not all*. However, *only some* clearly does imply *not all*, while *at least some* clearly doesn't. *Some* with a plural usually means *more than one*. In contrast, *some* with a singular usually means *exactly one*. For example, "some dogs" usually means "more than one dog," while "some dog" usually means "exactly one dog." But "some dog or dogs" means "at least one dog."

   iv. A quantifier like *no* or *none of* means something is being denied about all the individuals in a category, or about all of some whole.

   v. Other common quantifiers have more nuanced meanings. For example, *a few* vaguely means a small number more than two. The upper limit of what counts as *a few* depends on context. For example, "a few Europeans" might mean thousands of people (still a tiny part of Europe's population). But "a few residents in our building" might mean only three or four people if the building has only fifteen residents.

B. The table below classifies some quantifier words by their meanings.

Basic Quantifier Words

"All" and similar quantifier words	"Most" and similar quantifier words	"Some" and similar quantifier words	"No" and similar quantifier words
all	generally	a number	never
always	a majority	a portion	no
any	most	any	none
both	more than half	at least one	not any
each	usually	occasionally	not one
every		one or more	nowhere
everywhere		some	
whenever		sometimes	
wherever		somewhere	

Notice the table shows *any* both as a quantifier like *all* and as a quantifier like *some*. That's because *any* can have either meaning. For example, *Any of the students would prefer chocolate ice cream* means *Each of the students would prefer chocolate ice cream*. However, *I don't know if any of the students would prefer chocolate ice cream* means *I don't know if even one of the students would prefer chocolate ice cream*.

C. A quantifier used with a category usually implies the category isn't empty. But this doesn't always hold in hypothetical statements, in conditionals, or with the quantifier *any*.

Examples:

(i) **All** life forms native to planets other than Earth **are** carbon-based.

(ii) **Any** life forms native to planets other than Earth **would be** carbon-based.

In (i), the words *all* and *are* show the author is claiming there really are life forms native to planets other than Earth. But in (ii), the words *any* and *would be* show the author is carefully avoiding that claim.

D. Statements with two or more quantifiers sometimes look alike but differ in meaning because of word order and phrasing.

Example:

(i) Some beverage must be the favorite of every student in the class.

(ii) Each student in the class must have some favorite beverage.

Statement (i) suggests that every student in the class must have **the same** favorite beverage. In contrast, statement (ii) can be true even if each student has a **different** favorite beverage.

6. Reasoning with Quantifiers

A. Here's a list of some logically equivalent statement forms with quantifiers. In this list, *some* means **one or more**. The forms in the list use plurals, but similar equivalences can hold without plurals. For example, *No water is fire* is logically equivalent to *No fire is water*, even though those two statements don't have plurals like the forms in the list do.

Logical Equivalences with Quantifiers		
All As are Bs	is logically equivalent to	*No As are not Bs.*
Some As are Bs	is logically equivalent to	*Some Bs are As.*
No As are Bs	is logically equivalent to	*No Bs are As.*
Some As are not Bs	is logically equivalent to	*Not all As are Bs.*

However, *All As are Bs* is **not** equivalent to *All Bs are As*. And *Some As are not Bs* is **not** equivalent to *Some Bs are not As*.

Examples:

(i) The true statement *All ostriches are birds* is not equivalent to the false statement *All birds are ostriches*.

(ii) The true statement *Some birds are not ostriches* is not equivalent to the false statement *Some ostriches are not birds*.

B. As explained above, either of two logically equivalent statements can be a premise supporting the other as a conclusion in a valid deductive argument. This works for equivalences with quantifiers just like it does for equivalences with logical operators.

C. A *syllogism* is a type of simple deductive argument whose two premises have one quantifier apiece, and whose conclusion also has one quantifier.

Here's a list of some valid syllogism forms along with invalid forms sometimes confused with them. As above, in this list, **some** means **one or more**.

Valid and Invalid Syllogisms	
Valid: *All As are Bs. All Bs are Cs. So, all As are Cs.*	**Invalid:** *All As are Bs. All Bs are Cs. So, all Cs are As.* **Invalid:** *All As are Bs. All Cs are Bs. So, all As are Cs.* **Invalid:** *All Bs are As. All Bs are Cs. So, all As are Cs.*
Valid: *Some As are Bs. All Bs are Cs. So, some As are Cs.*	**Invalid:** *All As are Bs. Some Bs are Cs. So, some As are Cs.* **Invalid:** *Some As are Bs. Some Bs are Cs. So, some As are Cs.*
Valid: *All As are Bs. No Bs are Cs. So, no As are Cs.*	**Invalid:** *No As are Bs. All Bs are Cs. So, no As are Cs.* **Invalid:** *No As are Bs. No Bs are Cs. So, all As are Cs.* **Invalid:** *No As are Bs. All Bs are Cs. So, some As are not Cs.*

Examples:

The list's first line says that ***All As are Bs. All Bs are Cs. So, all As are Cs*** is valid. And here's a **valid** syllogism of that form:

(i) All the trees in the local park were planted by the town arborist. All the trees the arborist planted have been labeled by her. So, all the trees in the park must have been labeled by the arborist.

A similar-looking but **invalid** syllogism has the form ***All As are Bs. All Bs are Cs. So, all Cs are As*** from the list's second line:

(ii) All the trees in the local park were planted by the town arborist. All the trees the arborist planted have been labeled by her. So, all the trees the arborist has labeled must be in the park.

To see that argument (ii) is invalid, notice that even if both premises are true, the arborist might also have labeled trees outside the park—maybe even trees she didn't plant.

Another **invalid** syllogism has the form ***All As are Bs. All Cs are Bs. So, all As are Cs*** from the list's third line:

(iii) All the trees in the local park were planted by the town arborist. All the trees the arborist has labeled are trees she planted. So, all the trees in the park must have been labeled by the arborist.

To see that argument (iii) is invalid, notice that even if both premises are true, the arborist might not have labeled every tree she planted, nor even every tree she planted in the park.

The form in the list's fourth line (***All Bs are As. All Bs are Cs. So, all As are Cs***) gives us yet another **invalid** syllogism:

(iv) All the trees the town arborist has planted are in the local park. All the trees the arborist planted have been labeled by her. So, all the trees in the park must have been labeled by the arborist.

To see that argument (iv) is invalid, notice that even if both premises are true, the park might have many trees that the arborist neither planted nor labeled.

D. Some quantifier words in the table "Basic Quantifier Words" in Section 3.3.5.B above refer to time or place. For example, *whenever* means *every time,* *usually* means *most times*, and *never* means *at no time*. Understanding these meanings can help you rewrite deductive arguments using these words into standard syllogisms to check their validity.

> *Example:*
>
> Max never goes running when the sidewalks are icy. The sidewalks are usually icy on January mornings, so Max must not go running on most January mornings.
>
> We can rewrite this argument in the valid syllogism form *No As are Bs. Most Cs are Bs. So, most Cs are not As*:
>
> No occasions when Max goes running are occasions when the sidewalks are icy. Most January mornings are occasions when the sidewalks are icy. So, most January mornings are not occasions when Max goes running.
>
> Since arguments in this syllogism form are valid, we can tell that the argument in this example is valid.

4.0 Verbal Reasoning

4.0 Verbal Reasoning

The Verbal Reasoning section of the GMAT™ exam uses multiple-choice questions to measure your skill in reasoning, understanding what you read, and evaluating arguments. This section has passages about many topics, but it doesn't assume you already know about the topics. Mingled throughout the section are questions of two main types: Reading Comprehension and Critical Reasoning.

Reading Comprehension questions are based on passages of around 200 to 350 words. With each passage are several questions asking you to understand, analyze, apply, and evaluate that passage's information and concepts. On the left side of your screen, the passage stays visible as you answer the questions about it. On the right side of your screen, one question appears at a time, along with its answer choices. Different passages may have different numbers of questions.

Critical Reasoning questions are based on passages usually of fewer than 100 words. Unlike Reading Comprehension passages, each Critical Reasoning passage has just one question. This question asks you to logically analyze, evaluate, or reason about an argument, situation, or plan the passage presents. Only one passage and its single question appear at a time.

You have 45 minutes to answer the 23 questions in the Verbal Reasoning section, an average of just under two minutes per question.

To prepare for the Verbal Reasoning section, first review basic concepts of text analysis and logical reasoning. Read Chapter 3, "Verbal Review," which briefly covers these concepts. After reviewing, practice on questions from past GMAT exams.

4.1 What Is Measured

The Verbal Reasoning section measures how well you understand, analyze, apply, evaluate, and reason about information and ideas in texts. Specifically, it tests the following skills:

Skill Category	Details	Examples
Recognize stated ideas	Understand, restate, and summarize information and ideas	• Find a passage's overall theme or point • Find a specific detail • Summarize a set of statements • Tell if an idea is stated or implied • Tell what a word or phrase means in context
Analyze reasoning structure	Identify premises, conclusions, explanations, argument techniques, reasons for plans, and background information	• Tell what argument technique someone uses • Tell a statement's role in a passage
Apply ideas in new contexts	Use general ideas in new situations the passage doesn't discuss	• Decide which new situation is most like one in the passage • Tell which new action would follow or break a rule in the passage • Decide which new example would best illustrate an idea in the passage

Skill Category	Details	Examples
Infer	Draw an unstated conclusion from a passage	• Decide which conclusion a passage most strongly supports • Tell what follows logically from information given • Decide what a stated opinion implies • Recognize an author's attitude from word choices
Identify unstated assumptions	Find an assumption that fills a logical gap in an argument, explanation, or plan	• Find an assumption an argument depends on • Find an assumption that makes an argument's conclusion follow logically • Tell what must happen for a plan to succeed
Evaluate hypotheses	Judge explanations for a situation	• Decide what would most help explain why a plan failed • Decide what most likely caused an observed effect
Resolve discrepancies	Explain or justify an apparent conflict between two statements or situations	• Explain why a factor didn't cause its usual effect • Decide which principle resolves a conflict between two opinions
Strengthen or weaken reasoning	Identify new information that either supports or undermines an argument, explanation, plan, or claim	• Tell which discovery would cast the most doubt on an argument's reasoning • Tell what added evidence would best support a causal explanation
Identify reasoning flaws	Identify mistakes such as confusing correlation with causation or confusing a sufficient assumption with a necessary one	• Decide which observation points to a reasoning flaw • Tell which criticism an argument is most vulnerable to
Identify points of disagreement	Tell what two parties disagree about, based on their statements	• Find the main implied point of disagreement in a dialogue
Solve a practical problem	Recognize a good strategy for solving a problem	• Find a way of sampling a population accurately despite an obstacle

4.2 Question Types

Reading Comprehension and Critical Reasoning are the two main Verbal Reasoning question types. Each has several subtypes. During the test, the subtypes aren't labeled. Each question tells you what you need to do.

1. Reading Comprehension

The five Reading Comprehension question subtypes are Main Idea, Supporting Idea, Inference, Application, and Evaluation. Each tests a different main skill, but sometimes the skills overlap. For example, to find a passage's main idea, you must understand the passage's logical and rhetorical structure. To make inferences or apply ideas from a passage, you often must find its main and supporting ideas.

Below, we discuss the Reading Comprehension question subtypes.

A. Main Idea

- In each passage, all the sentences and paragraphs develop one central point or share one overall purpose. A Main Idea question asks you to find this central point or purpose. Sometimes the passage tells you its central point. Other times you must infer it from the passage's structure and content.

- A Main Idea question may ask which answer option best restates the central point, best explains the author's main goal for the passage, or works best as a title for the passage.

- Main Idea questions use phrases like these:

    . . . most accurately expresses the main idea . . .,

    The primary purpose of the passage as a whole is to . . ., or

    In the passage, the author seeks primarily to. . . .

- The right answer to a Main Idea question about an argumentative passage often restates or describes the main conclusion of the main argument. To find the main conclusion, you must notice which statements in the passage are given as reasons to accept which other statements. The main conclusion is an idea that the whole passage gives reasons to accept, but that isn't in turn given as a reason to accept some further conclusion.

- When the passage isn't argumentative, the right answer to a Main Idea question usually gives the passage's overall theme or purpose. The overall theme is often an idea repeated in different paragraphs. The overall purpose is usually a goal toward which all the paragraphs work. If the passage has no overall theme or purpose, the right answer may just summarize the passage. For example, the right answer to a Main Idea question about a narrative passage might summarize the events described or state their overall outcome.

- Wrong answer choices often repeat passage details that aren't the main point, make claims that look like the main point but are different, or state ideas not mentioned in the passage but related to it.

B. Supporting Idea

- Supporting Idea questions may ask you about anything the passage states except for the main point. To answer a Supporting Idea question, you must understand individual statements and their roles in the passage.

- Answers to Supporting Idea questions almost never directly quote the passage. They usually rephrase statements from the passage or describe them abstractly. A Supporting Idea question may ask which statement plays a specific role in the passage. For example, it may ask you to find a premise, an intermediate conclusion, a described viewpoint, an objection, an example or counterexample, a causal claim, background information, a descriptive detail, or part of an explanation or narrative. Or it may also ask what a word or phrase in the passage means in context.

- Supporting Idea questions often use phrases like these:

  According to the passage . . .,

  Which of the following does the author cite as . . .,

  Which of the following does the author offer as an objection to . . .,

  The passage compares . . .,

  The passage mentions . . ., or

  Which of the following does the author propose. . . .

C. Inference

- Inference questions ask about ideas the passage suggests or supports but doesn't state. Some of these questions ask about ideas the author clearly meant the passage to imply. Others ask about logical implications, which the author may not have noticed.

- An Inference question may ask you to find:

  a likely cause or effect of a situation the passage describes,

  a specific implication of a generalization in the passage, or

  a statement that someone discussed in the passage would likely accept or reject.

- Sometimes the inference follows from one small part of the passage. Other times it depends on several statements scattered through different paragraphs. Sometimes the question says where to look in the passage, but not always.

- Inference questions often use phrases like these:

  Which of the following statements about . . . is most strongly supported by . . .,

  It can be inferred from the passage that . . .,

  If the claims about . . . are true, which of the following is most likely also true?

  The passage implies that . . ., or

  The information in the passage suggests that. . . .

- Wrong answer choices may be true, and related to the passage, but not supported by it. Conversely, the right answer choice may be false but follow logically from false statements in the passage. For example, even if the passage rightly says a theory is mistaken, a question might ask what would follow if the theory were true.

D. Application

- Application questions ask how situations or ideas the passage discusses relate to other situations or ideas the passage doesn't mention.

- Application questions may use words like *would*, *could*, *might*, or *should*, or phrases like *most clearly exemplifies*, *most similar to*, or *most likely ruled out by*.

- Some Application questions ask you to reason by analogy. They may ask which of several roles, methods, goals, or relationships is most like one the passage mentions. Review Section 3.2.4, "Analogies," which explains reasoning by analogy.

- Other Application questions ask you to apply general rules. For example, they may ask:

  which rule's enforcement would help achieve a goal the passage mentions, which principle a judgment in the passage relies on,

which action would break or follow a rule the passage states,

which generalization the evidence in the passage best fits, or

which general strategy could solve a problem the passage describes.

- The third type of Application question asks you to extend the passage. Questions of this type may ask for:

the best topic for a new paragraph added to the end of the passage,

a good example of a point the author makes, or

the author's most likely response to a possible objection.

- The fourth type of Application question asks about "what-if" scenarios. These questions may ask:

how different experimental results might affect a researcher's conclusions,

how a trend the passage mentions might be disrupted, or

how events might have gone differently if a situation had never occurred.

- Don't rule out answer choices just because they're not about the passage. Because Application questions relate the passage to new topics, the right answers are often about topics the passage never mentions. For instance, the right answer to an analogy question about a water-treatment process the passage explains might be about book publishing.

E. Evaluation

- Evaluation questions ask you to assess the passage's organization and logic.
- They often use phrases like these:

  The purpose of . . .,

  . . . most accurately describes the structure of . . .,

  . . . most strengthens . . .,

  . . . would most justify . . .,

  . . . is most vulnerable to the objection that . . ., or

  Which . . . additional information would most help. . . .

- An Evaluation question's answer choices are often abstract. They may not use specific words or ideas from the passage. For example, a question about a paragraph's function might have this answer choice: *It rejects a theory presented in the preceding paragraph and offers some criteria that an alternative theory would need to meet.*

- Some Evaluation questions ask about the roles of different parts of the passage. They may ask:

  how the whole passage or part of it is structured,

  why the author put a specific detail in the passage,

  what purpose a statement in the passage serves,

  how the author tries to persuade readers to accept a claim, or

  what attitude most likely motivated an opinion the passage mentions.

- Other Evaluation questions ask about:

    the strengths, weaknesses, relevance, or effectiveness of parts of the passage,

    implicit assumptions in the passage,

    what would best resolve apparent conflicts between parts of the passage, or

    potential objections, justifications, supporting evidence, or counterexamples.

These questions are often similar to Critical Reasoning questions, discussed below.

2. Critical Reasoning

The four subtypes of Critical Reasoning question are Analysis, Construction, Critique, and Plan. We discuss each below.

A. Analysis

- Analysis questions ask about a passage's logical structure and the roles that statements play in it.
- Analysis questions often use phrases like these:

    *... the two portions in **boldface** play which of the following roles?*

    The argument proceeds by . . .,

    A technique used in the argument is to . . .,

    . . . responds to . . . by . . .,

    The statements above can best serve as part of an argument against . . ., or

    Which of the following is the main point of disagreement between. . . .

- Some Analysis questions ask about the roles of one or two statements in the passage. Often the passage shows these statements in **boldface**.
- Other Analysis questions ask about an argumentative method in the passage. Sometimes the passage itself is an argument, and the question asks how it works. Other times, the passage is a dialogue, and the question asks what argumentative technique one speaker uses in replying to the other.
- Another type of Analysis question asks about an unstated point in the passage. This point may be a conclusion the passage is meant to support. Or it may be a point of agreement or disagreement between the two speakers in a dialogue.

B. Construction

- Construction questions ask how to best complete partial arguments or explanations.
- Construction questions often use phrases like these:

    . . . most logically completes . . .,

    If the statements above are true . . .,

    . . . most strongly support . . .,

    . . . best explains the discrepancy . . .,

    . . . depends on the assumption that . . .,

    . . . enables the conclusion to be properly drawn? or

    . . . provides the strongest justification for. . . .

- Some Construction questions ask what conclusion a set of premises best supports. These questions may ask for a conclusion that logically follows from the premises, or for a conclusion that the premises merely give evidence for.

- Other Construction questions ask for a missing premise to support a given conclusion. A question like this usually says whether the premise must be a necessary assumption, a sufficient assumption, a relevant observation, or a justification for a position. The passage may state only the conclusion, or it may also give other premises to combine with the missing premise.

- Another type of Construction question asks what would best explain either an observation or a puzzling discrepancy between observations.

C. Critique

- Critique questions ask you to judge reasoning in passages, find its strengths or weaknesses, and decide how it could be improved.

- Critique questions often use phrases like these:

    . . . most vulnerable to the criticism that . . .,

    . . . logically flawed in that . . .,

    . . . most seriously weakens . . .,

    . . . casts the most serious doubt on . . .,

    . . . most strengthens . . .,

    . . . most strongly supports . . ., or

    . . . would be most useful to know in order to evaluate. . . .

- Some Critique questions ask how an argument is flawed or weak. These questions are often about arguments with standard reasoning flaws, like the flaws discussed in Sections 3.2, "Inductive Reasoning," and 3.3, "Deductive Reasoning." In other cases, the arguments have no standard flaw but don't work because they rely on some obviously implausible assumption.

- Other Critique questions ask what new evidence would most strengthen or weaken an argument. These arguments are always inductive because evidence can't strengthen or weaken a deductive argument. Section 3.2, "Inductive Reasoning," explains how evidence can strengthen and weaken arguments.

- Finally, some Critique questions ask you what would be most helpful to know in order to assess a hypothesis or argument in the passage. The answer choices for these questions start with the word *Whether*, followed by an idea whose truth is unknown. The right answer choice gives the idea whose truth or falsehood would be most helpful to know in order to decide whether the hypothesis in the passage is true. The wrong answer choices give ideas that, whether true or false, are less relevant to the hypothesis.

D. Plan

- Plan questions ask you to construct or judge reasoning about actual or proposed courses of action, or plans. Section 3.1.2.D briefly explains this type of reasoning.

- Plan questions use many of the same phrases found in Construction and Critique questions, but the questions are always about plans, strategies, or courses of action.

- Plan questions may ask:

    what must be true for a plan to succeed,

what conditions would make a plan more or less likely to succeed,

what would be most helpful to know in order to judge a plan,

what evidence would best support an opinion about a plan,

how a plan is flawed,

what strategy would most help overcome a problem,

what policy would most help reach a goal under certain conditions, or

why a plan succeeded, failed, or had some unexpected effect.

4.3 Tips for Answering Verbal Reasoning Questions

1. Answer using only the information given and common knowledge.

The passages and common knowledge tell you everything you need to answer correctly. If you already know about the passage topic, don't use that knowledge to answer. Answer based on what the passage states or implies, and on common knowledge. For example, if the passage says something happened during a snowstorm, you can use common knowledge about snowstorms to infer that the weather wasn't hot.

2. Look for cue words marking statements' roles.

Section 3.1, "Analyzing Passages," explains how certain cue words often mark premises, conclusions, causal explanations, and narrative sequences. These cue words tell you what roles statements near them play. Also notice transition words marking a shift from one topic to another, and how those words suggest the topics are related. Usually, you can tell a statement's role even without a cue word. For example, if the passage clearly gives one statement as a reason to accept another, you don't need cue words to tell that the first statement is a premise and the second a conclusion.

3. Analyze the passage's structure and purpose.

Once you know the roles individual statements play, you can find the passage's overall structure and purpose. Does the passage mainly report facts and events? Does it argue for a conclusion? Does it discuss competing causal explanations? Does it comment on situations or other writers' views? Notice which premises are given to support which conclusions, and which causes are said to produce which effects. Notice also if the passage uses intermediate conclusions to support a main conclusion. Finally, notice any clear but unstated implications of the passage.

4. Use basic principles of good reasoning to judge the passage's reasoning.

Sections 3.2, "Inductive Reasoning," and 3.3, "Deductive Reasoning," review some principles of good reasoning. When a question asks you to judge the reasoning in the passage, use these basic principles. You don't need advanced knowledge of logic or any other subject to answer correctly.

5. Notice exactly what the question asks.

Often the wrong answer to one question would be the right answer to another question that looks similar. You need to pick the right answer to the specific question asked. To do that, focus on the question. For example, if the question asks about one part of the passage, don't pick an answer choice about some other part of the passage. As another example, these two questions could easily be confused:

i) Which of the following crops is grown by *the most farms* in Nation X?

ii) Farms in Nation X grow *the most of* which of the following crops?

The nation's farms may grow the most of a crop that's not grown by the most farms. If many small farms grow potatoes while a few huge farms grow wheat, the right answer to (i) could be *potatoes* even if the right answer to (ii) is *wheat*.

6. Read all the answer choices before picking one.

Verbal Reasoning questions often ask you to pick the best answer choice of those given. To tell which answer choice is best, read them all.

7. If you're not sure which answer choice is right, try ruling out some that are clearly wrong.

Ruling out some clearly wrong answer choices can help you find the right answer choice. If you're still undecided between two answer choices, study the passage again for clues you may have missed.

8. Pace yourself.

You have less than two minutes per question. You need to spend much of that time reading the passages. To avoid running out of time, don't spend too long on any one question. If you get stuck on a question for a couple of minutes after you've ruled out some of the answer choices, just pick the remaining choice that seems best. Then go to the next question.

To register for the GMAT™ exam, go to www.mba.com/register

4.4 Practice Questions: Reading Comprehension

Each of the Reading Comprehension questions is based on the content of a passage. After reading the passage, answer all questions pertaining to it on the basis of what is stated or implied in the passage. For each question, select the best answer of the choices given. On the actual GMAT exam, you will see no more than four questions per passage.

Questions 1 to 47 — Difficulty: Easy

Line Human beings, born with a drive to explore and experiment, thrive on learning. Unfortunately, corporations are oriented predominantly toward controlling employees, not fostering their learning.
(5) Ironically, this orientation creates the very conditions that predestine employees to mediocre performances. Over time, superior performance requires superior learning, because long-term corporate survival depends on continually exploring
(10) new business and organizational opportunities that can create new sources of growth.
   To survive in the future, corporations must become "learning organizations," enterprises that are constantly able to adapt and expand their
(15) capabilities. To accomplish this, corporations must change how they view employees. The traditional view that a single charismatic leader should set the corporation's direction and make key decisions is rooted in an individualistic worldview. In an
(20) increasingly interdependent world, such a view is no longer viable. In learning organizations, thinking and acting are integrated at all job levels. Corporate leadership is shared, and leaders become designers, teachers, and stewards, roles requiring
(25) new skills: the ability to build shared vision, to reveal and challenge prevailing mental models, and to foster broader, more integrated patterns of thinking. In short, leaders in learning organizations are responsible for building organizations in which
(30) employees are continually learning new skills and expanding their capabilities to shape their future.

Questions 1–4 refer to the passage.

1. According to the passage, traditional corporate leaders differ from leaders in learning organizations in that the former

   (A) encourage employees to concentrate on developing a wide range of skills
   (B) enable employees to recognize and confront dominant corporate models and to develop alternative models
   (C) make important policy decisions alone and then require employees in the corporation to abide by those decisions
   (D) instill confidence in employees because of their willingness to make risky decisions and accept their consequences
   (E) are concerned with offering employees frequent advice and career guidance

2. Which of the following best describes employee behavior encouraged within learning organizations, as such organizations are described in the passage?

   (A) Carefully defining one's job description and taking care to avoid deviations from it
   (B) Designing mentoring programs that train new employees to follow procedures that have been used for many years
   (C) Concentrating one's efforts on mastering one aspect of a complicated task
   (D) Studying an organizational problem, preparing a report, and submitting it to a corporate leader for approval
   (E) Analyzing a problem related to productivity, making a decision about a solution, and implementing that solution

3. According to the author of the passage, corporate leaders of the future should do which of the following?

(A) They should encourage employees to put long-term goals ahead of short-term profits.
(B) They should exercise more control over employees in order to constrain production costs.
(C) They should redefine incentives for employees' performance improvement.
(D) They should provide employees with opportunities to gain new skills and expand their capabilities.
(E) They should promote individual managers who are committed to established company policies.

4. The primary purpose of the passage is to

(A) endorse a traditional corporate structure
(B) introduce a new approach to corporate leadership and evaluate criticisms of it
(C) explain competing theories about management practices and reconcile them
(D) contrast two typical corporate organizational structures
(E) propose an alternative to a common corporate approach

Line   For many years, historians thought that the development of capitalism had not faced serious challenges in the United States. Writing in the early twentieth century, Progressive historians
(5) sympathized with the battles waged by farmers and small producers against large capitalists in the late nineteenth century, but they did not question the widespread acceptance of laissez-faire (unregulated) capitalism throughout American history. Similarly,
(10) Louis Hartz, who sometimes disagreed with the Progressives, argued that Americans accepted laissez-faire capitalism without challenge because they lacked a feudal, precapitalist past. Recently, however, some scholars have argued that even
(15) though laissez-faire became the prevailing ethos in nineteenth-century America, it was not accepted without struggle. Laissez-faire capitalism, they suggest, clashed with existing religious and communitarian norms that imposed moral constraints
(20) on acquisitiveness to protect the weak from the predatory, the strong from corruption, and the entire culture from materialist excess. Buttressed by mercantilist notions that government should be both regulator and promoter of economic activity, these
(25) norms persisted long after the American Revolution helped unleash the economic forces that produced capitalism. These scholars argue that even in the late nineteenth century, with the government's role in the economy considerably diminished, laissez-faire had
(30) not triumphed completely. Hard times continued to revive popular demands for regulating business and softening the harsh edges of laissez-faire capitalism.

Questions 5–7 refer to the passage.

5. The passage suggests that the scholars mentioned in line 14 would agree with which of the following statements regarding the "norms" mentioned in line 19?

    (A) They provided a primary source of opposition to the development of laissez-faire capitalism in the United States in the nineteenth century.
    (B) Their appeal was undermined by difficult economic times in the United States at the end of the nineteenth century.
    (C) They disappeared in the United States in the late nineteenth century because of the triumph of laissez-faire capitalism.
    (D) They facilitated the successful implementation of mercantilist notions of government in the United States in the nineteenth century.
    (E) They are now recognized by historians as having been an important part of the ideology of the American Revolution.

6. The author of the passage mentions the Progressives as examples of historians who

    (A) saw farmers and small producers as having the potential to become a powerful force in American society
    (B) did not question the widespread acceptance of laissez-faire capitalism in the United States in spite of their sympathy for farmers and small producers
    (C) did not agree that religious and communitarian norms were needed to soften the harsh edges of laissez-faire capitalism
    (D) saw the development of laissez-faire capitalism in the United States as a historical inevitability in spite of their lack of sympathy for large capitalists
    (E) were somewhat out of the mainstream of the American historical profession

7. The primary purpose of the passage is to

   (A) reveal the underlying similarities of certain arguments regarding the development of capitalism in the United States
   (B) synthesize two competing arguments regarding the development of capitalism in the United States
   (C) defend an established argument regarding the development of capitalism in the United States
   (D) summarize a scholarly refutation of an argument regarding the development of capitalism in the United States
   (E) discuss a new methodology for the study of the development of capitalism in the United States

Line　　Ecoefficiency (measures to minimize environmental impact through the reduction or elimination of waste from production processes) has become a goal for companies worldwide, with many realizing significant
(5)　cost savings from such innovations. Peter Senge and Goran Carstedt see this development as laudable but suggest that simply adopting ecoefficiency innovations could actually worsen environmental stresses in the future. Such innovations reduce production waste but
(10)　do not alter the number of products manufactured nor the waste generated from their use and discard; indeed, most companies invest in ecoefficiency improvements in order to increase profits and growth. Moreover, there is no guarantee that increased
(15)　economic growth from ecoefficiency will come in similarly ecoefficient ways, since in today's global markets, greater profits may be turned into investment capital that could easily be reinvested in traditionally eco-inefficient industries. Even a vastly more
(20)　ecoefficient industrial system could, were it to grow much larger, generate more total waste and destroy more habitat and species than would a smaller, less ecoefficient economy. Senge and Carstedt argue that to preserve the global environment and sustain
(25)　economic growth, businesses must develop a new systemic approach that reduces total material use and total accumulated waste. Focusing exclusively on ecoefficiency, which offers a compelling business case according to established thinking, may distract
(30)　companies from pursuing radically different products and business models.

Questions 8–10 refer to the passage.

8. The primary purpose of the passage is to

   (A) explain why a particular business strategy has been less successful than was once anticipated
   (B) propose an alternative to a particular business strategy that has inadvertently caused ecological damage
   (C) present a concern about the possible consequences of pursuing a particular business strategy
   (D) make a case for applying a particular business strategy on a larger scale than is currently practiced
   (E) suggest several possible outcomes of companies' failure to understand the economic impact of a particular business strategy

9. The passage mentions which of the following as a possible consequence of a company's realization of greater profits through ecoefficiency?

   (A) The companies may be able to sell a greater number of products by lowering prices.
   (B) The companies may be better able to attract investment capital in the global market.
   (C) The profits may be reinvested to increase economic growth through ecoefficiency.
   (D) The profits may be used as investment capital for industries that are not ecoefficient.
   (E) The profits may encourage companies to make further innovations in reducing production waste.

10. The passage implies that which of the following is a possible consequence of a company's adoption of innovations that increase its ecoefficiency?

    (A) Company profits resulting from such innovations may be reinvested in that company with no guarantee that the company will continue to make further improvements in ecoefficiency.

    (B) Company growth fostered by cost savings from such innovations may allow that company to manufacture a greater number of products that will be used and discarded, thus worsening environmental stress.

    (C) A company that fails to realize significant cost savings from such innovations may have little incentive to continue to minimize the environmental impact of its production processes.

    (D) A company that comes to depend on such innovations to increase its profits and growth may be vulnerable in the global market to competition from traditionally eco-inefficient industries.

    (E) A company that meets its ecoefficiency goals is unlikely to invest its increased profits in the development of new and innovative ecoefficiency measures.

In 1971 researchers hoping to predict earthquakes in the short term by identifying precursory phenomena (those that occur a few days before large quakes but not otherwise) turned their attention to changes
(5) in seismic waves that had been detected prior to earthquakes. An explanation for such changes was offered by "dilatancy theory," based on a well-known phenomenon observed in rocks in the laboratory: as stress builds, microfractures in rock close,
(10) decreasing the rock's volume. But as stress continues to increase, the rock begins to crack and expand in volume, allowing groundwater to seep in, weakening the rock. According to this theory, such effects could lead to several precursory phenomena in
(15) the field, including a change in the velocity of seismic waves, and an increase in small, nearby tremors.

Researchers initially reported success in identifying these possible precursors, but subsequent analyses of their data proved disheartening. Seismic waves
(20) with unusual velocities were recorded before some earthquakes, but while the historical record confirms that most large earthquakes are preceded by minor tremors, these foreshocks indicate nothing about the magnitude of an impending quake and are
(25) indistinguishable from other minor tremors that occur without large earthquakes.

In the 1980s, some researchers turned their efforts from short-term to long-term prediction. Noting that earthquakes tend to occur repeatedly in
(30) certain regions, Lindh and Baker attempted to identify patterns of recurrence, or earthquake cycles, on which to base predictions. In a study of earthquake-prone sites along the San Andreas Fault, they determined that quakes occurred at intervals of approximately 22
(35) years near one site and concluded that there was a 95 percent probability of an earthquake in that area by 1992. The earthquake did not occur within the time frame predicted, however.

Evidence against the kind of regular
(40) earthquake cycles that Lindh and Baker tried to establish has come from a relatively new field, paleoseismology. Paleoseismologists have unearthed and dated geological features such as fault scarps that were caused by
(45) earthquakes thousands of years ago. They have determined that the average interval between ten earthquakes that took place at one site along the San Andreas Fault in the past two millennia was 132 years, but individual intervals ranged greatly,
(50) from 44 to 332 years.

Questions 11–16 refer to the passage.

11. The passage is primarily concerned with

    (A) explaining why one method of earthquake prediction has proven more practicable than an alternative method
    (B) suggesting that accurate earthquake forecasting must combine elements of long-term and short-term prediction
    (C) challenging the usefulness of dilatancy theory for explaining the occurrence of precursory phenomena
    (D) discussing the deficiency of two methods by which researchers have attempted to predict the occurrence of earthquakes
    (E) describing the development of methods for establishing patterns in the occurrence of past earthquakes

12. According to the passage, laboratory evidence concerning the effects of stress on rocks might help account for

    (A) differences in magnitude among earthquakes
    (B) certain phenomena that occur prior to earthquakes
    (C) variations in the intervals between earthquakes in a particular area
    (D) differences in the frequency with which earthquakes occur in various areas
    (E) the unreliability of short-term earthquake predictions

13. It can be inferred from the passage that one problem with using precursory phenomena to predict earthquakes is that minor tremors

    (A) typically occur some distance from the sites of the large earthquakes that follow them
    (B) are directly linked to the mechanisms that cause earthquakes
    (C) are difficult to distinguish from major tremors
    (D) have proven difficult to measure accurately
    (E) are not always followed by large earthquakes

14. According to the passage, some researchers based their research about long-term earthquake prediction on which of the following facts?

    (A) The historical record confirms that most earthquakes have been preceded by minor tremors.
    (B) The average interval between earthquakes in one region of the San Andreas Fault is 132 years.
    (C) Some regions tend to be the site of numerous earthquakes over the course of many years.
    (D) Changes in the volume of rock can occur as a result of building stress and can lead to the weakening of rock.
    (E) Paleoseismologists have been able to unearth and date geological features caused by past earthquakes.

15. The passage suggests which of the following about the paleoseismologists' findings described in lines 42–50?

    (A) They suggest that the frequency with which earthquakes occurred at a particular site decreased significantly over the past two millennia.
    (B) They suggest that paleoseismologists may someday be able to make reasonably accurate long-term earthquake predictions.
    (C) They suggest that researchers may someday be able to determine which past occurrences of minor tremors were actually followed by large earthquakes.
    (D) They suggest that the recurrence of earthquakes in earthquake-prone sites is too irregular to serve as a basis for earthquake prediction.
    (E) They indicate that researchers attempting to develop long-term methods of earthquake prediction have overlooked important evidence concerning the causes of earthquakes.

16. The author implies which of the following about the ability of the researchers mentioned in line 17 to predict earthquakes?

    (A) They can identify when an earthquake is likely to occur but not how large it will be.
    (B) They can identify the regions where earthquakes are likely to occur but not when they will occur.
    (C) They are unable to determine either the time or the place that earthquakes are likely to occur.
    (D) They are likely to be more accurate at short-term earthquake prediction than at long-term earthquake prediction.
    (E) They can determine the regions where earthquakes have occurred in the past but not the regions where they are likely to occur in the future.

Line A key decision required of advertising managers is whether a "hard-sell" or "soft-sell" strategy is appropriate for a specific target market. The hard-sell approach involves the use of direct, forceful
(5) claims regarding the benefits of the advertised brand over competitors' offerings. In contrast, the soft-sell approach involves the use of advertising claims that imply superiority more subtly.

One positive aspect of the hard-sell approach is
(10) its use of very simple and straightforward product claims presented as explicit conclusions, with little room for confusion regarding the advertiser's message. However, some consumers may resent being told what to believe, and some may distrust
(15) the message. Resentment and distrust often lead to counterargumentation and to boomerang effects where consumers come to believe conclusions diametrically opposed to conclusions endorsed in advertising claims. By contrast, the risk of
(20) boomerang effects is greatly reduced with soft-sell approaches. One way to implement the soft-sell approach is to provide information that implies the main conclusions the advertiser wants the consumer to draw but leave the conclusions
(25) themselves unstated. Because consumers are invited to make up their own minds, implicit conclusions reduce the risk of resentment, distrust, and counterargumentation.

Recent research on consumer memory and
(30) judgment suggests another advantage of implicit conclusions. Beliefs or conclusions that are self-generated are more accessible from memory than beliefs from conclusions provided explicitly by other individuals and thus have a greater impact on
(35) judgment and decision making. Moreover, self-generated beliefs are often perceived as more accurate and valid than the beliefs of others, because other individuals may be perceived as less knowledgeable or may be perceived as
(40) manipulative or deliberately misleading.

Despite these advantages, implicit conclusions may not always be more effective than explicit conclusions. One risk is that some consumers may fail to draw their own conclusions and thus miss the
(45) point of the message. Inferential activity is likely only when consumers are motivated and able to engage in effortful cognitive processes. Another risk is that some consumers may draw conclusions other than the one intended. Even if inferential
(50) activity is likely, there is no guarantee that consumers will follow the path provided by the advertiser. Finally, a third risk is that consumers may infer the intended conclusion but question the validity of their inference.

Questions 17–23 refer to the passage.

17. It can be inferred from the passage that one reason an advertiser might prefer a hard-sell approach to a soft-sell approach is that

    (A) the risks of boomerang effects are minimized when the conclusions an advertiser wants the consumer to draw are themselves left unstated
    (B) counterargumentation is likely from consumers who fail to draw their own conclusions regarding an advertising claim
    (C) inferential activity is likely to occur even if consumers perceive themselves to be more knowledgeable than the individuals presenting product claims
    (D) research on consumer memory suggests that the explicit conclusions provided by an advertiser using the hard-sell approach have a significant impact on decision making
    (E) the information presented by an advertiser using the soft-sell approach may imply different conclusions to different consumers

18. Each of the following is mentioned in the passage as a characteristic of the hard-sell approach EXCEPT:

    (A) Its overall message is readily grasped.
    (B) It appeals to consumers' knowledge about the product.
    (C) It makes explicit claims that the advertised brand is superior to other brands.
    (D) It uses statements that are expressed very clearly.
    (E) It makes claims in the form of direct conclusions.

19. It can be inferred from the passage that advertisers could reduce one of the risks discussed in the last paragraph if they were able to provide

    (A) motivation for consumers to think about the advertisement's message
    (B) information that implies the advertiser's intended conclusion but leaves that conclusion unstated
    (C) subtle evidence that the advertised product is superior to that of competitors
    (D) information comparing the advertised product with its competitors
    (E) opportunity for consumers to generate their own beliefs or conclusions

20. The primary purpose of the passage is to

    (A) point out the risks involved in the use of a particular advertising strategy
    (B) make a case for the superiority of one advertising strategy over another
    (C) illustrate the ways in which two advertising strategies may be implemented
    (D) present the advantages and disadvantages of two advertising strategies
    (E) contrast the types of target markets for which two advertising strategies are appropriate

21. Which of the following best describes the function of the sentence in lines 25–28 in the context of the passage as a whole?

    (A) It reiterates a distinction between two advertising strategies that is made in the first paragraph.
    (B) It explains how a particular strategy avoids a drawback described earlier in the paragraph.
    (C) It suggests that a risk described earlier in the paragraph is less serious than some researchers believe it to be.
    (D) It outlines why the strategy described in the previous sentence involves certain risks for an advertiser.
    (E) It introduces an argument that will be refuted in the following paragraph.

22. It can be inferred from the passage that one situation in which the boomerang effect often occurs is when consumers

    (A) have been exposed to forceful claims that are diametrically opposed to those in an advertiser's message
    (B) have previous self-generated beliefs or conclusions that are readily accessible from memory
    (C) are subjected to advertising messages that are targeted at specific markets to which those consumers do not belong
    (D) are confused regarding the point of the advertiser's message
    (E) come to view the advertiser's message with suspicion

23. It can be inferred from the passage that the research mentioned in line 29 supports which of the following statements?

    (A) Implicit conclusions are more likely to capture accurately the point of the advertiser's message than are explicit conclusions.
    (B) Counterargumentation is less likely to occur if an individual's beliefs or conclusions are readily accessible from memory.
    (C) The hard-sell approach results in conclusions that are more difficult for the consumer to recall than are conclusions resulting from the soft-sell approach.
    (D) When the beliefs of others are presented as definite and forceful claims, they are perceived to be as accurate as self-generated beliefs.
    (E) Despite the advantages of implicit conclusions, the hard-sell approach involves fewer risks for the advertiser than does the soft-sell approach.

Line Suppose we were in a spaceship in free fall, where objects are weightless, and wanted to know a small solid object's mass. We could not simply balance that object against another of known weight, as we
(5) would on Earth. The unknown mass could be determined, however, by placing the object on a spring scale and swinging the scale in a circle at the end of a string. The scale would measure the tension in the string, which would depend on both
(10) the speed of revolution and the mass of the object. The tension would be greater, the greater the mass or the greater the speed of revolution. From the measured tension and speed of whirling, we could determine the object's mass.
(15) Astronomers use an analogous procedure to "weigh" double-star systems. The speed with which the two stars in a double-star system circle one another depends on the gravitational force between them, which holds the system together. This
(20) attractive force, analogous to the tension in the string, is proportional to the stars' combined mass, according to Newton's law of gravitation. By observing the time required for the stars to circle each other (the period) and measuring the distance
(25) between them, we can deduce the restraining force and hence the masses.

Questions 24–28 refer to the passage.

24. It can be inferred from the passage that the two procedures described in the passage have which of the following in common?

    (A) They have been applied in practice.
    (B) They rely on the use of a device that measures tension.
    (C) Their purpose is to determine an unknown mass.
    (D) They can only be applied to small solid objects.
    (E) They involve attraction between objects of similar mass.

25. According to the passage, the tension in the string mentioned in lines 8–9 is analogous to which of the following aspects of a double-star system?

    (A) The speed with which one star orbits the other
    (B) The gravitational attraction between the stars
    (C) The amount of time it takes for the stars to circle one another
    (D) The distance between the two stars
    (E) The combined mass of the two stars

26. Which of the following best describes the relationship between the first and the second paragraph of the passage?

    (A) The first paragraph provides an illustration useful for understanding a procedure described in the second paragraph.
    (B) The first paragraph describes a hypothetical situation whose plausibility is tested in the second paragraph.
    (C) The first paragraph evaluates the usefulness of a procedure whose application is described further in the second paragraph.
    (D) The second paragraph provides evidence to support a claim made in the first paragraph.
    (E) The second paragraph analyzes the practical implications of a methodology proposed in the first paragraph.

27. The author of the passage mentions observations regarding the period of a double-star system as being useful for determining

   (A) the distance between the two stars in the system
   (B) the time it takes for each star to rotate on its axis
   (C) the size of the orbit the system's two stars occupy
   (D) the degree of gravitational attraction between the system's stars
   (E) the speed at which the star system moves through space

28. The primary purpose of the passage is to

   (A) analyze a natural phenomenon in terms of its behavior under special conditions
   (B) describe the steps by which a scientific measurement is carried out
   (C) point out the conditions under which a scientific procedure is most useful
   (D) contrast two different uses of a methodological approach in science
   (E) explain a method by which scientists determine an unknown quantity

The following is based on material written in 1996.

The Montreal Protocol on Substances that Deplete the Ozone Layer, signed in 1987 by more than 150 nations, has attained its short-term goals:
(5) It has decreased the rate of increase in amounts of most ozone-depleting chemicals reaching the atmosphere and has even reduced the atmospheric levels of some of them. The projection that the ozone layer will substantially recover from ozone
(10) depletion by 2050 is based on the assumption that the protocol's regulations will be strictly followed. Yet there is considerable evidence of violations, particularly in the form of the release of ozone-depleting chlorofluorocarbons (CFCs), which are
(15) commonly used in the refrigeration, heating, and air-conditioning industries. These violations reflect industry attitudes; for example, in the United States, 48% of respondents in a recent survey of subscribers to *Air Conditioning, Heating, and Refrigeration News*,
(20) an industry trade journal, said that they did not believe that CFCs damage the ozone layer. Moreover, some in the industry apparently do not want to pay for CFC substitutes, which can run five times the cost of CFCs. Consequently, a black market in imported
(25) illicit CFCs has grown. Estimates of the contraband CFC trade range from 10,000 to 22,000 tons a year, with most of the CFCs originating in India and China, whose agreements under the Protocol still allow them to produce CFCs. In fact, the United States Customs
(30) Service reports that CFCs are a contraband problem second only to illicit drugs.

Questions 29–31 refer to the passage.

29. The passage suggests which of the following about the illicit trade in CFCs?

    (A) It would cease if manufacturers in India and China stopped producing CFCs.
    (B) Most people who participate in such trade do not believe that CFCs deplete the ozone layer.
    (C) It will probably surpass illicit drugs as the largest contraband problem faced by the United States Customs Service.
    (D) It is fostered by people who do not want to pay the price of CFC substitutes.
    (E) It has grown primarily because of the expansion of the refrigeration, heating, and air-conditioning industries in other countries.

30. According to the passage, which of the following best describes most ozone-depleting chemicals in 1996 as compared to those in 1987?

    (A) The levels of such chemicals in the atmosphere had decreased.
    (B) The number of such chemicals that reached the atmosphere had declined.
    (C) The amounts of such chemicals released had increased, but the amounts that reached the atmosphere had decreased.
    (D) The rate of increase in amounts of such chemicals reaching the atmosphere had decreased.
    (E) The rate at which such chemicals were being reduced in the atmosphere had slowed.

31. The author of the passage compares the smuggling of CFCs to the illicit drug trade most likely for which of the following reasons?

    (A) To qualify a previous claim
    (B) To emphasize the extent of a problem
    (C) To provide an explanation for an earlier assertion
    (D) To suggest that the illicit CFC trade, like the illicit drug trade, will continue to increase
    (E) To suggest that the consequences of a relatively little-known problem are as serious as those of a well-known one

Most pre-1990 literature on businesses' use of information technology (IT)—defined as any form of computer-based information system—focused on spectacular IT successes and reflected a general
(5) optimism concerning IT's potential as a resource for creating competitive advantage. But toward the end of the 1980s, some economists spoke of a "productivity paradox": despite huge IT investments, most notably in the service sectors, productivity
(10) stagnated. In the retail industry, for example, in which IT had been widely adopted during the 1980s, productivity (average output per hour) rose at an average annual rate of 1.1 percent between 1973 and 1989, compared with 2.4 percent in the preceding
(15) 25-year period. Proponents of IT argued that it takes both time and a critical mass of investment for IT to yield benefits, and some suggested that growth figures for the 1990s proved these benefits were finally being realized. They also argued that measures
(20) of productivity ignore what would have happened without investments in IT—productivity gains might have been even lower. There were even claims that IT had improved the performance of the service sector significantly, although macroeconomic measures of
(25) productivity did not reflect the improvement.

But some observers questioned why, if IT had conferred economic value, it did not produce direct competitive advantages for individual firms. Resource-based theory offers an answer, asserting
(30) that, in general, firms gain competitive advantages by accumulating resources that are economically valuable, relatively scarce, and not easily replicated. According to a recent study of retail firms, which confirmed that IT has become pervasive and
(35) relatively easy to acquire, IT by itself appeared to have conferred little advantage. In fact, though little evidence of any direct effect was found, the frequent negative correlations between IT and performance suggested that IT had probably weakened some
(40) firms' competitive positions. However, firms' human resources, in and of themselves, did explain improved performance, and some firms gained IT-related advantages by merging IT with complementary resources, particularly human resources. The findings
(45) support the notion, founded in resource-based theory, that competitive advantages do not arise from easily replicated resources, no matter how impressive or economically valuable they may be, but from complex, intangible resources.

Questions 32–39 refer to the passage.

32. The passage is primarily concerned with

    (A) describing a resource and indicating various methods used to study it
    (B) presenting a theory and offering an opposing point of view
    (C) providing an explanation for unexpected findings
    (D) demonstrating why a particular theory is unfounded
    (E) resolving a disagreement regarding the uses of a technology

33. The author of the passage discusses productivity in the retail industry in the first paragraph primarily in order to

    (A) suggest a way in which IT can be used to create a competitive advantage
    (B) provide an illustration of the "productivity paradox"
    (C) emphasize the practical value of the introduction of IT
    (D) cite an industry in which productivity did not stagnate during the 1980s
    (E) counter the argument that IT could potentially create competitive advantage

34. The passage suggests that proponents of resource-based theory would be likely to explain IT's inability to produce direct competitive advantages for individual firms by pointing out that

    (A) IT is not a resource that is difficult to obtain
    (B) IT is not an economically valuable resource
    (C) IT is a complex, intangible resource
    (D) economic progress has resulted from IT only in the service sector
    (E) changes brought about by IT cannot be detected by macroeconomic measures

35. Which of the following best describes the content of the first paragraph?

   (A) It presents two explanations for the success of IT.
   (B) It provides evidence that decreases in productivity will continue.
   (C) It presents reasons for a decline in productivity.
   (D) It demonstrates the effect IT has had on productivity.
   (E) It contrasts views concerning the degree of IT's success.

36. The passage suggests that the recent study of retail firms discussed in the second paragraph supports which of the following conclusions regarding a firm's competitive advantage?

   (A) Human resources alone are more likely to contribute to competitive advantage than is IT alone.
   (B) Human resources combined with IT are more likely than human resources alone to have a negative effect on competitive advantage.
   (C) Human resources combined with IT often have a negative effect on competitive advantage.
   (D) IT by itself is much more likely to have a positive effect than a negative effect on competitive advantage.
   (E) The positive effect of IT on competitive advantage increases with time.

37. According to the passage, most pre-1990 literature on businesses' use of IT included which of the following?

   (A) Recommendations regarding effective ways to use IT to gain competitive advantage
   (B) Explanations of the advantages and disadvantages of adopting IT
   (C) Information about ways in which IT combined with human resources could be used to increase competitive advantage
   (D) A warning regarding the negative effect on competitive advantage that would occur if IT were not adopted
   (E) A belief in the likelihood of increased competitive advantage for firms using IT

38. The author of the passage implies that toward the end of the 1980s, some economists described which of the following as a "productivity paradox" (see line 8)?

   (A) Investments in IT would not result in increases in productivity until the 1990s.
   (B) Investments in IT did not lead to expected gains in productivity.
   (C) Productivity in the retail industry rose less rapidly than did productivity in other industries.
   (D) The gains in productivity due to the introduction of IT were not reflected in macroeconomic measures of productivity.
   (E) Most gains in productivity occurred in the service sector and were therefore particularly difficult to measure.

39. According to the passage, the recent study of retail firms discussed in the second paragraph (lines 33–36) best supports which of the following assessments of IT's potential?

   (A) Even when IT gives a firm a temporary competitive advantage, that firm is unlikely to continue to achieve productivity gains.
   (B) The competitive advantages conferred by a firm's introduction of IT are outweighed by IT's development costs.
   (C) A firm's introduction of IT is less likely to limit its ability to achieve productivity gains than to enhance that ability.
   (D) Although IT by itself is unlikely to give a firm a competitive advantage, IT combined with other resources may do so.
   (E) Although IT by itself is unlikely to give a firm a competitive advantage, a firm that does not employ IT cannot achieve a competitive advantage.

Line   The Black Death, a severe epidemic that ravaged fourteenth-century Europe, has intrigued scholars ever since Francis Gasquet's 1893 study contending that this epidemic greatly intensified the political
(5) and religious upheaval that ended the Middle Ages. Thirty-six years later, historian George Coulton agreed but, paradoxically, attributed a silver lining to the Black Death: prosperity engendered by diminished competition for food, shelter, and work led survivors
(10) of the epidemic into the Renaissance and subsequent rise of modern Europe.
     In the 1930s, however, Evgeny Kosminsky and other Marxist historians claimed the epidemic was merely an ancillary factor contributing to a general
(15) agrarian crisis stemming primarily from the inevitable decay of European feudalism. In arguing that this decline of feudalism was economically determined, the Marxist asserted that the Black Death was a relatively insignificant factor. This became the prevailing view
(20) until after the Second World War, when studies of specific regions and towns revealed astonishing mortality rates ascribed to the epidemic, thus restoring the central role of the Black Death in history.
     This central role of the Black Death (traditionally
(25) attributed to bubonic plague brought from Asia) has been recently challenged from another direction. Building on bacteriologist John Shrewsbury's speculations about mislabeled epidemics, zoologist Graham Twigg employs urban case studies suggesting
(30) that the rat population in Europe was both too sparse and insufficiently migratory to have spread plague. Moreover, Twigg disputes the traditional trade-ship explanation for plague transmissions by extrapolating from data on the number of dead rats aboard Nile
(35) sailing vessels in 1912. The Black Death, which he conjectures was anthrax instead of bubonic plague, therefore caused far less havoc and fewer deaths than historians typically claim.
     Although correctly citing the exacting conditions
(40) needed to start or spread bubonic plague, Twigg ignores virtually a century of scholarship contradictory to his findings and employs faulty logic in his single-minded approach to the Black Death. His speculative generalizations about the numbers of rats in medieval
(45) Europe are based on isolated studies unrepresentative of medieval conditions, while his unconvincing trade-ship argument overlooks land-based caravans, the overland migration of infected rodents, and the many other animals that carry plague.

Questions 40–43 refer to the passage.

40. The passage suggests that Twigg believes that rats could not have spread the Black Death unless which of the following were true?

   (A) The rats escaped from ships that had been in Asia.
   (B) The rats were immune to the diseases that they carried.
   (C) The rat population was larger in medieval Europe than Twigg believes it actually was.
   (D) The rat population primarily infested densely populated areas.
   (E) The rats interacted with other animals that Twigg believes could have carried plague.

41. According to the passage, the post–Second World War studies that altered the prevailing view of the Black Death involved which of the following?

   (A) Determining the death rates caused by the Black Death in specific regions and towns
   (B) Demonstrating how the Black Death intensified the political and religious upheaval that ended the Middle Ages
   (C) Presenting evidence to prove that many medieval epidemics were mislabeled
   (D) Arguing that the consequences of the Black Death led to the Renaissance and the rise of modern Europe
   (E) Employing urban case studies to determine the number of rats in medieval Europe

42. The "silver lining to the Black Death" (lines 7–8) refers to which of the following?

    (A) The decay of European feudalism precipitated by the Black Death
    (B) Greater availability of employment, sustenance, and housing for survivors of the epidemic
    (C) Strengthening of the human species through natural selection
    (D) Better understanding of how to limit the spread of contagious diseases
    (E) Immunities and resistance to the Black Death gained by later generations

43. The author's attitude toward Twigg's work is best characterized as which of the following?

    (A) Dismissive
    (B) Indifferent
    (C) Vindictive
    (D) Cautious
    (E) Ambivalent

This passage is based on an article written in 2000.

The traditional model of employer-employee relations in the United States was a "psychological contract" in which employees made long-term
(5) commitments to organizations in exchange for long-term job security, training and development, and internal opportunities for promotion. Beginning mainly with the recession in the early 1970s, this paradigm began to unravel. Organizations began
(10) using extensive downsizing and outsourcing to decrease the number of permanent employees in the workforce. Among employees, this situation has resulted in a decided shift in desire: instead of working their way up in an organization, many now
(15) prefer to work their way out. Entrepreneurship and small business administration are now the fastest-growing majors in business schools.

Several factors have generated movement from the old paradigm to the new one. Organizations have
(20) had legitimate and pressing reasons to shift to a new paradigm of employer-employee relations. Large numbers of permanent employees make it difficult for organizations to respond quickly to downturns in demand by decreasing payroll costs. The enormous
(25) rise in wrongful discharge suits has created incentives for organizations to use temporary, contract, and leased employees in order to distance themselves from potential litigation problems. Moreover, top management is under increased pressure from
(30) shareholders to generate higher and higher levels of return on investment in the short run, resulting in declines in hiring, increases in layoffs, and shortage of funds for employee development.

At the same time, a lack of forthrightness on the
(35) part of organizations has led to increased cynicism among employees about management's motivation and competence. Employees are now working 15 percent more hours per week than they were 20 years ago, but organizations acknowledge this fact only
(40) by running stress-management workshops to help employees to cope. Salespeople are being asked to increase sales at the same time organizations have cut travel, phone, and advertising budgets. Employees could probably cope effectively with changes in the
(45) psychological contract if organizations were more forthright about how they were changing it. But the euphemistic jargon used by executives to justify the changes they are implementing frequently backfires; rather than engendering sympathy for management's
(50) position, it sparks employees' desire to be free of the organization altogether. In a recent study of employees' attitudes about management, 49 percent of the sample strongly agreed that "management will take advantage of you if given the chance."

Questions 44–47 refer to the passage.

44. Which of the following is NOT mentioned in the passage as a characteristic of the traditional model of employer-employee relations in the United States?

   (A) Attractive compensation packages for employees
   (B) Opportunities for employees to receive training
   (C) Long-term job security for employees
   (D) Opportunities for employee advancement within a company
   (E) Long-term commitment toward a company by employees

45. According to the passage, managers' motivation for engaging in measures such as increased layoffs is often a result of

   (A) the hope that a smaller workforce will decrease the managers' own workloads
   (B) shareholder pressure to generate increased short-term financial gains
   (C) a desire to eradicate the idea of a "psychological contract"
   (D) dissatisfaction with the performance of disgruntled employees
   (E) a desire to appear to be following modern organizational trends

46. The passage suggests that which of the following is a legitimate reason for organizations' shift to the new model of employer-employee relations?

    (A) Organizations tend to operate more effectively when they have a high manager-to-employee ratio.
    (B) Organizations can move their operations to less-expensive locations more easily when they have fewer permanent employees.
    (C) Organizations have found that they often receive higher-quality work when they engage in outsourcing.
    (D) Organizations with large pools of permanent workers risk significant financial losses if the demand for their product or service decreases.
    (E) Organizations are under increasing pressure to adopt new technologies that often obviate the need for certain workers.

47. Which of the following best characterizes the function of the final sentence of the passage?

    (A) It suggests an alternative explanation for a phenomenon discussed earlier in the passage.
    (B) It provides data intended to correct a common misconception.
    (C) It further weakens an argument that is being challenged by the author.
    (D) It introduces a specific piece of evidence in support of a claim made at the beginning of the final paragraph.
    (E) It answers a question that is implicit in the preceding sentence.

Questions 48 to 109 — Difficulty: Medium

Line   The dry mountain ranges of the western United
       States contain rocks dating back 440 to 510 million
       years, to the Ordovician period, and teeming with
       evidence of tropical marine life. This rock record
(5)   provides clues about one of the most significant
       radiations (periods when existing life-forms gave rise
       to variations that would eventually evolve into entirely
       new species) in the history of marine invertebrates.
       During this radiation the number of marine biological
(10)   families increased greatly, and these families included
       species that would dominate the marine ecosystems
       of the area for the next 215 million years. Although
       the radiation spanned tens of millions of years,
       major changes in many species occurred during a
(15)   geologically short time span within the radiation and,
       furthermore, appear to have occurred worldwide,
       suggesting that external events were major factors
       in the radiation. In fact, there is evidence of major
       ecological and geological changes during this period:
(20)   the sea level dropped drastically and mountain ranges
       were formed. In this instance, rather than leading to
       large-scale extinctions, these kinds of environmental
       changes may have resulted in an enriched pattern of
       habitats and nutrients, which in turn gave rise to the
(25)   Ordovician radiation. However, the actual relationship
       between these environmental factors and the
       diversification of life-forms is not yet fully understood.

Questions 48–50 refer to the passage.

48. The passage is primarily concerned with

   (A) evaluating the evidence of a major geologic period and determining its duration
   (B) describing an evolutionary phenomenon and speculating about its cause
   (C) explaining the mechanisms through which marine life-forms evolved during a particular period
   (D) analyzing the impact on later life-forms of an important evolutionary development
   (E) contrasting a period of evolutionary change with other such periods

49. Which of the following can be inferred from the passage regarding the geologic changes that occurred during the Ordovician period?

   (A) They were more drastic than those associated with other radiations.
   (B) They may have created conditions favorable to the evolution of many new life-forms.
   (C) They may have caused the extinction of many of the marine species living in shallow waters.
   (D) They may have been a factor in the development of new species adapted to living both on land and in water.
   (E) They hastened the formation of the extensive dry regions found in the western United States.

50. Which of the following best describes the function of the last sentence of the passage?

   (A) It points out that the events described in the passage may be atypical.
   (B) It alludes to the fact that there is disagreement in the scientific community over the importance of the Ordovician radiation.
   (C) It concludes that the evidence presented in the passage is insufficient to support the proposed hypothesis because it comes from a limited geographic area.
   (D) It warns the reader against seeing a connection between the biological and geologic changes described in the passage.
   (E) It alerts the reader that current knowledge cannot completely explain the relationship suggested by the evidence presented in the passage.

Line   Seventeenth-century philosopher John Locke stated that as much as 99 percent of the value of any useful product can be attributed to "the effects of labor." For Locke's intellectual heirs, it was only a short step
(5) to the "labor theory of value," whose formulators held that 100 percent of the value of any product is generated by labor (the human work needed to produce goods) and that therefore the employer who appropriates any part of the product's value as profit
(10) is practicing theft.
    Although human effort is required to produce goods for the consumer market, effort is also invested in making capital goods (tools, machines, etc.), which are used to facilitate the production of consumer
(15) goods. In modern economies about one-third of the total output of consumer goods is attributable to the use of capital goods. Approximately two-thirds of the income derived from this total output is paid out to workers as wages and salaries, the remaining
(20) third serving as compensation to the owners of the capital goods. Moreover, part of this remaining third is received by workers who are shareholders, pension beneficiaries, and the like. The labor theory of value systematically disregards the productive contribution
(25) of capital goods—a failing for which Locke must bear part of the blame.

Questions 51–56 refer to the passage.

51. The author of the passage is primarily concerned with

    (A) criticizing Locke's economic theories
    (B) discounting the contribution of labor in a modern economy
    (C) questioning the validity of the labor theory of value
    (D) arguing for a more equitable distribution of business profits
    (E) contending that employers are overcompensated for capital goods

52. According to the author of the passage, which of the following is true of the distribution of the income derived from the total output of consumer goods in a modern economy?

    (A) Workers receive a share of this income that is significantly smaller than the value of their labor as a contribution to total output.
    (B) Owners of capital goods receive a share of this income that is significantly greater than the contribution to total output attributable to the use of capital goods.
    (C) Owners of capital goods receive a share of this income that is no greater than the proportion of total output attributable to the use of capital goods.
    (D) Owners of capital goods are not fully compensated for their investment because they pay out most of their share of this income to workers as wages and benefits.
    (E) Workers receive a share of this income that is greater than the value of their labor because the labor theory of value overestimates their contribution to total output.

53. Which of the following statements, if true, would most effectively counter the author's criticism of Locke at the end of the passage?

    (A) Locke was unfamiliar with the labor theory of value as it was formulated by his intellectual heirs.
    (B) In Locke's day, there was no possibility of ordinary workers becoming shareholders or pension beneficiaries.
    (C) During Locke's lifetime, capital goods did not make a significant productive contribution to the economy.
    (D) The precise statistical calculation of the productive contributions of labor and capital goods is not possible without computers.
    (E) The terms "capital goods" and "consumer goods" were coined by modern economists and do not appear in Locke's writings.

54. Which of the following best describes the organization of the passage?

    (A) The author explores the origins of a theory and explains why the theory never gained widespread acceptance.
    (B) The author introduces the premise of a theory, evaluates the premise by relating it to objective reality, then proposes a modification of the theory.
    (C) After quoting a well-known authority, the author describes the evolution of a theory, then traces its modern form back to the original quotation.
    (D) After citing a precursor of a theory, the author outlines and refutes the theory, then links its flaw to the precursor.
    (E) After tracing the roots of a theory, the author attempts to undermine the theory by discrediting its originator.

55. Which of the following arguments would a proponent of the labor theory of value, as it is presented in the first paragraph, be most likely to use in response to lines 23–25?

    (A) The productive contributions of workers and capital goods cannot be compared because the productive life span of capital goods is longer than that of workers.
    (B) The author's analysis of the distribution of income is misleading because only a small percentage of workers are also shareholders.
    (C) Capital goods are valuable only insofar as they contribute directly to the production of consumer goods.
    (D) The productive contribution of capital goods must be discounted because capital goods require maintenance.
    (E) The productive contribution of capital goods must be attributed to labor because capital goods are themselves products of labor.

56. The author of the passage implies which of the following regarding the formulators of the labor theory of value?

    (A) They came from a working-class background.
    (B) Their views were too radical to have popular appeal.
    (C) At least one of them was a close contemporary of Locke.
    (D) They were familiar with Locke's views on the relationship between labor and the value of products.
    (E) They underestimated the importance of consumer goods in a modern economy.

Line   Exactly when in the early modern era Native
Americans began exchanging animal furs with
Europeans for European-made goods is uncertain.
What is fairly certain, even though they left
(5)   no written evidence of having done so, is that
the first Europeans to conduct such trade during
the modern period were fishing crews working the
waters around Newfoundland. Archaeologists had
noticed that sixteenth-century Native American
(10)   sites were strewn with iron bolts and metal
pins. Only later, upon reading Nicolas Denys's
1672 account of seventeenth-century European
settlements in North America, did archaeologists
realize that sixteenth-century European fishing
(15)   crews had dismantled and exchanged parts of their
ships for furs.
    By the time Europeans sailing the Atlantic coast
of North America first documented the fur trade, it
was apparently well underway. The first to record
(20)   such trade—the captain of a Portuguese vessel
sailing from Newfoundland in 1501—observed that a
Native American aboard the ship wore Venetian silver
earrings. Another early chronicler noted in 1524 that
Native Americans living along the coast of what is now
(25)   New England had become selective about European
trade goods: they accepted only knives, fishhooks,
and sharp metal. By the time Cartier sailed the Saint
Lawrence River ten years later, Native Americans had
traded with Europeans for more than thirty years,
(30)   perhaps half a century.

Questions 57–65 refer to the passage.

57. The author of the passage draws conclusions about the fur trade in North America from all of the following sources EXCEPT

    (A) Cartier's accounts of trading with Native Americans
    (B) a seventeenth-century account of European settlements
    (C) a sixteenth-century account written by a sailing vessel captain
    (D) archaeological observations of sixteenth-century Native American sites
    (E) a sixteenth-century account of Native Americans in what is now New England

58. The passage suggests that which of the following is partially responsible for the difficulty in establishing the precise date when the fur trade in North America began?

    (A) A lack of written accounts before that of Nicolas Denys in 1672
    (B) A lack of written documentation before 1501
    (C) Ambiguities in the evidence from Native American sources
    (D) Uncertainty about Native American trade networks
    (E) Uncertainty about the origin of artifacts supposedly traded by European fishing crews for furs

59. Which of the following, if true, most strengthens the author's assertion in the first sentence of the second paragraph?

    (A) When Europeans retraced Cartier's voyage in the first years of the seventeenth century, they frequently traded with Native Americans.
    (B) Furs from beavers, which were plentiful in North America but nearly extinct in Europe, became extremely fashionable in Europe in the final decades of the sixteenth century.
    (C) Firing arms were rarely found on sixteenth-century Native American sites or on European lists of trading goods since such arms required frequent maintenance and repair.
    (D) Europeans and Native Americans had established trade protocols, such as body language assuring one another of their peaceful intentions, that antedate the earliest records of trade.
    (E) During the first quarter of the sixteenth century, an Italian explorer recorded seeing many Native Americans with what appeared to be copper beads, though they may have been made of indigenous copper.

60. Which of the following best describes the primary function of lines 11–16?

    (A) It offers a reconsideration of a claim made in the preceding sentence.
    (B) It reveals how archaeologists arrived at an interpretation of the evidence mentioned in the preceding sentence.
    (C) It shows how scholars misinterpreted the significance of certain evidence mentioned in the preceding sentence.
    (D) It identifies one of the first significant accounts of seventeenth-century European settlements in North America.
    (E) It explains why Denys's account of seventeenth-century European settlements is thought to be significant.

61. It can be inferred from the passage that the author would agree with which of the following statements about the fur trade between Native Americans and Europeans in the early modern era?

    (A) This trade may have begun as early as the 1480s.
    (B) This trade probably did not continue much beyond the 1530s.
    (C) This trade was most likely at its peak in the mid-1520s.
    (D) This trade probably did not begin prior to 1500.
    (E) There is no written evidence of this trade prior to the seventeenth century.

62. Which of the following can be inferred from the passage about the Native Americans mentioned in line 24?

    (A) They had little use for decorative objects such as earrings.
    (B) They became increasingly dependent on fishing between 1501 and 1524.
    (C) By 1524, only certain groups of Europeans were willing to trade with them.
    (D) The selectivity of their trading choices made it difficult for them to engage in widespread trade with Europeans.
    (E) The selectivity of their trading choices indicates that they had been trading with Europeans for a significant period of time prior to 1524.

63. The passage supports which of the following statements about sixteenth-century European fishing crews working the waters off Newfoundland?

    (A) They wrote no accounts of their fishing voyages.
    (B) They primarily sailed under the flag of Portugal.
    (C) They exchanged ship parts with Native Americans for furs.
    (D) They commonly traded jewelry with Native Americans for furs.
    (E) They carried surplus metal implements to trade with Native Americans for furs.

64. Which of the following can be inferred from the passage about evidence pertaining to the fur trade between Native Americans and Europeans in the early modern era?

    (A) A lack of written evidence has made it difficult to establish which Europeans first participated in this trade.
    (B) In general, the physical evidence pertaining to this trade has been more useful than the written evidence has been.
    (C) There is more written evidence pertaining to this trade from the early part of the sixteenth century than from later in that century.
    (D) The earliest written evidence pertaining to this trade dates from a time when the trade was already well established.
    (E) Some important pieces of evidence pertaining to this trade, such as Denys's 1672 account, were long overlooked by archaeologists.

65. The passage suggests which of the following about the sixteenth-century Native Americans who traded with Europeans on the coast of what is now called New England?

    (A) By 1524, they had become accustomed to exchanging goods with Europeans.
    (B) They were unfamiliar with metals before encountering Europeans.
    (C) They had no practical uses for European goods other than metals and metal implements.
    (D) By 1524, they had become disdainful of European traders because such traders had treated them unfairly in the past.
    (E) By 1524, they demanded only the most prized European goods because they had come to realize how valuable furs were on European markets.

Line   Determining whether a given population of animals constitutes a distinct species can be difficult because no single accepted definition of the term exists. One approach, called the biological species
(5) concept, bases the definition on reproductive compatibility. According to this view, a species is a group of animals that can mate with one another to produce fertile offspring but cannot mate successfully with members of a different
(10) group. Yet this idea can be too restrictive. First, mating between groups labeled as different species (hybridization), as often occurs in the canine family, is quite common in nature. Second, sometimes the differences between two populations might not
(15) prevent them from interbreeding, even though they are dissimilar in traits unrelated to reproduction; some biologists question whether such disparate groups should be considered a single species. A third problem with the biological species concept is
(20) that investigators cannot always determine whether two groups that live in different places are capable of interbreeding.
    When the biological species concept is difficult to apply, some investigators use phenotype, an
(25) organism's observable characteristics, instead. Two groups that have evolved separately are likely to display measurable differences in many of their traits, such as skull size or width of teeth. If the distribution of measurements from one group does
(30) not overlap with those of another, the two groups might reasonably be considered distinct species.

Questions 66–69 refer to the passage.

66. The passage is primarily concerned with

    (A) describing the development of the biological species concept
    (B) responding to a critique of reproductive compatibility as a criterion for defining a species
    (C) considering two different approaches to identifying biological species
    (D) pointing out the advantage of one method of distinguishing related species
    (E) identifying an obstacle to the classification of biological species

67. The author of the passage mentions "groups that live in different places" (line 21) most probably in order to

    (A) point out a theoretical inconsistency in the biological species concept
    (B) offer evidence in support of the biological species concept
    (C) identify an obstacle to the application of the biological species concept
    (D) note an instance in which phenotype classification is customarily used
    (E) describe an alternative to the biological species concept

68. With which of the following statements regarding the classification of individual species would the author most likely agree?

    (A) Phenotype comparison may help to classify species when application of the biological species concept proves inconclusive.

    (B) Because no standard definition exists for what constitutes a species, the classification of animal populations is inevitably an arbitrary process.

    (C) The criteria used by biologists to classify species have not been based on adequate research.

    (D) The existence of hybrids in wild animal species is the chief factor casting doubt on the usefulness of research into reproductive compatibility as a way of classifying species.

    (E) Phenotype overlap should be used as the basic criterion for standardizing species classification.

69. Which of the following best describes the function of lines 10–13?

    (A) It elaborates the definition of the biological species concept given in a previous sentence.

    (B) It develops a point about the biological species concept made in the previous sentence.

    (C) It states the author's central point about the biological species concept.

    (D) It identifies a central assumption underlying the biological species concept.

    (E) It demonstrates why the biological species concept is invalid.

Researchers studying how genes control animal behavior have had to deal with many uncertainties. In the first place, most behaviors are governed by more than one gene, and until recently geneticists
(5) had no method for identifying the multiple genes involved. In addition, even when a single gene is found to control a behavior, researchers in different fields do not necessarily agree that it is a "behavioral gene." Neuroscientists, whose interest
(10) in genetic research is to understand the nervous system (which generates behavior), define the term broadly. But ethologists—specialists in animal behavior—are interested in evolution, so they define the term narrowly. They insist that mutations
(15) in a behavioral gene must alter a specific normal behavior and not merely make the organism ill, so that the genetically induced behavioral change will provide variation that natural selection can act upon, possibly leading to the evolution of a new species.
(20) For example, in the fruit fly, researchers have identified the gene Shaker, mutations in which cause flies to shake violently under anesthesia. Since shaking is not healthy, ethologists do not consider Shaker a behavioral gene. In contrast, ethologists
(25) do consider the gene period (per), which controls the fruit fly's circadian (24-hour) rhythm, a behavioral gene because flies with mutated per genes are healthy; they simply have different rhythms.

Questions 70–72 refer to the passage.

70. The primary purpose of the passage is to

   (A) summarize findings in an area of research
   (B) discuss different perspectives on a scientific question
   (C) outline the major questions in a scientific discipline
   (D) illustrate the usefulness of investigating a research topic
   (E) reconcile differences between two definitions of a term

71. The passage suggests that neuroscientists would most likely consider Shaker to be which of the following?

   (A) An example of a behavioral gene
   (B) One of multiple genes that control a single behavior
   (C) A gene that, when mutated, causes an alteration in a specific normal behavior without making the organism ill
   (D) A gene of interest to ethologists but of no interest to neuroscientists
   (E) A poor source of information about the nervous system

72. It can be inferred from the passage that which of the following, if true, would be most likely to influence ethologists' opinions about whether a particular gene in a species is a behavioral gene?

   (A) The gene is found only in that species.
   (B) The gene is extremely difficult to identify.
   (C) The only effect of mutations in the gene is to make the organism ill.
   (D) Neuroscientists consider the gene to be a behavioral gene.
   (E) Geneticists consider the gene to be a behavioral gene.

Line   For most species of animals, the number of individuals in the species is inversely proportional to the average body size for members of the species: the smaller the body size, the larger the number of individual animals.
(5)   The tamarin, a small South American monkey, breaks this rule. Of the ten primate species studied in Peru's Manu National Park, for example, the two species of tamarins, saddle-backed and emperor, are the eighth and ninth least abundant, respectively. Only the pygmy
(10)   marmoset, which is even smaller, is less abundant. The tamarin's scarcity is not easily explained; it cannot be dismissed as a consequence of diet, because tamarins feed on the same mixture of fruit, nectar, and small prey as do several of their more numerous larger
(15)   counterparts, including the two capuchins known as the squirrel monkey and the night monkey. Although the relative proportions of fruits consumed varies somewhat among species, it is hard to imagine that such subtle differences are crucial to understanding
(20)   the relative rarity of tamarins.
    To emphasize just how anomalously rare tamarins are, we can compare them to the other omnivorous primates in the community. In terms of numbers of individuals per square kilometer, they rank well below
(25)   the two capuchins, the squirrel monkey and the night monkey. And in terms of biomass, or the total weight of the individuals that occupy a unit area of habitat, each tamarin species is present at only one-twentieth the mass of brown capuchins or one-tenth that of
(30)   squirrel monkeys. To gain another perspective, consider the spatial requirements of tamarins. Tamarins are rigidly territorial, vigorously expelling any intruders that may stray within the sharply defined boundaries of their domains. Groups invest an
(35)   appreciable part of their time and energy in patrolling their territorial boundaries, announcing their presence to their neighbors with shrill, sweeping cries. Such concerted territoriality is rather exceptional among primates, though the gibbons and siamangs of Asia
(40)   show it, as do a few other New World species such as the titi and night monkeys. What is most surprising about tamarin territories is their size. Titi monkeys routinely live within territories of 6 to 8 hectares, and night monkeys seldom defend more
(45)   than 10 hectares, but tamarin groups routinely occupy areas of 30 to 120 hectares. Contrast this with the 1 to 2 hectares needed by the common North American gray squirrel, a nonterritorial mammal of about the same size. A group of tamarins uses about as much
(50)   space as a troop of brown capuchins, though the latter weighs 15 times as much. Thus, in addition to being rare, tamarins require an amount of space that seems completely out of proportion to their size.

Questions 73–79 refer to the passage.

73. The author indicates that tamarin territories are

    (A) surprisingly large
    (B) poorly situated
    (C) unusually abundant in food resources
    (D) incapable of supporting large troops of tamarins
    (E) larger in Peru than in other parts of South America

74. The author mentions the spatial requirements of the gray squirrel in order to

    (A) explain why they are so common
    (B) demonstrate the consequences of their nonterritoriality
    (C) emphasize the unusual territorial requirements of the tamarin
    (D) provide an example of a major difference between squirrels and monkeys
    (E) provide an example of an animal with requirements similar to those of the tamarin

75. The author regards the differences between the diets of the tamarins and several larger species as

    (A) generally explicable in terms of territory size
    (B) apparently too small to explain the rarity of tamarins
    (C) wholly predictable on the basis of differences in body size
    (D) a result of the rigid territoriality of tamarins
    (E) a significant factor in determining behavioral differences

76. Which of the following would most probably be regarded by the author as anomalous?

    (A) A large primate species that eats mostly plants
    (B) A species of small mammals that is fiercely territorial
    (C) Two species of small primates that share the same territories
    (D) A species of small birds that is more abundant than many species of larger birds
    (E) A species of small rodents that requires more living space per individual than most species of larger rodents

77. The author most probably regards the tamarins studied in Manu National Park as

    (A) an endangered species
    (B) typical tamarins
    (C) unusually docile
    (D) the most unusual primates anywhere
    (E) too small a sample to be significant

78. Which of the following is NOT mentioned in the passage as a species whose groups display territoriality?

    (A) Gibbons
    (B) Siamangs
    (C) Titi monkeys
    (D) Squirrel monkeys
    (E) Night monkeys

79. The primary concern of the passage is to

    (A) recommend a policy
    (B) evaluate a theory
    (C) describe an unusual condition
    (D) explain the development of a hypothesis
    (E) support one of several competing hypotheses

Line   According to many analysts, labor-management relations in the United States are undergoing a fundamental change: traditional adversarialism is giving way to a new cooperative relationship between the
(5) two sides and even to concessions from labor. These analysts say the twin shocks of nonunion competition in this country and low-cost, high-quality imports from abroad are forcing unions to look more favorably at a variety of management demands: the need for
(10) wage restraint and reduced benefits as well as the abolition of "rigid" work rules, seniority rights, and job classifications.
    Sophisticated proponents of these new developments cast their observations in a prolabor
(15) light. In return for their concessions, they point out, some unions have bargained for profit sharing, retraining rights, and job-security guarantees. Unions can also trade concessions for more say on the shop floor, where techniques such as quality circles and
(20) quality-of-work-life programs promise workers greater control over their own jobs. Unions may even win a voice in investment and pricing strategy, plant location, and other major corporate policy decisions previously reserved to management.
(25)   Opponents of these concessions from labor argue that such concessions do not save jobs, but either prolong the agony of dying plants or finance the plant relocations that employers had intended anyway. Companies make investment decisions to fit their
(30) strategic plans and their profit objectives, opponents point out, and labor costs are usually just a small factor in the equation. Moreover, unrestrained by either loyalty to their work force or political or legislative constraints on their mobility, the companies eventually
(35) cut and run, concessions or no concessions.
    Wage-related concessions have come under particular attack, since opponents believe that high union wages underlay much of the success of United States industry in this century. They point out that a
(40) long-standing principle, shared by both management and labor, has been that workers should earn wages that give them the income they need to buy what they make. Moreover, high wages have given workers the buying power to propel the economy forward.
(45) If proposals for pay cuts, two-tier wage systems, and subminimum wages for young workers continue to gain credence, opponents believe the U.S. social structure will move toward that of a less-developed nation: a small group of wealthy investors, a sizable
(50) but still minority bloc of elite professionals and highly skilled employees, and a huge mass of marginal workers and unskilled laborers. Further, they argue that if unions willingly engage in concession bargaining on the false grounds that labor costs are the source
(55) of a company's problems, unions will find themselves competing with Third World pay levels—a competition they cannot win.

Questions 80–86 refer to the passage.

80. It can be inferred from the passage that opponents of labor concessions would most likely describe many plant-relocation decisions made by United States companies as

    (A) capricious
    (B) self-serving
    (C) naive
    (D) impulsive
    (E) illogical

81. It can be inferred from the passage that, until recently, which of the following has been true of United States industry in the twentieth century?

    (A) Unions have consistently participated in major corporate policy decisions.
    (B) Maintaining adequate quality control in manufacturing processes has been a principal problem.
    (C) Union workers have been paid relatively high wages.
    (D) Two-tier wage systems have been the norm.
    (E) Goods produced have been priced beyond the means of most workers.

82. The passage provides information to answer which of the following questions?

    (A) What has caused unions to consider wage restraints and reduced benefits?
    (B) Why do analysts study United States labor-management relations?
    (C) How do job-security guarantees operate?
    (D) Are investment and pricing strategies effective in combating imports?
    (E) Do quality circles improve product performance and value?

83. The passage is primarily concerned with the

    (A) reasons for adversarialism between labor and management
    (B) importance of cooperative labor-management relations
    (C) consequences of labor concessions to management
    (D) effects of foreign competition on the United States economy
    (E) effects of nonunion competition on union bargaining strategies

84. The sentence "If proposals for pay cuts . . . unskilled laborers" (lines 45–52) serves primarily to

    (A) disprove a theory
    (B) clarify an ambiguity
    (C) reconcile opposing views
    (D) present a hypothesis
    (E) contradict accepted data

85. It can be inferred from the passage that opponents of labor concessions believe that if concession bargaining continues, then

    (A) plants will close instead of relocating
    (B) young workers will need continued job retraining
    (C) professional workers will outnumber marginal workers
    (D) wealthy investors will invest in Third World countries instead of the United States
    (E) the social structure of the United States will be negatively affected

86. According to the author, "Sophisticated proponents" (line 13) of concessions do which of the following?

    (A) Support the traditional adversarialism characteristic of labor-management relations.
    (B) Emphasize the benefits unions can gain by granting concessions.
    (C) Focus on thorough analyses of current economic conditions.
    (D) Present management's reasons for demanding concessions.
    (E) Explain domestic economic developments in terms of worldwide trends.

Line   Historians who study European women of the
        Renaissance try to measure "independence,"
        "options," and other indicators of the degree to which
        the expression of women's individuality was either
(5)   permitted or suppressed. Influenced by Western
        individualism, these historians define a peculiar form
        of personhood: an innately bounded unit, autonomous
        and standing apart from both nature and society. An
        anthropologist, however, would contend that a person
(10)   can be conceived in ways other than as an "individual."
        In many societies a person's identity is not intrinsically
        unique and self-contained but instead is defined within
        a complex web of social relationships.
        In her study of the fifteenth-century Florentine
(15)   widow Alessandra Strozzi, a historian who specializes
        in European women of the Renaissance attributes
        individual intention and authorship of actions to her
        subject. This historian assumes that Alessandra had
        goals and interests different from those of her sons,
(20)   yet much of the historian's own research reveals
        that Alessandra acted primarily as a champion of
        her sons' interests, taking their goals as her own.
        Thus Alessandra conforms more closely to the
        anthropologist's notion that personal motivation is
(25)   embedded in a social context. Indeed, one could argue
        that Alessandra did not distinguish her personhood
        from that of her sons. In Renaissance Europe the
        boundaries of the conceptual self were not always firm
        and closed and did not necessarily coincide with the
(30)   boundaries of the bodily self.

Questions 87–91 refer to the passage.

87. According to the passage, much of the research on Alessandra Strozzi done by the historian mentioned in the second paragraph supports which of the following conclusions?

    (A) Alessandra used her position as her sons' sole guardian to further interests different from those of her sons.
    (B) Alessandra unwillingly sacrificed her own interests in favor of those of her sons.
    (C) Alessandra's actions indicate that her motivations and intentions were those of an independent individual.
    (D) Alessandra's social context encouraged her to take independent action.
    (E) Alessandra regarded her sons' goals and interests as her own.

88. In the first paragraph, the author of the passage mentions a contention that would be made by an anthropologist most likely in order to

    (A) present a theory that will be undermined in the discussion of a historian's study later in the passage
    (B) offer a perspective on the concept of personhood that can usefully be applied to the study of women in Renaissance Europe
    (C) undermine the view that the individuality of European women of the Renaissance was largely suppressed
    (D) argue that anthropologists have applied the Western concept of individualism in their research
    (E) lay the groundwork for the conclusion that Alessandra's is a unique case among European women of the Renaissance whose lives have been studied by historians

89. The passage suggests that the historians referred to in line 1 make which of the following assumptions about Renaissance Europe?

    (A) That anthropologists overestimate the importance of the individual in Renaissance European society
    (B) That in Renaissance Europe, women were typically allowed to express their individuality
    (C) That European women of the Renaissance had the possibility of acting independently of the social context in which they lived
    (D) That studying an individual such as Alessandra is the best way to draw general conclusions about the lives of women in Renaissance Europe
    (E) That people in Renaissance Europe had greater personal autonomy than people do currently

90. It can be inferred that the author of the passage believes which of the following about the study of Alessandra Strozzi done by the historian mentioned in the second paragraph?

    (A) Alessandra was atypical of her time and was therefore an inappropriate choice for the subject of the historian's research.
    (B) In order to bolster her thesis, the historian adopted the anthropological perspective on personhood.
    (C) The historian argues that the boundaries of the conceptual self were not always firm and closed in Renaissance Europe.
    (D) In her study, the historian reverts to a traditional approach that is out of step with the work of other historians of Renaissance Europe.
    (E) The interpretation of Alessandra's actions that the historian puts forward is not supported by much of the historian's research.

91. The passage suggests that the historian mentioned in the second paragraph would be most likely to agree with which of the following assertions regarding Alessandra Strozzi?

    (A) Alessandra was able to act more independently than most women of her time because she was a widow.
    (B) Alessandra was aware that her personal motivation was embedded in a social context.
    (C) Alessandra had goals and interests similar to those of many other widows in her society.
    (D) Alessandra is an example of a Renaissance woman who expressed her individuality through independent action.
    (E) Alessandra was exceptional because she was able to effect changes in the social constraints placed upon women in her society.

Line   In the fourteenth and fifteenth centuries, many Western Pueblo settlements in what is now the southwestern United States may have possessed distinctly hierarchical organizational structures.
(5)   These communities' agricultural systems—which were "intensive" in the use of labor rather than "extensive" in area—may have given rise to political leadership that managed both labor and food resources. That formal management of food resources
(10)   was needed is suggested by the large size of storage spaces located around some communal Great Kivas (underground ceremonial chambers). Though no direct evidence exists that such spaces were used to store food, Western Pueblo communities lacking sufficient
(15)   arable land to support their populations could have preserved the necessary extra food, including imported foodstuffs, in such apparently communal spaces.
        Moreover, evidence of specialization in procuring raw materials and in manufacturing ceramics and
(20)   textiles indicates differentiation of labor within and between communities. The organizational and managerial demands of such specialization strengthen the possibility that a decision-making elite existed, an elite whose control over labor, the use of community
(25)   surpluses, and the acquisition of imported goods would have led to a concentration of economic resources in their own hands. Evidence for differential distribution of wealth is found in burials of the period: some include large quantities of pottery, jewelry, and
(30)   other artifacts, whereas others from the same sites lack any such materials.

Questions 92–94 refer to the passage.

92. The primary purpose of the passage is to

    (A) outline the methods by which resources were managed within a particular group of communities
    (B) account for the distribution of wealth within a particular group of communities
    (C) provide support for a hypothesis concerning the social structure of a particular society
    (D) explain how political leadership changed in a particular historical situation
    (E) present new evidence that contradicts previous theories about a particular historical situation

93. According to the passage, which of the following is probably true of the storage spaces mentioned in lines 10–11?

    (A) They were used by the community elite for storage of their own food supplies.
    (B) They served a ceremonial as well as a practical function.
    (C) Their size is an indication of the wealth of the particular community to which they belonged.
    (D) Their existence proves that the community to which they belonged imported large amounts of food.
    (E) They belonged to and were used by the community as a whole.

94. Which of the following, if true, would most clearly undermine the author's statement in the last sentence of the passage regarding the distribution of wealth in Western Pueblo settlements?

    (A) Only community members of exceptional wealth are likely to have been buried with their personal possessions.
    (B) Members of communities with extensive agricultural systems are usually buried without personal possessions.
    (C) Most artifacts found in burial sites were manufactured locally rather than imported from other communities.
    (D) Burial artifacts are often ritual objects associated with religious practices rather than being the deceased's personal possessions.
    (E) The quality of burial artifacts varies depending on the site with which they are associated.

Line   In its 1903 decision in the case of *Lone Wolf v. Hitchcock*, the United States Supreme Court rejected the efforts of three Native American tribes to prevent the opening of tribal lands to non-Indian settlement without
(5)   tribal consent. In his study of the *Lone Wolf* case, Blue Clark properly emphasizes the Court's assertion of a virtually unlimited unilateral power of Congress (the House of Representatives and the Senate) over Native American affairs. But he fails to note the decision's
(10)   more far-reaching impact: shortly after *Lone Wolf*, the federal government totally abandoned negotiation and execution of formal written agreements with Indian tribes as a prerequisite for the implementation of federal Indian policy. Many commentators believe that this change had
(15)   already occurred in 1871 when—following a dispute between the House and the Senate over which chamber should enjoy primacy in Indian affairs—Congress abolished the making of treaties with Native American tribes. But in reality, the federal government continued to
(20)   negotiate formal tribal agreements past the turn of the century, treating these documents not as treaties with sovereign nations requiring ratification by the Senate but simply as legislation to be passed by both houses of Congress. The *Lone Wolf* decision ended this era of
(25)   formal negotiation and finally did away with what had increasingly become the empty formality of obtaining tribal consent.

Questions 95–97 refer to the passage.

95. According to the passage, which of the following was true of relations between the federal government and Native American tribes?

    (A) Some Native American tribes approved of the congressional action of 1871 because it simplified their dealings with the federal government.
    (B) Some Native American tribes were more eager to negotiate treaties with the United States after the *Lone Wolf* decision.
    (C) Prior to the *Lone Wolf* decision, the Supreme Court was reluctant to hear cases involving agreements negotiated between Congress and Native American tribes.
    (D) Prior to 1871, the federal government sometimes negotiated treaties with Native American tribes.
    (E) Following 1871, the House exercised more power than did the Senate in the government's dealings with Native American tribes.

96. According to the passage, in the case of *Lone Wolf v. Hitchcock*, the Supreme Court decided that

    (A) disputes among Native American tribes over the ownership of tribal lands were beyond the jurisdiction of the Court
    (B) Congress had the power to allow outsiders to settle on lands occupied by a Native American tribe without obtaining permission from that tribe
    (C) Congress had exceeded its authority in attempting to exercise sole power over Native American affairs
    (D) the United States was not legally bound by the provisions of treaties previously concluded with Native American tribes
    (E) formal agreements between the federal government and Native American tribes should be treated as ordinary legislation rather than as treaties

97. The author of the passage is primarily concerned with

    (A) identifying similarities in two different theories
    (B) evaluating a work of scholarship
    (C) analyzing the significance of a historical event
    (D) debunking a revisionist interpretation
    (E) exploring the relationship between law and social reality

Line   Some historians contend that conditions in the
United States during the Second World War gave rise
to a dynamic wartime alliance between trade unions
and the African American community, an alliance that
(5)   advanced the cause of civil rights. They conclude that
the postwar demise of this vital alliance constituted
a lost opportunity for the civil rights movement that
followed the war. Other scholars, however, have
portrayed organized labor as defending all along
(10)   the relatively privileged position of White workers
relative to African American workers. Clearly, these
two perspectives are not easily reconcilable, but the
historical reality is not reducible to one or the other.
    Unions faced a choice between either maintaining
(15)   the prewar status quo or promoting a more inclusive
approach that sought for all members the right
to participate in the internal affairs of unions,
access to skilled and high-paying positions within
the occupational hierarchy, and protection against
(20)   management's arbitrary authority in the workplace.
While union representatives often voiced this
inclusive ideal, in practice unions far more often
favored entrenched interests. The accelerating
development of the civil rights movement following
(25)   the Second World War exacerbated the unions'
dilemma, forcing trade unionists to confront
contradictions in their own practices.

Questions 98–100 refer to the passage.

98. According to the passage, the historians mentioned in line 1 and the scholars mentioned in line 8 disagree about the

    (A) contribution made by organized labor to the war effort during the Second World War
    (B) issues that union members considered most important during the Second World War
    (C) relationship between unions and African Americans during the Second World War
    (D) effect of the Second World War on the influence of unions in the workplace
    (E) extent to which African Americans benefited from social and political changes following the Second World War

99. Which of the following best summarizes a point of view attributed to the historians mentioned in line 1?

    (A) Trade unions were weakened during the Second World War by their failure to establish a productive relationship with the African American community.
    (B) Trade unions and the African American community forged a lasting relationship after the Second World War based on their wartime alliance.
    (C) The cause of civil rights was not significantly affected by the wartime alliance between trade unions and the African American community.
    (D) The civil rights movement that followed the Second World War forced trade unions to confront contradictions in their practices.
    (E) The civil rights movement would have benefited from a postwar continuation of the wartime alliance between trade unions and the African American community.

100. The passage is primarily concerned with

    (A) providing a context within which to evaluate opposing viewpoints about a historical phenomenon
    (B) identifying a flawed assumption underlying one interpretation of a historical phenomenon
    (C) assessing the merits and weaknesses of a controversial theory about a historical phenomenon
    (D) discussing the historical importance of the development of a wartime alliance
    (E) evaluating evidence used to support a particular interpretation of a historical phenomenon

Line *This passage was excerpted from material published in 1993.*

Like many other industries, the travel industry is under increasing pressure to expand globally in order
(5) to keep pace with its corporate customers, who have globalized their operations in response to market pressure, competitor actions, and changing supplier relations. But it is difficult for service organizations to globalize. Global expansion through acquisition
(10) is usually expensive, and expansion through internal growth is time-consuming and sometimes impossible in markets that are not actively growing. Some service industry companies, in fact, regard these traditional routes to global expansion as inappropriate for
(15) service industries because of their special need to preserve local responsiveness through local presence and expertise. One travel agency has eschewed the traditional route altogether. A survivor of the changes that swept the travel industry as a result of the
(20) deregulation of the airlines in 1978—changes that included dramatic growth in the corporate demand for travel services, as well as extensive restructuring and consolidation within the travel industry—this agency adopted a unique structure for globalization. Rather
(25) than expand by attempting to develop its own offices abroad, which would require the development of local travel management expertise sufficient to capture foreign markets, the company solved its globalization dilemma effectively by forging alliances with the best
(30) foreign partners it could find. The resulting cooperative alliance of independent agencies now comprises 32 partners spanning 37 countries.

Questions 101–103 refer to the passage.

101. According to the passage, which of the following is true of the traditional routes to global expansion?

    (A) They have been supplanted in most service industries by alternative routes.
    (B) They are less attractive to travel agencies since deregulation of the airlines.
    (C) They may represent the most cost-effective means for a travel agency to globalize.
    (D) They may be unsuitable for service agencies that are attempting to globalize.
    (E) They are most likely to succeed in markets that are not actively growing.

102. The passage suggests that one of the effects of the deregulation of the airlines was

    (A) a decline in the services available to noncommercial travelers
    (B) a decrease in the size of the corporate travel market
    (C) a sharp increase in the number of cooperative alliances among travel agencies
    (D) increased competition in a number of different service industries
    (E) the merging of some companies within the travel industry

103. The author discusses a particular travel agency in the passage most likely in order to

    (A) provide evidence of the pressures on the travel industry to globalize
    (B) demonstrate the limitations of the traditional routes to global expansion
    (C) illustrate an unusual approach to globalizing a service organization
    (D) highlight the difficulties confronting travel agencies that attempt to globalize
    (E) underscore the differences between the service industry and other industries

Line   Many economists believe that a high rate of business savings in the United States is a necessary precursor to investment, because business savings, as opposed to personal savings,
(5) comprise almost three-quarters of the national savings rate. The national savings rate heavily influences the overall rate of business investment. These economists further postulate that real interest rates—the difference between the rates
(10) charged by lenders and the inflation rate—will be low when national savings exceed business investment (creating a savings surplus), and high when national savings fall below the level of business investment (creating a savings deficit).
(15) However, during the 1960s real interest rates were often higher when the national savings surplus was large. Counterintuitive behavior also occurred when real interest rates skyrocketed from 2 percent in 1980 to 7 percent in 1982, even though national
(20) savings and investments were roughly equal throughout the period. Clearly, real interest rates respond to influences other than the savings/investment nexus. Indeed, real interest rates may themselves influence swings in the savings
(25) and investment rates. As real interest rates shot up after 1979, foreign investors poured capital into the United States, the price of domestic goods increased prohibitively abroad, and the price of foreign-made goods became lower in the
(30) United States. As a result, domestic economic activity and the ability of businesses to save and invest were restrained.

Questions 104–106 refer to the passage.

104. The passage suggests that the economists mentioned in line 1 would have expected which of the following to occur during the 1960s in the United States?

    (A) Savings and investment rates to be equal in spite of high real interest rates
    (B) Real interest rates to remain low when the national savings surplus was large
    (C) Investment rates to remain constant while the national savings rate changed
    (D) The national economy to suffer a decline as a result of high national savings rates
    (E) Businesses to be encouraged to save due to high real interest rates

105. The author of the passage would be most likely to agree with which of the following statements regarding the economists mentioned in line 1?

    (A) Their beliefs are contradicted by certain economic phenomena that occurred in the United States during the 1960s and the 1980s.
    (B) Their theory fails to predict under what circumstances the prices of foreign and domestic goods are likely to increase.
    (C) They incorrectly identify the factors other than savings and investment rates that affect real interest rates.
    (D) Their belief is valid only for the United States economy and not necessarily for other national economies.
    (E) They overestimate the impact of the real interest rate on the national savings and investment rates.

106. The passage is primarily concerned with

    (A) contrasting trends in two historical periods
    (B) presenting evidence that calls into question certain beliefs
    (C) explaining the reasons for a common phenomenon
    (D) criticizing evidence offered in support of a well-respected belief
    (E) comparing conflicting interpretations of a theory

Line	Traditional social science models of class groups in the United States are based on economic status and assume that women's economic status derives from association with men, typically fathers or
(5)	husbands, and that women therefore have more compelling common interests with men of their own economic class than with women outside it. Some feminist social scientists, by contrast, have argued that the basic division in American
(10)	society is instead based on gender, and that the total female population, regardless of economic status, constitutes a distinct class. Social historian Mary Ryan, for example, has argued that in early-nineteenth-century America, the identical legal
(15)	status of working-class and middle-class free women outweighed the differences between women of these two classes: Married women, regardless of their family's wealth, did essentially the same unpaid domestic work, and none could own property or
(20)	vote. Recently, though, other feminist analysts have questioned this model, examining ways in which the condition of working-class women differs from that of middle-class women as well as from that of working-class men. Ann Oakley notes, for example,
(25)	that the gap between women of different economic classes widened in the late nineteenth century: Most working-class women, who performed wage labor outside the home, were excluded from the emerging middle-class ideal of femininity centered around
(30)	domesticity and volunteerism.

Questions 107–109 refer to the passage.

107. The primary purpose of the passage is to

   (A) offer sociohistorical explanations for the cultural differences between men and women in the United States
   (B) examine how the economic roles of women in the United States changed during the nineteenth century
   (C) consider differing views held by social scientists concerning women's class status in the United States
   (D) propose a feminist interpretation of class structure in the United States
   (E) outline specific distinctions between working-class women and women of the upper and middle classes

108. It can be inferred from the passage that the most recent feminist social science research on women and class seeks to do which of the following?

   (A) Introduce a divergent new theory about the relationship between legal status and gender
   (B) Illustrate an implicit middle-class bias in earlier feminist models of class and gender
   (C) Provide evidence for the position that gender matters more than wealth in determining class status
   (D) Remedy perceived inadequacies of both traditional social science models and earlier feminist analyses of class and gender
   (E) Challenge the economic definitions of class used by traditional social scientists

109. Which of the following statements best characterizes the relationship between traditional social science models of class and Ryan's model, as described in the passage?

    (A) Ryan's model differs from the traditional model by making gender, rather than economic status, the determinant of women's class status.

    (B) The traditional social science model of class differs from Ryan's in its assumption that women are financially dependent on men.

    (C) Ryan's model of class and the traditional social science model both assume that women work, either within the home or for pay.

    (D) The traditional social science model of class differs from Ryan's in that each model focuses on a different period of American history.

    (E) Both Ryan's model of class and the traditional model consider multiple factors, including wealth, marital status, and enfranchisement, in determining women's status.

Questions 110 to 143 — Difficulty: Hard

Line   In addition to conventional galaxies, the universe
       contains very dim galaxies that until recently went
       unnoticed by astronomers. Possibly as numerous
       as conventional galaxies, these galaxies have the
(5)   same general shape and even the same
       approximate number of stars as a common type of
       conventional galaxy, the spiral, but tend to be much
       larger. Because these galaxies' mass is spread out
       over larger areas, they have far fewer stars per unit
(10)   volume than do conventional galaxies. Apparently
       these low-surface-brightness galaxies, as they are
       called, take much longer than conventional galaxies
       to condense their primordial gas and convert it to
       stars—that is, they evolve much more slowly.
(15)   These galaxies may constitute an answer to the
       long-standing puzzle of the missing baryonic mass
       in the universe. Baryons—subatomic particles that
       are generally protons or neutrons—are the source
       of stellar, and therefore galactic, luminosity, and so
(20)   their numbers can be estimated based on how
       luminous galaxies are. However, the amount of
       helium in the universe, as measured by
       spectroscopy, suggests that there are far more
       baryons in the universe than estimates based on
(25)   galactic luminosity indicate. Astronomers have long
       speculated that the missing baryonic mass might
       eventually be discovered in intergalactic space or as
       some large population of galaxies that are difficult
       to detect.

Questions 110–116 refer to the passage.

110. According to the passage, conventional spiral galaxies differ from low-surface-brightness galaxies in which of the following ways?

   (A) They have fewer stars than do low-surface-brightness galaxies.
   (B) They evolve more quickly than low-surface-brightness galaxies.
   (C) They are more diffuse than low-surface-brightness galaxies.
   (D) They contain less helium than do low-surface-brightness galaxies.
   (E) They are larger than low-surface-brightness galaxies.

111. It can be inferred from the passage that which of the following is an accurate physical description of typical low-surface-brightness galaxies?

   (A) They are large spiral galaxies containing fewer stars than conventional galaxies.
   (B) They are compact but very dim spiral galaxies.
   (c) They are diffuse spiral galaxies that occupy a large volume of space.
   (D) They are small, young spiral galaxies that contain a high proportion of primordial gas.
   (E) They are large, dense spirals with low luminosity.

112. It can be inferred from the passage that the "longstanding puzzle" refers to which of the following?

   (A) The difference between the rate at which conventional galaxies evolve and the rate at which low-surface-brightness galaxies evolve
   (B) The discrepancy between estimates of total baryonic mass derived from measuring helium and estimates based on measuring galactic luminosity
   (C) The inconsistency between the observed amount of helium in the universe and the number of stars in typical low-surface-brightness galaxies
   (D) Uncertainties regarding what proportion of baryonic mass is contained in intergalactic space and what proportion in conventional galaxies
   (E) Difficulties involved in detecting very distant galaxies and in investigating their luminosity

113. The author implies that low-surface-brightness galaxies could constitute an answer to the puzzle discussed in the second paragraph primarily because

    (A) they contain baryonic mass that was not taken into account by researchers using galactic luminosity to estimate the number of baryons in the universe
    (B) they, like conventional galaxies that contain many baryons, have evolved from massive, primordial gas clouds
    (C) they may contain relatively more helium, and hence more baryons, than do galaxies whose helium content has been studied using spectroscopy
    (D) they have recently been discovered to contain more baryonic mass than scientists had thought when low-surface-brightness galaxies were first observed
    (E) they contain stars that are significantly more luminous than would have been predicted on the basis of initial studies of luminosity in low-surface-brightness galaxies

114. The author mentions the fact that baryons are the source of stars' luminosity primarily in order to explain

    (A) how astronomers determine that some galaxies contain fewer stars per unit volume than do others
    (B) how astronomers are able to calculate the total luminosity of a galaxy
    (C) why astronomers can use galactic luminosity to estimate baryonic mass
    (D) why astronomers' estimates of baryonic mass based on galactic luminosity are more reliable than those based on spectroscopic studies of helium
    (E) how astronomers know bright galaxies contain more baryons than do dim galaxies

115. The author of the passage would be most likely to disagree with which of the following statements?

    (A) Low-surface-brightness galaxies are more difficult to detect than are conventional galaxies.
    (B) Low-surface-brightness galaxies are often spiral in shape.
    (C) Astronomers have advanced plausible ideas about where missing baryonic mass might be found.
    (D) Astronomers have devised a useful way of estimating the total baryonic mass in the universe.
    (E) Astronomers have discovered a substantial amount of baryonic mass in intergalactic space.

116. The primary purpose of the passage is to

    (A) describe a phenomenon and consider its scientific significance
    (B) contrast two phenomena and discuss a puzzling difference between them
    (C) identify a newly discovered phenomenon and explain its origins
    (D) compare two classes of objects and discuss the physical properties of each
    (E) discuss a discovery and point out its inconsistency with existing theory

Line   Antonia Castañeda has utilized scholarship from
women's studies and Mexican-American history to
examine nineteenth-century literary portrayals of
Mexican women. As Castañeda notes, scholars of
(5)   women's history observe that in the United States,
male novelists of the period—during which, according
to these scholars, women's traditional economic role
in home-based agriculture was threatened by the
transition to a factory-based industrial economy—
(10)   define women solely in their domestic roles of wife and
mother. Castañeda finds that during the same period
that saw non-Hispanic women being economically
displaced by industrialization, Hispanic law in territorial
California protected the economic position of
(15)   "Californianas" (the Mexican women of the territory) by
ensuring them property rights and inheritance rights
equal to those of males.
       For Castañeda, the laws explain a stereotypical
plot created primarily by male, non-Hispanic novelists:
(20)   the story of an ambitious non-Hispanic merchant or
trader desirous of marrying an elite Californiana.
These novels' favorable portrayal of such women
is noteworthy, since Mexican-American historians
have concluded that unflattering literary depictions
(25)   of Mexicans were vital in rallying the United States
public's support for the Mexican-American War
(1846–1848). The importance of economic alliances
forged through marriages with Californianas explains
this apparent contradiction. Because of their real-
(30)   life economic significance, the Californianas were
portrayed more favorably than were others of the
same nationality.

Questions 117–120 refer to the passage.

117. The primary purpose of the passage is to

   (A) trace historical influences on the depiction of Mexican Americans in the nineteenth century
   (B) explain how research in history has been affected by scholarship in women's studies
   (C) describe the historical origins of a literary stereotype
   (D) discuss ways in which minority writers have sought to critique a dominant culture through their writing
   (E) evaluate both sides in a scholarly debate about a prominent literary stereotype

118. The "apparent contradiction" mentioned in line 29 refers to the discrepancy between the

   (A) legal status of Mexican women in territorial California and their status in the United States
   (B) unflattering depiction of Mexicans in novels and the actual public sentiment about the Mexican-American War
   (C) existence of many marriages between Californianas and non-Hispanic merchants and the strictures against them expressed in novels
   (D) literary depiction of elite Californianas and the literary depiction of other Mexican individuals
   (E) novelistic portrayals of elite Californianas' privileged lives and the actual circumstances of those lives

119. Which of the following could best serve as an example of the kind of fictional plot discussed by Antonia Castañeda?

    (A) A land speculator of English ancestry weds the daughter of a Mexican vineyard owner after the speculator has migrated to California to seek his fortune.
    (B) A Californian woman of Hispanic ancestry finds that her agricultural livelihood is threatened when her husband is forced to seek work in a textile mill.
    (C) A Mexican rancher who loses his land as a result of the Mexican-American War migrates to the northern United States and marries an immigrant schoolteacher.
    (D) A wealthy Californiana whose father has bequeathed her all his property contends with avaricious relatives for her inheritance.
    (E) A poor married couple emigrate from French Canada and gradually become wealthy as merchants in territorial California.

120. Which of the following, if true, would provide the most support for Castañeda's explanation of the "stereotypical plot" mentioned in the lines 18–19?

    (A) Non-Hispanic traders found business more profitable in California while it was a territory than when it became a state.
    (B) Very few marriages between Hispanic women and non-Hispanic men in nineteenth-century territorial California have actually been documented.
    (C) Records from the nineteenth century indicate that some large and valuable properties were owned by elite Californianas in their own right.
    (D) Unmarried non-Hispanic women in the nineteenth-century United States were sometimes able to control property in their own right.
    (E) Most of the property in nineteenth-century territorial California was controlled by Hispanic men.

Line *This passage is excerpted from material published in 1997.*

Scientists have been puzzled by the seeming disparity between models of global warming based on
(5) greenhouse gas emissions and actual climatological data. In short, the world is not warming up as much as these models have predicted. In the early 1990s, Pat Michaels sought to explain this disparity, suggesting that sulfate emissions in industrial areas had a cooling
(10) effect, thus temporarily retarding global warming. Michaels later came to doubt this idea, however, pointing out that since most sulfate is emitted in the Northern Hemisphere, its cooling influence should be largely limited to that hemisphere. Yet, since 1987,
(15) warming in the Southern Hemisphere, which had been relatively intense, has virtually ceased, while warming in the north has accelerated. Thus, Michaels not only doubted the idea of sulfate cooling, but came to feel that global warming models themselves may be
(20) flawed.

Ben Santer disagrees. Santer contends that, in general, global warming occurs more slowly in the south because this hemisphere is dominated by oceans, which warm more slowly than the landmasses
(25) that dominate the Northern Hemisphere. But, according to Santer, the situation remains complicated by sulfate cooling, which peaked in the north in the mid-twentieth century. It drastically slowed warming in the Northern Hemisphere, and warming in the
(30) Southern Hemisphere raced ahead. Since 1987, Santer argues, the greenhouse effect has reasserted itself, and the north has taken the lead. Thus, Santer disputes Michaels's claim that model predictions and observed data differ fundamentally.

Questions 121–123 refer to the passage.

121. The passage suggests that, in the early 1990s, Michaels would have been most likely to agree with which of the following statements about the disparity mentioned in lines 3–4?

    (A) This disparity is relatively less extreme in the Northern Hemisphere because of sulfate cooling.
    (B) This disparity is only a short-term phenomenon brought about by sulfate cooling.
    (C) This disparity is most significant in those parts of the world dominated by oceans.
    (D) The extent of this disparity is being masked by the temporary effect of sulfate cooling.
    (E) The disparity confirms that current models of global warming are correct.

122. According to the passage, Santer asserts which of the following about global warming?

    (A) It will become a more serious problem in the Southern Hemisphere than in the Northern Hemisphere in spite of the cooling influence of oceans in the south.
    (B) It is unlikely to be a serious problem in the future because of the pervasive effect of sulfate cooling.
    (C) It will proceed at the same general rate in the Northern and Southern Hemispheres once the temporary influence of sulfate cooling comes to an end.
    (D) Until the late 1980s, it was moderated in the Northern Hemisphere by the effect of sulfate cooling.
    (E) Largely because of the cooling influence of oceans, it has had no discernible impact on the Southern Hemisphere.

123. The passage suggests that Santer and Michaels would be most likely to DISAGREE over which of the following issues?

    (A) Whether climatological data invalidates global warming models
    (B) Whether warming in the Northern Hemisphere has intensified since 1987
    (C) Whether disparities between global warming models and climatological data can be detected
    (D) Whether landmasses warm more rapidly than oceans
    (E) Whether oceans have a significant effect on global climate patterns

Line Micro-wear patterns found on the teeth of long-extinct specimens of the primate species australopithecine may provide evidence about their diets. For example, on the basis of tooth micro-wear
(5) patterns, Walker dismisses Jolly's hypothesis that australopithecines ate hard seeds. He also disputes Szalay's suggestion that the heavy enamel of australopithecine teeth is an adaptation to bone crunching, since both seed cracking and bone
(10) crunching produce distinctive micro-wear characteristics on teeth. His conclusion that australopithecines were frugivores (fruit eaters) is based upon his observation that the tooth micro-wear characteristics of east African
(15) australopithecine specimens are indistinguishable from those of chimpanzees and orangutans, which are commonly assumed to be frugivorous primates.

However, research on the diets of contemporary primates suggests that micro-wear
(20) studies may have limited utility in determining the foods that are actually eaten. For example, insect eating, which can cause distinct micro-wear patterns, would not cause much tooth abrasion in modern baboons, who eat only soft-bodied insects
(25) rather than hard-bodied insects. In addition, the diets of current omnivorous primates vary considerably depending on the environments that different groups within a primate species inhabit; if australopithecines were omnivores too, we might
(30) expect to find considerable population variation in their tooth micro-wear patterns. Thus, Walker's description of possible australopithecine diets may need to be expanded to include a much more diverse diet.

Questions 124–131 refer to the passage.

124. According to the passage, Walker and Szalay disagree on which of the following points?

    (A) The structure and composition of australopithecine teeth
    (B) The kinds of conclusions that can be drawn from the micro-wear patterns on australopithecine teeth
    (C) The idea that fruit was a part of the australopithecine diet
    (D) The extent to which seed cracking and bone crunching produce similar micro-wear patterns on teeth
    (E) The function of the heavy enamel on australopithecine teeth

125. The passage suggests that Walker's research indicated which of the following about australopithecine teeth?

    (A) They had micro-wear characteristics indicating that fruit constituted only a small part of their diet.
    (B) They lacked micro-wear characteristics associated with seed eating and bone crunching.
    (C) They had micro-wear characteristics that differed in certain ways from the micro-wear patterns of chimpanzees and orangutans.
    (D) They had micro-wear characteristics suggesting that the diet of australopithecines varied from one region to another.
    (E) They lacked the micro-wear characteristics distinctive of modern frugivores.

126. The passage suggests that which of the following would be true of studies of tooth micro-wear patterns conducted on modern baboons?

    (A) They would inaccurately suggest that some baboons eat more soft-bodied than hard-bodied insects.
    (B) They would suggest that insects constitute the largest part of some baboons' diets.
    (C) They would reveal that there are no significant differences in tooth micro-wear patterns among baboon populations.
    (D) They would inadequately reflect the extent to which some baboons consume certain types of insects.
    (E) They would indicate that baboons in certain regions eat only soft-bodied insects, whereas baboons in other regions eat hard-bodied insects.

127. The passage suggests which of the following about the micro-wear patterns found on the teeth of omnivorous primates?

    (A) The patterns provide information about what kinds of foods are not eaten by the particular species of primate, but not about the foods actually eaten.
    (B) The patterns of various primate species living in the same environment resemble one another.
    (C) The patterns may not provide information about the extent to which a particular species' diet includes seeds.
    (D) The patterns provide more information about these primates' diet than do the tooth micro-wear patterns of primates who are frugivores.
    (E) The patterns may differ among groups within a species depending on the environment within which a particular group lives.

128. It can be inferred from the passage that if studies of tooth micro-wear patterns were conducted on modern baboons, which of the following would most likely be true of the results obtained?

    (A) There would be enough abrasion to allow a determination of whether baboons are frugivorous or insectivorous.
    (B) The results would suggest that insects constitute the largest part of the baboons' diet.
    (C) The results would reveal that there are no significant differences in tooth micro-wear patterns from one regional baboon population to another.
    (D) The results would provide an accurate indication of the absence of some kinds of insects from the baboons' diet.
    (E) The results would be unlikely to provide any indication of what inferences about the australopithecine diet can or cannot be drawn from micro-wear studies.

129. It can be inferred from the passage that Walker's conclusion about the australopithecine diet would be called into question under which of the following circumstances?

    (A) The tooth enamel of australopithecines is found to be much heavier than that of modern frugivorous primates.
    (B) The micro-wear patterns of australopithecine teeth from regions other than east Africa are analyzed.
    (C) Orangutans are found to have a much broader diet than is currently recognized.
    (D) The environment of east Africa at the time australopithecines lived there is found to have been far more varied than is currently thought.
    (E) The area in which the australopithecine specimens were found is discovered to have been very rich in soft-bodied insects during the period when australopithecines lived there.

130. The passage is primarily concerned with

   (A) comparing two research methods for determining a species' dietary habits
   (B) describing and evaluating conjectures about a species' diet
   (C) contrasting several explanations for a species' dietary habits
   (D) discussing a new approach and advocating its use in particular situations
   (E) arguing that a particular research methodology does not contribute useful data

131. The author of the passage mentions the diets of baboons and other living primates most likely in order to

   (A) provide evidence that refutes Walker's conclusions about the foods making up the diets of australopithecines
   (B) suggest that studies of tooth micro-wear patterns are primarily useful for determining the diets of living primates
   (C) suggest that australopithecines were probably omnivores rather than frugivores
   (D) illustrate some of the limitations of using tooth micro-wear patterns to draw definitive conclusions about a group's diet
   (E) suggest that tooth micro-wear patterns are caused by persistent, as opposed to occasional, consumption of particular foods

In current historiography, the picture of a consistent, unequivocal decline in women's status with the advent of capitalism and industrialization is giving way to an analysis that not only emphasizes both change (whether
(5) improvement or decline) and continuity but also accounts for geographical and occupational variation. The history of women's work in English farmhouse cheese making between 1800 and 1930 is a case in point. In her influential *Women Workers and the Industrial*
(10) *Revolution* (1930), Pinchbeck argued that the agricultural revolution of the eighteenth and early nineteenth centuries, with its attendant specialization and enlarged scale of operation, curtailed women's participation in the business of cheese production. Earlier, she
(15) maintained, women had concerned themselves with feeding cows, rearing calves, and even selling the cheese in local markets and fairs. Pinchbeck thought that the advent of specialization meant that women's work in cheese dairying was reduced simply to
(20) processing the milk. "Dairymen" (a new social category) raised and fed cows and sold the cheese through factors, who were also men. With this narrowing of the scope of work, Pinchbeck believed, women lost business ability, independence, and initiative.
(25) Though Pinchbeck portrayed precapitalist, preindustrial conditions as superior to what followed, recent scholarship has seriously questioned the notion of a golden age for women in precapitalist society. For example, scholars note that women's control seldom
(30) extended to the disposal of the proceeds of their work. In the case of cheese, the rise of factors may have compromised women's ability to market cheese at fairs. But merely selling the cheese did not necessarily imply access to the money: Davidoff cites
(35) the case of an Essex man who appropriated all but a fraction of the money from his wife's cheese sales.
By focusing on somewhat peripheral operations, moreover, Pinchbeck missed a substantial element of continuity in women's participation: throughout the
(40) period women did the central work of actually making cheese. Their persistence in English cheese dairying contrasts with women's early disappearance from arable agriculture in southeast England and from American cheese dairying. Comparing these
(45) three divergent developments yields some reasons for the differences among them. English cheese-making women worked in a setting in which cultural values, agricultural conditions, and the nature of their work combined to support their continued
(50) participation. In the other cases, one or more of these elements was lacking.

Questions 132–135 refer to the passage.

132. The primary purpose of the passage is to

    (A) present recently discovered evidence that supports a conventional interpretation of a historical period

    (B) describe how reinterpretations of available evidence have reinvigorated a once-discredited scholarly position

    (C) explain why some historians have tended to emphasize change rather than continuity in discussing a particular period

    (D) explore how changes in a particular occupation serve to counter the prevailing view of a historical period

    (E) examine a particular area of historical research in order to exemplify a general scholarly trend

133. Regarding English local markets and fairs, which of the following can be inferred from the passage?

    (A) Both before and after the agricultural revolution, the sellers of agricultural products at these venues were men.

    (B) Knowing who the active sellers were at these venues may not give a reliable indication of who controlled the revenue from the sales.

    (C) There were no parallel institutions at which American cheese makers could sell their own products.

    (D) Prior to the agricultural revolution, the sellers of agricultural products at these venues were generally the producers themselves.

    (E) Prior to the agricultural revolution, women sold not only cheese but also products of arable agriculture at these venues.

134. The passage describes the work of Pinchbeck primarily in order to

    (A) demonstrate that some of the conclusions reached by recent historians were anticipated in earlier scholarship
    (B) provide an instance of the viewpoint that, according to the passage's author, is being superseded
    (C) illustrate the ways in which recent historians have built on the work of their predecessors
    (D) provide a point of reference for subsequent scholarship on women's work during the agricultural revolution
    (E) show the effect that the specialization introduced in the agricultural and industrial revolutions had on women's work

135. It can be inferred from the passage that women did work in

    (A) American cheesemaking at some point prior to industrialization
    (B) arable agriculture in northern England both before and after the agricultural revolution
    (C) arable agriculture in southeast England after the agricultural revolution, in those locales in which cultural values supported their participation
    (D) the sale of cheese at local markets in England even after the agricultural revolution
    (E) some areas of American cheese dairying after industrialization

Line   The ultimate pendulum clock, indeed the ultimate mechanical clock of any kind, was invented by a British engineer, William Shortt. The first was installed in the Royal Observatory in Edinburgh in 1921. The Shortt
(5)   clock had two pendulums, primary and secondary. The primary pendulum swung freely in a vacuum chamber. Its only job was to synchronize the swing of the secondary pendulum, which was housed in a neighboring cabinet and drove the time-indicating mechanism. Every 30
(10)   seconds, the secondary pendulum sent an electrical signal to give a nudge to the primary pendulum. In return, via an elaborate electromechanical linkage, the primary pendulum ensured that the secondary pendulum never got out of step.
(15)   Shortt clocks were standard provision in astronomical observatories of the 1920s and 1930s and are credited with keeping time to better than two milliseconds in a day. Many were on record as losing or gaining no more than one second in a year—a
(20)   stability of one part in 30 million. The first indications of seasonal variations in the earth's rotation were gleaned by the use of Shortt clocks.
        In 1984, Pierre Boucheron carried out a study of a Shortt clock which had survived in the basement
(25)   of the United States Naval Observatory since 1932. After replacing the electromechanical linkage with modern optical sensing equipment, he measured the Shortt clock's rate against the observatory's atomic clocks for a month. He found that it was stable to 200
(30)   microseconds a day over this period, equivalent to two to three parts in a billion. What is more, the data also revealed that the clock was responding to the slight tidal distortion of the earth due to the gravitational pull of the moon and sun.
(35)   In addition to causing the familiar ocean tides, both the sun and the moon raise tides in the solid body of the earth. The effect is to raise and lower the surface of the earth by about 30 centimeters. Since the acceleration due to gravity depends on distance
(40)   from the center of the earth, this slight tidal movement affects the period of swing of a pendulum. In each case, the cycle of the tides caused the clock to gain or lose up to 140 microseconds.

Questions 136–139 refer to the passage.

136. According to the passage, the use of Shortt clocks led to the discovery that

    (A) optical sensing equipment can be used effectively in timekeeping systems
    (B) atomic clocks can be used in place of pendulum clocks in observatories
    (C) tides occur in solid ground as well as in oceans
    (D) the earth's rotation varies from one time of year to another
    (E) pendulums can be synchronized with one another electronically

137. The passage most strongly suggests that which of the following is true of the chamber in which a Shortt clock's primary pendulum was housed?

    (A) It contained elaborate mechanisms that were attached to, and moved by, the pendulum.
    (B) It was firmly sealed during normal operation of the clock.
    (C) It was at least partly transparent so as to allow for certain types of visual data output.
    (D) It housed both the primary pendulum and another pendulum.
    (E) It contained a transmitter that was activated at irregular intervals to send a signal to the secondary pendulum.

138. The passage most strongly suggests that its author would agree with which of the following statements about clocks?

   (A) Before 1921, no one had designed a clock that used electricity to aid in its timekeeping functions.
   (B) Atomic clocks depend on the operation of mechanisms that were invented by William Shortt and first used in the Shortt clock.
   (C) No type of clock that keeps time more stably and accurately than a Shortt clock relies fundamentally on the operation of a pendulum.
   (D) Subtle changes in the earth's rotation slightly reduce the accuracy of all clocks used in observatories after 1921.
   (E) At least some mechanical clocks that do not have pendulums are almost identical to Shortt clocks in their mode of operation.

139. The passage most strongly suggests that the study described in the third paragraph would not have been possible in the absence of

   (A) accurate information regarding the times at which high and low ocean tides occurred at various locations during 1984
   (B) comparative data regarding the use of Shortt clocks in observatories between 1921 and 1932
   (C) a non-Shortt clock that was known to keep time extremely precisely and reliably
   (D) an innovative electric-power source that was not available in the 1920s and 1930s
   (E) optical data-transmission devices to communicate between the U.S. Naval Observatory and other research facilities

Line　　Comparable worth, as a standard applied to eliminate inequities in pay, insists that the values of certain tasks performed in dissimilar jobs can be compared. In the last decade, this approach has become a critical
(5)　social policy issue, as large numbers of private-sector firms and industries as well as federal, state, and local governmental entities have adopted comparable worth policies or begun to consider doing so.

　　This widespread institutional awareness of comparable
(10)　worth indicates increased public awareness that pay inequities—that is, situations in which pay is not "fair" because it does not reflect the true value of a job—exist in the labor market. However, the question still remains: have the gains already made in pay equity
(15)　under comparable worth principles been of a precedent-setting nature, or are they mostly transitory, a function of concessions made by employers to mislead female employees into believing that they have made long-term pay equity gains?

(20)　Comparable worth pay adjustments are indeed precedent-setting. Because of the principles driving them, other mandates that can be applied to reduce or eliminate unjustified pay gaps between male and female workers have not remedied perceived pay
(25)　inequities satisfactorily for the litigants in cases in which men and women hold different jobs. But whenever comparable worth principles are applied to pay schedules, perceived unjustified pay differences are eliminated. In this sense, then, comparable worth
(30)　is more comprehensive than other mandates, such as the Equal Pay Act of 1963 and Title VII of the Civil Rights Act of 1964. Neither compares tasks in dissimilar jobs (that is, jobs across occupational categories) in an effort to determine whether or not
(35)　what is necessary to perform these tasks—know-how, problem-solving, and accountability—can be quantified in terms of its dollar value to the employer. Comparable worth, on the other hand, takes as its premise that certain tasks in dissimilar jobs may
(40)　require a similar amount of training, effort, and skill; may carry similar responsibility; may be carried on in an environment having a similar impact upon the worker; and may have a similar dollar value to the employer.

Questions 140–143 refer to the passage.

140. According to the passage, comparable worth principles are different in which of the following ways from other mandates intended to reduce or eliminate pay inequities?

   (A) Comparable worth principles address changes in the pay schedules of male as well as female workers.
   (B) Comparable worth principles can be applied to employees in both the public and the private sector.
   (C) Comparable worth principles emphasize the training and skill of workers.
   (D) Comparable worth principles require changes in the employer's resource allocation.
   (E) Comparable worth principles can be used to quantify the value of elements of dissimilar jobs.

141. According to the passage, which of the following is true of comparable worth as a policy?

   (A) Comparable worth policy decisions in pay-inequity cases have often failed to satisfy the complainants.
   (B) Comparable worth policies have been applied to both public-sector and private-sector employee pay schedules.
   (C) Comparable worth as a policy has come to be widely criticized in the past decade.
   (D) Many employers have considered comparable worth as a policy, but very few have actually adopted it.
   (E) Early implementations of comparable worth policies resulted in only transitory gains in pay equity.

142. It can be inferred from the passage that application of "other mandates" (see line 22) would be unlikely to result in an outcome satisfactory to the female employees in which of the following situations?

   I. Males employed as long-distance truck drivers for a furniture company make $3.50 more per hour than do females with comparable job experience employed in the same capacity.
   II. Women working in the office of a cement company contend that their jobs are as demanding and valuable as those of the men working outside in the cement factory, but the women are paid much less per hour.
   III. A law firm employs both male and female paralegals with the same educational and career backgrounds, but the starting salary for male paralegals is $5,000 more than for female paralegals.

   (A) I only
   (B) II only
   (C) III only
   (D) I and II only
   (E) I and III only

143. Which of the following best describes an application of the principles of comparable worth as they are described in the passage?

   (A) The current pay, rates of increase, and rates of promotion for female mechanics are compared with those of male mechanics.
   (B) The training, skills, and job experience of computer programmers in one division of a corporation are compared to those of programmers making more money in another division.
   (C) The number of women holding top executive positions in a corporation is compared to the number of women available for promotion to those positions, and both tallies are matched to the tallies for men in the same corporation.
   (D) The skills, training, and job responsibilities of the clerks in the township tax assessor's office are compared to those of the much better paid township engineers.
   (E) The working conditions of female workers in a hazardous-materials environment are reviewed and their pay schedules compared to those of all workers in similar environments across the nation.

4.5 Answer Key: Reading Comprehension

1.	C	30.	D	59.	D	88.	B	117.	C
2.	E	31.	B	60.	B	89.	C	118.	D
3.	D	32.	C	61.	A	90.	E	119.	A
4.	E	33.	B	62.	E	91.	D	120.	C
5.	A	34.	A	63.	C	92.	C	121.	B
6.	B	35.	E	64.	D	93.	E	122.	D
7.	D	36.	A	65.	A	94.	D	123.	A
8.	C	37.	E	66.	C	95.	D	124.	E
9.	D	38.	B	67.	C	96.	B	125.	B
10.	B	39.	D	68.	A	97.	C	126.	D
11.	D	40.	C	69.	B	98.	C	127.	E
12.	B	41.	A	70.	B	99.	E	128.	D
13.	E	42.	B	71.	A	100.	A	129.	C
14.	C	43.	A	72.	C	101.	D	130.	B
15.	D	44.	A	73.	A	102.	E	131.	D
16.	C	45.	B	74.	C	103.	C	132.	E
17.	E	46.	D	75.	B	104.	B	133.	B
18.	B	47.	D	76.	E	105.	A	134.	B
19.	A	48.	B	77.	B	106.	B	135.	A
20.	D	49.	B	78.	D	107.	C	136.	D
21.	B	50.	E	79.	C	108.	D	137.	B
22.	E	51.	C	80.	B	109.	A	138.	C
23.	C	52.	C	81.	C	110.	B	139.	C
24.	C	53.	C	82.	A	111.	C	140.	E
25.	B	54.	D	83.	C	112.	B	141.	B
26.	A	55.	E	84.	D	113.	A	142.	B
27.	D	56.	D	85.	E	114.	C	143.	D
28.	E	57.	A	86.	B	115.	E		
29.	D	58.	B	87.	E	116.	A		

4.6 Answer Explanations: Reading Comprehension

The following discussion of Reading Comprehension is intended to familiarize you with the most efficient and effective approaches to the kinds of problems common to Reading Comprehension. The particular questions in this chapter are generally representative of the kinds of Reading Comprehension questions you will encounter on the GMAT exam. Remember that it is the problem-solving strategy that is important, not the specific details of a particular question.

Questions 1 to 47 — Difficulty: Easy

Questions 1–4 refer to the passage on page 52.

1. According to the passage, traditional corporate leaders differ from leaders in learning organizations in that the former

    (A) encourage employees to concentrate on developing a wide range of skills
    (B) enable employees to recognize and confront dominant corporate models and to develop alternative models
    (C) make important policy decisions alone and then require employees in the corporation to abide by those decisions
    (D) instill confidence in employees because of their willingness to make risky decisions and accept their consequences
    (E) are concerned with offering employees frequent advice and career guidance

Supporting Idea

This question requires understanding of the contrast the passage draws between leaders of traditional corporations and leaders of learning organizations. According to the second paragraph, the former are traditionally charismatic leaders who set policy and make decisions, while the latter foster integrated thinking at all levels of the organization.

   A   According to the passage, it is leaders in learning organizations, not traditional corporate leaders, who encourage the development of a wide range of skills.

   B   Leaders in learning organizations are those who want their employees to challenge dominant models.

   C   **Correct.** The second paragraph states that traditional corporate leaders are individualistic; they alone *set the corporation's direction and make key decisions*.

   D   The passage does not address the question of whether traditional corporate leaders instill confidence in employees. In fact, the first paragraph suggests that they may not; rather, they might come across as objectionably controlling.

   E   The passage suggests that advice and guidance are more likely to be offered by leaders of learning organizations than by leaders of traditional corporations.

The correct answer is C.

2. Which of the following best describes employee behavior encouraged within learning organizations, as such organizations are described in the passage?

    (A) Carefully defining one's job description and taking care to avoid deviations from it
    (B) Designing mentoring programs that train new employees to follow procedures that have been used for many years
    (C) Concentrating one's efforts on mastering one aspect of a complicated task
    (D) Studying an organizational problem, preparing a report, and submitting it to a corporate leader for approval
    (E) Analyzing a problem related to productivity, making a decision about a solution, and implementing that solution

Application

The second paragraph of the passage indicates that employees of learning organizations are encouraged to think and act for themselves; they learn new skills and expand their capabilities.

A. Avoiding deviations from one's carefully defined job description would more likely be encouraged in a traditional corporation, as described in the first paragraph, than in a learning organization.

B. Any employee training that involves following long-standing procedures would more likely be encouraged in a traditional corporation than a learning organization.

C. According to the passage, mastering only one aspect of a task, no matter how complicated, would be insufficient in a learning organization, in which broad patterns of thinking are encouraged.

D. As described in the passage, the role of corporate leaders in learning organizations is not, characteristically, to approve employees' solutions to problems, but rather to enable and empower employees to implement solutions on their own.

E. **Correct.** Employees in learning organizations are expected to act on their own initiative; thus, they would be encouraged to analyze and solve problems on their own, implementing whatever solutions they devised.

The correct answer is E.

3. According to the author of the passage, corporate leaders of the future should do which of the following?

(A) They should encourage employees to put long-term goals ahead of short-term profits.
(B) They should exercise more control over employees in order to constrain production costs.
(C) They should redefine incentives for employees' performance improvement.
(D) They should provide employees with opportunities to gain new skills and expand their capabilities.
(E) They should promote individual managers who are committed to established company policies.

Supporting Idea

This question focuses on what the author recommends in the passage for future corporate leaders. In the second paragraph, the author states that, among other things, corporate leaders need to be teachers to provide challenges to their employees and create an atmosphere where *employees are continually learning new skills and expanding their capabilities to shape their future.*

A. The passage does not directly discuss the issue of corporate goals and profitability in the long or short term.

B. The passage does not address the topic of production costs, and it suggests that its author would favor reducing, rather than increasing, corporate leaders' control over employees. The first paragraph states that leaders who attempt to control employees lead those employees to perform in mediocre fashion.

C. The passage does not discuss incentivizing employees' performance; rather, employees' performance will improve, the passage suggests, under different corporate leadership.

D. **Correct.** The final sentence of the passage states directly that leaders must build organizations in which employees can learn new skills and expand their capabilities.

E. The first paragraph indicates that clinging to established company policies is a strategy for the future that is likely to be unproductive.

The correct answer is D.

4. The primary purpose of the passage is to

(A) endorse a traditional corporate structure
(B) introduce a new approach to corporate leadership and evaluate criticisms of it
(C) explain competing theories about management practices and reconcile them
(D) contrast two typical corporate organizational structures
(E) propose an alternative to a common corporate approach

Main Idea

This question depends on understanding the passage as a whole. The first paragraph explains the way in which corporations fail to facilitate how humans learn. The second paragraph suggests that corporations should change the way they view employees in order to promote learning, and it explains the positive outcomes that would result from that shift in thinking.

A The first paragraph explains that the traditional corporate structure leads to mediocre performance; it does not endorse that structure.

B The second paragraph introduces the concept of a *learning organization* and its attendant approach to corporate leadership. Rather than identifying any criticisms of that approach, the passage endorses it wholeheartedly.

C The passage discusses the difference between the idea of a single charismatic leader and that of a shared corporate leadership, but it does not attempt to reconcile these two ideas.

D The passage's main focus is on advocating a particular approach, not on merely contrasting it with another. Furthermore, it portrays only one of the approaches as typical. It suggests that the organizational structure that relies on a single charismatic leader is typical but that another approach, that in which leadership is shared, should instead become typical.

E **Correct.** The passage identifies a common corporate approach, one based on controlling employees, and proposes that corporations should instead become *learning organizations*.

The correct answer is E.

Questions 5–7 refer to the passage on page 54.

5. The passage suggests that the scholars mentioned in line 14 would agree with which of the following statements regarding the "norms" mentioned in line 19?

(A) They provided a primary source of opposition to the development of laissez-faire capitalism in the United States in the nineteenth century.

(B) Their appeal was undermined by difficult economic times in the United States at the end of the nineteenth century.

(C) They disappeared in the United States in the late nineteenth century because of the triumph of laissez-faire capitalism.

(D) They facilitated the successful implementation of mercantilist notions of government in the United States in the nineteenth century.

(E) They are now recognized by historians as having been an important part of the ideology of the American Revolution.

Evaluation

The passage describes phases in the development of laissez-faire capitalism in the United States. It tells us that this kind of unfettered capitalism *was not accepted without struggle*. The present question asks us to relate the view attributed to *some scholars* to how the *norms* mentioned affected a phase in the history of capitalism in the United States.

A **Correct.** The passage tells us that, according to some scholars, *religious and communitarian norms* were in tension with values underlying unrestrained capitalism and were an important source of opposition to it into the late nineteenth century. At that time, these scholars argue, laissez-faire capitalism *had not triumphed completely*.

B The passage attributes to the scholars cited a suggestion that by the end of the nineteenth century, in economically difficult times, there was a popular sentiment that the government should regulate business, in accordance with the *norms* mentioned and contrary to the ideology of laissez-faire capitalism.

C On the contrary, the passage suggests that, in the view of the scholars cited, the norms being discussed persisted and provided some opposition to unrestrained capitalism.

D The passage does not state or imply that the scholars regarded the *norms* as facilitating the implementation of *mercantilist notions*. The view ascribed to the scholars is that mercantilist notions helped support the norms. The passage does not imply that such notions were implemented in the nineteenth century.

E The passage attributes to the scholars mentioned in line 14 no view concerning how the norms in question may have figured in the ideology of the American Revolution, which, the passage tells us, *helped unleash the economic forces* that led to laissez-faire capitalism.

The correct answer is A.

6. The author of the passage mentions the Progressives as examples of historians who

(A) saw farmers and small producers as having the potential to become a powerful force in American society

(B) did not question the widespread acceptance of laissez-faire capitalism in the United States in spite of their sympathy for farmers and small producers

(C) did not agree that religious and communitarian norms were needed to soften the harsh edges of laissez-faire capitalism

(D) saw the development of laissez-faire capitalism in the United States as a historical inevitability in spite of their lack of sympathy for large capitalists

(E) were somewhat out of the mainstream of the American historical profession

Application

The author discusses the views of historians, including Progressive historians, regarding late-nineteenth-century capitalism in the United States.

A The author does not attribute to Progressive historians the view that the resistance mounted by farmers and small producers against large capitalist businesses could pose a powerful challenge to entrenched laissez-faire capitalism.

B **Correct.** The author tells us that historians ideologically aligned with the Progressive movement sympathized with farmers and small producers who struggled against large capitalist entities. But these historians accepted the reality of laissez-faire capitalism as the dominant economic force throughout United States history.

C The author provides no information on the attitude of Progressive historians to a possible role for religious and communitarian norms to oppose laissez-faire capitalism.

D While the author's view is that Progressive historians recognized the reality that laissez-faire capitalism predominated since the founding of the United States, we are not told that they saw its triumph as historically inevitable.

E The passage indicates that the views of the Progressive historians regarding laissez-faire capitalism were not universally accepted in every detail by other historians, but this does not imply that their views were *out of the mainstream* among American historians.

The correct answer is B.

7. The primary purpose of the passage is to

(A) reveal the underlying similarities of certain arguments regarding the development of capitalism in the United States

(B) synthesize two competing arguments regarding the development of capitalism in the United States

(C) defend an established argument regarding the development of capitalism in the United States

(D) summarize a scholarly refutation of an argument regarding the development of capitalism in the United States

(E) discuss a new methodology for the study of the development of capitalism in the United States

Main Idea

For many years, the passage tells us, the orthodox view among historians was that capitalism faced no serious resistance in the

United States. But the passage makes the case that other historians challenged that orthodoxy, arguing that unrestrained capitalism *was not accepted without struggle*.

A   The primary purpose of the passage is not to reveal underlying similarities but rather to show historical arguments against an entrenched orthodoxy among some historians regarding the rise of unrestrained capitalism in the United States.
B   The passage does not aim to meld two competing arguments into a single consistent argument.
C   On the contrary, the passage does not try to *defend an established argument* regarding capitalism in the United States but rather to present the arguments of historians who contest an established argument.
D   **Correct.** More than half of the passage is devoted to a scholarly argument that unrestrained capitalism in the United States never enjoyed unqualified support.
E   It is not a purpose of the passage to discuss a methodology for the study of capitalism's rise in the United States.

The correct answer is D.

Questions 8–10 refer to the passage on page 56.

8. The primary purpose of the passage is to

   (A) explain why a particular business strategy has been less successful than was once anticipated
   (B) propose an alternative to a particular business strategy that has inadvertently caused ecological damage
   (C) present a concern about the possible consequences of pursuing a particular business strategy
   (D) make a case for applying a particular business strategy on a larger scale than is currently practiced
   (E) suggest several possible outcomes of companies' failure to understand the economic impact of a particular business strategy

Main Idea

Ecoefficient processes involve reducing waste from industrial production to minimize environmental impact, and they have resulted in cost savings for companies. However, the passage cites the views of Senge and Carstedt, who argue that such a strategy, if not prudently pursued, can worsen environmental outcomes.

A   The passage does not indicate that implementing ecoefficient processes has been less successful than anticipated in reducing environmental impact. Rather, the primary focus of the passage is to present ways that, according to Senge and Carstedt, ecoefficient strategies can go wrong.
B   The passage does not suggest that implementing ecoefficient processes has caused ecological damage. In describing recommendations made by Senge and Carstedt, the passage indicates ways that ecoefficiency approaches can be moderated to improve environmental outcomes.
C   **Correct.** The passage, drawing on the views of Senge and Carstedt, argues that use of ecoefficient processes in industrial production, however commendable, can have bad environmental effects if exclusively pursued.
D   The passage cautions against more extensive use of an ecoefficiency approach than currently exists in industrial production.
E   The passage is not focused on exploring the economic impact of pursuing ecoefficiency in industrial production. The focus is on possible environmental outcomes.

The correct answer is C.

9. The passage mentions which of the following as a possible consequence of a company's realization of greater profits through ecoefficiency?

   (A) The companies may be able to sell a greater number of products by lowering prices.
   (B) The companies may be better able to attract investment capital in the global market.
   (C) The profits may be reinvested to increase economic growth through ecoefficiency.

(D) The profits may be used as investment capital for industries that are not ecoefficient.

(E) The profits may encourage companies to make further innovations in reducing production waste.

Supporting Idea

The passage tells us that ecoefficient practices by industrial companies can result in higher profits. But according to the views of Senge and Carstedt cited by the passage, higher profits are a mixed blessing with respect to possible environmental impact. Note that the question concerns something that the passage *mentions* (as opposed to suggests or implies).

A   Although this could result from higher profits, the passage does not mention it.
B   No doubt higher profits could make this more likely, but it is not mentioned in the passage.
C   The company could reinvest some of its higher profits to grow in an ecoefficient manner, but this is not mentioned in the passage.
D   **Correct.** The passage states: *greater profits may be turned into investment capital that could easily be reinvested in traditionally eco-inefficient industries.*
E   This possibility is consistent with what is conveyed in the passage, but it is not mentioned in the passage.

The correct answer is D.

10. The passage implies that which of the following is a possible consequence of a company's adoption of innovations that increase its ecoefficiency?

    (A) Company profits resulting from such innovations may be reinvested in that company with no guarantee that the company will continue to make further improvements in ecoefficiency.
    (B) Company growth fostered by cost savings from such innovations may allow that company to manufacture a greater number of products that will be used and discarded, thus worsening environmental stress.
    (C) A company that fails to realize significant cost savings from such innovations may have little incentive to continue to minimize the environmental impact of its production processes.
    (D) A company that comes to depend on such innovations to increase its profits and growth may be vulnerable in the global market to competition from traditionally eco-inefficient industries.
    (E) A company that meets its ecoefficiency goals is unlikely to invest its increased profits in the development of new and innovative ecoefficiency measures.

Inference

The question concerns something implied but not stated in the passage. The passage states that ecoefficient innovations, no matter how effective in reducing production waste, do not *alter the number of products manufactured nor the waste generated from their use and discard*. In fact, as the passage says, growth in profits allow a company *to generate more total waste*, with increased damage to the environment.

A   The passage contains no implication as to whether a company's profits from ecoefficient innovation, if reinvested in the company, would necessarily lead to further ecoefficiency gains.
B   **Correct.** The passage implies that cost savings from ecoefficient production can enable a company to expand production, thus generating more total waste, not just from production itself, but also from the greater number of products eventually discarded after use.
C   Although such a failure to achieve cost saving through ecoefficiency in production might well be a disincentive for further efforts to improve ecoefficiency, such an effect is not addressed in the passage either explicitly or by implication.
D   The information in the passage suggests that ecoefficient production would improve a company's competitive edge over companies that did not enjoy gains from ecoefficient approaches.
E   The passage suggests that some companies may not reinvest profits from ecoefficient production in further boosting their ecoefficiency, but the passage does not imply that such reinvestment is unlikely.

The correct answer is B.

Questions 11–16 refer to the passage on page 58.

11. The passage is primarily concerned with

    (A) explaining why one method of earthquake prediction has proven more practicable than an alternative method
    (B) suggesting that accurate earthquake forecasting must combine elements of long-term and short-term prediction
    (C) challenging the usefulness of dilatancy theory for explaining the occurrence of precursory phenomena
    (D) discussing the deficiency of two methods by which researchers have attempted to predict the occurrence of earthquakes
    (E) describing the development of methods for establishing patterns in the occurrence of past earthquakes

Main Idea

To answer this question, focus on what the passage as a whole is trying to do. The first paragraph describes a method for predicting the occurrence of earthquakes, and the second paragraph explains problems with that method. The third paragraph describes a second method for predicting the occurrence of earthquakes, and the fourth paragraph explains problems with that method. Thus, the passage as a whole is primarily concerned with explaining the deficiencies of two methods for predicting the occurrence of earthquakes.

A The passage does not compare the practicability of the two methods.
B The passage does not discuss combining long-term and short-term methods.
C Only the first half of the passage discusses dilatancy theory; the second half discusses a different method for predicting the occurrence of earthquakes.
D **Correct.** The passage describes two methods for predicting the occurrence of earthquakes and explains the shortcomings of each method.
E Only the second half of the passage discusses patterns in the occurrence of past earthquakes; the first half discusses a different method for predicting the occurrence of earthquakes.

The correct answer is D.

12. According to the passage, laboratory evidence concerning the effects of stress on rocks might help account for

    (A) differences in magnitude among earthquakes
    (B) certain phenomena that occur prior to earthquakes
    (C) variations in the intervals between earthquakes in a particular area
    (D) differences in the frequency with which earthquakes occur in various areas
    (E) the unreliability of short-term earthquake predictions

Supporting Idea

This question asks for information explicitly stated in the passage. The first paragraph explains that rocks subjected to stress in the laboratory undergo multiple changes. According to *dilatancy theory*, such changes happening to rocks in the field could lead to earthquake precursors—phenomena that occur before large earthquakes.

A The passage explains how laboratory evidence might be used to predict the occurrence of large earthquakes, not to differentiate between earthquakes' magnitudes.
B **Correct.** According to dilatancy theory, the sort of changes that have been observed in laboratories to occur in rocks might lead to earthquake precursors in the field.
C Although the passage discusses variation in earthquake intervals, that evidence is based on historical records, not laboratory evidence.
D The passage does not refer in any way to differences in the frequency of earthquakes in various regions.

E   The unreliability of one method for making short-term earthquake predictions is implied by information gathered in the field, not by laboratory evidence.

The correct answer is B.

13. It can be inferred from the passage that one problem with using precursory phenomena to predict earthquakes is that minor tremors

    (A) typically occur some distance from the sites of the large earthquakes that follow them
    (B) are directly linked to the mechanisms that cause earthquakes
    (C) are difficult to distinguish from major tremors
    (D) have proven difficult to measure accurately
    (E) are not always followed by large earthquakes

Inference

This question asks what can be inferred from certain information in the passage. The second paragraph explains two problems with using minor tremors to predict earthquakes. First, minor tremors provide no information about how large an impending earthquake will be. Second, the minor tremors that occur prior to a large earthquake are indistinguishable from other minor tremors. Thus, it can be inferred that minor tremors sometimes occur when no large earthquake follows.

A   The passage does not mention the distance between minor tremors and ensuing earthquakes.

B   The passage implies that minor tremors sometimes occur without an ensuing earthquake, so the phenomena are most likely not directly linked.

C   The passage suggests no difficulty in distinguishing between minor tremors and major tremors.

D   The passage does not mention any difficulties in the measurement of minor tremors.

E   **Correct.** The passage indicates that minor tremors occurring prior to a large earthquake are indistinguishable from minor tremors that are not followed by large earthquakes. So the fact that minor tremors are not always followed by large earthquakes, together with the inability to distinguish between those that are and those that are not, poses a problem for any attempt to predict large earthquakes on the basis of this type of precursory phenomena.

The correct answer is E.

14. According to the passage, some researchers based their research about long-term earthquake prediction on which of the following facts?

    (A) The historical record confirms that most earthquakes have been preceded by minor tremors.
    (B) The average interval between earthquakes in one region of the San Andreas Fault is 132 years.
    (C) Some regions tend to be the site of numerous earthquakes over the course of many years.
    (D) Changes in the volume of rock can occur as a result of building stress and can lead to the weakening of rock.
    (E) Paleoseismologists have been able to unearth and date geological features caused by past earthquakes.

Supporting Idea

This question asks for information explicitly provided in the passage. The question asks what the basis is for the research into long-term earthquake prediction described in the third paragraph. Based on the fact that numerous earthquakes occur in some regions over the course of many years, the researchers tried to identify regular earthquake intervals that would assist in making long-term predictions. Thus, the basis of their research is the occurrence of numerous earthquakes at particular sites.

A   The passage indicates that minor tremors are used by some scientists to make short-term earthquake predictions, not that they were the basis for research about long-term predictions.

B   This fact about the San Andreas Fault was used by paleoseismologists to show the inadequacy of the long-term prediction research, since actual earthquake intervals varied greatly from the average.

C   **Correct.** Since earthquakes occur repeatedly in certain regions, researchers tried to identify regular cycles in earthquake intervals.

D   The passage indicates that changes in rock volume have been used by some scientists to make short-term earthquake predictions, not that they were the basis for research about long-term predictions.

E   Paleoseismologists' research provided evidence against the existence of regular earthquake cycles used in making long-term predictions.

The correct answer is C.

15. The passage suggests which of the following about the paleoseismologists' findings described in lines 42–50?

    (A) They suggest that the frequency with which earthquakes occurred at a particular site decreased significantly over the past two millennia.

    (B) They suggest that paleoseismologists may someday be able to make reasonably accurate long-term earthquake predictions.

    (C) They suggest that researchers may someday be able to determine which past occurrences of minor tremors were actually followed by large earthquakes.

    (D) They suggest that the recurrence of earthquakes in earthquake-prone sites is too irregular to serve as a basis for earthquake prediction.

    (E) They indicate that researchers attempting to develop long-term methods of earthquake prediction have overlooked important evidence concerning the causes of earthquakes.

Inference

This question asks about what can be inferred from a particular portion of the passage (lines 42–50). The third paragraph describes research that attempted to identify regular patterns of recurrence in earthquake-prone regions, to aid in long-term earthquake prediction. The fourth paragraph describes evidence discovered by paleoseismologists that undermines this idea that regular earthquake cycles exist. The paragraph indicates that in one region along the San Andreas Fault, the average interval between earthquakes was 132 years, but individual intervals varied widely—from 44 to 332 years. This information implies that earthquake intervals are too irregular to be used for accurate long-term earthquake prediction.

A   The evidence suggests that the earthquake intervals are irregular, not that they have become shorter over time.

B   The findings provide evidence against the use of regular earthquake cycles in long-term earthquake prediction.

C   The findings do not clearly pertain to minor tremors.

D   **Correct.** The great variation in intervals between earthquakes suggests that recurrence is too irregular to serve as the basis for long-term earthquake prediction.

E   The paleoseismologists studied evidence showing when earthquakes occurred. The passage does not suggest that the evidence has any implications regarding the causes of earthquakes.

The correct answer is D.

16. The author implies which of the following about the ability of the researchers mentioned in line 17 to predict earthquakes?

    (A) They can identify when an earthquake is likely to occur but not how large it will be.

    (B) They can identify the regions where earthquakes are likely to occur but not when they will occur.

    (C) They are unable to determine either the time or the place that earthquakes are likely to occur.

    (D) They are likely to be more accurate at short-term earthquake prediction than at long-term earthquake prediction.

(E) They can determine the regions where earthquakes have occurred in the past but not the regions where they are likely to occur in the future.

Supporting Idea

The question asks for information explicitly provided in the passage. The second paragraph indicates that researchers at first reported success in identifying earthquake precursors, but further analysis of the data undermined their theory. The passage then explains that atypical seismic waves were recorded before some earthquakes; this evidence at first seemed to support the researchers' theory, before further analysis proved the evidence inadequate.

A   Although earthquakes are caused by stress on rock, the passage does not indicate that this fact encouraged researchers to believe that precursors could be used to predict earthquakes.

B   This fact would undermine the theory that changes in seismic waves are precursory phenomena that can be used to predict earthquakes.

C   **Correct.** Seismic waves with unusual velocities occurring before earthquakes at first seemed to provide support for researchers' theory that earthquakes could be predicted by precursory phenomena.

D   Though earthquakes' recurrence in certain regions is mentioned as being important to researchers seeking to make long-term earthquake predictions, it is not mentioned as being relevant to researchers' theory that earthquakes can be predicted by precursory phenomena.

E   This is not mentioned as being relevant to scientists' belief that earthquakes could be predicted on the basis of precursory phenomena.

The correct answer is C.

Questions 17–23 refer to the passage on page 60.

17. It can be inferred from the passage that one reason an advertiser might prefer a hard-sell approach to a soft-sell approach is that

(A) the risks of boomerang effects are minimized when the conclusions an advertiser wants the consumer to draw are themselves left unstated

(B) counterargumentation is likely from consumers who fail to draw their own conclusions regarding an advertising claim

(C) inferential activity is likely to occur even if consumers perceive themselves to be more knowledgeable than the individuals presenting product claims

(D) research on consumer memory suggests that the explicit conclusions provided by an advertiser using the hard-sell approach have a significant impact on decision making

(E) the information presented by an advertiser using the soft-sell approach may imply different conclusions to different consumers

Inference

This question relies on what the passage suggests about the difference between the hard-sell and soft-sell approaches—and why the hard-sell approach might be preferred. The hard-sell approach, according to the second paragraph, presents explicit conclusions. The soft-sell approach, on the other hand, does not explicitly state conclusions about products; instead, consumers make up their own minds.

A   While the passage makes clear that boomerang effects are minimized when conclusions are left unstated, this is an advantage of the soft-sell approach over the hard-sell approach.

B   According to the second paragraph, counterargumentation is a disadvantage, not an advantage, of the hard-sell approach. This is a reason not to prefer the hard sell.

119

C   The third paragraph suggests that in cases in which consumers may perceive themselves as more knowledgeable than individuals presenting product claims, the soft-sell approach offers an advantage over the hard-sell approach.

D   According to the third paragraph, self-generated conclusions that are associated with the soft-sell approach have a greater impact on decision making than explicit conclusions. The passage does not allude to any research on memory that would favor the hard-sell approach.

E   **Correct.** The fourth paragraph suggests that one problem with the soft-sell approach is that consumers could miss the point; they may not come to the conclusions that the advertiser would prefer. Thus an advertiser might prefer a hard-sell approach.

The correct answer is E.

18. Each of the following is mentioned in the passage as a characteristic of the hard-sell approach EXCEPT:

    (A) Its overall message is readily grasped.
    (B) It appeals to consumers' knowledge about the product.
    (C) It makes explicit claims that the advertised brand is superior to other brands.
    (D) It uses statements that are expressed very clearly.
    (E) It makes claims in the form of direct conclusions.

Supporting Idea

This question asks about what is directly stated in the passage about the hard-sell approach. The first and second paragraphs provide the details about this approach, including that it uses *direct, forceful claims* about benefits of a brand over competitors' brands; its claims are simple and straightforward, in the form of explicit conclusions; and consumers are generally left with little room for confusion about the message.

A   The second paragraph states that there is little room for confusion about the message.

B   **Correct.** The extent of consumers' knowledge about the product is not mentioned in the passage.

C   The first paragraph indicates that in the hard-sell approach advertisers make direct claims regarding the benefits of the advertised brand over other offerings.

D   The first and second paragraphs say that hard-sell claims are direct, simple, and straightforward.

E   The second paragraph emphasizes that the hard-sell approach presents its claims in the form of explicit conclusions.

The correct answer is B.

19. It can be inferred from the passage that advertisers could reduce one of the risks discussed in the last paragraph if they were able to provide

    (A) motivation for consumers to think about the advertisement's message
    (B) information that implies the advertiser's intended conclusion but leaves that conclusion unstated
    (C) subtle evidence that the advertised product is superior to that of competitors
    (D) information comparing the advertised product with its competitors
    (E) opportunity for consumers to generate their own beliefs or conclusions

Inference

This question requires understanding the risks discussed in the last paragraph of the passage. Those risks are, first, that consumers would not be motivated to think about the advertisement and thus would miss the message's point; second, that consumers may draw conclusions that the advertiser did not intend; and finally, that consumers could question the validity of the conclusions they reach, even if those conclusions are what advertisers intend.

A   **Correct.** Providing motivation for consumers to think about an advertisement's message would reduce the first risk discussed in the last paragraph: that consumers would fail to draw any conclusions because they would lack motivation to engage with advertisements.

B Providing *information that implies a conclusion but leaves it unstated* is the very definition of the soft-sell approach, and it is this approach that gives rise to the risks discussed in the last paragraph.

C Providing subtle evidence that a product is superior is most likely to give rise to all three of the risks identified in the last paragraph, in that its subtlety would leave consumers free to draw their own conclusions, to fail to draw those conclusions, or to question the validity of their own conclusions.

D A direct comparison of the advertised product with its competitors would run all the risks identified in the last paragraph: consumers might not find the comparison motivating; they could draw conclusions that the advertiser did not intend (e.g., that the competing products are superior); or they could question whatever conclusions they do draw.

E Giving consumers the opportunity *to generate their own beliefs or conclusions* is an intrinsic part of the soft-sell approach, which produces the risks discussed in the last paragraph.

The correct answer is A.

20. The primary purpose of the passage is to

    (A) point out the risks involved in the use of a particular advertising strategy
    (B) make a case for the superiority of one advertising strategy over another
    (C) illustrate the ways in which two advertising strategies may be implemented
    (D) present the advantages and disadvantages of two advertising strategies
    (E) contrast the types of target markets for which two advertising strategies are appropriate

Inference

Overall, the passage is concerned with two advertising strategies. The first paragraph introduces the strategies. The second paragraph explains how a particular aspect of one approach may be both positive and negative and how the second approach mitigates these problems. The third paragraph continues this discussion of mitigation, while the fourth paragraph points out that there are drawbacks to this approach, too. Thus, according to the passage, both strategies have positive and negative aspects.

A The passage is concerned not with one particular advertising strategy but with two, and it discusses benefits, as well as risks, involved with both strategies.

B The passage does not suggest that one strategy is superior to the other but rather that each has positive and negative aspects.

C The passage does not discuss how to implement either of the strategies it is concerned with; instead, it deals with how consumers are likely to respond once the implementation has already taken place.

D **Correct.** The passage is primarily concerned with showing that both of the strategies described have advantages and disadvantages.

E The passage provides some indirect grounds for inferring the target markets for which each advertising strategy might be appropriate, but it is not primarily concerned with contrasting those markets.

The correct answer is D.

21. Which of the following best describes the function of the sentence in lines 25–28 in the context of the passage as a whole?

    (A) It reiterates a distinction between two advertising strategies that is made in the first paragraph.
    (B) It explains how a particular strategy avoids a drawback described earlier in the paragraph.
    (C) It suggests that a risk described earlier in the paragraph is less serious than some researchers believe it to be.

(D) It outlines why the strategy described in the previous sentence involves certain risks for an advertiser.

(E) It introduces an argument that will be refuted in the following paragraph.

Evaluation

The sentence in lines 25–28 explains how the kinds of conclusions consumers are invited to draw based on the soft-sell approach reduce the risk that consumers will respond with *resentment, distrust, and counterargumentation*—that is, the possible *boomerang effect* identified earlier in the paragraph as a drawback of the hard-sell approach.

A The sentence does not reiterate the distinction between the hard- and soft-sell approaches; rather, it explains an advantage of the soft-sell approach.

B **Correct.** The sentence explains how the soft-sell approach avoids the problems that can arise from the hard-sell approach's explicitly stated conclusions.

C The sentence suggests that the risk of boomerang effects described earlier in the paragraph is serious but that a different approach can mitigate it.

D The sentence outlines why the strategy described in the previous sentence reduces advertisers' risks, not why it involves risks.

E At no point does the passage refute the idea that implicit conclusions reduce the risk of boomerang effects. It does say that there could be drawbacks to the soft-sell approach, but those drawbacks are related to the problem with implicit conclusions themselves and how people reach them. In addition, the *following paragraph* does not mention the drawbacks, only the advantages of implicit conclusions.

The correct answer is B.

22. It can be inferred from the passage that one situation in which the boomerang effect often occurs is when consumers

(A) have been exposed to forceful claims that are diametrically opposed to those in an advertiser's message

(B) have previous self-generated beliefs or conclusions that are readily accessible from memory

(C) are subjected to advertising messages that are targeted at specific markets to which those consumers do not belong

(D) are confused regarding the point of the advertiser's message

(E) come to view the advertiser's message with suspicion

Inference

The passage discusses the boomerang effect in the second paragraph. This effect is defined as consumers deriving conclusions from advertising that are the opposite of those that advertisers intended to present, and it occurs when consumers resent and/or distrust what they are being told.

A The passage provides no grounds for inferring that consumers need to be exposed to opposing claims in order to believe such claims; they may reach opposing claims on their own.

B The passage indicates that the boomerang effect can be reduced by using a soft-sell approach, which can result in self-generated conclusions, but it provides no evidence about any possible effects of preexisting self-generated beliefs or conclusions on the boomerang effect.

C The passage does not address how consumers who are subjected to advertising messages not intended for them might respond.

D Confusion regarding the point of the advertiser's message is more likely to occur, the passage suggests, when advertisers use a soft-sell approach—but it is the hard-sell approach, not the soft-sell, that is likely to result in the boomerang effect.

E **Correct.** The second paragraph indicates that consumers who resent being told what to believe and come to distrust the advertiser's message—that is, those who view the message with suspicion—may experience a boomerang effect, believing the opposite of the conclusions offered.

The correct answer is E.

23. It can be inferred from the passage that the research mentioned in line 29 supports which of the following statements?

    (A) Implicit conclusions are more likely to capture accurately the point of the advertiser's message than are explicit conclusions.
    (B) Counterargumentation is less likely to occur if an individual's beliefs or conclusions are readily accessible from memory.
    (C) The hard-sell approach results in conclusions that are more difficult for the consumer to recall than are conclusions resulting from the soft-sell approach.
    (D) When the beliefs of others are presented as definite and forceful claims, they are perceived to be as accurate as self-generated beliefs.
    (E) Despite the advantages of implicit conclusions, the hard-sell approach involves fewer risks for the advertiser than does the soft-sell approach.

Inference

The research this item refers to—research on consumer memory and judgment—indicates that beliefs are more memorable when they are self-generated and so matter when making judgments and decisions. Further, self-generated beliefs seem more believable to those who have them than beliefs that come from elsewhere.

A The fourth paragraph indicates that implicit conclusions are more likely to fail to replicate the advertiser's message than explicit conclusions are.

B The research discussed in the passage does not address when counterargumentation is more or less likely to occur. Even though counterargumentation is a risk when consumers distrust the advertiser's message—as they may do when harder-to-recall explicit conclusions are given—it may be as much of a risk when consumers reach an implicit conclusion that is readily accessible from memory.

C **Correct.** The research indicates that it is easier for consumers to recall conclusions they have reached on their own—that is, the sorts of conclusions that are encouraged by the soft-sell approach—than conclusions that have been provided explicitly, as happens in the hard-sell approach.

D The research does not show that the forcefulness with which claims are presented increases perceptions of the accuracy of those claims. Indeed, it is most likely the opposite, as the forcefulness of others' claims may make them seem even less related to any conclusions the consumer might generate for him- or herself.

E The research suggests that it is the soft-sell, not the hard-sell, approach that has fewer risks. The fourth paragraph indicates that there could be some risks to the implicit conclusions that consumers draw, but this is not part of the research in question.

The correct answer is C.

Questions 24–28 refer to the passage on page 62.

24. It can be inferred from the passage that the two procedures described in the passage have which of the following in common?

    (A) They have been applied in practice.
    (B) They rely on the use of a device that measures tension.
    (C) Their purpose is to determine an unknown mass.
    (D) They can only be applied to small solid objects.
    (E) They involve attraction between objects of similar mass.

Inference

The procedures described in the passage are introduced by the suggestion in the first paragraph that someone in a spaceship who wanted to determine a solid object's mass could do so in a particular way. The second paragraph uses the word *weigh* in quotes to refer to a similar procedure for determining the mass of a double-star system.

A   The language of the first paragraph is hypothetical: we *could* do particular things. Thus, there is no way to determine from the passage whether that procedure has been applied in practice.
B   The first procedure relies on a spring scale, which measures tension, but the second procedure measures time and distance to determine restraining force.
C   **Correct.** Both procedures determine mass: the first procedure can determine the mass of a small solid object on a spaceship in free fall, and the second can determine the mass of a double-star system.
D   The first procedure would, according to the passage, be applied to a small solid object, but the second *weighs* double-star systems, which are clearly not small objects.
E   The second procedure involves attraction between two stars, which could be of similar mass, in the same system, but the first procedure involves measuring tension in a string and speed of whirling, not attraction between objects.

The correct answer is C.

25. According to the passage, the tension in the string mentioned in lines 8–9 is analogous to which of the following aspects of a double-star system?

    (A) The speed with which one star orbits the other
    (B) The gravitational attraction between the stars
    (C) The amount of time it takes for the stars to circle one another
    (D) The distance between the two stars
    (E) The combined mass of the two stars

Supporting Idea

The second paragraph states that an *attractive force* is analogous to the tension in the string. This attractive force is identified in the previous sentence as the gravitational force between the two stars in a double-star system.

A   The second paragraph states that the speed with which the stars circle each other depends on the gravitational force between them, but it is that force that is analogous to the tension in the string.
B   **Correct.** The second paragraph clearly identifies the gravitational force between the two stars as the attractive force that is analogous to the tension in the spring scale's string.
C   The amount of time it takes for the stars to circle one another is necessary for calculating the force that holds them together, but it is the force itself that is analogous to the string's tension.
D   The distance between the stars must be measured if the attraction between them is to be determined, but the attraction, not the distance, is analogous to the string's tension.
E   The combined mass of the two stars is what the procedure is designed to determine; it is analogous to the mass of the small solid object, as described in the first paragraph.

The correct answer is B.

26. Which of the following best describes the relationship between the first and the second paragraph of the passage?

    (A) The first paragraph provides an illustration useful for understanding a procedure described in the second paragraph.
    (B) The first paragraph describes a hypothetical situation whose plausibility is tested in the second paragraph.
    (C) The first paragraph evaluates the usefulness of a procedure whose application is described further in the second paragraph.
    (D) The second paragraph provides evidence to support a claim made in the first paragraph.

(E) The second paragraph analyzes the practical implications of a methodology proposed in the first paragraph.

Evaluation

This question requires understanding that the second paragraph describes a somewhat difficult-to-understand procedure that the first paragraph illustrates in smaller, and simpler, terms.

A **Correct.** The first paragraph illustrates, hypothetically, a simple procedure for determining mass, and this illustration provides the grounds on which the passage explains the procedure of the second paragraph.

B The first paragraph describes a situation in hypothetical terms, but the second paragraph does not test that situation's plausibility. Instead, the second paragraph draws an analogy between the initial situation and another procedure.

C The first paragraph does not evaluate the usefulness of the procedure for determining a small solid object's mass while in a spaceship in freefall; it simply describes how that procedure would work.

D The second paragraph provides no evidence; it describes a procedure analogous to what is described in the first paragraph.

E The second paragraph does not discuss the practical implications of the first paragraph's methodology but rather a procedure that is analogous to the hypothetical situation of the first paragraph.

The correct answer is A.

27. The author of the passage mentions observations regarding the period of a double-star system as being useful for determining

    (A) the distance between the two stars in the system
    (B) the time it takes for each star to rotate on its axis
    (C) the size of the orbit the system's two stars occupy
    (D) the degree of gravitational attraction between the system's stars
    (E) the speed at which the star system moves through space

Supporting Idea

The author mentions the period of a double-star system in the final sentence of the second paragraph, defining it as the time required for stars to circle each other. Knowing this time, in combination with the distance between the stars, enables the determination of the restraining force between the stars.

A The final sentence of the second paragraph indicates that the period of a double-star system is measured independently of the distance between the two stars in the system.

B The passage is not concerned with how long it takes each star to rotate on its axis.

C The passage does not mention anyone's trying to determine the size of the orbit of a system's two stars. It does mention the related topic of distance between the stars but indicates that knowing such distance is required for measuring the stars' mass, not that it can be inferred from the period of the system.

D **Correct.** According to the passage, the restraining force, or gravitational attraction, between the two stars can be deduced based on the period and the distance between them.

E The passage does not mention the speed at which the star system moves through space.

The correct answer is D.

28. The primary purpose of the passage is to

    (A) analyze a natural phenomenon in terms of its behavior under special conditions
    (B) describe the steps by which a scientific measurement is carried out
    (C) point out the conditions under which a scientific procedure is most useful
    (D) contrast two different uses of a methodological approach in science
    (E) explain a method by which scientists determine an unknown quantity

Evaluation

What is the primary purpose of the passage? What we call the weight of an object is its weight as measured in Earth's gravitational field; that weight is a function of gravity and the mass of the object. How is the mass of an object determined in a weightless, zero-gravity environment? The first paragraph of the passage explains a method to determine this. The second paragraph explains an analogous method that astronomers use to measure the masses of stars in a double-star system.

A   Although the passage has portions containing analysis and references to characteristics of natural phenomena, these portions are merely subsidiary to explanations of measurement methods.

B   A description of steps in a measurement procedure occurs in the first paragraph, but this is merely preliminary to an explanation of how masses of stars in double-star systems can be measured. The passage mentions two aspects of the method used to measure the masses of double stars—measuring the period and measuring the distance—but it does not tell whether these are separate steps of the process, and it does not primarily focus on these as a main topic.

C   The passage describes some conditions under which a particular measurement method is valid, but that description is merely subsidiary to an explanation meant to show why the method is valid.

D   The structure of the passage is based on analogy rather than contrast.

E   **Correct.** The primary purpose of the passage is to explain, using analogy, methods for determining mass independently of Earth's gravity.

The correct answer is E.

Questions 29–31 refer to the passage on page 64.

29. The passage suggests which of the following about the illicit trade in CFCs?

    (A) It would cease if manufacturers in India and China stopped producing CFCs.
    (B) Most people who participate in such trade do not believe that CFCs deplete the ozone layer.
    (C) It will probably surpass illicit drugs as the largest contraband problem faced by the United States Customs Service.
    (D) It is fostered by people who do not want to pay the price of CFC substitutes.
    (E) It has grown primarily because of the expansion of the refrigeration, heating, and air-conditioning industries in other countries.

Supporting Idea

The Montreal Protocol projects that the depleted ozone layer would substantially recover by 2050. This assumes that internationally agreed regulations on limiting the use of chlorofluorocarbons (CFCs) for refrigeration and air-conditioning would be observed. CFCs damage the ozone layer. Illicit trade in CFCs made in China and India suggests the agreed regulations are not being observed. Substitutes for CFCs are up to five times as expensive as CFCs. Also, about half of industry professionals believe that CFCs do not damage the ozone layer.

A   The passage neither states nor implies that this would occur.

B   The passage does not attribute such a belief to the majority of those engaged in the illicit trade of CFCs.

C   The passage cites the United States Customs Service as reporting that illicit CFC-12 imports are the second most serious contraband problem they find, only illicit-drug contraband being more serious. The passage provides no specific quantitative information about growth in either form of contraband to support such an inference.

D **Correct.** The passage tells us that CFCs have a competitive price advantage over suitable replacements, which can cost five times as much, and this advantage has boosted the illicit trade in CFCs.

E The passage contains no information about expansion in other areas.

The correct answer is D.

30. According to the passage, which of the following best describes most ozone-depleting chemicals in 1996 as compared to those in 1987?

    (A) The levels of such chemicals in the atmosphere had decreased.
    (B) The number of such chemicals that reached the atmosphere had declined.
    (C) The amounts of such chemicals released had increased, but the amounts that reached the atmosphere had decreased.
    (D) The rate of increase in amounts of such chemicals reaching the atmosphere had decreased.
    (E) The rate at which such chemicals were being reduced in the atmosphere had slowed.

Supporting Idea

To answer the question, it is important to notice the distinction implied in the passage between a reduction in the rate of increase of CFCs in the atmosphere and a reduction in the level, i.e., total quantity, of CFCs in the atmosphere. CFCs can persist and accumulate in the atmosphere.

A The passage neither states nor implies that the amounts of most ozone-depleting chemicals had decreased. The passage states that the rate of increase had decreased, as well as the atmospheric levels of "some" individual ozone-depleting chemicals. But that is consistent with an ongoing increase in the overall level of CFCs in the atmosphere.

B The passage neither states nor implies this. CFCs are a category of chemicals, but we are given no count of the number of ozone-depleting chemicals in this category.

C There is a contrast here between the amount released and the amount reaching the atmosphere. However, the passage addresses only the amount of such chemicals reaching the atmosphere, implying that this amount increased, but more slowly. See the first sentence of the passage.

D **Correct.** This is stated clearly in the first sentence of the passage.

E The passage provides no information regarding changes in how quickly CFCs were being reduced in the atmosphere. The first sentence of the passage does mention reductions in levels of some atmospheric CFCs but gives no information about the rate at which those levels are being reduced.

The correct answer is D.

31. The author of the passage compares the smuggling of CFCs to the illicit drug trade most likely for which of the following reasons?

    (A) To qualify a previous claim
    (B) To emphasize the extent of a problem
    (C) To provide an explanation for an earlier assertion
    (D) To suggest that the illicit CFC trade, like the illicit drug trade, will continue to increase
    (E) To suggest that the consequences of a relatively little-known problem are as serious as those of a well-known one

Application

In the final sentence of the passage, the author cites a report from the United States Customs Service, comparing the illicit importation of CFCs with the illicit importation of drugs. Why? Note that the preceding sentence of the passage gives estimated quantities of CFCs illegally imported.

A The comparison cited does not "qualify" a preceding claim in the sense of limiting it or moderating it.

B **Correct.** The comparison is meant to show the seriousness of the illicit importation of CFCs, both quantitatively (the amounts) and qualitatively (the difficulty of solution).

C   The comparison presents not so much an "explanation" of a previous assertion as a brief and memorable way of conveying the seriousness of the problem posed by illicit importation of CFCs.

D   The point of the comparison is not to forecast how the problem of illicit importation of CFCs might change quantitatively.

E   The point of the comparison is not to suggest that the serious consequences of illicit importation of CFCs are on a par with the serious consequences of illicit importation of drugs.

The correct answer is B.

Questions 32–39 refer to the passage on page 65.

32. The passage is primarily concerned with

    (A) describing a resource and indicating various methods used to study it
    (B) presenting a theory and offering an opposing point of view
    (C) providing an explanation for unexpected findings
    (D) demonstrating why a particular theory is unfounded
    (E) resolving a disagreement regarding the uses of a technology

Main Idea

What issue, problem, or puzzle is the passage primarily meant to address? The passage discusses whether—and if so why or under what conditions—adoption of information technology (IT) benefits businesses. The first paragraph provides background information by summarizing opinions and data concerning the extent to which businesses can benefit by adopting IT. It details pre-1990 findings showing that, contrary to some experts' expectations, overall productivity in business sectors that adopted IT did not improve. It summarizes contrasting attempts by proponents of IT to explain how, by different performance measures, IT may have actually yielded business benefits other than competitive advantage. The second paragraph discusses the puzzle that the passage primarily addresses: why, if IT had *conferred economic value*, the pre-1990 findings indicated that, contrary to expectations, IT failed to *produce direct competitive advantage for individual firms*. The passage invokes *resource-based theory* to help resolve this puzzle.

A   IT is accurately described as *a resource,* but the passage is not concerned at all with *describing* IT, except in its very brief parenthetical definition of IT. Neither is it directly concerned with methods used to study IT.

B   Opinions are presented in the passage. But the only perspective or point of view that is referred to and characterized as a *theory* is *resource-based theory*. A possible application of that theory is described, but neither that theory nor any other theory is *presented*.

C   **Correct.** As explained above, the passage is primarily concerned with explaining why findings based on pre-1990 data suggested that, contrary to expectations, adoption of IT failed to produce direct competitive advantage for many businesses.

D   The only *theory* referred to in the passage is *resource-based theory*, but the passage neither opposes nor attempts to refute that theory.

E   The first paragraph indicates that there was some disagreement as to the magnitude or nature of any business benefits possibly produced by IT. But the passage is not aimed at resolving any such disagreements; it is aimed, rather, at explaining why expectations regarding certain business benefits of IT were not fulfilled.

The correct answer is C.

33. The author of the passage discusses productivity in the retail industry in the first paragraph primarily in order to

(A) suggest a way in which IT can be used to create a competitive advantage
(B) provide an illustration of the "productivity paradox"
(C) emphasize the practical value of the introduction of IT
(D) cite an industry in which productivity did not stagnate during the 1980s
(E) counter the argument that IT could potentially create competitive advantage

Evaluation

Why does the author, in the first paragraph of the passage, discuss productivity in the retail industry? In the first paragraph, the information concerning *productivity in the retail industry* is presented as an example that seemed to provide support for what some economists termed *the "productivity paradox."* The passage describes the paradox as follows: *despite huge IT investments, . . . productivity stagnated.* As an example of this, pre-1990 data is cited for the retail industry, which had widely adopted IT; the data indicated that productivity increases had significantly slowed relative to the average for the 25 years preceding 1973.

A The data in the first paragraph regarding productivity in the retail industry does not suggest that IT can be used to create a competitive advantage. In fact, the data presented could provide reason to doubt whether, in the retail sector, IT would fulfill expectations regarding its potential for creating competitive advantage.

B **Correct.** As explained above, the primary purpose of the author's first paragraph of productivity in the retail industry is to illustrate the "productivity paradox."

C This could not be the author's purpose in the discussion of productivity in the retail industry in the first paragraph, since that discussion casts doubt on whether IT would fulfill expectations regarding its potential for creating competitive advantage.

D This cannot be the primary purpose of the discussion of productivity in the retail industry in the first paragraph. The data concerning the retail industry is cited as an instance supporting and illustrating the general point that when there were huge IT investments, especially *in the service sectors, productivity stagnated.*

E The author's purpose in the discussion of productivity in the retail sector is not to *counter the argument that IT could potentially create competitive advantage.* In the first paragraph, the author neither argues for nor endorses the view that IT lacked potential to create competitive advantage.

The correct answer is B.

34. The passage suggests that proponents of resource-based theory would be likely to explain IT's inability to produce direct competitive advantages for individual firms by pointing out that

(A) IT is not a resource that is difficult to obtain
(B) IT is not an economically valuable resource
(C) IT is a complex, intangible resource
(D) economic progress has resulted from IT only in the service sector
(E) changes brought about by IT cannot be detected by macroeconomic measures

Inference

How would a proponent of resource-based theory be likely to explain the pre-1990 failure of IT to produce direct competitive advantage for firms that adopted it? According to the passage, resource-based theory implies that *in general, firms gain competitive advantages by accumulating resources that are economically valuable, relatively scarce, and not easily replicated.* However, the passage cites a study indicating that IT had become *pervasive and relatively easy to acquire* but did not seem sufficient by itself to confer competitive advantage. Based on this information, a proponent of resource-based theory would likely claim that since IT proved to be *easily replicated*, one of the conditions stipulated by resource-based theory for gaining competitive advantage was violated.

A **Correct.** According to the study mentioned in the second paragraph, IT was *relatively easy to acquire*. According to the conditions for gaining competitive advantage as attributed in the passage to resource-based theory, a proponent of resource-based theory would likely claim that the ease of acquiring IT could help explain why adoption of IT was not by itself sufficient for gaining competitive advantage.

B The passage suggests neither that IT lacks economic value nor that resource-based theory assumes or implies that it does. Rather, resource-based theory suggests that the economic value of IT during the period discussed in the passage typically did not provide competitive advantages to any company that adopted it over others that did so.

C Although IT may in some respects be both complex and intangible, the passage does not suggest that resource-based theory entails that resources need to be simple or tangible in order to confer competitive advantage.

D This is not a view that the passage attributes, even by implication, to proponents of resource-based theory.

E The first paragraph of the passage indicates that some IT advocates claimed that macroeconomic measures of productivity failed to reflect the economic benefits of IT. But the passage neither endorses this viewpoint nor attributes it to proponents of resource-based theory.

The correct answer is A.

35. Which of the following best describes the content of the first paragraph?

    (A) It presents two explanations for the success of IT.
    (B) It provides evidence that decreases in productivity will continue.
    (C) It presents reasons for a decline in productivity.
    (D) It demonstrates the effect IT has had on productivity.
    (E) It contrasts views concerning the degree of IT's success.

Evaluation

Among the choices given, which one best describes the content of the first paragraph of the passage? The first paragraph provides background information by summarizing opinions and data concerning the extent to which businesses benefited by adopting IT. It details pre-1990 findings showing that, contrary to some experts' expectations, overall productivity in business sectors that adopted IT did not significantly improve. It summarizes contrasting attempts by proponents of IT to explain how, judged by different performance measures, IT may have actually yielded business benefits other than competitive advantage.

A The first paragraph provides information suggesting that IT did not provide the expected benefits. In other words, it casts doubt on whether IT succeeded.

B The first paragraph considers neither past nor future decreases in productivity. (It does, however, describe past decreases in the rate of increase in productivity).

C The first paragraph discusses certain pre-1990 decreases in the average rate of productivity growth, but it does not discuss declines in productivity.

D The first paragraph suggests that IT may have had little or no effect in producing productivity growth. The passage does not claim that IT actually had an effect on productivity and does not demonstrate any way in which IT had such an effect.

E **Correct.** The first paragraph describes differing views concerning whether IT may have met expectations in enhancing competitiveness or providing other economic benefits for business.

The correct answer is E.

36. The passage suggests that the recent study of retail firms discussed in the second paragraph supports which of the following conclusions regarding a firm's competitive advantage?

    (A) Human resources alone are more likely to contribute to competitive advantage than is IT alone.
    (B) Human resources combined with IT are more likely than human resources alone to have a negative effect on competitive advantage.
    (C) Human resources combined with IT often have a negative effect on competitive advantage.
    (D) IT by itself is much more likely to have a positive effect than a negative effect on competitive advantage.
    (E) The positive effect of IT on competitive advantage increases with time.

Inference

The second paragraph describes a study of retail firms. The study confirmed that IT, having become relatively easy to acquire, by itself conferred little advantage. Negative correlations between IT and performance suggest that IT likely weakened some retail firms' competitive positions. Firms' human resources, however, did explain improved performance, both in and of themselves and when merged with IT.

A   **Correct.** As explained above, the study indicated that human resources in and of themselves led to improved performance, whereas there were negative correlations between IT and performance.

B   The passage indicates that some firms gained IT-related advantages when IT was merged with human resources. The passage gives no indication whether this—or human resources alone—ever has negative effects on performance.

C   The passage indicates that some firms gained IT-related advantages when IT was merged with human resources. The passage gives no indication whether this ever has negative effects on performance.

D   The passage states that the study found that IT by itself conferred little advantage, but the study found frequent negative correlations between IT and performance.

E   The first paragraph states that some people have argued that it takes time for IT to yield results, but the study discussed in the second paragraph provides no evidence to support this. The finding of the study that indicates that IT can yield results when merged with human resources says nothing about whether all the effects are immediate or whether they instead increase with time.

The correct answer is A.

37. According to the passage, most pre-1990 literature on businesses' use of IT included which of the following?

    (A) Recommendations regarding effective ways to use IT to gain competitive advantage
    (B) Explanations of the advantages and disadvantages of adopting IT
    (C) Information about ways in which IT combined with human resources could be used to increase competitive advantage
    (D) A warning regarding the negative effect on competitive advantage that would occur if IT were not adopted
    (E) A belief in the likelihood of increased competitive advantage for firms using IT

Supporting Idea

The passage begins by stating that most pre-1990 literature on businesses' use of IT was optimistic about IT's ability to create competitive advantage and focused on dramatic success stories.

A   The passage does not state that pre-1990 literature on businesses' use of IT made recommendations regarding ways IT could be used to gain competitive advantage.

B The passage indicates that most pre-1990 literature on businesses' use of IT focused on the advantages IT was believed to confer. The passage does indicate that some literature at the end of the 1980s discussed some disadvantages of adopting IT; but the passage suggests that most of the literature of this period did not discuss any disadvantages.

C The passage does not clearly indicate whether any pre-1990 literature discussed the results of combining human resources and IT. The study described as "recent" in the second paragraph does discuss such results, but the study was not pre-1990 and does not discuss any specific ways IT combined with human resources could be used to increase competitive advantage.

D Pre-1990 literature on businesses' use of IT expressed optimism that IT could confer competitive advantage, but the passage does not mention whether this literature presented a warning about negative effects on performance if IT was not adopted.

E **Correct.** The first paragraph of the passage states that most pre-1990 literature on businesses' use of IT was optimistic about IT's ability to create competitive advantage.

The correct answer is E.

38. The author of the passage implies that toward the end of the 1980s, some economists described which of the following as a "productivity paradox" (see line 8)?

(A) Investments in IT would not result in increases in productivity until the 1990s.

(B) Investments in IT did not lead to expected gains in productivity.

(C) Productivity in the retail industry rose less rapidly than did productivity in other industries.

(D) The gains in productivity due to the introduction of IT were not reflected in macroeconomic measures of productivity.

(E) Most gains in productivity occurred in the service sector and were therefore particularly difficult to measure.

Inference

The passage indicates in the first paragraph that toward the end of the 1980s, economists noticed that productivity was not increasing, as it had been expected to do as a result of significant investments in IT. The economists referred to this as a *productivity paradox*.

A Although the first paragraph does indicate that productivity growth did occur in the 1990s, this is not what is referred to by the term *productivity paradox*.

B **Correct.** The passage begins by indicating that before 1990 there was general optimism that investments in IT would lead to competitive advantages. However, by the late 1980s some economists had identified a *productivity paradox*, noting that *despite huge IT investments . . . productivity stagnated*; that is, the IT investments had not resulted in the expected gains in productivity.

C The passage does not indicate that productivity rose less rapidly in the retail industry than in other industries. It merely indicates that it rose less rapidly than had been expected and less rapidly than it did prior to large IT investments.

D The *productivity paradox* refers to a lack of gains in productivity due to IT, not to a failure of macroeconomic measures to capture actual productivity gains.

E The passage indicates that the service sector failed to show significant gains, and it makes no mention of any difficulty related to measuring productivity gains in the service sector.

The correct answer is B.

39. According to the passage, the recent study of retail firms discussed in the second paragraph (lines 33–36) best supports which of the following assessments of IT's potential?

   (A) Even when IT gives a firm a temporary competitive advantage, that firm is unlikely to continue to achieve productivity gains.
   (B) The competitive advantages conferred by a firm's introduction of IT are outweighed by IT's development costs.
   (C) A firm's introduction of IT is less likely to limit its ability to achieve productivity gains than to enhance that ability.
   (D) Although IT by itself is unlikely to give a firm a competitive advantage, IT combined with other resources may do so.
   (E) Although IT by itself is unlikely to give a firm a competitive advantage, a firm that does not employ IT cannot achieve a competitive advantage.

Supporting Idea

Answering this question correctly involves an understanding of what the second paragraph says about a particular study of retail firms, specifically, what that study has to say about IT's potential. The study confirmed that IT, having become relatively easy to acquire, by itself conferred little advantage. Negative correlations between IT and performance suggest that IT likely weakened some retail firms' competitive positions. On the other hand, the second paragraph states that *some firms gained IT-related advantages by merging IT with complementary resources.*

A   The study reveals that IT by itself does not give firms a competitive advantage, but that it does give some firms such an advantage when IT is merged with complementary resources. The study does not indicate that any productivity gains that are achieved in this way are short lived.

B   The passage does not indicate whether any competitive advantages conferred by a firm's introduction of IT (for instance, those that arise when merged with other resources) are outweighed by IT's development costs.

C   The study indicates that a firm's introduction of IT is likely to limit its ability to achieve productivity when it is not merged with complementary resources, but that it can enhance that ability when it is merged with such resources. The passage does not indicate the relative likelihood of those outcomes.

D   **Correct.** The study as described in the passage's second paragraph states that IT by *itself conferred little advantage* but that *some firms gained IT-related advantages by merging IT with complementary resources.*

E   This statement correctly indicates that the study states that IT by itself is unlikely to give a firm a competitive advantage. However, the passage does not indicate that the study states that firms that do not employ IT are unable to achieve a competitive advantage.

The correct answer is D.

Questions 40–43 refer to the passage on page 67.

40. The passage suggests that Twigg believes that rats could not have spread the Black Death unless which of the following were true?

   (A) The rats escaped from ships that had been in Asia.
   (B) The rats were immune to the diseases that they carried.
   (C) The rat population was larger in medieval Europe than Twigg believes it actually was.
   (D) The rat population primarily infested densely populated areas.
   (E) The rats interacted with other animals that Twigg believes could have carried plague.

Inference

The question requires recognizing information that is strongly implied, but not directly stated, in the passage. The passage states that Graham Twigg claims the rat population in medieval Europe was too sparse to spread plague; therefore, it follows that he believes a larger rat population would have been required for rats to have spread the Black Death.

A The passage states that Twigg disputes the idea that plague-carrying rats came on ships from Asia, but it does not suggest that Twigg believes either an Asian provenance or transport on ships was a necessary condition for rats to bring plague.

B The passage states that Twigg believes there weren't enough rats, but it suggests nothing regarding the immunity to disease of those rats.

C **Correct.** The passage states that Twigg believes there weren't enough rats to spread plague in medieval Europe; it would follow that he believes a larger rat population would have been necessary to spread plague.

D The passage makes no mention of population density in relation to Twigg's ideas.

E The passage states that Twigg overlooks the possibility that animals other than rats carried plague; it does not suggest that he believes rat interactions with other species would have been necessary for those other species to spread plague.

The correct answer is C.

41. According to the passage, the post–Second World War studies that altered the prevailing view of the Black Death involved which of the following?

    (A) Determining the death rates caused by the Black Death in specific regions and towns

    (B) Demonstrating how the Black Death intensified the political and religious upheaval that ended the Middle Ages

    (C) Presenting evidence to prove that many medieval epidemics were mislabeled

    (D) Arguing that the consequences of the Black Death led to the Renaissance and the rise of modern Europe

    (E) Employing urban case studies to determine the number of rats in medieval Europe

Supporting Idea

The question requires recognizing specific information mentioned in the passage. The passage states that studies conducted after World War II changed then-common ideas regarding the Black Death, when examination of data from specific regions and towns revealed extremely high mortality rates at the time of the epidemic; this revelation of the plague's toll restored ideas of its historical significance.

A **Correct.** The passage states that the post–WWII discovery of exceptionally high death rates in specific regions and towns during the time of the plague restored ideas of the plague's historical importance.

B The passage states that a study in 1893—not the studies after WWII—made an argument for the plague's contribution to religious and political upheaval.

C The passage refers to speculations regarding mislabeled epidemics, but not in connection with the post–WWII studies.

D The passage attributes this argument regarding the rise of the Renaissance to George Coulton, not to the post–WWII studies.

E The passage states that Graham Twigg employed such case studies to determine rat populations, not that the post–WWII studies did so.

The correct answer is A.

42. The "silver lining to the Black Death" (lines 7–8) refers to which of the following?

    (A) The decay of European feudalism precipitated by the Black Death

    (B) Greater availability of employment, sustenance, and housing for survivors of the epidemic

(C) Strengthening of the human species through natural selection
(D) Better understanding of how to limit the spread of contagious diseases
(E) Immunities and resistance to the Black Death gained by later generations

Supporting Idea

The question requires recognizing the specific significance of the text: a "silver lining to the Black Death" in lines 7–8. The passage attributes the idea that there was such a silver lining to historian George Coulton, then expands on the idea by stating that Coulton believed reduced competition for resources and work—that is, increased sustenance, employment, and housing becoming available to survivors—led to prosperity and cultural development.

A   The passage discusses the plague's relationship with the decline of feudalism, but it does not do so in connection with lines 7–8.
B   **Correct.** The passage attributes the idea of a "silver lining to the Black Death" to historian George Coulton, then states that he believed that the silver lining consisted of reduced competition for resources among epidemic survivors, leading to prosperity and cultural blossoming.
C   The passage makes no mention of strengthening the human species through natural selection.
D   The passage discusses various possible mechanisms for the spread of the plague but never mentions ideas for how to limit the spread of disease.
E   The passage makes no mention of immunity gained by the generations following the Black Death.

The correct answer is B.

43. The author's attitude toward Twigg's work is best characterized as which of the following?

(A) Dismissive
(B) Indifferent
(C) Vindictive
(D) Cautious
(E) Ambivalent

Evaluation

The question requires assessing the overall attitude the author holds toward the work of Graham Twigg. That attitude can be inferred through specific phrases the author uses to characterize Twigg's work, such as "faulty logic," "speculative generalizations," "isolated studies," and "unconvincing . . . argument." Taken together, these phrases suggest an attitude of irritated disdain and the belief that Twigg's work is insufficiently rigorous to be worthy of serious consideration by scholars of the Black Death.

A   **Correct.** The author describes Twigg's work in terms including "faulty logic," "speculative generalizations," and "unconvincing . . . argument," strongly suggesting that the author believes Twigg's work deserves dismissal.
B   The author's attitude toward Twigg's work is strongly negative, not indifferent.
C   While the author's attitude toward Twigg's work verges on disrespect, there is no suggestion in the passage that it is motivated by revenge.
D   The author's tone in regard to Twigg's work is confidently negative rather than cautious.
E   While the author acknowledges a single merit in Twigg's work—that it "correctly cites the exacting conditions" necessary for an epidemic of plague—the preponderance of the author's remarks on Twigg are so negative that an overall attitude of ambivalence is unlikely.

The correct answer is A.

Questions 44–47 refer to the passage on page 69.

44. Which of the following is NOT mentioned in the passage as a characteristic of the traditional model of employer-employee relations in the United States?

    (A) Attractive compensation packages for employees
    (B) Opportunities for employees to receive training
    (C) Long-term job security for employees
    (D) Opportunities for employee advancement within a company
    (E) Long-term commitment toward a company by employees

Supporting Idea

The question requires recognizing specific details included in the passage. The passage specifies several benefits workers received from the traditional model of employer-employee relations, including long-term job security, training, and opportunities for promotion, and also states that these benefits led workers to form a corresponding long-term commitment to their companies. However, the passage does not mention good compensation packages among the listed benefits.

A **Correct.** The passage does not mention attractive compensation packages for employees as one of the characteristics of traditional employee-employer relations.
B The passage specifies training for employees as one characteristic of traditional employment models.
C The passage includes long-term job security in its list of the characteristics of traditional employment models.
D The passage mentions opportunities for promotion, or advancement, as a characteristic feature of traditional employment models.
E The passage states that the benefits of traditional employment models generally led employees to make long-term commitments to their companies.

The correct answer is A.

45. According to the passage, managers' motivation for engaging in measures such as increased layoffs is often a result of

    (A) the hope that a smaller workforce will decrease the managers' own workloads
    (B) shareholder pressure to generate increased short-term financial gains
    (C) a desire to eradicate the idea of a "psychological contract"
    (D) dissatisfaction with the performance of disgruntled employees
    (E) a desire to appear to be following modern organizational trends

Supporting Idea

The item requires recognizing specific information presented in the passage. In the second paragraph, the passage states that top management is under pressure from shareholders to generate high short-term returns on investment, and that this pressure drives measures such as layoffs and decreased hiring.

A The passage makes no mention of managers seeking to decrease their workloads through layoffs.
B **Correct.** The passage states that pressure from shareholders to generate high short-term returns on investment drives cost-cutting measures such as layoffs.
C The passage makes no mention of a desire to eradicate the "psychological contract" but rather suggests that such eradication is the result of decreasing job security, training, and promotions.
D The passage makes no mention of the performance of disgruntled employees.
E The passage does not cite a desire to appear to be modern as a motive for layoffs.

The correct answer is B.

46. The passage suggests that which of the following is a legitimate reason for organizations' shift to the new model of employer-employee relations?

   (A) Organizations tend to operate more effectively when they have a high manager-to-employee ratio.
   (B) Organizations can move their operations to less-expensive locations more easily when they have fewer permanent employees.
   (C) Organizations have found that they often receive higher-quality work when they engage in outsourcing.
   (D) Organizations with large pools of permanent workers risk significant financial losses if the demand for their product or service decreases.
   (E) Organizations are under increasing pressure to adopt new technologies that often obviate the need for certain workers.

Supporting Idea

The question requires recognizing specific information presented in the passage. The second paragraph describes as "legitimate and pressing" three reasons that employers have shifted to a paradigm of decreased commitment to their workers: that large numbers of permanent employees make it difficult for companies to avoid losses in downturns, that there has been an increase in wrongful discharge suits, and that there is shareholder pressure for short-term gains.

   A The passage does not include manager-to-employee ratio in its list of legitimate reasons for employers to decrease their commitment to employees.
   B The passage does not mention ease of relocating companies as a legitimate reason for decreasing employer commitment to employees.
   C The passage does not state that companies receive better work through outsourcing.
   D **Correct.** The passage states that companies with large numbers of permanent employees are susceptible to losses in downturns when demand decreases, and it characterizes this susceptibility as a legitimate reason for adopting the new model of lower employer commitment to employees.
   E The passage does not mention pressure to adopt new technologies as a reason for the new model of employer-employee relations.

The correct answer is D.

47. Which of the following best characterizes the function of the final sentence of the passage?

   (A) It suggests an alternative explanation for a phenomenon discussed earlier in the passage.
   (B) It provides data intended to correct a common misconception.
   (C) It further weakens an argument that is being challenged by the author.
   (D) It introduces a specific piece of evidence in support of a claim made at the beginning of the final paragraph.
   (E) It answers a question that is implicit in the preceding sentence.

Evaluation

The question requires assessing the function of a specific detail included in the passage. The final sentence discusses a study of employee attitudes toward management and includes the fact that nearly half of those surveyed agreed that management is eager to take advantage of workers. The survey result provides evidence for the earlier claim that employees are increasingly cynical regarding management's motivations.

   A The perceived tendency of management to exploit workers discussed in the last sentence would help explain phenomena mentioned earlier—such as increasing interest in entrepreneurship—but it is not presented as an alternative explanation for such phenomena.
   B Nothing in the passage suggests a common misconception that would be corrected by data regarding employee attitudes.
   C The passage does not include any explicit argument that is being challenged by the author.

D **Correct.** The survey result cited in the final sentence provides specific evidence for the idea that employees often distrust management; in other words, it supports the claim made at the beginning of the final paragraph that employees have grown cynical about management's motivations.

E There is no question implicit in the preceding sentence; rather, it advances the claim that employers' attitudes are alienating their employees.

The correct answer is D.

Questions 48 to 109 — Difficulty: Medium

Questions 48–50 refer to the passage on page 71.

48. The passage is primarily concerned with

    (A) evaluating the evidence of a major geologic period and determining its duration
    (B) describing an evolutionary phenomenon and speculating about its cause
    (C) explaining the mechanisms through which marine life-forms evolved during a particular period
    (D) analyzing the impact on later life-forms of an important evolutionary development
    (E) contrasting a period of evolutionary change with other such periods

Main Idea

This question asks for an assessment of what the passage as a whole is doing. The passage is mainly concerned with a possible link between certain geological and ecological changes that occurred during the Ordovician period and the Ordovician radiation (when existing marine invertebrate life-forms gave rise to new variations that would eventually lead to new species).

A The passage is not particularly concerned with determining the length of the period in question.

B **Correct.** The passage is mainly concerned with a possible link between the evolutionary phenomenon of the Ordovician radiation and certain environmental changes that may have resulted in an enriched pattern of habitats and nutrients that could have fostered that radiation.

C The passage indicates that the particular mechanisms through which marine life-forms evolved are not well understood.

D Although the passage indicates that the changes it discusses ultimately did lead to new life-forms, it does not analyze that relationship.

E The passage does not discuss any period of evolutionary change besides the Ordovician radiation.

The correct answer is B.

49. Which of the following can be inferred from the passage regarding the geologic changes that occurred during the Ordovician period?

    (A) They were more drastic than those associated with other radiations.
    (B) They may have created conditions favorable to the evolution of many new life-forms.
    (C) They may have caused the extinction of many of the marine species living in shallow waters.
    (D) They may have been a factor in the development of new species adapted to living both on land and in water.
    (E) They hastened the formation of the extensive dry regions found in the western United States.

Inference

The question asks what can be inferred from the passage's claims regarding the geologic changes that took place during the Ordovician period. The passage indicates that during this period the sea level dropped and mountain ranges were formed and that these changes, rather than leading to large-scale extinctions, may have created more favorable habitats providing greater nutrients, which would likely have been favorable to newly evolved life-forms.

A The passage does not mention other radiations and does not compare the Ordovician geologic changes to geologic changes associated with other radiations.
B **Correct.** The passage does suggest that certain geologic changes that occurred during the Ordovician period may have created conditions favorable to the new life-forms associated with the Ordovician radiation.
C The passage does not indicate whether any marine species became extinct; in fact, it explicitly denies that the geologic changes led to any large-scale extinctions.
D The passage does not indicate that any new species were adapted to living both on land and in water. It merely discusses marine life-forms.
E Although these geologic changes did likely create newly dry areas in the western United States, it does not indicate that these areas are *extensive*.

The correct answer is B.

50. Which of the following best describes the function of the last sentence of the passage?

    (A) It points out that the events described in the passage may be atypical.
    (B) It alludes to the fact that there is disagreement in the scientific community over the importance of the Ordovician radiation.
    (C) It concludes that the evidence presented in the passage is insufficient to support the proposed hypothesis because it comes from a limited geographic area.
    (D) It warns the reader against seeing a connection between the biological and geologic changes described in the passage.
    (E) It alerts the reader that current knowledge cannot completely explain the relationship suggested by the evidence presented in the passage.

Evaluation

The last sentence of the passage functions primarily to indicate that, though certain evidence from the geologic record suggests a possible cause of the Ordovician radiation, the current level of knowledge regarding the relationship between environmental factors and that radiation is not sufficient for a full understanding of that relationship.

A Although there may be certain geologic or evolutionary aspects of the Ordovician period that are atypical, the final sentence of the passage does not address them.
B Neither the final sentence nor the rest of the passage addresses any disagreements within the scientific community.
C Although the final sentence of the passage does indicate that current understanding of the relationship between the environmental factors discussed and the Ordovician radiation is incomplete, it does not indicate that it is because the evidence comes from a limited geographic area that the evidence is insufficient.
D The last sentence does not advise against seeing a connection between the biological and geologic changes discussed; it merely advises that such a connection is not yet fully understood.
E **Correct.** The last sentence indicates to the reader that current knowledge is insufficient for fully explaining the relationships among the evidence provided in the passage regarding geologic, ecological, and evolutionary changes.

The correct answer is E.

Questions 51–56 refer to the passage on page 72.

51. The author of the passage is primarily concerned with

    (A) criticizing Locke's economic theories
    (B) discounting the contribution of labor in a modern economy
    (C) questioning the validity of the labor theory of value
    (D) arguing for a more equitable distribution of business profits
    (E) contending that employers are overcompensated for capital goods

Main Idea

This question depends on an understanding of the passage as a whole. The first paragraph describes the labor theory of value and the theory's historical origins in the philosophy of John Locke. The second paragraph provides some analysis of the theory and uses the analysis to support a critique.

A   The passages describes a historical connection between the labor theory of value and Locke's economic theories and suggests that the influence of Locke on the labor theory of value is one reason why, according to the author, the theory may be inadequate. This perhaps suggests an indirect criticism of Locke and his theories, via his influence on more recent theories. However, Locke's economic theories are not criticized directly and are not the focus of the passage.

B   Although the passage may suggest that a particular economic theory—the labor theory of value—may exaggerate the "contribution of labor in a modern economy" because the theory may neglect the importance of capital goods, the author does not suggest that the contribution of labor is unimportant.

C   **Correct.** The second paragraph—more than half of the passage—is almost entirely focused on critiquing the labor theory of value. The first paragraph, by introducing the theory and providing some historical context, can be seen as supporting the critique, by introducing the theory to readers who may not be familiar with it.

D   The passage offers no argument for or against a more equitable distribution of business profits.

E   The point at issue in this answer choice is similar to the point at issue in answer choice D, to do with what might be right or wrong, or more equitable, in matters concerning the distribution of money or "compensation." The passage makes no argument as to what might be right or wrong in this respect.

The correct answer is C.

52. According to the author of the passage, which of the following is true of the distribution of the income derived from the total output of consumer goods in a modern economy?

(A) Workers receive a share of this income that is significantly smaller than the value of their labor as a contribution to total output.

(B) Owners of capital goods receive a share of this income that is significantly greater than the contribution to total output attributable to the use of capital goods.

(C) Owners of capital goods receive a share of this income that is no greater than the proportion of total output attributable to the use of capital goods.

(D) Owners of capital goods are not fully compensated for their investment because they pay out most of their share of this income to workers as wages and benefits.

(E) Workers receive a share of this income that is greater than the value of their labor because the labor theory of value overestimates their contribution to total output.

Supporting Idea

This question asks us to identify something that is true of the distribution of the income derived from all of the consumer goods that are produced in the modern economy.

A   The passage makes certain claims about the relative distribution of income between workers and the owners of capital goods, with respect to the income derived from the total output of consumer goods. However, no clear comparison is made between the share thus received by workers and the "value" of their labor.

B   The passage states that roughly one-third of the total output of consumer goods is attributable to the use of capital goods and that the owners of capital receive one-third of the income from this total output. The shares of income are roughly the same.

C   **Correct.** As explained in answer choice B, the share of income to the owners of capital goods is roughly equal to the proportion of total output of consumer goods that can be attributed to the use of capital goods.

D   Although the passage mentions that some workers, because they are shareholders or pension beneficiaries, receive some of the income that "serves as compensation to the owners of capital goods," there is no indication that this is *most* of the share that serves as the compensation to these owners. Furthermore, the workers who are, say, shareholders, may be owners of capital themselves. Therefore, the income that these workers receive as shareholders may be no reduction at all to the income received by the owners of capital.

E   The passage does not suggest that workers receive a share of the income derived from the total output of consumer goods that is greater than the value of their labor. And it provides no explanation of such a phenomenon.

The correct answer is C.

53. Which of the following statements, if true, would most effectively counter the author's criticism of Locke at the end of the passage?

    (A) Locke was unfamiliar with the labor theory of value as it was formulated by his intellectual heirs.
    (B) In Locke's day, there was no possibility of ordinary workers becoming shareholders or pension beneficiaries.
    (C) During Locke's lifetime, capital goods did not make a significant productive contribution to the economy.
    (D) The precise statistical calculation of the productive contributions of labor and capital goods is not possible without computers.
    (E) The terms "capital goods" and "consumer goods" were coined by modern economists and do not appear in Locke's writings.

Application

The question asks us to identify the most effective counter to the criticism of Locke that he is at least somewhat responsible for the fact, according to the author of the passage, that the labor theory of value "systematically disregards" the contribution of capital goods to production.

A   The criticism of Locke in question has to do with his supposed responsibility for a supposed flaw in a certain theory, presumably because of his influence on later theorizers. That Locke was "unfamiliar" with this theory, which did not exist at the time of Locke, does not significantly mitigate Locke's (supposed) responsibility for the (supposed) flaw in the theory.

B   Once we see what the criticism of Locke is, to do with a claim that he is responsible for a "systematic disregard" of a certain theory of the productive contribution of capital goods, we can see that this answer choice is irrelevant.

C   **Correct.** Whatever the flaws in Locke's theories, it would seem wrong to hold him responsible for "neglecting" something—capital goods in this case—that was not a significant factor in his day. Given the fact (assuming that it is a fact) that capital goods were not a significant factor when Locke was alive, the responsibility for neglecting them (assuming that they have been neglected by economic theorists) may seem to rest with those who have neglected them after they have become a significant factor.

D   The precision of the calculation of the productive contributions of labor and capital goods—to the degree for which a computer would be necessary—is not a factor anywhere in the passage, and it would not be relevant to the criticism of Locke.

E   That certain terms are used today that were not used in the past does not indicate that there were not other terms that were used to refer to the same thing. And the mere fact of the word we happen to use to refer to capital goods is not relevant to the criticism of Locke.

The correct answer is C.

54. Which of the following best describes the organization of the passage?

    (A) The author explores the origins of a theory and explains why the theory never gained widespread acceptance.
    (B) The author introduces the premise of a theory, evaluates the premise by relating it to objective reality, then proposes a modification of the theory.
    (C) After quoting a well-known authority, the author describes the evolution of a theory, then traces its modern form back to the original quotation.
    (D) After citing a precursor of a theory, the author outlines and refutes the theory, then links its flaw to the precursor.
    (E) After tracing the roots of a theory, the author attempts to undermine the theory by discrediting its originator.

Evaluation

The question asks us to identify the statement that most accurately describes the organization of the passage.

A The author indeed explores an aspect of the origin of the labor theory of value, to do with the philosopher John Locke. However, the author neither claims that the theory never gained widespread acceptance nor tries to explain a supposed fact that the theory never gained widespread acceptance.

B Although the author explains a fundamental aspect of a theory—the labor theory of value—and then may seem to evaluate this aspect by "relating it to objective reality," she or he does not propose a modification of the theory.

C The passage indeed quotes John Locke, who is well known and may be considered an authority on certain matters. However, Locke would not be considered an authority on the contents of the labor theory of value, which, the passage suggests, did not exist at the time of Locke. Furthermore, much of the passage is devoted to developing a criticism of the theory. A good characterization of the passage would need to at least mention this criticism.

D **Correct.** The author begins the passage by describing a theory of John Locke that is, according to the author, a precursor to the labor theory of value. Most of the second paragraph is devoted to a criticism of the theory, which the author ends by claiming that Locke is somewhat responsible for the supposed flaw.

E The criticism of the labor theory of value is based on certain purported claims, made by the theory, about the economy that, according to the author, do not agree with the theory. The criticism of John Locke is then based on this critique of the theory, and the claim that Locke is somewhat responsible for the flaw in the theory that the author claims to identify. Because the critique of the theory is thus not based on the critique of Locke, and thus not on something that would purportedly "discredit" him, this answer choice is clearly incorrect.

The correct answer is D.

55. Which of the following arguments would a proponent of the labor theory of value, as it is presented in the first paragraph, be most likely to use in response to lines 23–25?

    (A) The productive contributions of workers and capital goods cannot be compared because the productive life span of capital goods is longer than that of workers.
    (B) The author's analysis of the distribution of income is misleading because only a small percentage of workers are also shareholders.
    (C) Capital goods are valuable only insofar as they contribute directly to the production of consumer goods.
    (D) The productive contribution of capital goods must be discounted because capital goods require maintenance.
    (E) The productive contribution of capital goods must be attributed to labor because capital goods are themselves products of labor.

Application

The passage asks us to identify the most likely response of a proponent of the labor theory of value, as the theory is described in the passage, to lines 23–25. Because the statement in lines 23–25 is a criticism of the theory, it is reasonable to expect that a likely response of a proponent of the theory may be to defend the theory against this criticism.

A   The labor theory of value, as described by the author, would suggest that the relative contributions of workers and capital goods can be compared. According to the theory (as described by the author), it is labor that makes the fundamental contribution—a clear comparison. So the statement that the relative contributions cannot be so compared would not defend the theory.

B   Although this answer choice may offer a reasonable criticism of an aspect of the passage, it does not offer a criticism of the point that is made in lines 23–25.

C   This answer choice may seem to describe how, according to the author, capital goods get their value. Restating this point of the author would not defend the labor theory of value against the author's arguments.

D   This statement is consistent with the content of the passage; for example, the discount due to maintenance could already be figured into the calculations behind the author's claims as to the relative importance of capital goods and labor.

E   **Correct.** If the productive contribution of capital goods is attributed to labor, then the author's claim, against the labor theory of value, that this productive contribution should not be attributed to labor, would be incorrect. The labor theory of value might therefore be justified when, according to lines 23–25, it "systematically disregards the productive contribution of capital goods."

The correct answer is E.

56.   The author of the passage implies which of the following regarding the formulators of the labor theory of value?

(A)   They came from a working-class background.
(B)   Their views were too radical to have popular appeal.
(C)   At least one of them was a close contemporary of Locke.
(D)   They were familiar with Locke's views on the relationship between labor and the value of products.
(E)   They underestimated the importance of consumer goods in a modern economy.

Inference

The question asks us to identify an inference that can be made regarding the people who formulated the labor theory of value.

A   Although it is plausible that the formulators of the theory may have been sympathetic with the interests of people who may be described as working class, there is no indication that the author of the passage actually has a working-class background.

B   Although at least some proponents of the theory have been considered radical, there is nothing in the passage that indicates this, or indicates whether or not the theory had popular appeal.

C   The "short step," mentioned in the passage, from Locke's theory of value to the labor theory of value, could seem to indicate a short step in time, whereby at least one of the formulators of the theory would be a rough contemporary of Locke. However, this would be an incorrect reading. Rather than a "step" in time, the "short step" in the passage refers to a logical step, whereby it would be a "short step" from one theory to another that resembles it in fundamental respects.

D   **Correct.** The passage strongly suggests that the formulators of the labor theory of value were influenced by Locke's views in certain fundamental respects. This indicates that the formulators would likely have been familiar with these views.

E   Although the author suggests that proponents of the labor theory of value may have significantly underestimated the importance of capital goods in the economy, no such suggestion is made about the importance of consumer goods.

The correct answer is D.

Questions 57–65 refer to the passage on page 74.

57. The author of the passage draws conclusions about the fur trade in North America from all of the following sources EXCEPT

   (A) Cartier's accounts of trading with Native Americans
   (B) a seventeenth-century account of European settlements
   (C) a sixteenth-century account written by a sailing vessel captain
   (D) archaeological observations of sixteenth-century Native American sites
   (E) a sixteenth-century account of Native Americans in what is now New England

Supporting Idea

This question asks about the sources mentioned by the author of the passage. Answering the question correctly requires determining which answer choice is NOT referred to in the passage as a source of evidence regarding the North American fur trade.

A   **Correct.** The passage mentions Cartier's voyage but does not refer to Cartier's accounts of his trading.
B   In the first paragraph, Nicolas Denys's 1672 account of European settlements provides evidence of fur trading by sixteenth-century European fishing crews.
C   In the second paragraph, a Portuguese captain's records provide evidence that the fur trade was going on for some time prior to his 1501 account.
D   In the first paragraph, archaeologists' observations of sixteenth-century Native American sites provide evidence of fur trading at that time.
E   In the second paragraph, a 1524 account provides evidence that Native Americans living in what is now New England had become selective about which European goods they would accept in trade for furs.

The correct answer is A.

58. The passage suggests that which of the following is partially responsible for the difficulty in establishing the precise date when the fur trade in North America began?

   (A) A lack of written accounts before that of Nicolas Denys in 1672
   (B) A lack of written documentation before 1501
   (C) Ambiguities in the evidence from Native American sources
   (D) Uncertainty about Native American trade networks
   (E) Uncertainty about the origin of artifacts supposedly traded by European fishing crews for furs

Inference

The question asks about information implied by the passage. The first paragraph points out the difficulty of establishing exactly when the fur trade between Native Americans and Europeans began. The second paragraph explains that the first written record of the fur trade (at least the earliest known to scholars who study the history of the trade) dates to 1501, but that trading was already well established by that time. Thus, it can be inferred that lack of written records prior to 1501 contributes to the difficulty in establishing an exact date for the beginning of the fur trade.

A   Two written records of the fur trade prior to the account by Nicolas Denys are mentioned in the passage. The passage does not suggest that a lack of written records from before 1672 is a source of the difficulty in establishing the date.

B   **Correct.** The passage indicates that the fur trade was well established by the time of the documentation dating from 1501 but strongly suggests that there is no known earlier documentation regarding that trade, so a lack of records before that time contributes to the difficulty in establishing an exact date.

C   The only Native American sources mentioned in the passage are archaeological sites, and there is no indication of ambiguities at those sites.

D   Native American trade networks are not mentioned in the passage.

E   The passage mentions that fishing crews exchanged parts of their ships for furs and does not suggest any uncertainty about the origin of those artifacts.

The correct answer is B.

59. Which of the following, if true, most strengthens the author's assertion in the first sentence of the second paragraph?

    (A) When Europeans retraced Cartier's voyage in the first years of the seventeenth century, they frequently traded with Native Americans.

    (B) Furs from beavers, which were plentiful in North America but nearly extinct in Europe, became extremely fashionable in Europe in the final decades of the sixteenth century.

    (C) Firing arms were rarely found on sixteenth-century Native American sites or on European lists of trading goods since such arms required frequent maintenance and repair.

    (D) Europeans and Native Americans had established trade protocols, such as body language assuring one another of their peaceful intentions, that antedate the earliest records of trade.

    (E) During the first quarter of the sixteenth century, an Italian explorer recorded seeing many Native Americans with what appeared to be copper beads, though they may have been made of indigenous copper.

Evaluation

The question depends on evaluating an assertion made in the passage and determining which additional evidence would most strengthen it.

The first sentence of the second paragraph claims that the fur trade was well established by the time Europeans sailing the Atlantic coast of America first documented it. The passage then indicates that the first written documentation of the trade dates to 1501. Thus, evidence showing that trade had been going on for some time before 1501 would strengthen (support) the assertion.

A   This evidence shows trade occurring in the first years of the seventeenth century, not prior to the first records from 1501.

B   This evidence shows trade occurring in the final decades of the sixteenth century, not prior to the first records from 1501.

C   This evidence does not indicate that trade took place prior to the first records from 1501.

D   **Correct.** Evidence that trade protocols had developed before the trade was first recorded in 1501 would strengthen support for the assertion that trade was taking place prior to the earliest documentation.

E   Because the copper beads may have been made by Native Americans rather than acquired through trade with other societies, this observation would not provide evidence that trade with Europeans took place prior to 1501.

The correct answer is D.

60. Which of the following best describes the primary function of lines 11–16?

    (A) It offers a reconsideration of a claim made in the preceding sentence.

    (B) It reveals how archaeologists arrived at an interpretation of the evidence mentioned in the preceding sentence.

    (C) It shows how scholars misinterpreted the significance of certain evidence mentioned in the preceding sentence.

    (D) It identifies one of the first significant accounts of seventeenth-century European settlements in North America.

    (E) It explains why Denys's account of seventeenth-century European settlements is thought to be significant.

Evaluation

This question depends on understanding how the last sentence of the first paragraph functions in relation to the larger passage. The first paragraph explains that the earliest Europeans to trade with Native Americans were fishing crews near Newfoundland. The second-to-last sentence of the paragraph describes archaeological artifacts from Native American sites. The last sentence then explains that Nicolas Denys's 1672 account helped archaeologists realize that the artifacts were evidence of trade with fishing crews. Thus, the last sentence of the passage shows how archaeologists learned to interpret the evidence mentioned in the previous sentence.

A   The only claim made in the previous sentence is that archaeologists found a particular type of evidence. The final sentence of the paragraph does not suggest that this claim should be reconsidered.

B   Correct. After reading Denys's account, archaeologists were able to interpret the archaeological evidence mentioned in the previous sentence.

C   The passage suggests that archaeologists correctly interpreted the evidence, not misinterpreted it.

D   Denys's account is mentioned primarily to explain how archaeologists learned to interpret the archaeological evidence, not primarily to identify an important early account of settlements.

E   The passage does not discuss why Denys's account is significant, only that archaeologists used it to help understand the evidence mentioned in the previous sentence.

The correct answer is B.

61. It can be inferred from the passage that the author would agree with which of the following statements about the fur trade between Native Americans and Europeans in the early modern era?

    (A) This trade may have begun as early as the 1480s.

    (B) This trade probably did not continue much beyond the 1530s.

    (C) This trade was most likely at its peak in the mid-1520s.

    (D) This trade probably did not begin prior to 1500.

    (E) There is no written evidence of this trade prior to the seventeenth century.

Inference

The question requires determining which statement can most reasonably be inferred from the information in the passage. The passage argues that it is difficult to determine when the fur trade between Native Americans and Europeans began, since the earliest people to participate in that trade apparently left no written records. The second paragraph notes that at the time of the earliest known record in 1501, trade was already *well underway*. In the final two sentences of the passage, the author mentions an event that occurred in 1534 and then says that by that time the trade may have been going on for *perhaps half a century*.

A   Correct. The next-to-last sentence of the passage cites evidence of fur trade between Native Americans and Europeans in 1524. In the final sentence of the passage, the author mentions an event that happened a decade after that date—thus in 1534—and expresses the opinion that the trade started *perhaps half a century* (fifty years) before that later date. Fifty years before 1534 would be 1484. This implies that the author accepts that the trade may have begun by the 1480s.

B   The passage gives no indication that the author believes trade ended shortly after the 1530s.

C   The passage does not discuss when the fur trade was at its peak.

D   To the contrary, the passage argues that trade began well before 1501.

E   The passage mentions written evidence of the trade from 1501 and 1524.

The correct answer is A.

62. Which of the following can be inferred from the passage about the Native Americans mentioned in line 24?

(A) They had little use for decorative objects such as earrings.
(B) They became increasingly dependent on fishing between 1501 and 1524.
(C) By 1524, only certain groups of Europeans were willing to trade with them.
(D) The selectivity of their trading choices made it difficult for them to engage in widespread trade with Europeans.
(E) The selectivity of their trading choices indicates that they had been trading with Europeans for a significant period of time prior to 1524.

Inference

The question asks about information that can be inferred from the passage. The Native Americans mentioned in the 1524 chronicles accepted only certain kinds of European goods in trade. The passage indicates that these Native Americans *had become selective* about which goods they would accept, which implies that by 1524 they had been trading long enough to determine which European goods were most valuable to them.

A The passage does not imply that these Native Americans had no use for decorative objects, only that they did not desire to obtain such items through trade with Europeans.
B The passage does not suggest that the Native Americans' dependency on fishing changed over time.
C There is no indication that any groups of Europeans were unwilling to trade with these Native Americans.
D The passage notes that the Native Americans were selective in their trade choices but does not suggest that such selectivity made widespread trade difficult.
E **Correct.** The passage notes that by 1524, the Native Americans had become selective about which European goods they would accept, and the passage takes this to indicate that the trade with Europeans significantly predated 1524.

The correct answer is E.

63. The passage supports which of the following statements about sixteenth-century European fishing crews working the waters off Newfoundland?

(A) They wrote no accounts of their fishing voyages.
(B) They primarily sailed under the flag of Portugal.
(C) They exchanged ship parts with Native Americans for furs.
(D) They commonly traded jewelry with Native Americans for furs.
(E) They carried surplus metal implements to trade with Native Americans for furs.

Inference

The question asks which statement is supported by information provided in the passage. The first paragraph states that European fishing crews around Newfoundland were the first Europeans to trade goods for furs with Native Americans in the modern period. The last sentence of the paragraph states that archaeological evidence indicates the crews had dismantled their ships to trade ship parts for furs.

A The second sentence states that the crews left no written accounts of their trade with Native Americans, but it does not suggest that they left no written accounts of their voyages.
B The passage mentions one Portuguese vessel but does not suggest that the European crews who fished off Newfoundland were mostly on Portuguese vessels.
C **Correct.** The last sentence of the first paragraph supports the conclusion that the crews traded ship parts for furs.
D The passage mentions one instance of a Native American acquiring earrings from Europeans but does not suggest that trades for such goods were common.
E The passage indicates that fishing crews traded metal implements with Native Americans but does not suggest that they brought surplus implements for that purpose—and in fact mentions that sometimes traded metal articles had been parts of their own ships.

The correct answer is C.

64. Which of the following can be inferred from the passage about evidence pertaining to the fur trade between Native Americans and Europeans in the early modern era?

   (A) A lack of written evidence has made it difficult to establish which Europeans first participated in this trade.
   (B) In general, the physical evidence pertaining to this trade has been more useful than the written evidence has been.
   (C) There is more written evidence pertaining to this trade from the early part of the sixteenth century than from later in that century.
   (D) The earliest written evidence pertaining to this trade dates from a time when the trade was already well established.
   (E) Some important pieces of evidence pertaining to this trade, such as Denys's 1672 account, were long overlooked by archaeologists.

Inference

This question asks about information that can be inferred from the passage. Any suggestion that Native Americans may have produced written evidence of the early-modern trade with Europeans is absent from the passage. The second paragraph states that by the time Europeans first documented the fur trade, it was already well underway. This statement, in the context of the passage, implies that the earliest written records of the trade date to a time after it was well established.

   A The first paragraph indicates that the first Europeans to participate in the trade were quite certainly fishing crews near Newfoundland.
   B The passage gives no indication that physical evidence of the trade has been more useful than written evidence.
   C Although the passage does not cite written evidence from the late sixteenth century, the passage gives no reason to believe that less written evidence exists from that time.

   D **Correct.** According to the passage, the fur trade was well underway when written evidence of the trade was first documented by Europeans. The passage contains no suggestion that there might have been earlier documentation of that trade by anybody other than Europeans.
   E The passage does not imply that archaeologists overlooked evidence for long periods of time.

The correct answer is D.

65. The passage suggests which of the following about the sixteenth-century Native Americans who traded with Europeans on the coast of what is now called New England?

   (A) By 1524, they had become accustomed to exchanging goods with Europeans.
   (B) They were unfamiliar with metals before encountering Europeans.
   (C) They had no practical uses for European goods other than metals and metal implements.
   (D) By 1524, they had become disdainful of European traders because such traders had treated them unfairly in the past.
   (E) By 1524, they demanded only the most prized European goods because they had come to realize how valuable furs were on European markets.

Inference

The question asks about what is implied in the passage. The Native Americans trading with Europeans on the coast of what is now called New England are discussed in the 1524 chronicles mentioned in the second paragraph. The passage indicates that these Native Americans *had become selective* about which European goods they would accept in trade, which suggests they had become accustomed to trading with Europeans.

   A **Correct.** By the time the chronicle was written, the Native Americans were familiar enough with trade to be able to specify which European goods they would accept.

B Although the Native Americans chose to trade furs for European metal goods, the passage does not imply they were unfamiliar with any metals prior to encountering Europeans.
C The passage does not suggest why Native Americans preferred certain goods over others.
D The passage does not attribute disdain for European traders to Native Americans.
E There is no indication in the passage that Native Americans were aware of furs' value in European markets.

The correct answer is A.

Questions 66–69 refer to the passage on page 77.

66. The passage is primarily concerned with

(A) describing the development of the biological species concept
(B) responding to a critique of reproductive compatibility as a criterion for defining a species
(C) considering two different approaches to identifying biological species
(D) pointing out the advantage of one method of distinguishing related species
(E) identifying an obstacle to the classification of biological species

Main Idea

This question depends on understanding the passage as a whole. The passage begins by explaining that identifying a species can be difficult, because there are different ways of defining the term. The biological species concept is one approach, but it has problems. Phenotype is another approach that can be used when the biological species concept proves difficult.

A The first paragraph defines the biological species concept and identifies some problems with its application, but it does not explain how that concept developed.
B The passage presents some critiques of reproductive compatibility as a way of identifying a biological species; it does not concern itself with responding to those critiques.
C **Correct.** The passage considers the biological species concept and the idea of phenotype as ways of identifying biological species.
D While the passage identifies two ways of distinguishing species and states that some investigators use one of those methods—the phenotype method—when the biological method is difficult to apply, the passage is not primarily concerned with pointing out that either one is better than the other.
E The passage does discuss certain obstacles to the classification of species. First, it points out that there is no single accepted definition of *distinct species*. Second, it points out obstacles related to one particular approach to the classification of species. However, the passage considers these obstacles in service of its primary concern, namely considering two different approaches to identifying biological species.

The correct answer is C.

67. The author of the passage mentions "groups that live in different places" (line 21) most probably in order to

(A) point out a theoretical inconsistency in the biological species concept
(B) offer evidence in support of the biological species concept
(C) identify an obstacle to the application of the biological species concept
(D) note an instance in which phenotype classification is customarily used
(E) describe an alternative to the biological species concept

Evaluation

The author's mention of *groups that live in different places* comes at the end of the first paragraph, in the context of discussing a third problem with the biological species concept: that investigators may not know whether animals in such groups are able to interbreed.

A The author does not address theoretical inconsistencies in the biological species concept.

149

B   The author mentions groups that live in different places in order to address a problem with the biological species concept, not to support it.

C   **Correct.** One obstacle to applying the biological species concept is that those attempting to distinguish among species may not be able to determine whether geographically separated groups of animals can interbreed.

D   The passage does mention that some investigators use phenotype classification when the biological species concept is difficult to apply, but it does not mention specifically that a situation in which groups live in different places is an instance in which phenotype classification is customarily used.

E   Animal groups that live in different places pose a problem for the application of the biological species concept, according to the author. The author does not mention these groups in order to describe an alternative to that concept.

The correct answer is C.

68. With which of the following statements regarding the classification of individual species would the author most likely agree?

    (A) Phenotype comparison may help to classify species when application of the biological species concept proves inconclusive.

    (B) Because no standard definition exists for what constitutes a species, the classification of animal populations is inevitably an arbitrary process.

    (C) The criteria used by biologists to classify species have not been based on adequate research.

    (D) The existence of hybrids in wild animal species is the chief factor casting doubt on the usefulness of research into reproductive compatibility as a way of classifying species.

    (E) Phenotype overlap should be used as the basic criterion for standardizing species classification.

Inference

This question depends on understanding the general points the author makes with regard to classification of individual species. The author explains that there is no single definition of species and then describes the biological species concept, which depends on reproductive compatibility. This approach has several problems, however, and the author goes on to say that phenotype may be used when the biological species concept is difficult to apply.

A   **Correct.** The author states at the beginning of the second paragraph that some investigators use phenotype when they find it difficult to apply the biological species concept, and the passage provides no reason to believe that the author would disagree with the idea that phenotype comparison can be helpful in these situations.

B   The author would most likely not agree that classification of animal populations is arbitrary. Investigators use clearly defined approaches, such as the biological species concept and phenotype classification, to make such classifications. That there may be problems with an approach does not make it arbitrary.

C   The author states that the biological species concept can be too restrictive, but there is no suggestion that the author finds this approach, or phenotype classification, to be inadequately researched.

D   The author mentions hybridization first as a factor casting doubt on the usefulness of the biological species concept, but nothing in the passage suggests that the author thinks that it is more significant than the other reasons offered for finding the biological species concept too restrictive.

E   Phenotype overlap does not receive the author's endorsement as the best, or most basic, way of classifying species; instead, the author states merely that some investigators rely on this approach when they cannot apply the biological species concept.

The correct answer is A.

69. Which of the following best describes the function of lines 10–13?

(A) It elaborates the definition of the biological species concept given in a previous sentence.
(B) It develops a point about the biological species concept made in the previous sentence.
(C) It states the author's central point about the biological species concept.
(D) It identifies a central assumption underlying the biological species concept.
(E) It demonstrates why the biological species concept is invalid.

Evaluation

The sentence in question discusses hybridization as a first factor complicating the applicability of the biological species concept. Thus its function is to help explain why, as the previous sentence states, that concept is too restrictive.

A   The sentence in question brings up a problem with the biological species concept; it does not elaborate the definition of that concept.
B   **Correct.** According to the sentence that precedes the sentence in question, the biological species concept can be too restrictive. The author offers three reasons to develop this point, and the first reason is given in the sentence in question.
C   The sentence in question could be said to support the author's central point about the biological species concept—that it is one (flawed) way of determining whether a population is a species—but it does not state that central point.
D   The sentence in question expresses a problem with the biological species concept, not a central assumption of it.
E   The sentence in question serves to indicate a problem with the biological species concept, but it does not go so far as to demonstrate that it is invalid.

The correct answer is B.

Questions 70–72 refer to the passage on page 79.

70. The primary purpose of the passage is to

(A) summarize findings in an area of research
(B) discuss different perspectives on a scientific question
(C) outline the major questions in a scientific discipline
(D) illustrate the usefulness of investigating a research topic
(E) reconcile differences between two definitions of a term

Main Idea

The passage discusses two problems confronting researchers studying the genetic bases of animal behavior: the complexity of the control of most behaviors by multiple genes, and divergence between research fields in what counts as a behavioral gene. The passage focuses mainly on the latter issue, discussing how ethologists define "behavioral gene" in a narrower manner than neuroscientists, who define the term broadly. To elucidate the ethologists' approach, two genes are discussed, one a behavioral gene, the other not.

A   The passage primarily aims to explain how researchers in two different research areas define "behavioral gene." It does not try to summarize the research findings of either area.
B   **Correct.** The primary purpose of the passage is to identify differing perspectives on the scientific question of how genes control animal behavior.
C   The scientific disciplines of genetics, neuroscience, and ethology—all subdisciplines of biology—contain many different "major questions," and the passage does not try to outline the great variety of such questions in any one of those subdisciplines.
D   The topic of the utility of doing research is not part of the passage discussion.

E   An important purpose of the passage is to illustrate divergence among scientific fields in how a key term is defined, but the point is to show how the definitions differ rather than to "reconcile" the difference.

The correct answer is B.

71. The passage suggests that neuroscientists would most likely consider Shaker to be which of the following?

    (A) An example of a behavioral gene
    (B) One of multiple genes that control a single behavior
    (C) A gene that, when mutated, causes an alteration in a specific normal behavior without making the organism ill
    (D) A gene of interest to ethologists but of no interest to neuroscientists
    (E) A poor source of information about the nervous system

Application

The passage asserts that ethologists do not regard *Shaker* as a behavioral gene because it merely makes fruit flies exhibit unhealthy behavior (shaking under anesthesia). But neuroscientists, according to the passage, are mainly interested in how genes, via the nervous system, contribute to behavior. The passage suggests that neuroscientists, unlike ethologists, have no reservation about using the term *behavioral gene* to apply to any gene that contributes to behavior. The implication is that neuroscientists would probably regard *Shaker* as a behavioral gene.

A   **Correct.** The passage suggests that neuroscientists would probably regard *Shaker* as a behavioral gene.

B   The passage indicates that research shows *Shaker* is a sufficient cause, in fruit flies, of shaking under anesthesia. Although some organism might display a behavior controlled by *Shaker* in concert with other genes, the passage is silent on any such possibility.

C   The passage lacks information as to whether there is any alteration—one that neuroscientists would likely consider healthy—in a normal behavior if the alteration is caused by a mutation in *Shaker*.

D   The passage indicates that neuroscientists' interest in genetics is part of their effort to understand the nervous system. This seems to imply that neuroscientists might be interested in *Shaker*.

E   The passage is silent on how neuroscientists would evaluate the potential for *Shaker* to contribute to understanding of the nervous system.

The correct answer is A.

72. It can be inferred from the passage that which of the following, if true, would be most likely to influence ethologists' opinions about whether a particular gene in a species is a behavioral gene?

    (A) The gene is found only in that species.
    (B) The gene is extremely difficult to identify.
    (C) The only effect of mutations in the gene is to make the organism ill.
    (D) Neuroscientists consider the gene to be a behavioral gene.
    (E) Geneticists consider the gene to be a behavioral gene.

Application

The passage identifies two criteria that ethologists use in deciding whether a gene should count as a behavioral gene: a mutation in the gene alters a specific normal behavior and the mutation does not merely make the organism ill.

A   The passage is silent on whether either of two genes identified by ethologists in fruit flies are to be found only in fruit flies. The two criteria mentioned used by ethologists carry no implication as to whether any gene unique to a given species would count as a behavioral gene.

B The difficulty of identifying a gene can obviously be due to many factors, such as limitations in existing scientific techniques, and the passage does not imply that such difficulty increases the likelihood that a gene would count as a behavioral gene for ethologists.

C **Correct.** The passage implies that if this were found to be true, ethologists would regard it as sufficient reason for not counting the gene as a behavioral gene.

D A central theme of the passage is that whether ethologists would count a gene as a behavioral gene is largely unaffected by whether neuroscientists do so, given the divergent perspectives of the scientists' respective disciplines.

E The main contrast in the passage with respect to definitions of the term *behavioral gene* is between ethologists and neuroscientists, and no specific definitional criteria for this term are explicitly attributed to geneticists. However, there is a slight suggestion that since geneticists find that most behaviors are governed by multiple genes, geneticists might regard any gene involved in the governance of a behavior as a behavioral gene. This approach, however, would be unlikely to influence the opinions of ethologists concerning definition.

The correct answer is C.

Questions 73–79 refer to the passage on page 80.

73. The author indicates that tamarin territories are

(A) surprisingly large
(B) poorly situated
(C) unusually abundant in food resources
(D) incapable of supporting large troops of tamarins
(E) larger in Peru than in other parts of South America

Supporting Idea

This question depends on understanding what the passage says about tamarin territories. In the second paragraph, the passage claims that the most surprising thing about tamarins is the size of their territories, and it indicates how large these territories are by comparing them to the territories of certain other animals.

A **Correct.** The passage indicates that the size of tamarins' territories—large in comparison to the territories of several other species—is surprising.

B The passage gives no indication as to whether tamarin territories are poorly situated.

C Although the passage does discuss the tamarin diet, it does not indicate how abundant in food sources tamarin territories are.

D The passage does indicate that relatively few tamarins live per square kilometer, but it does not claim that this is so because the territories are incapable of supporting a larger number of tamarins. In fact, there is some suggestion that the territories would seem to be capable of supporting more, which is one reason the size of the territories is so surprising.

E The passage does not compare the size of tamarin territories in Peru to tamarin territories elsewhere in South America.

The correct answer is A.

74. The author mentions the spatial requirements of the gray squirrel in order to

(A) explain why they are so common
(B) demonstrate the consequences of their nonterritoriality
(C) emphasize the unusual territorial requirements of the tamarin
(D) provide an example of a major difference between squirrels and monkeys
(E) provide an example of an animal with requirements similar to those of the tamarin

Evaluation

The passage mentions the spatial requirements of the gray squirrel as part of its discussion of the surprising size of tamarin territories. Gray squirrel territories are mentioned for the specific purpose of highlighting how much more space tamarins require compared to another animal of roughly equal size.

A The passage does refer to "the common gray squirrel," but it does not explain why they are so common.

B The passage does not say anything about the consequences of the gray squirrel's nonterritoriality.

C **Correct.** The spatial requirements of gray squirrels are mentioned to highlight, by contrast, how expansive the spatial requirements of tamarins are.

D Although the passage mentions the spatial requirements of the gray squirrel to highlight how different the spatial requirements of one particular type of monkey, the tamarin, are from those of other animals, the passage does not mention the squirrels' spatial requirements to provide an example of a difference between squirrels and monkeys in general.

E The passage actually does the opposite of this—it mentions the gray squirrel's spatial requirements to provide an example of an animal with requirements vastly different from those of the tamarin.

The correct answer is C.

75. The author regards the differences between the diets of the tamarins and several larger species as

    (A) generally explicable in terms of territory size
    (B) apparently too small to explain the rarity of tamarins
    (C) wholly predictable on the basis of differences in body size
    (D) a result of the rigid territoriality of tamarins
    (E) a significant factor in determining behavioral differences

Supporting Idea

This question depends on recognizing that the passage rejects the idea that any differences between the diets of tamarins and those of certain larger animals are large enough to explain tamarins' relative rarity. The passage points out that these animals feed on the same fruits, nectar, and small prey, and claims that though the proportions of the fruits consumed varies somewhat, this variation is not sufficient to explain the tamarin's rarity.

A The author does not seek to explain why these differences in diet—which the passage indicates are minimal—exist. Given that the author indicates that differences in territory size are large and differences in diet are small, it is unlikely, in any case, that the author would regard the former as explaining the latter.

B **Correct.** The passage indicates that the differences in diet among these animals are too small to explain the rarity of tamarins.

C The author does not give any indication that the differences in the diets of these animals are predictable based on differences in body size.

D The author does indicate that tamarins are rather unusual among primates in their rigid territoriality, but there is no indication that this rigid territoriality explains the small differences in diet among tamarins and certain larger animals.

E The author mentions differences in diet merely to rule out that these differences are large enough to explain tamarins' rarity; these differences are not mentioned as a factor in determining behavioral differences.

The correct answer is B.

76. Which of the following would most probably be regarded by the author as anomalous?

    (A) A large primate species that eats mostly plants
    (B) A species of small mammals that is fiercely territorial
    (C) Two species of small primates that share the same territories
    (D) A species of small birds that is more abundant than many species of larger birds

(E) A species of small rodents that requires more living space per individual than most species of larger rodents

Application

This question requires you to understand an underlying principle of the passage and to apply that principle to an instance that is not specifically discussed in the passage. The passage is concerned with how anomalous tamarins are: they are exceptions to the general rule that in general the number of animals in a species is proportional to the average body size of individuals within the species. The author also points out that tamarins are unusual in that the amount of space they require is out of proportion to their body size, suggesting the principle that an animal's spatial requirement is generally proportional to the animal's body size. And, though the passage is generally concerned with comparing tamarins to other primates, the author also compares tamarins' spatial requirements to those of gray squirrels, a type of rodent.

A   The author does not give any indication whether it would be anomalous for a species of large primates to eat mostly plants. The author does not present a general principle about the diets of primates, and says nothing specific about species of large primates.

B   Although the author indicates that the "rigid" territoriality of tamarins is "rather exceptional among primates," the author lists several other primate species that are also territorial. The author does not indicate whether such territoriality is rare among small mammals in general.

C   The author indicates that most primates do not have "such concerted territoriality" as tamarins do, suggesting that the author may not think that two other species of small primates sharing territories would be anomalous.

D   Given that the author indicates that generally the number of individuals within a species is inversely proportional to the average body size of the members of the species, the author would probably expect that a species of small birds would be more abundant than most species of larger birds and would not regard this as anomalous.

E   **Correct.** The author would generally expect that smaller animals would require less living space than larger animals.

The correct answer is E.

77. The author most probably regards the tamarins studied in Manu National Park as

(A) an endangered species
(B) typical tamarins
(C) unusually docile
(D) the most unusual primates anywhere
(E) too small a sample to be significant

Inference

This question requires you to make an inference from what the author says about the tamarins studied in Manu National Park to a claim about how the author most likely regards these tamarins. The author considers certain information that has been gathered about the two tamarin species studied in the park, and on the basis of that, makes claims about tamarins in general (note that the author elsewhere in the passage simply refers to "tamarins" without qualification, i.e., without referring specifically to "the tamarins studied in Manu National Park"). This suggests that the author would regard the tamarins studied in the park as being typical of tamarins generally, at least in the ways discussed.

A   It is possible that the two tamarin species studied in the park are endangered, but apart from noting the surprisingly small number of individuals belonging to the species, there is no information that would suggest that they are endangered, and the mere fact that the number of members is relatively small compared to the number of members in other species is not sufficient to indicate that they are endangered, as that number could nonetheless be stable or even growing.

B **Correct.** The author does not specifically mention anything that would indicate that these tamarins are atypical of tamarins in general, and appears to make inferences about tamarins in general on the basis of the two species studied in the park. The author would not be justified in making such inferences if the author believed that the tamarins observed in the park were not in fact typical.

C The author does not give any indication that these species are unusually docile, and in fact suggests the opposite by indicating that tamarins vigorously expel any intruders from their territories.

D The author does note some ways in which these tamarin species are unusual among primates, but does not indicate that they are "the most unusual primates anywhere." The author, in fact, indicates that in one of the ways that these species are unusual—their relative scarcity despite their small body size—another primate species, the pygmy marmoset, is even more unusual.

E Because the author appears to make some inferences from information about the tamarins studied in the park to claims about tamarins in general, the author does not seem to regard the tamarins studied in the park as too small a sample to be significant.

The correct answer is B.

78. Which of the following is NOT mentioned in the passage as a species whose groups display territoriality?

    (A) Gibbons
    (B) Siamangs
    (C) Titi monkeys
    (D) Squirrel monkeys
    (E) Night monkeys

Inference

This question requires you, by process of elimination, to identify the species that is NOT explicitly mentioned as being a species displaying territoriality. Each of the species given in the answer choices is explicitly mentioned in the passage, and all but one of these species are explicitly described as displaying territoriality. In lines 38–41, the author states, "concerted territoriality [like that of tamarins] is rather exceptional among primates, though the gibbons and siamangs of Asia show it, as do a few other New World species such as the titi and night monkeys." So, clearly, gibbons, siamangs, titi monkeys, and night monkeys are each said to display territoriality. Squirrel monkeys, the remaining answer choice, are mentioned three different times in the passage (see lines 16, 25, 30), but never as displaying territoriality.

A Gibbons are identified as displaying "concerted territoriality" (line 39).

B Siamangs are identified as displaying "concerted territoriality" (line 39).

C Titi monkeys are identified as displaying "concerted territoriality" (line 41).

D **Correct.** Although squirrel monkeys are mentioned three times in the passage (lines 16, 25, and 30), in none of the instances are they mentioned as displaying territoriality.

E Night monkeys are identified as displaying "concerted territoriality" (line 41).

The correct answer is D.

79. The primary concern of the passage is to

    (A) recommend a policy
    (B) evaluate a theory
    (C) describe an unusual condition
    (D) explain the development of a hypothesis
    (E) support one of several competing hypotheses

Main Idea

Answering this question requires identifying an abstract description of the primary purpose of the passage. The passage focuses in different ways on an unusual condition, namely, the anomalous relationship between tamarins' relatively small average body size and the number of individuals in the species.

A   The passage is not concerned with recommending any policy.

B   The passage does not focus on any theory; it considers a phenomenon, but proposes no theory to explain that phenomenon.

C   **Correct.** The passage's primary concern is to describe an unusual phenomenon, namely, how tamarins "break the rule" that, in general, the number of individuals in a species is inversely proportional to the average body size of members of the species.

D   The passage is primarily concerned with a particular, unusual phenomenon, but it offers no hypothesis regarding it, nor does it discuss the development of any such hypothesis.

E   Although the passage gives passing consideration to some hypotheses, its primary concern is to note certain characteristics of tamarins. The passage does not primarily concern itself with any hypotheses.

The correct answer is C.

Questions 80–86 refer to the passage on page 82.

80. It can be inferred from the passage that opponents of labor concessions would most likely describe many plant-relocation decisions made by United States companies as

    (A) capricious
    (B) self-serving
    (C) naive
    (D) impulsive
    (E) illogical

Evaluation

This question requires you to pick a word that the passage suggests opponents of labor concessions would apply to many plant-relocation decisions made by U.S. companies. The passage indicates that those who oppose labor concessions often do so on the grounds that companies will move their production overseas if it matches their perceived self-interest—regardless of any concessions labor has made in order to preserve jobs. According to the passage, opponents of labor concessions therefore tend to view such plant-relocation decisions as self-serving.

A   The passage does not attribute to opponents of labor concessions the view that corporate decisions are variable in a way that makes them unpredictable.

B   **Correct.** According to the passage, the opponents of labor concessions believe that companies make investment decisions that fit their strategic plans and profit objectives.

C   The passage suggests that the opponents may view plant managers' relocation decisions as based on realistic assessments of corporate interests.

D   The passage does not attribute to the opponents the view that companies make plant-relocation decisions on impulse; rather, it suggests that these opponents tend to see relocation decisions as based on analysis of how relocation would advance predetermined strategies and objectives.

E   According to the passage, the opponents see an inflexible logic governing such relocation decisions, which are based on an assessment of how best to serve companies' interests, as judged by reference to predetermined investment strategies and profit objectives.

The correct answer is B.

81. It can be inferred from the passage that, until recently, which of the following has been true of United States industry in the twentieth century?

    (A) Unions have consistently participated in major corporate policy decisions.
    (B) Maintaining adequate quality control in manufacturing processes has been a principal problem.
    (C) Union workers have been paid relatively high wages.
    (D) Two-tier wage systems have been the norm.
    (E) Goods produced have been priced beyond the means of most workers.

Inference

This question requires you to draw a conclusion about United States industry in the twentieth century from the information in the passage. The passage indicates that even opponents of labor concessions believe that union workers have traditionally been paid relatively high wages and that high wages underlay much of the success of industry in the United States in the twentieth century.

A The passage suggests otherwise. It tells us that advocates of labor concessions believe it may eventually be possible for labor to participate in management decisions in a way that was not traditionally the case.

B The passage mentions "quality circles" as a benefit that, according to some proponents of labor concessions, may eventually be gained in the context of having more say on the shop floor. But that does not imply that quality control in manufacturing has been a major problem.

C **Correct.** The passage attributes a belief that this was so to opponents of labor concessions.

D The passage tells us that opponents of labor concessions believe that proposals for two-tier wage systems could become a reality—which indicates that such systems have not been the norm.

E According to the passage, opponents of labor concessions admit that wages have been relatively high for union workers and that labor and management have long been committed to the idea that workers should be able to afford to purchase the products they make.

The correct answer is C.

82. The passage provides information to answer which of the following questions?

   (A) What has caused unions to consider wage restraints and reduced benefits?
   (B) Why do analysts study United States labor-management relations?
   (C) How do job-security guarantees operate?
   (D) Are investment and pricing strategies effective in combating imports?
   (E) Do quality circles improve product performance and value?

Evaluation

This question requires you to identify a question that the passage provides an answer to. In paragraph 1, the passage indicates some factors ("twin shocks") that have contributed to a change in the approach of labor unions to negotiations with management.

A **Correct.** The passage claims that competition from non-union companies and imports of low-priced high-quality products from abroad have induced labor unions to be more flexible in meeting the demands of management.

B The passage does not address this question either directly or indirectly.

C According to the passage, proponents of labor concessions claim that job-security guarantees can be negotiated if concessions are made, but the passage provides no further detail that would shed light on how such guarantees operate.

D The passage is silent on the effectiveness of investment and pricing strategies in combating imports.

E The passage mentions quality circles, but provides no information on their impact. Presumably, quality circles aim to improve quality, and such improvements would be pointless absent any payoff in "performance and value."

The correct answer is A.

83. The passage is primarily concerned with the

   (A) reasons for adversarialism between labor and management
   (B) importance of cooperative labor-management relations
   (C) consequences of labor concessions to management

- (D) effects of foreign competition on the United States economy
- (E) effects of nonunion competition on union bargaining strategies

Main Idea

This question asks us to identify the overall theme of the passage, i.e., the topic that motivates the discussion of various subtopics.

- A The traditionally adversarial relationship between labor and management is mentioned in passing, but the reasons for that relationship are not probed.
- B The passage details benefits that some labor unionists perceive in cooperative labor-management relations, but does not assess the importance of such relations.
- **C Correct.** The passage explores this theme by looking at the new approach of some labor unions by discussing the pros and cons of labor concessions as perceived by proponents and opponents of such concessions.
- D The passage alludes to these effects, but no sustained exploration of this topic is present in the passage.
- E The passage alludes to these effects, but no sustained exploration of this topic is present in the passage.

The correct answer is C.

84. The sentence "If proposals for pay cuts . . . unskilled laborers" (lines 45–52) serves primarily to
    - (A) disprove a theory
    - (B) clarify an ambiguity
    - (C) reconcile opposing views
    - (D) present a hypothesis
    - (E) contradict accepted data

Evaluation

This question asks you to determine the intended purpose of one of the passage's sentences. This sentence, found in the final paragraph, describes what opponents of labor concessions predict are possible consequences if labor unions agree to pay cuts, two-tier wage systems, or lower wages for newly hired workers. These hypothesized consequences can be summarized as a significant degradation in the overall material welfare of large sections of the population because of grossly unequal distribution of wealth and income such as exist in some less-developed societies.

- A The sentence describes what is perceived as something that could occur if labor unions were to make concessions resulting in reductions in wages. It is not framed as evidence to refute a theory, since it is merely a prediction of what could occur.
- B The sentence does not function in resolving an ambiguity; no ambiguity that the sentence could be meant to resolve is described or suggested.
- C The sentence does nothing to reconcile opposing views; it articulates a vision of a possible future that it attributes to those who oppose wage-reduction concessions by labor unions.
- **D Correct.** The sentence presents a hypothesis about the possible long-term consequences of labor-union concessions that would result in significantly lower wages.
- E Accepted data can be contradicted only by alternative datasets, but the sentence in question does not provide alternative data, only a prediction of what the future might bring for workers' material welfare if drastic wage reductions were to be conceded by labor unions.

The correct answer is D.

85. It can be inferred from the passage that opponents of labor concessions believe that if concession bargaining continues, then
    - (A) plants will close instead of relocating
    - (B) young workers will need continued job retraining
    - (C) professional workers will outnumber marginal workers

(D) wealthy investors will invest in Third World countries instead of the United States

(E) the social structure of the United States will be negatively affected

Inference

This question concerns the beliefs of opponents of labor concessions, as those beliefs are represented in the passage. The passage attributes to those opponents the view that if the idea of reducing wages gains credence, the U.S. social structure will begin to decline and will eventually be on a par with the social structures of less-developed nations. Moreover, the passage represents the opponents as believing that if labor unions negotiate on the premise that high labor costs are causing a company's problems, eventually wages will be reduced drastically—potentially to Third World levels. In paragraph 1, the passage reports that analysts say that labor unions are currently forced to favorably consider management demands for "wage restraint" and concessions on benefits.

A   The passage indicates that the opponents believe companies relocate their plants whenever companies perceive this as in accord with their investment strategies and profit objectives.
B   A need for continued retraining of young workers is not a belief attributed by the passage to opponents of labor concessions.
C   The passage, in referring to "a huge mass of marginal workers," attributes a contrary view to opponents of labor concessions.
D   The passage does not attribute this view to opponents of labor concessions.
E   **Correct.** We learn from the passage that labor unions are engaged in concession bargaining, on topics that include wage restraint. The opponents of labor concessions believe, according to the passage, that eventually the result will be wage reductions, and the ultimate result will be degradation of the U.S. social structure, resulting in a social structure more like that of a less-developed nation.

The correct answer is E.

86. According to the author, "Sophisticated proponents" (line 13) of concessions do which of the following?

(A) Support the traditional adversarialism characteristic of labor-management relations.
(B) Emphasize the benefits unions can gain by granting concessions.
(C) Focus on thorough analyses of current economic conditions.
(D) Present management's reasons for demanding concessions.
(E) Explain domestic economic developments in terms of worldwide trends.

Supporting Idea

This question requires you to identify what the passage says "sophisticated proponents" of concessions do. According to the passage, these sophisticated proponents represent their concessions in a "prolabor light." They suggest that concessions by labor can bargain for profit sharing, retraining rights, and job-security guarantees—and can even bargain for "more say on the shop floor" and a voice in company strategy and decision making.

A   According to the passage, analysts say that labor-management relations are increasingly cooperative rather than adversarial.
B   **Correct.** As explained above, the proponents of labor concessions represent concessions in a prolabor light by detailing the types of labor gains that can come from such concessions.
C   The proponents probably conduct such analyses, but no information about this is given in the passage.
D   Sophisticated proponents may sometimes do this, but the passage emphasizes their focus on the opportunities for labor gains.
E   Sophisticated proponents may sometimes do this, but the passage emphasizes their focus on the opportunities for labor gains.

The correct answer is B.

Questions 87–91 refer to the passage on page 84.

87. According to the passage, much of the research on Alessandra Strozzi done by the historian mentioned in the second paragraph supports which of the following conclusions?

    (A) Alessandra used her position as her sons' sole guardian to further interests different from those of her sons.
    (B) Alessandra unwillingly sacrificed her own interests in favor of those of her sons.
    (C) Alessandra's actions indicate that her motivations and intentions were those of an independent individual.
    (D) Alessandra's social context encouraged her to take independent action.
    (E) Alessandra regarded her sons' goals and interests as her own.

Supporting Idea

According to the passage, a historian of women in Renaissance Europe attributes to a Florentine widow Alessandra Strozzi "individual intention and authorship of actions" and argues that she had significant individual goals and interests other than those of her sons. But the passage states that much of the historian's research indicates otherwise.

A According to the passage, the historian's research provides much evidence that Alessandra Strozzi acted primarily to further her sons' interests.
B The passage does not cite any of the historian's research to suggest that Strozzi was an unwilling champion of her sons' interest.
C A theme of the passage is that the historian's research provides weak, if any, support for this claim.
D The historian's research is not invoked in the passage to support this. The passage suggests that such a claim is more compatible with an anthropologist's idea that identity is socially and culturally determined and not necessarily "independent," as various historians assume.
E **Correct.** The passage states: "much of the historian's own research reveals that Alessandra acted primarily as a champion of her sons' interests, taking their goals as her own."

The correct answer is E.

88. In the first paragraph, the author of the passage mentions a contention that would be made by an anthropologist most likely in order to

    (A) present a theory that will be undermined in the discussion of a historian's study later in the passage
    (B) offer a perspective on the concept of personhood that can usefully be applied to the study of women in Renaissance Europe
    (C) undermine the view that the individuality of European women of the Renaissance was largely suppressed
    (D) argue that anthropologists have applied the Western concept of individualism in their research
    (E) lay the groundwork for the conclusion that Alessandra's is a unique case among European women of the Renaissance whose lives have been studied by historians

Evaluation

The passage asserts that an anthropologist would contend that "a person can be conceived in ways other than as an 'individual.'" Immediately preceding this assertion, the passage asserts that certain historians think of a person as "an innately bounded unit, autonomous and standing apart from both nature and society." The passage invokes anthropology to support the view that perhaps the findings of those historians regarding individualism among women in Renaissance Europe are biased.

A Anthropology is invoked to provide a corrective to the findings of the historians mentioned—not to provide a critique of any anthropological theory.
B **Correct.** The passage makes the case that the anthropological view may be more useful than the historian's in the study of women in Renaissance Europe.

C The passage cites no claim by historians that individuality of women in Renaissance Europe was largely suppressed, and the passage presents no argument to critique or refute such a claim.

D The passage makes no such claim about anthropologists, but does make a similar claim about certain historians.

E The passage does not state or imply that Strozzi was atypical of women in Renaissance Europe that historians have studied, nor is the anthropological conception of personhood invoked to underpin any such view.

The correct answer is B.

89. The passage suggests that the historians referred to in line 1 make which of the following assumptions about Renaissance Europe?

    (A) That anthropologists overestimate the importance of the individual in Renaissance European society
    (B) That in Renaissance Europe, women were typically allowed to express their individuality
    (C) That European women of the Renaissance had the possibility of acting independently of the social context in which they lived
    (D) That studying an individual such as Alessandra is the best way to draw general conclusions about the lives of women in Renaissance Europe
    (E) That people in Renaissance Europe had greater personal autonomy than people do currently

Evaluation

The passage suggests that the historians, in their studies of women in Renaissance Europe, held a preconceived notion of personhood—a notion that implied at least the possibility of individual autonomous action unaffected by social context. By implication, the passage ascribes a similar preconception to the historian whose study of Strozzi is discussed.

A No view concerning anthropologists or their work is attributed, even by implication, to the historians.

B Even if the historians held a view regarding the scope of what women in Renaissance Europe were typically allowed to do, the passage does not attribute such a view to them.

C **Correct.** The passage implies that the historians assumed it was at least sometimes possible for women in Renaissance Europe to act autonomously, unaffected by social context.

D The passage does not indicate that the historians assumed study of a single individual was the best approach to study of women's lives in Renaissance Europe.

E The passage neither explicitly nor implicitly claims that the historians assumed women had more personal autonomy in Renaissance Europe than women have currently.

The correct answer is C.

90. It can be inferred that the author of the passage believes which of the following about the study of Alessandra Strozzi done by the historian mentioned in the second paragraph?

    (A) Alessandra was atypical of her time and was therefore an inappropriate choice for the subject of the historian's research.
    (B) In order to bolster her thesis, the historian adopted the anthropological perspective on personhood.
    (C) The historian argues that the boundaries of the conceptual self were not always firm and closed in Renaissance Europe.
    (D) In her study, the historian reverts to a traditional approach that is out of step with the work of other historians of Renaissance Europe.
    (E) The interpretation of Alessandra's actions that the historian puts forward is not supported by much of the historian's research.

Inference

The passage tells us that the historian who studied Strozzi "attributes individual intention and authorship of actions" to her. But the passage author claims that much of the historian's own research supports the view that, contrary to the historian's interpretation, "Alessandra did not distinguish her personhood from that of her sons"—and therefore that her actions did not primarily express personal autonomy.

- A Nothing in the passage implies that this is true or that the passage author believes it was so.
- B The passage is in direct contradiction with this claim about the historian, and it strongly suggests that the author of the passage would reject this claim.
- C The passage author makes this point concerning "the boundaries of the conceptual self" as part of the critique of the historian's approach.
- D The passage author characterizes the historian's approach neither as traditional nor as nontraditional; nor does the passage author contrast the historian's approach with that of any other historian.
- E **Correct.** The passage author suggest that much of the historian's research provides support for an interpretation that is incompatible with the historian's own interpretation.

The correct answer is E.

91. The passage suggests that the historian mentioned in the second paragraph would be most likely to agree with which of the following assertions regarding Alessandra Strozzi?

    (A) Alessandra was able to act more independently than most women of her time because she was a widow.
    (B) Alessandra was aware that her personal motivation was embedded in a social context.
    (C) Alessandra had goals and interests similar to those of many other widows in her society.
    (D) Alessandra is an example of a Renaissance woman who expressed her individuality through independent action.
    (E) Alessandra was exceptional because she was able to effect changes in the social constraints placed upon women in her society.

Application

According to the passage, the historian whose study of Strozzi is discussed "attributes individual intention and authorship of actions" to her. The passage does not discuss whether, or how, the historian may have regarded Strozzi's widowhood as relevant to her exercise of autonomy; nor does the passage discuss the extent to which, if at all, the historian regarded Strozzi's actions, goals, or interests as typical of women in Renaissance Europe.

- A The passage provides no evidence as to whether the historian would agree with this.
- B The passage does not attribute to the historian, even implicitly, a view that Strozzi's personal motivation was primarily "embedded in a social context"; so the historian would likely believe that Strozzi herself did not see her personal motivation as so embedded.
- C The passage provides no evidence as to whether the historian would regard Strozzi's goals and interests as resembling those of other widows in her society.
- D **Correct.** The first sentence of the second paragraph indicates that the historian treats Strozzi as an example of a Renaissance woman who expressed her individuality through independent action.
- E The passage provides no evidence that the historian viewed Strozzi as exceptional in effecting any kind of social change.

The correct answer is D.

Questions 92–94 refer to the passage on page 86.

92. The primary purpose of the passage is to

    (A) outline the methods by which resources were managed within a particular group of communities
    (B) account for the distribution of wealth within a particular group of communities
    (C) provide support for a hypothesis concerning the social structure of a particular society
    (D) explain how political leadership changed in a particular historical situation
    (E) present new evidence that contradicts previous theories about a particular historical situation

163

Main Idea

This question requires understanding the passage as a whole. The passage proposes that Western Pueblo settlements may have had a hierarchical organizational structure. The passage presents evidence suggesting the existence of a decision-making elite and a differential distribution of wealth, both of which lend support for the existence of this hierarchical structure.

A The passage argues that labor and food resources may have been managed by a political elite in Western Pueblo settlements, but it does not outline the methods by which these resources were managed.

B The passage discusses evidence that suggests that there may have been a differential distribution of wealth within the Western Pueblo settlements, but it does not provide any account or explanation of why or how this distribution arose.

C **Correct.** The passage claims that the Western Pueblo settlements may have had a distinctly hierarchical structure, and it provides evidence to support that claim.

D The passage does not discuss any change among the political leadership in the Western Pueblo settlements or anywhere else.

E The passage presents evidence for a particular hypothesis, but it does not consider any previous theories.

The correct answer is C.

93. According to the passage, which of the following is probably true of the storage spaces mentioned in lines 10–11?

    (A) They were used by the community elite for storage of their own food supplies.
    (B) They served a ceremonial as well as a practical function.
    (C) Their size is an indication of the wealth of the particular community to which they belonged.
    (D) Their existence proves that the community to which they belonged imported large amounts of food.
    (E) They belonged to and were used by the community as a whole.

Supporting Idea

Answering this question requires recognizing something that the passage says about the storage spaces mentioned in lines 10–11. In the final sentence of the first paragraph, the passage describes these storage spaces as "apparently communal spaces," that is, spaces that belonged to and were used by the community as a whole.

A The passage does suggest that an elite may have managed food resources and may also have stored such resources in the large spaces mentioned; however, the passage does not indicate that the elite stored their own supplies there but rather says that the spaces were "communal" and suggests that food stored in them likely belonged to the community as a whole.

B The passage indicates that these storage spaces were located around communal ceremonial chambers known as great kivas; it does not indicate that the storage spaces themselves had any ceremonial function.

C The passage indicates that the large size of these storage spaces suggests the need for formal management of food resources, but it does not claim that the size of these spaces gives any indication of the community's overall wealth.

D The passage states that the spaces could have been used to preserve imported foods, but it gives no indication of how much food was imported. The passage merely suggests that imports are one possible source of the "necessary extra food" stored in the spaces.

E **Correct.** The passage does refer to these storage spaces as "apparently communal spaces."

The correct answer is E.

94. Which of the following, if true, would most clearly undermine the author's statement in the last sentence of the passage regarding the distribution of wealth in Western Pueblo settlements?

(A) Only community members of exceptional wealth are likely to have been buried with their personal possessions.
(B) Members of communities with extensive agricultural systems are usually buried without personal possessions.
(C) Most artifacts found in burial sites were manufactured locally rather than imported from other communities.
(D) Burial artifacts are often ritual objects associated with religious practices rather than being the deceased's personal possessions.
(E) The quality of burial artifacts varies depending on the site with which they are associated.

Evaluation

Answering this question requires identifying what information would undermine the author's claim made in the last sentence of the passage. That sentence asserts that the fact that some burials, but not others at the same site, include large quantities of pottery, jewelry, and other artifacts is evidence for differential distribution of wealth. This claim would be undermined if these artifacts included in the burials were not the personal possessions of the people buried but were something else, e.g., ritual objects associated with religious practices, in which case the presence of the artifacts may simply indicate that the buried person was a religious leader and not necessarily a person of wealth.

A   If only community members of exceptional wealth are likely to have been buried with their personal possessions, and if the artifacts found in certain burials were indeed the personal property of the people interred, then this statement would support, not undermine, the author's statement in the last sentence of the passage.

B   The passage claims that the Western Pueblo settlements had intensive rather than extensive agricultural systems, so this claim about extensive systems is not relevant to the author's statement about the Western Pueblo settlements.
C   The statement makes no claims regarding the artifacts' places of origin.
D   **Correct.** If these burial artifacts were not personal possessions but rather were ritual objects associated with religious practices, then the fact that some burials included the artifacts and others did not may indicate that those who were buried with such artifacts played some part in rituals rather than that they possessed greater wealth.
E   The statement in the passage's final sentence deals with comparing different burials at the same site, not comparing the quality of artifacts found at different sites.

The correct answer is D.

Questions 95–97 refer to the passage on page 87.

95. According to the passage, which of the following was true of relations between the federal government and Native American tribes?

(A) Some Native American tribes approved of the congressional action of 1871 because it simplified their dealings with the federal government.
(B) Some Native American tribes were more eager to negotiate treaties with the United States after the *Lone Wolf* decision.
(C) Prior to the *Lone Wolf* decision, the Supreme Court was reluctant to hear cases involving agreements negotiated between Congress and Native American tribes.
(D) Prior to 1871, the federal government sometimes negotiated treaties with Native American tribes.
(E) Following 1871, the House exercised more power than did the Senate in the government's dealings with Native American tribes.

Supporting Idea

The question depends on recognizing information implicit in the passage. The passage states that a change occurred when Congress abolished the making of treaties with Native American tribes in 1871. Since that decision represented a change, it would follow that such treaties were negotiated at least sometimes prior to that date.

A   The passage does not suggest that some tribes approved of the decision to abolish making treaties.

B   The passage does not suggest that some tribes were more eager to negotiate treaties after *Lone Wolf*, but it does say such treaties were banned well before then.

C   The passage suggests nothing about the Supreme Court's willingness to hear cases related to Native American tribes before the *Lone Wolf* case.

D   **Correct.** The passage states that the 1871 federal ban on negotiating treaties with Native American tribes represented a change, which suggests that such treaties had been negotiated, at least sometimes, prior to 1871.

E   The passage states that the House and Senate disputed control over Native American affairs and that this dispute led to the 1871 ban on treaties, but it does not suggest that the House exercised more power than did the Senate after that date.

The correct answer is D.

96. According to the passage, in the case of *Lone Wolf v. Hitchcock*, the Supreme Court decided that

   (A) disputes among Native American tribes over the ownership of tribal lands were beyond the jurisdiction of the Court

   (B) Congress had the power to allow outsiders to settle on lands occupied by a Native American tribe without obtaining permission from that tribe

   (C) Congress had exceeded its authority in attempting to exercise sole power over Native American affairs

   (D) the United States was not legally bound by the provisions of treaties previously concluded with Native American tribes

   (E) formal agreements between the federal government and Native American tribes should be treated as ordinary legislation rather than as treaties

Supporting Idea

The question requires recognizing specific information presented in the passage. The passage states that in *Lone Wolf*, the Supreme Court rejected an effort by Native American tribes to refuse settlement of their territory by outsiders without their consent. According to the passage, this decision represented an assertion of Congress's power over Native American affairs, in deciding that Congress could allow settlement of Native American lands without the permission of the tribes.

A   The passage does not concern disputes among Native American tribes but rather an effort by those tribes to retain control over their territory and the Supreme Court's rejection of that control.

B   **Correct.** The passage states that the Supreme Court rejected an effort by the tribes to exclude settlers who did not have the tribes' permission and that this represented an assertion of Congress's power over Native American affairs. In other words, the Court decided that Congress could allow such settlement without the tribes' consent.

C   The passage states that the Supreme Court expanded Congress's authority over Native American affairs, not that it decided Congress had exceeded such authority.

D   The passage describes a decision by Congress to abolish making new treaties, but it does not say that the Supreme Court decided that earlier treaties were not binding.

E   According to the passage, *Lone Wolf* concerned questions of tribal sovereignty, not issues of whether agreements between the government and the tribes should be treated as legislation or as treaties.

The correct answer is B.

97. The author of the passage is primarily concerned with

   (A) identifying similarities in two different theories
   (B) evaluating a work of scholarship
   (C) analyzing the significance of a historical event
   (D) debunking a revisionist interpretation
   (E) exploring the relationship between law and social reality

Evaluation

The question requires recognizing the main purpose of the passage. The passage describes a historical event—the Supreme Court's decision in *Lone Wolf*—and goes on to discuss the ramifications of that decision: ending formal negotiation with Native American tribes and rejecting the need for tribal consent, instead asserting Congress's control over the tribes' affairs.

A The passage mentions two different views of the relevant history: the contention that the federal government's usurpation of tribal control occurred in 1871 and the author's belief that it occurred in 1903 with *Lone Wolf*. These ideas are presented in opposition, however, and the passage does not point out similarities between them.
B The passage is mainly concerned with evaluating a historical event, not a work of scholarship.
C **Correct.** The passage is primarily concerned with analyzing the impact of the *Lone Wolf* decision on the federal government's relationship with Native American tribes.
D The passage disputes the contention that 1871 marked the end of formal negotiation between Native American tribes and the federal government, but that contention is nowhere characterized as a revisionist interpretation.
E While the legal decisions discussed in the passage likely affected social reality, those impacts are not explored in the passage.

The correct answer is C.

Questions 98–100 refer to the passage on page 88.

98. According to the passage, the historians mentioned in line 1 and the scholars mentioned in line 8 disagree about the

   (A) contribution made by organized labor to the war effort during the Second World War
   (B) issues that union members considered most important during the Second World War
   (C) relationship between unions and African Americans during the Second World War
   (D) effect of the Second World War on the influence of unions in the workplace
   (E) extent to which African Americans benefited from social and political changes following the Second World War

Supporting Idea

The item requires identifying the central disagreement between two competing views described in the passage. One view holds that African Americans and labor unions were allied during World War II, while the other believes that unions at the period were not supportive of African Americans but rather favored White workers. The common concern of both these views is the nature of the relationship between unions and African Americans during World War II, so that is the focus of their disagreement.

A The passage never mentions the contribution of organized labor to the war effort.
B The passage mentions the issues affecting union members, but those issues and their relative importance are not the subject of the disagreement between the historians and scholars in line 1 and line 8 of the text.
C **Correct.** The passage describes conflicting views held by the scholars and historians mentioned in line 1 and line 8 of the text; the subject of that disagreement is the relationship between African Americans and unions during the Second World War.

D   The passage does not discuss the effect of the Second World War on the influence of unions.

E   While the passage implies that the relationship between unions and African Americans likely affected the social well-being of African Americans, the extent of any benefits to African Americans is not the subject of the disagreement the passage ascribes to the highlighted historians and scholars.

The correct answer is C.

99. Which of the following best summarizes a point of view attributed to the historians mentioned in line 1?

    (A) Trade unions were weakened during the Second World War by their failure to establish a productive relationship with the African American community.
    (B) Trade unions and the African American community forged a lasting relationship after the Second World War based on their wartime alliance.
    (C) The cause of civil rights was not significantly affected by the wartime alliance between trade unions and the African American community.
    (D) The civil rights movement that followed the Second World War forced trade unions to confront contradictions in their practices.
    (E) The civil rights movement would have benefited from a postwar continuation of the wartime alliance between trade unions and the African American community.

Inference

The question requires recognizing what the passage implies about ideas held by those historians mentioned in the highlighted text. The passage states that such historians believe a wartime alliance between African Americans and trade unions helped advance the civil rights of African Americans and that the end of that alliance after the war's conclusion was unfortunate for the later civil rights movement. While the passage does not directly state that such historians believe African Americans would have benefited from a postwar continuation of a wartime alliance with labor, it seems implied that they did believe so.

A   The passage states that the highlighted historians believe African Americans and unions had a dynamic alliance, not that the lack of such an alliance weakened unions.

B   The passage states that these historians believe there was a positive relationship between unions and African Americans but also that such historians believe the relationship did not last.

C   The passage states that the highlighted historians believe the alliance between unions and African Americans advanced the cause of civil rights, not that the alliance had no significant effects.

D   The passage describes the contradictions confronting unions after the war, but it does not attribute a view on the subject to the historians mentioned in line 1 of the text.

E   **Correct.** The passage states in line 1 of the text that the historians believe that the end of the wartime alliance between African Americans and trade unions represented a lost opportunity to advance the cause of civil rights; it would follow that such historians believe a continued alliance would have benefited the cause of civil rights.

The correct answer is E.

100. The passage is primarily concerned with

    (A) providing a context within which to evaluate opposing viewpoints about a historical phenomenon
    (B) identifying a flawed assumption underlying one interpretation of a historical phenomenon
    (C) assessing the merits and weaknesses of a controversial theory about a historical phenomenon
    (D) discussing the historical importance of the development of a wartime alliance
    (E) evaluating evidence used to support a particular interpretation of a historical phenomenon

Evaluation

The item requires evaluating the passage's primary purpose. The passage describes two opposing views on the relationship between African Americans and trade unions during World War II: one view that considers the relationship an alliance and another view that believes organized labor always favored White workers. The passage then provides additional context to suggest that neither view completely reflects the reality of that relationship but that the inclusive ideals of the labor movement were in conflict with entrenched habits of favoring established interests, i.e. White workers.

A **Correct.** The passage describes two conflicting views on the relationship between unions and African Americans during WWII, then provides additional context to advance a more nuanced view.

B The passage suggests that both views are incomplete, not that either view relies on a flawed assumption.

C The passage does not characterize either of the views it criticizes as controversial, nor is it concerned with assessing their merits and weaknesses; rather, it suggests that the truth is more complex than either view can encompass.

D The passage describes a view characterizing the wartime relationship between unions and African Americans as a historically important alliance; however, the passage does not endorse that view, and discussing it is not the primary purpose.

E The passage includes some evidence to support its interpretation of the relationship between unions and African Americans, but it is not primarily concerned with evaluating that evidence.

The correct answer is A.

Questions 101–103 refer to the passage on page 90.

101. According to the passage, which of the following is true of the traditional routes to global expansion?

(A) They have been supplanted in most service industries by alternative routes.

(B) They are less attractive to travel agencies since deregulation of the airlines.

(C) They may represent the most cost-effective means for a travel agency to globalize.

(D) They may be unsuitable for service agencies that are attempting to globalize.

(E) They are most likely to succeed in markets that are not actively growing.

Supporting Idea

The question requires recognizing a specific view advanced by the passage. The passage states that service industries face challenges when attempting to globalize that are not addressed by the traditional expansion strategies of acquisition and internal expansion. Also, some service industries perceive a need to rely on local presence and expertise. Therefore, such traditional routes may be unsuitable, and other routes such as partnerships may be preferable.

A The passage suggests that some service industries are seeking alternative routes, not that traditional routes have been supplanted in most service industries.

B The passage suggests that the deregulation of airlines had a major impact on the travel industry, not that the deregulation made traditional routes to global expansion less attractive.

C The passage nowhere suggests that traditional routes are more cost-effective; on the contrary, it notes that high costs are a disadvantage of one traditional route, acquisition.

D **Correct.** The passage suggests that traditional routes to global expansion may be unsuitable for some service agencies, because providing good service requires local expertise.

169

E   The passage states that the traditional route of internal expansion may be impossible in markets that are not actively growing, not that traditional routes fare better in markets that are not growing.

The correct answer is D.

102. The passage suggests that one of the effects of the deregulation of the airlines was

    (A) a decline in the services available to noncommercial travelers
    (B) a decrease in the size of the corporate travel market
    (C) a sharp increase in the number of cooperative alliances among travel agencies
    (D) increased competition in a number of different service industries
    (E) the merging of some companies within the travel industry

Supporting Idea

The item requires recognizing specific information included in the passage. The passage states that the deregulation of airlines in 1978 led to changes including increased corporate demand for travel services and widespread restructuring and *consolidation* in the travel industry. In other words, some companies in the travel industry merged in the aftermath of airline deregulation.

A   The passage makes no mention of any effects on noncommercial travelers.
B   The passage states, on the contrary, that the corporate travel market grew dramatically.
C   The passage states that one result was increased restructuring and consolidation among travel agencies, not that they formed cooperating alliances.
D   The passage does not mention increased competition in a variety of service industries as a result of airline deregulation.
E   **Correct.** The passage states that there was extensive consolidation in the travel industry as a result of the deregulation of airlines; in other words, some travel companies merged.

The correct answer is E.

103. The author discusses a particular travel agency in the passage most likely in order to

    (A) provide evidence of the pressures on the travel industry to globalize
    (B) demonstrate the limitations of the traditional routes to global expansion
    (C) illustrate an unusual approach to globalizing a service organization
    (D) highlight the difficulties confronting travel agencies that attempt to globalize
    (E) underscore the differences between the service industry and other industries

Evaluation

The item requires assessing the author's purpose in discussing a specific travel agency. The only agency discussed on an individual basis rejected traditional routes to global expansion in favor of forming cooperative partnerships with foreign travel companies. This example illustrates an alternative strategy to global expansion for service companies that find the traditional routes impracticable.

A   The passage discusses pressures on the travel industry to globalize, but it does not mention such pressures in relation to the travel agency discussed as an example.
B   The travel agency used as an example may have adopted their alternative strategy in response to the limitations of traditional routes to globalization, but the agency does not demonstrate such limitations.
C   **Correct.** After a discussion of the drawbacks to traditional globalization strategies for service industries, the author uses the travel agency to illustrate an alternative approach that might be more appropriate.
D   The passage discusses the difficulties facing travel agencies that attempt to globalize, but not in relation to the travel agency brought up as an example.
E   The passage suggests that there are differences between service and other industries, but it does not do so in relation to the travel agency used as an example.

The correct answer is C.

Questions 104–106 refer to the passage on page 91.

104. The passage suggests that the economists mentioned in line 1 would have expected which of the following to occur during the 1960s in the United States?

 (A) Savings and investment rates to be equal in spite of high real interest rates
 (B) Real interest rates to remain low when the national savings surplus was large
 (C) Investment rates to remain constant while the national savings rate changed
 (D) The national economy to suffer a decline as a result of high national savings rates
 (E) Businesses to be encouraged to save due to high real interest rates

Application

The thinking of many economists about business savings, business investment, and real interest rates is explained in the passage. However, the passage tells us, an event occurred in the 1960s that these economists would have not expected. We are asked what the economists would have expected based on their thinking about interest-rate dynamics.

 A   The passage does not explain what the economists would have expected regarding the rates (as opposed to the amounts) of national savings and business investment. The passage does not indicate that if real interest rates were high, the economists' theory would have predicted the rates of national savings and industrial investment to be equal.
 B   **Correct.** If total national savings exceeded total business investment, there would be a savings surplus. This occurred during the 1960s. Consistent with their theory, the economists would have expected real interest rates to be low. On the contrary, real interest rates were high.

 C   According to the economists' theory as explained in the passage, if total national savings changed while total business investment remained unchanged, real interest rates would have changed. But the passage does not address what the economists would have predicted regarding changes in the rates (as opposed to the totals) of national saving and business investment.
 D   The passage provides no information about any implications of the economists' theory regarding the impact on the national economy of high national savings rates.
 E   The passage provides no information about what the economists' theory would have predicted regarding the likely response of businesses to high real interest rates.

The correct answer is B.

105. The author of the passage would be most likely to agree with which of the following statements regarding the economists mentioned in line 1?

 (A) Their beliefs are contradicted by certain economic phenomena that occurred in the United States during the 1960s and the 1980s.
 (B) Their theory fails to predict under what circumstances the prices of foreign and domestic goods are likely to increase.
 (C) They incorrectly identify the factors other than savings and investment rates that affect real interest rates.
 (D) Their belief is valid only for the United States economy and not necessarily for other national economies.
 (E) They overestimate the impact of the real interest rate on the national savings and investment rates.

Evaluation

The passage indicates that economic phenomena that occurred in the United States during the 1960s and the 1980s were contrary to the predictions of many economists' theory regarding savings, investment, and real interest rates.

A **Correct.** In the 1960s, real interest rates were higher even with a large national savings surplus; in the period 1980-82, real interest rates went from 2 percent to 7 percent even with national savings and business investment roughly equal. The author of the passage believes that both occurrences were contrary to what the economists' theory predicted.

B Although the passage describes the actual consequences of a drastic rise in real interest rates after 1979, the author also indicates that the economists' theory would have failed to predict correctly how a drastic rise in real interest rates would affect the prices of goods produced in the United States or elsewhere. The passage is silent on whether the economists' theory addressed factors claimed to be predictive of changes in the prices of goods.

C The passage does not indicate that the economists identified any factors other than savings and investment rates that would affect real interest rates. Therefore, it does not indicate that they misidentified any such factors.

D The passage indicates no such restriction on the scope of application of the economists' theory, which is represented in the passage as highly general.

E The author states that *real interest rates may themselves influence swings in the savings and investment rates*. The context of the statement suggests that the author believes that economists may have underestimated how real interest rates impact savings and investment.

The correct answer is A.

106. The passage is primarily concerned with

    (A) contrasting trends in two historical periods
    (B) presenting evidence that calls into question certain beliefs
    (C) explaining the reasons for a common phenomenon
    (D) criticizing evidence offered in support of a well-respected belief
    (E) comparing conflicting interpretations of a theory

Main Idea

The passage discusses a theory held by *many economists* regarding the relationships among business investment, national savings, and real interest rates. The passage presents evidence from economic events in the United States to show that the theory is flawed.

A The passage does not contrast trends in two historical periods. It discusses two historical periods, though not with the goal of contrasting them.

B **Correct.** The passage presents evidence from economic events in the 1960s and the 1980s and concludes that this evidence indicates that *real interest rates respond to influences other than the savings/investment nexus*. The evidence of these events is contrary to predictions of the economists' theory. The main conclusion of the argumentation in the passage is that the theory is flawed.

C The passage cites economic events in the 1960s and 1980s that were not characterized as "common phenomena," and the passage does not explore specific factors that contributed to these phenomena.

D The passage is not primarily focused on debunking the evidence that the economists based their theory on—a theory which may have been "well-respected" at some time but is not characterized as such in the passage.

E The passage does not compare any conflicting interpretations of a theory.

The correct answer is B.

Questions 107–109 refer to the passage on page 92.

107. The primary purpose of the passage is to

 (A) offer sociohistorical explanations for the cultural differences between men and women in the United States
 (B) examine how the economic roles of women in the United States changed during the nineteenth century
 (C) consider differing views held by social scientists concerning women's class status in the United States
 (D) propose a feminist interpretation of class structure in the United States
 (E) outline specific distinctions between working-class women and women of the upper and middle classes

Main Idea

Various social science models of class in the United States, based on economic status, gender, or occupation, are presented in the passage as differing in their implications regarding women's class status. We are asked what the primary purpose of the passage is.

 A The passage is not focused on cultural differences between women and men.
 B The passage cites a view that *the gap between women of different economic classes widened in the late nineteenth century*. However, the passage does not primarily address changes in women's economic roles during the nineteenth century.
 C **Correct.** The passage surveys a variety of social science analyses of women's class status in the United States.
 D Although the passage examines accounts from *some feminist social scientists* concerning women's class status, the primary purpose of the passage is not to propose a feminist interpretation of United States class structure.
 E The passage examines views of various feminist analysts regarding class distinctions among women. However, this is not the main purpose of the passage.

The correct answer is C.

108. It can be inferred from the passage that the most recent feminist social science research on women and class seeks to do which of the following?

 (A) Introduce a divergent new theory about the relationship between legal status and gender
 (B) Illustrate an implicit middle-class bias in earlier feminist models of class and gender
 (C) Provide evidence for the position that gender matters more than wealth in determining class status
 (D) Remedy perceived inadequacies of both traditional social science models and earlier feminist analyses of class and gender
 (E) Challenge the economic definitions of class used by traditional social scientists

Inference

What does the passage imply about the primary goal of most recent feminist social research on women and class? One would expect such more recent research to seek to adjust earlier accounts, both in traditional social science models and feminist models.

 A Historian Mary Ryan points out that identical legal status of working-class and middle-class free married women outweighed any other distinctions. But the passage does not present this as the primary theme of the most recent feminist social science research.
 B The passage does not attribute to the most recent feminist social research, explicitly or by implication, any attempt to illustrate a middle-class bias in earlier feminist models.
 C The passage cites a recent feminist analyst as noting that *the gap between women of different economic classes widened in the late nineteenth century*. This goes against the notion that recent feminist analysts sought to argue that gender outweighed economic position in determining women's class status.

D **Correct.** The passage represents the most recent feminist social science analysts as seeking to amend the views of traditional social science models and earlier feminist models regarding women's class status. We read: *Recently, though, other feminist analysts have questioned this model*—namely, the feminist model that regarded women's class as predominantly determined by gender alone. Ann Oakley contests this, arguing that, in the late nineteenth century, differences of economic standing among women contributed to determining women's relative class statuses.

E This does not reflect what the passage implies about the primary goal of recent feminist social science analysts. One of the most recent feminist analysts, Ann Oakley, suggests that from the late nineteenth century, distinct economic statuses were reflected in distinct social class statuses for women.

The correct answer is D.

109. Which of the following statements best characterizes the relationship between traditional social science models of class and Ryan's model, as described in the passage?

(A) Ryan's model differs from the traditional model by making gender, rather than economic status, the determinant of women's class status.

(B) The traditional social science model of class differs from Ryan's in its assumption that women are financially dependent on men.

(C) Ryan's model of class and the traditional social science model both assume that women work, either within the home or for pay.

(D) The traditional social science model of class differs from Ryan's in that each model focuses on a different period of American history.

(E) Both Ryan's model of class and the traditional model consider multiple factors, including wealth, marital status, and enfranchisement, in determining women's status.

Application

How does Ryan's model differ from the traditional social science models? According to the passage, the traditional models were based on women's economic status as derived from their association with men. Ryan advocated a model that regarded women's class as based on gender alone.

A **Correct.** The passage indicates that Ryan's model involved cleaving women's class status from their association with men and regarding women as one distinct class.

B The passage does not describe Ryan's model as assuming that women are never "financially dependent on men." According to the passage, Ryan's view is that women's class status is determined by gender and not based on financial dependence on men.

C The passage does not ascribe to the traditional social science models of class the assumption that all women work either in the home or outside of it for pay. For example, the model as described in the passage would have been consistent with some women who were not themselves employed having all the work in their home done by other people.

D The passage does not support this view. Ryan's opinions in the passage are represented as applying to the early nineteenth century and later, whereas the *traditional social science model of class* is not clearly located in time.

E The passage indicates that neither the traditional model nor Ryan's model consider multiple factors in determining women's class status. Ryan is cited as illustrating the view that gender, not economic standing, was the crucial determinant of women's class status in American society. According to the passage, the traditional social science models held that the class status of women was derived exclusively from their economic situation, which was determined, in turn, by their association with men (fathers or husbands).

The correct answer is A.

Questions 110 to 143 — Difficulty: Hard

Questions 110–116 refer to the passage on page 94.

110. According to the passage, conventional spiral galaxies differ from low-surface-brightness galaxies in which of the following ways?

    (A) They have fewer stars than do low-surface-brightness galaxies.
    (B) They evolve more quickly than low-surface-brightness galaxies.
    (C) They are more diffuse than low-surface-brightness galaxies.
    (D) They contain less helium than do low-surface-brightness galaxies.
    (E) They are larger than low-surface-brightness galaxies.

Supporting Idea

This question requires recognizing information that is provided in the passage. The first paragraph describes and compares two types of galaxies: conventional galaxies and dim, or low-surface-brightness, galaxies. It states that dim galaxies have the same approximate number of stars as a common type of conventional galaxy but tend to be larger and more diffuse because their mass is spread over wider areas (lines 4-10). The passage also indicates that dim galaxies take longer than conventional galaxies to convert their primordial gases into stars, meaning that dim galaxies evolve much more slowly than conventional galaxies (lines 10-14), which entails that conventional galaxies evolve more quickly than dim galaxies.

    A   The passage states that dim galaxies have approximately the same numbers of stars as a common type of conventional galaxy.
    B   **Correct.** The passage indicates that dim galaxies evolve much more slowly than conventional galaxies, which entails that conventional galaxies evolve more quickly.
    C   The passage states that dim galaxies are more spread out, and therefore more diffuse, than conventional galaxies.
    D   The passage does not mention the relative amounts of helium in the two types of galaxies under discussion.
    E   The passage states that dim galaxies tend to be much larger than conventional galaxies.

The correct answer is B.

111. It can be inferred from the passage that which of the following is an accurate physical description of typical low-surface-brightness galaxies?

    (A) They are large spiral galaxies containing fewer stars than conventional galaxies.
    (B) They are compact but very dim spiral galaxies.
    (C) They are diffuse spiral galaxies that occupy a large volume of space.
    (D) They are small, young spiral galaxies that contain a high proportion of primordial gas.
    (E) They are large, dense spirals with low luminosity.

Inference

This question requires drawing an inference from information given in the passage. The first paragraph compares dim galaxies and conventional galaxies. Dim galaxies are described as having the same general shape (lines 4–5) as a common type of conventional galaxy, the spiral galaxy, suggesting that dim galaxies are, themselves, spiral shaped. The passage also indicates that, although both types of galaxies tend to have approximately the same number of stars, dim galaxies tend to be much larger and spread out over larger areas of space (lines 4–10) than conventional galaxies.

    A   The passage states that the two types of galaxies have approximately the same number of stars.
    B   The passage indicates that dim galaxies are relatively large and spread out.
    C   **Correct.** The passage indicates that dim galaxies have the same general shape as spiral galaxies and that their mass is spread out over large areas of space.
    D   The passage indicates that dim galaxies are relatively large and spread out.

E The passage states that dim galaxies have few stars per unit of volume, suggesting that they are not dense but diffuse.

The correct answer is C.

112. It can be inferred from the passage that the "longstanding puzzle" refers to which of the following?

    (A) The difference between the rate at which conventional galaxies evolve and the rate at which low-surface-brightness galaxies evolve
    (B) The discrepancy between estimates of total baryonic mass derived from measuring helium and estimates based on measuring galactic luminosity
    (C) The inconsistency between the observed amount of helium in the universe and the number of stars in typical low-surface-brightness galaxies
    (D) Uncertainties regarding what proportion of baryonic mass is contained in intergalactic space and what proportion in conventional galaxies
    (E) Difficulties involved in detecting very distant galaxies and in investigating their luminosity

Inference

This question requires drawing an inference from information given in the passage. The second paragraph describes *the long-standing puzzle of the missing baryonic mass in the universe*. The passage states that baryons are the source of galactic luminosity, and so scientists can estimate the amount of baryonic mass in the universe by measuring the luminosity of galaxies (lines 17–21). The puzzle is that spectroscopic measures of helium in the universe suggest that the baryonic mass in the universe is much higher than measures of luminosity would indicate (21–25).

A The differences between the rates of evolution of the two types of galaxies is not treated as being controversial in the passage.
B **Correct.** The passage indicates that measurements using spectroscopy and measurements using luminosity result in puzzling differences in estimates of the universe's baryonic mass.

C The passage does not suggest how helium might relate to the numbers of stars in dim galaxies.
D The passage indicates that astronomers have speculated that the missing baryonic mass might be discovered in intergalactic space or hard-to-detect galaxies but does not suggest that these speculations are constituents of the long-standing puzzle.
E The passage does not mention how the distance to galaxies affects scientists' ability to detect these galaxies.

The correct answer is B.

113. The author implies that low-surface-brightness galaxies could constitute an answer to the puzzle discussed in the second paragraph primarily because

    (A) they contain baryonic mass that was not taken into account by researchers using galactic luminosity to estimate the number of baryons in the universe
    (B) they, like conventional galaxies that contain many baryons, have evolved from massive, primordial gas clouds
    (C) they may contain relatively more helium, and hence more baryons, than do galaxies whose helium content has been studied using spectroscopy
    (D) they have recently been discovered to contain more baryonic mass than scientists had thought when low-surface-brightness galaxies were first observed
    (E) They contain stars that are significantly more luminous than would have been predicted on the basis of initial studies of luminosity in low-surface-brightness galaxies

Inference

This question requires drawing an inference from information given in the passage. The puzzle is that estimates of the baryonic mass of the universe based on luminosity are lower than those based on spectroscopy (lines 21–25). The passage states that astronomers did not notice dim galaxies until recently (lines 2–3) and that these galaxies may help account for the missing baryonic mass in the universe (lines 15–17). The passage also suggests that astronomers measure the luminosity of specific galaxies (lines 19–21). Thus it can be inferred that, prior to their being noticed by astronomers, the luminosity of these dim galaxies was not measured, and their baryonic mass was not taken into account in the estimates of luminosity that led to the long-standing puzzle.

- A **Correct.** The passage states that the missing baryonic mass in the universe may be discovered in the dim galaxies that have only recently been noticed by astronomers.
- B The passage does not suggest that dim and conventional galaxies both originating from primordial gas clouds help solve the longstanding puzzle of the missing baryonic mass in the universe.
- C The passage does not suggest that dim galaxies might contain more helium than do conventional galaxies or that measures of baryonic mass using spectroscopy do not take some dim galaxies into account.
- D The passage does not suggest that dim galaxies contain more baryonic mass than scientists originally believed upon discovering these galaxies.
- E The passage suggests that scientists measured the luminosity of galaxies, not of individual stars.

The correct answer is A.

114. The author mentions the fact that baryons are the source of stars' luminosity primarily in order to explain

    (A) how astronomers determine that some galaxies contain fewer stars per unit volume than do others
    (B) how astronomers are able to calculate the total luminosity of a galaxy
    (C) why astronomers can use galactic luminosity to estimate baryonic mass
    (D) why astronomers' estimates of baryonic mass based on galactic luminosity are more reliable than those based on spectroscopic studies of helium
    (E) how astronomers know bright galaxies contain more baryons than do dim galaxies

Evaluation

This question requires understanding how one aspect of the passage relates to the reasoning in a larger portion of the passage. The second paragraph explains that scientists have been puzzled over missing baryonic mass in the universe as measured by luminosity (lines 21–25). Given that baryons are the source of luminosity in the galaxy (lines 17–19), astronomers can estimate the baryonic mass of a galaxy by measuring its luminosity.

- A The passage discussion of baryons does not address the number of stars in individual galaxies.
- B The passage discusses how the luminosity of galaxies can be used to estimate baryonic mass but does not address how total luminosity is measured.
- C **Correct.** The passage indicates that because baryons are the source of galactic luminosity, measuring luminosity can be used to estimate baryonic mass of galaxies.
- D The passage suggests that estimates based on luminosity may have been less accurate, not more accurate, than those based on spectroscopy.
- E The passage does not indicate that bright galaxies contain more baryons than do dim galaxies.

The correct answer is C.

115. The author of the passage would be most likely to disagree with which of the following statements?

    (A) Low-surface-brightness galaxies are more difficult to detect than are conventional galaxies.
    (B) Low-surface-brightness galaxies are often spiral in shape.
    (C) Astronomers have advanced plausible ideas about where missing baryonic mass might be found.
    (D) Astronomers have devised a useful way of estimating the total baryonic mass in the universe.
    (E) Astronomers have discovered a substantial amount of baryonic mass in intergalactic space.

Inference

This question involves identifying which answer choice potentially conflicts with the information the author has provided in the passage. The second paragraph indicates that astronomers' estimates of the baryonic mass of the universe is lower when measured using luminosity than it is when measured using spectroscopy (lines 21–25). The final sentence states that astronomers have speculated that the missing baryonic mass might be discovered in intergalactic space or in hard-to-detect galaxies (lines 25–29). Although the passage does indicate that the discovery of dim, low-surface-brightness galaxies might help account for the missing baryonic mass (lines 15–17), the passage provides no support for the possibility that baryonic mass has been discovered in intergalactic space.

A   The passage indicates that low-surface-brightness galaxies went unnoticed until recently, unlike conventional galaxies.

B   The passage indicates that low-surface-brightness galaxies have the same general shape as spiral galaxies.

C   The passage describes two possible explanations astronomers have given for the missing baryonic mass, one of which was made more plausible by the discovery of low-surface-brightness galaxies.

D   The passage indicates that astronomers have used spectroscopy to estimate baryonic mass and gives no reason to suspect that this method is not useful.

E   **Correct.** The passage does not indicate that astronomers have found any baryonic mass in intergalactic space.

The correct answer is E.

116. The primary purpose of the passage is to

(A) describe a phenomenon and consider its scientific significance

(B) contrast two phenomena and discuss a puzzling difference between them

(C) identify a newly discovered phenomenon and explain its origins

(D) compare two classes of objects and discuss the physical properties of each

(E) discuss a discovery and point out its inconsistency with existing theory

Main Idea

This question requires understanding, in broad terms, the purpose of the passage as a whole. The first paragraph describes a phenomenon: the discovery of dim galaxies and some of their general attributes. The second paragraph describes how this discovery may help astronomers to solve a long-standing puzzle about the baryonic mass of the universe.

A   **Correct.** The passage describes the phenomenon of dim galaxies and describes their significance in solving the longstanding puzzle of the missing baryonic mass in the universe.

B   Although the passage discusses the puzzling difference between the two estimates of baryonic mass, this answer choice does not account for the broader topic of dim galaxies.

C   While the passage identifies the newly discovered phenomenon of dim galaxies, it does not offer a significant explanation for these galaxies' origins.

D   Although the passage compares dim and conventional galaxies in the first paragraph, this answer choice does not account for the important detail that dim galaxies may help solve a long-standing puzzle.

E   The discovery of dim galaxies discussed in the passage is not said to be inconsistent with any existing scientific theory.

The correct answer is A.

Questions 117–120 refer to the passage on page 96.

117. The primary purpose of the passage is to

(A) trace historical influences on the depiction of Mexican Americans in the nineteenth century
(B) explain how research in history has been affected by scholarship in women's studies
(C) describe the historical origins of a literary stereotype
(D) discuss ways in which minority writers have sought to critique a dominant culture through their writing
(E) evaluate both sides in a scholarly debate about a prominent literary stereotype

Main Idea

Answering this question requires understanding, in general terms, the passage as a whole. The passage discusses Antonia Castañeda's scholarship concerning the historical economic conditions underlying the portrayal by male, non-Hispanic novelists writing in the United States of "Californianas," that is, Mexican women living in territorial California. Certain Hispanic laws in this territory protected these women's property and inheritance rights. These laws, Castañeda claims, explain a stereotypical plot, used by these novelists, depicting a non-Hispanic trader or merchant who wishes to marry an elite Californiana.

A The passage is more narrowly focused than this answer choice indicates; it primarily investigates depictions of Californianas, Mexican women living in territorial California.
B The passage primarily deals with how both women's studies and Mexican-American history can illuminate literary portrayals of Mexican women, and, in particular, Californianas. The passage does not provide a broad examination of how research in history has been affected by women's studies.
C **Correct.** As explained above, the passage is focused on examining the historical origins of the stereotypical plot, employed by nineteenth-century non-Hispanic male novelists in the United States, in which a non-Hispanic male seeks to marry a Californiana.
D The passage is focused on a plot used by nineteenth-century non-Hispanic male writers in the nineteenth century. There is no indication that these were minority writers.

E The passage discusses only Castaneda's scholarship regarding this particular literary stereotype.

The correct answer is C.

118. The "apparent contradiction" mentioned in line 29 refers to the discrepancy between the

(A) legal status of Mexican women in territorial California and their status in the United States
(B) unflattering depiction of Mexicans in novels and the actual public sentiment about the Mexican-American War
(C) existence of many marriages between Californianas and non-Hispanic merchants and the strictures against them expressed in novels
(D) literary depiction of elite Californianas and the literary depiction of other Mexican individuals
(E) novelistic portrayals of elite Californianas' privileged lives and the actual circumstances of those lives

Supporting Idea

The *apparent contradiction* in line 29 refers to the difference, noted in the previous sentence, between favorable literary portrayals of elite Californianas—that is, Mexican women of the California territory—on the one hand and novels' generally unflattering depictions of Mexicans on the other.

A The passage discusses the difference between the legal rights of Mexican women in the California territory and those of non-Hispanic women. The legal rights of Mexican women outside territorial California are not mentioned.
B The passage suggests that there is no contradiction between unflattering depictions of Mexicans in novels and public sentiment about the Mexican-American War: such depictions of Mexicans served to stir up sentiment in support of the war.
C According to the passage, novels expressed no strictures against marriages between Californianas and non-Hispanic merchants. Instead, the novels portrayed such marriages favorably.

D **Correct.** Non-Hispanic novelists glorified elite Californianas based on the importance of forging economic alliances with them, whereas novelists depicted other Mexicans in unflattering terms.

E The passage indicates that elite Californianas' lives were in fact privileged, at least in comparison to those of non-Hispanic women. It does not suggest that there was any contradiction between elite Californianas' lives and how those lives were portrayed in novels.

The correct answer is D.

119. Which of the following could best serve as an example of the kind of fictional plot discussed by Antonia Castañeda?

    (A) A land speculator of English ancestry weds the daughter of a Mexican vineyard owner after the speculator has migrated to California to seek his fortune.

    (B) A Californian woman of Hispanic ancestry finds that her agricultural livelihood is threatened when her husband is forced to seek work in a textile mill.

    (C) A Mexican rancher who loses his land as a result of the Mexican-American War migrates to the northern United States and marries an immigrant schoolteacher.

    (D) A wealthy Californiana whose father has bequeathed her all his property contends with avaricious relatives for her inheritance.

    (E) A poor married couple emigrate from French Canada and gradually become wealthy as merchants in territorial California.

Application

According to the passage, Castaneda focuses on a particular plot in which an elite Californiana is pursued by a non-Hispanic merchant or trader for the purpose of gaining economic advantage.

A **Correct.** The story of a non-Hispanic land speculator wedding a Californiana who is likely, based on the inheritance rights granted her by the Hispanic law in territorial California, to inherit her father's vineyard would precisely fit the plot that Castañeda discusses.

B This description fails to identify the ethnicity of the Californiana's husband and the reason he married her, so there is no way to determine whether the story would fit Castañeda's plot.

C Castañeda's plot involves a non-Hispanic male protagonist, so a Mexican rancher could not play the main male role in such a story.

D The presence of a wealthy Californiana who inherits property might make this story seem to be an example of the fictional plot that Castañeda discusses, but there is no mention of a non-Hispanic merchant or trader who seeks her hand in marriage.

E Simply taking place in territorial California would not make a story an appropriate example of the plot discussed by Castañeda.

The correct answer is A.

120. Which of the following, if true, would provide the most support for Castañeda's explanation of the "stereotypical plot" mentioned in the lines 18–19?

    (A) Non-Hispanic traders found business more profitable in California while it was a territory than when it became a state.

    (B) Very few marriages between Hispanic women and non-Hispanic men in nineteenth-century territorial California have actually been documented.

    (C) Records from the nineteenth century indicate that some large and valuable properties were owned by elite Californianas in their own right.

    (D) Unmarried non-Hispanic women in the nineteenth-century United States were sometimes able to control property in their own right.

    (E) Most of the property in nineteenth-century territorial California was controlled by Hispanic men.

Evaluation

Castañeda explains the *stereotypical plot* of a non-Hispanic merchant seeking to marry an elite Californiana based on economics: these women had property and inheritance rights equal to men. Novelists based their plots on the women's *real-life* economic power, which resulted in men's wishing to build economic alliances with them. Supporting this explanation requires supporting these economic ideas in some way.

A   The profitability of non-Hispanic traders' business is not an issue in Castañeda's explanation; thus the change described has no significant relevance to that explanation.

B   The lack of the type of documentation described, rather than providing support for Castañeda's explanation, signifies a deficit in documentary support for that explanation.

C   **Correct.** If elite Californianas did in fact own valuable properties, Castañeda's economic explanation gains force. The women did have the real economic significance upon which Castañeda suggests the novelists drew.

D   If it were true that some non-Hispanic women controlled property in this way, Castañeda's explanation of Californianas' uniqueness would be somewhat undermined.

E   If most of the property in nineteenth-century territorial California was controlled by Hispanic men, that suggests that Californianas were less likely to possess the kind of economic power described in Castañeda's argument.

The correct answer is C.

Questions 121–123 refer to the passage on page 98.

121. The passage suggests that, in the early 1990s, Michaels would have been most likely to agree with which of the following statements about the disparity mentioned in lines 3–4?

   (A)   This disparity is relatively less extreme in the Northern Hemisphere because of sulfate cooling.

   (B)   This disparity is only a short-term phenomenon brought about by sulfate cooling.

   (C)   This disparity is most significant in those parts of the world dominated by oceans.

   (D)   The extent of this disparity is being masked by the temporary effect of sulfate cooling.

   (E)   The disparity confirms that current models of global warming are correct.

Inference

The disparity highlighted in this question is between global warming models and actual climate data—that is, that the models predicted warming that has not occurred. In the early 1990s, according to the passage, Michaels tried to explain this disparity by saying that industrial sulfate emissions had a cooling effect that slowed global warming briefly.

A   The passage does not indicate that Michaels came to distinguish between the Northern and Southern Hemispheres until he began to doubt his early 1990s explanation for the mentioned disparity.

B   **Correct.** Michaels claimed in the early 1990s that the disparity was temporary, and that it occurred due to the cooling effect of sulfate emissions.

C   Santer's contention, not Michaels's, is based on the effect of oceans on global warming.

D   In the early 1990s, Michaels used the idea of sulfate cooling to explain the observed disparity, not to suggest that the disparity itself was larger than observed.

E   In seeking to explain the disparity, Michaels seems to have assumed, in the early 1990s at least, that the models of global warming were correct. But he did not take the disparity as evidence of their correctness.

The correct answer is B.

122. According to the passage, Santer asserts which of the following about global warming?

   (A)   It will become a more serious problem in the Southern Hemisphere than in the Northern Hemisphere in spite of the cooling influence of oceans in the south.

   (B)   It is unlikely to be a serious problem in the future because of the pervasive effect of sulfate cooling.

   (C)   It will proceed at the same general rate in the Northern and Southern Hemispheres once the temporary influence of sulfate cooling comes to an end.

(D) Until the late 1980s, it was moderated in the Northern Hemisphere by the effect of sulfate cooling.

(E) Largely because of the cooling influence of oceans, it has had no discernible impact on the Southern Hemisphere.

Supporting Idea

The second paragraph of the passage discusses Santer's take on global warming. He is concerned with the effect of oceans and of sulfate cooling on this process, and he argues that the rate of warming in the Southern and Northern Hemispheres has been differently affected by each of these. In general, oceans slow warming in the south, while sulfate cooling temporarily slowed warming in the north until the late 1980s.

A According to the passage, Santer has argued that since 1987 the Northern Hemisphere has warmed more significantly than the Southern Hemisphere.

B Santer maintains that sulfate cooling complicates our attempts to understand global warming. He notes, however, that sulfate cooling peaked in the Northern Hemisphere in the mid-1900s, and that that hemisphere's warming has increased considerably. So sulfate cooling's effect is not pervasive and has not mitigated the medium- and long-term problem of global warming.

C Santer argues that, in the absence of sulfate cooling, global warming would occur more slowly in the Southern Hemisphere due to the greater ocean coverage there.

D **Correct.** Santer says that sulfate cooling slowed warming in the Northern Hemisphere, but that in 1987, the influence of sulfate cooling was no longer significant.

E Santer maintains that global warming happens more slowly in the Southern Hemisphere due to the greater ocean coverage there, not that it has no discernible impact there.

The correct answer is D.

123. The passage suggests that Santer and Michaels would be most likely to DISAGREE over which of the following issues?

(A) Whether climatological data invalidates global warming models

(B) Whether warming in the Northern Hemisphere has intensified since 1987

(C) Whether disparities between global warming models and climatological data can be detected

(D) Whether landmasses warm more rapidly than oceans

(E) Whether oceans have a significant effect on global climate patterns

Inference

According to the end of the first paragraph, Michaels began to doubt that sulfate cooling had an effect on global warming, and, further, based on the fact that he could not find an answer for why climatological data did not line up with global warming models, he questioned the accuracy of those models. The second paragraph explains that Santer, in contrast, offered a more nuanced explanation for the effect of sulfate cooling, and that based on this explanation, he disputed the claim that climatological data were inconsistent with the models' predictions.

A **Correct.** Based on the passage, Santer and Michaels would clearly disagree about whether climatological data invalidate global warming models: Michaels came to question the models on the basis of those data, while Santer found the model predictions were in fact ultimately consistent with the observed data.

B Both Santer and Michaels accept the idea that warming in the north has accelerated since 1987.

C Santer and Michaels both offered reasons for why the seeming disparity between models and data occurred—thus they agreed that such disparities were in fact detected.

D According to the second paragraph, Santer holds that landmasses warm more rapidly than oceans. But the passage offers no indication that Michaels disagrees with this.

E   Santer's argument is based in large part on the effect of oceans on global climate patterns, but nothing in the passage's discussion of Michaels's work indicates that Michaels would disagree that oceans have such an effect.

The correct answer is A.

Questions 124–131 refer to the passage on page 100.

124. According to the passage, Walker and Szalay disagree on which of the following points?

    (A) The structure and composition of australopithecine teeth
    (B) The kinds of conclusions that can be drawn from the micro-wear patterns on australopithecine teeth
    (C) The idea that fruit was a part of the australopithecine diet
    (D) The extent to which seed cracking and bone crunching produce similar micro-wear patterns on teeth
    (E) The function of the heavy enamel on australopithecine teeth

Supporting Idea

This question refers to the first paragraph, which states that Walker does not agree with Szalay's idea that *the heavy enamel of australopithecine teeth is an adaptation to bone crunching.*

A   According to the passage, Walker and Szalay disagree about the function of heavy enamel on the teeth, not the structure and composition of the teeth.
B   The passage does not indicate that Szalay has anything to say about the micro-wear patterns on the teeth.
C   Walker does, according to the passage, believe that australopithecines ate fruit, but it gives no evidence about whether Szalay believes that they ate at least some fruit.
D   According to the passage, Walker believes that seed cracking and bone crunching produce distinctive micro-wear patterns on teeth, but he does not necessarily believe that they are similar. The passage does not indicate Szalay's position on the difference between micro-wear patterns.

E   **Correct.** The function of the heavy enamel on the teeth is the only idea about which the passage clearly indicates that Walker and Szalay disagree.

The correct answer is E.

125. The passage suggests that Walker's research indicated which of the following about australopithecine teeth?

    (A) They had micro-wear characteristics indicating that fruit constituted only a small part of their diet.
    (B) They lacked micro-wear characteristics associated with seed eating and bone crunching.
    (C) They had micro-wear characteristics that differed in certain ways from the micro-wear patterns of chimpanzees and orangutans.
    (D) They had micro-wear characteristics suggesting that the diet of australopithecines varied from one region to another.
    (E) They lacked the micro-wear characteristics distinctive of modern frugivores.

Inference

According to the passage, Walker's research focuses on micro-wear patterns on the teeth of australopithecines. He draws several conclusions on the basis of these patterns: first, that australopithecines did not eat hard seeds; next, that they did not crunch bones; and finally, that they ate fruit.

A   The passage indicates that Walker's observation of micro-wear patterns led him to conclude that australopithecines ate mostly fruit, not that *fruit constituted only a small part of their diet.*
B   **Correct.** The first paragraph explains that Walker concluded from micro-wear patterns that australopithecines did not eat hard seeds and did not crunch bones; thus, his research must have indicated that they lacked micro-wear characteristics associated with such activities.

C According to the passage, the opposite is true: based on the observation that their micro-wear patterns were indistinguishable from those of chimpanzees and orangutans, Walker concluded that australopithecines ate fruit.

D The second paragraph of the passage complicates Walker's view by suggesting that australopithecines' diet might have varied from one region to another, but the passage says nothing about Walker's research from which to infer that it indicated such variation.

E Chimpanzees and orangutans are assumed to be frugivores, according to the passage, and Walker's research indicated that australopithecine teeth had micro-wear characteristics identical to theirs.

The correct answer is B.

126. The passage suggests that which of the following would be true of studies of tooth micro-wear patterns conducted on modern baboons?

    (A) They would inaccurately suggest that some baboons eat more soft-bodied than hard-bodied insects.
    (B) They would suggest that insects constitute the largest part of some baboons' diets.
    (C) They would reveal that there are no significant differences in tooth micro-wear patterns among baboon populations.
    (D) They would inadequately reflect the extent to which some baboons consume certain types of insects.
    (E) They would indicate that baboons in certain regions eat only soft-bodied insects, whereas baboons in other regions eat hard-bodied insects.

Inference

The second paragraph states that modern baboons eat *only soft-bodied insects* and so would not exhibit tooth abrasion to indicate that they were insectivores. Thus, it would be difficult to determine exactly which soft-bodied insects they ate.

A The passage states that baboons eat only soft-bodied insects—so it is in fact accurate to suggest that all baboons eat more soft-bodied than hard-bodied insects.

B The passage says that baboons eat only soft-bodied insects. It also suggests that soft-bodied insects do not leave significant enough abrasions on baboons' teeth to provide evidence of this aspect of their diet. Therefore, the tooth-wear patterns would give little or no information regarding what proportion of the baboons' overall diet consists of insects.

C The passage does not provide grounds for inferring anything about the differences, or lack thereof, among baboon populations in terms of tooth micro-wear patterns.

D Correct. Because soft-bodied insects cause little tooth abrasion, micro-wear patterns would most likely not reflect the extent to which baboons consume soft-bodied insects.

E The passage states that baboons eat *only soft-bodied insects*. Nothing in the passage suggests that baboons in certain regions eat hard-bodied insects.

The correct answer is D.

127. The passage suggests which of the following about the micro-wear patterns found on the teeth of omnivorous primates?

    (A) The patterns provide information about what kinds of foods are not eaten by the particular species of primate, but not about the foods actually eaten.
    (B) The patterns of various primate species living in the same environment resemble one another.
    (C) The patterns may not provide information about the extent to which a particular species' diet includes seeds.
    (D) The patterns provide more information about these primates' diet than do the tooth micro-wear patterns of primates who are frugivores.
    (E) The patterns may differ among groups within a species depending on the environment within which a particular group lives.

Inference

This question focuses mainly on the end of the second paragraph, which states that *the diets of current omnivorous primates vary considerably depending on the environments* in which they live. It goes on to conclude that australopithecines, if they were omnivores, would similarly consume varied diets, depending on environment, and exhibit varied tooth micro-wear patterns as well. Thus, it is reasonable to conclude that any omnivorous primates living in different environments and consuming different diets would exhibit varied micro-wear patterns.

A   The passage indicates that the absence of certain types of micro-wear patterns can provide evidence about what foods a species does not eat. It also says that among omnivorous primates, one might expect to find considerable population variation in their tooth micro-wear patterns. Wherever micro-wear patterns are present, they provide evidence about what kinds of foods are eaten.

B   The passage suggests that various primate species living in the same environment might consume a variety of different diets, so there is no reason to conclude that their micro-wear patterns would resemble one another.

C   The passage indicates that seed-eating produces distinctive micro-wear patterns, so the patterns, or lack thereof, on the teeth of any species would most likely provide information about the extent to which the species' diet includes seeds.

D   The end of the first paragraph suggests that frugivores' micro-wear patterns are distinctive; the passage provides no reason to believe that omnivores' diets provide more information.

E   **Correct.** According to the passage, omnivorous primates of a particular species may consume different diets depending on where they live. Thus, their micro-wear patterns may differ on this basis.

The correct answer is E.

128. It can be inferred from the passage that if studies of tooth micro-wear patterns were conducted on modern baboons, which of the following would most likely be true of the results obtained?

(A)   There would be enough abrasion to allow a determination of whether baboons are frugivorous or insectivorous.

(B)   The results would suggest that insects constitute the largest part of the baboons' diet.

(C)   The results would reveal that there are no significant differences in tooth micro-wear patterns from one regional baboon population to another.

(D)   The results would provide an accurate indication of the absence of some kinds of insects from the baboons' diet.

(E)   The results would be unlikely to provide any indication of what inferences about the australopithecine diet can or cannot be drawn from micro-wear studies.

Inference

The second paragraph states that modern baboons eat soft-bodied insects but not hard-bodied ones—and it is hard-bodied insects, the passage suggests, that would cause particular micro-wear patterns on teeth. So the patterns on modern baboons' teeth most likely do not exhibit the patterns indicating hard-bodied insect consumption.

A   The passage states that baboons' consumption of soft-bodied insects would not show up in the patterns on their teeth—so the abrasion would most likely not provide enough information for a determination of whether baboons are frugivorous or insectivorous.

B   Since soft-bodied insects do not abrade the teeth significantly, it would be difficult to determine, based on micro-wear patterns, the part such insects play in the baboons' diet. Furthermore, the passage does not suggest that micro-wear patterns can indicate the quantity of food an animal might have eaten.

C There could be differences in tooth micro-wear patterns from one regional baboon population to another if they consumed anything in addition to soft-bodied insects.

D **Correct.** Studying tooth micro-wear patterns on baboons' teeth would most likely show that their teeth do not exhibit patterns typical of creatures that consume hard-bodied insects.

E The passage suggests that based on results from micro-wear patterns on modern baboons' teeth, one cannot infer from micro-wear studies whether australopithecines ate soft-bodied insects.

The correct answer is D.

129. It can be inferred from the passage that Walker's conclusion about the australopithecine diet would be called into question under which of the following circumstances?

(A) The tooth enamel of australopithecines is found to be much heavier than that of modern frugivorous primates.

(B) The micro-wear patterns of australopithecine teeth from regions other than east Africa are analyzed.

(C) Orangutans are found to have a much broader diet than is currently recognized.

(D) The environment of east Africa at the time australopithecines lived there is found to have been far more varied than is currently thought.

(E) The area in which the australopithecine specimens were found is discovered to have been very rich in soft-bodied insects during the period when australopithecines lived there.

Inference

The passage explains that Walker bases his conclusion about the frugivorous nature of the australopithecine diet on the fact that the micro-wear patterns on australopithecine teeth are indistinguishable from those of chimpanzees and orangutans, both of which are presumed to have frugivorous diets.

A The passage indicates that Walker took into account the fact that australopithecines had relatively heavy tooth enamel and that he rejected the view that this heaviness was evidence against the hypothesis that they were frugivorous. For all we can tell from the information in the passage, the australopithecines' tooth enamel was already known to be much heavier than that of modern frugivorous primates.

B It could be the case that analyzing the micro-wear patterns of australopithecine teeth from other regions would yield the same data as those from east Africa.

C **Correct.** According to the passage, Walker bases the conclusion that australopithecines were frugivorous on the similarity between their micro-wear patterns and those of modern chimpanzees and orangutans. If orangutans were found to have a diet that included a greater range of non-fruit foods than is currently recognized, then the correspondence between their micro-wear patterns and australopithecines' micro-wear patterns would be consistent with the hypothesis that australopithecines' diet was broader as well.

D Even if the environment of east Africa were more varied, that would not mean the australopithecines necessarily ate a more varied diet. Many species that live in very varied environments specialize narrowly on particular foods in those environments.

E Just because many soft-bodied insects might have been available to australopithecines does not mean that australopithecines ate them.

The correct answer is C.

130. The passage is primarily concerned with

(A) comparing two research methods for determining a species' dietary habits

(B) describing and evaluating conjectures about a species' diet

(C) contrasting several explanations for a species' dietary habits

(D) discussing a new approach and advocating its use in particular situations

(E) arguing that a particular research methodology does not contribute useful data

Main Idea

Answering this question depends on identifying the main point of the passage and requires an understanding of the passage as a whole. The passage discusses Walker's dismissal of certain other researchers' hypotheses regarding the diet of the primate species australopithecine. Walker does so on the basis of tooth micro-wear patterns, which lead him to the hypothesis that australopithecines were fruit eaters. However, the passage goes on to point out limitations of the utility of micro-wear studies, and discusses certain considerations which suggest that the australopithecines may have had a more diverse diet.

A   The passage primarily focuses on using an analysis of micro-wear patterns to determine australopithecines' dietary habits, so it is not the case that the passage is primarily concerned with comparing two research methods.

B   **Correct.** The passage considers Walker's evidence against certain hypotheses regarding the australopithecine diet, as well as his evidence for his own hypothesis, and presents considerations that suggest an alternative hypothesis. Thus, the passage is primarily concerned with describing and evaluating conjectures about the diet of a species—the australopithecines.

C   The passage is not so much concerned with contrasting explanations for a species' dietary habits as with describing and evaluating evidence for such explanations.

D   The passage gives no indication that the analysis of micro-wear patterns is a new approach.

E   The passage does not argue that micro-wear analysis fails to contribute useful data. It merely points out that such analysis has certain limitations.

The correct answer is B.

131. The author of the passage mentions the diets of baboons and other living primates most likely in order to

(A) provide evidence that refutes Walker's conclusions about the foods making up the diets of australopithecines

(B) suggest that studies of tooth micro-wear patterns are primarily useful for determining the diets of living primates

(C) suggest that australopithecines were probably omnivores rather than frugivores

(D) illustrate some of the limitations of using tooth micro-wear patterns to draw definitive conclusions about a group's diet

(E) suggest that tooth micro-wear patterns are caused by persistent, as opposed to occasional, consumption of particular foods

Evaluation

The passage discusses the diets of baboons and other living primates mainly in the second paragraph, which is concerned with explaining the limited utility of micro-wear studies.

A   The author raises some doubts about Walker's conclusions but does not go as far as to try to refute them outright. The author argues only that, as the final sentence of the passage states, they may need to be expanded.

B   The author discusses the diets of baboons and other living primates in relation to micro-wear research on extinct primates. Nothing in the discussion suggests that micro-wear studies would be more useful for determining the diets of living primates than for providing evidence regarding the diets of earlier primates or of other types of animals. Furthermore, the mention of baboon diets suggests that micro-wear studies may not be very useful for determining the diets of some living primates.

C   The author leaves open the question of whether australopithecines were omnivores or frugivores. The passage suggests that some australopithecines might have been omnivores, if australopithecines' diets varied according to the environments they inhabited. Walker's conclusion regarding east African australopithecines' being frugivores might still hold, however.

D   **Correct.** The author refers to baboons' diets and those of current omnivorous primates in order to suggest that there might be limitations to Walker's use of tooth micro-wear patterns to determine australopithecines' diet.

E   The passage does not make a distinction between persistent and occasional consumption of particular foods.

The correct answer is D.

Questions 132–135 refer to the passage on page 103.

132. The primary purpose of the passage is to

(A) present recently discovered evidence that supports a conventional interpretation of a historical period

(B) describe how reinterpretations of available evidence have reinvigorated a once-discredited scholarly position

(C) explain why some historians have tended to emphasize change rather than continuity in discussing a particular period

(D) explore how changes in a particular occupation serve to counter the prevailing view of a historical period

(E) examine a particular area of historical research in order to exemplify a general scholarly trend

Main Idea

This question asks about the passage's main purpose. The first paragraph initially describes a way in which historiography is changing: the idea of a consistent, monolithic decline in women's status is being complicated by *recent research*. The rest of the passage uses the example of Pinchbeck's interpretation of women's work in English cheesemaking to show the limits of earlier ideas about women's status: Pinchbeck's work illustrates the idea of consistent decline, but recent scholarship has called that work into question.

A   The first paragraph suggests that Pinchbeck's work represents the conventional position that women's status declined consistently with the advent of capitalism; according to the passage, recent evidence undermines, rather than supports, that position.

B   According to the passage, reinterpretations of evidence have inspired new interpretations; they have not reinvigorated a discredited position.

C   The passage is concerned with noting both change and continuity, as stated in the first sentence.

D   In the passage, continuity, not change, in a particular occupation—English farmhouse cheesemaking—helps to counter the prevailing view.

E   **Correct.** The passage's main purpose is to examine women's work in English farmhouse cheesemaking so as to illustrate a trend in historiography of women's status under capitalism and industrialization.

The correct answer is E.

133. Regarding English local markets and fairs, which of the following can be inferred from the passage?

(A) Both before and after the agricultural revolution, the sellers of agricultural products at these venues were men.

(B) Knowing who the active sellers were at these venues may not give a reliable indication of who controlled the revenue from the sales.

(C) There were no parallel institutions at which American cheese makers could sell their own products.

(D) Prior to the agricultural revolution, the sellers of agricultural products at these venues were generally the producers themselves.

(E) Prior to the agricultural revolution, women sold not only cheese but also products of arable agriculture at these venues.

Inference

The passage discusses English local markets and fairs in the first and second paragraphs: the first paragraph states that before the agricultural revolution, women had sold cheese in such venues but that after that, factors, who were men, sold the cheese. The second paragraph argues that even though English women in precapitalist, preindustrial times may have at one point sold cheese at fairs, evidence indicates that in at least one case, a man appropriated most of the money his wife made from her sales.

A   The first paragraph states that prior to the agricultural revolution, women sold cheese at local markets and fairs.

B   **Correct.** As the second paragraph indicates, women may have sold the cheese, but there is evidence to suggest that they did not necessarily control the revenue from its sale.

C   The passage does not provide evidence regarding any institutions at which American cheese makers sold their products.

D   While the passage indicates that the producers of English farmhouse cheese may have been the ones who sold that cheese at local markets and fairs, there is no evidence to suggest that this was necessarily the case for other agricultural products.

E   The passage provides no information regarding whether women sold products of arable agriculture in any venue.

The correct answer is B.

134. The passage describes the work of Pinchbeck primarily in order to

(A) demonstrate that some of the conclusions reached by recent historians were anticipated in earlier scholarship

(B) provide an instance of the viewpoint that, according to the passage's author, is being superseded

(C) illustrate the ways in which recent historians have built on the work of their predecessors

(D) provide a point of reference for subsequent scholarship on women's work during the agricultural revolution

(E) show the effect that the specialization introduced in the agricultural and industrial revolutions had on women's work

Evaluation

This question focuses on the function of Pinchbeck's work in the passage. Pinchbeck's study of women's work in cheese production is, according to the passage, an illustration of the view that women's status declined consistently with the advent of industrialization. That view, the author claims, is being challenged by current historiography.

A   The passage indicates that the conclusions of Pinchbeck, who represents earlier scholarship, did not anticipate recent work, but rather that recent work argues against those conclusions.

B   **Correct.** Pinchbeck's work illustrates earlier trends in historiography, trends that the author suggests are now giving way to newer ideas.

C   The passage does not focus on any ways in which recent historians have built on Pinchbeck's work; instead, it discusses how they have argued against its conclusions.

D   Pinchbeck's work provides a point of reference only insofar as subsequent scholarship is arguing against it.

E   Pinchbeck makes the argument that specialization caused women's status to decline, but the passage is concerned with undermining this argument.

The correct answer is B.

135. It can be inferred from the passage that women did work in

(A) American cheesemaking at some point prior to industrialization

(B) arable agriculture in northern England both before and after the agricultural revolution

(C) arable agriculture in southeast England after the agricultural revolution, in those locales in which cultural values supported their participation

(D) the sale of cheese at local markets in England even after the agricultural revolution

(E) some areas of American cheese dairying after industrialization

Inference

This question focuses mainly on the final paragraph of the passage, in which women's continued work in English cheese dairying is contrasted with what the passage calls their *disappearance from arable agriculture in southeast England and from American cheese dairying*, presumably during the period of industrialization. The correct answer will be a conclusion that can be drawn from this information.

A **Correct.** That women "disappeared" from American cheese dairying during industrialization provides grounds for inferring that they did such dairying work at some point prior to industrialization.

B The passage says that women disappeared from arable agriculture in southeast England, but it gives no information about their participation in arable agriculture in northern England.

C The passage makes a blanket statement about women's *disappearance from arable agriculture in southeast England*, so there is no reason to infer that any locales supported women's participation in agriculture.

D The first paragraph states that factors, who were men, sold cheese after the agricultural revolution.

E The final paragraph explicitly states that women disappeared from American cheese dairying; thus, there is no basis for inferring that women worked in any areas of that field after industrialization.

The correct answer is A.

Questions 136–139 refer to the passage on page 105.

136. According to the passage, the use of Shortt clocks led to the discovery that

(A) optical sensing equipment can be used effectively in timekeeping systems

(B) atomic clocks can be used in place of pendulum clocks in observatories

(C) tides occur in solid ground as well as in oceans

(D) the earth's rotation varies from one time of year to another

(E) pendulums can be synchronized with one another electronically

Supporting Idea

The item requires recognizing information stated in the passage. The second paragraph describes the use of Shortt clocks in astronomical observatories and attributes one discovery to the use of Shortt clocks: "the first indications of seasonal variations in the Earth's rotation." In other words, Shortt clocks enabled the discovery that the Earth's rotation varies at different times of year.

A The passage mentions the use of optical sensing equipment in a Shortt clock, but it does not characterize the effectiveness of that use as a discovery.

B The passage refers to the use of atomic clocks in observatories, but it does not suggest that Shortt clocks led to the discovery that atomic clocks could be used instead of pendulum clocks.

C The passage discusses the fact that tides occur in solid ground, but it does not suggest that the discovery of this phenomenon was enabled by Shortt clocks.

D **Correct.** The passage states that the use of Shortt clocks revealed the first evidence of seasonal variations in the rotation of the Earth; in other words, Shortt clocks led to the discovery that the Earth's rotation varies at different times of year.

E The passage mentions the pendulums in a Shortt clock synchronizing by means of an electrical signal, but it does not suggest that Shortt clocks led to the discovery of such synchronization.

The correct answer is D.

137. The passage most strongly suggests that which of the following is true of the chamber in which a Shortt clock's primary pendulum was housed?

(A) It contained elaborate mechanisms that were attached to, and moved by, the pendulum.
(B) It was firmly sealed during normal operation of the clock.
(C) It was at least partly transparent so as to allow for certain types of visual data output.
(D) It housed both the primary pendulum and another pendulum.
(E) It contained a transmitter that was activated at irregular intervals to send a signal to the secondary pendulum.

Inference

The question requires recognizing information strongly implied, but not directly stated, in the passage. The first paragraph states that the primary pendulum in a Shortt clock swung freely in a vacuum chamber. To maintain a vacuum, that chamber necessarily would have been tightly sealed when the clock was operating normally.

A   The passage states that the primary pendulum swung freely, which does not suggest that it was attached to and moving an elaborate mechanism.
B   **Correct.** The passage states that the primary pendulum swung freely in a vacuum chamber. Maintaining a vacuum would necessitate a tight seal, so it follows that the chamber was firmly sealed when the clock was operating normally.
C   The passage implies nothing about the transparency of the chamber housing the primary pendulum.
D   The passage states that the secondary pendulum was housed in a separate cabinet, so a second pendulum in the same cabinet with the primary pendulum is not suggested.
E   The passage describes a signal sent from the secondary pendulum to the primary pendulum, not the other way around.

The correct answer is B.

138. The passage most strongly suggests that its author would agree with which of the following statements about clocks?

(A) Before 1921, no one had designed a clock that used electricity to aid in its timekeeping functions.
(B) Atomic clocks depend on the operation of mechanisms that were invented by William Shortt and first used in the Shortt clock.
(C) No type of clock that keeps time more stably and accurately than a Shortt clock relies fundamentally on the operation of a pendulum.
(D) Subtle changes in the earth's rotation slightly reduce the accuracy of all clocks used in observatories after 1921.
(E) At least some mechanical clocks that do not have pendulums are almost identical to Shortt clocks in their mode of operation.

Inference

The question requires recognizing information implied, but not directly stated, in the passage. The author characterizes Shortt's clock as the "ultimate pendulum clock, indeed the ultimate mechanical clock of any kind," which strongly suggests the view that any type of clock superior to a Shortt clock—that is, any clock which kept time more reliably and accurately—must not be mechanical or rely on the operation of a pendulum.

A   The passage states that Shortt clocks were first used in 1921, but it does not imply that earlier clocks did not use electricity.
B   The passage does not suggest that the mechanisms in an atomic clock have any relation to those in a Shortt clock.
C   **Correct.** The author describes Shortt clocks as the ultimate, or best, in the class of pendulum clocks; therefore, the author likely would agree that any clock that kept time more accurately than a Shortt clock would not rely on a pendulum.
D   The passage suggests nothing about the subtle changes in the Earth's rotation affecting all clocks; rather, it states that Shortt clocks first allowed such subtle seasonal changes to be detected.

E The passage does not discuss mechanical clocks without pendulums, nor would such clocks be almost identical to a pendulum clock, such as a Shortt clock, in their mode of operation.

The correct answer is C.

139. The passage most strongly suggests that the study described in the third paragraph would not have been possible in the absence of

    (A) accurate information regarding the times at which high and low ocean tides occurred at various locations during 1984
    (B) comparative data regarding the use of Shortt clocks in observatories between 1921 and 1932
    (C) a non-Shortt clock that was known to keep time extremely precisely and reliably
    (D) an innovative electric-power source that was not available in the 1920s and 1930s
    (E) optical data-transmission devices to communicate between the U.S. Naval Observatory and other research facilities

Inference

The item requires recognizing information strongly implied, but not directly stated, in the passage. The study discussed in the third paragraph compared a Shortt clock's functioning against that of atomic clocks. Atomic clocks are known to be extraordinarily precise, allowing for the precise comparisons made by the study; it follows that the study would have been impossible without an atomic clock or another non-Shortt clock that was equally precise and reliable.

A The study discovered slight deviations in the functioning of the Shortt clock caused by tidal distortion in the earth itself, but it did not rely on information regarding ocean tides.
B The study compared a Shortt clock against atomic clocks; it did not compare the use of Shortt clocks in observatories during a specific period.
C **Correct.** The study compared a Shortt clock against atomic clocks to determine exactly how accurate a Shortt clock is. Atomic clocks are known to be extremely precise and reliable. It follows that such precise comparisons would have been impossible without either an atomic clock or another non-Shortt clock that was as precise and reliable as an atomic clock.
D Nothing suggests that the study in question required an innovative power source.
E The passage states that the study used optical sensing equipment but makes no mention of optical data transmission devices used to communicate between various research facilities.

The correct answer is C.

Questions 140–143 refer to the passage on page 107.

140. According to the passage, comparable worth principles are different in which of the following ways from other mandates intended to reduce or eliminate pay inequities?

    (A) Comparable worth principles address changes in the pay schedules of male as well as female workers.
    (B) Comparable worth principles can be applied to employees in both the public and the private sector.
    (C) Comparable worth principles emphasize the training and skill of workers.
    (D) Comparable worth principles require changes in the employer's resource allocation.
    (E) Comparable worth principles can be used to quantify the value of elements of dissimilar jobs.

Supporting Idea

The question requires recognizing specific claims presented in the passage. The passage notes that two mandates—the Equal Pay Act of 1963 and Title VII of the Civil Rights Act of 1964—do not compare the value of similar tasks in dissimilar jobs, and then contrasts that limitation with comparable worth principles, which attempt to quantify the value of specific elements of diverse jobs in order to assert that similar work elements, even when found in dissimilar jobs, should be regarded as comparable in value and therefore receive comparable remuneration.

- A The passage mentions comparable worth principles in relation to pay schedules, but it does not specify pay schedules as a point of difference with other mandates.
- B The passage states that both public- and private-sector employers have adopted comparable worth principles, but it does not contrast that adoption with the application of other mandates.
- C The passage suggests that comparable worth principles emphasize the similar training and skills of workers performing dissimilar jobs, but it does not suggest that comparable worth principles differ from other mandates in emphasizing skills and training.
- D While comparable worth principles are likely to require changes in resource allocation, nothing in the passage suggests that other mandates would not also require such changes.
- E **Correct.** The passage notes that other mandates do not attempt to compare the value of tasks performed in dissimilar jobs, then states that comparable worth principles are different because they quantify the value of such job elements as training, responsibility, and work environment, even across different categories of work.

The correct answer is E.

141. According to the passage, which of the following is true of comparable worth as a policy?

    (A) Comparable worth policy decisions in pay-inequity cases have often failed to satisfy the complainants.
    (B) Comparable worth policies have been applied to both public-sector and private-sector employee pay schedules.
    (C) Comparable worth as a policy has come to be widely criticized in the past decade.
    (D) Many employers have considered comparable worth as a policy, but very few have actually adopted it.
    (E) Early implementations of comparable worth policies resulted in only transitory gains in pay equity.

Supporting Idea

The question requires recognizing specific information presented in the passage. In the first paragraph, the passage states that over the last decade, comparable worth policies have been adopted or considered by both private-sector companies and governments on the federal, state, and local levels. In other words, such policies have been applied to both public-sector and private-sector employee pay schedules by the companies and governmental entities discussed.

- A The passage states that other mandates meant to address inequity have failed to satisfy litigants and contrasts this dissatisfaction with the greater perceived fairness of comparable worth policies.
- B **Correct.** The passage states in the first paragraph that comparable worth policies have been adopted by both private companies and governmental entities, which would mean that such policies were applied to both private-sector and public-sector employee pay.
- C The passage does not mention widespread criticisms of comparable worth policies.
- D The passage states that large numbers of employers have adopted or begun to consider comparable worth policies; nowhere does it suggest that very few employers have adopted such policies after considering them.
- E The passage mentions concerns that the pay gains brought about by comparable worth policies will be transitory, but it goes on to suggest that such concerns are misplaced.

The correct answer is B.

142. It can be inferred from the passage that application of "other mandates" (see line 22) would be unlikely to result in an outcome satisfactory to the female employees in which of the following situations?

   I. Males employed as long-distance truck drivers for a furniture company make $3.50 more per hour than do females with comparable job experience employed in the same capacity.
   II. Women working in the office of a cement company contend that their jobs are as demanding and valuable as those of the men working outside in the cement factory, but the women are paid much less per hour.
   III. A law firm employs both male and female paralegals with the same educational and career backgrounds, but the starting salary for male paralegals is $5,000 more than for female paralegals.

   (A) I only
   (B) II only
   (C) III only
   (D) I and II only
   (E) I and III only

Inference

The question requires applying the information supplied by the passage to hypothetical scenarios. The passage states that the "other mandates" referred to in line 22 of the text—such as the Equal Pay Act of 1963 and Title VII of the Civil Rights Act of 1964—do not address the issue of similarly valuable work in dissimilar jobs. Therefore, it can be inferred that they *do* address the issue of pay disparities in similar or identical jobs, like the scenarios described in I and III. It would follow that the female employees described in scenarios I and III would be more likely to be satisfied with the results of applying those mandates, and only the female employees described in scenario II—who seek to correct pay inequities across dissimilar but equally demanding jobs—would likely be dissatisfied.

A   The male and female employees in scenario I are performing identical work with comparable experience but receiving unequal pay—a situation that the passage implies "other mandates" can address adequately.

B   **Correct.** The male and female employees in scenario II are performing different but equally demanding jobs—exactly the situation that the passage suggests the "other mandates" referred to in line 22 of the text do not address. Therefore, the female employees in this scenario are likely to find the application of such other mandates unsatisfying.

C   The male and female employees in scenario III are performing identical work with identical credentials but receiving unequal pay—a situation that the passage implies "other mandates" can address satisfactorily.

D   As discussed above, the female employees in scenario II are likely to be dissatisfied by the application of "other mandates," but those in scenario I are more likely to be satisfied.

E   As discussed above, the female employees in scenarios I and III are most likely to find that the "other mandates" are sufficient to address their situations.

The correct answer is B.

143. Which of the following best describes an application of the principles of comparable worth as they are described in the passage?

   (A) The current pay, rates of increase, and rates of promotion for female mechanics are compared with those of male mechanics.
   (B) The training, skills, and job experience of computer programmers in one division of a corporation are compared to those of programmers making more money in another division.
   (C) The number of women holding top executive positions in a corporation is compared to the number of women available for promotion to those positions, and both tallies are matched to the tallies for men in the same corporation.

(D) The skills, training, and job responsibilities of the clerks in the township tax assessor's office are compared to those of the much better paid township engineers.

(E) The working conditions of female workers in a hazardous-materials environment are reviewed and their pay schedules compared to those of all workers in similar environments across the nation.

Main Idea

The question requires grasping the central principle behind comparable worth policies and then assessing if application of that principle is illustrated by hypothetical scenarios. The passage describes comparable worth as the idea that jobs requiring similar levels of skill, training, and responsibility, or involving similar tasks, should receive similar remuneration, even when those jobs differ from each other in other respects. Therefore, the scenario that illustrates the application of comparable worth will involve the comparison of such elements as skills, training, and responsibilities in two jobs that are otherwise broadly different.

A Comparable worth principles apply in situations where people are doing work of similar value in dissimilar jobs; in this scenario, the male and female mechanics are doing the same job.

B Comparable worth principles do not apply in situations where people are doing the same work—programming—in different divisions of a company.

C Assessing the availability of male and female employees for promotion is not an application of comparable worth principles.

D **Correct.** Comparable worth principles are demonstrated in scenarios such as this one, where skills, training, and responsibilities are compared across jobs that are otherwise different; in this case, a comparison between the work performed by tax clerks and by engineers.

E Comparable worth principles apply to comparisons of the value of work performed in different jobs, not to comparisons of working conditions.

The correct answer is D.

4.7 Practice Questions: Critical Reasoning

Each of the Critical Reasoning questions is based on a short argument, a set of statements, or a plan of action. For each question, select the best answer of the choices given.

Questions 144 to 187 — Difficulty: Easy

144. Stockholders have been critical of the Flyna Company, a major furniture retailer, because most of Flyna's furniture is manufactured in Country X from local wood, and illegal logging is widespread there. However, Flyna has set up a certification scheme for lumber mills. It has hired a staff of auditors and forestry professionals who review documentation of the wood supply of Country X's lumber mills to ensure its legal origin, make surprise visits to mills to verify documents, and certify mills as approved sources of legally obtained lumber. Flyna uses only lumber from certified mills. Thus, Flyna's claim that its Country X wood supply is obtained legally is justified.

Which of the following, if true, would most undermine the justification provided for Flyna's claim?

(A) Only about one-third of Flyna's inspectors were hired from outside the company.

(B) Country X's government recently reduced its subsidies for lumber production.

(C) Flyna has had to pay higher than expected salaries to attract qualified inspectors.

(D) The proportion of Country X's lumber mills inspected each year by Flyna's staff is about 10 percent, randomly selected.

(E) Illegal logging costs Country X's government a significant amount in lost revenue each year.

145. Companies O and P each have the same number of employees who work the same number of hours per week. According to records maintained by each company, the employees of Company O had fewer job-related accidents last year than did the employees of Company P. Therefore, employees of Company O are less likely to have job-related accidents than are employees of Company P.

Which of the following, if true, would most weaken the conclusion?

(A) The employees of Company P lost more time at work due to job-related accidents than did the employees of Company O.

(B) Company P considered more types of accidents to be job-related than did Company O.

(C) The employees of Company P were sick more often than were the employees of Company O.

(D) Several employees of Company O each had more than one job-related accident.

(E) The majority of job-related accidents at Company O involved a single machine.

146. The *XCT* automobile is considered less valuable than the *ZNK* automobile, because insurance companies pay less, on average, to replace a stolen *XCT* than a stolen *ZNK*. Surprisingly, the average amount insurance companies will pay to repair a car involved in a collision is typically higher for the *XCT* than for the *ZNK*. One insurance expert explained that repairs to *XCT* automobiles are especially labor-intensive, and labor is a significant factor in collision repair costs.

Which of the following, if true, most strongly supports the insurance expert's explanation?

(A) *ZNK* automobiles are involved in accidents more frequently than *XCT* automobiles.
(B) The cost of routine maintenance for the *ZNK* is about the same as for the *XCT*.
(C) There are more automobile mechanics who specialize in *XCT* repairs than in *ZNK* repairs.
(D) The ease of repair of *ZNK* automobiles is one factor that adds to their value.
(E) *XCT* automobiles are more likely to be stolen than *ZNK* automobiles.

147. The sustained massive use of pesticides in farming has two effects that are especially pernicious. First, it often kills off the pests' natural enemies in the area. Second, it often unintentionally gives rise to insecticide-resistant pests, since those insects that survive a particular insecticide will be the ones most resistant to it, and they are the ones left to breed.

From the passage above, it can be properly inferred that the effectiveness of the sustained massive use of pesticides can be extended by doing which of the following, assuming that each is a realistic possibility?

(A) Using only chemically stable insecticides
(B) Periodically switching the type of insecticide used
(C) Gradually increasing the quantities of pesticides used
(D) Leaving a few fields fallow every year
(E) Breeding higher-yielding varieties of crop plants

148. Editorial: The mayor plans to deactivate the city's fire alarm boxes, because most calls received from them are false alarms. The mayor claims that the alarm boxes are no longer necessary, since most people now have access to cell phones. But the city's commercial district, where there is the greatest risk of fire, has few residents and few cell towers, so some alarm boxes are still necessary.

Which of the following, if true, most seriously weakens the editorial's argument?

(A) Maintaining the fire alarm boxes costs the city more than 5 million dollars annually.
(B) Commercial buildings have automatic fire alarm systems that are linked directly to the fire department.
(C) The fire department gets less information from an alarm box than it does from a telephone call.
(D) The city's fire department is located much closer to the residential areas than to the commercial district.
(E) On average, almost 25 percent of the cell towers in the city are out of order.

149. Which of the following, if true, most logically completes the argument?

Some dairy farmers in the province of Takandia want to give their cows a synthetic hormone that increases milk production. Many Takandians, however, do not want to buy milk from cows given the synthetic hormone. For this reason Takandia's legislature is considering a measure requiring milk from cows given the hormone to be labeled as such. Even if the measure is defeated, dairy farmers who use the hormone will probably lose customers, since _____.

(A) it has not been proven that any trace of the synthetic hormone exists in the milk of cows given the hormone
(B) some farmers in Takandia who plan to use the synthetic hormone will probably not do so if the measure were passed
(C) milk from cows that have not been given the synthetic hormone can be labeled as such without any legislative action
(D) the legislature's consideration of the bill has been widely publicized
(E) milk that comes from cows given the synthetic hormone looks and tastes the same as milk from cows that have not received the hormone

150. Which of the following most logically completes the passage?

A business analysis of the Appenian railroad system divided its long-distance passenger routes into two categories: rural routes and interurban routes. The analysis found that, unlike the interurban routes, few rural routes carried a high enough passenger volume to be profitable. Closing unprofitable rural routes, however, will not necessarily enhance the profitability of the whole system, since _____.

(A) a large part of the passenger volume on interurban routes is accounted for by passengers who begin or end their journeys on rural routes

(B) within the last two decades several of the least used rural routes have been closed and their passenger services have been replaced by buses

(C) the rural routes were all originally constructed at least one hundred years ago, whereas some of the interurban routes were constructed recently for new high-speed express trains

(D) not all of Appenia's large cities are equally well served by interurban railroad services

(E) the greatest passenger volume, relative to the routes' capacity, is not on either category of long-distance routes but is on suburban commuter routes

151. Although Ackerburg's subway system is currently operating at a deficit, the transit authority will lower subway fares next year. The authority projects that the lower fares will result in a ten percent increase in the number of subway riders. Since the additional income from the larger ridership will more than offset the decrease due to lower fares, the transit authority actually expects the fare reduction to reduce or eliminate the subway system's operating deficit for next year.

Which of the following, if true, provides the most support for the transit authority's expectation of reducing the subway system's operating deficit?

(A) Throughout the years that the subway system has operated, fares have never before been reduced.

(B) The planned fare reduction will not apply to students, who can already ride the subway for a reduced fare.

(C) Next year, the transit authority will have to undertake several large-scale track maintenance projects.

(D) The subway system can accommodate a ten percent increase in ridership without increasing the number of trains it runs each day.

(E) The current subway fares in Ackerburg are higher than subway fares in other cities in the region.

152. At several locations on the northwest coast of North America are formations known as chevrons—wedge-shaped formations of mounded sediment—pointing toward the ocean. Most geologists take them to have been formed by erosion, but recently other scientists have proposed that they were thrown up from the ocean by massive waves triggered by meteor impacts in the Pacific Ocean.

    Which of the following, if discovered, would most help in deciding which hypothesis is correct?

    (A) Chevron-like structures which are not currently near glaciers, large rivers, or other bodies of water
    (B) The presence, in chevrons, of deposits of ocean microfossils containing metals typically formed by meteor impacts
    (C) Oral-history evidence for flooding that could have been caused by ocean waves
    (D) The fact that exact data about the location and depth of any meteor impact craters on the Pacific seabed is lacking
    (E) The fact that certain changes in the shape and location of maritime sand dunes have been produced by the action of wind and waves

153. Sparrow Airlines is planning to reduce its costs by cleaning its planes' engines once a month, rather than the industry standard of every six months. With cleaner engines, Sparrow can postpone engine overhauls, which take planes out of service for up to 18 months. Furthermore, cleaning an engine reduces its fuel consumption by roughly 1.2 percent.

    The airline's plan assumes that

    (A) fuel prices are likely to rise in the near future and therefore cutting fuel consumption is an important goal
    (B) the cost of monthly cleaning of an airplane's engines is not significantly greater in the long run than is the cost of an engine overhaul
    (C) engine cleaning does not remove an airplane from service
    (D) Sparrow Airlines has had greater problems with engine overhauls and fuel consumption than other airlines have
    (E) cleaning engines once a month will give Sparrow Airlines a competitive advantage over other airlines

154. Patrick usually provides child care for six children. Parents leave their children at Patrick's house in the morning and pick them up after work. At the end of each workweek, the parents pay Patrick at an hourly rate for the child care provided that week. The weekly income Patrick receives is usually adequate but not always uniform, particularly in the winter, when children are likely to get sick and be unpredictably absent.

    Which of the following plans, if put into effect, has the best prospect of making Patrick's weekly income both uniform and adequate?

    (A) Pool resources with a neighbor who provides child care under similar arrangements, so that the two of them cooperate in caring for twice as many children as Patrick currently does.
    (B) Replace payment by actual hours of child care provided with a fixed weekly fee based upon the number of hours of child care that Patrick would typically be expected to provide.
    (C) Hire a full-time helper and invest in facilities for providing child care to sick children.
    (D) Increase the hourly rate to a level that would provide adequate income even in a week when half of the children Patrick usually cares for are absent.
    (E) Increase the number of hours made available for child care each day, so that parents can leave their children in Patrick's care for a longer period each day at the current hourly rate.

155. Film director: It is true that certain characters and plot twists in my newly released film *The Perfect Heist* are strikingly similar to characters and plot twists in *Thieves*, a movie that came out last year. Based on these similarities, the film studio that produced *Thieves* is now accusing me of taking ideas from that film. The accusation is clearly without merit. All production work on *The Perfect Heist* was actually completed months before *Thieves* was released.

    Which of the following, if true, provides the strongest support for the director's rejection of the accusation?

    (A) Before *Thieves* began production, its script had been circulating for several years among various film studios, including the studio that produced *The Perfect Heist*.
    (B) The characters and plot twists that are most similar in the two films have close parallels in many earlier films of the same genre.
    (C) The film studio that produced *Thieves* seldom produces films in this genre.
    (D) The director of *Thieves* worked with the director of *The Perfect Heist* on several earlier projects.
    (E) The time it took to produce *The Perfect Heist* was considerably shorter than the time it took to produce *Thieves*.

156. The rate at which a road wears depends on various factors, including climate, amount of traffic, and the size and weight of the vehicles using it. The only land transportation to Rittland's seaport is via a divided highway, one side carrying traffic to the seaport and one carrying traffic away from it. The side leading to the seaport has worn faster, even though each side has carried virtually the same amount of traffic, consisting mainly of large trucks.

    Which of the following, if true, most helps to explain the difference in the rate of wear?

    (A) The volume of traffic to and from Rittland's seaport has increased beyond the intended capacity of the highway that serves it.
    (B) Wear on the highway that serves Rittland's seaport is considerably greater during the cold winter months.
    (C) Wear on the side of the highway that leads to Rittland's seaport has encouraged people to take buses to the seaport rather than driving there in their own automobiles.
    (D) A greater tonnage of goods is exported from Rittland's seaport than is imported through it.
    (E) All of Rittland's automobiles are imported by ship.

157. Ythex has developed a small diesel engine that produces 30 percent less particulate pollution than the engine made by its main rival, Onez, now widely used in Marania; Ythex's engine is well-suited for use in the thriving warehousing businesses in Marania, though it costs more than the Onez engine. The Maranian government plans to ban within the next two years the use of diesel engines with more than 80 percent of current diesel engine particulate emissions in Marania, and Onez will probably not be able to retool its engine to reduce emissions to reach this target. So if the ban is passed, the Ythex engine ought to sell well in Marania after that time.

Which of the following is an assumption on which the argument above depends?

(A) Marania's warehousing and transshipment business buys more diesel engines of any size than other types of engines.

(B) Ythex is likely to be able to reduce the cost of its small diesel engine within the next two years.

(C) The Maranian government is generally favorable to anti-pollution regulations.

(D) The government's ban on high levels of pollution caused by diesel engines, if passed, will not be difficult to enforce.

(E) The other manufacturers of small diesel engines in Marania, if there are any, have not produced an engine as popular and clean running as Ythex's new engine.

158. In parts of South America, vitamin-A deficiency is a serious health problem, especially among children. In one region, agriculturists are attempting to improve nutrition by encouraging farmers to plant a new variety of sweet potato called SPK004 that is rich in beta-carotene, which the body converts into vitamin A. The plan has good chances of success, since sweet potato is a staple of the region's diet and agriculture, and the varieties currently grown contain little beta-carotene.

Which of the following, if true, most strongly supports the prediction that the plan will succeed?

(A) The growing conditions required by the varieties of sweet potato currently cultivated in the region are conditions in which SPK004 can flourish.

(B) The flesh of SPK004 differs from that of the currently cultivated sweet potatoes in color and texture, so traditional foods would look somewhat different when prepared from SPK004.

(C) There are no other varieties of sweet potato that are significantly richer in beta-carotene than SPK004 is.

(D) The varieties of sweet potato currently cultivated in the region contain some important nutrients that are lacking in SPK004.

(E) There are other vegetables currently grown in the region that contain more beta-carotene than the currently cultivated varieties of sweet potato do.

159. Which of the following most logically completes the argument?

The last members of a now-extinct species of a European wild deer called the giant deer lived in Ireland about 16,000 years ago. Prehistoric cave paintings in France depict this animal as having a large hump on its back. Fossils of this animal, however, do not show any hump. Nevertheless, there is no reason to conclude that the cave paintings are therefore inaccurate in this regard, since _____.

(A) some prehistoric cave paintings in France also depict other animals as having a hump

(B) fossils of the giant deer are much more common in Ireland than in France

(C) animal humps are composed of fatty tissue, which does not fossilize

(D) the cave paintings of the giant deer were painted well before 16,000 years ago

(E) only one currently existing species of deer has any anatomical feature that even remotely resembles a hump

160. Super Express Shipping Company has implemented a new distribution system that can get almost every package to its destination the day after it is sent. The company worries that this more efficient system will result in lower sales of its premium next-day delivery service, because its two-day service will usually arrive the following day anyway. The company plans to encourage sales of its next-day service by intentionally delaying delivery of its two-day packages so that they will not be delivered the following day, even if the package arrives at its destination city in time for next-day delivery.

The company's plan assumes that

(A) deliberate delay of packages will not affect the company's image in a way that significantly reduces its ability to attract and retain customers

(B) most people do not have a preference for either two-day or next-day delivery

(C) if the plan is not implemented, the company would lose more money in lost sales of overnight deliveries than it would save with its new efficient distribution system

(D) the overnight service is too expensive to be attractive to most customers currently

(E) competing companies' delivery services rarely deliver packages to their destination earlier than their promised time

161. Psychologists conducted an experiment in which half of the volunteers were asked to describe an unethical action they had performed, while the other half were asked to describe an ethical action they had performed. Some of the volunteers, chosen at random from each of the two groups, were encouraged to wash their hands afterward. Among those who described unethical actions, those who washed their hands were significantly less likely to volunteer for another, similar experiment than those who did not wash their hands. The researchers concluded that some of the subjects failed to volunteer again in part because of their having described an unethical action.

    Which of the following would, if true, most help to support the researchers' conclusion?

    (A) Among the volunteers who described ethical actions, those who washed their hands were significantly less likely to volunteer for another, similar experiment than those who did not wash their hands.
    (B) The average likelihood of volunteering for another, similar experiment was higher among those who described ethical actions than among those who described unethical actions.
    (C) Most of the volunteers who were encouraged to wash their hands did so.
    (D) The volunteers in the study were not more disposed to washing their hands under normal circumstances than the general population was.
    (E) Equal numbers of volunteers from both groups were encouraged to wash their hands.

162. High levels of fertilizer and pesticides, needed when farmers try to produce high yields of the same crop year after year, pollute water supplies. Experts therefore urge farmers to diversify their crops and to rotate their plantings yearly.

    To receive governmental price-support benefits for a crop, farmers must have produced that same crop for the past several years.

    The statements above, if true, best support which of the following conclusions?

    (A) The rules for governmental support of farm prices work against efforts to reduce water pollution.
    (B) The only solution to the problem of water pollution from fertilizers and pesticides is to take farmland out of production.
    (C) Farmers can continue to make a profit by rotating diverse crops, thus reducing costs for chemicals, but not by planting the same crop each year.
    (D) New farming techniques will be developed to make it possible for farmers to reduce the application of fertilizers and pesticides.
    (E) Governmental price supports for farm products are set at levels that are not high enough to allow farmers to get out of debt.

163. The interview is an essential part of a successful hiring program because, with it, job applicants who have personalities that are unsuited to the requirements of the job will be eliminated from consideration.

    The argument above logically depends on which of the following assumptions?

    (A) A hiring program will be successful if it includes interviews.
    (B) The interview is a more important part of a successful hiring program than is the development of a job description.
    (C) Interviewers can accurately identify applicants whose personalities are unsuited to the requirements of the job.
    (D) The only purpose of an interview is to evaluate whether job applicants' personalities are suited to the requirements of the job.
    (E) The fit of job applicants' personalities to the requirements of the job was once the most important factor in making hiring decisions.

164. Many leadership theories have provided evidence that leaders affect group success rather than the success of particular individuals. So it is irrelevant to analyze the effects of supervisor traits on the attitudes of individuals whom they supervise. Instead, assessment of leadership effectiveness should occur only at the group level.

    Which of the following would it be most useful to establish in order to evaluate the argument?

    (A) Whether supervisors' documentation of individual supervisees' attitudes toward them is usually accurate
    (B) Whether it is possible to assess individual supervisees' attitudes toward their supervisors without thereby changing those attitudes
    (C) Whether any of the leadership theories in question hold that leaders should assess other leaders' attitudes
    (D) Whether some types of groups do not need supervision in order to be successful in their endeavors
    (E) Whether individuals' attitudes toward supervisors affect group success

165. A major health insurance company in Lagolia pays for special procedures prescribed by physicians only if the procedure is first approved as "medically necessary" by a company-appointed review panel. The rule is intended to save the company the money it might otherwise spend on medically unnecessary procedures. The company has recently announced that in order to reduce its costs, it will abandon this rule.

    Which of the following, if true, provides the strongest justification for the company's decision?

    (A) Patients often register dissatisfaction with physicians who prescribe nothing for their ailments.
    (B) Physicians often prescribe special procedures that are helpful but not altogether necessary for the health of the patient.
    (C) The review process is expensive and practically always results in approval of the prescribed procedure.
    (D) The company's review process does not interfere with the prerogative of physicians, in cases where more than one effective procedure is available, to select the one they personally prefer.
    (E) The number of members of the company-appointed review panel who review a given procedure depends on the cost of the procedure.

166. Automobile ownership was rare in Sabresia as recently as 30 years ago, but with continuing growth of personal income there, automobile ownership has become steadily more common. Consequently, there are now far more automobiles on Sabresia's roads than there were 30 years ago, and the annual number of automobile accidents has increased significantly. Yet the annual number of deaths and injuries resulting from automobile accidents has not increased significantly.

Which of the following, if true, most helps to explain why deaths and injuries resulting from automobile accidents have not increased significantly?

(A) Virtually all of the improvements in Sabresia's roads that were required to accommodate increased traffic were completed more than ten years ago.

(B) With more and more people owning cars, the average number of passengers in a car on the road has dropped dramatically.

(C) The increases in traffic volume have been most dramatic on Sabresia's highways, where speeds are well above those of other roads.

(D) Because of a vigorous market in used cars, the average age of cars on the road has actually increased throughout the years of steady growth in automobile ownership.

(E) Automobile ownership is still much less common in Sabresia than it is in other countries.

167. A child learning to play the piano will not succeed unless the child has an instrument at home on which to practice. However, good-quality pianos, whether new or secondhand, are costly. Buying one is justified only if the child has the necessary talent and perseverance, which is precisely what one cannot know in advance. Consequently, parents should buy an inexpensive secondhand instrument at first and upgrade if and when the child's ability and inclination are proven.

Which of the following, if true, casts the most serious doubt on the course of action recommended for parents?

(A) Learners, particularly those with genuine musical talent, are apt to lose interest in the instrument if they have to play on a piano that fails to produce a pleasing sound.

(B) Reputable piano teachers do not accept children as pupils unless they know that the children can practice on a piano at home.

(C) Ideally, the piano on which a child practices at home should be located in a room away from family activities going on at the same time.

(D) Very young beginners often make remarkable progress at playing the piano at first, but then appear to stand still for a considerable period of time.

(E) In some parents, spending increasing amounts of money on having their children learn to play the piano produces increasing anxiety to hear immediate results.

168. Nutritionists are advising people to eat more fish, since the omega-3 fatty acids in fish help combat many diseases. If everyone took this advice, however, there would not be enough fish in oceans, rivers, and lakes to supply the demand; the oceans are already being overfished. The obvious method to ease the pressure on wild fish populations is for people to increase their consumption of farmed fish.

    Which of the following, if true, raises the most serious doubt concerning the prospects for success of the solution proposed above?

    (A) Aquaculture, or fish farming, raises more fish in a given volume of water than are generally present in the wild.

    (B) Some fish farming, particularly of shrimp and other shellfish, takes place in enclosures in the ocean.

    (C) There are large expanses of ocean waters that do not contain enough nutrients to support substantial fish populations.

    (D) The feed for farmed ocean fish is largely made from small wild-caught fish, including the young of many popular food species.

    (E) Some of the species that are now farmed extensively were not commonly eaten when they were only available in the wild.

169. Which of the following most logically completes the market forecaster's argument?

    Market forecaster: The price of pecans is high when pecans are comparatively scarce but drops sharply when pecans are abundant. Thus, in high-yield years, growers often store part of their crop in refrigerated warehouses until after the next year's harvest, hoping for higher prices then. Because of bad weather, this year's pecan crop will be very small. Nevertheless, pecan prices this year will not be significantly higher than last year, since _____.

    (A) the last time the pecan crop was as small as it was this year, the practice of holding back part of one year's crop had not yet become widely established

    (B) last year's pecan harvest was the largest in the last 40 years

    (C) pecan prices have remained relatively stable in recent years

    (D) pecan yields for some farmers were as high this year as they had been last year

    (E) the quality of this year's pecan crop is as high as the quality of any pecan crop in the previous five years

170. Which of the following most logically completes the reasoning?

    Either food scarcity or excessive hunting can threaten a population of animals. If the group faces food scarcity, individuals in the group will reach reproductive maturity later than otherwise. If the group faces excessive hunting, individuals that reach reproductive maturity earlier will come to predominate. Therefore, it should be possible to determine whether prehistoric mastodons became extinct because of food scarcity or human hunting, since there are fossilized mastodon remains from both before and after mastodon populations declined, and _____.

    (A) there are more fossilized mastodon remains from the period before mastodon populations began to decline than from after that period
    (B) the average age at which mastodons from a given period reached reproductive maturity can be established from their fossilized remains
    (C) it can be accurately estimated from fossilized remains when mastodons became extinct
    (D) it is not known when humans first began hunting mastodons
    (E) climate changes may have gradually reduced the food available to mastodons

171. Many office buildings designed to prevent outside air from entering have been shown to have elevated levels of various toxic substances circulating through the air inside, a phenomenon known as sick building syndrome. Yet the air in other office buildings does not have elevated levels of these substances, even though those buildings are the same age as the "sick" buildings and have similar designs and ventilation systems.

    Which of the following, if true, most helps to explain why not all office buildings designed to prevent outside air from entering have air that contains elevated levels of toxic substances?

    (A) Certain adhesives and drying agents used in particular types of furniture, carpets, and paint contribute the bulk of the toxic substances that circulate in the air of office buildings.
    (B) Most office buildings with sick building syndrome were built between 1950 and 1990.
    (C) Among buildings designed to prevent outside air from entering, houses are no less likely than office buildings to have air that contains elevated levels of toxic substances.
    (D) The toxic substances that are found in the air of "sick" office buildings are substances that are found in at least small quantities in nearly every building.
    (E) Office buildings with windows that can readily be opened are unlikely to suffer from sick building syndrome.

172. Newsletter: **A condominium generally offers more value for its cost than an individual house because of economies of scale.** The homeowners in a condominium association can collectively buy products and services that they could not afford on their own. And since a professional management company handles maintenance of common areas, **condominium owners spend less time and money on maintenance than individual homeowners do.**

    The two portions in **boldface** play which of the following roles in the newsletter's argument?

    (A) The first is the argument's main conclusion; the second is another conclusion supporting the first.
    (B) The first is a premise, for which no evidence is provided; the second is the argument's only conclusion.
    (C) The first is a conclusion supporting the second; the second is the argument's main conclusion.
    (D) The first is the argument's only conclusion; the second is a premise, for which no evidence is provided.
    (E) Both are premises, for which no evidence is provided, and both support the argument's only conclusion.

173. Platinum is a relatively rare metal vital to a wide variety of industries. Xagor Corporation, a major producer of platinum, has its production plant in a country that will soon begin imposing an export tax on platinum sold and shipped to customers abroad. As a consequence, the price of platinum on the world market is bound to rise.

    Which of the following, if true, tends to confirm the conclusion above?

    (A) An inexpensive substitute for platinum has been developed and will be available to industry for the first time this month.
    (B) The largest of the industries that depend on platinum reported a drop in sales last month.
    (C) The producers of platinum in other countries taken together cannot supply enough platinum to meet worldwide demand.
    (D) Xagor produced more platinum last month than in any previous month.
    (E) New deposits of platinum have been found in the country in which Xagor has its production plant.

174. From 1973 to 1986, growth in the United States economy was over 33 percent, while the percent growth in United States energy consumption was zero. The number of barrels of oil being saved per day by energy-efficiency improvements made since 1973 is now 13 million.

    If the information above is correct, which of the following conclusions can properly be drawn on the basis of it?

    (A) It is more difficult to find new sources of oil than to institute new energy-conservation measures.
    (B) Oil imports cannot be reduced unless energy consumption does not grow at all.
    (C) A reduction in the consumption of gasoline was the reason overall energy consumption remained steady.
    (D) It is possible for an economy to grow without consuming additional energy.
    (E) The development of nontraditional energy sources will make it possible for the United States economy to grow even faster.

175. Although many customers do not make a sufficient effort to conserve water, water companies must also be held responsible for wasteful consumption. Their own policies, in fact, encourage excessive water use, and attempts at conservation will succeed only if the water companies change their practices.

    Which of the following, if true, would most strongly support the view above?

    (A) Most water companies reduce the cost per unit of water as the amount of water used by a customer increases.
    (B) Most water companies keep detailed records of the quantity of water used by different customers.
    (C) Most water companies severely curtail the use of water during periods of drought.
    (D) Federal authorities limit the range of policies that can be enforced by the water companies.
    (E) The price per unit of water charged by the water companies has risen steadily in the last 10 years.

176. Despite legislation designed to stem the accumulation of plastic waste, the plastics industry continued to grow rapidly last year, as can be seen from the fact that sales of the resin that is the raw material for manufacturing plastics grew by 10 percent to $28 billion.

    In assessing the support provided by the evidence cited above for the statement that the plastics industry continued to grow, in addition to the information above it would be most useful to know

    (A) whether the resin has other uses besides the manufacture of plastics
    (B) the dollar amount of resin sales the year before last
    (C) the plastics industry's attitude toward the legislation concerning plastic waste
    (D) whether sales of all goods and services in the economy as a whole were increasing last year
    (E) what proportion of the plastics industry's output eventually contributes to the accumulation of plastic waste

177. Studies of the political orientations of 1,055 college students revealed that the plurality of students in an eastern, big-city, private university was liberal, whereas in a state-supported, southern college, the plurality was conservative. Orientations were independent of the student's region of origin, and the trends were much more pronounced in seniors than in beginning students.

    Which of the following hypotheses is best supported by the observations stated above?

    (A) The political orientations of college students are more similar to the political orientations of their parents when the students start college than when the students are seniors.
    (B) The political orientations of college seniors depend significantly on experiences they have had while in college.
    (C) A college senior originally from the South is more likely to be politically conservative than is a college senior originally from the East.
    (D) Whether their college is state-supported or private is the determining factor in college students' political orientations.
    (E) College students tend to become more conservative politically as they become older and are confronted with pressures for financial success.

178. Diabetics often suffer dangerously low blood sugar levels, which they can correct safely if they notice the symptoms quickly. It has been suggested that **diabetics should be advised to drink moderate amounts of coffee**, since doing so improves their ability to recognize symptoms of low blood sugar quickly. That would be bad advice, however, since drinking even small amounts of coffee can increase the body's need for sugar in unpredictable ways.

    In the argument being made, the part that is in **boldface** plays which of the following roles?

    (A) Presenting the conclusion toward which the argument as a whole is directed
    (B) Providing support for the conclusion of the argument
    (C) Offering a reason to take a course of action recommended in the argument
    (D) Stating the position to be refuted by the argument
    (E) Providing an instance of a general principle articulated in the argument

179. Trancorp currently transports all its goods to Burland Island by truck. The only bridge over the channel separating Burland from the mainland is congested, and trucks typically spend hours in traffic. Trains can reach the channel more quickly than trucks, and freight cars can be transported to Burland by barges that typically cross the channel in an hour. Therefore, to reduce shipping time, Trancorp plans to switch to trains and barges to transport goods to Burland.

    Which of the following, if true, casts the most serious doubt on whether Trancorp's plan will succeed?

    (A) It does not cost significantly more to transport goods to Burland by truck than it does to transport goods by train and barge.
    (B) The number of cars traveling over the bridge into Burland is likely to increase slightly over the next two years.
    (C) Because there has been so much traffic on the roads leading to the bridge between Burland and the mainland, these roads are in extremely poor condition.
    (D) Barges that arrive at Burland typically wait several hours for their turn to be unloaded.
    (E) Most trucks transporting goods into Burland return to the mainland empty.

180. When ducklings are exposed to music, they gain about 6 percent more weight for a given amount of feed than ducklings that are not exposed to music.

    Which of the following, if true, most helps to explain the extra weight gains referred to above?

    (A) Music played for ducklings must be kept at a low level because ducklings exposed to loud music gain less weight than ducklings exposed to no music.
    (B) Ducklings exposed to classical music gained more weight than ducklings exposed to popular music.
    (C) Ducklings are less active when they hear music, so that less of the food they eat is expended in movement and more contributes directly to the ducklings' growth.
    (D) When ducklings gain 6 percent more weight on a given amount of grain, the farmers' profits increase because they can spend less money on grain to feed the ducklings.
    (E) When female ducklings were exposed to music, the percentage of fertile eggs that they laid as adults increased by over 27 percent in comparison to ducklings not exposed to music.

181. X: In order to reduce the amount of plastic in landfills, legislatures should impose a ban on the use of plastics for packaging goods.

    Y: Impossible! Plastic packaging is necessary for public safety. Consumers will lose all of the safety features that plastic offers, chiefly tamper-resistant closures and shatterproof bottles.

    Which of the following best describes the weak point in Y's response to X's proposal?

    (A) Y ignores the possibility that packaging goods in materials other than plastic might provide the same safety features that packaging in plastic offers.

    (B) The economic disadvantages of using plastics as a means of packaging goods are not taken into consideration.

    (C) Y attempts to shift the blame for the large amount of plastic in landfills from the users of plastic packaging to the legislators.

    (D) Y does not consider the concern of some manufacturers that safety features spoil package appearances.

    (E) Y wrongly assumes that X defends the interests of the manufacturers rather than the interests of the consumers.

182. United Lumber will use trees from its forests for two products. The tree trunks will be used for lumber and the branches converted into wood chips to make fiberboard. The cost of this conversion would be the same whether done at the logging site, where the trees are debranched, or at United's factory. However, wood chips occupy less than half the volume of the branches from which they are made.

    The information given, if accurate, most strongly supports which of the following?

    (A) Converting the branches into wood chips at the logging site would require transporting a fully assembled wood-chipping machine to and from the site.

    (B) It would be more economical to debranch the trees at the factory where the fiberboard is manufactured.

    (C) The debranching of trees and the conversion of the branches into chips are the only stages in the processing of branches that would be in United's economic advantage to perform at the logging site.

    (D) Transportation costs from the logging site to the factory that are determined by volume of cargo would be lower if the conversion into chips is done at the logging site rather than at the factory.

    (E) In the wood-processing industry, branches are used only for the production of wood chips for fiberboard.

183. Which of the following most logically completes the passage?

For the past several years, a certain technology has been widely used to transmit data among networked computers. Recently, two data transmission companies, Aptron and Gammatech, have each developed separate systems that allow network data transmission at rates ten times faster than the current technology allows. Although the systems are similarly priced and are equally easy to use, Aptron's product is likely to dominate the market, because _____.

(A) Gammatech has been in the business of designing data transmission systems for several years more than Aptron has

(B) the number of small businesses that need computer networking systems is likely to double over the next few years

(C) it is much more likely that Gammatech's system will be expandable to meet future needs

(D) unlike many data transmission companies, Aptron and Gammatech develop computers in addition to data transmission systems

(E) it is easier for users of the current data transmission technology to switch to Aptron's product than to Gammatech's

184. In Brindon County, virtually all of the fasteners—such as nuts, bolts, and screws—used by workshops and manufacturing firms have for several years been supplied by the Brindon Bolt Barn, a specialist wholesaler. In recent months, many of Brindon County's workshops and manufacturing firms have closed down, and no new ones have opened. Therefore, the Brindon Bolt Barn will undoubtedly show a sharp decline in sales volume and revenue for this year as compared to last year.

The argument depends on assuming which of the following?

(A) Last year, the Brindon Bolt Barn's sales volume and revenue were significantly higher than they had been the previous year.

(B) The workshops and manufacturing firms that have remained open have a smaller volume of work to do this year than they did last year.

(C) Soon the Brindon Bolt Barn will no longer be the only significant supplier of fasteners to Brindon County's workshops.

(D) The Brindon Bolt Barn's operating expenses have not increased this year.

(E) The Brindon Bolt Barn is not a company that gets the great majority of its business from customers outside Brindon County.

185. Healthy lungs produce a natural antibiotic that protects them from infection by routinely killing harmful bacteria on airway surfaces. People with cystic fibrosis, however, are unable to fight off such bacteria, even though their lungs produce normal amounts of the antibiotic. The fluid on airway surfaces in the lungs of people with cystic fibrosis has an abnormally high salt concentration; accordingly, scientists hypothesize that the high salt concentration is what makes the antibiotic ineffective.

    Which of the following, if true, most strongly supports the scientists' hypothesis?

    (A) When the salt concentration of the fluid on the airway surfaces of healthy people is raised artificially, the salt concentration soon returns to normal.
    (B) A sample of the antibiotic was capable of killing bacteria in an environment with an unusually low concentration of salt.
    (C) When lung tissue from people with cystic fibrosis is maintained in a solution with a normal salt concentration, the tissue can resist bacteria.
    (D) Many lung infections can be treated by applying synthetic antibiotics to the airway surfaces.
    (E) High salt concentrations have an antibiotic effect in many circumstances.

186. Eurasian water milfoil, a weed not native to Frida Lake, has reproduced prolifically since being accidentally introduced there. In order to eliminate the weed, biologists proposed treating infested parts of the lake with a certain herbicide that is nontoxic for humans and aquatic animals. However, the herbicide might damage populations of certain rare plant species that the lake contains. For this reason, local officials rejected the proposal.

    Which of the following, if true, points out the most serious weakness in the officials' grounds for rejecting the biologists' proposal?

    (A) The continuing spread of Eurasian water milfoil in Frida Lake threatens to choke out the lake's rare plant species.
    (B) Because of ecological conditions prevailing in its native habitat, Eurasian water milfoil is not as dominant there as it is in Frida Lake.
    (C) The proliferation of Eurasian water milfoil in Frida Lake has led to reductions in the populations of some species of aquatic animals.
    (D) Although Eurasian water milfoil could be mechanically removed from Frida Lake, eliminating the weed would take far longer this way than it would using herbicides.
    (E) Unless Eurasian water milfoil is completely eliminated from Frida Lake, it will quickly spread again once herbicide treatments or other control measures cease.

187. Columnist: People should completely avoid using a certain artificial fat that has been touted as an alternative for those whose medical advisers have advised them to reduce their fat intake. The artificial fat can be used in place of ordinary fats in prepared foods and has none of the negative health effects of fat, but it does have a serious drawback: it absorbs certain essential vitamins, thereby preventing them from being used by the body.

    In evaluating the columnist's position, it would be most useful to determine which of the following?

    (A) Whether increasing one's intake of the vitamins can compensate for the effects of the artificial fat
    (B) Whether any of the vitamins that the artificial fat absorbs are destroyed by prolonged cooking
    (C) Whether having an extremely low fat intake for an extended period can endanger a person's health
    (D) Whether there are any foods that cannot be prepared using the artificial fat as a substitute for other fats
    (E) Whether people are generally able to detect differences in taste between foods prepared using the artificial fat and foods that are similar except for the use of other fats

Questions 188 to 235 — Difficulty: Medium

188. Donations of imported food will be distributed to children in famine-stricken countries in the form of free school meals. The process is efficient because the children are easy to reach at the schools and cooking facilities are often available on site.

    Which of the following, if true, casts the most serious doubt on the efficiency of the proposed process?

    (A) The emphasis on food will detract from the major function of the schools, which is to educate the children.
    (B) A massive influx of donated food will tend to lower the price of food in the areas near the schools.
    (C) Supplies of fuel needed for cooking at the schools arrive there only intermittently and in inadequate quantities.
    (D) The reduction in farm surpluses in donor countries benefits the donor countries to a greater extent than the recipient countries are benefited by the donations.
    (E) The donation of food tends to strengthen the standing of the political party that happens to be in power when the donation is made.

189. *John:* You told me once that no United States citizen who supports union labor should buy an imported car. Yet you are buying an Alma. Since Alma is one of the biggest makers of imports, I infer that you no longer support unions.

    Harry: I still support labor unions. Even though Alma is a foreign car company, the car I am buying, the Alma Deluxe, is designed, engineered, and manufactured in the United States.

    Harry's method of defending his purchase of an Alma is to

    (A) disown the principle he formerly held
    (B) show that John's argument involves a false unstated assumption
    (C) contradict John's conclusion without challenging John's reasoning in drawing that conclusion
    (D) point out that one of the statements John makes in support of his argument is false
    (E) claim that his is a special case in which the rule need not apply

190. Public-sector (government-owned) companies are often unprofitable and a drain on the taxpayer. Such enterprises should be sold to the private sector, where competition will force them either to be efficient and profitable or else to close.

    Which of the following, if true, identifies a flaw in the policy proposed above?

    (A) The revenue gained from the sale of public-sector companies is likely to be negligible compared to the cost of maintaining them.
    (B) By buying a public-sector company and then closing the company and selling its assets, a buyer can often make a profit.
    (C) The services provided by many public-sector companies must be made available to citizens, even when a price that covers costs cannot be charged.
    (D) Some unprofitable private-sector companies have become profitable after being taken over by the government to prevent their closing.
    (E) The costs of environmental protection, contributions to social programs, and job-safety measures are the same in the public and private sectors.

191. After receiving numerous complaints from residents about loud, highly amplified music played at local clubs, Middletown is considering a law that would prohibit clubs located in residential areas from employing musical groups that consist of more than three people.

    The likelihood that the law would be effective in reducing noise would be most seriously diminished if which of the following were true?

    (A) Groups that consist of more than three musicians are usually more expensive for clubs to hire than are groups that consist of fewer than three musicians.
    (B) In towns that have passed similar laws, many clubs in residential areas have relocated to nonresidential areas.
    (C) Most of the complaints about the music have come from people who do not regularly attend the clubs.
    (D) Much of the music popular at the local clubs can be played only by groups of at least four musicians.
    (E) Amplified music played by fewer than three musicians generally is as loud as amplified music played by more than three musicians.

192. From enlargements that are commonly found on the ulna bones of the forearms of Ice Age human skeletons, anthropologists have drawn the conclusion that the Ice Age humans represented by those skeletons frequently hunted by throwing spears. The bone enlargements, the anthropologists believe, resulted from the stresses of habitual throwing.

    Which of the following, if true, would be the LEAST appropriate to use as support for the conclusion drawn by the anthropologists?

    (A) Humans typically favor one arm over the other when throwing, and most Ice Age human skeletons have enlargements on the ulna bone of only one arm.

    (B) Such enlargements on the ulna bone do not appear on skeletons from other human cultures of the same time period whose diets are believed to have been mainly vegetarian.

    (C) Cave paintings dating from approximately the same time period and located not far from where the skeletons were found show hunters carrying and throwing spears.

    (D) Damaged bones in the skeletons show evidence of diseases that are believed to have afflicted most people living during the Ice Age.

    (E) Twentieth-century athletes who use a throwing motion similar to that of a hunter throwing a spear often develop enlargements on the ulna bone similar to those detected on the Ice Age skeletons.

193. The town council of North Tarrytown favored changing the name of the town to Sleepy Hollow. Council members argued that making the town's association with Washington Irving and his famous "legend" more obvious would increase tourism and result immediately in financial benefits for the town's inhabitants.

    The council members' argument requires the assumption that

    (A) most of the inhabitants would favor a change in the name of the town

    (B) many inhabitants would be ready to supply tourists with information about Washington Irving and his "legend"

    (C) the town can accomplish, at a very low cost per capita, the improvements in tourist facilities that an increase in tourism would require

    (D) other towns in the region have changed their names to reflect historical associations and have, as a result, experienced a rise in tourism

    (E) the immediate per capita cost to inhabitants of changing the name of the town would be less than the immediate per capita revenue they would receive from the change

194. Premature babies who receive regular massages are more active than premature babies who do not. Even when all the babies drink the same amount of milk, the massaged babies gain more weight than do the unmassaged babies. This is puzzling because a more active person generally requires a greater food intake to maintain or gain weight.

    Which of the following, if true, best reconciles the apparent discrepancy described above?

    (A) Increased activity leads to increased levels of hunger, especially when food intake is not also increased.
    (B) Massage increases premature babies' curiosity about their environment, and curiosity leads to increased activity.
    (C) Increased activity causes the intestines of premature babies to mature more quickly, enabling the babies to digest and absorb more of the nutrients in the milk they drink.
    (D) Massage does not increase the growth rate of babies over one year old, if the babies had not been previously massaged.
    (E) Premature babies require a daily intake of nutrients that is significantly higher than that required by babies who were not born prematurely.

195. In Australia, in years with below-average rainfall, less water goes into rivers and more water is extracted from rivers for drinking and irrigation. Consequently, in such years, water levels drop considerably and the rivers flow more slowly. Because algae grow better the more slowly the water in which they are growing moves, such years are generally beneficial to populations of algae. But, by contrast, populations of algae drop in periods of extreme drought.

    Which of the following, if true, does most to explain the contrast?

    (A) Algae grow better in ponds and lakes than in rivers.
    (B) The more slowly water moves, the more conducive its temperature is to the growth of algae.
    (C) Algae cannot survive in the absence of water.
    (D) Algae must be filtered out of water before it can be used for drinking.
    (E) The larger the population of algae in a body of water, the less sunlight reaches below the surface of the water.

196. Which of the following, if true, most logically completes the politician's argument?

    United States politician: Although the amount of United States goods shipped to Mexico doubled in the year after tariffs on trade between the two countries were reduced, it does not follow that the reduction in tariffs caused the sales of United States goods to companies and consumers in Mexico to double that year, because ____.

    (A) many of the United States companies that produced goods that year had competitors based in Mexico that had long produced the same kind of goods
    (B) most of the increase in goods shipped by United States companies to Mexico was in parts shipped to the companies' newly relocated subsidiaries for assembly and subsequent shipment back to the United States
    (C) marketing goods to a previously unavailable group of consumers is most successful when advertising specifically targets those consumers, but developing such advertising often takes longer than a year
    (D) the amount of Mexican goods shipped to the United States remained the same as it had been before the tariff reductions
    (E) there was no significant change in the employment rate in either of the countries that year

197. Budget constraints have made police officials consider reassigning a considerable number of officers from traffic enforcement to work on higher-priority, serious crimes. Reducing traffic enforcement for this reason would be counterproductive, however, in light of the tendency of criminals to use cars when engaged in the commission of serious crimes. An officer stopping a car for a traffic violation can make a search that turns up evidence of serious crime.

    Which of the following, if true, most strengthens the argument given?

    (A) An officer who stops a car containing evidence of the commission of a serious crime risks a violent confrontation, even if the vehicle was stopped only for a traffic violation.
    (B) When the public becomes aware that traffic enforcement has lessened, it typically becomes lax in obeying traffic rules.
    (C) Those willing to break the law to commit serious crimes are often in committing such crimes unwilling to observe what they regard as the lesser constraints of traffic law.
    (D) The offenders committing serious crimes who would be caught because of traffic violations are not the same group of individuals as those who would be caught if the arresting officers were reassigned from traffic enforcement.
    (E) The great majority of persons who are stopped by officers for traffic violations are not guilty of any serious crimes.

198. Conventional wisdom suggests vaccinating elderly people first in flu season, because they are at greatest risk of dying if they contract the virus. This year's flu virus poses particular risk to elderly people and almost none at all to younger people, particularly children. Nevertheless, health professionals are recommending vaccinating children first against the virus rather than elderly people.

    Which of the following, if true, provides the strongest reason for the health professionals' recommendation?

    (A) Children are vulnerable to dangerous infections when their immune systems are severely weakened by other diseases.
    (B) Children are particularly unconcerned with hygiene and therefore are the group most responsible for spreading the flu virus to others.
    (C) The vaccinations received last year will confer no immunity to this year's flu virus.
    (D) Children who catch one strain of the flu virus and then recover are likely to develop immunity to at least some strains with which they have not yet come in contact.
    (E) Children are no more likely than adults to have immunity to a particular flu virus if they have never lived through a previous epidemic of the same virus.

199. Pro-Tect Insurance Company has recently been paying out more on car-theft claims than it expected. Cars with special antitheft devices or alarm systems are much less likely to be stolen than are other cars. Consequently Pro-Tect, as part of an effort to reduce its annual payouts, will offer a discount to holders of car-theft policies if their cars have antitheft devices or alarm systems.

    Which of the following, if true, provides the strongest indication that the plan is likely to achieve its goal?

    (A) The decrease in the risk of car theft conferred by having a car alarm is greatest when only a few cars have such alarms.
    (B) The number of policyholders who have filed a claim in the past year is higher for Pro-Tect than for other insurance companies.
    (C) In one or two years, the discount that Pro-Tect is offering will amount to more than the cost of buying certain highly effective antitheft devices.
    (D) Currently, Pro-Tect cannot legally raise the premiums it charges for a given amount of insurance against car theft.
    (E) The amount Pro-Tect has been paying out on car-theft claims has been greater for some models of car than for others.

200. While the total enrollment of public elementary and secondary schools in Sondland is one percent higher this academic year than last academic year, the number of teachers there increased by three percent. Thus, the Sondland Education Commission's prediction of a teacher shortage as early as next academic year is unfounded.

Which of the following, if true, most seriously weakens the claim that the prediction of a teacher shortage as early as next academic year is unfounded?

(A) Funding for public elementary schools in Sondland is expected to increase over the next ten years.

(B) Average salaries for Sondland's teachers increased at the rate of inflation from last academic year to this academic year.

(C) A new law has mandated that there be ten percent more teachers per pupil in Sondland's public schools next academic year than there were this academic year.

(D) In the past, increases in enrollments in public elementary and secondary schools in Sondland have generally been smaller than increases in the number of teachers.

(E) Because of reductions in funding, the number of students enrolling in teacher-training programs in Sondland is expected to decline beginning in the next academic year.

201. Art restorers who have been studying the factors that cause Renaissance oil paintings to deteriorate physically when subject to climatic changes have found that the oil paint used in these paintings actually adjusts to these changes well. The restorers therefore hypothesize that it is a layer of material called gesso, which is under the paint, that causes the deterioration.

Which of the following, if true, most strongly supports the restorers' hypothesis?

(A) Renaissance oil paintings with a thin layer of gesso are less likely to show deterioration in response to climatic changes than those with a thicker layer.

(B) Renaissance oil paintings are often painted on wooden panels, which swell when humidity increases and contract when it declines.

(C) Oil paint expands and contracts readily in response to changes in temperature, but it absorbs little water and so is little affected by changes in humidity.

(D) An especially hard and nonabsorbent type of gesso was the raw material for moldings on the frames of Renaissance oil paintings.

(E) Gesso layers applied by Renaissance painters typically consisted of a coarse base layer onto which several increasingly fine-grained layers were applied.

202. A newly discovered painting seems to be the work of one of two 17th-century artists, either the northern German Johannes Drechen or the Frenchman Louis Birelle, who sometimes painted in the same style as Drechen. Analysis of the carved picture frame, which has been identified as the painting's original 17th-century frame, showed that it is made of wood found widely in northern Germany at the time, but rare in the part of France where Birelle lived. This shows that the painting is most likely the work of Drechen.

Which of the following is an assumption that the argument requires?

(A) The frame was made from wood local to the region where the picture was painted.

(B) Drechen is unlikely to have ever visited the home region of Birelle in France.

(C) Sometimes a painting so closely resembles others of its era that no expert is able to confidently decide who painted it.

(D) The painter of the picture chose the frame for the picture.

(E) The carving style of the picture frame is not typical of any specific region of Europe.

203. Archaeologists working in the Andes Mountains recently excavated a buried 4,000-year-old temple containing structures that align with a stone carving on a distant hill to indicate the direction of the rising sun at the summer solstice. Alignments in the temple were also found to point toward the position, at the summer solstice, of a constellation known in Andean culture as the Fox. Since the local mythology represents the fox as teaching people how to cultivate and irrigate plants, the ancient Andeans may have built the temple as a religious representation of the fox.

Which of the following is an assumption on which the argument is based?

(A) The constellation known as the Fox has the same position at the summer solstice as it did 4,000 years ago.

(B) In the region around the temple, the summer solstice marks the time for planting.

(C) The temple was protected from looters by dirt and debris built up over thousands of years.

(D) Other structural alignments at the temple point to further constellations with agricultural significance.

(E) The site containing the temple was occupied for a significant amount of time before abandonment.

204. Meat from chickens contaminated with salmonella bacteria can cause serious food poisoning. Capsaicin, the chemical that gives chili peppers their hot flavor, has antibacterial properties. Chickens do not have taste receptors for capsaicin and will readily eat feed laced with capsaicin. When chickens were fed such feed and then exposed to salmonella bacteria, relatively few of them became contaminated with salmonella.

    In deciding whether the feed would be useful in raising salmonella-free chicken for retail sale, it would be most helpful to determine which of the following?

    (A) Whether feeding capsaicin to chickens affects the taste of their meat
    (B) Whether eating capsaicin reduces the risk of salmonella poisoning for humans
    (C) Whether chicken is more prone to salmonella contamination than other kinds of meat
    (D) Whether appropriate cooking of chicken contaminated with salmonella can always prevent food poisoning
    (E) Whether capsaicin can be obtained only from chili peppers

205. Which of the following most logically completes the argument below?

    When mercury-vapor streetlights are used in areas inhabited by insect-eating bats, the bats feed almost exclusively around the lights, because the lights attract flying insects. In Greenville, the mercury-vapor streetlights are about to be replaced with energy-saving sodium streetlights, which do not attract insects. This change is likely to result in a drop in the population of insect-eating bats in Greenville, since _____.

    (A) the bats do not begin to hunt until after sundown
    (B) the bats are unlikely to feed on insects that do not fly
    (C) the highway department will be able to replace mercury-vapor streetlights with sodium streetlights within a relatively short time and without disrupting the continuity of lighting at the locations of the streetlights
    (D) in the absence of local concentrations of the flying insects on which bats feed, the bats expend much more energy on hunting for food, requiring much larger quantities of insects to sustain each bat
    (E) bats use echolocation to catch insects and therefore gain no advantage from the fact that insects flying in the vicinity of streetlights are visible at night

206. Rats injected with morphine exhibit decreased activity of the immune system, the bodily system that fights off infections. These same rats exhibited heightened blood levels of corticosteroids, chemicals secreted by the adrenal glands. Since corticosteroids can interfere with immune-system activity, scientists hypothesized that the way morphine reduces immune responses in rats is by stimulating the adrenal glands to secrete additional corticosteroids into the bloodstream.

Which of the following experiments would yield the most useful results for evaluating the scientists' hypothesis?

(A) Injecting morphine into rats that already have heightened blood levels of corticosteroids and then observing their new blood levels of corticosteroids

(B) Testing the level of immune-system activity of rats, removing their adrenal glands, and then testing the rats' immune-system activity levels again

(C) Injecting rats with corticosteroids and then observing how many of the rats contracted infections

(D) Removing the adrenal glands of rats, injecting the rats with morphine, and then testing the level of the rats' immune-system responses

(E) Injecting rats with a drug that stimulates immune-system activity and then observing the level of corticosteroids in their bloodstreams

207. Curator: If our museum lends *Venus* to the Hart Institute for their show this spring, they will lend us their Rembrandt etchings for our print exhibition next fall. Having those etchings will increase attendance to the exhibition and hence increase revenue from our general admission fee.

Museum Administrator: But *Venus* is our biggest attraction. Moreover the Hart's show will run for twice as long as our exhibition. So on balance the number of patrons may decrease.

The point of the administrator's response to the curator is to question

(A) whether getting the Rembrandt etchings from the Hart Institute is likely to increase attendance at the print exhibition

(B) whether the Hart Institute's Rembrandt etchings will be appreciated by those patrons of the curator's museum for whom the museum's biggest attraction is *Venus*

(C) whether the number of patrons attracted by the Hart Institute's Rembrandt etchings will be larger than the number of patrons who do not come in the spring because *Venus* is on loan

(D) whether, if *Venus* is lent, the museum's revenue from general admission fees during the print exhibition will exceed its revenue from general admission fees during the Hart Institute's exhibition

(E) whether the Hart Institute or the curator's museum will have the greater financial gain from the proposed exchange of artworks

208. Which of the following most logically completes the passage?

Leaf beetles damage willow trees by stripping away their leaves, but a combination of parasites and predators generally keeps populations of these beetles in check. Researchers have found that severe air pollution results in reduced predator populations. The parasites, by contrast, are not adversely affected by pollution; nevertheless, the researchers' discovery probably does explain why leaf beetles cause particularly severe damage to willows in areas with severe air pollution, since _____.

(A) neither the predators nor the parasites of leaf beetles themselves attack willow trees

(B) the parasites that attack leaf beetles actually tend to be more prevalent in areas with severe air pollution than they are elsewhere

(C) the damage caused by leaf beetles is usually not enough to kill a willow tree outright

(D) where air pollution is not especially severe, predators have much more impact on leaf-beetle populations than parasites do

(E) willows often grow in areas where air pollution is especially severe

209. On May first, in order to reduce the number of overdue books, a children's library instituted a policy of forgiving fines and giving bookmarks to children returning all of their overdue books. On July first there were twice as many overdue books as there had been on May first, although a record number of books had been returned during the interim.

Which of the following, if true, most helps to explain the apparent inconsistency in the results of the library's policy?

(A) The librarians did not keep accurate records of how many children took advantage of the grace period, and some of the children returning overdue books did not return all of their overdue books.

(B) Although the grace period enticed some children to return all of their overdue books, it did not convince all of the children with overdue books to return all of their books.

(C) The bookmarks became popular among the children, so in order to collect the bookmarks, many children borrowed many more books than they usually did and kept them past their due date.

(D) The children were allowed to borrow a maximum of five books for a two-week period, and hence each child could keep a maximum of fifteen books beyond their due date within a two-month period.

(E) Although the library forgave overdue fines during the grace period, the amount previously charged the children was minimal; hence, the forgiveness of the fines did not provide enough incentive for them to return their overdue books.

210. A certain species of desert lizard digs tunnels in which to lay its eggs. The eggs must incubate inside the tunnel for several weeks before hatching, and they fail to hatch if they are disturbed at any time during this incubation period. Yet these lizards guard their tunnels for only a few days after laying their eggs.

    Which of the following, if true, most helps explain why there is no need for lizards to guard their tunnels for more than a few days?

    (A) The eggs are at risk of being disturbed only during the brief egg-laying season when many lizards are digging in a relatively small area.

    (B) The length of the incubation period varies somewhat from one tunnel to another.

    (C) Each female lizard lays from 15 to 20 eggs, only about 10 of which hatch even if the eggs are not disturbed at any time during the incubation period.

    (D) The temperature and humidity within the tunnels will not be suitable for the incubating eggs unless the tunnels are plugged with sand immediately after the eggs are laid.

    (E) The only way to disturb the eggs of this lizard species is by opening up one of the tunnels in which they are laid.

211. Most banks that issue credit cards charge interest rates on credit card debt that are ten percentage points higher than the rates those banks charge for ordinary consumer loans. These banks' representatives claim the difference is fully justified, since it simply covers the difference between the costs to these banks associated with credit card debt and those associated with consumer loans.

    Which of the following, if true, most seriously calls into question the reasoning offered by the banks' representatives?

    (A) Some lenders that are not banks offer consumer loans at interest rates that are even higher than most banks charge on credit card debt.

    (B) Most car rental companies require that their customers provide signed credit card charge slips or security deposits.

    (C) Two to three percent of the selling price of every item bought with a given credit card goes to the bank that issued that credit card.

    (D) Most people need not use credit cards to buy everyday necessities, but could buy those necessities with cash or pay by check.

    (E) People who pay their credit card bills in full each month usually pay no interest on the amounts they charge.

212. Often patients with ankle fractures that are stable, and thus do not require surgery, are given follow-up x-rays because their orthopedists are concerned about possibly having misjudged the stability of the fracture. When a number of follow-up x-rays were reviewed, however, all the fractures that had initially been judged stable were found to have healed correctly. Therefore, it is a waste of money to order follow-up x-rays of ankle fractures initially judged stable.

Which of the following, if true, most strengthens the argument?

(A) Doctors who are general practitioners rather than orthopedists are less likely than orthopedists to judge the stability of an ankle fracture correctly.

(B) Many ankle injuries for which an initial x-ray is ordered are revealed by the x-ray not to involve any fracture of the ankle.

(C) X-rays of patients of many different orthopedists working in several hospitals were reviewed.

(D) The healing of ankle fractures that have been surgically repaired is always checked by means of a follow-up x-ray.

(E) Orthopedists routinely order follow-up x-rays for fractures of bones other than ankle bones.

213. In setting environmental standards for industry and others to meet, it is inadvisable to require the best results that state-of-the-art technology can achieve. Current technology is able to detect and eliminate even extremely minute amounts of contaminants, but at a cost that is exorbitant relative to the improvement achieved. So it would be reasonable instead to set standards by taking into account all of the current and future risks involved.

The argument given concerning the reasonable way to set standards presupposes that

(A) industry currently meets the standards that have been set by environmental authorities

(B) there are effective ways to take into account all of the relevant risks posed by allowing different levels of contaminants

(C) the only contaminants worth measuring are generated by industry

(D) it is not costly to prevent large amounts of contaminants from entering the environment

(E) minute amounts of some contaminants can be poisonous

214. The chemical adenosine is released by brain cells when those cells are active. Adenosine then binds to more and more sites on cells in certain areas of the brain, as the total amount released gradually increases during wakefulness. During sleep, the number of sites to which adenosine is bound decreases. Some researchers have hypothesized that it is the cumulative binding of adenosine to a large number of sites that causes the onset of sleep.

Which of the following, if true, provides the most support for the researchers' hypothesis?

(A) Even after long periods of sleep when adenosine is at its lowest concentration in the brain, the number of brain cells bound with adenosine remains very large.

(B) Caffeine, which has the effect of making people remain wakeful, is known to interfere with the binding of adenosine to sites on brain cells.

(C) Besides binding to sites in the brain, adenosine is known to be involved in biochemical reactions throughout the body.

(D) Some areas of the brain that are relatively inactive nonetheless release some adenosine.

(E) Stress resulting from a dangerous situation can preserve wakefulness even when brain levels of bound adenosine are high.

215. A two-year study beginning in 1977 found that, among 85-year-old people, those whose immune systems were weakest were twice as likely to die within two years as others in the study. The cause of their deaths, however, was more often heart disease, against which the immune system does not protect, than cancer or infections, which are attacked by the immune system.

Which of the following, if true, would offer the best prospects for explaining deaths in which weakness of the immune system, though present, played no causal role?

(A) There were twice as many infections among those in the study with the weakest immune systems as among those with the strongest immune systems.

(B) The majority of those in the study with the strongest immune systems died from infection or cancer by 1987.

(C) Some of the drugs that had been used to treat the symptoms of heart disease had a side effect of weakening the immune system.

(D) Most of those in the study who survived beyond the two-year period had recovered from a serious infection sometime prior to 1978.

(E) Those in the study who survived into the 1980s had, in 1976, strengthened their immune systems through drug therapy.

216. Most scholars agree that King Alfred (A.D. 849–899) personally translated a number of Latin texts into Old English. One historian contends that Alfred also personally penned his own law code, arguing that the numerous differences between the language of the law code and Alfred's translations of Latin texts are outweighed by the even more numerous similarities. Linguistic similarities, however, are what one expects in texts from the same language, the same time, and the same region. Apart from Alfred's surviving translations and law code, there are only two other extant works from the same dialect and milieu, so it is risky to assume here that linguistic similarities point to common authorship.

The passage above proceeds by

(A) providing examples that underscore another argument's conclusion

(B) questioning the plausibility of an assumption on which another argument depends

(C) showing that a principle if generally applied would have anomalous consequences

(D) showing that the premises of another argument are mutually inconsistent

(E) using argument by analogy to undermine a principle implicit in another argument

217. Parland's alligator population has been declining in recent years, primarily because of hunting. Alligators prey heavily on a species of freshwater fish that is highly valued as food by Parlanders, who had hoped that the decline in the alligator population would lead to an increase in the numbers of these fish available for human consumption. Yet the population of this fish species has also declined, even though the annual number caught for human consumption has not increased.

    Which of the following, if true, most helps to explain the decline in the population of the fish species?

    (A) The decline in the alligator population has meant that fishers can work in some parts of lakes and rivers that were formerly too dangerous.

    (B) Over the last few years, Parland's commercial fishing enterprises have increased the number of fishing boats they use.

    (C) Many Parlanders who hunt alligators do so because of the high market price of alligator skins, not because of the threat alligators pose to the fish population.

    (D) During Parland's dry season, holes dug by alligators remain filled with water long enough to provide a safe place for the eggs of this fish species to hatch.

    (E) In several neighboring countries through which Parland's rivers also flow, alligators are at risk of extinction as a result of extensive hunting.

218. A company plans to develop a prototype weeding machine that uses cutting blades with optical sensors and microprocessors that distinguish weeds from crop plants by differences in shade of color. The inventor of the machine claims that it will reduce labor costs by virtually eliminating the need for manual weeding.

    Which of the following is a consideration in favor of the company's implementing its plan to develop the prototype?

    (A) There is a considerable degree of variation in shade of color between weeds of different species.

    (B) The shade of color of some plants tends to change appreciably over the course of their growing season.

    (C) When crops are weeded manually, overall size and leaf shape are taken into account in distinguishing crop plants from weeds.

    (D) Selection and genetic manipulation allow plants of virtually any species to be economically bred to have a distinctive shade of color without altering their other characteristics.

    (E) Farm laborers who are responsible for the manual weeding of crops carry out other agricultural duties at times in the growing season when extensive weeding is not necessary.

219. Aroca City currently funds its public schools through taxes on property. **In place of this system, the city plans to introduce a sales tax of 3 percent on all retail sales in the city.** Critics protest that 3 percent of current retail sales falls short of the amount raised for schools by property taxes. The critics are correct on this point. **Nevertheless, implementing the plan will probably not reduce the money going to Aroca's schools.** Several large retailers have selected Aroca City as the site for huge new stores, and these are certain to draw large numbers of shoppers from neighboring municipalities, where sales are taxed at rates of 6 percent and more. In consequence, retail sales in Aroca City are bound to increase substantially.

In the argument given, the two portions in **boldface** play which of the following roles?

(A) The first presents a plan that the argument concludes is unlikely to achieve its goal; the second expresses that conclusion.

(B) The first presents a plan that the argument concludes is unlikely to achieve its goal; the second presents evidence in support of that conclusion.

(C) The first presents a plan that the argument contends is the best available; the second is a conclusion drawn by the argument to justify that contention.

(D) The first presents a plan one of whose consequences is at issue in the argument; the second is the argument's conclusion about that consequence.

(E) The first presents a plan that the argument seeks to defend against a certain criticism; the second is that criticism.

220. Which of the following most logically completes the argument?

A photograph of the night sky was taken with the camera shutter open for an extended period. The normal motion of stars across the sky caused the images of the stars in the photograph to appear as streaks. However, one bright spot was not streaked. Even if the spot were caused, as astronomers believe, by a celestial object, that object could still have been moving across the sky during the time the shutter was open, since _____.

(A) the spot was not the brightest object in the photograph

(B) the photograph contains many streaks that astronomers can identify as caused by noncelestial objects

(C) stars in the night sky do not appear to shift position relative to each other

(D) the spot could have been caused by an object that emitted a flash that lasted for only a fraction of the time that the camera shutter was open

(E) if the camera shutter had not been open for an extended period, it would have recorded substantially fewer celestial objects

221. Economist: Paying extra for fair-trade coffee—coffee labeled with the Fairtrade logo—is intended to help poor farmers, because they receive a higher price for the fair-trade coffee they grow. But this practice may hurt more farmers in developing nations than it helps. By raising average prices for coffee, it encourages more coffee to be produced than consumers want to buy. This lowers prices for non-fair-trade coffee and thus lowers profits for non-fair-trade coffee farmers.

    To evaluate the strength of the economist's argument, it would be most helpful to know which of the following?

    (A) Whether there is a way of alleviating the impact of the increased average prices for coffee on non-fair-trade coffee farmers' profits
    (B) What proportion of coffee farmers in developing nations produce fair-trade coffee
    (C) Whether many coffee farmers in developing nations also derive income from other kinds of farming
    (D) Whether consumers should pay extra for fair-trade coffee if doing so lowers profits for non-fair-trade coffee farmers
    (E) How fair-trade coffee farmers in developing nations could be helped without lowering profits for non-fair-trade coffee farmers

222. Since smoking-related illnesses are a serious health problem in Country X, and since addiction to nicotine prevents many people from quitting smoking, the government of Country X plans to reduce the maximum allowable quantity of nicotine per cigarette by half over the next five years. However, reducing the quantity of nicotine per cigarette will probably cause people addicted to nicotine to smoke more cigarettes. Therefore, implementing this plan is unlikely to reduce the incidence of smoking-related illnesses.

    Which of the following, if true, most strongly supports the argument about the consequences of implementing the Country X government's plan?

    (A) Over half of the nonsmoking adults in Country X have smoked cigarettes in the past.
    (B) If the Country X government's plan is implemented, the brands of cigarettes sold in Country X will differ less from each other than they do now in terms of their nicotine content.
    (C) Inexpensive, smoke-free sources of nicotine, such as nicotine gum and nicotine skin patches, have recently become available in Country X.
    (D) Many smokers in Country X already spend a large proportion of their disposable income on cigarettes.
    (E) The main cause of smoking-related illnesses is not nicotine but the tar in cigarette smoke.

223. In 1983, Argonia's currency, the argon, underwent a reduction in value relative to the world's strongest currencies. This reduction resulted in a significant increase in Argonia's exports over 1982 levels. In 1987, a similar reduction in the value of the argon led to another increase in Argonia's exports. Faced with the need to increase exports yet again, Argonia's finance minister has proposed another reduction in the value of the argon.

Which of the following, if true, most strongly supports the prediction that the finance minister's plan will NOT result in a significant increase in Argonia's exports next year?

(A) The value of the argon rose sharply last year against the world's strongest currencies.

(B) In 1988, the argon lost a small amount of its value, and Argonian exports rose slightly in 1989.

(C) The value of Argonia's exports was lower last year than it was the year before.

(D) All of Argonia's export products are made by factories that were operating at full capacity last year, and new factories would take years to build.

(E) Reductions in the value of the argon have almost always led to significant reductions in the amount of goods and services that Argonians purchase from abroad.

224. Transnational cooperation among corporations is experiencing a modest resurgence among United States firms, even though projects undertaken by two or more corporations under a collaborative agreement are less profitable than projects undertaken by a single corporation. The advantage of transnational cooperation is that such joint international projects may allow United States firms to win foreign contracts that they would not otherwise be able to win.

Which of the following is information provided by the passage?

(A) Transnational cooperation involves projects too big for a single corporation to handle.

(B) Transnational cooperation results in a pooling of resources leading to high-quality performance.

(C) Transnational cooperation has in the past been both more common and less common than it is now among United States firms.

(D) Joint projects between United States and foreign corporations are not profitable enough to be worth undertaking.

(E) Joint projects between United States and foreign corporations benefit only those who commission the projects.

225. In many corporations, employees are being replaced by automated equipment in order to save money. However, many workers who lose their jobs to automation will need government assistance to survive, and the same corporations that are laying people off will eventually pay for that assistance through increased taxes and unemployment insurance payments.

Which of the following, if true, most strengthens the author's argument?

(A) Many workers who have already lost their jobs to automation have been unable to find new jobs.

(B) Many corporations that have failed to automate have seen their profits decline.

(C) Taxes and unemployment insurance are also paid by corporations that are not automating.

(D) Most of the new jobs created by automation pay less than the jobs eliminated by automation did.

(E) The initial investment in machinery for automation is often greater than the short-term savings in labor costs.

226. Theatergoer: In January of last year, the Megaplex chain of movie theaters started popping its popcorn in canola oil instead of the less healthful coconut oil that it had been using until then. Now Megaplex is planning to switch back, saying that the change has hurt popcorn sales. That claim is false, however, since according to Megaplex's own sales figures, Megaplex sold 5 percent more popcorn last year than in the previous year.

Which of the following, if true, most seriously weakens the theatergoer's argument?

(A) When it switched from using coconut oil to using canola oil, Megaplex made sure that the chain received a great deal of publicity stressing the health benefits of the change.

(B) Megaplex makes more money on food and beverages sold at its theaters than it does on sales of movie tickets.

(C) In a survey to determine public response to the change to canola oil, very few of Megaplex's customers said that the change had affected their popcorn-buying habits.

(D) Total sales of all food and beverage items at Megaplex's movie theaters increased by less than 5 percent last year.

(E) Total attendance at Megaplex's movie theaters was more than 20 percent higher last year than the year before.

227. Temporary-services firms supply trained workers to other companies on a temporary basis. Temporary-services firms lose business when the economy shows signs of beginning to weaken. They gain business when the economy begins to recover but often lose business again when the economy stabilizes. These firms have begun to gain business in the present weak economy. The economy therefore must be beginning to recover.

Which of the following is an assumption on which the argument depends?

(A) Temporary-services firms are more likely to regain old clients than to acquire new ones when the economy begins to recover.

(B) Temporary-services firms do not gain business when an already weak economy worsens.

(C) New companies do not often hire temporary help until they have been in business for some time.

(D) Companies that use workers from temporary-services firms seldom hire those workers to fill permanent positions.

(E) Temporary-services firms can most easily find qualified new workers when the economy is at its weakest.

228. Wolves generally avoid human settlements. For this reason, domestic sheep, though essentially easy prey for wolves, are not usually attacked by them. In Hylantia prior to 1910, farmers nevertheless lost considerable numbers of sheep to wolves each year. Attributing this to the large number of wolves, in 1910, the government began offering rewards to hunters for killing wolves. From 1910 to 1915, large numbers of wolves were killed. Yet wolf attacks on sheep increased significantly.

Which of the following, if true, most helps to explain the increase in wolf attacks on sheep?

(A) Populations of deer and other wild animals that wolves typically prey on increased significantly in numbers from 1910 to 1915.

(B) Prior to 1910, there were no legal restrictions in Hylantia on the hunting of wolves.

(C) After 1910, hunters shot and wounded a substantial number of wolves, thereby greatly diminishing these wolves' ability to prey on wild animals.

(D) Domestic sheep are significantly less able than most wild animals to defend themselves against wolf attacks.

(E) The systematic hunting of wolves encouraged by the program drove many wolves in Hylantia to migrate to remote mountain areas uninhabited by humans.

229. Paint on a new airliner is usually applied in two stages: first, a coat of primer, and then a top coat. A new process requires no primer, but instead uses two layers of the same newly developed coating, with each layer of the new coating having the same thickness and weight as a traditional top coat. Using the new process instead of the old process increases the price of a new aircraft considerably.

Which of the following, if true, most strongly indicates that it is in an airline's long-term economic interest to purchase new airliners painted using the new process rather than the old process?

(A) Although most new airliners are still painted using the old process, aircraft manufacturers now offer a purchaser of any new airliner the option of having it painted using the new process instead.

(B) A layer of primer on an airliner weighs more than a layer of the new coating would by an amount large enough to make a difference to that airliner's load-bearing capacity.

(C) A single layer of the new coating provides the aluminum skin of the airliner with less protection against corrosion than does a layer of primer of the usual thickness.

(D) Unlike the old process, the new process was originally invented for use on spacecraft, which are subject to extremes of temperature to which airliners are never exposed.

(E) Because the new coating has a viscosity similar to that of a traditional top coat, aircraft manufacturers can apply it using the same equipment as is used for a traditional top coat.

230. Unless tiger hunting decreases, tigers will soon be extinct in the wild. The countries in which the tigers' habitats are located are currently debating joint legislation that would ban tiger hunting. Thus, if these countries can successfully enforce this legislation, the survival of tigers in the wild will be ensured.

The reasoning in the argument is most vulnerable to criticism on the grounds that the argument

(A) assumes without sufficient warrant that a ban on tiger hunting could be successfully enforced

(B) considers the effects of hunting on tigers without also considering the effects of hunting on other endangered animal species

(C) fails to take into account how often tiger hunters are unsuccessful in their attempts to kill tigers

(D) neglects to consider the results of governmental attempts in the past to limit tiger hunting

(E) takes the removal of an impediment to the tigers' survival as a guarantee of their survival

231. Because of steep increases in the average price per box of cereal over the last 10 years, overall sales of cereal have recently begun to drop. In an attempt to improve sales, one major cereal manufacturer reduced the wholesale prices of its cereals by 20 percent. Since most other cereal manufacturers have announced that they will follow suit, it is likely that the level of overall sales of cereal will rise significantly.

Which of the following would it be most useful to establish in evaluating the argument?

(A) Whether the high marketing expenses of the highly competitive cereal market led to the increase in cereal prices

(B) Whether cereal manufacturers use marketing techniques that encourage brand loyalty among consumers

(C) Whether the variety of cereals available on the market has significantly increased over the last 10 years

(D) Whether the prices that supermarkets charge for these cereals will reflect the lower prices the supermarkets will be paying the manufacturers

(E) Whether the sales of certain types of cereal have declined disproportionately over the last 10 years

232. Crowding on Mooreville's subway frequently leads to delays, because it is difficult for passengers to exit from the trains. Over the next ten years, the Mooreville Transit Authority projects that subway ridership will increase by 20 percent. The authority plans to increase the number of daily train trips by only 5 percent over the same period. Officials predict that this increase is sufficient to ensure that the incidence of delays due to crowding does not increase.

Which of the following, if true, provides the strongest grounds for the officials' prediction?

(A) The population of Mooreville is not expected to increase significantly in the next ten years.

(B) The Transit Authority also plans a 5 percent increase in the number of bus trips on routes that connect to subways.

(C) The Transit Authority projects that the number of Mooreville residents who commute to work by automobile will increase in the next ten years.

(D) Most of the projected increase in ridership is expected to occur in off-peak hours when trains now are sparsely used.

(E) The 5 percent increase in the number of train trips can be achieved without an equal increase in Transit Authority operational costs.

233. Though sucking zinc lozenges has been promoted as a treatment for the common cold, research has revealed no consistent effect. Recently, however, a zinc gel applied nasally has been shown to greatly reduce the duration of colds. Since the gel contains zinc in the same form and concentration as the lozenges, the greater effectiveness of the gel must be due to the fact that cold viruses tend to concentrate in the nose, not the mouth.

Which of the following, if true, most seriously weakens the argument?

(A) Experimental subjects who used the zinc gel not only had colds of shorter duration but also had less severe symptoms than did those who used a gel that did not contain zinc.

(B) The mechanism by which zinc affects the viruses that cause the common cold has not been conclusively established.

(C) To make them palatable, zinc lozenges generally contain other ingredients, such as citric acid, that can interfere with the chemical activity of zinc.

(D) No zinc-based cold remedy can have any effect unless it is taken or applied within 48 hours of the initial onset of cold symptoms.

(E) Drug-company researchers experimenting with a nasal spray based on zinc have found that it has much the same effect on colds as the gel does.

234. In each of the past five years, Barraland's prison population has increased. Yet, according to official government statistics, for none of those years has there been either an increase in the number of criminal cases brought to trial or an increase in the rate at which convictions have been obtained. Clearly, therefore, the percentage of people convicted of crimes who are being given prison sentences is on the increase.

Which of the following, if true, most seriously weakens the argument?

(A) In Barraland, the range of punishments that can be imposed instead of a prison sentence is wide.

(B) Over the last ten years, overcrowding in the prisons of Barraland has essentially been eliminated as a result of an ambitious program of prison construction.

(C) Ten years ago, Barraland reformed its criminal justice system, imposing longer minimum sentences for those crimes for which a prison sentence had long been mandatory.

(D) Barraland has been supervising convicts on parole more closely in recent years, with the result that parole violations have become significantly less frequent.

(E) The number of people in Barraland who feel that crime is on the increase is significantly greater now than it was five years ago.

235. TrueSave is a mail-order company that ships electronic products from its warehouses to customers worldwide. The company's shipping manager is proposing that customer orders be packed with newer, more expensive packing materials that virtually eliminate damage during shipping. The manager argues that overall costs would essentially remain unaffected, since the extra cost of the new packing materials roughly equals the current cost of replacing products returned by customers because they arrived in damaged condition.

Which of the following would it be most important to ascertain in determining whether implementing the shipping manager's proposal would have the argued-for effect on costs?

(A) Whether the products shipped by TrueSave are more vulnerable to incurring damage during shipping than are typical electronic products

(B) Whether electronic products are damaged more frequently in transit than are most other products shipped by mail-order companies

(C) Whether a sizable proportion of returned items are returned because of damage already present when those items were packed for shipping

(D) Whether there are cases in which customers blame themselves for product damage that, though present on arrival of the product, is not discovered until later

(E) Whether TrueSave continually monitors the performance of the shipping companies it uses to ship products to its customers

Questions 236 to 290 — Difficulty: **Hard**

236. Twenty-five years ago, 2,000 married people were asked to rank four categories—spouses, friends, jobs, and housework—according to the amount of time each category demanded. A recent follow-up survey indicates that a majority of those same people rank housework higher on the list now than they did twenty-five years ago. Yet most of the respondents also claim that housework has become less demanding of their time over the last twenty-five years.

Which of the following, if true, helps to explain the apparent discrepancy?

(A) Some of the people surveyed were married to other people in the survey.

(B) Many of the most time-consuming aspects of people's lives do not appear as categories on either survey.

(C) Most of those who responded to the follow-up survey have retired in the last twenty-five years.

(D) At the time of the follow-up survey, some of the people surveyed did no housework.

(E) Many of the respondents to the follow-up survey claim that they now spend much more time with their friends than they did twenty-five years ago.

237. In order to achieve self-sufficiency in electricity production, **the Hasarian government proposes to construct eleven huge hydroelectric power plants.** Although this is a massive project, it is probably not massive enough to achieve the goal. It is true that **adding the projected output of the new hydroelectric plants to the output that Hasaria can achieve now would be enough to meet the forecast demand for electricity.** It will, however, take at least fifteen years to complete the project and by then the majority of Hasaria's current power plants will be too old to function at full capacity.

In the argument given, the two portions in **boldface** play which of the following roles?

(A) The first introduces a proposed course of action for which the argument provides support; the second gives evidence in support of that course of action.

(B) The first introduces a proposed course of action for which the argument provides support; the second gives a reason for not adopting a possible alternative course of action.

(C) The first introduces a plan that the argument evaluates; the second provides evidence that is used to support that plan against possible alternatives.

(D) The first introduces a proposed plan for achieving a certain goal; the second is a claim that has been used in support of the plan but that the argument maintains is inaccurate.

(E) The first introduces a proposed plan for achieving a certain goal; the second provides evidence that is used to support the argument's evaluation of that plan.

238. In Cecropia, inspections of fishing boats that estimate the number of fish they are carrying are typically conducted upon their return to port. The high numbers so obtained have led the government to conclude that the coastal waters are being overfished. To allow commercial fishing stocks to recover, the government is considering introducing annual quotas on the number of fish that each fishing boat can catch. Compliance with the quotas would be determined by the established system of inspections.

Which of the following, if true, raises the most serious doubts about whether the government's proposed plan would succeed?

(A) Some commercial fishing boats in Cecropia are large enough to catch their entire annual quota in only a few months of fishing.

(B) The quotas would have to be reduced if more boats began fishing in Cecropia's coastal waters.

(C) Because fish prices will rise if the quotas go into effect, it is unlikely that the quotas will significantly change the number of boats fishing Cecropia's coastal waters.

(D) The procedure that inspectors use to estimate the number of fish a boat is carrying often results in a slight overcount.

(E) Quotas encourage fishers to bring only the most commercially valuable fish into port and to discard less valuable fish, most of them dead or dying.

239. Consultant: **A significant number of complex repair jobs carried out by Ace Repairs have to be redone under the company's warranty, but when those repairs are redone they are invariably successful.** Since we have definitely established that **there is no systematic difference between the mechanics who are assigned to do the initial repairs and those who are assigned to redo unsatisfactory jobs**, it is clear that inadequacies in the initial repairs cannot be attributed to the mechanics' lack of competence. Rather, it is likely that complex repairs require a level of focused attention that the company's mechanics apply consistently only to repair jobs that have been inadequately done on the first try.

    In the consultant's reasoning, the two portions in **boldface** play which of the following roles?

    (A) The first is a claim that the consultant rejects as false; the second is evidence that forms the basis for that rejection.

    (B) The first is part of an explanation that the consultant offers for a certain finding; the second is that finding.

    (C) The first presents a pattern whose explanation is at issue in the reasoning; the second provides evidence to rule out one possible explanation of that pattern.

    (D) The first presents a pattern whose explanation is at issue in the reasoning; the second is evidence that has been used to challenge the explanation presented by the consultant.

    (E) The first is the position the consultant seeks to establish; the second is offered as evidence for that position.

240. Half of Metroburg's operating budget comes from a payroll tax of 2 percent on salaries paid to people who work in the city. Recently, a financial services company, one of Metroburg's largest private-sector employers, announced that it will be relocating just outside the city. All the company's employees, amounting to 1 percent of all people now employed in Metroburg, will be employed at the new location.

    From the information given, which of the following can most properly be concluded?

    (A) Unless other employers add a substantial number of jobs in Metroburg, the company's relocation is likely to result in a 1 percent reduction in the revenue for the city's operating budget.

    (B) Although the company's relocation will have a negative effect on the city's tax revenue, the company's departure will not lead to any increase in the unemployment rate among city residents.

    (C) One of the benefits that the company will realize from its relocation is a reduction in the taxes paid by itself and its employees.

    (D) Revenue from the payroll tax will decline by 1 percent if there is no increase in jobs within the city to compensate, fully or partially, for the company's departure.

    (E) The company's relocation will tend to increase the proportion of jobs in Metroburg that are in the public sector, unless it results in a contraction of the public-sector payroll.

241. A library currently has only coin-operated photocopy machines, which cost 10 cents per copy. Library administrators are planning to refit most of those machines with card readers. The library will sell prepaid copy cards that allow users to make 50 copies at 9 cents per copy. Administrators believe that, despite the convenience of copy cards and their lower per-copy cost, the number of copies made in the library will be essentially unchanged after the refit.

On the assumption that administrators' assessment is correct, which of the following predictions about the effect of the refit is most strongly supported by the information given?

(A) Library patrons will only purchase a copy card on days when they need to make 50 or more copies.

(B) No library patrons will increase their usage of the library's photocopy machines once the refit has been made.

(C) If most of the copy cards sold in the library are used to their full capacity, the number of people using the library's photocopy machines over a given period will fall.

(D) Revenues from photocopying will decrease unless most library patrons choose to use the remaining coin-operated machines in preference to the card-reader equipped ones.

(E) Revenues from photocopying will increase if copy cards that are purchased are, on average, used to significantly less than 90 percent of their capacity.

242. Harvester-ant colonies live for fifteen to twenty years, though individual worker ants live only a year. The way a colony behaves changes steadily in a predictable pattern as the colony grows older and larger. For the first few years, the foragers behave quite aggressively, searching out and vigorously defending new food sources, but once a colony has reached a certain size, its foragers become considerably less aggressive.

If the statements above are true, which of the following can most properly be concluded on the basis of them?

(A) As a result of pressure from neighbors, some colonies do not grow larger as they become older.

(B) Unpredictable changes in a colony's environment can cause changes in the tasks that the colony must perform if it is to continue to survive.

(C) The reason a mature colony goes out of existence is that younger, more aggressive colonies successfully outcompete it for food.

(D) The pattern of changing behavior that a colony displays does not arise from a change in the behavior of any individual worker ant or group of worker ants.

(E) A new colony comes into existence when a group of young, aggressive workers leaves a mature colony and sets up on its own.

243. Trucking company owner: Theft of trucks containing valuable cargo is a serious problem. A new device produces radio signals that allow police to track stolen vehicles, and the recovery rate for stolen cargo in trucks equipped with the device is impressive. The device is too expensive to install in every truck, so we plan to install it in half of our trucks. Using those trucks for the most valuable cargo should largely eliminate losses from theft.

Which of the following, if true, most strongly supports the trucking company owner's expectation about the results of implementing the plan?

(A) For thieves, a cargo is valuable only if it is easy for them to dispose of profitably.

(B) Some insurance companies charge less to insure cargoes transported in trucks protected by the device.

(C) Most stolen trucks are eventually found, but unless a stolen truck is found very soon after it is taken, the likelihood that the trucking company will recover any of its cargo is very low.

(D) Thieves generally avoid trucks belonging to trucking companies that are known to have installed the device in a large proportion of their trucks.

(E) The manufacturer of the device offers a five-year warranty on each unit sold, a longer warranty than any that is offered on any competing antitheft device.

244. To improve customer relations, several big retailers have recently launched "smile initiatives," requiring their employees to smile whenever they have contact with customers. These retailers generally have low employee morale, which is why they have to enforce smiling. However, studies show that customers can tell fake smiles from genuine smiles and that fake smiles prompt negative feelings in customers. So the smile initiatives are unlikely to achieve their goal.

The argument relies on which of the following as an assumption?

(A) The smile initiatives have achieved nearly complete success in getting employees to smile while they are around customers.

(B) Customers' feelings about fake smiles are no better than their feelings about the other facial expressions employees with low morale are likely to have.

(C) The feelings that employees generate in retail customers are a principal determinant of the amount of money customers will spend at a retailer.

(D) At the retailers who have launched the smile initiatives, none of the employees gave genuine smiles to customers before the initiatives were launched.

(E) Customers rarely, if ever, have a negative reaction to a genuine smile from a retail employee.

245. Many economists hold that keeping taxes low helps to spur economic growth, and that low taxes thus lead to greater national prosperity. But Country X, which has unusually high taxes, has greater per-capita income than the neighboring Country Y, which has much lower taxes. Some politicians have concluded from this that high taxes do not hinder national prosperity.

The politicians' reasoning is most vulnerable to criticism on which of the following grounds?

(A) It overlooks the possibility that even if Country X reduced its taxes, it would not experience greater national prosperity in the long term.

(B) It confuses a claim that a factor does not hinder a given development with the claim that the same factor promotes that development.

(C) It fails to adequately address the possibility that Country X and Country Y differ in relevant respects other than taxation.

(D) It fails to take into account that the per-capita income of a country does not determine its rate of economic growth.

(E) It assumes that the economists' thesis must be correct despite a clear counterexample to that thesis.

246. Urban rail systems have been proposed to alleviate traffic congestion, but results in many cities have been cited as evidence that this approach to traffic management is ineffective. For example, a U.S. city that opened three urban rail branches experienced a net decline of 3,100 urban rail commuters during a period when employment increased by 96,000. Officials who favor urban rail systems as a solution to traffic congestion have attempted to counter this argument by noting that commuting trips in that city represent just 20 percent of urban travel.

The response of the officials to the claim that urban rail systems are ineffective is most vulnerable to criticism on the grounds that it

(A) presents no evidence to show that the statistics are incorrect

(B) relies solely on general data about U.S. cities rather than data about the city in question

(C) fails to consider that commuting trips may cause significantly more than 20 percent of the traffic congestion

(D) fails to show that the decline in the number of urban rail commuters in one U.S. city is typical of U.S. cities generally

(E) provides no statistics on the use of urban rail systems by passengers other than commuters

247. Mayor: The financial livelihood of our downtown businesses is in jeopardy. There are few available parking spaces close to the downtown shopping area, so if we are to spur economic growth in our city, we must build a large parking ramp no more than two blocks from downtown.

Which of the following, if true, most seriously weakens the mayor's reasoning?

(A) The city budget is not currently large enough to finance the construction of a new parking ramp.

(B) There are other more significant reasons for the financial woes of downtown businesses in addition to a lack of nearby parking spaces.

(C) Building a parking ramp as much as four blocks from downtown would be sufficient to greatly increase the number of shoppers to downtown businesses.

(D) Explosive growth is most often associated with large suburban shopping malls, not small businesses.

(E) Some additional parking spaces could be added to the downtown area without the construction of a parking ramp.

248. Compact fluorescent light (CFL) bulbs are growing in market share as a replacement for the standard incandescent light bulb. However, an even newer technology is emerging: the light-emitting diode (LED) bulb. Like CFL bulbs, LED bulbs are energy efficient, and they can last around fifty thousand hours, about five times as long as most CFL bulbs. Yet, a single LED bulb costs much more than five CFL bulbs.

The information in the passage above most supports which of the following conclusions?

(A) LED bulbs are most likely to be used in locations where light bulbs would be difficult or costly to replace.

(B) CFL bulbs will need to come down further in price in order to compete with LED bulbs.

(C) LED bulbs are most likely to be used in locations where there is frequent accidental breakage of bulbs.

(D) CFL bulb designs are likely to advance to the point where they can last as long as LED bulbs.

(E) LED bulbs are likely to drop in price, to the point of being competitive with CFL bulbs.

249. Tanco, a leather manufacturer, uses large quantities of common salt to preserve animal hides. New environmental regulations have significantly increased the cost of disposing of salt water that results from this use, and, in consequence, Tanco is considering a plan to use potassium chloride in place of common salt. Research has shown that Tanco could reprocess the by-product of potassium chloride use to yield a crop fertilizer, leaving a relatively small volume of waste for disposal.

In determining the impact on company profits of using potassium chloride in place of common salt, it would be important for Tanco to research all of the following EXCEPT:

(A) What difference, if any, is there between the cost of the common salt needed to preserve a given quantity of animal hides and the cost of the potassium chloride needed to preserve the same quantity of hides?

(B) To what extent is the equipment involved in preserving animal hides using common salt suitable for preserving animal hides using potassium chloride?

(C) What environmental regulations, if any, constrain the disposal of the waste generated in reprocessing the by-product of potassium chloride?

(D) How closely does leather that results when common salt is used to preserve hides resemble that which results when potassium chloride is used?

(E) Are the chemical properties that make potassium chloride an effective means for preserving animal hides the same as those that make common salt an effective means for doing so?

250. Colorless diamonds can command high prices as gemstones. A type of less valuable diamonds can be treated to remove all color. Only sophisticated tests can distinguish such treated diamonds from naturally colorless ones. However, only 2 percent of diamonds mined are of the colored type that can be successfully treated, and many of those are of insufficient quality to make the treatment worthwhile. Surely, therefore, the vast majority of colorless diamonds sold by jewelers are naturally colorless.

    A serious flaw in the reasoning of the argument is that

    (A) comparisons between the price diamonds command as gemstones and their value for other uses are omitted
    (B) information about the rarity of treated diamonds is not combined with information about the rarity of naturally colorless, gemstone diamonds
    (C) the possibility that colored diamonds might be used as gemstones, even without having been treated, is ignored
    (D) the currently available method for making colorless diamonds from colored ones is treated as though it were the only possible method for doing so
    (E) the difficulty that a customer of a jeweler would have in distinguishing a naturally colorless diamond from a treated one is not taken into account

251. The Sumpton town council recently voted to pay a prominent artist to create an abstract sculpture for the town square. Critics of this decision protested that town residents tend to dislike most abstract art, and any art in the town square should reflect their tastes. But a town council spokesperson dismissed this criticism, pointing out that other public abstract sculptures that the same sculptor has installed in other cities have been extremely popular with those cities' local residents.

    The statements above most strongly suggest that the main point of disagreement between the critics and the spokesperson is whether

    (A) it would have been reasonable to consult town residents on the decision
    (B) most Sumpton residents will find the new sculpture to their taste
    (C) abstract sculptures by the same sculptor have truly been popular in other cities
    (D) a more traditional sculpture in the town square would be popular among local residents
    (E) public art that the residents of Sumpton would find desirable would probably be found desirable by the residents of other cities

252. Jay: Of course there are many good reasons to support the expansion of preventive medical care, but arguments claiming that it will lead to greater societal economic gains are misguided. Some of the greatest societal expenses arise from frequent urgent-care needs for people who have attained a long life due to preventive care.

Sunil: Your argument fails because you neglect economic gains outside the health care system: society suffers an economic loss when any of its productive members suffer preventable illnesses.

Sunil's response to Jay makes which of the following assumptions?

(A) Those who receive preventive care are not more likely to need urgent care than are those who do not receive preventive care.

(B) Jay intends the phrase "economic gains" to refer only to gains accruing to institutions within the health care system.

(C) Productive members of society are more likely than others to suffer preventable illnesses.

(D) The economic contributions of those who receive preventive medical care may outweigh the economic losses caused by preventive care.

(E) Jay is incorrect in stating that patients who receive preventive medical care are long-lived.

253. Boreal owls range over a much larger area than do other owls of similar size. The reason for this behavior is probably that the small mammals on which owls feed are especially scarce in the forests where boreal owls live, and the relative scarcity of prey requires the owls to range more extensively to find sufficient food.

Which of the following, if true, most helps to confirm the explanation above?

(A) Some boreal owls range over an area eight times larger than the area over which any other owl of similar size ranges.

(B) Boreal owls range over larger areas in regions where food of the sort eaten by small mammals is sparse than they do in regions where such food is abundant.

(C) After their young hatch, boreal owls must hunt more often than before in order to feed both themselves and their newly hatched young.

(D) Sometimes individual boreal owls hunt near a single location for many weeks at a time and do not range farther than a few hundred yards.

(E) The boreal owl requires less food, relative to its weight, than is required by members of other owl species.

254. Microbiologist: A lethal strain of salmonella recently showed up in a European country, causing an outbreak of illness that killed two people and infected twenty-seven others. Investigators blame the severity of the outbreak on the overuse of antibiotics, since the salmonella bacteria tested were shown to be drug-resistant. But this is unlikely because patients in the country where the outbreak occurred cannot obtain antibiotics to treat illness without a prescription, and the country's doctors prescribe antibiotics less readily than do doctors in any other European country.

    Which of the following, if true, would most weaken the microbiologist's reasoning?

    (A) Physicians in the country where the outbreak occurred have become hesitant to prescribe antibiotics since they are frequently in short supply.
    (B) People in the country where the outbreak occurred often consume foods produced from animals that eat antibiotics-laden livestock feed.
    (C) Use of antibiotics in two countries that neighbor the country where the outbreak occurred has risen over the past decade.
    (D) Drug-resistant strains of salmonella have not been found in countries in which antibiotics are not generally available.
    (E) Salmonella has been shown to spread easily along the distribution chains of certain vegetables, such as raw tomatoes.

255. Economist: Construction moves faster in good weather than in bad, so mild winters in areas that usually experience harsh conditions can appear to create construction booms as builders complete projects that would otherwise have to wait. But forecasting one mild winter or even two for such areas generally does not lead to overall increases in construction during these periods, because construction loans are often obtained more than a year in advance, and because ———.

    Which of the following, if true, most logically completes the economist's argument?

    (A) construction workers often travel to warmer climates in the wintertime in search of work
    (B) construction materials are often in short supply during construction booms
    (C) many builders in these areas are likely to apply for construction loans at the same time
    (D) it is frequently the case that forecasted weather trends do not actually occur
    (E) mild winters are generally followed by spring and summer weather that promotes more rapid construction

256. Historian: Newton developed mathematical concepts and techniques that are fundamental to modern calculus. Leibniz developed closely analogous concepts and techniques. It has traditionally been thought that these discoveries were independent. Researchers have, however, recently discovered notes of Leibniz's that discuss one of Newton's books on mathematics. Several scholars have argued that since **the book includes a presentation of Newton's calculus concepts and techniques**, and since the notes were written before Leibniz's own development of calculus concepts and techniques, it is virtually certain **that the traditional view is false.** A more cautious conclusion than this is called for, however. Leibniz's notes are limited to early sections of Newton's book, sections that precede the ones in which Newton's calculus concepts and techniques are presented.

In the historian's reasoning, the two portions in **boldface** play which of the following roles?

(A) The first is a claim that the historian rejects; the second is a position that that claim has been used to support.

(B) The first is evidence that has been used to support a conclusion about which the historian expresses reservations; the second is that conclusion.

(C) The first provides evidence in support of a position that the historian defends; the second is that position.

(D) The first and the second each provide evidence in support of a position that the historian defends.

(E) The first has been used in support of a position that the historian rejects; the second is a conclusion that the historian draws from that position.

257. For over two centuries, no one had been able to make Damascus blades—blades with a distinctive serpentine surface pattern—but a contemporary sword maker may just have rediscovered how. Using iron with trace impurities that precisely matched those present in the iron used in historic Damascus blades, this contemporary sword maker seems to have finally hit on an intricate process by which he can produce a blade indistinguishable from a true Damascus blade.

Which of the following, if true, provides the strongest support for the hypothesis that trace impurities in the iron are essential for the production of Damascus blades?

(A) There are surface features of every Damascus blade—including the blades produced by the contemporary sword maker—that are unique to that blade.

(B) The iron with which the contemporary sword maker made Damascus blades came from a source of iron that was unknown two centuries ago.

(C) Almost all the tools used by the contemporary sword maker were updated versions of tools that were used by sword makers over two centuries ago.

(D) Production of Damascus blades by sword makers of the past ceased abruptly after those sword makers' original source of iron became exhausted.

(E) Although Damascus blades were renowned for maintaining a sharp edge, the blade made by the contemporary sword maker suggests that they may have maintained their edge less well than blades made using what is now the standard process for making blades.

258. Images from ground-based telescopes are invariably distorted by the Earth's atmosphere. Orbiting space telescopes, however, operating above Earth's atmosphere, should provide superbly detailed images. Therefore, ground-based telescopes will soon become obsolete for advanced astronomical research purposes.

    Which of the following statements, if true, would cast the most doubt on the conclusion drawn above?

    (A) An orbiting space telescope due to be launched this year is far behind schedule and over budget, whereas the largest ground-based telescope was both within budget and on schedule.

    (B) Ground-based telescopes located on mountain summits are not subject to the kinds of atmospheric distortion which, at low altitudes, make stars appear to twinkle.

    (C) By careful choice of observatory location, it is possible for large-aperture telescopes to avoid most of the kind of wind turbulence that can distort image quality.

    (D) When large-aperture telescopes are located at high altitudes near the equator, they permit the best Earth-based observations of the center of the Milky Way Galaxy, a prime target of astronomical research.

    (E) Detailed spectral analyses, upon which astronomers rely for determining the chemical composition and evolutionary history of stars, require telescopes with more light-gathering capacity than space telescopes can provide.

259. Generally scientists enter their field with the goal of doing important new research and accept as their colleagues those with similar motivation. Therefore, when any scientist wins renown as an expounder of science to general audiences, most other scientists conclude that this popularizer should no longer be regarded as a true colleague.

    The explanation offered above for the low esteem in which scientific popularizers are held by research scientists assumes that

    (A) serious scientific research is not a solitary activity, but relies on active cooperation among a group of colleagues

    (B) research scientists tend not to regard as colleagues those scientists whose renown they envy

    (C) a scientist can become a famous popularizer without having completed any important research

    (D) research scientists believe that those who are well known as popularizers of science are not motivated to do important new research

    (E) no important new research can be accessible to or accurately assessed by those who are not themselves scientists

260. Urban planner: When a city loses population due to migration, property taxes in that city tend to rise. This is because there are then fewer residents paying to maintain an infrastructure that was designed to support more people. Rising property taxes, in turn, drive more residents away, compounding the problem. Since the city of Stonebridge is starting to lose population, the city government should therefore refrain from raising property taxes.

Which of the following, if true, would most weaken the urban planner's argument?

(A) If Stonebridge does not raise taxes on its residents to maintain its infrastructure, the city will become much less attractive to live in as that infrastructure decays.

(B) Stonebridge at present benefits from grants provided by the national government to help maintain certain parts of its infrastructure.

(C) If there is a small increase in property taxes in Stonebridge and a slightly larger proportion of total revenue than at present is allocated to infrastructure maintenance, the funding will be adequate for that purpose.

(D) Demographers project that the population of a region that includes Stonebridge will start to increase substantially within the next several years.

(E) The property taxes in Stonebridge are significantly lower than those in many larger cities.

261. Which of the following most logically completes the argument?

Utrania was formerly a major petroleum exporter, but in recent decades economic stagnation and restrictive regulations inhibited investment in new oil fields. In consequence, Utranian oil exports dropped steadily as old fields became depleted. Utrania's currently improving economic situation, together with less-restrictive regulations, will undoubtedly result in the rapid development of new fields. However, it would be premature to conclude that the rapid development of new fields will result in higher oil exports, because _____.

(A) the price of oil is expected to remain relatively stable over the next several years

(B) the improvement in the economic situation in Utrania is expected to result in a dramatic increase in the proportion of Utranians who own automobiles

(C) most of the investment in new oil fields in Utrania is expected to come from foreign sources

(D) new technology is available to recover oil from old oil fields formerly regarded as depleted

(E) many of the new oil fields in Utrania are likely to be as productive as those that were developed during the period when Utrania was a major oil exporter

262. The use of growth-promoting antibiotics in hog farming can weaken their effectiveness in treating humans because such use can spread resistance to those antibiotics among microorganisms. But now the Smee Company, one of the largest pork marketers, may stop buying pork raised on feed containing these antibiotics. Smee has 60 percent of the pork market, and farmers who sell to Smee would certainly stop using antibiotics in order to avoid jeopardizing their sales. So if Smee makes this change, it will probably significantly slow the decline in antibiotics' effectiveness for humans.

Which of the following, if true, would most strengthen the argument above?

(A) Other major pork marketers will probably stop buying pork raised on feed containing growth-promoting antibiotics if Smee no longer buys such pork.

(B) The decline in hog growth due to discontinuation of antibiotics can be offset by improved hygiene.

(C) Authorities are promoting the use of antibiotics to which microorganisms have not yet developed resistance.

(D) A phaseout of use of antibiotics for hogs in one country reduced usage by over 50 percent over five years.

(E) If Smee stops buying pork raised with antibiotics, the firm's costs will probably increase.

263. In an experiment, volunteers walked individually through a dark, abandoned theater. Half of the volunteers had been told that the theater was haunted and the other half that it was under renovation. The first half reported significantly more unusual experiences than the second did. The researchers concluded that reports of encounters with ghosts and other supernatural entities generally result from prior expectations of such experiences.

Which of the following, if true, would most seriously weaken the researchers' reasoning?

(A) None of the volunteers in the second half believed that the unusual experiences they reported were supernatural.

(B) All of the volunteers in the first half believed that the researchers' statement that the theater was haunted was a lie.

(C) Before being told about the theater, the volunteers within each group varied considerably in their prior beliefs about supernatural experiences.

(D) Each unusual experience reported by the volunteers had a cause that did not involve the supernatural.

(E) The researchers did not believe that the theater was haunted.

264. In order to reduce dependence on imported oil, the government of Jalica has imposed minimum fuel-efficiency requirements on all new cars, beginning this year. The more fuel-efficient a car, the less pollution it produces per mile driven. As Jalicans replace their old cars with cars that meet the new requirements, annual pollution from car traffic is likely to decrease in Jalica.

Which of the following, if true, most seriously weakens the argument?

(A) In Jalica, domestically produced oil is more expensive than imported oil.

(B) The Jalican government did not intend the new fuel-efficiency requirement to be a pollution-reduction measure.

(C) Some pollution-control devices mandated in Jalica make cars less fuel-efficient than they would be without those devices.

(D) The new regulation requires no change in the chemical formulation of fuel for cars in Jalica.

(E) Jalicans who get cars that are more fuel-efficient tend to do more driving than before.

265. Plantings of cotton bioengineered to produce its own insecticide against bollworms, a major cause of crop failure, sustained little bollworm damage until this year. This year the plantings are being seriously damaged by bollworms. Bollworms, however, are not necessarily developing resistance to the cotton's insecticide. Bollworms breed on corn, and last year more corn than usual was planted throughout cotton-growing regions. So it is likely that the cotton is simply being overwhelmed by corn-bred bollworms.

    In evaluating the argument, which of the following would it be most useful to establish?

    (A) Whether corn could be bioengineered to produce the insecticide

    (B) Whether plantings of cotton that does not produce the insecticide are suffering unusually extensive damage from bollworms this year

    (C) Whether other crops that have been bioengineered to produce their own insecticide successfully resist the pests against which the insecticide was to protect them

    (D) Whether plantings of bioengineered cotton are frequently damaged by insect pests other than bollworms

    (E) Whether there are insecticides that can be used against bollworms that have developed resistance to the insecticide produced by the bioengineered cotton

266. Typically during thunderstorms most lightning strikes carry a negative electric charge; only a few carry a positive charge. Thunderstorms with unusually high proportions of positive-charge strikes tend to occur in smoky areas near forest fires. The fact that smoke carries positively charged smoke particles into the air above a fire suggests the hypothesis that the extra positive strikes occur because of the presence of such particles in the storm clouds.

    Which of the following, if discovered to be true, most seriously undermines the hypothesis?

    (A) Other kinds of rare lightning also occur with unusually high frequency in the vicinity of forest fires.

    (B) The positive-charge strikes that occur near forest fires tend to be no more powerful than positive strikes normally are.

    (C) A positive-charge strike is as likely to start a forest fire as a negative-charge strike is.

    (D) Thunderstorms that occur in drifting clouds of smoke have extra positive-charge strikes weeks after the charge of the smoke particles has dissipated.

    (E) The total number of lightning strikes during a thunderstorm is usually within the normal range in the vicinity of a forest fire.

267. Since 1990 the percentage of bacterial sinus infections in Aqadestan that are resistant to the antibiotic perxicillin has increased substantially. Bacteria can quickly develop resistance to an antibiotic when it is prescribed indiscriminately or when patients fail to take it as prescribed. Since perxicillin has not been indiscriminately prescribed, health officials hypothesize that the increase in perxicillin-resistant sinus infections is largely due to patients' failure to take this medication as prescribed.

Which of the following, if true of Aqadestan, provides most support for the health officials' hypothesis?

(A) Resistance to several other commonly prescribed antibiotics has not increased since 1990 in Aqadestan.
(B) A large number of Aqadestanis never seek medical help when they have a sinus infection.
(C) When it first became available, perxicillin was much more effective in treating bacterial sinus infections than any other antibiotic used for such infections at the time.
(D) Many patients who take perxicillin experience severe side effects within the first few days of their prescribed regimen.
(E) Aqadestani health clinics provide antibiotics to their patients at cost.

268. Psychologist: In a study, researchers gave 100 volunteers a psychological questionnaire designed to measure their self-esteem. The researchers then asked each volunteer to rate the strength of his or her own social skills. The volunteers with the highest levels of self-esteem consistently rated themselves as having much better social skills than did the volunteers with moderate levels. This suggests that attaining an exceptionally high level of self-esteem greatly improves one's social skills.

The psychologist's argument is most vulnerable to criticism on which of the following grounds?

(A) It fails to adequately address the possibility that many of the volunteers may not have understood what the psychological questionnaire was designed to measure.
(B) It takes for granted that the volunteers with the highest levels of self-esteem had better social skills than did the other volunteers, even before the former volunteers had attained their high levels of self-esteem.
(C) It overlooks the possibility that people with very high levels of self-esteem may tend to have a less accurate perception of the strength of their own social skills than do people with moderate levels of self-esteem.
(D) It relies on evidence from a group of volunteers that is too small to provide any support for any inferences regarding people in general.
(E) It overlooks the possibility that factors other than level of self-esteem may be of much greater importance in determining the strength of one's social skills.

269. Political advertisement: Mayor Delmont's critics complain about the jobs that were lost in the city under Delmont's leadership. Yet the fact is that not only were more jobs created than were eliminated, but each year since Delmont took office the average pay for the new jobs created has been higher than that year's average pay for jobs citywide. So it stands to reason that throughout Delmont's tenure the average paycheck in this city has been getting steadily bigger.

Which of the following, if true, most seriously weakens the argument in the advertisement?

(A) The unemployment rate in the city is higher today than it was when Mayor Delmont took office.

(B) The average pay for jobs in the city was at a ten-year low when Mayor Delmont took office.

(C) Each year during Mayor Delmont's tenure, the average pay for jobs that were eliminated has been higher than the average pay for jobs citywide.

(D) Most of the jobs eliminated during Mayor Delmont's tenure were in declining industries.

(E) The average pay for jobs in the city is currently lower than it is for jobs in the suburbs surrounding the city.

270. To prevent a newly built dam on the Chiff River from blocking the route of fish migrating to breeding grounds upstream, the dam includes a fish pass, a mechanism designed to allow fish through the dam. Before the construction of the dam and fish pass, several thousand fish a day swam upriver during spawning season. But in the first season after the project's completion, only 300 per day made the journey. Clearly, the fish pass is defective.

Which of the following, if true, most seriously weakens the argument?

(A) Fish that have migrated to the upstream breeding grounds do not return down the Chiff River again.

(B) On other rivers in the region, the construction of dams with fish passes has led to only small decreases in the number of fish migrating upstream.

(C) The construction of the dam stirred up potentially toxic river sediments that were carried downstream.

(D) Populations of migratory fish in the Chiff River have been declining slightly over the last 20 years.

(E) During spawning season, the dam releases sufficient water for migratory fish below the dam to swim upstream.

271. Music critic: Fewer and fewer musicians are studying classical music, decreasing the likelihood that those with real aptitude for such music will be performing it. Audiences who hear these performances will not appreciate classical music's greatness and will thus decamp to other genres. So to maintain classical music's current meager popularity, we must encourage more young musicians to enter the field.

    Which of the following, if true, most weakens the music critic's reasoning?

    (A) Musicians who choose to study classical music do so because they believe they have an aptitude for the music.
    (B) Classical music's current meager popularity is attributable to the profusion of other genres of music available to listeners.
    (C) Most people who appreciate classical music come to do so through old recordings rather than live performances.
    (D) It is possible to enjoy the music in a particular genre even when it is performed by musicians who are not ideally suited for that genre.
    (E) The continued popularity of a given genre of music depends in part on the audiences being able to understand why that genre attained its original popularity.

272. People with a college degree are more likely than others to search for a new job while they are employed. There are proportionately more people with college degrees among managers and other professionals than among service and clerical workers. Surprisingly, however, 2009 figures indicate that people employed as managers and other professionals were no more likely than people employed as service and clerical workers to have searched for a new job.

    Which of the following, if true, most helps to resolve the apparent paradox?

    (A) People generally do not take a new job that is offered to them while they are employed unless the new job pays better.
    (B) Some service and clerical jobs pay more than some managerial and professional jobs.
    (C) People who felt they were overqualified for their current positions were more likely than others to search for a new job.
    (D) The percentage of employed people who were engaged in job searches declined from 2005 to 2009.
    (E) In 2009 employees with no college degree who retired were more likely to be replaced by people with a college degree if they retired from a managerial or professional job than from a service or clerical job.

273. To reduce traffic congestion, City X's transportation bureau plans to encourage people who work downtown to sign a form pledging to carpool or use public transportation for the next year. Everyone who signs the form will get a coupon for a free meal at any downtown restaurant.

For the transportation bureau's plan to succeed in reducing traffic congestion, which of the following must be true?

(A) Everyone who signs the pledge form will fully abide by the pledge for the next year.
(B) At least some people who work downtown prefer the restaurants downtown to those elsewhere.
(C) Most downtown traffic congestion in City X results from people who work downtown.
(D) The most effective way to reduce traffic congestion downtown would be to persuade more people who work there to carpool or use public transportation.
(E) At least some people who receive the coupon for a free meal will sometimes carpool or use public transportation during the next year.

274. Commemorative plaques cast from brass are a characteristic art form of the Benin culture of West Africa. Some scholars, noting that the oldest surviving plaques date to the 1400s, hypothesize that brass-casting techniques were introduced by the Portuguese, who came to Benin in 1485 A.D. But Portuguese records of that expedition mention cast-brass jewelry sent to Benin's king from neighboring Ife. So it is unlikely that Benin's knowledge of brass casting derived from the Portuguese.

Which of the following, if true, most strengthens the argument?

(A) The Portuguese records do not indicate whether their expedition of 1485 included metalworkers.
(B) The Portuguese had no contact with Ife until the 1500s.
(C) In the 1400s the Portuguese did not use cast brass for commemorative plaques.
(D) As early as 1500 A.D., Benin artists were making brass plaques incorporating depictions of Europeans.
(E) Copper, which is required for making brass, can be found throughout Benin territory

275. When new laws imposing strict penalties for misleading corporate disclosures were passed, they were hailed as initiating an era of corporate openness. As an additional benefit, given the increased amount and accuracy of information disclosed under the new laws, it was assumed that analysts' predictions of corporate performance would become more accurate. Since the passage of the laws, however, the number of inaccurate analysts' predictions has not in fact decreased.

Which of the following would, if true, best explain the discrepancy outlined above?

(A) The new laws' definition of "misleading information" can be interpreted in more than one way.
(B) The new laws require corporations in all industries to release information at specific times of the year.
(C) Even before the new laws were passed, the information most corporations released was true.
(D) Analysts base their predictions on information they gather from many sources, not just corporate disclosures.
(E) The more pieces of information corporations release, the more difficult it becomes for anyone to organize them in a manageable way.

276. Economist: Even with energy conservation efforts, current technologies cannot support both a reduction in carbon dioxide emissions and an expanding global economy. Attempts to restrain emissions without new technology will stifle economic growth. Therefore, increases in governmental spending on research into energy technology will be necessary if we wish to reduce carbon dioxide emissions without stifling economic growth.

    Which of the following is an assumption the economist's argument requires?

    (A) If research into energy technology does not lead to a reduction in carbon dioxide emissions, then economic growth will be stifled.
    (B) Increased governmental spending on research into energy technology will be more likely to reduce carbon dioxide emissions without stifling growth than will nongovernmental spending.
    (C) An expanding global economy may require at least some governmental spending on research into energy technology.
    (D) Attempts to restrain carbon dioxide emissions without new technology could ultimately cost more than the failure to reduce those emissions would cost.
    (E) Restraining carbon dioxide emissions without stifling economic growth would require both new energy technology and energy conservation efforts.

277. Researchers have developed a technology that uses sound as a means of converting heat into electrical energy. Converters based on this technology can be manufactured small enough to be integrated into consumer electronics, where they will absorb significant quantities of heat. A group of engineers is now designing converters to be sold to laptop computer manufacturers, who are expected to use the electrical output of the converters to conserve battery power in their computers.

    Which of the following would, if true, provide the strongest evidence that the engineers' plan will be commercially successful for their group?

    (A) The sound that is used by the converters is generated by the converters themselves.
    (B) Most laptop computer manufacturers today receive fewer complaints than in previous years regarding shortness of operating time on a single battery charge.
    (C) The overheating of microprocessors in laptop computers presents a major technological challenge that manufacturers are prepared to meet at significant expense.
    (D) Although battery technology has improved significantly, the average capacity of laptop computer batteries has not.
    (E) Electrical power generated by the converters can be used to power the fans installed to cool computers' components.

278. According to a widely held economic hypothesis, imposing strict environmental regulations reduces economic growth. This hypothesis is undermined by the fact that the states with the strictest environmental regulations also have the highest economic growth. This fact does not show that environmental regulations promote growth, however, since _____.

Which of the following, if true, provides evidence that most logically completes the argument above?

(A) those states with the strictest environmental regulations invest the most in education and job training

(B) even those states that have only moderately strict environmental regulations have higher growth than those with the least-strict regulations

(C) many states that are experiencing reduced economic growth are considering weakening their environmental regulations

(D) after introducing stricter environmental regulations, many states experienced increased economic growth

(E) even those states with very weak environmental regulations have experienced at least some growth

279. The prairie vole, a small North American grassland rodent, breeds year-round, and a group of voles living together consists primarily of an extended family, often including two or more litters. Voles commonly live in large groups from late autumn through winter; from spring through early autumn, however, most voles live in far smaller groups. The seasonal variation in group size can probably be explained by a seasonal variation in mortality among young voles.

Which of the following, if true, provides the strongest support for the explanation offered?

(A) It is in the spring and early summer that prairie vole communities generally contain the highest proportion of young voles.

(B) Prairie vole populations vary dramatically in size from year to year.

(C) The prairie vole subsists primarily on broad-leaved plants that are abundant only in spring.

(D) Winters in the prairie voles' habitat are often harsh, with temperatures that drop well below freezing.

(E) Snakes, a major predator of young prairie voles, are active only from spring through early autumn.

280. From 1980 to 1989, total consumption of fish in the country of Jurania increased by 4.5 percent, and total consumption of poultry products there increased by 9.0 percent. During the same period, the population of Jurania increased by 6 percent, in part due to immigration to Jurania from other countries in the region.

If the statements above are true, which of the following must also be true on the basis of them?

(A) During the 1980s in Jurania, profits of wholesale distributors of poultry products increased at a greater rate than did profits of wholesale distributors of fish.

(B) For people who immigrated to Jurania during the 1980s, fish was less likely to be a major part of their diet than was poultry.

(C) In 1989, Juranians consumed twice as much poultry as fish.

(D) For a significant proportion of Jurania's population, both fish and poultry products were a regular part of their diet during the 1980s.

(E) Per capita consumption of fish in Jurania was lower in 1989 than in 1980.

281. Junior biomedical researchers have long assumed that their hirings and promotions depend significantly on the amount of their published work. People responsible for making hiring and promotion decisions in the biomedical research field, however, are influenced much more by the overall impact that a candidate's scientific publications have on his or her field than by the number of those publications.

The information above, if accurate, argues most strongly AGAINST which of the following claims?

(A) Even biomedical researchers who are just beginning their careers are expected to already have published articles of major significance to the field.

(B) Contributions to the field of biomedical research are generally considered to be significant only if the work is published.

(C) The potential scientific importance of not-yet-published work is sometimes taken into account in decisions regarding the hiring or promotion of biomedical researchers.

(D) People responsible for hiring or promoting biomedical researchers can reasonably be expected to make a fair assessment of the overall impact of a candidate's publications on his or her field.

(E) Biomedical researchers can substantially increase their chances of promotion by fragmenting their research findings so that they are published in several journals instead of one.

282. Rabbits were introduced to Tambor Island in the nineteenth century. Overgrazing by the enormous rabbit population now menaces the island's agriculture. The government proposes to reduce the population by using a virus that has caused devastating epidemics in rabbit populations elsewhere. There is, however, a small chance that the virus will infect the bilby, an endangered native herbivore. The government's plan, therefore, may serve the interests of agriculture but will clearly increase the threat to native wildlife.

The argument above assumes which of the following?

(A) There is less chance that the virus will infect domestic animals on Tambor than that it will infect wild animals of species native to the island.

(B) Overgrazing by rabbits does not pose the most significant current threat to the bilby.

(C) There is at least one alternative means of reducing the rabbit population that would not involve any threat to the bilby.

(D) There are no species of animals on the island that prey on the rabbits.

(E) The virus that the government proposes to use has been successfully used elsewhere to control populations of rabbits.

283. Telomerase is an enzyme that is produced only in cells that are actively dividing. Thus, as a rule, it is not present in adult tissue. Bone marrow is an exception to this rule, however, since even in adults, bone marrow cells continually divide to replace old blood cells. Cancers are another exception, because their cells are rapidly dividing.

    The information provided most strongly supports which of the following?

    (A) Telomerase is the only enzyme that is present in cancerous cells but absent from cells that are not actively dividing.
    (B) Embryonic tissue is less likely to become cancerous than tissue that has ceased to actively divide.
    (C) The presence of telomerase in bone marrow is no indication of bone marrow cancer.
    (D) Cancer of the bone marrow develops more rapidly than cancer growing in any other kind of adult tissue.
    (E) The level of telomerase production is always higher in cancerous tissue than in noncancerous tissue.

284. Which of the following provides the most logical completion of the argument?

    Many of Vebrol Corporation's department heads will retire this year. The number of junior employees with the qualifications Vebrol will require for promotion to department head is equal to only half the expected vacancies. Vebrol is not going to hire department heads from outside the company, have current department heads take over more than one department, or reduce the number of its departments. So some departments will be without department heads next year, since Vebrol will not _____.

    (A) promote more than one employee from any department to serve as heads of departments
    (B) promote any current department heads to higher-level managerial positions
    (C) have any managers who are currently senior to department heads serve as department heads
    (D) reduce the responsibilities of each department
    (E) reduce the average number of employees per department

285. Ecologist: The Scottish Highlands were once the site of extensive forests, but these forests have mostly disappeared and been replaced by peat bogs. The common view is that the Highlands' deforestation was caused by human activity, especially agriculture. However, **agriculture began in the Highlands less than 2,000 years ago.** Peat bogs, which consist of compressed decayed vegetable matter, build up by only about one foot per 1,000 years and, **throughout the Highlands, remains of trees in peat bogs are almost all at depths greater than four feet.** Since climate changes that occurred between 7,000 and 4,000 years ago favored the development of peat bogs rather than the survival of forests, the deforestation was more likely the result of natural processes than of human activity.

    In the ecologist's argument, the two portions in **boldface** play which of the following roles?

    (A) The first is evidence that has been used in support of a position that the ecologist rejects; the second is a finding that the ecologist uses to counter that evidence.

    (B) The first is evidence that, in light of the evidence provided in the second, serves as grounds for the ecologist's rejection of a certain position.

    (C) The first is a position that the ecologist rejects; the second is evidence that has been used in support of that position.

    (D) The first is a position that the ecologist rejects; the second provides evidence in support of that rejection.

    (E) The first is a position for which the ecologist argues; the second provides evidence to support that position.

286. Background information: This year, each film submitted to the Barbizon Film Festival was submitted in one of ten categories. For each category, there was a panel that decided which submitted films to accept.

    Fact 1: Within each category, the rate of acceptance for domestic films was the same as that for foreign films.

    Fact 2: The overall rate of acceptance of domestic films was significantly higher than that of foreign films.

    In light of the background information, which of the following, if true, can account for fact 1 and fact 2 both being true of the submissions to this year's Barbizon Film Festival?

    (A) In each category, the selection panel was composed of filmmakers, and some selection panels included no foreign filmmakers.

    (B) Significantly more domestic films than foreign films were submitted to the festival.

    (C) In each of the past three years, the overall acceptance rate was higher for foreign than for domestic films, an outcome that had upset some domestic filmmakers.

    (D) The number of films to be selected in each category was predetermined, but in no category was it required that the acceptance rate of foreign films should equal that of domestic films.

    (E) Most foreign films, unlike most domestic films, were submitted in categories with high prestige, but with correspondingly low rates of acceptance.

287. Beets and carrots are higher in sugar than many other vegetables. They are also high on the glycemic index, a scale that measures the rate at which a food increases blood sugar levels. But while nutritionists usually advise people to avoid high-sugar and high-glycemic-index foods, despite any nutritional benefits they may confer, they are not very concerned about the consumption of beets and carrots.

Which of the following, if true, would best explain the nutritionists' lack of concern?

(A) Foods with added sugar are much higher in sugar, and have a larger effect on blood sugar levels, than do beets and carrots.

(B) Most consumption of beets and carrots occurs in combination with higher-protein foods, which reduce blood sugar fluctuations.

(C) Beets and carrots contain many nutrients, such as folate, beta-carotene, and vitamin C, of which many people fail to consume optimal quantities.

(D) The glycemic index measures the extent to which a food increases blood sugar levels as compared to white bread, a food that is much less healthy than beets and carrots.

(E) Nutritionists have only recently come to understand that a food's effect on blood sugar levels is an important determinant of that food's impact on a person's health.

288. Biologist: Species with broad geographic ranges probably tend to endure longer than species with narrow ranges. The broader a species' range, the more likely that species is to survive the extinction of populations in a few areas. Therefore, it is likely that the proportion of species with broad ranges tends to gradually increase with time.

The biologist's conclusion follows logically from the above if which of the following is assumed?

(A) There are now more species with broad geographic ranges than with narrow geographic ranges.

(B) Most species can survive extinctions of populations in a few areas as long as the species' geographic range is not very narrow.

(C) If a population of a species in a particular area dies out, that species generally does not repopulate that area.

(D) If a characteristic tends to help species endure longer, then the proportion of species with that characteristic tends to gradually increase with time.

(E) Any characteristic that makes a species tend to endure longer will make it easier for that species to survive the extinction of populations in a few areas.

289. Mashika: We already know from polling data that some segments of the electorate provide significant support to Ms. Puerta. If those segments also provide significant support to Mr. Quintana, then no segment of the electorate that provides significant support to Mr. Quintana provides significant support to Mr. Ramirez.

    Salim: But actually, as the latest polling data conclusively shows, at least one segment of the electorate does provide significant support to both Mr. Quintana and Mr. Ramirez.

    Assuming Mashika and Salim's statements are all true, which of the following can be most reasonably inferred from them?

    (A) At least one segment of the electorate provides significant support to neither Mr. Quintana nor to Mr. Ramirez.
    (B) At least one segment of the electorate provides significant support to Ms. Puerta but not to Mr. Quintana.
    (C) Each segment of the electorate provides significant support to Ms. Puerta.
    (D) Each segment of the electorate provides significant support to Mr. Quintana.
    (E) Each segment of the electorate provides significant support to Mr. Ramirez.

290. In a certain rural area, people normally dispose of household garbage by burning it. Burning household garbage releases toxic chemicals known as dioxins. New conservation regulations will require a major reduction in packaging—specifically, paper and cardboard packaging—for products sold in the area. Since such packaging materials contain dioxins, one result of the implementation of the new regulations will surely be a reduction in dioxin pollution in the area.

    Which of the following, if true, most seriously weakens the argument?

    (A) Garbage containing large quantities of paper and cardboard can easily burn hot enough for some portion of the dioxins that it contains to be destroyed.
    (B) Packaging materials typically make up only a small proportion of the weight of household garbage, but a relatively large proportion of its volume.
    (C) Per-capita sales of products sold in paper and cardboard packaging are lower in rural areas than in urban areas.
    (D) The new conservation regulations were motivated by a need to cut down on the consumption of paper products in order to bring the harvesting of timber into a healthier balance with its regrowth.
    (E) It is not known whether the dioxins released by the burning of household garbage have been the cause of any serious health problems.

4.8 Answer Key: Critical Reasoning

144.	D	174.	D	204.	A	234.	C	264.	E
145.	B	175.	A	205.	D	235.	C	265.	B
146.	D	176.	A	206.	D	236.	C	266.	D
147.	B	177.	B	207.	C	237.	E	267.	D
148.	B	178.	D	208.	D	238.	E	268.	C
149.	C	179.	D	209.	C	239.	C	269.	C
150.	A	180.	C	210.	A	240.	E	270.	C
151.	D	181.	A	211.	C	241.	E	271.	C
152.	B	182.	D	212.	C	242.	D	272.	C
153.	B	183.	E	213.	B	243.	D	273.	E
154.	B	184.	E	214.	B	244.	B	274.	B
155.	B	185.	C	215.	C	245.	C	275.	E
156.	D	186.	A	216.	B	246.	C	276.	B
157.	E	187.	A	217.	D	247.	C	277.	C
158.	A	188.	C	218.	D	248.	A	278.	A
159.	C	189.	B	219.	D	249.	E	279.	E
160.	A	190.	C	220.	D	250.	B	280.	E
161.	B	191.	E	221.	B	251.	B	281.	E
162.	A	192.	D	222.	E	252.	D	282.	B
163.	C	193.	E	223.	D	253.	B	283.	C
164.	E	194.	C	224.	C	254.	B	284.	C
165.	C	195.	C	225.	A	255.	D	285.	B
166.	B	196.	B	226.	E	256.	B	286.	B
167.	A	197.	C	227.	B	257.	D	287.	B
168.	D	198.	B	228.	C	258.	E	288.	D
169.	B	199.	C	229.	B	259.	D	289.	B
170.	B	200.	C	230.	E	260.	A	290.	A
171.	A	201.	A	231.	D	261.	B		
172.	A	202.	A	232.	D	262.	A		
173.	C	203.	A	233.	C	263.	B		

4.9 Answer Explanations: Critical Reasoning

The following discussion is intended to familiarize you with the most efficient and effective approaches to Critical Reasoning questions. The particular questions in this chapter are generally representative of the kinds of Critical Reasoning questions you will encounter on the GMAT exam. Remember that it is the problem-solving strategy that is important, not the specific details of a particular question.

Questions 144 to 187 — Difficulty: Easy

144. Stockholders have been critical of the Flyna Company, a major furniture retailer, because most of Flyna's furniture is manufactured in Country X from local wood, and illegal logging is widespread there. However, Flyna has set up a certification scheme for lumber mills. It has hired a staff of auditors and forestry professionals who review documentation of the wood supply of Country X's lumber mills to ensure its legal origin, make surprise visits to mills to verify documents, and certify mills as approved sources of legally obtained lumber. Flyna uses only lumber from certified mills. Thus, Flyna's claim that its Country X wood supply is obtained legally is justified.

    Which of the following, if true, would most undermine the justification provided for Flyna's claim?

    (A) Only about one-third of Flyna's inspectors were hired from outside the company.
    (B) Country X's government recently reduced its subsidies for lumber production.
    (C) Flyna has had to pay higher than expected salaries to attract qualified inspectors.
    (D) The proportion of Country X's lumber mills inspected each year by Flyna's staff is about 10 percent, randomly selected.
    (E) Illegal logging costs Country X's government a significant amount in lost revenue each year.

    Argument Evaluation

    Situation   The Flyna Company sells furniture mostly made in Country X from local wood. Illegal logging is widespread in Country X. Flyna has set up a certification scheme for lumber mills. Specialized staff make surprise visits to Country X mills, inspect documentation to ensure that the wood supply has a legal origin, and certify mills as approved sources for legally obtained lumber. Flyna uses only lumber from certified mills. According to the argument, Flyna's claim that its wood supply is legally obtained is justified.

    Reasoning   *What additional information would, if true, most undermine the justification for Flyna' claim that its Country X wood is legally obtained?* Clearly, much depends on the thoroughness of the certification scheme. For example, the staff auditing the mills would need to be qualified for the job and meticulous in meeting their responsibilities. The auditing visits would need to be frequent enough, and not predictable by mill management. Flyna would need to be genuinely committed to ensuring legality of wood sources; it would need to monitor its staff to ensure that they were doing their jobs effectively.

    A   This suggests that Flyna could make good judgments as to the competence and trustworthiness of most of the inspectors hired to certify lumber mills.

    B   This could provide a perverse incentive to loggers to violate legal restrictions on logging. However, this would not undercut Flyna's justification for its claim that its system ensures that all its lumber is legally sourced.

C   This has no bearing on whether Flyna's certification system will be effective in guaranteeing that Flyna's lumber is legally sourced. We are not told, for example, that Flyna has been unable to find enough qualified inspectors for the certification system to be effective.

D   **Correct**. This means that 90 percent of Country X's certified lumber mills are not inspected in any particular year. Moreover, since the selection of the 10 percent of lumber mills to be inspected in a given year is random, some lumber mills might go for much longer than ten years without inspection; during this period, many of those mills might fall below certification standards and even use lumber illegally obtained.

E   This indicates that a significant amount of illegal logging occurs in Country X; this suggests that it is possible that some illegally sourced wood could find its way to lumber mills that Flyna uses and has certified. But the information given here is not sufficiently specific to indicate that the Flyna certification system would fail to prevent the company's use of illegally sourced wood.

The correct answer is D.

145. Companies O and P each have the same number of employees who work the same number of hours per week. According to records maintained by each company, the employees of Company O had fewer job-related accidents last year than did the employees of Company P. Therefore, employees of Company O are less likely to have job-related accidents than are employees of Company P.

Which of the following, if true, would most weaken the conclusion?

(A) The employees of Company P lost more time at work due to job-related accidents than did the employees of Company O.
(B) Company P considered more types of accidents to be job-related than did Company O.
(C) The employees of Company P were sick more often than were the employees of Company O.
(D) Several employees of Company O each had more than one job-related accident.
(E) The majority of job-related accidents at Company O involved a single machine.

Argument Evaluation

Situation Two companies, O and P, have identical numbers of employees working identical numbers of hours. According to the companies' records, O's workers experienced fewer job-related accidents than did P's workers over the same period. According to the argument, it follows that O's workers are less likely to suffer job-related accidents than are P's workers.

Reasoning *Which of the statements provided would weaken the argument that workers at O are safer from job-related accidents than are workers at P?* In reviewing the statements, the key phrase here is *According to records maintained at each company*. On the face of it, differing numbers of job-related accidents among identical numbers of workers over an identical timeframe would necessarily imply differing *rates* of such accidents—unless the two companies construe what counts as a job-related accident differently. O's workers may not actually have a lower rate of such accidents, or be safer from such accidents in the future, if their company chooses not to class their accidents as job-related. Therefore, identifying such a discrepancy in how the two companies classify accidents would weaken the conclusion.

A P's workers losing more time to job-related injuries would be a reasonable expectation if the conclusion is correct; it does not weaken support for that conclusion.

B **Correct.** If P defines job-related accidents more broadly than does O, that fact would undermine the argument for the conclusion that O's workers genuinely suffer job-related accidents at a lower rate.

C Relative rates of sickness at the two companies have no bearing on their relative rates of accidents.

D Absent detailed information about whether P's workers also suffer multiple accidents per worker, this fact does not affect the conclusion that O's workers are safer than P's.

E The fact that a specific machine was particularly dangerous would not affect the conclusion about rates of accidents at the two companies.

The correct answer is B.

146. The *XCT* automobile is considered less valuable than the *ZNK* automobile, because insurance companies pay less, on average, to replace a stolen *XCT* than a stolen *ZNK*. Surprisingly, the average amount insurance companies will pay to repair a car involved in a collision is typically higher for the *XCT* than for the *ZNK*. One insurance expert explained that repairs to *XCT* automobiles are especially labor-intensive, and labor is a significant factor in collision repair costs.

Which of the following, if true, most strongly supports the insurance expert's explanation?

(A) *ZNK* automobiles are involved in accidents more frequently than *XCT* automobiles.
(B) The cost of routine maintenance for the *ZNK* is about the same as for the *XCT*.
(C) There are more automobile mechanics who specialize in *XCT* repairs than in *ZNK* repairs.
(D) The ease of repair of *ZNK* automobiles is one factor that adds to their value.
(E) *XCT* automobiles are more likely to be stolen than *ZNK* automobiles.

Argument Evaluation

Situation Two automobile models *XCT* and *ZNK* are compared with respect to (1) what insurance companies pay on average to replace a stolen vehicle and (2) what insurance companies pay on average to repair a crashed vehicle. On (1), insurance companies pay less for XCTs than for ZNKs. On (2), insurance companies pay more for repairing XCTs than ZNKs. An insurance expert explains that repairs to XCTs are especially labor-intensive; this tends to raise the cost of repairs.

Reasoning *Which piece of new information most strongly supports the expert's explanation for the fact that the replacement value is greater for the car that has lower repair costs?* We should look for information that supplements the explanation in a way that shows the coherence of the two facts given regarding insurance payments for the two cars.

A The frequency of accidents is not directly relevant to the higher cost of collision repair for those *XCT*s that are involved in collisions.

B This information is not directly relevant to the higher cost of collision repair for *XCT*s. It neither undermines nor supports the claim that *XCT* labor costs are higher per crashed vehicle and does not help support that claim as an explanation for the discrepancy in question.

C This neither supports nor undermines the expert's explanation. If we had information concerning the supply of *XCT* mechanics and *ZNK* mechanics relative to the demand for each, we would have some evidence that could throw light on differences in labor costs.

D **Correct.** *ZNK*s are more valuable because buyers know that total repair costs will be lower. This is reflected in the market value of *ZNK*s compared to that of *XCT*s. Replacing a stolen *XCT* costs insurance companies less than replacing a stolen *ZNK* because the lower market value of *XCT*s is related in the high cost of collision repair.

E This is unlikely to lower the market value of *XCT*s. The market value of *XCT*s is the factor that determines how much it costs to replace a stolen *XCT*.

The correct answer is D.

147. The sustained massive use of pesticides in farming has two effects that are especially pernicious. First, it often kills off the pests' natural enemies in the area. Second, it often unintentionally gives rise to insecticide-resistant pests, since those insects that survive a particular insecticide will be the ones most resistant to it, and they are the ones left to breed.

From the passage above, it can be properly inferred that the effectiveness of the sustained massive use of pesticides can be extended by doing which of the following, assuming that each is a realistic possibility?

(A) Using only chemically stable insecticides
(B) Periodically switching the type of insecticide used
(C) Gradually increasing the quantities of pesticides used
(D) Leaving a few fields fallow every year
(E) Breeding higher-yielding varieties of crop plants

Evaluation of a Plan

Situation Continued high-level pesticide use often kills off the targeted pests' natural enemies. In addition, the pests that survive the application of the pesticide may become resistant to it, and these pesticide-resistant pests will continue breeding.

Reasoning What can be done to prolong the effectiveness of pesticide use? *It can be inferred that the ongoing* use of a particular pesticide will not continue to be effective against the future generations of pests with an inherent resistance to that pesticide. What would be effective against these future generations? If farmers periodically change the particular pesticide they use, then pests resistant to one kind of pesticide might be killed by another. This would continue, with pests being killed off in cycles as the pesticides are changed. It is also possible that this rotation might allow some of the pests' natural enemies to survive, at least until the next cycle.

A   Not enough information about chemically stable insecticides is given to make a sound inference.
B   Correct. This statement properly identifies an action that could extend the effectiveness of pesticide use.
C   Gradually increasing the amount of the pesticides being used will not help the situation since the pests are already resistant to it.
D   Continued use of pesticides is assumed as part of the argument. Since pesticides would be unnecessary for fallow fields, this suggestion is irrelevant.
E   Breeding higher-yielding varieties of crops does nothing to extend the effectiveness of the use of pesticides.

The correct answer is B.

148. Editorial: The mayor plans to deactivate the city's fire alarm boxes, because most calls received from them are false alarms. The mayor claims that the alarm boxes are no longer necessary, since most people now have access to cell phones. But the city's commercial district, where there is the greatest risk of fire, has few residents and few cell towers, so some alarm boxes are still necessary.

Which of the following, if true, most seriously weakens the editorial's argument?

(A) Maintaining the fire alarm boxes costs the city more than 5 million dollars annually.
(B) Commercial buildings have automatic fire alarm systems that are linked directly to the fire department.
(C) The fire department gets less information from an alarm box than it does from a telephone call.
(D) The city's fire department is located much closer to the residential areas than to the commercial district.
(E) On average, almost 25 percent of the cell towers in the city are out of order.

Argument Evaluation

Situation Due to many false alarms from fire alarm boxes, the mayor intends to turn off the boxes and rely on cell phones for reporting fires. A shortage of cell towers in the commercial district suggests some alarm boxes are still necessary.

Reasoning *What would weaken the argument that alarm boxes are necessary?* The argument relies on the dearth of cell towers in the commercial district to conclude that alarm boxes are needed in order to report fires. If, however, there was some alternative way to alert the fire department to fires in the commercial district, that fact would undermine the suggestion that the commercial district needs alarm boxes.

A The cost of the alarm boxes has no bearing on whether or not they are necessary.

B **Correct.** The argument relies on a shortage of cell towers in the commercial district to conclude that alarm boxes are necessary for reporting fires; if, however, commercial buildings have an alternative way to alert the fire department, such as the alarm systems described here, then that would undermine the argument that the commercial district needs alarm boxes.

C The lack of detailed information conveyed by alarm boxes does not undermine the contention that such boxes are still necessary in some areas.

D The location of the fire department is not relevant to the question of whether the city needs alarm boxes.

E A high percentage of nonfunctional cell towers would tend to strengthen an argument for alarm boxes, not weaken it.

The correct answer is B.

149. Which of the following, if true, most logically completes the argument?

Some dairy farmers in the province of Takandia want to give their cows a synthetic hormone that increases milk production. Many Takandians, however, do not want to buy milk from cows given the synthetic hormone. For this reason Takandia's legislature is considering a measure requiring milk from cows given the hormone to be labeled as such. Even if the measure is defeated, dairy farmers who use the hormone will probably lose customers, since _____.

(A) it has not been proven that any trace of the synthetic hormone exists in the milk of cows given the hormone
(B) some farmers in Takandia who plan to use the synthetic hormone will probably not do so if the measure were passed
(C) milk from cows that have not been given the synthetic hormone can be labeled as such without any legislative action
(D) the legislature's consideration of the bill has been widely publicized
(E) milk that comes from cows given the synthetic hormone looks and tastes the same as milk from cows that have not received the hormone

Argument Construction

Situation   In Takandia, some of the dairy farmers are interested in increasing the amount of milk their cows produce by giving the animals a synthetic hormone. A significant percentage of consumers prefer not to buy milk from cows dosed with the hormone; lawmakers are considering a requirement that such milk carry an identifying label. Even without the labels, however, farmers using the hormone on their cows are likely to have fewer customers buy their milk.

Reasoning   *What would cause a declining share of customers?* The argument states that even if the milk from hormone-dosed cows continues to be unlabeled, fewer customers will probably buy it. That outcome would be likely if customers had another way to identify the milk they prefer—for example, labels on milk from *untreated* cows—so that they could choose the milk from untreated cows instead of milk that does not provide any information about whether the cows were treated. In other words, labeling the untreated milk provides that milk a competitive advantage over treated milk, and that advantage will probably reduce market share for treated milk.

A   Lack of proof that the hormone is in the milk would not be expected to *decrease* market share of such milk; indeed, farmers could use that fact to try to persuade customers to buy it.

B   The fact that required labels might dissuade farmers from using the hormone would have no effect on their potential sales in the *absence* of required labels.

C   **Correct.** If farmers who *don't* use the hormone can label their milk and thereby allow customers to identify the milk they prefer, those labels would provide milk from untreated cows with a competitive advantage. That advantage would be likely to reduce the share of customers who would buy milk from treated cows, even if that milk was not specifically labeled.

D   Publicity regarding potential label requirements would not be likely to cause declining sales in the absence of such requirements.

E   The fact that milk from treated cows looks and tastes the same would not be expected to reduce its share of customers.

The correct answer is C.

150. Which of the following most logically completes the passage?

A business analysis of the Appenian railroad system divided its long-distance passenger routes into two categories: rural routes and interurban routes. The analysis found that, unlike the interurban routes, few rural routes carried a high enough passenger volume to be profitable. Closing unprofitable rural routes, however, will not necessarily enhance the profitability of the whole system, since _____.

(A) a large part of the passenger volume on interurban routes is accounted for by passengers who begin or end their journeys on rural routes

(B) within the last two decades several of the least used rural routes have been closed and their passenger services have been replaced by buses

(C) the rural routes were all originally constructed at least one hundred years ago, whereas some of the interurban routes were constructed recently for new high-speed express trains

(D) not all of Appenia's large cities are equally well served by interurban railroad services

(E) the greatest passenger volume, relative to the routes' capacity, is not on either category of long-distance routes but is on suburban commuter routes

Argument Construction

Situation   In the Appenian railroad system, interurban routes generally carry enough passengers to be profitable, but few rural routes do.

Reasoning   *What would suggest that closing unprofitable rural routes would not enhance the railroad system's profitability?* Any evidence that closing the unprofitable rural routes would indirectly reduce the profitability of other components of the railroad system would support the conclusion that closing those rural routes will not enhance the system's profitability. Thus, a statement providing such evidence would logically complete the passage.

A   **Correct.** This suggests that closing the rural routes could discourage many passengers from traveling on the profitable interurban routes as well, thus reducing the profitability of the railroad system as a whole.

B   Even if some of the least used rural routes have already been closed, it remains true that most of the remaining rural routes are too little used to be profitable.

C   Closing very old routes would be at least as likely to enhance the railroad system's profitability as closing newer routes would be.

D   Even if there is better railroad service to some large cities than others, closing unprofitable rural routes could still enhance the system's profitability.

E   Even if suburban routes are the most heavily used and profitable, closing underused, unprofitable rural routes could still enhance the system's profitability.

The correct answer is A.

151. Although Ackerburg's subway system is currently operating at a deficit, the transit authority will lower subway fares next year. The authority projects that the lower fares will result in a ten percent increase in the number of subway riders. Since the additional income from the larger ridership will more than offset the decrease due to lower fares, the transit authority actually expects the fare reduction to reduce or eliminate the subway system's operating deficit for next year.

    Which of the following, if true, provides the most support for the transit authority's expectation of reducing the subway system's operating deficit?

    (A) Throughout the years that the subway system has operated, fares have never before been reduced.
    (B) The planned fare reduction will not apply to students, who can already ride the subway for a reduced fare.
    (C) Next year, the transit authority will have to undertake several large-scale track maintenance projects.
    (D) The subway system can accommodate a ten percent increase in ridership without increasing the number of trains it runs each day.
    (E) The current subway fares in Ackerburg are higher than subway fares in other cities in the region.

    Argument Evaluation

    Situation   Ackerburg's transit authority plans to lower subway fares, projecting that this will increase ridership by 10 percent and thereby reduce or eliminate the subway system's operating deficit.

    Reasoning   *What evidence would support the expectation that lowering subway fares will reduce the operating deficit?* The passage says the additional income from the projected increase in ridership will more than offset the decrease due to the lowered fares. The claim that lowering fares will reduce the operating deficit could be supported either by additional evidence that lowering the fares will increase ridership at least as much as projected or by evidence that the plan will not increase overall operating expenses.

    A   The fact that fares have never been reduced provides no evidence about what would happen if they were reduced.
    B   This suggests that the planned fare reduction would not affect revenue from student riders, but it does not suggest how it would affect revenue from all other riders.
    C   These maintenance projects will probably increase the operating deficit, making it less likely that the fare reduction will reduce or eliminate that deficit.
    D   **Correct.** This indicates that the plan will not involve extra operating expenses for running trains and thus increases the likelihood that the plan will reduce the operating deficit.
    E   Ackerburg may differ from other cities in the region in ways that make the higher fares optimal for Ackerburg's subway system.

    The correct answer is D.

152. At several locations on the northwest coast of North America are formations known as chevrons—wedge-shaped formations of mounded sediment—pointing toward the ocean. Most geologists take them to have been formed by erosion, but recently other scientists have proposed that they were thrown up from the ocean by massive waves triggered by meteor impacts in the Pacific Ocean.

    Which of the following, if discovered, would most help in deciding which hypothesis is correct?

    (A) Chevron-like structures which are not currently near glaciers, large rivers, or other bodies of water
    (B) The presence, in chevrons, of deposits of ocean microfossils containing metals typically formed by meteor impacts
    (C) Oral-history evidence for flooding that could have been caused by ocean waves
    (D) The fact that exact data about the location and depth of any meteor impact craters on the Pacific seabed is lacking
    (E) The fact that certain changes in the shape and location of maritime sand dunes have been produced by the action of wind and waves

Argument Evaluation

Situation   The northwest coast of North America has chevrons—large wedge-shaped mounds of sediment—pointing toward the ocean. Two explanations have been offered for these phenomena: (1) they were formed by erosion, according to most geologists; and (2) meteor impacts caused massive waves that threw the formations up from the Pacific Ocean.

Reasoning   *Which of the answer choices most helps to decide which explanation is correct?* If (2) is the true explanation, then one would expect evidence such as residues of ocean matter to be present in chevrons. If (1) is the true explanation, the chevrons would need to be analyzed to determine the sources of the eroded material, and the factors, such as wind or water, that produced the erosion.

A   This information neither confirms nor conclusively eliminates either explanation (1) or explanation (2). The scientists hypothesize is that these chevrons, at these locations on the coast, were caused by meteor impacts, not that geological structures with a similar shape are generally formed in that way. The scientists' reasoning is consistent with the hypothesis that different wedge-shaped geological structures are formed in many different ways.

B   **Correct.** The ocean microfossils containing metals typically found in meteors would indicate that the metals were found in fossils that originated in the ocean. This provides strong evidence that meteors landed in the ocean; the fact that the metals are now found in the chevrons strongly supports explanation (2).

C   The oral-history testimony concerning flooding by ocean waves provides weak evidence consistent with each of the two explanations. Erosion of rocks can deposit sediment, and ocean waves could form mounds of such sediment.

D   This information points out that some additional bits of evidence that might help confirm explanation (2) are currently lacking, but such evidence might be discovered later, and the impacts might have occurred so long ago that all evidence of their exact locations has been obliterated. The fact that such evidence happens to be lacking now does not significantly count for or against either of the proposed explanations.

E   This indicates that some types of sedimentary structures (such as sand dunes) can be shaped by ocean waves, but it gives no evidence of whether the chevrons might have originated as sand dunes. It also gives no indication of whether the dunes in question have a chevron shape or some other shape. So this does not provide information to significantly support either of the explanations.

The correct answer is B.

153. Sparrow Airlines is planning to reduce its costs by cleaning its planes' engines once a month, rather than the industry standard of every six months. With cleaner engines, Sparrow can postpone engine overhauls, which take planes out of service for up to 18 months. Furthermore, cleaning an engine reduces its fuel consumption by roughly 1.2 percent.

    The airline's plan assumes that

    (A) fuel prices are likely to rise in the near future and therefore cutting fuel consumption is an important goal
    (B) the cost of monthly cleaning of an airplane's engines is not significantly greater in the long run than is the cost of an engine overhaul
    (C) engine cleaning does not remove an airplane from service
    (D) Sparrow Airlines has had greater problems with engine overhauls and fuel consumption than other airlines have
    (E) cleaning engines once a month will give Sparrow Airlines a competitive advantage over other airlines

    Evaluation of a Plan

    Situation   Sparrow Airlines plans to clean the engines of its planes monthly rather than every six months. The goal is to reduce its costs.

    Reasoning   *Which statement provides an assumption underlying the plan?* The plan will enable Sparrow to postpone engine overhauls, which put a plane out of service for up to 18 months. The monthly cleaning will reduce its fuel consumption by 1.2 percent. But suppose the long-run cost of monthly cleanings were greater than the cost of an engine overhaul, then the rationale for the airline's plan would fail.

    A   Nothing in the information provided indicates that this is assumed in the plan.

    B   **Correct.** The plan makes sense only if this is assumed. If the long-run total cost of monthly cleaning significantly exceeded the total cost of engine overhaul—which would include, in the long run, more frequent downtime of 18 months if the plan were not adopted—then it seems likely that the projected benefit of postponement of engine overhauls would not be compensated for by the 1.2 percent fuel-cost savings.

    C   The plan does not have to assume this. Perhaps monthly engine cleaning requires only one day of down time.

    D   This is perhaps a good reason for Sparrow to put in place the proposed cost-saving plan, but it is not an assumption that the plan requires for it to make sense.

    E   The plan does not have to assume this, even if Sparrow's cost saving were to result in a competitive advantage. Sparrow's plan could equally be aimed at simply removing a competitive disadvantage. The issue of competition is not addressed in the given information.

    The correct answer is B.

154. Patrick usually provides child care for six children. Parents leave their children at Patrick's house in the morning and pick them up after work. At the end of each workweek, the parents pay Patrick at an hourly rate for the child care provided that week. The weekly income Patrick receives is usually adequate but not always uniform, particularly in the winter, when children are likely to get sick and be unpredictably absent.

Which of the following plans, if put into effect, has the best prospect of making Patrick's weekly income both uniform and adequate?

(A) Pool resources with a neighbor who provides child care under similar arrangements, so that the two of them cooperate in caring for twice as many children as Patrick currently does.

(B) Replace payment by actual hours of child care provided with a fixed weekly fee based upon the number of hours of child care that Patrick would typically be expected to provide.

(C) Hire a full-time helper and invest in facilities for providing child care to sick children.

(D) Increase the hourly rate to a level that would provide adequate income even in a week when half of the children Patrick usually cares for are absent.

(E) Increase the number of hours made available for child care each day, so that parents can leave their children in Patrick's care for a longer period each day at the current hourly rate.

Evaluation of a Plan

Situation   At the end of the workweek, Patrick is paid a certain amount for each hour of child care he has provided. Patrick usually receives adequate weekly income under this arrangement, but in the winter Patrick's income fluctuates, because children are unpredictably absent due to illness.

Reasoning   *Which plan would be most likely to meet the two goals of uniform weekly income and adequate weekly income?* Patrick must find a way to ensure that his weekly income is both adequate—that is, not reduced significantly from current levels—and uniform—that is, not subject to seasonal or other fluctuations. A successful plan would thus most likely be one that does not increase Patrick's costs. Further, the plan need not increase Patrick's weekly income; it must merely ensure that that income is more reliable. It should therefore also provide some way to mitigate the unexpected loss of income from children's absences.

A   This plan might raise Patrick's income slightly, because he and the neighbor might pay out less in costs if they pool their resources. But this plan would have no effect on the problem that unpredictable absences pose for Patrick's weekly income.

B   **Correct.** This statement properly identifies a plan that would most likely keep Patrick's income adequate (he would probably receive approximately the same amount of money per child as he does now) and uniform (he would receive the money regardless of whether a child was present or absent).

C   While this plan might somewhat mitigate the unpredictability in Patrick's income that results from sick children's absences—because parents would be less likely to keep sick children at home—it would increase Patrick's costs. Paying a helper and investing in different facilities would reduce Patrick's income and might thus result in that income being inadequate.

D   Under this plan, if we assume that parents did not balk at the increase in Patrick's hourly rate and find alternative child care, Patrick's income would most likely be adequate. But this plan would not help make Patrick's weekly income uniform. His income would continue to fluctuate when children are absent. Remember, there are two goals with regard to Patrick's income: adequacy and uniformity.

E   This plan might increase Patrick's income, in that he might be paid for more hours of child care each week. The goals here, however, are to make Patrick's weekly income both adequate and uniform, and this plan does not address the issue of uniformity.

The correct answer is B.

155. Film director: It is true that certain characters and plot twists in my newly released film *The Perfect Heist* are strikingly similar to characters and plot twists in *Thieves*, a movie that came out last year. Based on these similarities, the film studio that produced *Thieves* is now accusing me of taking ideas from that film. The accusation is clearly without merit. All production work on *The Perfect Heist* was actually completed months before *Thieves* was released.

Which of the following, if true, provides the strongest support for the director's rejection of the accusation?

(A) Before *Thieves* began production, its script had been circulating for several years among various film studios, including the studio that produced *The Perfect Heist*.

(B) The characters and plot twists that are most similar in the two films have close parallels in many earlier films of the same genre.

(C) The film studio that produced *Thieves* seldom produces films in this genre.

(D) The director of *Thieves* worked with the director of *The Perfect Heist* on several earlier projects.

(E) The time it took to produce *The Perfect Heist* was considerably shorter than the time it took to produce *Thieves*.

Argument Evaluation

Situation A film director is accused of stealing ideas from a recent movie, *Thieves*, and using those ideas in their own newer movie, *The Perfect Heist*. The director admits that there are similarities but denies the charge of plagiarism on the grounds that work on *The Perfect Heist* was complete before *Thieves* came out.

Reasoning *What factor would support the contention that* The Perfect Heist *did not copy* Thieves? *If it can be shown that* The Perfect Heist *had likely sources for its ideas other than* Thieves, *that would tend to support the director's contention that* The Perfect Heist *did not steal ideas from the earlier film.*

A If the director could have read or heard about the *Thieves* script at any point in the last several years, that would tend to support the accusation of copying and to undermine the director's dismissal of that accusation.

B **Correct.** If the disputed ideas are tropes common to many earlier films, then that would tend to suggest that both *Thieves* and *The Perfect Heist* drew their ideas from those earlier films and support the assertion that *The Perfect Heist* did not copy *Thieves*.

C The fact that the studio behind *Thieves* rarely works in the heist genre has no bearing on whether or not *The Perfect Heist* copied *Thieves*.

D The fact that the two directors have worked together in the past neither supports nor undermines the accusation that one copied the other.

E The relative production time of the two movies is not relevant to the question of whether one copied the other.

The correct answer is B.

156. The rate at which a road wears depends on various factors, including climate, amount of traffic, and the size and weight of the vehicles using it. The only land transportation to Rittland's seaport is via a divided highway, one side carrying traffic to the seaport and one carrying traffic away from it. The side leading to the seaport has worn faster, even though each side has carried virtually the same amount of traffic, consisting mainly of large trucks.

Which of the following, if true, most helps to explain the difference in the rate of wear?

(A) The volume of traffic to and from Rittland's seaport has increased beyond the intended capacity of the highway that serves it.

(B) Wear on the highway that serves Rittland's seaport is considerably greater during the cold winter months.

(C) Wear on the side of the highway that leads to Rittland's seaport has encouraged people to take buses to the seaport rather than driving there in their own automobiles.

(D) A greater tonnage of goods is exported from Rittland's seaport than is imported through it.

(E) All of Rittland's automobiles are imported by ship.

Argument Construction

Situation   The side of a divided highway leading to a seaport has worn faster than the side leading away from the seaport. Both sides carry roughly the same amount of traffic, mainly consisting of large trucks.

Reasoning   *What could explain why the side of the highway leading to the seaport has worn faster than the other side?* We are told that climate, amount of traffic, and the size and weight of vehicles on a road affect how quickly the road wears. We are also told that the amounts of traffic on the two sides of the highway are almost identical. Probably the climate on the two sides is also almost identical. Thus, the most likely explanation for the different rates of wear is that the size or weight of the vehicles driving on the two sides differs significantly. So any factor that would make the vehicles' size or weight greater on the side leading to the seaport than on the other side could help explain the difference in wearing.

A   The increased traffic volume affects both sides of the highway, so it does not help explain why one side is wearing faster than the other.

B   The winter weather affects both sides of the highway, so it does not help explain why one side is wearing faster than the other.

C   The buses may contribute to wear on the side of the highway leading to the seaport, but not necessarily more than the car traffic they are replacing would (though the increased use of buses instead of cars may decrease the amount of traffic, buses would be heavier than cars and thus may result in an equal or greater amount of wear). Furthermore, the buses have to come back on the other side, probably carrying the returning travelers who have not left their cars at the airport.

D   **Correct**. This suggests that the many trucks visiting the seaport tend to be more heavily laden with goods when traveling on the side of the highway leading to the seaport than when returning on the other side. The resulting difference in the trucks' weight when traveling on the two sides could explain the different rates of wear.

E   These automobiles would be transported along the side of the highway leading from the seaport, but not along the side leading to it. This would likely create a pattern of wear opposite to the one observed.

The correct answer is D.

157. Ythex has developed a small diesel engine that produces 30 percent less particulate pollution than the engine made by its main rival, Onez, now widely used in Marania; Ythex's engine is well-suited for use in the thriving warehousing businesses in Marania, although it costs more than the Onez engine. The Maranian government plans to ban within the next two years the use of diesel engines with more than 80 percent of current diesel engine particulate emissions in Marania, and Onez will probably not be able to retool its engine to reduce emissions to reach this target. So if the ban is passed, the Ythex engine ought to sell well in Marania after that time.

Which of the following is an assumption on which the argument above depends?

(A) Marania's warehousing and transshipment business buys more diesel engines of any size than other types of engines.
(B) Ythex is likely to be able to reduce the cost of its small diesel engine within the next two years.
(C) The Maranian government is generally favorable to anti-pollution regulations.
(D) The government's ban on high levels of pollution caused by diesel engines, if passed, will not be difficult to enforce.
(E) The other manufacturers of small diesel engines in Marania, if there are any, have not produced an engine as popular and clean-running as Ythex's new engine.

Argument Evaluation

Situation Two companies, Ythex and Onez, produce diesel engines in Marania. Ythex has developed a small engine that produces less particulate pollution than the engine made by Onez, its main rival. The Maranian government will put a new maximum particulate-emission level in force within two years, but Onez will not be able to meet this target.

Reasoning *What would have to be assumed for the argument to support the prediction that Ythex's engine will sell well in two years when the new maximum particulate level is introduced?* To answer this, one might ask, for example: Will the maximum level be efficiently enforced? Will Ythex have any rivals other than Onez that will compete in the low-pollution diesel market?

A This tells us that there is a significant market for diesel engines, but this not an assumption that the reasoning depends on. The reasoning focuses only on the market for diesel engines and does not address the relative sizes of the market for diesel engines and that for non-diesel engines.

B If this is true, it provides additional support for the conclusion that Ythex's engine will sell well in two years. However, it is not an assumption on which the reasoning relies.

C This information is peripheral to the reasoning and not an assumption on which the reasoning relies. Adding it to the information given would not make the reasoning more logically compelling.

D The ban might be quite difficult to enforce, but a more important issue is whether the ban will be effectively enforced (so the reasoning does have to assume that the ban would be at least somewhat effective). No assumption about the relative difficulty of enforcing the ban needs to be made for the reasoning to be logically compelling.

E **Correct.** Are there one or more diesel engines from other companies that will be able to compete effectively with Ythex's engine when the ban is introduced? For the reasoning to be logically compelling, it needs to be assumed that the answer is no.

The correct answer is E.

158. In parts of South America, vitamin-A deficiency is a serious health problem, especially among children. In one region, agriculturists are attempting to improve nutrition by encouraging farmers to plant a new variety of sweet potato called SPK004 that is rich in beta-carotene, which the body converts into vitamin A. The plan has good chances of success, since sweet potato is a staple of the region's diet and agriculture, and the varieties currently grown contain little beta-carotene.

Which of the following, if true, most strongly supports the prediction that the plan will succeed?

(A) The growing conditions required by the varieties of sweet potato currently cultivated in the region are conditions in which SPK004 can flourish.

(B) The flesh of SPK004 differs from that of the currently cultivated sweet potatoes in color and texture, so traditional foods would look somewhat different when prepared from SPK004.

(C) There are no other varieties of sweet potato that are significantly richer in beta-carotene than SPK004 is.

(D) The varieties of sweet potato currently cultivated in the region contain some important nutrients that are lacking in SPK004.

(E) There are other vegetables currently grown in the region that contain more beta-carotene than the currently cultivated varieties of sweet potato do.

Evaluation of a Plan

Situation Agriculturists believe that if farmers in a particular South American region plant a new beta-carotene-rich variety of sweet potato, SPK004, the vitamin-A deficiency suffered in that region can be alleviated. Even though sweet potatoes are a staple of the region and the body can convert a sweet potato's beta-carotene into vitamin A, the varieties currently grown there contain little beta-carotene.

Reasoning *What would most support the success of the plan to improve nutrition by encouraging farmers to plant SPK004?* What, that is, would make farmers respond positively to encouragement to plant SPK004? Farmers in the region would probably be inclined to substitute SPK004 for the varieties of sweet potato they currently grow if they could be assured that SPK004 would grow as well as those other varieties do. This would in turn most likely lead to SPK004 being substituted for current varieties of sweet potato in staple dishes, and thus to an improvement in nutrition in the region.

A **Correct.** This statement properly identifies a factor that would support a prediction of the plan's success.

B If dishes made with SPK004 look different than traditional sweet potato dishes in the region do, people might be less likely to eat those dishes; in such a situation, the plan's success would be less likely, rather than more likely.

C It is SPK004's beta-carotene content relative to the beta-carotene content of the sweet potatoes currently grown in the region that is relevant here, so it does not matter if there are other varieties of sweet potato that are richer in beta-carotene than SPK004 is.

D This suggests that switching from currently grown sweet potatoes to SPK004 could negatively affect nutrition in the region; this undermines, rather than supports, the prediction that the plan to improve nutrition will succeed.

E These other vegetables, despite their beta-carotene content being higher than that of the currently cultivated varieties of sweet potato, are clearly not sufficient to prevent a vitamin-A deficiency in the region. This information does nothing to support the prediction that encouraging farmers to plant SPK004 will help to meet those beta-carotene needs.

The correct answer is A.

159. Which of the following most logically completes the argument?

The last members of a now-extinct species of a European wild deer called the giant deer lived in Ireland about 16,000 years ago. Prehistoric cave paintings in France depict this animal as having a large hump on its back. Fossils of this animal, however, do not show any hump. Nevertheless, there is no reason to conclude that the cave paintings are therefore inaccurate in this regard, since _____.

(A) some prehistoric cave paintings in France also depict other animals as having a hump
(B) fossils of the giant deer are much more common in Ireland than in France
(C) animal humps are composed of fatty tissue, which does not fossilize
(D) the cave paintings of the giant deer were painted well before 16,000 years ago
(E) only one currently existing species of deer has any anatomical feature that even remotely resembles a hump

Argument Construction

Situation Representations found in prehistoric cave paintings in France of the now-extinct giant deer species—the last members of which lived in Ireland about 16,000 years ago—depict the deer as having a hump on its back. Fossils of the deer, however, do not feature a hump.

Reasoning *What point would most logically complete the argument? That is, what would show that the cave paintings are not inaccurate even though fossils of the giant deer show no hump?* How could it be the case that the paintings show a hump while the fossils do not? One way in which this could be so is if the humps are not part of the fossils—that is, if there is some reason why a hump would not be preserved with the rest of an animal's remains.

A We do not know whether these other cave paintings accurately depict the animals as having humps, so this provides no reason to think that the depictions of giant deer are accurate.

B Where giant deer fossils are found has no bearing on whether cave paintings of giant deer that show a hump on the animal's back are inaccurate. It could be that this suggests that the painters responsible for the representations would not be very familiar with the species; if this were so, it would give some reason to conclude that the representations were inaccurate.

C **Correct.** This statement properly identifies a point that logically completes the argument. A hump would not be found as part of a giant deer's fossilized remains if the humps were fatty tissue that would not be fossilized.

D That the cave paintings were painted well before 16,000 years ago shows that they were executed before the giant deer became extinct, but this does not help to explain the discrepancy between the paintings' depiction of a hump on the deer's back and the fossil record's lack of such a hump. It could be that even though the cave painters coexisted with the giant deer, they were not sufficiently familiar with them to depict them accurately.

E That currently existing species of deer lack humps, or even that one species does have a feature resembling a hump, has little bearing on whether cave paintings in France accurately depict the giant deer as having a hump.

The correct answer is C.

160. Super Express Shipping Company has implemented a new distribution system that can get almost every package to its destination the day after it is sent. The company worries that this more efficient system will result in lower sales of its premium next-day delivery service, because its two-day service will usually arrive the following day anyway. The company plans to encourage sales of its next-day service by intentionally delaying delivery of its two-day packages so that they will not be delivered the following day, even if the package arrives at its destination city in time for next-day delivery.

The company's plan assumes that

(A) deliberate delay of packages will not affect the company's image in a way that significantly reduces its ability to attract and retain customers
(B) most people do not have a preference for either two-day or next-day delivery
(C) if the plan is not implemented, the company would lose more money in lost sales of overnight deliveries than it would save with its new efficient distribution system
(D) the overnight service is too expensive to be attractive to most customers currently
(E) competing companies' delivery services rarely deliver packages to their destination earlier than their promised time

Evaluation of a Plan

Situation Super Express, a shipping company, is concerned that a new level of efficiency in its delivery process, resulting in next-day delivery even with guaranteed two-day delivery, might sabotage the company's more expensive "premium" next-day delivery service. To promote the premium delivery service, the company plans to delay, for one day, two-day delivery packages that arrive one day early at a center near the customer and could be delivered that same day.

Reasoning *What does the company's plan assume?* The company's rationale for its plan is that without the planned delay, its next-day premium service would lose revenue if potential customers realized that the less expensive two-day delivery service usually results in next-day delivery. So the plan must assume that the planned delivery day will not damage the company's image in a way that would cause significant loss of customers.

A **Correct.** If it became public that the company was deliberately delaying packages, its brand and reputation would likely suffer major damage and its ability to promote its services—including its premium next-day delivery service—would probably be seriously impaired. Since presumably the company wants to retain existing customers and even attract new ones, its plan (including the rationale for it) would not make sense unless it were assumed that such catastrophic consequences would not result.

B The given information indicates that the company believes that a sizeable number of customers would, in certain circumstances, prefer guaranteed next-day delivery and pay more for it.

C Neither the plan nor its rationale is based on assuming that no other, equally good, plan could be devised to achieve the company's major objective and prevent the consequence of overall revenue loss.

D The given information gives no indication that the company believes this is so, and nothing related to its plan implies otherwise.

E Nothing is assumed in the company's plan about the frequency with which its competitors deliver packages to customers earlier than the promised delivery time.

The correct answer is A.

161. Psychologists conducted an experiment in which half of the volunteers were asked to describe an unethical action they had performed, while the other half were asked to describe an ethical action they had performed. Some of the volunteers, chosen at random from each of the two groups, were encouraged to wash their hands afterward. Among those who described unethical actions, those who washed their hands were significantly less likely to volunteer for another, similar experiment than those who did not wash their hands. The researchers concluded that some of the subjects failed to volunteer again in part because of their having described an unethical action.

    Which of the following would, if true, most help to support the researchers' conclusion?

    (A) Among the volunteers who described ethical actions, those who washed their hands were significantly less likely to volunteer for another, similar experiment than those who did not wash their hands.
    (B) The average likelihood of volunteering for another, similar experiment was higher among those who described ethical actions than among those who described unethical actions.
    (C) Most of the volunteers who were encouraged to wash their hands did so.
    (D) The volunteers in the study were not more disposed to washing their hands under normal circumstances than the general population was.
    (E) Equal numbers of volunteers from both groups were encouraged to wash their hands.

    Argument Evaluation

    Situation In an experiment, volunteers in one group were asked to describe an unethical action they had performed; volunteers in another group were asked to describe an ethical action they had performed. Some of the volunteers, randomly selected from each group, were encouraged to wash their hands afterwards. Among those who had described unethical actions, those who washed their hands were significantly less likely to volunteer for another, similar experiment than were those who did not wash their hands. The researchers concluded that some of the volunteers declined to volunteer again because of their having described an unethical action.

    Reasoning *Which new information most strongly supports the researchers' conclusion?* The researchers offered an answer to the following question in their conclusion: What caused some subjects not to volunteer again for another, similar experiment? The researchers concluded that one causal factor was having described an unethical action. This conclusion is based only on data about those who had described their unethical actions; the data showed that the hand washers among them were less likely to volunteer again than were those who did not wash their hands. This data, by itself, seems to provide at best weak support for the researchers' conclusion. The hypothesis could be strengthened by data comparing those who had described their ethical actions with those who had described their unethical ones.

    A This information slightly weakens the researchers' conclusion in that it suggests that the decision not to volunteer for future experiments could have been due entirely to the hand washing rather than partly to the participants' having described unethical actions.

    B **Correct.** This information does not refer to hand washing but provides a comparison between those who described an ethical action and those who described an unethical one, with respect to the likelihood of their volunteering for another, similar experiment. The fact that those who described ethical actions were more likely than the others to volunteer for subsequent experiments provides some evidence that describing an unethical action could have been a factor, along with the hand washing, that caused the observed difference in the volunteering rate. This additional evidence is only prima facie, though; it would be weakened if we also knew that among those who described ethical actions, the hand washers were just as unlikely to volunteer again as were those who washed their hands after describing unethical actions.

C   This information about hand washing is largely irrelevant to the researchers' conclusion, which is focused on the hypothesis that having described an unethical action made some participants less likely to volunteer again. It provides only very slight, conjectural support in that it is inconsistent with a hypothesis that so few actually washed their hands that they constituted a statistically insignificant sample.

D   The researchers' conclusion is not about the general population, so the information in this answer choice could only be relevant if such a generalization were the goal.

E   Like answer choice C, this information about hand washing is largely irrelevant to the researchers' conclusion, which is focused on the hypothesis that having described an unethical action made some participants less likely to volunteer again. It provides only very slight, conjectural support in that it is inconsistent with a hypothesis that one or more of the groups being compared was too small to be statistically significant.

The correct answer is B.

162. High levels of fertilizer and pesticides, needed when farmers try to produce high yields of the same crop year after year, pollute water supplies. Experts therefore urge farmers to diversify their crops and to rotate their plantings yearly.

To receive governmental price-support benefits for a crop, farmers must have produced that same crop for the past several years.

The statements above, if true, best support which of the following conclusions?

(A) The rules for governmental support of farm prices work against efforts to reduce water pollution.
(B) The only solution to the problem of water pollution from fertilizers and pesticides is to take farmland out of production.
(C) Farmers can continue to make a profit by rotating diverse crops, thus reducing costs for chemicals, but not by planting the same crop each year.
(D) New farming techniques will be developed to make it possible for farmers to reduce the application of fertilizers and pesticides.
(E) Governmental price supports for farm products are set at levels that are not high enough to allow farmers to get out of debt.

Argument Construction

Situation   Farmers are urged to rotate crops annually because the chemicals they must use when continuing to produce the same crops pollute water supplies. On the other hand, farmers may receive federal price-support benefits only if they have been producing the same crop for the past several years.

Reasoning   *What conclusion can be drawn from this information?* Farmers wish to receive the price-support benefits offered by the government, so they grow the same crop for several years. In order to continue getting good yields, they use the high levels of chemicals necessary when the same crop is grown from year to year. The result is water pollution. The government's rules for price-support benefits work against the efforts to reduce water pollution.

A   **Correct.** This statement properly identifies the conclusion supported by the evidence.
B   The experts cited in the passage believe that the rotation of crops is the solution, not the removal of farmland from production.
C   The conclusion that farmers cannot make a profit by producing the same crop year after year is not justified by the information given in the premises. The information given suggests that this conclusion would actually be false, since these farmers would benefit by price-support measures for such a crop.
D   No information in the passage supports a conclusion about farming techniques other than crop diversification and rotation, which are clearly existing farming techniques and not new or yet to be developed.
E   This conclusion is unwarranted because there is no information in the two statements about the levels of the price supports and of the farmers' debts.

The correct answer is A.

163. The interview is an essential part of a successful hiring program because, with it, job applicants who have personalities that are unsuited to the requirements of the job will be eliminated from consideration.

    The argument above logically depends on which of the following assumptions?

    (A) A hiring program will be successful if it includes interviews.
    (B) The interview is a more important part of a successful hiring program than is the development of a job description.
    (C) Interviewers can accurately identify applicants whose personalities are unsuited to the requirements of the job.
    (D) The only purpose of an interview is to evaluate whether job applicants' personalities are suited to the requirements of the job.
    (E) The fit of job applicants' personalities to the requirements of the job was once the most important factor in making hiring decisions.

    Argument Construction

    Situation   The interview is a necessary part of hiring because candidates with unsuitable personalities are eliminated from consideration.

    Reasoning   *What is being assumed in this argument?* The argument puts forth one reason that the interview is important: it eliminates candidates with unsuitable personalities. This presupposes that interviewers can, with a fair degree of accuracy, rule out those candidates whose personalities do not fit the needs of the job.

    A   The argument does not go so far as to say that interviews guarantee a successful hiring program.
    B   The argument does not prioritize the parts of a hiring program.
    C   **Correct.** This statement properly identifies the assumption underlying the argument.
    D   The argument gives one reason that the interview is important, but it does not say it is the only reason.
    E   This concerns past practices in hiring, and is irrelevant to the argument.

    The correct answer is C.

164. Many leadership theories have provided evidence that leaders affect group success rather than the success of particular individuals. So it is irrelevant to analyze the effects of supervisor traits on the attitudes of individuals whom they supervise. Instead, assessment of leadership effectiveness should occur only at the group level.

Which of the following would it be most useful to establish in order to evaluate the argument?

(A) Whether supervisors' documentation of individual supervisees' attitudes toward them is usually accurate
(B) Whether it is possible to assess individual supervisees' attitudes toward their supervisors without thereby changing those attitudes
(C) Whether any of the leadership theories in question hold that leaders should assess other leaders' attitudes
(D) Whether some types of groups do not need supervision in order to be successful in their endeavors
(E) Whether individuals' attitudes toward supervisors affect group success

Argument Evaluation

Situation   Many leadership theories have provided evidence that leaders affect the success of groups but not of individuals.

Reasoning   *What would be most helpful to know in order to evaluate how well the stated fact supports the conclusion that leadership effectiveness should be assessed only at the group level without considering supervisors' influence on the attitudes of the individuals they supervise?* Even if leaders do not affect the success of the individuals they lead, they might still affect those individuals' attitudes. And those attitudes in turn might affect group success. If so, the argument would be weak. So any evidence about the existence or strength of these possible effects in the relationship between supervisors and their supervisees would be helpful in evaluating the argument.

A   How accurately supervisors document their supervisees' attitudes is not clearly relevant to how much the supervisors affect those attitudes, nor to how much the attitudes affect group success.

B   Even if assessing supervisees' attitudes would in itself change those attitudes, the person doing the assessment might be able to predict this change and take it into account. Thus, considering individual supervisees' attitudes might still be worthwhile.

C   The argument is not about interactions among leaders, but rather about interactions between supervisors and supervisees.

D   The argument is not about groups without supervisors, or whether certain groups might be effective without a supervisor, but rather about how to assess the effectiveness of supervisors in groups that do have them.

E   **Correct**. As explained above, if individual supervisees' attitudes affect group success, the argument would be weak. And probably individual supervisees' attitudes toward their supervisors are influenced by those supervisors. So knowing whether individual attitudes toward supervisors affect group success would be helpful in evaluating the argument

The correct answer is E.

165. A major health insurance company in Lagolia pays for special procedures prescribed by physicians only if the procedure is first approved as "medically necessary" by a company-appointed review panel. The rule is intended to save the company the money it might otherwise spend on medically unnecessary procedures. The company has recently announced that in order to reduce its costs, it will abandon this rule.

Which of the following, if true, provides the strongest justification for the company's decision?

(A) Patients often register dissatisfaction with physicians who prescribe nothing for their ailments.
(B) Physicians often prescribe special procedures that are helpful but not altogether necessary for the health of the patient.
(C) The review process is expensive and practically always results in approval of the prescribed procedure.
(D) The company's review process does not interfere with the prerogative of physicians, in cases where more than one effective procedure is available, to select the one they personally prefer.
(E) The number of members of the company-appointed review panel who review a given procedure depends on the cost of the procedure.

Evaluation of a Plan

Situation   In order to cut costs, a major health insurance company is abandoning a rule stating that it will pay for special procedures only if the procedure is approved as medically necessary by a review panel.

Reasoning   *What piece of information would most help to justify the company's decision?* For the company to save money, it would need to be in some way cutting its costs by abandoning the rule. Under what circumstances might the rule cost, rather than save, the company money? The panel itself might be expensive to convene, for example. Further, the cost savings achieved by the panel might be minimal if the panel did not deny significant numbers of procedures.

A   This suggests that patients might be pressuring their physicians to prescribe certain unnecessary procedures for their ailments, which in turn suggests that the panel is reviewing these procedures and denying them. But if so, then the panel is probably saving the insurance company money, so abandoning the panel's review would not reduce the company's costs.

B   This suggests that certain procedures that are being prescribed by physicians are not medically necessary, which in turn suggests that the panel reviewing these procedures may be denying them. If this is the case, then the panel is probably saving the insurance company a significant amount of money, so abandoning the panel's review may well increase rather than decrease the company's costs.

C   **Correct.** This statement properly identifies information that would help to justify the company's decision.

D   Even if the panel does not interfere with physicians' choices when more than one medically effective procedure is available, the panel may still be denying pay for many procedures that are not medically necessary. In such cases the panel may be saving the insurance company money, and abandoning the review process would not reduce the company's costs.

E   This suggests that the more expensive the procedure under review, the more expensive the panel itself is. Even so, if the panel denies payment for very expensive procedures, it may nonetheless save the company significantly more than the company has to pay to convene the panel, so abandoning the review process would not reduce the company's costs.

The correct answer is C.

166. Automobile ownership was rare in Sabresia as recently as 30 years ago, but with continuing growth of personal income there, automobile ownership has become steadily more common. Consequently, there are now far more automobiles on Sabresia's roads than there were 30 years ago, and the annual number of automobile accidents has increased significantly. Yet the annual number of deaths and injuries resulting from automobile accidents has not increased significantly.

Which of the following, if true, most helps to explain why deaths and injuries resulting from automobile accidents have not increased significantly?

(A) Virtually all of the improvements in Sabresia's roads that were required to accommodate increased traffic were completed more than ten years ago.
(B) With more and more people owning cars, the average number of passengers in a car on the road has dropped dramatically.
(C) The increases in traffic volume have been most dramatic on Sabresia's highways, where speeds are well above those of other roads.
(D) Because of a vigorous market in used cars, the average age of cars on the road has actually increased throughout the years of steady growth in automobile ownership.
(E) Automobile ownership is still much less common in Sabresia than it is in other countries.

Argument Construction

Situation   Many more cars are on Sabresia's roads than 30 years ago; and there are also many more car accidents. Yet the annual number of deaths and injuries resulting from car accidents has not increased much, which is quite puzzling.

Reasoning   *What factor could help explain the puzzling fact that the increase in car accidents was not reflected in a similar increase in deaths and injuries from car accidents?* One (but perhaps unlikely) possibility is that a significantly greater proportion of the recent annual number of car accidents consisted of merely minor accidents, unlike 30 years ago. Another possibility is that cars are currently much better engineered for driver and passenger safety than 30 years ago. Yet a third possibility is that the total number of people traveling by car—passengers and drivers—has not increased significantly despite the large increase in the number of cars. This would mean that the average occupancy of a car has greatly decreased; so, even though the number of car accidents has significantly increased, the average number of people per car involved in an accident would have decreased significantly. On average, this would mean significantly fewer deaths and injuries per accident.

A   This throws little light on the central puzzle: why the current number of car accidents is significantly higher than 30 years ago, while the number of deaths and injuries in car accidents is not. The fact that there has been a significant increase in car accidents suggests that the roads were not made as safe as they could have been, and this just deepens the puzzle about the lack of a significant increase in deaths and injuries.

B   **Correct**. This implies that the average number of passengers per car accident is significantly less, and this helps explain why the total number of deaths and injuries has not increased significantly.

C   This information does not help explain the mismatch between increased accident numbers and relatively stable death-and-injury numbers. High-speed car accidents would likely have caused more fatalities, on average, than other car accidents; so, given that the increase in traffic volume has been greatest on Sabresia's high-speed roads, one would expect a significant increase in the number of accidents, and consequently in the number of deaths and injuries. But this expectation has not been fulfilled.

D   This does not help explain the surprisingly stable death-and-injury numbers in contrast with the significantly increased number of car accidents. The increase in average age of cars on the road might contribute to the increased number of accidents if older cars are more likely to be dangerously defective than newer ones.

E   The central puzzle already described involves no comparisons between Sabresia and other countries, so this information is irrelevant to explaining the puzzling discrepancy.

The correct answer is B.

167. A child learning to play the piano will not succeed unless the child has an instrument at home on which to practice. However, good-quality pianos, whether new or secondhand, are costly. Buying one is justified only if the child has the necessary talent and perseverance, which is precisely what one cannot know in advance. Consequently, parents should buy an inexpensive secondhand instrument at first and upgrade if and when the child's ability and inclination are proven.

Which of the following, if true, casts the most serious doubt on the course of action recommended for parents?

(A) Learners, particularly those with genuine musical talent, are apt to lose interest in the instrument if they have to play on a piano that fails to produce a pleasing sound.

(B) Reputable piano teachers do not accept children as pupils unless they know that the children can practice on a piano at home.

(C) Ideally, the piano on which a child practices at home should be located in a room away from family activities going on at the same time.

(D) Very young beginners often make remarkable progress at playing the piano at first, but then appear to stand still for a considerable period of time.

(E) In some parents, spending increasing amounts of money on having their children learn to play the piano produces increasing anxiety to hear immediate results.

Evaluation of a Plan

Situation   Children learning the piano need to have a piano on which to practice at home. Purchasing a high-quality piano is costly, and justified only if the child has talent and will persevere, which is hard to predict at an early stage. Parents should make do with a secondhand piano until the child's ability and inclination are proven.

Reasoning   *Which of the statements given would cast the most serious doubt on the recommendation given to parents?* Suppose that a child, because possessed of very high musical talent, is especially sensitive to imprecisions in tuning or imperfections of tone in a secondhand, less expensive piano (presumably Mozart would have been so!). This could, over time, make the child less interested in using the piano—especially if the child had the opportunity to hear music on far superior pianos. The result could be total loss of interest in learning to play the piano.

A   **Correct.** This, if true, would be a good reason to provide the child with the chance to practice regularly on a superior piano.

B   The issue is whether it would be best to provide the child with a superior piano at home, not whether it would be important to provide some piano at home.

C   This is irrelevant to the point at issue, which concerns how high a quality of piano should parents provide at home if they desire optimal development of the child's potential for piano musicianship.

D   Fluctuations in the pace of learning the piano are possible, but not relevant to the central question raised about the quality of the piano to be provided.

E   Investing so much in a piano, to the extent that doing so causes financial and psychological stress, might not be beneficial overall. However, if buying a new piano and buying a used piano are equally feasible financially for a given family, the question concerns which option would most achieve the objective of optimally developing the child's potential for piano musicianship.

The correct answer is A.

168. Nutritionists are advising people to eat more fish, since the omega-3 fatty acids in fish help combat many diseases. If everyone took this advice, however, there would not be enough fish in oceans, rivers, and lakes to supply the demand; the oceans are already being overfished. The obvious method to ease the pressure on wild fish populations is for people to increase their consumption of farmed fish.

Which of the following, if true, raises the most serious doubt concerning the prospects for success of the solution proposed above?

(A) Aquaculture, or fish farming, raises more fish in a given volume of water than are generally present in the wild.
(B) Some fish farming, particularly of shrimp and other shellfish, takes place in enclosures in the ocean.
(C) There are large expanses of ocean waters that do not contain enough nutrients to support substantial fish populations.
(D) The feed for farmed ocean fish is largely made from small wild-caught fish, including the young of many popular food species.
(E) Some of the species that are now farmed extensively were not commonly eaten when they were only available in the wild.

Argument Evaluation

Situation   Nutritionists advise people to eat fish for the omega-3 fatty acids, but there would not be enough fish to meet the demand if everyone followed this advice. Therefore, people should increase their consumption of farmed fish to ease pressure of wild fish populations.

Reasoning   *What evidence would suggest that increasing consumption of farmed fish would not ease pressure on wild fish populations?* Any evidence suggesting that significantly increasing consumption of farmed fish would diminish the habitat or food available for wild fish would also suggest that increasing consumption of farmed fish would not ease pressure on wild fish populations.

A   Probably the less space fish farming requires, the less pressure it creates on wild fish habitats and populations, other things being equal.

B   Whether any fish farming takes place in enclosures in the ocean is not clearly relevant to whether it eases pressure on wild fish populations.

C   Substantial fish populations may thrive in other large expanses of ocean water that contain more nutrients, and in rivers and lakes.

D   Correct. This suggests that increasing consumption of farmed fish would require increased use of wild fish as feed for farmed fish and therefore would not ease pressure on wild fish populations.

E   Even if some farmed fish are different species from the wild fish that are commonly eaten, increased consumption of the farmed fish could reduce demand for the wild fish and thereby ease pressure on wild fish populations.

The correct answer is D.

169. Which of the following most logically completes the market forecaster's argument?

> Market forecaster: The price of pecans is high when pecans are comparatively scarce but drops sharply when pecans are abundant. Thus, in high-yield years, growers often store part of their crop in refrigerated warehouses until after the next year's harvest, hoping for higher prices then. Because of bad weather, this year's pecan crop will be very small. Nevertheless, pecan prices this year will not be significantly higher than last year, since _____.

(A) the last time the pecan crop was as small as it was this year, the practice of holding back part of one year's crop had not yet become widely established
(B) last year's pecan harvest was the largest in the last 40 years
(C) pecan prices have remained relatively stable in recent years
(D) pecan yields for some farmers were as high this year as they had been last year
(E) the quality of this year's pecan crop is as high as the quality of any pecan crop in the previous five years

Argument Construction

Situation The price of pecans fluctuates based on the fluctuations in market supplies. When pecan farmers have a large harvest, they tend to save some of the crop in refrigerated storage until the following year, hoping to get higher prices then. This year's crop will be very small. But prices are not predicted to be significantly higher than last year.

Reasoning *What can most reasonably complete the argument by filling in the blank?* In other words, what would be the best reason for the prediction about this year's prices? This year's prices will be determined by the total market supply of pecans; this will include not only freshly harvested pecans but also pecans that were kept in storage from last year's harvest. Information about the relative size of last year's harvest could be partial evidence for a prediction about this year's prices.

A   What this tells us, in effect, is that previous experience with very poor harvests provide a poor guide about this year's total market supply, since the practice of refrigerated storage of pecans had not existed then.

B   **Correct.** This tells us that there was probably an unprecedented quantity of pecans in refrigerated storage from last year, so it is likely that the market supply of pecans this year will be relatively normal despite the poor harvest. This means that this year's prices will not be much higher than last year's; last year, the total pecan harvest was enormous and market supply probably relatively large.

C   This creates a general expectation of prices not being inordinately high this year, but since the harvest this year was "very small," such a general expectation could remain unfulfilled, absent countervailing factors.

D   This information is too vague to be useful. What percentage of farmers obtained satisfactory yields? Were these yields on farms that were by far the largest or the smallest?

E   The reasoning is silent on the issue of pecan quality, even though perceived quality could perhaps affect prices obtained. The additional information does not tell us that this year's quality is better than that found in recent harvests.

The correct answer is B.

170. Which of the following most logically completes the reasoning?

Either food scarcity or excessive hunting can threaten a population of animals. If the group faces food scarcity, individuals in the group will reach reproductive maturity later than otherwise. If the group faces excessive hunting, individuals that reach reproductive maturity earlier will come to predominate. Therefore, it should be possible to determine whether prehistoric mastodons became extinct because of food scarcity or human hunting, since there are fossilized mastodon remains from both before and after mastodon populations declined, and _____.

(A) there are more fossilized mastodon remains from the period before mastodon populations began to decline than from after that period

(B) the average age at which mastodons from a given period reached reproductive maturity can be established from their fossilized remains

(C) it can be accurately estimated from fossilized remains when mastodons became extinct

(D) it is not known when humans first began hunting mastodons

(E) climate changes may have gradually reduced the food available to mastodons

Argument Construction

Situation   In a population of animals, food scarcity causes later reproductive maturity; if that population is hunted excessively, earlier-maturing animals will be more numerous in the population.

Reasoning   *What point would most logically complete the argument?* For the information given to be of use in determining what caused mastodons' extinction, mastodon fossils would need to indicate the age at which mastodons reached reproductive maturity, since that is what the argument suggests can indicate cause of extinction. If fossilized remains exist from before and after mastodon populations began to decline, and if the age at which those fossilized mastodons reached reproductive maturity can be determined, then we will have a good idea of what caused their extinction: if they reached reproductive maturity late, it was probably food scarcity, but if they matured earlier, it was most likely hunting.

A   This fact only helps indicate that there was a decline; it tells us nothing about what caused the decline.

B   **Correct.** This statement properly identifies a point that logically completes the argument: it explains how the fossilized mastodon remains could be used to help determine what caused mastodons' extinction.

C   The point at which mastodons became extinct is not part of this argument, which is concerned with the cause of their extinction. The only way in which this could be relevant to the issue at hand is if mastodons became extinct before humans took up hunting mastodons—but the argument includes no information on whether this was so.

D   Not knowing when humans began hunting mastodons would have no effect on the argument, which is concerned with how mastodon fossils, combined with knowledge about how food scarcity and hunting affect mastodon reproductive maturity, can help determine how mastodons became extinct.

E   This fact only shows that food scarcity *may* have led to mastodon's decline. It tells us nothing about whether fossilized remains can help determine whether it was food scarcity or human hunting that actually led to the decline.

The correct answer is B.

171. Many office buildings designed to prevent outside air from entering have been shown to have elevated levels of various toxic substances circulating through the air inside, a phenomenon known as sick building syndrome. Yet the air in other office buildings does not have elevated levels of these substances, even though those buildings are the same age as the "sick" buildings and have similar designs and ventilation systems.

    Which of the following, if true, most helps to explain why not all office buildings designed to prevent outside air from entering have air that contains elevated levels of toxic substances?

    (A) Certain adhesives and drying agents used in particular types of furniture, carpets, and paint contribute the bulk of the toxic substances that circulate in the air of office buildings.
    (B) Most office buildings with sick building syndrome were built between 1950 and 1990.
    (C) Among buildings designed to prevent outside air from entering, houses are no less likely than office buildings to have air that contains elevated levels of toxic substances.
    (D) The toxic substances that are found in the air of "sick" office buildings are substances that are found in at least small quantities in nearly every building.
    (E) Office buildings with windows that can readily be opened are unlikely to suffer from sick building syndrome.

    Argument Evaluation

    Situation   Many office buildings designed to prevent outside air from entering have elevated levels of toxic substances in their interior air, but other such buildings similar in age, design, and ventilation do not.

    Reasoning   *What would help to explain the difference in air quality among buildings similar in age, design, and ventilation?* If office buildings are designed to prevent outside air from entering, toxic substances emitted into the interior air might not be ventilated out quickly, and thus might become more concentrated inside the building. But if such toxic substances are not emitted into a building's interior air in the first place, they will not become concentrated there, even if the building is poorly ventilated. So any factor that suggests why toxic substances are emitted into the interior air of some buildings but not others of similar age and design would help to explain the difference in the buildings' air quality.

    A **Correct.** Some buildings may have these types of furniture, carpets, and paint, while other buildings similar in age, design, and ventilation do not.
    B Since all these buildings were built during the same period, this does not help to explain the difference in air quality among buildings similar in age.
    C The passage concerns air quality in office buildings only, not in houses.
    D This does not help to explain why these toxic substances are more concentrated in some office buildings than in others.
    E The passage concerns the differences in air quality only among office buildings that were designed to prevent outside air from entering.

    The correct answer is A.

172. Newsletter: **A condominium generally offers more value for its cost than an individual house because of economies of scale.** The homeowners in a condominium association can collectively buy products and services that they could not afford on their own. And since a professional management company handles maintenance of common areas, **condominium owners spend less time and money on maintenance than individual homeowners do.**

The two portions in **boldface** play which of the following roles in the newsletter's argument?

(A) The first is the argument's main conclusion; the second is another conclusion supporting the first.
(B) The first is a premise, for which no evidence is provided; the second is the argument's only conclusion.
(C) The first is a conclusion supporting the second; the second is the argument's main conclusion.
(D) The first is the argument's only conclusion; the second is a premise, for which no evidence is provided.
(E) Both are premises, for which no evidence is provided, and both support the argument's only conclusion.

Argument Construction

Situation   Homeowners in a condominium association can buy products and services collectively. A management company handles maintenance of condominium common areas.

Reasoning   *What roles are played in the argument by the statement that a condominium generally offers more value for its cost than a house because of economies of scale and by the statement that condominium owners spend less time and money on maintenance than owners of individual homes do?* In the passage, the first sentence (the first **boldfaced** statement) is a generalization. The second sentence provides an example of the economies of scale mentioned in the first sentence, so it helps support the first sentence as a conclusion. In the third sentence, the word *since* indicates that the first clause is a premise supporting the second clause (the second **boldfaced** statement) as a conclusion. That conclusion itself provides another example of the economies of scale mentioned in the first sentence, so it also helps support that first sentence as a conclusion.

A   **Correct.** As explained above, the first **boldfaced** statement is supported by the rest of the statements in the argument, so it is the main conclusion. The second **boldfaced** statement supports the first, but is itself a conclusion supported by the *since* clause preceding it.

B   The second and third sentences in the argument provide examples of economies of scale. These examples are evidence supporting the first **boldfaced** statement as a conclusion.

C   Since the second **boldfaced** statement provides evidence of the economies of scale described by the first, it supports the first as a conclusion.

D   The *since* clause immediately preceding the second **boldfaced** statement provides evidence that supports it, so the second **boldfaced** statement is a conclusion.

E   Both the second and the third sentences of the argument support the first **boldfaced** statement as a conclusion. And the *since* clause immediately preceding the second **boldfaced** statement supports it as a conclusion.

The correct answer is A.

173. Platinum is a relatively rare metal vital to a wide variety of industries. Xagor Corporation, a major producer of platinum, has its production plant in a country that will soon begin imposing an export tax on platinum sold and shipped to customers abroad. As a consequence, the price of platinum on the world market is bound to rise.

    Which of the following, if true, tends to confirm the conclusion above?

    (A) An inexpensive substitute for platinum has been developed and will be available to industry for the first time this month.
    (B) The largest of the industries that depend on platinum reported a drop in sales last month.
    (C) The producers of platinum in other countries taken together cannot supply enough platinum to meet worldwide demand.
    (D) Xagor produced more platinum last month than in any previous month.
    (E) New deposits of platinum have been found in the country in which Xagor has its production plant.

    Argument Evaluation

    Situation   Xagor Corporation produces platinum, a rare metal vital to many industries. Xagor's plant is in a country that will soon impose an export tax on platinum. The world market price of platinum is predicted to rise.

    Reasoning   *Which of the pieces of information given, if true, would most tend to confirm the prediction given?* The conclusion of the argument is a causal prediction: the world market price of platinum will increase because of the export tax on platinum. The argument tells us that a wide range of industries need platinum, so the introduction of taxes on exported platinum would likely make that platinum more expensive for the importing industries. This, in turn, would likely raise the world market price of platinum. But what if those industries could get all their platinum from countries that did not tax platinum exports? Then the world market price might not rise if exports from those countries could adequately fulfill market demand.

    A   This information tends to undermine the reasoning and does not confirm the conclusion. If a less expensive platinum-substitute were to be developed, the world market price of platinum would tend to decline.

    B   This information somewhat weakens support for the conclusion. It suggests that overall demand for platinum might decline, at least temporarily, which would tend to lower the world market price of platinum.

    C   **Correct.** This information strengthens the support for the conclusion. It indicates that some platinum subject to the export tax will almost certainly be exported and will cost importers more than before. This would tend to cause the world market price of platinum to rise, especially since platinum producers in other countries could remain competitive and still raise their prices.

    D   This information could indicate a possible upswing in platinum production, which could increase the total world supply of platinum. If the supply increased relative to world demand, the world market price of platinum could decrease, not increase as the argument's conclusion predicts.

    E   This information suggests a possible increase in the world market supply of platinum, which would tend to reduce the world market price, provided world demand for platinum did not also increase at least proportionately.

    The correct answer is C.

174. From 1973 to 1986, growth in the United States economy was over 33 percent, while the percent growth in United States energy consumption was zero. The number of barrels of oil being saved per day by energy-efficiency improvements made since 1973 is now 13 million.

    If the information above is correct, which of the following conclusions can properly be drawn on the basis of it?

    (A) It is more difficult to find new sources of oil than to institute new energy-conservation measures.
    (B) Oil imports cannot be reduced unless energy consumption does not grow at all.
    (C) A reduction in the consumption of gasoline was the reason overall energy consumption remained steady.
    (D) It is possible for an economy to grow without consuming additional energy.
    (E) The development of nontraditional energy sources will make it possible for the United States economy to grow even faster.

Argument Construction

Situation   From 1973 to 1986, the United States economy grew over 33 percent while energy consumption did not grow. Energy improvements have made dramatic savings in annual oil consumption since 1973.

Reasoning   *If the given information in the passage is true, which answer choice must be true based on that information?* To find that statement, look for the one that has the closest relevance to the information given. All of the answer choices refer to topics at least loosely associated with the topics discussed in the given information. But four of them introduce extraneous information, while just one relies solely on the given information, simply making explicit something implicit in that information.

A   Nothing in the given information even implicitly depends on contrasting the relative difficulty of finding new oil with the difficulty of instituting new energy-conservation measures.

B   Nothing in the given information refers, even implicitly, to oil imports, so this statement does not follow logically from the given information.

C   This is new information that, if true, would help explain why there was zero percent growth in energy consumption in the period under discussion. But this new information could easily be false even if the given information is true. For instance, gasoline consumption could have held steady but the consumption of petroleum diesel or heating oil could have been reduced significantly.

D   **Correct.** This statement must be true if the given information is accurate. If something of a given kind has occurred, then it must be possible for that kind of thing to occur. The given information cites an example of an economy that had 33 percent economic growth along with zero percent growth in energy consumption.

E   The given information may be entirely accurate even if this claim is false. Even if this claim is true, the given information does not address, even implicitly, the development of nontraditional sources.

The correct answer is D.

175. Although many customers do not make a sufficient effort to conserve water, water companies must also be held responsible for wasteful consumption. Their own policies, in fact, encourage excessive water use, and attempts at conservation will succeed only if the water companies change their practices.

    Which of the following, if true, would most strongly support the view above?

    (A) Most water companies reduce the cost per unit of water as the amount of water used by a customer increases.
    (B) Most water companies keep detailed records of the quantity of water used by different customers.
    (C) Most water companies severely curtail the use of water during periods of drought.
    (D) Federal authorities limit the range of policies that can be enforced by the water companies.
    (E) The price per unit of water charged by the water companies has risen steadily in the last 10 years.

    Argument Evaluation

    Situation   Water companies have policies that encourage excessive water use. Water conservation cannot succeed unless water companies change their practices.

    Reasoning   *Which answer choice would indicate that water companies' policies and practices lead to wasteful water use?* If the companies have policies or practices that reduce customers' incentive to consume less water, then wasteful water consumption would be more likely to occur. Water companies would be contributing to wasteful water use and should be held accountable for that waste if water conservation is to succeed.

    A   **Correct.** Water companies' charging customers less per additional unit of water consumed is likely to reduce customers' incentive to avoid wasteful water use. So water companies bear some responsibility for wasteful water use.

    B   This shows that water companies have adequate data to indicate trends in customers' water consumption. But this does not, by itself, indicate that water companies incentivize wasteful consumption.

    C   This indicates that water companies likely curtail wasteful water use during droughts, which somewhat weakens the argument.

    D   This information is too nonspecific to allow us to judge whether the federal authorities' regulatory regime directly or indirectly contributes to wasteful water use.

    E   If anything, this information tends to weaken the argument. Over a 10-year period, because most economies experience inflation, increases in the price per unit of water would naturally occur, absent special countervailing factors. But if the increases were large, they would, if anything, tend to reduce wasteful water use.

    The correct answer is A.

176. Despite legislation designed to stem the accumulation of plastic waste, the plastics industry continued to grow rapidly last year, as can be seen from the fact that sales of the resin that is the raw material for manufacturing plastics grew by 10 percent to $28 billion.

In assessing the support provided by the evidence cited above for the statement that the plastics industry continued to grow, in addition to the information above it would be most useful to know

(A) whether the resin has other uses besides the manufacture of plastics
(B) the dollar amount of resin sales the year before last
(C) the plastics industry's attitude toward the legislation concerning plastic waste
(D) whether sales of all goods and services in the economy as a whole were increasing last year
(E) what proportion of the plastics industry's output eventually contributes to the accumulation of plastic waste

Argument Evaluation

Situation There is legislation meant to slow the accumulation of plastic waste. Last year, however, the plastics industry continued to grow rapidly. Sales of the resin that is the raw material for plastics grew in monetary terms by 10 percent.

Reasoning *What additional information should we seek in order to evaluate the evidence offered for the conclusion that the plastics industry continued to grow rapidly last year?* The evidence offered is that sales of resin from which plastics can be made increased 10 percent over the preceding year. For example, we could inquire whether the resin is used exclusively for plastics manufacture. If this were found NOT to be so, then the evidence presented would be of little use in showing that the plastics industry grew rapidly last year.

A **Correct.** Knowing whether this is so is crucial for judging the evidential value of last year's growth in sales of resin.

B This information is implicit in the given information and is therefore not additional information.

C The central issue is whether the information about last year's resin sales is good evidence of the plastics industry growth. The question as to whether that industry favors curtailment of plastics pollution has little if any relevance to that issue.

D If the answer to this *whether*-question is yes, there was presumably some inflation in the currency, so the increase in nominal monetary value of resin sales may or may not reflect very strong evidence of growth in the plastics industry. If the answer to the question is no, the increase in resin sales could be evidence of growth but is not necessarily so. In either case, we would need further information, so either answer to the question would not be useful for assessing the evidence.

E Knowing the answer to this could be important, but it is irrelevant in determining the evidential value of the information about growth in resin sales last year.

The correct answer is A.

177. Studies of the political orientations of 1,055 college students revealed that the plurality of students in an eastern, big-city, private university was liberal, whereas in a state-supported, southern college, the plurality was conservative. Orientations were independent of the student's region of origin, and the trends were much more pronounced in seniors than in beginning students.

Which of the following hypotheses is best supported by the observations stated above?

(A) The political orientations of college students are more similar to the political orientations of their parents when the students start college than when the students are seniors.

(B) The political orientations of college seniors depend significantly on experiences they have had while in college.

(C) A college senior originally from the South is more likely to be politically conservative than is a college senior originally from the East.

(D) Whether their college is state-supported or private is the determining factor in college students' political orientations.

(E) College students tend to become more conservative politically as they become older and are confronted with pressures for financial success.

Argument Evaluation

Situation Studies of a total of 1,055 college students in an eastern big-city private university and in a state-supported southern college found that, in the sample, the political orientation of most students in the private college was liberal and that of most students in the southern college was conservative. Among the liberal students identified in the private college and among the conservative students identified in the state-supported college, significantly more were seniors than beginning students.

Reasoning *What would best explain the trends observed in the college students' political orientations?* Five hypotheses to explain the trends are offered, and we are asked to identify the hypothesis that is most supported by the information already given about the studies. It should be noted that the information given is very limited, whereas the hypotheses offered involve quite broad generalizations, so whatever support is provided by the given information for any of these will at best be quite weak from a statistician's perspective. We should look for the hypothesis that makes the least ambitious claim and draws most closely on the given information.

A The given information, without unjustified introduction of unstated assumptions, provides no insight into the political orientations of the students' parents.

B **Correct.** Among the five hypotheses offered, this makes the least ambitious claim. Although its scope extends to college seniors in general (and in a statistical sense goes far beyond the evidence provided in the given information), it is the best supported of the five because it deviates least from the information we have. It is a good inference that the students' political re-orientation occurred as a result of the "experiences they have had while in college"—even if some of the truly mind-changing experiences were obtained in activities unrelated to their college life (e.g., speaking with fellow workers in a part-time restaurant job).

C We are given no information about the students' places of origin. The passage states: "orientations were independent of the student's region of origin."

D The given information provides no information regarding which among a multiplicity of conceivable influences contributed most strongly to the students' political orientations.

E We are not told in the given information that the students were "confronted with pressures for financial success"—although it is a truism that they were becoming older in their progress toward graduation.

The correct answer is B.

178. Diabetics often suffer dangerously low blood sugar levels, which they can correct safely if they notice the symptoms quickly. It has been suggested that **diabetics should be advised to drink moderate amounts of coffee**, since doing so improves their ability to recognize symptoms of low blood sugar quickly. That would be bad advice, however, since drinking even small amounts of coffee can increase the body's need for sugar in unpredictable ways.

In the argument being made, the part that is in **boldface** plays which of the following roles?

(A) Presenting the conclusion toward which the argument as a whole is directed
(B) Providing support for the conclusion of the argument
(C) Offering a reason to take a course of action recommended in the argument
(D) Stating the position to be refuted by the argument
(E) Providing an instance of a general principle articulated in the argument

Argument Evaluation

Situation   Diabetics need to recognize the signs of dangerously low blood sugar to address low sugar levels promptly. Because moderate coffee consumption heightens diabetics' awareness of symptoms indicating low blood sugar, some people advise that diabetics consume coffee. However, even limited coffee consumption can also destabilize blood sugar levels unpredictably.

Reasoning   *What role does the advice for diabetics to drink coffee play in an argument about safe strategies for avoiding dangerous drops in blood sugar?* Since drinking coffee heightens diabetics' awareness of the symptoms of low blood pressure, the argument might be expected to endorse the advice that diabetics should drink coffee in moderation. The following sentence, however, suggests that coffee consumption could be dangerous for diabetics by destabilizing their blood sugar levels.

A   The recommendation in **boldface** is described as bad advice in the following sentence, so it is not the argument's conclusion.

B   The advice for diabetics to drink coffee does not support the conclusion that drinking coffee could be risky for them.

C   The **boldfaced** text advises a course of action but does not offer a reason to follow any course of action.

D   **Correct.** The recommendation that diabetics should drink moderate amounts of coffee is refuted by the following sentence, which suggests that even small amounts of coffee could cause unpredictable shifts in their sugar requirements.

E   The recommendation for diabetics to drink moderate amounts of coffee is specific advice and not a general principle.

The correct answer is D.

179. Trancorp currently transports all its goods to Burland Island by truck. The only bridge over the channel separating Burland from the mainland is congested, and trucks typically spend hours in traffic. Trains can reach the channel more quickly than trucks, and freight cars can be transported to Burland by barges that typically cross the channel in an hour. Therefore, to reduce shipping time, Trancorp plans to switch to trains and barges to transport goods to Burland.

Which of the following, if true, casts the most serious doubt on whether Trancorp's plan will succeed?

(A) It does not cost significantly more to transport goods to Burland by truck than it does to transport goods by train and barge.
(B) The number of cars traveling over the bridge into Burland is likely to increase slightly over the next two years.
(C) Because there has been so much traffic on the roads leading to the bridge between Burland and the mainland, these roads are in extremely poor condition.
(D) Barges that arrive at Burland typically wait several hours for their turn to be unloaded.
(E) Most trucks transporting goods into Burland return to the mainland empty.

Evaluation of a Plan

Situation   Trancorp's shipments to Burland Island are slowed by congestion on the one bridge that connects the island to the mainland. To address this problem, the company plans to transport goods to Burland Island by a combination of trains and barges, which can reach the island more quickly.

Reasoning   *Since the goal of Trancorp's plan is to reduce shipping times by switching to trains and barges for transport, what would be most likely to interfere with that goal's achievement?* Trancorp is attempting to reduce shipping times to Burland Island by switching from trucks to trains and barges, so any factors that significantly slow shipping by trains and barges cast doubt on their plan's success.

A   Trancorp's goal is to reduce shipping times, not shipping costs, so the costs of different shipping methods do not cast doubt on the plan's success.

B   Increasing congestion on the bridge to Burland would make the plan to reduce shipping times by avoiding that bridge more likely to succeed, not less.

C   The poor condition of roads to Burland Island would make the plan to reduce shipping times by avoiding those roads more likely to succeed, not less.

D   **Correct.** If waiting time for barges to be unloaded adds several hours to the total shipping time by train and barge, that delay may cancel out the time otherwise saved by switching to trains and barges, making Trancorp's plan less likely to succeed.

E   The plan concerns having goods transported to Burland Island, not carrying goods back from there, so the emptiness of returning trucks has no bearing on that plan's success.

The correct answer is D.

180. When ducklings are exposed to music, they gain about 6 percent more weight for a given amount of feed than ducklings that are not exposed to music.

    Which of the following, if true, most helps to explain the extra weight gains referred to above?

    (A) Music played for ducklings must be kept at a low level because ducklings exposed to loud music gain less weight than ducklings exposed to no music.
    (B) Ducklings exposed to classical music gained more weight than ducklings exposed to popular music.
    (C) Ducklings are less active when they hear music, so that less of the food they eat is expended in movement, and more contributes directly to the ducklings' growth.
    (D) When ducklings gain 6 percent more weight on a given amount of grain, the farmers' profits increase because they can spend less money on grain to feed the ducklings.
    (E) When female ducklings were exposed to music, the percentage of fertile eggs that they laid as adults increased by over 27 percent in comparison to ducklings not exposed to music.

Argument Construction

Situation Ducklings that are exposed to music gain more weight from a given amount of feed than ducklings that aren't exposed to music.

Reasoning *What factor is most likely to contribute to the additional weight gains observed in ducklings exposed to music?* Because the amount of food given to ducklings exposed to music is the same as the amount given to ducklings not exposed to music, other factors must account for the music-exposed ducklings' greater weight gains.

A The effects of variable musical volume on ducklings' weight gains would not help explain those gains.

B Variable duckling weight gains promoted by different types of music does not provide an explanation for those gains.

C **Correct.** If ducklings exposed to music are less active and therefore burn fewer calories, then the lesser activity of such ducklings would provide a likely explanation for their higher weight gains.

D The greater profits of farmers is a consequence of the ducklings' increased weight gains and does not provide any explanation for those weight gains.

E The gain in egg fertility observed in ducks with early musical exposure does not explain the greater weight gains in music-exposed ducklings.

The correct answer is C.

181. X: In order to reduce the amount of plastic in landfills, legislatures should impose a ban on the use of plastics for packaging goods.

    Y: Impossible! Plastic packaging is necessary for public safety. Consumers will lose all of the safety features that plastic offers, chiefly tamper-resistant closures and shatterproof bottles.

    Which of the following best describes the weak point in Y's response to X's proposal?

    (A) Y ignores the possibility that packaging goods in materials other than plastic might provide the same safety features that packaging in plastic offers.
    (B) The economic disadvantages of using plastics as a means of packaging goods are not taken into consideration.
    (C) Y attempts to shift the blame for the large amount of plastic in landfills from the users of plastic packaging to the legislators.
    (D) Y does not consider the concern of some manufacturers that safety features spoil package appearances.
    (E) Y wrongly assumes that X defends the interests of the manufacturers rather than the interests of the consumers.

    Argument Evaluation

    Situation X believes that plastic packaging should be banned to reduce plastic waste in landfills, but Y argues that plastic packaging is essential for public safety because of the safety features offered by plastic.

    Reasoning *What is the weak point in Y's response to X's proposal, based on the claim that plastic packaging is necessary for public safety?* Since Y's argument is that plastic packaging offers essential safety features and therefore should not be eliminated, Y's argument would be undermined by information that those safety features could be provided without the use of plastic.

    A **Correct.** Y's argument states that plastic is essential for providing safety features, which would allow the argument to be refuted by any evidence that those features can be created with other materials.
    B Possible economic disadvantages of using plastic do not weaken Y's argument or undermine the claim that plastic is necessary for public safety.
    C Y's argument does not address the roles of either legislators or consumers in creating plastic waste in landfills.
    D Whether or not safety features spoil package appearance is irrelevant to the argument that plastic is necessary to provide such features.
    E Y's argument that plastic is essential for public safety does not imply that X favors the interests of manufacturers over those of consumers.

    The correct answer is A.

182. United Lumber will use trees from its forests for two products. The tree trunks will be used for lumber and the branches converted into wood chips to make fiberboard. The cost of this conversion would be the same whether done at the logging site, where the trees are debranched, or at United's factory. However, wood chips occupy less than half the volume of the branches from which they are made.

The information given, if accurate, most strongly supports which of the following?

(A) Converting the branches into wood chips at the logging site would require transporting a fully assembled wood-chipping machine to and from the site.

(B) It would be more economical to debranch the trees at the factory where the fiberboard is manufactured.

(C) The debranching of trees and the conversion of the branches into chips are the only stages in the processing of branches that would be in United's economic advantage to perform at the logging site.

(D) Transportation costs from the logging site to the factory that are determined by volume of cargo would be lower if the conversion into chips is done at the logging site rather than at the factory.

(E) In the wood-processing industry, branches are used only for the production of wood chips for fiberboard.

Argument Construction

Situation   United Lumber creates two products from trees: lumber from trunks and wood-chip-composed fiberboard from branches. Though converting the branches into wood chips costs the same whether done at the logging site or at the factory, the wood chips take up half the space that the branches take up before conversion.

Reasoning   *What is most likely to be true if the cost of converting branches to wood chips is equal at the logging site and the factory, but the total volume of the branches is greatly reduced by converting them into wood chips?* The information states that the cost of conversion is the same at both locations, so the significant variable is the reduced volume of the branches after conversion into chips.

A   While converting branches to chips might well require machinery onsite, nothing suggests that such machinery would require transport fully assembled.

B   No information is provided about the cost of debranching at the logging site compared to the cost of debranching at the factory.

C   The information states that converting branches to chips reduces volume, which might benefit United if performed at the logging site, but nothing implies that other steps in the process would not also be advantageous if performed at the site.

D   **Correct.** Since converting the branches into chips greatly reduces their total volume, it follows that shipping costs determined by volume would also be reduced if the conversion were done at the logging site.

E   The information states that United converts branches into wood chips for fiberboard, but it does not imply that the wood-processing industry in general uses branches exclusively to make fiberboard.

The correct answer is D.

183. Which of the following most logically completes the passage?

For the past several years, a certain technology has been widely used to transmit data among networked computers. Recently, two data transmission companies, Aptron and Gammatech, have each developed separate systems that allow network data transmission at rates ten times faster than the current technology allows. Although the systems are similarly priced and are equally easy to use, Aptron's product is likely to dominate the market, because _____.

(A) Gammatech has been in the business of designing data transmission systems for several years more than Aptron has
(B) the number of small businesses that need computer networking systems is likely to double over the next few years
(C) it is much more likely that Gammatech's system will be expandable to meet future needs
(D) unlike many data transmission companies, Aptron and Gammatech develop computers in addition to data transmission systems
(E) it is easier for users of the current data transmission technology to switch to Aptron's product than to Gammatech's

Argument Construction

Situation Two companies, Aptron and Gammatech, have both developed data transmission systems that are much faster than the previously available systems. Moreover, the two new systems are comparable in performance, price, and ease of use.

Reasoning *Since the systems developed by Gammatech and Aptron are similar in price and ease of use, what other factor supports the prediction that Aptron's system is more likely to dominate the market?* The statement predicts that Aptron's system will dominate the market but implicitly rules out two explanations—price and ease of use—for that prediction. Therefore, there is likely to be another factor that justifies the prediction.

A Gammatech's greater experience in the field would not make Aptron more likely to dominate the market.

B Increased demand for networking systems would be likely to benefit both companies, not Aptron in particular.

C If Gammatech's system is more likely to meet future needs, that would be a factor that might help Gammatech, not Aptron, dominate the market.

D If both companies make the same products in addition to data transmission systems, that would not be likely in itself to help one company outperform the other in the market.

E **Correct.** If it is easier to convert to Aptron's system than to Gammatech's, which might include some conversions from an earlier Gammatech system to the newest Aptron system, that would provide a logical reason for the prediction that Aptron will be likely to dominate the market.

The correct answer is E.

184. In Brindon County, virtually all of the fasteners—such as nuts, bolts, and screws—used by workshops and manufacturing firms have for several years been supplied by the Brindon Bolt Barn, a specialist wholesaler. In recent months, many of Brindon County's workshops and manufacturing firms have closed down, and no new ones have opened. Therefore, the Brindon Bolt Barn will undoubtedly show a sharp decline in sales volume and revenue for this year as compared to last year.

The argument depends on assuming which of the following?

(A) Last year, the Brindon Bolt Barn's sales volume and revenue were significantly higher than they had been the previous year.

(B) The workshops and manufacturing firms that have remained open have a smaller volume of work to do this year than they did last year.

(C) Soon the Brindon Bolt Barn will no longer be the only significant supplier of fasteners to Brindon County's workshops.

(D) The Brindon Bolt Barn's operating expenses have not increased this year.

(E) The Brindon Bolt Barn is not a company that gets the great majority of its business from customers outside Brindon County.

Argument Construction

Situation Brindon County has seen a recent steep decline in the number of its workshops and manufacturing firms. This will result in a significant decline in Brindon Bolt Barn's sales, given that Brindon Bolt Barn supplied these defunct businesses with parts.

Reasoning *What assumption underlies the argument that Brindon Bolt Barn's decreasing sales in Brindon County will necessarily lead to a steep decline in Brindon Bolt Barn's sales overall?* A sharp decline in overall sales due to reduced demand in Brindon County would be likely only if Brindon Bolt Barn did not have enough sales elsewhere to offset that reduction by a significant amount.

A Brindon Bolt Barn's higher sales last year would not be expected to lead to sharply lower sales this year.

B If Brindon Bolt Barn relies heavily on sales in Brindon County, then a large number of workshop closures in the county could well be enough to cause sharply declining sales, even without the additional factor of lower demand from the surviving workshops.

C The argument suggests that the decline is sales will be caused by decreasing demand, not by increasing competition.

D Steady operating expenses would not be expected to lead to sharply decreasing sales.

E **Correct.** The argument assumes that Brindon Bolt Barn relies heavily on sales in Brindon County; if a great majority of its products are sold outside the county, then a sharp decline in local sales would not necessarily lead to a sharp decline in overall sales.

The correct answer is E.

185. Healthy lungs produce a natural antibiotic that protects them from infection by routinely killing harmful bacteria on airway surfaces. People with cystic fibrosis, however, are unable to fight off such bacteria, even though their lungs produce normal amounts of the antibiotic. The fluid on airway surfaces in the lungs of people with cystic fibrosis has an abnormally high salt concentration; accordingly, scientists hypothesize that the high salt concentration is what makes the antibiotic ineffective.

    Which of the following, if true, most strongly supports the scientists' hypothesis?

    (A) When the salt concentration of the fluid on the airway surfaces of healthy people is raised artificially, the salt concentration soon returns to normal.
    (B) A sample of the antibiotic was capable of killing bacteria in an environment with an unusually low concentration of salt.
    (C) When lung tissue from people with cystic fibrosis is maintained in a solution with a normal salt concentration, the tissue can resist bacteria.
    (D) Many lung infections can be treated by applying synthetic antibiotics to the airway surfaces.
    (E) High salt concentrations have an antibiotic effect in many circumstances.

Argument Evaluation

Situation   Infection-fighting antibiotics occur naturally in both healthy lungs and in lungs affected by cystic fibrosis. However, in the lungs of people with cystic fibrosis, these antibiotics do not fight infection effectively. Some scientists propose that the higher levels of salt in lungs affected by cystic fibrosis may be the cause of the antibiotics' poor functioning.

Reasoning   *What evidence adds support to the hypothesis that, since people with cystic fibrosis have normal levels of naturally occurring antibiotics in their lungs, but abnormally high salt concentrations in their lungs, the extra salt is responsible for weakening the antibiotic's efficacy?* People with cystic fibrosis are vulnerable to lung infections despite normal levels of natural antibiotics, so the hypothesis that higher-than-normal salt concentrations in their lungs interfere with the antibiotic is reasonable; however, that hypothesis requires additional support.

A   The ability of healthy people's lungs to normalize salt levels would not support the hypothesis that high salt concentrations interfere with the natural antibiotics.

B   The antibiotic's ability to kill bacteria in a low-salt environment has no bearing on its performance in a high-salt environment.

C   **Correct.** If lung tissue from people with cystic fibrosis can fight infection in a low-salt environment, that would add support to the hypothesis that the high-salt environment present in their lungs reduces the effect of the antibiotics.

D   The effectiveness of synthetic antibiotics adds no support to the hypothesis that salt interferes with natural antibiotics.

E   The antibiotic effect of salt would tend to undermine the hypothesis that high salt levels lead to lung infections in people with cystic fibrosis, not support that hypothesis.

The correct answer is C.

186. Eurasian water milfoil, a weed not native to Frida Lake, has reproduced prolifically since being accidentally introduced there. In order to eliminate the weed, biologists proposed treating infested parts of the lake with a certain herbicide that is nontoxic for humans and aquatic animals. However, the herbicide might damage populations of certain rare plant species that the lake contains. For this reason, local officials rejected the proposal.

Which of the following, if true, points out the most serious weakness in the officials' grounds for rejecting the biologists' proposal?

(A) The continuing spread of Eurasian water milfoil in Frida Lake threatens to choke out the lake's rare plant species.

(B) Because of ecological conditions prevailing in its native habitat, Eurasian water milfoil is not as dominant there as it is in Frida Lake.

(C) The proliferation of Eurasian water milfoil in Frida Lake has led to reductions in the populations of some species of aquatic animals.

(D) Although Eurasian water milfoil could be mechanically removed from Frida Lake, eliminating the weed would take far longer this way than it would using herbicides.

(E) Unless Eurasian water milfoil is completely eliminated from Frida Lake, it will quickly spread again once herbicide treatments or other control measures cease.

Evaluation of a Plan

Situation Invasive Eurasian water milfoil is spreading rapidly in Frida Lake. Biologists want to control the milfoil with an herbicide safe for people and aquatic animals, but because it is potentially harmful to rare native plants, officials declined to use this herbicide.

Reasoning *Since officials rejected the plan to kill the invasive milfoil in Frida Lake with herbicide because of that herbicide's risk to rare plant species in the same lake, what factor would significantly weaken those grounds for rejection?* Rejecting the plan to use herbicide to kill milfoil because of the herbicide's risk to native plants only makes sense if the milfoil itself does not present a greater risk than the herbicide does.

A **Correct.** The risk that milfoil could completely choke out the rare native plant species might well be greater than the risk that the milfoil-killing herbicide could damage those rare species, which would present a serious weakness in the officials' grounds for rejecting the herbicide's use.

B Eurasian water milfoil's behavior in its native habitat has no bearing on the decision not to use herbicide against it in Frida Lake.

C The officials refused the use of milfoil-killing herbicide on the specific grounds that the herbicide could damage native plants, so milfoil's damage to native animal species might support the use of herbicide, but it does not weaken the officials' stated grounds for refusing to use it.

D The possibility of removing milfoil from Frida Lake by means other than the herbicide would tend to support the officials' decision, not weaken it.

E The possibility of milfoil quickly returning to Frida Lake if eradication is incomplete has no bearing on whether or not officials were right to reject the use of herbicide against milfoil.

The correct answer is A.

187. Columnist: People should completely avoid using a certain artificial fat that has been touted as an alternative for those whose medical advisers have advised them to reduce their fat intake. The artificial fat can be used in place of ordinary fats in prepared foods and has none of the negative health effects of fat, but it does have a serious drawback: it absorbs certain essential vitamins, thereby preventing them from being used by the body.

In evaluating the columnist's position, it would be most useful to determine which of the following?

(A) Whether increasing one's intake of the vitamins can compensate for the effects of the artificial fat
(B) Whether any of the vitamins that the artificial fat absorbs are destroyed by prolonged cooking
(C) Whether having an extremely low fat intake for an extended period can endanger a person's health
(D) Whether there are any foods that cannot be prepared using the artificial fat as a substitute for other fats
(E) Whether people are generally able to detect differences in taste between foods prepared using the artificial fat and foods that are similar except for the use of other fats

Argument Evaluation

Situation A columnist argues that everyone should avoid eating a certain artificial fat that has been touted by medical advisers. The columnist argues that, though the artificial fat can be used in place of ordinary foods, without any of natural fat's negative health effects, it absorbs certain essential vitamins, preventing their use by the body.

Reasoning *What information would be most useful in evaluating the columnist's argument?* Given that the sole reason the columnist gives for avoiding consumption of the artificial fat is its absorption of certain essential vitamins, it would be helpful to know whether this effect can be overcome in some way.

A **Correct.** The columnist's argument would be less compelling if one could compensate for the effects of the artificial fat by increasing one's intake of the essential vitamins the fat can absorb.

B The columnist's argument depends in no way on whether any vitamins are destroyed by prolonged cooking.

C The columnist's argument has to do with the problems the artificial fat creates for vitamin absorption; it has nothing to do with the effects of an extremely low intake of fat for an extended period of time.

D The columnist's argument does not depend in any way on whether there are any foods that cannot be prepared using the artificial fat.

E The columnist's argument does not depend on whether there are any detectable flavor differences between food prepared with the artificial fat and food prepared with other fats.

The correct answer is A.

Questions 188 to 235 — Difficulty: **Medium**

188. Donations of imported food will be distributed to children in famine-stricken countries in the form of free school meals. The process is efficient because the children are easy to reach at the schools and cooking facilities are often available on site.

    Which of the following, if true, casts the most serious doubt on the efficiency of the proposed process?

    (A) The emphasis on food will detract from the major function of the schools, which is to educate the children.
    (B) A massive influx of donated food will tend to lower the price of food in the areas near the schools.
    (C) Supplies of fuel needed for cooking at the schools arrive there only intermittently and in inadequate quantities.
    (D) The reduction in farm surpluses in donor countries benefits the donor countries to a greater extent than the recipient countries are benefited by the donations.
    (E) The donation of food tends to strengthen the standing of the political party that happens to be in power when the donation is made.

    Evaluation of a Plan

    Situation   On grounds of efficiency, it has been proposed that food donated to famine-stricken countries be distributed free to children through the schools. Many of the country's children attend school. Many schools have cooking facilities. Distributing the food through the schools is thus an efficient way of providing nutrition, at least to the children.

    Reasoning   *What would most cast doubt on the efficiency of the proposed distribution method?* The rationale offered for the method is twofold. First, many of the country's children attend school. Secondly, many schools have cooking facilities. Any additional information that weakens the significance of either of these two parts of the rationale would cast doubt on the efficiency of the proposed distribution process.

    A   This information does not cast significant doubt on the rationale. Of course, providing nutrition might take some time that could otherwise be devoted to teaching and would in that sense perhaps "detract" from the schools' main mission. However, the focus of the given information is on the efficiency of food distribution through the schools, presumably as compared with other methods of distribution that would provide children with adequate nutrition. The trade-off involving some loss of teaching time may be rendered less significant by the fact that children lacking adequate nutrition cannot learn well.

    B   This effect, if it occurred, could damage local markets but could also in the short term make locally grown food more available to those who need it. However, the point at issue is whether the rationale for distributing donated food through the schools to improve children's nutrition sufficiently indicates that this distribution method is efficient for that purpose.

    C   **Correct.** This information indicates that one part of the rationale given for the efficiency of the distribution method should carry less weight. If the "cooking facilities" at the schools are often inoperable due to lack of fuel, then some of the food to be distributed (for example, staples such as corn, millet, rice, or sorghum) may not be consumable.

    D   This information fails to address the central issue, which is the relative efficiency of the proposed distribution method for donated food, to improve children's nutrition.

    E   This addresses a possible effect of any food donation and fails to focus on the central issue identified in the foregoing discussion.

    The correct answer is C.

189. *John:* You told me once that no United States citizen who supports union labor should buy an imported car. Yet you are buying an Alma. Since Alma is one of the biggest makers of imports, I infer that you no longer support unions.

Harry: I still support labor unions. Even though Alma is a foreign car company, the car I am buying, the Alma Deluxe, is designed, engineered, and manufactured in the United States.

Harry's method of defending his purchase of an Alma is to

(A) disown the principle he formerly held
(B) show that John's argument involves a false unstated assumption
(C) contradict John's conclusion without challenging John's reasoning in drawing that conclusion
(D) point out that one of the statements John makes in support of his argument is false
(E) claim that his is a special case in which the rule need not apply

Evaluation of a Plan

Situation   Harry has bought a car manufactured by Alma, a company among the largest makers of cars imported to the United States. From that fact John infers that Harry no longer holds a principle he formerly professed: that nobody who supports U.S. union labor should buy an imported car. Harry responds by clarifying that the Alma Deluxe he is buying is entirely a U.S. product.

Reasoning   *What method has Harry used to show that his purchasing an Alma is not inconsistent with his principles?* Harry does this by showing that John is incorrectly assuming that the car Harry is purchasing has been imported.

A   Harry does not disown the principle he formerly held; rather, he tries to show that his purchase is consistent with it.

B   **Correct.** John mistakenly assumes—without asserting—that the Alma that Harry is buying must be an imported car, and Harry indicates that this assumption is false.

C   Harry challenges John's conclusion but he also challenges John's reasoning, by indicating that it relies on a false unstated assumption.

D   John does not state the assumption that Harry indicates is false, but Harry recognizes that the assumption in question is unstated.

E   Harry does not claim this; he claims, rather, that the new Alma he is purchasing is not imported and so his purchase does not violate his principle concerning union labor.

The correct answer is B.

190. Public-sector (government-owned) companies are often unprofitable and a drain on the taxpayer. Such enterprises should be sold to the private sector, where competition will force them either to be efficient and profitable or else to close.

    Which of the following, if true, identifies a flaw in the policy proposed above?

    (A) The revenue gained from the sale of public-sector companies is likely to be negligible compared to the cost of maintaining them.
    (B) By buying a public-sector company and then closing the company and selling its assets, a buyer can often make a profit.
    (C) The services provided by many public-sector companies must be made available to citizens, even when a price that covers costs cannot be charged.
    (D) Some unprofitable private-sector companies have become profitable after being taken over by the government to prevent their closing.
    (E) The costs of environmental protection, contributions to social programs, and job-safety measures are the same in the public and private sectors.

    Evaluation of a Plan

    Situation   A policy position is advocated, i.e., that unprofitable public-sector companies that burden taxpayers should be sold to the private sector. As private-sector companies, they would either become efficient and profitable or go out of business.

    Reasoning   *In what way is the policy position flawed?* The rationale given for the policy is that unprofitable public-sector companies burden taxpayers and privatizing them would subject them to competition—which would force them either to become efficient and profitable or to go out of business. But one of the characteristics of some public-sector companies is that they must provide certain services in market segments where provision of the services cannot become profitable. For example, provision of transportation services in sparsely populated rural areas is likely to be unprofitable because utilization of the services is insufficient to cover the cost of those services at a price that the market can bear.

    A   This information does not clearly indicate a flaw, since elimination of an exorbitant recurring cost by selling off, even at a very low price, an inefficient public company could be financially rational, even if not rational in other ways.

    B   This scenario could result in the non-provision of services that should be provided in the public interest, but it represents an aberration relative to the privatization policy described and does not indicate an essential flaw in that policy.

    C   **Correct.** This information indicates an essential flaw in the privatization policy described, since private companies are unlikely to provide services, even those needed by the public, in situations where provision of those services is unprofitable.

    D   This information indicates that some government-controlled companies can be profitable even when those companies were not profitable when in the private sector. But this does not indicate a flaw in the reasoning concerning privatization.

    E   This information offers no help in identifying a flaw in the argument. The types of costs listed are only some of the costs that companies incur and may not be the most significant cost factors in determining whether a company is profitable or not.

    The correct answer is C.

191. After receiving numerous complaints from residents about loud, highly amplified music played at local clubs, Middletown is considering a law that would prohibit clubs located in residential areas from employing musical groups that consist of more than three people.

The likelihood that the law would be effective in reducing noise would be most seriously diminished if which of the following were true?

(A) Groups that consist of more than three musicians are usually more expensive for clubs to hire than are groups that consist of fewer than three musicians.
(B) In towns that have passed similar laws, many clubs in residential areas have relocated to nonresidential areas.
(C) Most of the complaints about the music have come from people who do not regularly attend the clubs.
(D) Much of the music popular at the local clubs can be played only by groups of at least four musicians.
(E) Amplified music played by fewer than three musicians generally is as loud as amplified music played by more than three musicians.

Evaluation of a Plan

Situation   Middletown is considering a law to eliminate a nuisance that residents have complained about: loud, highly amplified music at local clubs. The proposed law would address this by prohibiting the clubs to have groups of more than three musicians playing at the club.

Reasoning   *Which statement, if true, would be the strongest indication that the proposed law would fail to reduce the noise that residents complained of?* The proposed limit on group size depends on the assumption that the music played by a group of three musicians or fewer would not be loud enough to bother Middletown's residents. If this assumption is false, for example if some of the smaller groups felt a need to use powerful amplification, the proposed law would be unlikely to be eliminate the nuisance by reducing the noise sufficiently.

A   We are given no information about whether Middletown, in framing its proposal, gave any consideration to the costs the clubs incur in hiring groups of various sizes. If the clubs' costs but not their revenues were to decrease by hiring smaller groups, they would likely obey the new law. However, this by itself would not indicate success for the noise abatement program.

B   If the Middletown clubs were to relocate to nonresidential areas as a result of the law, this would contribute to the law's effectiveness in alleviating the noise disturbance.

C   The proposal for the law is motivated by Middletown's need to respond to "numerous" resident complaints. If relatively few complaints come from residents who regularly attend the clubs, it may be because most of those residents either like loud music or are insensitive to it. But this has no bearing on whether the proposed law would be effective in addressing the noise level that bothers numerous other residents.

D   This could make the law less acceptable to the clubs or their patrons. If the law proved unacceptable, an unacceptable frequency of violation might result unless the law is well designed for effective enforcement. But perhaps the law will be well designed for effective enforcement. Nothing in the passage suggests otherwise.

E   **Correct.** This indicates that the size of a musical group generally has little impact on the volume of sound that the group produces. The proposed law is therefore likely to be ineffective in reducing the noise residents complained about.

The correct answer is E.

192. From enlargements that are commonly found on the ulna bones of the forearms of Ice Age human skeletons, anthropologists have drawn the conclusion that the Ice Age humans represented by those skeletons frequently hunted by throwing spears. The bone enlargements, the anthropologists believe, resulted from the stresses of habitual throwing.

Which of the following, if true, would be the LEAST appropriate to use as support for the conclusion drawn by the anthropologists?

(A) Humans typically favor one arm over the other when throwing, and most Ice Age human skeletons have enlargements on the ulna bone of only one arm.

(B) Such enlargements on the ulna bone do not appear on skeletons from other human cultures of the same time period whose diets are believed to have been mainly vegetarian.

(C) Cave paintings dating from approximately the same time period and located not far from where the skeletons were found show hunters carrying and throwing spears.

(D) Damaged bones in the skeletons show evidence of diseases that are believed to have afflicted most people living during the Ice Age.

(E) Twentieth-century athletes who use a throwing motion similar to that of a hunter throwing a spear often develop enlargements on the ulna bone similar to those detected on the Ice Age skeletons.

Evaluation of a Plan

Situation   The ulna-bone enlargements often found on forearms of skeletons of Ice Age humans have led anthropologists to conclude that those humans frequently hunted by throwing spears and that this practice caused the bone enlargement.

Reasoning   *Which of the additional pieces of information offered provide the weakest (if any) support for the anthropologists' conclusion?* A premise of the anthropologists' reasoning is that many Ice Age humans developed enlarged ulna bones. Another premise is that the bone enlargements resulted from the stresses of habitual [spear] throwing. The anthropologists' conclusion is that those Ice Age humans frequently hunted by throwing spears. Several of the five additional pieces of information provide additional support for the anthropologists' conclusion.

A   The information, if true, that the bone enlargement found on Ice Age skeletons is typically found on just one arm provides significant additional support for the argument's conclusion. Ice Age spear-throwing hunters would likely have been left-handed or right-handed and would have habitually used just one of their arms—either left or right—to throw spears.

B   This information, if true, provides significant additional support for the anthropologists' conclusion. Ice Age humans with mainly vegetarian diets would have hunted, if at all, only infrequently—and so would not have been habitual spear-throwing hunters. We would expect, then, that if the anthropologists' conclusion is correct, enlarged ulna bones would not be found among the remains of such populations—and that is what the archaeological evidence indicates.

C   This information, if true, provides compelling evidence that some Ice Age human populations hunted using spears, and so it provides significant additional support for the anthropologists' conclusion.

D   **Correct.** This information, if true, tends to weaken the support for the anthropologists' conclusion. It vaguely suggests that diseases that were endemic in the Ice Age and caused bone damage might adequately explain the enlargement of ulna bones found in the archaeological evidence. If this were correct, then that bone enlargement could no longer be regarded as compelling evidence of spear-throwing.

E   This information, if true, provides additional support for the anthropologists' conclusion. Twentieth-century athletes (perhaps javelin throwers, for example) use a throwing motion like that of spear throwers, and they often develop enlarged ulna bones like those found in the archaeological evidence.

The correct answer is D.

193. The town council of North Tarrytown favored changing the name of the town to Sleepy Hollow. Council members argued that making the town's association with Washington Irving and his famous "legend" more obvious would increase tourism and result immediately in financial benefits for the town's inhabitants.

The council members' argument requires the assumption that

(A) most of the inhabitants would favor a change in the name of the town
(B) many inhabitants would be ready to supply tourists with information about Washington Irving and his "legend"
(C) the town can accomplish, at a very low cost per capita, the improvements in tourist facilities that an increase in tourism would require
(D) other towns in the region have changed their names to reflect historical associations and have, as a result, experienced a rise in tourism
(E) the immediate per capita cost to inhabitants of changing the name of the town would be less than the immediate per capita revenue they would receive from the change

Evaluation of a Plan

Situation Members of the North Tarrytown town council argued for changing the town's name to Sleepy Hollow (the name of a fictitious place in stories by early nineteenth-century author Washington Irving). The goal was to increase tourism.

Reasoning *What unstated assumption is required for the council members' argument to be logically compelling?* Their argument was that people who associate the name Sleepy Hollow with the author Washington Irving would come to visit the town because of that association. The resulting influx of tourists would provide additional spending that would "immediately" result in financial benefits for the town's inhabitants. There would not be such immediate benefits if the additional spending did not outweigh the costs of the name change.

A   This information about the popular acceptability of the name-change strategy could provide additional logical support for the proposal, but the information is not strictly required for the council members' reasoning to logically succeed.

B   If this occurred, it could benefit tourists and help enhance the town's reputation as a tourist venue, thus helping the name-change plan attain its goals. But an assumption that this would occur is not necessary for the logical success of the council members' reasoning.

C   This could make it more likely that the proposed name-change strategy would attain its financial goals. But the council members' reasoning does not have to assume that the relevant costs would be "very low."

D   This information, if true, would help dispel any doubts as to whether the proposed name change would attain its goals. But it is not information that is necessary for the council members' reasoning to logically succeed.

E   **Correct.** To be logically successful, the council members' reasoning requires that this be assumed. Part of the council members' reasoning is that the proposed name change would "result immediately in financial benefits for the town's inhabitants." This result will not occur unless the immediate costs associated with implementing the change are less than the revenue accruing to the town's inhabitants as a result. In the medium and long term, the name change could provide increased financial benefits to the town's inhabitants, but the council members' reasoning requires that those benefits flow immediately.

The correct answer is E.

194. Premature babies who receive regular massages are more active than premature babies who do not. Even when all the babies drink the same amount of milk, the massaged babies gain more weight than do the unmassaged babies. This is puzzling because a more active person generally requires a greater food intake to maintain or gain weight.

Which of the following, if true, best reconciles the apparent discrepancy described above?

(A) Increased activity leads to increased levels of hunger, especially when food intake is not also increased.
(B) Massage increases premature babies' curiosity about their environment, and curiosity leads to increased activity.
(C) Increased activity causes the intestines of premature babies to mature more quickly, enabling the babies to digest and absorb more of the nutrients in the milk they drink.
(D) Massage does not increase the growth rate of babies over one year old, if the babies had not been previously massaged.
(E) Premature babies require a daily intake of nutrients that is significantly higher than that required by babies who were not born prematurely.

Argument Construction

Situation Premature babies who receive regular massages are more active and gain more weight than unmassaged premature babies do, even when they drink the same amount of milk.

Reasoning *What would help to explain how the massaged babies could be more active than the unmassaged babies and yet still gain more weight without consuming more milk?* If the massaged babies are burning more calories than unmassaged babies through their extra activity, but are not consuming more calories in the form of milk, then how are they gaining more weight than the unmassaged babies? Possible explanations could cite factors suggesting how the massaged babies might not actually burn more calories despite their greater activity; how they might consume or absorb more calories even without consuming more milk; or how they might gain more weight without extra calorie intake.

A Increased hunger without increased food intake would not help to explain why the massaged babies are gaining more weight.

B This only helps to explain why the massaged babies are more active, not why they are gaining more weight without consuming more milk.

C **Correct.** This suggests that the increased activity of the massaged babies could increase their calorie and nutrient intake from a given amount of milk, thereby explaining how they could gain extra weight without drinking more milk.

D This suggests that the apparent discrepancy is only present in premature babies under one year old, but it does not explain why that discrepancy exists.

E The passage does not compare premature babies to babies that were not born prematurely, but rather only compares premature babies that are massaged to premature babies that are not massaged.

The correct answer is C.

195. In Australia, in years with below-average rainfall, less water goes into rivers and more water is extracted from rivers for drinking and irrigation. Consequently, in such years, water levels drop considerably and the rivers flow more slowly. Because algae grow better the more slowly the water in which they are growing moves, such years are generally beneficial to populations of algae. But, by contrast, populations of algae drop in periods of extreme drought.

Which of the following, if true, does most to explain the contrast?

(A) Algae grow better in ponds and lakes than in rivers.
(B) The more slowly water moves, the more conducive its temperature is to the growth of algae.
(C) Algae cannot survive in the absence of water.
(D) Algae must be filtered out of water before it can be used for drinking.
(E) The larger the population of algae in a body of water, the less sunlight reaches below the surface of the water.

Argument Construction

Situation   The quantity of water in Australian rivers greatly diminishes in years of below-average rainfall. When river levels become very low, the rivers flow more slowly. The low flow favors rapid algae growth. However, in periods of extreme drought, algae populations drop.

Reasoning   *What information would most help to explain the two contrasting trends in algae growth?* The information given indicates that algae proliferate when rivers flow slowly. When the water levels become extremely low, algae populations decrease. In periods of extreme drought, presumably some rivers retain little or no water.

A   This has no obvious relevance to explaining the contrast in the algae growth trends.

B   Nothing in the given information is explicit about the effects of water temperature and how that changes in rivers with changes in rainfall rates.

C   **Correct.** This information could help explain the decrease in algae populations during periods of extreme drought. It seems quite probable that during such periods, at least parts of some riverbeds would dry out.

D   This information does not help explain the contrasting trends in algae growth. Algae filtered out of river water to be used for drinking might not be returned to rivers, and this conceivably could affect algae populations. But it seems likely, based on the given information, that this would occur mainly during low-rainfall non-drought periods, when proliferation of algae has increased, so the impact on algae populations would probably be minimal.

E   This information is clearly irrelevant to the contrast that needs to be explained.

The correct answer is C.

196. Which of the following, if true, most logically completes the politician's argument?

United States politician: Although the amount of United States goods shipped to Mexico doubled in the year after tariffs on trade between the two countries were reduced, it does not follow that the reduction in tariffs caused the sales of United States goods to companies and consumers in Mexico to double that year, because _____.

(A) many of the United States companies that produced goods that year had competitors based in Mexico that had long produced the same kind of goods
(B) most of the increase in goods shipped by United States companies to Mexico was in parts shipped to the companies' newly relocated subsidiaries for assembly and subsequent shipment back to the United States
(C) marketing goods to a previously unavailable group of consumers is most successful when advertising specifically targets those consumers, but developing such advertising often takes longer than a year
(D) the amount of Mexican goods shipped to the United States remained the same as it had been before the tariff reductions
(E) there was no significant change in the employment rate in either of the countries that year

Argument Construction

Situation The politician suggests that tariffs on trade between Mexico and the United States were reduced during a certain year and notes that, in the year after that year, the amount of United States goods shipped to Mexico doubled. It may seem from this that the decrease in tariffs, because they may have reduced the prices of United States goods to Mexican companies and consumers, caused Mexican companies and consumers to double their purchases of United States goods in the year after the reduction in tariffs. This might explain the doubling of shipments of goods to Mexico. However, the politician argues that the decrease in tariffs did *not* cause the purchase of United States goods by Mexican companies and consumers to double.

Reasoning *What possible facts would indicate that the decrease in tariffs may not have caused Mexican companies and consumers to double their purchases of United States goods?* The task in this question is to complete an argument that purports to show that a certain inference—that sales of United States goods to companies and consumers in Mexico increased as a result of the tariff decrease—does not follow logically from the fact that shipments of United States goods to Mexico doubled after the decrease in tariffs. Although it is not necessary to show that sales of United States goods to companies and consumers in Mexico did not double, any statement that would significantly decrease the strength of this inference may provide a reasonable answer to our question.

A The argument that the politician is criticizing concerns a change in a certain year that purportedly caused another purported change in the next year. This answer choice, about longstanding relationships between United States and Mexican companies, does not address these changes.

B **Correct.** If the statement in this answer choice is true, then we cannot, on the basis of an increase in shipments of goods to Mexico, infer that these goods were purchased by Mexican companies and consumers. The statement thus directly supports the politician's argument.

C The argument that the politician is criticizing has to do with purported changes in purchasing behavior by Mexican companies and consumers, due to an increase in tariffs. This answer choice, being entirely concerned with the effectiveness of marketing and advertising, does not address the argument.

D Although this answer choice may suggest that the change in tariffs did not cause a significant change in shipments of Mexican goods to the United States, it does not address the matter of shipments of United States goods to Mexico.

E This answer choice addresses an aspect that would be of interest when examining the effects of the change in tariffs. But it does not address the purported change that is addressed by the politician's argument.

The correct answer is B.

197. Budget constraints have made police officials consider reassigning a considerable number of officers from traffic enforcement to work on higher-priority, serious crimes. Reducing traffic enforcement for this reason would be counterproductive, however, in light of the tendency of criminals to use cars when engaged in the commission of serious crimes. An officer stopping a car for a traffic violation can make a search that turns up evidence of serious crime.

Which of the following, if true, most strengthens the argument given?

(A) An officer who stops a car containing evidence of the commission of a serious crime risks a violent confrontation, even if the vehicle was stopped only for a traffic violation.
(B) When the public becomes aware that traffic enforcement has lessened, it typically becomes lax in obeying traffic rules.
(C) Those willing to break the law to commit serious crimes are often in committing such crimes unwilling to observe what they regard as the lesser constraints of traffic law.
(D) The offenders committing serious crimes who would be caught because of traffic violations are not the same group of individuals as those who would be caught if the arresting officers were reassigned from traffic enforcement.
(E) The great majority of persons who are stopped by officers for traffic violations are not guilty of any serious crimes.

Argument Construction

Situation   Budget constraints have made police officials consider reassigning many officers from traffic enforcement to work on serious crimes. But criminals often drive when committing serious crimes, and police who stop cars for traffic violations can find evidence of those crimes.

Reasoning   *What additional information, when combined with the argument provided, would suggest that it would be counterproductive to reassign officers from traffic enforcement to work on serious crimes?* The argument implicitly reasons that because officers working on traffic enforcement can turn up evidence of serious crimes by searching cars that commit traffic violations, reassigning those officers would hinder police efforts to prevent serious crime, even if the officers were reassigned to work directly on serious crime. The argument could be strengthened by information suggesting that traffic enforcement may increase the probability that evidence relating to serious crimes will be discovered.

A   If anything, this risk of violence might discourage traffic enforcement officers from stopping and searching as many cars, thus reducing their effectiveness at preventing serious crimes.

B   This suggests that reassigning officers from traffic enforcement to work on serious crimes would increase the number of unpunished minor traffic violations, not the number of unpunished serious crimes.

C   **Correct.** This suggests that people committing serious crimes often commit traffic violations as well, increasing the likelihood that traffic enforcement officers will stop and search their cars and find evidence of those crimes.

D   The question at issue is not whether the same offenders would be caught if the officers were reassigned, but rather whether more or fewer offenders would be caught.

E   This weakens the argument by suggesting that most work by traffic enforcement officers is unrelated to preventing serious crimes.

The correct answer is C.

198. Conventional wisdom suggests vaccinating elderly people first in flu season, because they are at greatest risk of dying if they contract the virus. This year's flu virus poses particular risk to elderly people and almost none at all to younger people, particularly children. Nevertheless, health professionals are recommending vaccinating children first against the virus rather than elderly people.

Which of the following, if true, provides the strongest reason for the health professionals' recommendation?

(A) Children are vulnerable to dangerous infections when their immune systems are severely weakened by other diseases.

(B) Children are particularly unconcerned with hygiene and therefore are the group most responsible for spreading the flu virus to others.

(C) The vaccinations received last year will confer no immunity to this year's flu virus.

(D) Children who catch one strain of the flu virus and then recover are likely to develop immunity to at least some strains with which they have not yet come in contact.

(E) Children are no more likely than adults to have immunity to a particular flu virus if they have never lived through a previous epidemic of the same virus.

Argument Construction

Situation Although this year's flu virus poses particular risk to elderly people and almost no risk to children, health professionals are recommending vaccinating children before elderly people, contrary to what conventional wisdom recommends.

Reasoning *What would help justify the health professionals' recommendation?* Since children will experience almost no risk from the virus, vaccinating them first for their own sake appears unnecessary. However, individuals at no personal risk from a virus can still transmit it to more-vulnerable individuals. If children are especially likely to transmit the virus, it could be reasonable to vaccinate them first in order to protect others, including elderly people, by preventing the virus from spreading.

A This might be a reason to vaccinate certain children with severely weakened immune systems, if their weak immune systems would even respond effectively to the vaccine. However, it is not clearly a reason to vaccinate the vast majority of children.

B **Correct.** This suggests that children are especially likely to transmit the virus even if it does not endanger them. So as explained above, it provides a good reason for the health professionals' recommendation.

C This might be a good reason to vaccinate everyone, but it is not clearly a reason to vaccinate children before vaccinating elderly people.

D If anything, this would suggest that there might be a reason not to vaccinate children against this year's strain at all: unvaccinated children who catch this year's strain, which the argument claims is relatively harmless to children, may develop immunity to more dangerous strains that might arise in the future.

E The argument claims that this year's virus poses almost no risk to children. So even if they are not technically immune to it, it does not affect them significantly enough to justify vaccinating them before vaccinating elderly people.

The correct answer is B.

199. Pro-Tect Insurance Company has recently been paying out more on car-theft claims than it expected. Cars with special antitheft devices or alarm systems are much less likely to be stolen than are other cars. Consequently Pro-Tect, as part of an effort to reduce its annual payouts, will offer a discount to holders of car-theft policies if their cars have antitheft devices or alarm systems.

Which of the following, if true, provides the strongest indication that the plan is likely to achieve its goal?

(A) The decrease in the risk of car theft conferred by having a car alarm is greatest when only a few cars have such alarms.
(B) The number of policyholders who have filed a claim in the past year is higher for Pro-Tect than for other insurance companies.
(C) In one or two years, the discount that Pro-Tect is offering will amount to more than the cost of buying certain highly effective antitheft devices.
(D) Currently, Pro-Tect cannot legally raise the premiums it charges for a given amount of insurance against car theft.
(E) The amount Pro-Tect has been paying out on car-theft claims has been greater for some models of car than for others.

Evaluation of a Plan

Situation An insurance company is paying more money on car-theft claims than anticipated. To reduce these payments, the company is planning to offer discounts to customers whose cars have antitheft devices or alarm systems, because such cars are less likely to be stolen.

Reasoning *What piece of information would indicate that the plan is likely to succeed?* Pro-Tect wishes to reduce its annual payouts, and one way for that to happen is for fewer cars insured by Pro-Tect to be stolen. To help accomplish this, Pro-Tect is offering discounts to policyholders whose cars are so equipped, because cars equipped with antitheft devices or alarm systems are less likely to be stolen than are cars without such devices. What would interfere with the success of Pro-Tect's plan? Car owners would probably resist investing in antitheft devices or alarm systems if the cost of such systems is higher than the discount they will receive. So if Pro-Tect sets the discount at a level that makes installing antitheft devices seem like a bargain to car owners, the plan will most likely succeed.

A Pro-Tect's plan is designed to increase the number of cars equipped with car alarms. If having more cars equipped with car alarms reduces those alarms' effectivity in preventing thefts, then Pro-Tect's plan is unlikely to achieve its goal.

B Pro-Tect's claims in relation to those of other insurance companies are not relevant to whether Pro-Tect's plan to reduce its own car-theft claims will achieve its goal.

C **Correct.** This statement suggests that Pro-Tect's plan will provide an effective incentive for car owners to install antitheft devices; this statement therefore properly identifies information that indicates the plan is likely to achieve its goal.

D Because Pro-Tect's plan does not involve raising the premiums it charges, restrictions on its ability to do so are irrelevant to whether that plan will achieve its goal.

E Pro-Tect's plan does not distinguish among different models of car, so this statement indicates nothing about whether the proposed plan will succeed.

The correct answer is C.

200. While the total enrollment of public elementary and secondary schools in Sondland is one percent higher this academic year than last academic year, the number of teachers there increased by three percent. Thus, the Sondland Education Commission's prediction of a teacher shortage as early as next academic year is unfounded.

Which of the following, if true, most seriously weakens the claim that the prediction of a teacher shortage as early as next academic year is unfounded?

(A) Funding for public elementary schools in Sondland is expected to increase over the next ten years.

(B) Average salaries for Sondland's teachers increased at the rate of inflation from last academic year to this academic year.

(C) A new law has mandated that there be 10 percent more teachers per pupil in Sondland's public schools next academic year than there were this academic year.

(D) In the past, increases in enrollments in public elementary and secondary schools in Sondland have generally been smaller than increases in the number of teachers.

(E) Because of reductions in funding, the number of students enrolling in teacher-training programs in Sondland is expected to decline beginning in the next academic year.

Argument Evaluation

Situation   In Sondland's public schools this academic year, the number of students is one percent higher and the number of teachers three percent higher than they were last academic year. For this reason, the Sondland Education Commission's prediction of a teacher shortage as early as next academic year is questionable.

Reasoning   *What evidence would most weaken support for the claim that there will be no teacher shortage next academic year?* A teacher shortage will arise next academic year if the number of teachers needed will exceed the number of teachers employed. This will happen if the number of teachers needed increases without a sufficient increase in the number employed, or if the number employed decreases without a sufficient decrease in the number needed. Evidence that either or both of these changes will occur next academic year is evidence that the predicted shortage will occur, so any such evidence will weaken support for the claim that the prediction is unfounded.

A   Increased funding will likely allow more teachers to be hired but will not necessarily increase the need for teachers, so it does not support the prediction of a teacher shortage (and indeed it very slightly undermines the prediction). Also, the funding is expected to increase over ten years, not necessarily next year. Furthermore, we are not told who expects this increase or why. Their expectation may be unjustifiable.

B   A salary increase at the rate of inflation is equivalent to no change in the salary's actual value. The absence of a change in real salary in the past academic year does not by itself support any prediction of a change in the number of teachers needed or employed next academic year.

C   **Correct.** The schools will need a lot more teachers next academic year to satisfy this mandate. It may be difficult for the schools to hire enough teachers in time. This provides at least some reason to predict that a teacher shortage will result.

D   This means the number of students per teacher has been generally declining. It does not suggest that next academic year the number of teachers needed will increase, nor that the number employed will decrease.

E   This does support the prediction that a shortage of trained teachers will arise eventually. But the declining number of students in teacher-training programs next academic year probably will not reduce the number of teachers available to teach during that same year.

The correct answer is C.

201. Art restorers who have been studying the factors that cause Renaissance oil paintings to deteriorate physically when subject to climatic changes have found that the oil paint used in these paintings actually adjusts to these changes well. The restorers therefore hypothesize that it is a layer of material called gesso, which is under the paint, that causes the deterioration.

Which of the following, if true, most strongly supports the restorers' hypothesis?

(A) Renaissance oil paintings with a thin layer of gesso are less likely to show deterioration in response to climatic changes than those with a thicker layer.
(B) Renaissance oil paintings are often painted on wooden panels, which swell when humidity increases and contract when it declines.
(C) Oil paint expands and contracts readily in response to changes in temperature, but it absorbs little water and so is little affected by changes in humidity.
(D) An especially hard and nonabsorbent type of gesso was the raw material for moldings on the frames of Renaissance oil paintings.
(E) Gesso layers applied by Renaissance painters typically consisted of a coarse base layer onto which several increasingly fine-grained layers were applied.

Argument Evaluation

Situation   Renaissance paintings are subject to deterioration due to changes in climate, but their actual paint is not a factor in this deterioration. Instead, restorers hypothesize, it is gesso, the material under the paint, that causes problems for the paintings.

Reasoning   *What would most strongly support the hypothesis that gesso is causing the deterioration?* An indication that gesso is affected by climatic changes would be most helpful in supporting the hypothesis. What could show that gesso is affected in this way? If the extent of a painting's deterioration is directly related to the amount of gesso used under that painting, then the gesso clearly plays some part in that deterioration.

A   **Correct.** This statement properly identifies a point supporting the hypothesis.

B   This suggests that another factor—the wood of the panels—has a role in the paintings' deterioration. Thus it weakens the hypothesis that gesso causes the deterioration.

C   This merely reinforces given information, that the paint itself is not responsible for the paintings' deterioration.

D   Because this gives no information about any connection between this especially hard and nonabsorbent type of gesso and the type of gesso used under the paint in Renaissance paintings, the properties and usage of the former type of gesso are irrelevant to the question of whether gesso is responsible for the paintings' deterioration.

E   Because we are told nothing about whether this technique of gesso application increases or decreases the likelihood that gesso will be affected by climatic change, it does not support the restorers' hypothesis.

The correct answer is A.

202. A newly discovered painting seems to be the work of one of two 17th-century artists, either the northern German Johannes Drechen or the Frenchman Louis Birelle, who sometimes painted in the same style as Drechen. Analysis of the carved picture frame, which has been identified as the painting's original 17th-century frame, showed that it is made of wood found widely in northern Germany at the time, but rare in the part of France where Birelle lived. This shows that the painting is most likely the work of Drechen.

Which of the following is an assumption that the argument requires?

(A) The frame was made from wood local to the region where the picture was painted.
(B) Drechen is unlikely to have ever visited the home region of Birelle in France.
(C) Sometimes a painting so closely resembles others of its era that no expert is able to confidently decide who painted it.
(D) The painter of the picture chose the frame for the picture.
(E) The carving style of the picture frame is not typical of any specific region of Europe.

Argument Construction

Situation   A 17th-century painting has been discovered that was either by Johannes Drechen from northern Germany or by French artist Louis Birelle. The painting's original picture frame is made of wood widely found in 17th-century northern Germany but rare in the French region where Birelle lived. So the painting was probably the work of Drechen.

Reasoning   *Which answer choice is an assumption required by the argument?* If the painting is correctly attributed to Drechen, then the wood that the frame was made from probably came from the region where Drechen lived and did his painting. The argument assumes that the specific wood used in the frame came from northern Germany rather than from some other place where that wood might have been found, and where (for all we know) Birelle might have visited.

A **Correct.** Without an assumption equivalent to this, the argument would fail.
B This is not a required assumption (unlike, for example, the following: Drechen did not give the picture frame to Birelle as a gift).
C This is a truism but is not required to make the argument's conclusion well supported.
D This does not need to be assumed; Drechen could, for example, have simply asked a local frame-maker to make a frame for his picture.
E Neither the affirmation nor the denial of this statement is needed to underpin the argument.

The correct answer is A.

203. Archaeologists working in the Andes Mountains recently excavated a buried 4,000-year-old temple containing structures that align with a stone carving on a distant hill to indicate the direction of the rising sun at the summer solstice. Alignments in the temple were also found to point toward the position, at the summer solstice, of a constellation known in Andean culture as the Fox. Since the local mythology represents the fox as teaching people how to cultivate and irrigate plants, the ancient Andeans may have built the temple as a religious representation of the fox.

Which of the following is an assumption on which the argument is based?

(A) The constellation known as the Fox has the same position at the summer solstice as it did 4,000 years ago.
(B) In the region around the temple, the summer solstice marks the time for planting.
(C) The temple was protected from looters by dirt and debris built up over thousands of years.
(D) Other structural alignments at the temple point to further constellations with agricultural significance.
(E) The site containing the temple was occupied for a significant amount of time before abandonment.

Argument Construction

Situation   A recently excavated 4,000-year-old temple contains structures that point toward the positions at the summer solstice of both the rising sun and a constellation known in local culture as the Fox. Local mythology represents the fox as teaching people how to cultivate and irrigate plants.

Reasoning   *What must be true in order for the argument's premises to suggest that the temple was built to religiously represent the fox?* The argument's premises are all observations about current conditions: the current alignment at the summer solstice of the temple relative to the sunrise and to the constellation known as the Fox, the current local name for a constellation, and current local mythology. To support the conclusion about the temple's original purpose, the argument has to assume that all these conditions may still be essentially the same as they were 4,000 years ago when the temple was built.

A   **Correct.** If the constellation's position at the summer solstice relative to the temple is different from what it was 4,000 years ago, the temple must not have been aligned to point toward it when it was built. In that case, the argument's justification for associating the temple with that constellation and with the fox is undermined.

B   This does not have to be assumed for the argument to succeed, though if true, it might strengthen the argument by providing additional evidence associating the temple with the mythological fox as a teacher of agriculture. But the argument could be just as strong if the solstice were instead associated with agricultural activities other than planting.

C   Even if the temple was not protected from looters, the conditions described in the argument's premises may still be the same as they were 4,000 years ago.

D   This is not assumed. Additional structural alignments pointing to different constellations associated with mythological beings other than the fox might weaken or even undermine the argument's justification for associating the temple with the fox specifically.

E   The argument makes no assumption regarding how long the temple was occupied, or even regarding whether the temple was ever occupied.

The correct answer is A.

204. Meat from chickens contaminated with salmonella bacteria can cause serious food poisoning. Capsaicin, the chemical that gives chili peppers their hot flavor, has antibacterial properties. Chickens do not have taste receptors for capsaicin and will readily eat feed laced with capsaicin. When chickens were fed such feed and then exposed to salmonella bacteria, relatively few of them became contaminated with salmonella.

In deciding whether the feed would be useful in raising salmonella-free chicken for retail sale, it would be most helpful to determine which of the following?

(A) Whether feeding capsaicin to chickens affects the taste of their meat
(B) Whether eating capsaicin reduces the risk of salmonella poisoning for humans
(C) Whether chicken is more prone to salmonella contamination than other kinds of meat
(D) Whether appropriate cooking of chicken contaminated with salmonella can always prevent food poisoning
(E) Whether capsaicin can be obtained only from chili peppers

Argument Evaluation

Situation   Chickens will readily eat feed laced with capsaicin, which appears to protect them from contamination with salmonella bacteria that can cause food poisoning.

Reasoning   *What information would help determine whether using the feed would be an effective strategy for raising salmonella-free chicken for retail sale?* In order for the strategy to be effective, it must be economically feasible for farmers to raise chickens using the feed, and there must be enough consumer demand for chickens raised this way. So any information about factors likely to affect either the economic feasibility of raising the chickens or consumer demand for them could be helpful in determining how useful the feed would be.

A   **Correct.** If chicken producers tried to market meat from capsaicin-fed chickens without knowing whether the taste is affected, they would risk alienating consumers. Of course, if they found that the taste is affected, they would then need to do further investigations to determine how consumers would likely respond to the difference. If consumers did not like the taste, this could negatively affect demand for the chickens. In that case, using the feed would not be an effective way to raise chickens for retail sale.

B   There are two ways this might be considered relevant. First, it might be thought that because capsaicin reduces the risk of salmonella poisoning in humans, it will also do so in chickens; but we already have good evidence of that in the argument. Second, it might be thought that, if the capsaicin does not produce chickens that are totally salmonella free, then if any capsaicin remains in the chickens, it will help prevent any humans who consume the chicken from getting salmonella poisoning. But the relevant issue is whether the capsaicin will make the chickens salmonella free, not whether humans will be protected whether the chickens are salmonella free or not.

C   The susceptibility of other types of meat to salmonella contamination would not affect the usefulness of the feed for preventing such contamination in chicken.

D   Presumably many people do not cook contaminated chicken appropriately, so consumers could still benefit from salmonella-free chicken whether or not appropriate cooking methods could prevent food poisoning.

E   Regardless of whether capsaicin can be obtained from other sources, chili peppers may be a perfectly viable source.

The correct answer is A.

205. Which of the following most logically completes the argument below?

When mercury-vapor streetlights are used in areas inhabited by insect-eating bats, the bats feed almost exclusively around the lights, because the lights attract flying insects. In Greenville, the mercury-vapor streetlights are about to be replaced with energy-saving sodium streetlights, which do not attract insects. This change is likely to result in a drop in the population of insect-eating bats in Greenville, since _____.

(A) the bats do not begin to hunt until after sundown

(B) the bats are unlikely to feed on insects that do not fly

(C) the highway department will be able to replace mercury-vapor streetlights with sodium streetlights within a relatively short time and without disrupting the continuity of lighting at the locations of the streetlights

(D) in the absence of local concentrations of the flying insects on which bats feed, the bats expend much more energy on hunting for food, requiring much larger quantities of insects to sustain each bat

(E) bats use echolocation to catch insects and therefore gain no advantage from the fact that insects flying in the vicinity of streetlights are visible at night

Argument Construction

Situation   In areas with mercury-vapor streetlights, any insect-eating bats feed almost exclusively around the lights, which attract flying insects. In Greenville, mercury-vapor streetlights will soon be replaced with sodium streetlights that do not attract insects.

Reasoning   *What evidence would suggest that the change in streetlights will reduce Greenville's population of insect-eating bats?* Since the sodium streetlights will not attract flying insects, the bats will probably stop focusing their feeding around Greenville's streetlights after the lights are changed. A statement providing evidence that this will make it harder for the bats to get enough food to sustain themselves would support the conclusion that the change is likely to reduce Greenville's bat population and thus would logically complete the argument.

A   Insect-eating bats existed long before streetlights did, so they can probably find insects away from streetlights even if they hunt only after sundown.

B   Greenville will almost certainly still have flying insects for the bats to eat after the change, even if those insects no longer gather around the streetlights.

C   If anything, such a smooth transition would be less likely to disturb the bats and therefore less likely to reduce their population.

D   **Correct.** Since there will be no local concentrations of flying insects around Greenville streetlights after the change, the bats will most likely have more trouble getting enough to eat, and that their local population will therefore fall.

E   The advantage that the bats gain from mercury-vapor streetlights comes from the high concentration of insects. The fact that the bats get no additional advantage from the insects' visibility tells us nothing about what affect the change to a different type of light might have.

The correct answer is D.

206. Rats injected with morphine exhibit decreased activity of the immune system, the bodily system that fights off infections. These same rats exhibited heightened blood levels of corticosteroids, chemicals secreted by the adrenal glands. Since corticosteroids can interfere with immune-system activity, scientists hypothesized that the way morphine reduces immune responses in rats is by stimulating the adrenal glands to secrete additional corticosteroids into the bloodstream.

Which of the following experiments would yield the most useful results for evaluating the scientists' hypothesis?

(A) Injecting morphine into rats that already have heightened blood levels of corticosteroids and then observing their new blood levels of corticosteroids

(B) Testing the level of immune-system activity of rats, removing their adrenal glands, and then testing the rats' immune-system activity levels again

(C) Injecting rats with corticosteroids and then observing how many of the rats contracted infections

(D) Removing the adrenal glands of rats, injecting the rats with morphine, and then testing the level of the rats' immune-system responses

(E) Injecting rats with a drug that stimulates immune-system activity and then observing the level of corticosteroids in their bloodstreams

Argument Evaluation

Situation Rats injected with morphine exhibit decreased immune-system activity and increased levels of corticosteroids, which are secreted by the adrenal glands and can interfere with immune-system activity.

Reasoning *What further experiment would help determine whether morphine reduces immune responses in rats by stimulating the adrenal glands to release more corticosteroids?* Contrary to the scientists' hypothesis, the experimental results might have occurred because the morphine injections directly reduced immune-system activity. Or the injections might have blocked some mechanism that reduces corticosteroid levels in the blood, even if the morphine did not stimulate the adrenal glands to produce more corticosteroids. To evaluate whether the scientists' hypothesis is more plausible than these rival hypotheses, it would be helpful to know whether similar experimental results would occur after morphine injections even if adrenal gland activity did not change.

A Morphine could stimulate the adrenal glands of rats with normal corticosteroid levels to produce more corticosteroids, whether or not it does so in rats whose corticosteroid levels are already heightened.

B Such an experiment would not involve morphine and thus would not help to determine how morphine affects immune-system activity in rats.

C Whether or not rats contract infections may not reliably indicate their levels of immune-system activity.

D **Correct.** If the immune system responses decreased after the morphine injections in this experiment, the hypothesis that it was by stimulation of the adrenal glands that morphine reduced immune-system activity would be undermined. But if no decrease in immune-system responses occurred, the hypothesis would be confirmed.

E Even if the mechanism by which a drug other than morphine increases immune-system activity were discovered, this discovery would not necessarily reveal the mechanism by which morphine reduces immune-system activity.

The correct answer is D.

207. Curator: If our museum lends *Venus* to the Hart Institute for their show this spring, they will lend us their Rembrandt etchings for our print exhibition next fall. Having those etchings will increase attendance to the exhibition and hence increase revenue from our general admission fee.

Museum Administrator: But *Venus* is our biggest attraction. Moreover the Hart's show will run for twice as long as our exhibition. So on balance the number of patrons may decrease.

The point of the administrator's response to the curator is to question

(A) whether getting the Rembrandt etchings from the Hart Institute is likely to increase attendance at the print exhibition
(B) whether the Hart Institute's Rembrandt etchings will be appreciated by those patrons of the curator's museum for whom the museum's biggest attraction is *Venus*
(C) whether the number of patrons attracted by the Hart Institute's Rembrandt etchings will be larger than the number of patrons who do not come in the spring because *Venus* is on loan
(D) whether, if *Venus* is lent, the museum's revenue from general admission fees during the print exhibition will exceed its revenue from general admission fees during the Hart Institute's exhibition
(E) whether the Hart Institute or the curator's museum will have the greater financial gain from the proposed exchange of artworks

Argument Construction

Situation   A curator and a museum administrator debate whether lending a **particular** artwork to the Hart Institute in exchange for a loan of some of the Hart Institute's artworks would increase or decrease attendance and revenue at the museum.

Reasoning   *Which of the curator's explicit or implicit claims is the museum administrator questioning?* The administrator's statements that *Venus* is the museum's biggest attraction and that the Hart Institute's show will run twice as long as the museum's exhibition do not directly conflict with any statement or assumption made by the curator. However, the administrator's conclusion is that on balance the number of patrons at the museum may decrease if the curator's proposal is followed. This conclusion calls into question the curator's claim that the proposal will increase revenue from the general admission fee, since that claim presupposes that on balance the proposal will increase the number of visitors to the museum. (The context suggests that the administrator is using the term *patrons* to mean visitors rather than donors.)

A   The administrator does not dispute that the Rembrandt etchings would probably increase attendance at the print exhibition but rather suggests that this increase would be exceeded by the loss of visitors to the museum while the Hart Institute borrows *Venus*.

B   Neither the curator nor the administrator comments on whether the patrons attracted to the Rembrandt etchings would be the same people attracted to *Venus*.

C   **Correct.** The curator implicitly infers that the former number will be larger than the latter, whereas the administrator questions this by asserting that the latter number may be larger than the former.

D   The administrator does not question whether the revenue during the print exhibition will exceed the revenue during the Hart Institute's exhibition, but rather whether it will exceed the loss of revenue during the Hart Institute's exhibition.

E   Neither the curator nor the administrator comments on whether the museum would gain more or less from the exchange than the Hart Institute would.

The correct answer is C.

208. Which of the following most logically completes the passage?

Leaf beetles damage willow trees by stripping away their leaves, but a combination of parasites and predators generally keeps populations of these beetles in check. Researchers have found that severe air pollution results in reduced predator populations. The parasites, by contrast, are not adversely affected by pollution; nevertheless, the researchers' discovery probably does explain why leaf beetles cause particularly severe damage to willows in areas with severe air pollution, since _____.

(A) neither the predators nor the parasites of leaf beetles themselves attack willow trees
(B) the parasites that attack leaf beetles actually tend to be more prevalent in areas with severe air pollution than they are elsewhere
(C) the damage caused by leaf beetles is usually not enough to kill a willow tree outright
(D) where air pollution is not especially severe, predators have much more impact on leaf-beetle populations than parasites do
(E) willows often grow in areas where air pollution is especially severe

Argument Construction

Situation   Leaf beetles damage willow trees, but predators and parasites keep leaf beetle populations in check. Air pollution reduces populations of predators but not of parasites. Leaf beetles damage willows especially severely in areas with severe air pollution.

Reasoning   *What would support the conclusion that air pollution's effects on the predator populations (but not on the parasite populations) explains why leaf beetles damage willows the most in areas with severe air pollution?* The word *since* preceding the blank space at the end of the passage indicates that the space should be filled with a premise supporting the conclusion stated immediately before the *since*. To support this conclusion, it would help to have evidence that predators play a predominant role in keeping leaf beetle populations in check, and thus that the reduction of predator populations by air pollution could be sufficient to enable leaf beetle populations to grow and cause especially severe damage.

A   The fact that neither the predators nor the parasites directly contribute to harming the trees offers no reason to conclude that a difference in how they are affected by pollution would contribute to the harm that the beetles cause to the trees.

B   If the parasites are more prevalent in areas with severe air pollution, then they are more likely to keep leaf beetle populations in check in those areas, despite the reduced predator populations. Thus, the decline in predator populations would more likely be insufficient to explain why the leaf beetles cause more damage in those areas.

C   This observation is irrelevant to whether the decline in predator populations explains why leaf beetles damage willow trees more severely in areas with severe air pollution.

D   Correct. This indicates that predators play a predominant role in keeping leaf beetle populations in check, so, as explained above, it supports the argument's conclusion.

E   This is not clearly relevant to whether the decline in predator populations explains why leaf beetles damage willow trees more severely in areas with severe air pollution. The argument's conclusion could just as easily be true regardless of whether willows grow in such polluted areas frequently or infrequently.

The correct answer is D.

209. On May first, in order to reduce the number of overdue books, a children's library instituted a policy of forgiving fines and giving bookmarks to children returning all of their overdue books. On July first there were twice as many overdue books as there had been on May first, although a record number of books had been returned during the interim.

Which of the following, if true, most helps to explain the apparent inconsistency in the results of the library's policy?

(A) The librarians did not keep accurate records of how many children took advantage of the grace period, and some of the children returning overdue books did not return all of their overdue books.

(B) Although the grace period enticed some children to return all of their overdue books, it did not convince all of the children with overdue books to return all of their books.

(C) The bookmarks became popular among the children, so in order to collect the bookmarks, many children borrowed many more books than they usually did and kept them past their due date.

(D) The children were allowed to borrow a maximum of five books for a two-week period, and hence each child could keep a maximum of fifteen books beyond their due date within a two-month period.

(E) Although the library forgave overdue fines during the grace period, the amount previously charged the children was minimal; hence, the forgiveness of the fines did not provide enough incentive for them to return their overdue books.

Argument Construction

Situation   After a library started forgiving fines and giving bookmarks to children who returned all their overdue books, the number of books returned greatly increased, but so did the number of overdue books.

Reasoning   *Why might the policy have simultaneously increased the number of overdue books and the number of books being returned?* In order to increase both these numbers, the policy must have resulted in more books being checked out, kept past their due dates, and then returned. But why would the policy have promoted that behavior? One possibility is that it rewarded the behavior. The policy involved giving children bookmarks as rewards for returning overdue books, while removing the fines that penalized the children for doing so. If the children liked the bookmarks, they might have tried to get more of them by deliberately checking books out in order to keep them past their due dates before returning them to get the bookmarks.

A   Failing to keep accurate records of the number of children would not clearly increase the number of books being returned. And the policy change did not apply to children who returned only some of their overdue books.

B   This suggests that the policy had limited effects, but does not help to explain why it had apparently inconsistent effects.

C   **Correct.** This explains how the policy gave the children a motive to check out and return more books while also allowing them to keep more of the books past the due dates.

D   This restriction would have limited the number of overdue books and thus would not help to explain why that number increased.

E   This suggests that the policy had little effect but does not help to explain why it had apparently inconsistent effects.

The correct answer is C.

210. A certain species of desert lizard digs tunnels in which to lay its eggs. The eggs must incubate inside the tunnel for several weeks before hatching, and they fail to hatch if they are disturbed at any time during this incubation period. Yet these lizards guard their tunnels for only a few days after laying their eggs.

Which of the following, if true, most helps explain why there is no need for lizards to guard their tunnels for more than a few days?

(A) The eggs are at risk of being disturbed only during the brief egg-laying season when many lizards are digging in a relatively small area.

(B) The length of the incubation period varies somewhat from one tunnel to another.

(C) Each female lizard lays from 15 to 20 eggs, only about 10 of which hatch even if the eggs are not disturbed at any time during the incubation period.

(D) The temperature and humidity within the tunnels will not be suitable for the incubating eggs unless the tunnels are plugged with sand immediately after the eggs are laid.

(E) The only way to disturb the eggs of this lizard species is by opening up one of the tunnels in which they are laid.

Argument Construction

Situation Lizards of a certain species dig tunnels in which they lay their eggs. Although the eggs fail to hatch if disturbed during their several weeks of incubation, the lizards guard the tunnels for only a few days after laying the eggs.

Reasoning *What would help to explain why the lizards have to guard their tunnels for only a few days?* For the lizards to survive as a species, their behaviors must ensure that enough of their eggs hatch. Thus, they must successfully prevent enough of their eggs from being disturbed in the tunnels throughout the several weeks of incubation. If guarding the tunnels for only a few days accomplishes this, then some other factor must prevent the eggs from being disturbed during the remaining weeks. Evidence of any such factor would help to explain why the lizards do not have to guard the tunnels longer. For example, to protect the eggs without guarding them, the lizards might conceal the tunnel entrances after the first few days. Or animals likely to disturb the eggs might only be present for those first days, in which case there would be nothing for the lizards to guard against thereafter.

A **Correct.** This suggests that the only creatures likely to disturb the eggs are other lizards of the same species digging tunnels to lay their own eggs at around the same time. If so, each lizard can safely leave its eggs unguarded after a few days because all the other lizards will have finished digging.

B Even if the incubation period varies somewhat, the passage says it always lasts several weeks. So this does not explain why the lizards have to guard the tunnels for only a few days.

C If many eggs fail to hatch even when undisturbed, that is all the more reason for the lizards to protect the remaining eggs from disturbance throughout the incubation period so that at least some will hatch. So it does not explain why the lizards guard their tunnels only for a few days.

D Whether or not immediately plugging the tunnels with sand is enough to protect the eggs, this behavior does not explain why the lizards subsequently guard the tunnels for a few days and then leave for the rest of the incubation period.

E Even if it is impossible to disturb the eggs without opening the tunnels, that does not explain why the lizards guard the tunnels for a few days and then leave for the rest of the incubation period.

The correct answer is A.

211. Most banks that issue credit cards charge interest rates on credit card debt that are ten percentage points higher than the rates those banks charge for ordinary consumer loans. These banks' representatives claim the difference is fully justified, since it simply covers the difference between the costs to these banks associated with credit card debt and those associated with consumer loans.

    Which of the following, if true, most seriously calls into question the reasoning offered by the banks' representatives?

    (A) Some lenders that are not banks offer consumer loans at interest rates that are even higher than most banks charge on credit card debt.
    (B) Most car rental companies require that their customers provide signed credit card charge slips or security deposits.
    (C) Two to three percent of the selling price of every item bought with a given credit card goes to the bank that issued that credit card.
    (D) Most people need not use credit cards to buy everyday necessities, but could buy those necessities with cash or pay by check.
    (E) People who pay their credit card bills in full each month usually pay no interest on the amounts they charge.

    Argument Evaluation

    Situation   Banks that issue credit cards tend to charge interest rates on the associated debt that are ten percentage points higher than the rates associated with "ordinary" consumer loans (consumer loans that are not associated with credit cards). Representatives of these banks have offered a justification of this practice, based on a claim that this difference in interest rates "simply covers the difference" in costs, to the banks, associated with these respective types of loans (loans associated with credit cards and consumer loans that are not associated with credit cards).

    Reasoning   *What additional facts would indicate a flaw in the bank representatives' argument?* Given the description of the bank representatives' argument, we may assume that, by their estimation, the costs to banks associated with credit card debt are greater than the costs associated with other consumer loans. The representatives' argument, that the difference in interest rates "simply covers" this difference in costs, may then be seen as an argument that all of the extra money that the banks collect from the higher interest rates is *necessary* if the banks are to cover this difference in costs. If we can find a fact whereby the ten percentage point difference is not necessary to cover the difference in costs, then we may be able to "call into question" the bank representatives' argument.

    A   The point of this response to the bank representatives' argument would seem to be that the relatively high interest rates on credit debt may be justified because certain other businesses charge even higher interest rates on consumer loans. Regardless of the merits of this response, it appears intended to *support* the argument of the representatives, whereas our task is to identify a fact that could be used to criticize the argument.

    B   This purported fact does not address the argument concerning the interest rates on credit-card debt.

    C   **Correct.** If two to three percent of the value of purchases made on credit cards goes to the issuing banks, then this money could be used to cover some of the difference in costs described by the bank representatives. The interest rates on credit cards could therefore be somewhat lower than they actually are, with the difference in costs nevertheless still fully covered. The difference in interest rates of ten percentage points may therefore not be necessary.

    D   This point might be used in support of an argument that consumers have a genuine choice as to whether to use credit cards, and that they are therefore responsible for the higher rates of interest that they pay for credit-card debt. Such an argument would seem to *support* the position of bank representatives.

    E   As with the point in answer choice D, this point might seem to suggest that consumers bear some of the responsibility for the higher interest rates they pay, thus perhaps mitigating the responsibility of the banks. The point might thus seem to *support* the position of the banks' representatives.

    The correct answer is C.

212. Often patients with ankle fractures that are stable, and thus do not require surgery, are given follow-up x-rays because their orthopedists are concerned about possibly having misjudged the stability of the fracture. When a number of follow-up x-rays were reviewed, however, all the fractures that had initially been judged stable were found to have healed correctly. Therefore, it is a waste of money to order follow-up x-rays of ankle fractures initially judged stable.

Which of the following, if true, most strengthens the argument?

(A) Doctors who are general practitioners rather than orthopedists are less likely than orthopedists to judge the stability of an ankle fracture correctly.

(B) Many ankle injuries for which an initial x-ray is ordered are revealed by the x-ray not to involve any fracture of the ankle.

(C) X-rays of patients of many different orthopedists working in several hospitals were reviewed.

(D) The healing of ankle fractures that have been surgically repaired is always checked by means of a follow-up x-ray.

(E) Orthopedists routinely order follow-up x-rays for fractures of bones other than ankle bones.

Argument Evaluation

Situation   Often patients with ankle fractures that their orthopedists have judged not to require surgery are given follow-up x-rays to check whether the fracture healed correctly. An examination of a sample of those x-rays found that the ankle had, in each case, healed properly.

Reasoning   *The question is which of the answer choices, if true, would most strengthen the argument.* The argument is based on data concerning follow-up x-rays, each of which revealed no problem with the orthopedist's initial judgment that the ankle fracture was stable (and would heal without surgery). This invites the question whether the follow-up x-rays are really needed. The argument concludes that they are a waste of money. But was the x-ray data truly representative of orthopedists generally? After all, some orthopedists—perhaps more experienced, better-trained, or employed at a facility with better staff or facilities—may be much better than others at judging ankle fractures. If we add the information that the data for the conclusion comes from many orthopedists working at many different hospitals, we have greater assurance that the x-ray data is representative, and the argument will be made much stronger.

A   Neither the study nor the conclusion that is drawn from it concerns general practitioners, so this point is irrelevant.

B   Naturally many ankle injuries do not involve fractures—x-rays may sometimes be used to determine this—but the argument concerns only cases where there have been ankle fractures.

C   **Correct.** This shows that the sample of x-ray data examined was probably sufficiently representative of cases of ankle fracture judged to be stable by orthopedists.

D   The argument does not concern cases of ankle fracture that have been surgically repaired.

E   The argument concerns only x-rays of ankles. From the information given here, we cannot infer that orthopedists are generally wasteful in routinely ordering follow-up x-rays.

The correct answer is C.

213. In setting environmental standards for industry and others to meet, it is inadvisable to require the best results that state-of-the-art technology can achieve. Current technology is able to detect and eliminate even extremely minute amounts of contaminants, but at a cost that is exorbitant relative to the improvement achieved. So it would be reasonable instead to set standards by taking into account all of the current and future risks involved.

    The argument given concerning the reasonable way to set standards presupposes that

    (A) industry currently meets the standards that have been set by environmental authorities
    (B) there are effective ways to take into account all of the relevant risks posed by allowing different levels of contaminants
    (C) the only contaminants worth measuring are generated by industry
    (D) it is not costly to prevent large amounts of contaminants from entering the environment
    (E) minute amounts of some contaminants can be poisonous

Argument Construction

Situation   State-of-the-art technology can detect and eliminate even tiny amounts of environmental contaminants, but at a cost that is exorbitant relative to its benefits.

Reasoning   *What must be true in order for the argument's premises to support its conclusion?* The argument is that environmental standards requiring the best results that state-of-the-art technology can provide are unreasonably expensive relative to their benefits, so it would be reasonable instead to set environmental standards that take into account all present and future risks from contaminants. In order for the premise to support the conclusion, the environmental standards based on present and future risks would have to be less expensive relative to their benefits than the *best results* environmental standards are. Furthermore, setting the *current and future risks* environmental standards cannot be reasonable unless it is feasible to assess present and future risks as those standards require.

A   The argument does not say which standards, if any, environmental authorities have set. In any case, such standards could be reasonable or unreasonable regardless of whether industry currently meets them.

B   **Correct.** If taking future risks into account were infeasible, then applying the *current and future risks* standards would also be infeasible. And setting those standards would be unreasonable if they could not feasibly be applied.

C   According to the stimulus, the proposed *current and future risks* standards would apply to industry *and others*. So those standards could be reasonable even if the unspecified *others* also generated contaminants worth measuring, and even if the standards required measuring those contaminants.

D   Even if it were costly to prevent large amounts of contaminants from entering the environment, the benefits of doing so to prevent present and future risks might outweigh the costs.

E   The *current and future risks* standards could take into account any poisoning risks posed by minute amounts of contaminants.

The correct answer is B.

214. The chemical adenosine is released by brain cells when those cells are active. Adenosine then binds to more and more sites on cells in certain areas of the brain, as the total amount released gradually increases during wakefulness. During sleep, the number of sites to which adenosine is bound decreases. Some researchers have hypothesized that it is the cumulative binding of adenosine to a large number of sites that causes the onset of sleep.

Which of the following, if true, provides the most support for the researchers' hypothesis?

(A) Even after long periods of sleep when adenosine is at its lowest concentration in the brain, the number of brain cells bound with adenosine remains very large.

(B) Caffeine, which has the effect of making people remain wakeful, is known to interfere with the binding of adenosine to sites on brain cells.

(C) Besides binding to sites in the brain, adenosine is known to be involved in biochemical reactions throughout the body.

(D) Some areas of the brain that are relatively inactive nonetheless release some adenosine.

(E) Stress resulting from a dangerous situation can preserve wakefulness even when brain levels of bound adenosine are high.

Argument Evaluation

Situation   Adenosine is released from brain cells that are active. The amount of adenosine released increases during wakefulness, and it binds to more and more sites on cells in certain brain locations. The number of sites to which it is bound decreases during sleep. Researchers have hypothesized that the cumulative binding of adenosine to many sites causes the onset of sleep.

Reasoning   *Which answer choice most strongly supports the hypothesis?* If the hypothesis is correct, then some factor that impedes the binding of adenosine should be closely associated with wakefulness. Therefore, finding some such factor, and observing that it is accompanied by wakefulness when the factor operates, would tend to confirm the hypothesis.

A   Without further, more specific information, this piece of information suffices neither to confirm nor to refute the hypothesis.

B   **Correct.** A finding that caffeine, known to induce wakefulness, inhibits adenosine from binding to sites on brain cells helps confirm the hypothesis.

C   This piece of information lacks a clear relevance to the hypothesized impact on sleep, and therefore does not help confirm the hypothesis.

D   This information lacks a clear relevance to the hypothesized impact on sleep, and therefore does not help confirm the hypothesis.

E   What this indicates is that stress may impede the hypothesized sleep-inducing effect of adenosine. It does not refute the hypothesis but does not confirm it either.

The correct answer is B.

215. A two-year study beginning in 1977 found that, among 85-year-old people, those whose immune systems were weakest were twice as likely to die within two years as others in the study. The cause of their deaths, however, was more often heart disease, against which the immune system does not protect, than cancer or infections, which are attacked by the immune system.

Which of the following, if true, would offer the best prospects for explaining deaths in which weakness of the immune system, though present, played no causal role?

(A) There were twice as many infections among those in the study with the weakest immune systems as among those with the strongest immune systems.
(B) The majority of those in the study with the strongest immune systems died from infection or cancer by 1987.
(C) Some of the drugs that had been used to treat the symptoms of heart disease had a side effect of weakening the immune system.
(D) Most of those in the study who survived beyond the two-year period had recovered from a serious infection sometime prior to 1978.
(E) Those in the study who survived into the 1980s had, in 1976, strengthened their immune systems through drug therapy.

Argument Construction

Situation This question presents a puzzling scenario and asks us to find a possible fact that could make the situation less puzzling. The scenario involves a study that was conducted a few decades ago on a certain group of older adults. Those with the weakest immune systems were much more likely to die within two years than were the other individuals in the study. However, among the individuals with the weakest immune systems, death was more often by heart disease, from which the immune system does not protect, than from cancer or infections, for which a strong immune system is protective.

Reasoning *For the participants in the study with the weakest immune systems, what might best explain the deaths that were not due to weakness of the immune system?* We might expect that the people with the weakest immune systems would be more likely to die from diseases that a strong immune system would protect them from than from other diseases. An explanation of the deaths that were not due to weakness of the immune system would explain why this is not the case.

A This point is irrelevant. The hypothesis that the participants in the study with the weakest immune systems had more infections than did the other participants does not explain why those participants died from conditions that were not infections.

B Our question involves identifying a possible explanation for the deaths of the participants in the study with the weakest immune systems. This answer choice, about the deaths of those with strong immune systems, is thus irrelevant.

C **Correct.** This answer choice suggests that those with heart disease—which would not have been due to weakness of the immune system—would have nevertheless had a weaker immune system due to the administration of certain drugs. Those with heart disease may for this reason have been among those with the weakest immune systems. If the individuals with weak immune systems due to treatment for heart disease formed a large-enough portion of the patients with the weakest immune systems, then we would have an explanation for why those with the weakest immune systems were more likely to die from heart disease than from infections or cancer.

D This answer choice is not specific enough for us to use in the explanation we are looking for. For example, the "serious" infections in question may have occurred well before the 1977 study. Furthermore, there may appear to be no significant relationship between having had a serious infection and death from a condition that was not an infection.

E This answer choice is also not specific enough to be a factor that might reasonably offer the explanation we are looking for. For example, given the information in this answer choice, it could have been the case that all of the participants had the drug therapy.

The correct answer is C.

216. Most scholars agree that King Alfred (A.D. 849–899) personally translated a number of Latin texts into Old English. One historian contends that Alfred also personally penned his own law code, arguing that the numerous differences between the language of the law code and Alfred's translations of Latin texts are outweighed by the even more numerous similarities. Linguistic similarities, however, are what one expects in texts from the same language, the same time, and the same region. Apart from Alfred's surviving translations and law code, there are only two other extant works from the same dialect and milieu, so it is risky to assume here that linguistic similarities point to common authorship.

The passage above proceeds by

(A) providing examples that underscore another argument's conclusion
(B) questioning the plausibility of an assumption on which another argument depends
(C) showing that a principle if generally applied would have anomalous consequences
(D) showing that the premises of another argument are mutually inconsistent
(E) using argument by analogy to undermine a principle implicit in another argument

Argument Evaluation

Situation A historian argues that King Alfred must have written his own law code, since there are more similarities than differences between the language in the law code and that in Alfred's translations of Latin texts. Apart from Alfred's translations and law code, there are only two other extant works in the same dialect and from the same milieu.

Reasoning *How does the reasoning in the passage proceed?* The first sentence presents a claim that is not disputed in the passage. The second sentence presents a historian's argument. Implicitly citing the undisputed claim in the passage's first sentence as evidence, the historian proposes an analogy between the law code and Alfred's translations, arguing on the basis of this analogy that Alfred wrote the law code. The third sentence of the passage casts doubt on this analogy, pointing out that it could plausibly apply to texts that Alfred did not write. The fourth sentence suggests that too few extant texts are available as evidence to rule out the possibility raised in the third sentence. Thus, the third and fourth sentences are intended to undermine the historian's argument.

A As explained above, the passage is intended to undermine the conclusion of the historian's argument, not to *underscore* (emphasize) it.

B **Correct.** The passage's third and fourth sentences question the plausibility of the historian's assumption that no one but Alfred would have been likely to write a text whose language has more similarities to than differences from the language in Alfred's translations.

C Although there might well be anomalous consequences from generalizing the assumption on which the historian's argument relies, the passage does not mention or allude to any such consequences.

D The passage does not mention, or suggest the existence of, any inconsistencies among the premises of the historian's argument.

E Although the historian argues by analogy, the passage does not itself argue by analogy; it does not suggest any specific counteranalogy to undermine the historian's argument.

The correct answer is B.

217. Parland's alligator population has been declining in recent years, primarily because of hunting. Alligators prey heavily on a species of freshwater fish that is highly valued as food by Parlanders, who had hoped that the decline in the alligator population would lead to an increase in the numbers of these fish available for human consumption. Yet the population of this fish species has also declined, even though the annual number caught for human consumption has not increased.

Which of the following, if true, most helps to explain the decline in the population of the fish species?

(A) The decline in the alligator population has meant that fishers can work in some parts of lakes and rivers that were formerly too dangerous.

(B) Over the last few years, Parland's commercial fishing enterprises have increased the number of fishing boats they use.

(C) Many Parlanders who hunt alligators do so because of the high market price of alligator skins, not because of the threat alligators pose to the fish population.

(D) During Parland's dry season, holes dug by alligators remain filled with water long enough to provide a safe place for the eggs of this fish species to hatch.

(E) In several neighboring countries through which Parland's rivers also flow, alligators are at risk of extinction as a result of extensive hunting.

Argument Construction

Situation The alligators in a certain region prey heavily on a certain species of fish that is prized for human consumption. However, although in recent years hunting has reduced the population of alligators in the region, the population of the prized freshwater fish species has declined. The annual number caught for human consumption has not increased.

Reasoning *What might explain the decline in the population of the prized fish species, despite both the decrease in population of another species that preys heavily on the prized fish and the lack of increase in fishing for the species for human consumption?* The population of the fish species declined, despite both the presence of a factor that we might be expected to produce an increase in the population of the species and the absence of a factor that we might ordinarily expect to explain the decrease. This situation may seem puzzling, and we may thus wish to find an explanation for it.

A Given that fishers can work in parts of lakes and rivers that were formerly too dangerous to work in, we might expect fishing of the prized species to increase and thus expect the population of the species to decrease. Although this might explain a decrease in the population of the fish species if fishing for the species increased, we have been given reason to believe that fishing for the species *decreased*.

B As with answer choice A, answer choice B suggests that fishing in the region may have increased and thus that fishing for the prized fish species for human consumption may have increased. This might explain the decrease in the population of the fish species if the statement were correct. However, we have been given that fishing for the prized fish species for human consumption has decreased.

C The statement in this answer choice provides an explanation of why the alligator hunting has occurred. Given that the alligators prey on the fish, this might help to explain an increase in the population of the prized fish species, had such an increase occurred. However, we are given that the population of the fish species in the region has decreased.

D **Correct.** Despite the fact that alligators prey on the prized fish species, this statement describes a way in which the fish species may be dependent on the alligators, in such a way that a decline in the population of the alligators could contribute to a decline in the fish species.

E The statement in this answer choice serves to amplify a point that is given in the puzzling situation of a decline in the population of the fish species *despite* (among other factors) a decrease in the population of the alligators. It does not explain why a decline in the population of the alligator species may have contributed to a decline in the population of the fish species.

The correct answer is D.

218. A company plans to develop a prototype weeding machine that uses cutting blades with optical sensors and microprocessors that distinguish weeds from crop plants by differences in shade of color. The inventor of the machine claims that it will reduce labor costs by virtually eliminating the need for manual weeding.

Which of the following is a consideration in favor of the company's implementing its plan to develop the prototype?

(A) There is a considerable degree of variation in shade of color between weeds of different species.

(B) The shade of color of some plants tends to change appreciably over the course of their growing season.

(C) When crops are weeded manually, overall size and leaf shape are taken into account in distinguishing crop plants from weeds.

(D) Selection and genetic manipulation allow plants of virtually any species to be economically bred to have a distinctive shade of color without altering their other characteristics.

(E) Farm laborers who are responsible for the manual weeding of crops carry out other agricultural duties at times in the growing season when extensive weeding is not necessary.

Evaluation of a Plan

Situation   A company plans to develop an automated weeding machine that would distinguish weeds from crop plants by differences in shade of color. It is supposed to reduce labor costs by eliminating the need for manual weeding.

Reasoning   *Which answer choice describes a consideration that would favor the company's plan?* The passage supports the plan by claiming that the machine would reduce labor costs by virtually eliminating weeding by hand. The correct answer choice will be one that adds to this support. Labor costs will be reduced only if the machine works well. The machine relies on shade of color to distinguish between weeds and crop plants. If crop plants can be bred to have distinctive color without sacrificing other qualities, it would be more likely that the machine could be used effectively.

A   Greater variation among weed plants would make it more difficult for the machine to distinguish between weeds and crop plants, and this would make it less likely that the machine would be effective.

B   This answer choice tends to disfavor the effectiveness of the machine. The more changeable the colors of the plants to be distinguished, the more complex the task of distinguishing between weeds and crop plants based on their color.

C   This answer choice tends to disfavor the likely benefits of the machine because it indicates that manual weeding distinguishes weeds from crop plants by using criteria that the machine does not take into account. If the machine does not distinguish weeds from crop plants as accurately and reliably as manual weeding does, then the machine is less apt to make manual weeding unnecessary.

D   **Correct.** Making crop plants easily distinguishable from weeds would facilitate the effective use of the weeding machine.

E   This does not favor the company's implementing the plan to develop the machine. There would still be tasks other than weeding that would require hiring staff. Thus there would still be labor costs even if the need for manual weeding were eliminated.

The correct answer is D.

219. Aroca City currently funds its public schools through taxes on property. **In place of this system, the city plans to introduce a sales tax of 3 percent on all retail sales in the city.** Critics protest that 3 percent of current retail sales falls short of the amount raised for schools by property taxes. The critics are correct on this point. **Nevertheless, implementing the plan will probably not reduce the money going to Aroca's schools.** Several large retailers have selected Aroca City as the site for huge new stores, and these are certain to draw large numbers of shoppers from neighboring municipalities, where sales are taxed at rates of 6 percent and more. In consequence, retail sales in Aroca City are bound to increase substantially.

In the argument given, the two portions in **boldface** play which of the following roles?

(A) The first presents a plan that the argument concludes is unlikely to achieve its goal; the second expresses that conclusion.

(B) The first presents a plan that the argument concludes is unlikely to achieve its goal; the second presents evidence in support of that conclusion.

(C) The first presents a plan that the argument contends is the best available; the second is a conclusion drawn by the argument to justify that contention.

(D) The first presents a plan one of whose consequences is at issue in the argument; the second is the argument's conclusion about that consequence.

(E) The first presents a plan that the argument seeks to defend against a certain criticism; the second is that criticism.

Argument Evaluation

Situation   Aroca City plans to switch the source of its public school funding from property taxes to a new local sales tax.

Reasoning   *What argumentative roles do the two portions in **boldface** play in the passage?* The first **boldfaced** portion simply describes the city's plan. The next two sentences in the passage describe an observation some critics have made in objecting to the plan and say that the observation is correct. But then the second **boldfaced** portion rejects the critics' implicit conclusion that the plan will reduce school funding. The final two sentences in the passage present reasons to accept the statement in the second **boldfaced** portion, so they are premises supporting it as a conclusion.

A   The argument concludes that the plan is unlikely to reduce funding for the schools. The passage does not mention the plan's goal, but presumably that goal is not to reduce school funding.

B   The second **boldfaced** portion presents the argument's conclusion, not evidence to support the conclusion. The passage does not mention the plan's goal, but presumably that goal is not to reduce school funding.

C   The passage does not say whether the plan is better than any other possible school funding plans.

D   **Correct.** The plan's likely effect on the amount of school funding is at issue in the argument, whose conclusion is that the plan probably will not reduce that funding.

E   The second **boldfaced** portion does not criticize the plan, but rather rejects a criticism of the plan by stating that the plan will probably not reduce school funding.

The correct answer is D.

220. Which of the following most logically completes the argument?

A photograph of the night sky was taken with the camera shutter open for an extended period. The normal motion of stars across the sky caused the images of the stars in the photograph to appear as streaks. However, one bright spot was not streaked. Even if the spot were caused, as astronomers believe, by a celestial object, that object could still have been moving across the sky during the time the shutter was open, since _____.

- (A) the spot was not the brightest object in the photograph
- (B) the photograph contains many streaks that astronomers can identify as caused by noncelestial objects
- (C) stars in the night sky do not appear to shift position relative to each other
- (D) the spot could have been caused by an object that emitted a flash that lasted for only a fraction of the time that the camera shutter was open
- (E) if the camera shutter had not been open for an extended period, it would have recorded substantially fewer celestial objects

Argument Construction

Situation   In a photograph of the night sky taken with the camera shutter open for an extended period, the images of stars appeared as streaks because of the stars' normal motion across the sky, but one bright spot was not streaked.

Reasoning   *What would most strongly suggest that a celestial object moving across the sky could have caused the spot?* An object moving across the sky that was bright throughout the time the camera shutter was open should have appeared as a streak in the photograph, just as the stars did. But if the moving object was bright for only a very brief moment, and thus not for an extended time while the camera shutter was open, the object's movement may not have been captured in the photograph, and thus would appear in the photograph as an unstreaked bright spot.

A   The argument is not about how bright the spot was compared to other objects in the photograph.

B   Streaks caused by noncelestial objects such as satellites or airplanes do not explain how only one of many celestial objects moving across the sky could have produced the unstreaked spot.

C   The passage indicates that the stars were shifting position relative to the camera, not relative to one another. In any case, this observation does not help to explain how a celestial object that may not have been a star but that was moving across the sky could have produced the unstreaked spot in the photograph.

D   **Correct.** As explained above, a moving celestial object that only produced a momentary flash of light would produce an unstreaked bright spot in the photograph.

E   This may be true, given that fewer celestial objects might have moved into the camera's range of view if the camera shutter had not been open as long. But it does not provide any evidence that a moving celestial object could have produced the unstreaked spot.

The correct answer is D.

221. Economist: Paying extra for fair-trade coffee—coffee labeled with the Fairtrade logo—is intended to help poor farmers, because they receive a higher price for the fair-trade coffee they grow. But this practice may hurt more farmers in developing nations than it helps. By raising average prices for coffee, it encourages more coffee to be produced than consumers want to buy. This lowers prices for non-fair-trade coffee and thus lowers profits for non-fair-trade coffee farmers.

To evaluate the strength of the economist's argument, it would be most helpful to know which of the following?

(A) Whether there is a way of alleviating the impact of the increased average prices for coffee on non-fair-trade coffee farmers' profits
(B) What proportion of coffee farmers in developing nations produce fair-trade coffee
(C) Whether many coffee farmers in developing nations also derive income from other kinds of farming
(D) Whether consumers should pay extra for fair-trade coffee if doing so lowers profits for non-fair-trade coffee farmers
(E) How fair-trade coffee farmers in developing nations could be helped without lowering profits for non-fair-trade coffee farmers

Argument Evaluation

Situation   Poor farmers receive higher prices for fair-trade coffee. But paying extra for fair-trade coffee lowers prices for non-fair-trade coffee and thus lowers profits for non-fair-trade coffee farmers.

Reasoning   *What would be most helpful to know to evaluate how well the economist's observations support the conclusion that buying fair-trade coffee hurts more farmers in developing nations than it helps?* The economist suggests that buying fair-trade coffee benefits farmers who grow it because they receive higher prices, but that it hurts non-fair-trade coffee farmers by reducing their profits. So to know whether the practice hurts more farmers in developing nations than it helps, it would be helpful to know whether developing nations have more farmers who produce non-fair-trade coffee than produce fair-trade coffee.

A   Even if there were some potential way of alleviating the negative impact from buying fair-trade coffee on non-fair-trade coffee farmers, it still could be that the practice hurts more developing-nation farmers than it helps. Alleviating the negative impact does not entail that there is no negative impact.

B   **Correct.** If fewer than half of these farmers produce fair-trade coffee, then the economist's observations do suggest that buying fair-trade coffee hurts more coffee farmers in developing nations than it helps. But if more than half do, those observations suggest the contrary.

C   Although knowing this could be helpful in determining how intensely many farmers are economically affected by people buying fair-trade coffee, it is not helpful in determining whether more farmers are hurt than are helped.

D   The argument's conclusion is only about the economic impact of buying fair-trade coffee, not about how consumers should or should not respond to that impact.

E   Knowing how the fair-trade coffee farmers could potentially be helped without hurting the other coffee farmers is irrelevant to assessing whether the practice of buying fair-trade coffee hurts more developing-nation farmers than it helps.

The correct answer is B.

222. Since smoking-related illnesses are a serious health problem in Country X, and since addiction to nicotine prevents many people from quitting smoking, the government of Country X plans to reduce the maximum allowable quantity of nicotine per cigarette by half over the next five years. However, reducing the quantity of nicotine per cigarette will probably cause people addicted to nicotine to smoke more cigarettes. Therefore, implementing this plan is unlikely to reduce the incidence of smoking-related illnesses.

Which of the following, if true, most strongly supports the argument about the consequences of implementing the Country X government's plan?

(A) Over half of the nonsmoking adults in Country X have smoked cigarettes in the past.
(B) If the Country X government's plan is implemented, the brands of cigarettes sold in Country X will differ less from each other than they do now in terms of their nicotine content.
(C) Inexpensive, smoke-free sources of nicotine, such as nicotine gum and nicotine skin patches, have recently become available in Country X.
(D) Many smokers in Country X already spend a large proportion of their disposable income on cigarettes.
(E) The main cause of smoking-related illnesses is not nicotine but the tar in cigarette smoke.

Argument Construction

Situation Country X plans to mandate that the nicotine content of cigarettes be reduced by half to encourage a reduction in smoking. The goal is to reduce the incidence of illnesses caused by cigarette smoking. Is there information given that suggests a likelihood that this goal will not be attained?

Reasoning We're given the information that people addicted to nicotine would probably smoke more cigarettes after Country X's plan has been implemented. The argument concludes that the incidence of smoking-related illnesses is therefore unlikely to be reduced. The option providing the strongest support for that conclusion is (E): the information that tar, not nicotine, is the main contributor to smoking-related illnesses.

A This information suggests that cigarette smoking is a well-established practice in Country X. But it does not address the question of whether the government's plan will succeed.

B This information indicates that cigarette smokers in Country X will have less choice regarding the average quantity of nicotine per cigarette smoked, but it does not suggest that addicted smokers will smoke less, on average, than they do now. Having greater uniformity in the average quantity of nicotine per cigarette, however, does not support the contention that the government's plan to reduce smoking-related illness will fail.

C This information suggests a way in which cigarette smoking rates could decline, though it does not indicate any likelihood that such a decline would occur.

D This information suggests how strong the incentive to smoke cigarettes is for many smokers in Country X. But it does not indicate that mandating lower nicotine levels will reduce smoking or smoking-related illnesses.

E **Correct.** This option adds important information to the argument regarding a key causal factor showing that smoking even nicotine-reduced cigarettes would likely not reduce the incidence of illnesses caused by cigarette smoking in Country X, unless the average rate of cigarette smoking were to decline significantly. A premise of the argument indicates that people addicted to nicotine would probably smoke more cigarettes, on average, to feed their addiction. If this occurred, more tar from cigarette smoking would enter the lungs, which suggests that a reduction in illnesses caused by smoking cigarettes would be unlikely to occur.

The correct answer is E.

223. In 1983, Argonia's currency, the argon, underwent a reduction in value relative to the world's strongest currencies. This reduction resulted in a significant increase in Argonia's exports over 1982 levels. In 1987, a similar reduction in the value of the argon led to another increase in Argonia's exports. Faced with the need to increase exports yet again, Argonia's finance minister has proposed another reduction in the value of the argon.

Which of the following, if true, most strongly supports the prediction that the finance minister's plan will NOT result in a significant increase in Argonia's exports next year?

(A) The value of the argon rose sharply last year against the world's strongest currencies.
(B) In 1988, the argon lost a small amount of its value, and Argonian exports rose slightly in 1989.
(C) The value of Argonia's exports was lower last year than it was the year before.
(D) All of Argonia's export products are made by factories that were operating at full capacity last year, and new factories would take years to build.
(E) Reductions in the value of the argon have almost always led to significant reductions in the amount of goods and services that Argonians purchase from abroad.

Argument Construction

Situation   Two drops in the value of Argonia's currency, the argon, during the 1980s both led to increased exports. To stimulate a new surge in exports, the finance minister suggests lowering the value of the argon again.

Reasoning   *What supports the prediction that a weak argon may not increase exports?* Drops in the value of the argon have led to increases in Argonian exports in the past, so the finance minister's plan to increase exports by weakening the currency is reasonable *unless* some additional factor undermines the plan's odds of success. Therefore, identifying such a factor would support the prediction that the finance minister's plan will not increase exports.

A   The fact that the argon's value rose last year does not in itself support the prediction that lowering the argon's value will not increase exports.

B   A small decline in the argon's value leading to a slight increase in Argonian exports would tend to support the idea that the minister's plan to increase exports by weakening the currency will succeed; it does not support the prediction that the plan will fail.

C   Recent decreases in the value of Argonia's exports have no bearing on whether the finance minister's plan to increase exports will succeed or fail.

D   **Correct.** The prediction that the finance minister's plan to increase exports will fail would be more likely to be correct *if* the factories which make exports are already working at full capacity, and therefore would be unable to make significantly more goods to meet the increased demand stimulated by a weaker currency. Exports could not increase without additional goods to export.

E   The fact that a weaker argon reduces Argonia's imports has no bearing on whether a weaker argon would successfully stimulate exports.

The correct answer is D.

224. Transnational cooperation among corporations is experiencing a modest resurgence among United States firms, even though projects undertaken by two or more corporations under a collaborative agreement are less profitable than projects undertaken by a single corporation. The advantage of transnational cooperation is that such joint international projects may allow United States firms to win foreign contracts that they would not otherwise be able to win.

Which of the following is information provided by the passage?

(A) Transnational cooperation involves projects too big for a single corporation to handle.
(B) Transnational cooperation results in a pooling of resources leading to high-quality performance.
(C) Transnational cooperation has in the past been both more common and less common than it is now among United States firms.
(D) Joint projects between United States and foreign corporations are not profitable enough to be worth undertaking.
(E) Joint projects between United States and foreign corporations benefit only those who commission the projects.

Argument Construction

Situation   The passage states that cooperative transnational projects have recently had a resurgence among US firms; the advantage of such cooperative projects is that companies working together may win international contracts they could not win separately, and the disadvantage is that profits for each firm are lower than profits derived from independent projects.

Reasoning   *Which fact is included in the passage?* The key phrase in the passage is *modest resurgence*. A resurgence, or rebirth, in any area can only occur if that area previously enjoyed more popularity, then fell out of favor. If it had never been popular in the past, its increase would be a novelty and not a resurgence. Moreover, if the current resurgence equaled or surpassed previous levels of transnational cooperation, that increase would be robust, not modest. Therefore, the passage includes the information that transnational cooperation was first more popular than currently, then less so, before making the modest resurgence discussed.

A   The passage states that corporations may be more likely to win contracts for cooperative projects, not that they could not handle those projects on their own.

B   The passage states that transnational cooperation helps firms secure contracts, not that it results in quality work.

C   **Correct**. If transnational cooperation among corporations is experiencing a *modest resurgence*, as stated in the passage, then, by definition, such cooperation must have once been more common, experienced a falling-off, and then increased again to a current level somewhere between the two previous levels. In other words, such cooperation was both more common and less common at different points in the past.

D   The passage states that joint projects are less profitable than individual projects, not that they are not profitable enough to be worthwhile.

E   The passage never states that joint projects benefit only those who commission them.

The correct answer is C.

225. In many corporations, employees are being replaced by automated equipment in order to save money. However, many workers who lose their jobs to automation will need government assistance to survive, and the same corporations that are laying people off will eventually pay for that assistance through increased taxes and unemployment insurance payments.

Which of the following, if true, most strengthens the author's argument?

(A) Many workers who have already lost their jobs to automation have been unable to find new jobs.
(B) Many corporations that have failed to automate have seen their profits decline.
(C) Taxes and unemployment insurance are also paid by corporations that are not automating.
(D) Most of the new jobs created by automation pay less than the jobs eliminated by automation did.
(E) The initial investment in machinery for automation is often greater than the short-term savings in labor costs.

Argument Construction

Situation   Companies are replacing workers with automation to cut costs. But the argument states that replaced workers will rely on government assistance after losing their jobs, and the companies will pay for that assistance through taxes and unemployment insurance.

Reasoning   *What would strengthen the argument that companies will ultimately pay to support their laid-off workers?* The author implies that replacing workers with machines is not necessarily cost effective, because companies will ultimately pay to support unemployed workers via increased government assistance. If such workers find new jobs, they would not require as much government assistance, and the argument would be weakened. On the other hand, if such workers cannot find new jobs, that would strengthen the author's argument that companies will pay indirectly for the support of workers they replace.

A   **Correct.** If many workers who lose their jobs to automation cannot find new jobs, that would strengthen the argument that such workers will be forced to rely on government assistance and therefore increase the tax burden on the companies which replaced their workers.

B   Declining profits among companies that do not automate does not affect the argument that there may be hidden costs associated with automation, namely increased taxes to support replaced workers.

C   The fact that taxes and unemployment insurance are also paid by companies that do *not* automate has no bearing on the argument that companies which *do* automate will pay for that decision via increased taxes.

D   While reduced labor costs associated with automation would be an additional factor affecting the companies, it does not counter the argument that their taxes will increase.

E   Short-term costs associated with automation have no relevance to the argument that automation will lead to increased taxes and unemployment insurance costs.

The correct answer is A.

226. Theatergoer: In January of last year, the Megaplex chain of movie theaters started popping its popcorn in canola oil instead of the less healthful coconut oil that it had been using until then. Now Megaplex is planning to switch back, saying that the change has hurt popcorn sales. That claim is false, however, since according to Megaplex's own sales figures, Megaplex sold 5 percent more popcorn last year than in the previous year.

Which of the following, if true, most seriously weakens the theatergoer's argument?

(A) When it switched from using coconut oil to using canola oil, Megaplex made sure that the chain received a great deal of publicity stressing the health benefits of the change.

(B) Megaplex makes more money on food and beverages sold at its theaters than it does on sales of movie tickets.

(C) In a survey to determine public response to the change to canola oil, very few of Megaplex's customers said that the change had affected their popcorn-buying habits.

(D) Total sales of all food and beverage items at Megaplex's movie theaters increased by less than 5 percent last year.

(E) Total attendance at Megaplex's movie theaters was more than 20 percent higher last year than the year before.

Argument Evaluation

Situation Megaplex movie theaters switched from coconut oil to canola oil for their popcorn at the beginning of the previous year. They intend to revert to using coconut oil, on the grounds that using canola oil hurts popcorn sales. The author claims these reduced sales did not occur, because the company's records show a 5 percent increase in popcorn sales last year over the year before.

Reasoning *What additional fact would demonstrate that popcorn sales were indeed hurt?* The argument states that a 5 percent increase in popcorn sales last year, relative to the year previous, proves that Megaplex's claim of hurt popcorn sales owing to the use of canola oil is false. But Megaplex claims that sales were *hurt*, not that sales were *lower*. If, therefore, some additional fact suggested that the rate of popcorn sales was in fact less than would be expected, then that fact would weaken the argument that Megaplex is making a false claim.

A Publicity regarding the switch to healthier canola oil has no bearing on the claim that canola oil did not hurt popcorn sales.

B The question of where Megaplex earns its money is not relevant to the argument that Megaplex's claim—that canola oil hurts popcorn sales—is necessarily false.

C This survey result would tend to support, not weaken, the argument that Megaplex is giving inaccurate information about hurt popcorn sales.

D The fact that overall food and beverage sales increased at a lower rate than did popcorn sales specifically has no impact on the argument that Megaplex is giving inaccurate information about canola oil hurting popcorn sales.

E **Correct.** If attendance at Megaplex was over 20 percent higher last year than the year previous, then that would be expected to produce a corresponding over 20 percent increase in popcorn sales. The fact that the actual increase in popcorn sales was much lower, just 5 percent, suggests that Megaplex may be correct in their claim that canola oil hurts popcorn sales. Therefore, this fact weakens the argument that Megaplex's claims regarding hurt sales are false.

The correct answer is E.

227. Temporary-services firms supply trained workers to other companies on a temporary basis. Temporary-services firms lose business when the economy shows signs of beginning to weaken. They gain business when the economy begins to recover but often lose business again when the economy stabilizes. These firms have begun to gain business in the present weak economy. The economy therefore must be beginning to recover.

Which of the following is an assumption on which the argument depends?

(A) Temporary-services firms are more likely to regain old clients than to acquire new ones when the economy begins to recover.
(B) Temporary-services firms do not gain business when an already weak economy worsens.
(C) New companies do not often hire temporary help until they have been in business for some time.
(D) Companies that use workers from temporary-services firms seldom hire those workers to fill permanent positions.
(E) Temporary-services firms can most easily find qualified new workers when the economy is at its weakest.

Argument Construction

Situation   Temporary-services firms lose business when the economy appears to be starting to weaken, but they gain business when the economy begins to recover (though as the economy stabilizes, in many instances the firms will lose business again). Because these firms have started gaining new business in the current weak economy, an economic recovery must have begun.

Reasoning   *On what assumption does the argument depend?* The argument states that temporary-services firms will *lose* business as the economy *begins* to weaken and *gain* business as the economy *begins* to recover. Nothing in the argument rules out the possibility that these firms may also gain business during a period of increased weakening. If these firms did gain business during times when a weak economy gets even worse, then the argument's conclusion—that the economy must be strengthening—would not follow. So, the argument must assume that these firms do *not* gain business during such times.

A   Whether the clients are old or new is not relevant to the argument that an overall increase in hiring temporary workers necessarily implies an improving economy.

B   **Correct.** If the argument did not assume this—that temporary-services firms do not at least sometimes gain business when an already weak economy worsens—then the mere fact that such firms *have* gained business recently would not be good reason to infer that the economy is recovering.

C   Even if new companies regularly hire temporary help before they have been in business for some time, it still could be the case that the gaining of business by temporary-services firms indicates economic recovery.

D   Nothing in the argument makes any assumptions about the frequency with which companies that use temporary-services workers hire those workers to fill permanent positions.

E   The *availability* of temporary workers has no bearing on whether or not *demand* for such workers necessarily implies that the weak economy is improving.

The correct answer is B.

228. Wolves generally avoid human settlements. For this reason, domestic sheep, though essentially easy prey for wolves, are not usually attacked by them. In Hylantia prior to 1910, farmers nevertheless lost considerable numbers of sheep to wolves each year. Attributing this to the large number of wolves, in 1910, the government began offering rewards to hunters for killing wolves. From 1910 to 1915, large numbers of wolves were killed. Yet wolf attacks on sheep increased significantly.

Which of the following, if true, most helps to explain the increase in wolf attacks on sheep?

(A) Populations of deer and other wild animals that wolves typically prey on increased significantly in numbers from 1910 to 1915.

(B) Prior to 1910, there were no legal restrictions in Hylantia on the hunting of wolves.

(C) After 1910, hunters shot and wounded a substantial number of wolves, thereby greatly diminishing these wolves' ability to prey on wild animals.

(D) Domestic sheep are significantly less able than most wild animals to defend themselves against wolf attacks.

(E) The systematic hunting of wolves encouraged by the program drove many wolves in Hylantia to migrate to remote mountain areas uninhabited by humans.

Argument Construction

Situation   Significant numbers of wolf attacks on sheep in Hylantia prior to 1910 led the Hylantia government to adopt a wolf-reduction program that year. Although large numbers of wolves were killed over the next five years, wolf attacks on sheep nonetheless increased.

Reasoning   *Since Hylantia's wolf population was presumably reduced by significant killing of wolves from 1910 to 1915, what other factor would help explain increasing wolf attacks on sheep during the same period?* Hylantia's reduction of its wolf population did not lead to the desired result of reducing wolf attacks on sheep, but on the contrary increased such attacks. Therefore, some additional factor should account for the unexpected increase.

A   Increasing availability of other prey animals would be likely to decrease wolf attacks on sheep, not increase such attacks.

B   A lack of hunting restrictions before 1910 would not help explain increasing attacks after 1910.

C   **Correct.** If the population of injured wolves with a limited ability to hunt wild prey greatly increased after 1910, that would help explain why wolves increased their attacks on easier prey such as sheep at that time.

D   The ability of sheep to defend themselves would not change in the period from 1910–1915 and so would not have any effect on the rate of wolf attacks during that time.

E   Driving wolves to remote regions far from human populations would probably decrease, not increase, attacks on domestic animals such as sheep.

The correct answer is C.

229. Paint on a new airliner is usually applied in two stages: first, a coat of primer, and then a top coat. A new process requires no primer, but instead uses two layers of the same newly developed coating, with each layer of the new coating having the same thickness and weight as a traditional top coat. Using the new process instead of the old process increases the price of a new aircraft considerably.

Which of the following, if true, most strongly indicates that it is in an airline's long-term economic interest to purchase new airliners painted using the new process rather than the old process?

(A) Although most new airliners are still painted using the old process, aircraft manufacturers now offer a purchaser of any new airliner the option of having it painted using the new process instead.

(B) A layer of primer on an airliner weighs more than a layer of the new coating would by an amount large enough to make a difference to that airliner's load-bearing capacity.

(C) A single layer of the new coating provides the aluminum skin of the airliner with less protection against corrosion than does a layer of primer of the usual thickness.

(D) Unlike the old process, the new process was originally invented for use on spacecraft, which are subject to extremes of temperature to which airliners are never exposed.

(E) Because the new coating has a viscosity similar to that of a traditional top coat, aircraft manufacturers can apply it using the same equipment as is used for a traditional top coat.

Evaluation of a Plan

Situation A new coating for airliners has been developed. Instead of a coat of primer followed by a top coat, the new coating is applied in two coats, each of which is equal in weight and thickness to an application of top coat. Coating the airliner in this way makes purchasing a new airliner more expensive.

Reasoning *Since the new painting process adds significant expense, what additional factors could make that expense economically beneficial in the long term?* The added expense of the new painting process would seem to make it a poor economic choice for airlines, unless some other factor would be likely to make using the new paint increase revenue over time, sufficiently to justify the added cost.

A The ready availability of the new process does not make that process economically beneficial to airlines.

B **Correct.** If the new process reduces an airliner's weight enough to increase its load-bearing capacity, the extra revenue generated by the greater loads might be enough to outweigh, over time, the additional upfront cost.

C If the new process provides inferior protection than does the old process, that would not help make the new process economically beneficial.

D The new process's utility in space has no bearing on its economic advantages for airlines.

E The ability of aircraft manufacturers to use their old equipment for the new process might help keep the cost of the new process from going even higher, but it does not provide airlines with an incentive to choose the more expensive paint.

The correct answer is B.

230. Unless tiger hunting decreases, tigers will soon be extinct in the wild. The countries in which the tigers' habitats are located are currently debating joint legislation that would ban tiger hunting. Thus, if these countries can successfully enforce this legislation, the survival of tigers in the wild will be ensured.

The reasoning in the argument is most vulnerable to criticism on the grounds that the argument

(A) assumes without sufficient warrant that a ban on tiger hunting could be successfully enforced
(B) considers the effects of hunting on tigers without also considering the effects of hunting on other endangered animal species
(C) fails to take into account how often tiger hunters are unsuccessful in their attempts to kill tigers
(D) neglects to consider the results of governmental attempts in the past to limit tiger hunting
(E) takes the removal of an impediment to the tigers' survival as a guarantee of their survival

Evaluation of a Plan

Situation   Tiger hunting threatens wild tigers with extinction. Accordingly, countries with native tiger populations are considering a collective ban on tiger hunting to ensure the survival of wild tigers.

Reasoning   *What weakness is present in the argument that successfully enforcing a ban on tiger hunting will guarantee the survival of wild tigers?* A ban on tiger hunting does not guarantee that no other causes could lead to the extinction of wild tigers, so the argument that effectively banning hunting will save wild tigers is vulnerable to criticism on the grounds that it assumes removal of one risk to tigers is sufficient to ensure their survival.

A   The argument posits that tigers will be saved if the ban is enforced effectively, but it does not assert that the ban could be enforced effectively.

B   The effects of hunting on other species are not relevant to the claim that enforcing a ban on tiger hunting will ensure wild tigers' survival.

C   If hunters often fail to kill tigers, that could conceivably weaken the claim that tiger hunting will lead to tiger extinction, but it does not weaken the claim that the ban on hunting will save tigers.

D   The results of previous bans on tiger hunting would not in themselves weaken the claim that enforcing this new ban will be sufficient to save wild tigers.

E   **Correct.** Removing one impediment to the tigers' survival would not remove all potential impediments to their survival, so the argument is vulnerable to criticism pointing out that oversight.

The correct answer is E.

231. Because of steep increases in the average price per box of cereal over the last 10 years, overall sales of cereal have recently begun to drop. In an attempt to improve sales, one major cereal manufacturer reduced the wholesale prices of its cereals by 20 percent. Since most other cereal manufacturers have announced that they will follow suit, it is likely that the level of overall sales of cereal will rise significantly.

Which of the following would it be most useful to establish in evaluating the argument?

(A) Whether the high marketing expenses of the highly competitive cereal market led to the increase in cereal prices
(B) Whether cereal manufacturers use marketing techniques that encourage brand loyalty among consumers
(C) Whether the variety of cereals available on the market has significantly increased over the last 10 years
(D) Whether the prices that supermarkets charge for these cereals will reflect the lower prices the supermarkets will be paying the manufacturers
(E) Whether the sales of certain types of cereal have declined disproportionately over the last 10 years

Evaluation of a Plan

Situation Increasing cereal prices over the past decade have led to decreasing sales. In an effort to reverse this trend, one cereal manufacturer is significantly lowering wholesale prices. Because other manufacturers have said they will do the same, lower wholesale prices will lead to higher cereal sales.

Reasoning *What additional factor would be likely to affect the argument that lower wholesale cereal prices will lead to higher cereal sales?* To determine whether the lower wholesale cereal prices set by manufacturers will indeed lead to higher retail sales of cereal, it would be useful to determine if any other factors would be likely to interfere in the expected causative relation between lower wholesale prices and higher demand. Since the information specifies that the lower prices are wholesale, one variable that could affect the argument is retail pricing.

A Even if increased marketing expenses was one factor that contributed to higher cereal prices, this would not affect the argument that lowering wholesale prices will lead to higher sales.

B Brand loyalty might affect the market share of various cereal brands, but it would not be likely to lead to decreases or increases in cereal sales overall.

C The variety of available cereals is not relevant to the question of whether decreasing wholesale prices will promote cereal sales.

D Correct. If supermarkets failed to lower their retail prices to reflect the decrease in wholesale prices, retail sales and ultimately wholesale sales would probably not increase. On the other hand, a lowering of retail cereal prices would likely boost retail and wholesale sales volume.

E The greater sales decreases of specific cereals would not affect the argument that lower wholesale prices will lead to higher total sales of cereals.

The correct answer is D.

232. Crowding on Mooreville's subway frequently leads to delays, because it is difficult for passengers to exit from the trains. Over the next ten years, the Mooreville Transit Authority projects that subway ridership will increase by 20 percent. The authority plans to increase the number of daily train trips by only 5 percent over the same period. Officials predict that this increase is sufficient to ensure that the incidence of delays due to crowding does not increase.

Which of the following, if true, provides the strongest grounds for the officials' prediction?

(A) The population of Mooreville is not expected to increase significantly in the next ten years.

(B) The Transit Authority also plans a 5 percent increase in the number of bus trips on routes that connect to subways.

(C) The Transit Authority projects that the number of Mooreville residents who commute to work by automobile will increase in the next ten years.

(D) Most of the projected increase in ridership is expected to occur in off-peak hours when trains now are sparsely used.

(E) The 5 percent increase in the number of train trips can be achieved without an equal increase in Transit Authority operational costs.

Evaluation of a Plan

Situation Crowding on Mooreville's subway makes it difficult for passengers to exit the trains, which in turn leads to delays. Officials plan to address an anticipated 20 percent increase in ridership over the coming decade with a 5 percent increase in trains, and these officials predict that this increase in trains will be sufficient to prevent more crowding-related delays.

Reasoning *What factor could support the prediction that a greater increase in ridership than in the number of trains over the next ten years will not lead to increased crowding over the same period?* A 20 percent increase in ridership, with only a 5 percent increase in train trips to accommodate the additional passengers, would be expected to significantly increase crowding, unless an additional reason justified the prediction that it would not increase, and might even reduce, crowding and the resulting delays.

A Constant population does not support the prediction that a larger percentage increase in ridership than in available trains will not lead to increased crowding.

B An increase in bus trips that connect to subways would not necessarily affect crowding caused by a 20 percent increase in ridership on those subways.

C An increase in commuting by car, without a corresponding decrease in subway ridership, would not support the prediction that subway crowding won't increase.

D Correct. If the projected increase in ridership mainly affects trains that have space available to accommodate the added passengers, then that would provide support for the prediction that a greater percentage increase in riders than in train trips will not lead to greater crowding and delays.

E Constant operational costs would not support the prediction that crowding will not increase.

The correct answer is D.

233. Though sucking zinc lozenges has been promoted as a treatment for the common cold, research has revealed no consistent effect. Recently, however, a zinc gel applied nasally has been shown to greatly reduce the duration of colds. Since the gel contains zinc in the same form and concentration as the lozenges, the greater effectiveness of the gel must be due to the fact that cold viruses tend to concentrate in the nose, not in the mouth.

Which of the following, if true, most seriously weakens the argument?

(A) Experimental subjects who used the zinc gel not only had colds of shorter duration but also had less severe symptoms than did those who used a gel that did not contain zinc.
(B) The mechanism by which zinc affects the viruses that cause the common cold has not been conclusively established.
(C) To make them palatable, zinc lozenges generally contain other ingredients, such as citric acid, that can interfere with the chemical activity of zinc.
(D) No zinc-based cold remedy can have any effect unless it is taken or applied within 48 hours of the initial onset of cold symptoms.
(E) Drug-company researchers experimenting with a nasal spray based on zinc have found that it has much the same effect on colds as the gel does.

Argument Evaluation

Situation   Sucking zinc lozenges has not been shown to fight colds effectively, but application of a nasal zinc gel is demonstrably effective. Both the gel and the lozenges contain the same type and concentration of zinc, so the greater efficacy of the nasal gel must be because cold viruses are present in higher levels in the nose than in the mouth.

Reasoning   *What additional factor could weaken the argument that, since zinc-based remedies fight colds, but nasal-gel zinc fights colds more effectively than does oral-lozenge zinc, that difference must be explained by higher concentrations of cold virus in the nose than in the mouth?* The argument that the virus's high concentrations in the nose must account for the greater effectiveness of nasal zinc gel over oral zinc lozenges only holds if no other factor could explain that difference in effectiveness; therefore, identifying another explanation for that difference weakens the argument.

A   The greater effectiveness of zinc gel versus a control would not explain the greater effectiveness of zinc gel versus zinc lozenges.

B   Uncertainty regarding the mechanism by which zinc fights colds is not relevant to the question of why zinc lozenges are less effective than zinc gel.

C   **Correct.** The presence of other ingredients in zinc lozenges that can interfere with zinc's activity could help explain why zinc lozenges are less effective than zinc gel and thereby weaken the argument that the virus's distribution must be the reason for differences in effectiveness.

D   The importance of early treatment with zinc has no bearing on the question of why nasal zinc gel works better than oral zinc lozenges.

E   The equal effectiveness of nasal spray and nasal gel does not provide any explanation for why nasal gel is more effective than oral lozenges.

The correct answer is C.

234. In each of the past five years, Barraland's prison population has increased. Yet, according to official government statistics, for none of those years has there been either an increase in the number of criminal cases brought to trial or an increase in the rate at which convictions have been obtained. Clearly, therefore, the percentage of people convicted of crimes who are being given prison sentences is on the increase.

Which of the following, if true, most seriously weakens the argument?

(A) In Barraland, the range of punishments that can be imposed instead of a prison sentence is wide.
(B) Over the last ten years, overcrowding in the prisons of Barraland has essentially been eliminated as a result of an ambitious program of prison construction.
(C) Ten years ago, Barraland reformed its criminal justice system, imposing longer minimum sentences for those crimes for which a prison sentence had long been mandatory.
(D) Barraland has been supervising convicts on parole more closely in recent years, with the result that parole violations have become significantly less frequent.
(E) The number of people in Barraland who feel that crime is on the increase is significantly greater now than it was five years ago.

Argument Evaluation

Situation: Barraland has seen annual increases in its prison population over a five-year period. However, over the same period, there has not been a corresponding increase in the number of people convicted of crimes, which indicates that a larger percentage of prison sentences handed down to convicted people must account for the increase.

Reasoning: *What additional factor could weaken the argument that, since the annual number of convicted people in Barraland has not increased over the last five years, a greater percentage of such convicts receiving prison sentences must be responsible for the increasing prison population during the same period?* The argument that a higher rate of prison sentences must be responsible for a higher prison population only holds if there are no other factors contributing to that increase in population, so identifying such an additional factor weakens the argument.

A Sentencing options other than prison would not account for an increasing prison population over the last five years.

B The lack of overcrowding in Barraland's prisons is not relevant to the question of why its prison population has increased.

C **Correct.** Longer prison sentences would provide an alternative explanation for increasing prison population and thereby weaken the argument that an increasing percentage of the people sentenced to prison must be responsible.

D Lower rates of parole violations would not account for the increasing prison population.

E A general sense that crime is increasing, absent a corresponding increase in criminal convictions, would not explain an increasing prison population.

The correct answer is C.

235. TruSave is a mail-order company that ships electronic products from its warehouses to customers worldwide. The company's shipping manager is proposing that customer orders be packed with newer, more expensive packing materials that virtually eliminate damage during shipping. The manager argues that overall costs would essentially remain unaffected, since the extra cost of the new packing materials roughly equals the current cost of replacing products returned by customers because they arrived in damaged condition.

Which of the following would it be most important to ascertain in determining whether implementing the shipping manager's proposal would have the argued-for effect on costs?

(A) Whether the products shipped by TrueSave are more vulnerable to incurring damage during shipping than are typical electronic products

(B) Whether electronic products are damaged more frequently in transit than are most other products shipped by mail-order companies

(C) Whether a sizable proportion of returned items are returned because of damage already present when those items were packed for shipping

(D) Whether there are cases in which customers blame themselves for product damage that, though present on arrival of the product, is not discovered until later

(E) Whether TrueSave continually monitors the performance of the shipping companies it uses to ship products to its customers

Evaluation of a Plan

Situation   TruSave's shipping manager wants to switch to new, more costly packing materials that will prevent their products from being damaged during shipping. The manager argues that the additional cost will be offset by a reduction in returns of broken items.

Reasoning   *If the increased cost of switching to better packing materials is roughly equal to the cost of items returned due to damage, what additional factors might affect the cost-effectiveness of the proposed switch?* Returns due to damage cost TrueSave roughly the same amount as would better packaging. Since the better packaging only protects against damage during shipping, returns due to damage prior to shipping would add support to the manager's argument that switching to better packaging would not affect overall costs.

A   Higher rates of damage to TrueSave's shipments would not affect the overall cost of switching to better packaging.

B   The comparative rates of damage to electronics versus other products would not affect the overall cost of switching to better packaging.

C   **Correct.** If a significant proportion of total damage is found to occur before shipping, and therefore would not be prevented by better packaging during shipping, that finding would support the manager's argument that the switch to better packaging would not affect total costs.

D   Cases of consumers wrongly blaming themselves for damage would not affect the question of whether or not switching to better packaging would affect total costs, since those consumers presumably do not return their items.

E   TrueSave's attentiveness to the performance of its shipping companies would not affect the overall cost of switching to better packaging.

The correct answer is C.

Questions 236 to 290 — Difficulty: Hard

236. Twenty-five years ago, 2,000 married people were asked to rank four categories—spouses, friends, jobs, and housework—according to the amount of time each category demanded. A recent follow-up survey indicates that a majority of those same people rank housework higher on the list now than they did twenty-five years ago. Yet most of the respondents also claim that housework has become less demanding of their time over the last twenty-five years.

Which of the following, if true, helps to explain the apparent discrepancy?

(A) Some of the people surveyed were married to other people in the survey.
(B) Many of the most time-consuming aspects of people's lives do not appear as categories on either survey.
(C) Most of those who responded to the follow-up survey have retired in the last twenty-five years.
(D) At the time of the follow-up survey, some of the people surveyed did no housework.
(E) Many of the respondents to the follow-up survey claim that they now spend much more time with their friends than they did twenty-five years ago.

Argument Construction

Situation Twenty-five years ago, 2,000 married people were asked in a survey to rank four categories—spouse, friends, jobs, and housework—with respect to the average amount of time demanded by activities in each category. In a recent survey, most of the same people were asked to rank those activities again. Many ranked housework higher than they had ranked it in the first survey. Yet most claimed that housework had become less demanding of their time over the past twenty-five years. In light of the higher ranking of housework, this claim is initially puzzling.

Reasoning *Which answer choice provides the best explanation for the apparent inconsistency between the two findings cited from the recent survey?* A rise in the ranking of housework could occur either because the amount of time taken by housework increased or because the amount of time taken by one or more of the other categories declined over the twenty-five years. For example, suppose housework ranked fourth, i.e., lowest, in the first survey. If most of those surveyed had been fulltime employees twenty-five years ago, the category *jobs* would probably have ranked much higher than the category *housework*. But if those people were retired twenty-five years later, then the time demanded by jobs would be much less or even zero. Housework might then rank higher than jobs in the second survey even if it did not demand as many hours as it did previously.

A The information that some people surveyed were spouses of others surveyed would not, by itself, indicate statistical error in the survey. Single people in the surveys would obviously have ranked the category *spouse* lower than did married people. We are given no information as to how many of those people who were single when first surveyed had since married. But even if we had such information, a rise in the ranking for the category *spouse* would not, without further information, explain the rise in the ranking for *housework*.

B The surveys asked only for a ranking of activities in the four categories. Each ranking reflects the proportion of total time spent on those four categories, not including other kinds of activity.

C **Correct.** Housework could move up in the ranking if the category *jobs*, for example, had drastically declined in the ranking below even housework. As explained above, this could occur if many or most of those surveyed had been employed fulltime twenty-five years ago but had retired in the meantime; this would be consistent with a rise in the ranking of housework as well as a reduction in the proportion of total time spent on housework.

D This information is nonspecific about how many people did no housework. It is also nonspecific about how many of those who were surveyed ranked housework lowest or reported doing no housework. It does not help explain the apparent inconsistency in the overall survey results.

E In the absence of further information about the ranking of the categories *housework* and *friends* in the two surveys, this new information does little to explain the apparent inconsistency. In fact, without some indication that many respondents do housework with their friends, this suggests that the ranking for the category *housework* should have declined if it changed at all.

The correct answer is C.

237. In order to achieve self-sufficiency in electricity production, **the Hasarian government proposes to construct eleven huge hydroelectric power plants.** Although this is a massive project, it is probably not massive enough to achieve the goal. It is true that **adding the projected output of the new hydroelectric plants to the output that Hasaria can achieve now would be enough to meet the forecast demand for electricity.** It will, however, take at least fifteen years to complete the project and by then the majority of Hasaria's current power plants will be too old to function at full capacity.

In the argument given, the two portions in **boldface** play which of the following roles?

(A) The first introduces a proposed course of action for which the argument provides support; the second gives evidence in support of that course of action.

(B) The first introduces a proposed course of action for which the argument provides support; the second gives a reason for not adopting a possible alternative course of action.

(C) The first introduces a plan that the argument evaluates; the second provides evidence that is used to support that plan against possible alternatives.

(D) The first introduces a proposed plan for achieving a certain goal; the second is a claim that has been used in support of the plan but that the argument maintains is inaccurate.

(E) The first introduces a proposed plan for achieving a certain goal; the second provides evidence that is used to support the argument's evaluation of that plan.

Argument Construction

Situation   To achieve self-sufficiency in electricity production, the Hasarian government proposes to construct eleven large hydroelectric power plants. But the project might not be large enough to achieve its goal. It will take fifteen years to complete, but by then many of the existing power plants will not be able to function at full capacity.

Reasoning   *What logical roles in the argument do the **boldfaced** portions play?* The first reports the proposed plan. But it is argued that the plan might not achieve its goal. It is conceded that the amount of power projected to be generated by the new plants might be sufficient if added to the existing power generation capacity. But since it will take fifteen years to complete the project, some of the existing power generation capacity will no longer be fully available.

A   The first introduces a proposed plan. But the argument is critical of that proposal and indicates that the plan, if adopted, might ultimately NOT achieve its goal. The second does not give evidence in support of the plan.

B   The first introduces a proposed plan. The second does not give evidence against adopting an alternative course of action. No alternative plan is considered.

C   The first does introduce a plan that the argument evaluates, but the second does not provide evidence to support that plan against possible alternatives. No possible alternative plan is considered.

D   The first introduces a proposed plan for achieving a goal of energy self-sufficiency. The second gives a claim that the argument treats as accurate.

E   **Correct.** The first introduces a proposed plan for achieving a goal of energy self-sufficiency. The second provides support for the argument's evaluation of the plan. It provides information to indicate that the planned new energy generation capacity would provide energy self-sufficiency if existing generation capacity were added. However, the argument indicates a flaw in the plan: Hasaria's existing power plants will have significantly reduced generation capacity in fifteen years, the time it will take for the new plants to become operational.

The correct answer is E.

238. In Cecropia, inspections of fishing boats that estimate the number of fish they are carrying are typically conducted upon their return to port. The high numbers so obtained have led the government to conclude that the coastal waters are being overfished. To allow commercial fishing stocks to recover, the government is considering introducing annual quotas on the number of fish that each fishing boat can catch. Compliance with the quotas would be determined by the established system of inspections.

Which of the following, if true, raises the most serious doubts about whether the government's proposed plan would succeed?

(A) Some commercial fishing boats in Cecropia are large enough to catch their entire annual quota in only a few months of fishing.

(B) The quotas would have to be reduced if more boats began fishing in Cecropia's coastal waters.

(C) Because fish prices will rise if the quotas go into effect, it is unlikely that the quotas will significantly change the number of boats fishing Cecropia's coastal waters.

(D) The procedure that inspectors use to estimate the number of fish a boat is carrying often results in a slight overcount.

(E) Quotas encourage fishers to bring only the most commercially valuable fish into port and to discard less valuable fish, most of them dead or dying.

Evaluation of a Plan

Situation The government of Cecropia is considering introducing annual catch quotas for fishing boats in order to allow commercial fishing stocks in coastal waters to recover. The quotas would be enforced by inspectors who will estimate the number of fish brought into port by each boat.

Reasoning *What new information raises the most serious doubts about whether the plan would succeed if it is implemented?* The quota restrictions could raise problems associated with enforcement, economic viability, and acceptance by those whose livelihood depends, directly or indirectly, on the fishing industry. The restrictions would be pointless and would not attain the goal of protecting fishing stocks unless they could be effectively enforced. Other issues would have to be resolved for the proposed quotas to pass into law.

A For large commercial fishing boats, the quota system could pose difficulties. Large capital investment would likely be tied up in such boats, and such boats might have to supplement their catches by fishing in waters not controlled by any nation. But large boats could presumably do so.

B We are given no information as to whether possible reduction of fishing quotas is envisaged in the government's proposed plan—or whether quota reduction would count as a different proposal superseding the one under discussion.

C This is a consideration in favor of the proposal. It suggests that the proposed quota system would succeed and that the viability of commercial fishing boats and the livelihoods of fishers would not be negatively affected.

D This information does not suggest that the quota system is likely to fail. If fish counts are adjusted using a reasonable margin of error and there are appeal procedures to resolve disputes about fish counts, such disputes, by themselves, would then be unlikely to cause the quota system to fail.

E **Correct.** The information about the proposed quota system indicates that the fish catch of each boat is monitored only in port. Boats could circumvent the quota system by indiscriminately catching and letting die all available fish but discarding the least valuable fish out at sea before submitting to the inspections in port. The non-survival of this part of the catch could, over time, impair the recovery of the coastal fish populations.

The correct answer is E.

239. Consultant: **A significant number of complex repair jobs carried out by Ace Repairs have to be redone under the company's warranty, but when those repairs are redone they are invariably successful.** Since we have definitely established that **there is no systematic difference between the mechanics who are assigned to do the initial repairs and those who are assigned to redo unsatisfactory jobs**, it is clear that inadequacies in the initial repairs cannot be attributed to the mechanics' lack of competence. Rather, it is likely that complex repairs require a level of focused attention that the company's mechanics apply consistently only to repair jobs that have been inadequately done on the first try.

In the consultant's reasoning, the two portions in **boldface** play which of the following roles?

(A) The first is a claim that the consultant rejects as false; the second is evidence that forms the basis for that rejection.
(B) The first is part of an explanation that the consultant offers for a certain finding; the second is that finding.
(C) The first presents a pattern whose explanation is at issue in the reasoning; the second provides evidence to rule out one possible explanation of that pattern.
(D) The first presents a pattern whose explanation is at issue in the reasoning; the second is evidence that has been used to challenge the explanation presented by the consultant.
(E) The first is the position the consultant seeks to establish; the second is offered as evidence for that position.

Argument Evaluation

Situation   The following information is attributed to a consultant. Some complex repair jobs done by Ace Repairs have to be redone under warranty and the repairs, when redone, are usually successful. But the mechanics who do the initial repairs and those who redo them are, overall, equally competent to do the repairs successfully.

Reasoning   *What role in the consultant's reasoning do the **boldfaced** statements play?* The first sentence describes a situation that is puzzling and needs explanation. One might be inclined to argue that the mechanics who redo the repairs are more competent that those who did the initial repairs. But the second **boldfaced** statement rebuts this explanation by telling us that it has been *definitely established* that there are no systematic differences in competence. The final sentence of the consultant's reasoning offers another explanation: that the redoing of a repair elicits from mechanics a higher level of focused attention than did the performance of the initial repair.

A   The first is an assertion made by the consultant concerning a puzzling phenomenon. It does not attribute a denial of any claim to the consultant; so the second does not provide a reason for a denial made by the consultant in the first **boldfaced** portion.

B   The first is not an explanation, or even part of one, for a finding, but rather, a description of a puzzling finding concerning a difference between success rates of initial repairs and those of repairs that are redone. The first, not the second, describes the finding itself.

C   **Correct.** The first is a statement of a puzzling fact that the consultant seems to have found and that needs explanation. The second provides evidence to exclude the hypothesis that the higher success rates in redoing repairs than in the initial doing of the repairs is explainable by reference to different levels of competence in the mechanics in each case.

D   The first is a statement of a puzzling fact that the consultant seems to believe needs explanation. Regarding the second, first note that the explanation that the consultant offers is to be found in the final sentence of the passage. The second **boldfaced** portion is part of the reasoning on which the consultant bases the explanation, not a claim that someone else has made in opposition to the consultant's explanation.

E   The first is an assertion by the consultant; the consultant presents it as established fact, not as a position that the consultant seeks to establish (i.e., provide evidence for). The second does not give evidence that helps establish the consultant's initial assertion.

The correct answer is C.

240. Half of Metroburg's operating budget comes from a payroll tax of 2 percent on salaries paid to people who work in the city. Recently, a financial services company, one of Metroburg's largest private-sector employers, announced that it will be relocating just outside the city. All the company's employees, amounting to 1 percent of all people now employed in Metroburg, will be employed at the new location.

From the information given, which of the following can most properly be concluded?

(A) Unless other employers add a substantial number of jobs in Metroburg, the company's relocation is likely to result in a 1 percent reduction in the revenue for the city's operating budget.

(B) Although the company's relocation will have a negative effect on the city's tax revenue, the company's departure will not lead to any increase in the unemployment rate among city residents.

(C) One of the benefits that the company will realize from its relocation is a reduction in the taxes paid by itself and its employees.

(D) Revenue from the payroll tax will decline by 1 percent if there is no increase in jobs within the city to compensate, fully or partially, for the company's departure.

(E) The company's relocation will tend to increase the proportion of jobs in Metroburg that are in the public sector, unless it results in a contraction of the public-sector payroll.

Argument Construction

Situation Metroburg funds half of its operating budget with a 2 percent payroll tax for each person who works in the city. A large private-sector firm will soon relocate outside the city; all its current employees will be employed at the new location.

Reasoning *Which answer choice is most strongly supported by the information provided?* The firm's employees comprise 1 percent of all employees working in Metroburg. But we have no information about the company's salaries; for all we can tell, they might be far higher or far lower than the Metroburg average. So we do not know what proportion of the city's total operating budget is funded by the taxes paid by the firm's employees.

A As explained above, we do not know how much of the revenue for Metroburg's operating budget comes from the payroll taxes paid by the firm's employees.

B We lack the information needed to predict what the downstream economic effects of the firm's departure will be. These effects could include an increase in the unemployment rate among city residents. We do not know whether all the firm's employees are city residents; perhaps none are. But it is conceivable that some of the spending now occurring in the city would migrate to the firm's new location; this loss of commercial business could presumably result in job losses and increased unemployment in the city, but there is little reason to suppose that it would do so.

C We have no information to support this. The given information does not imply that the firm is relocating in order to avoid city taxes.

D As explained, we do not know how much of the revenue for Metroburg's operating budget is currently funded by taxes on the firm's payroll.

E **Correct.** The firm that will relocate is a private-sector employer, and its employees currently comprise 1 percent of the total workforce employed in Metroburg. As a city that collects taxes, Metroburg presumably has public-sector employees. The migration of jobs to a location outside the city will entail that the proportion of all those working in the city who are private-sector employees will decrease, and—all things being equal—this, in turn, will cause an increase in the proportion of all employees in the city that are public-sector employees. However, this consequence would not necessarily occur if the firm's relocation indirectly resulted in a sufficiently large reduction in the city's public-sector workforce.

The correct answer is E.

241. A library currently has only coin-operated photocopy machines, which cost 10 cents per copy. Library administrators are planning to refit most of those machines with card readers. The library will sell prepaid copy cards that allow users to make 50 copies at 9 cents per copy. Administrators believe that, despite the convenience of copy cards and their lower per-copy cost, the number of copies made in the library will be essentially unchanged after the refit.

On the assumption that administrators' assessment is correct, which of the following predictions about the effect of the refit is most strongly supported by the information given?

(A) Library patrons will only purchase a copy card on days when they need to make 50 or more copies.
(B) No library patrons will increase their usage of the library's photocopy machines once the refit has been made.
(C) If most of the copy cards sold in the library are used to their full capacity, the number of people using the library's photocopy machines over a given period will fall.
(D) Revenues from photocopying will decrease unless most library patrons choose to use the remaining coin-operated machines in preference to the card-reader equipped ones.
(E) Revenues from photocopying will increase if copy cards that are purchased are, on average, used to significantly less than 90 percent of their capacity.

Evaluation of a Plan

Situation   A library's photocopiers are coin-operated; a copy costs 10 cents. The library's management plans to refit most of the photocopiers to accept copy cards that allow 50 copies to be made at 9 cents each. The administrators believe that the refit will not result in fewer copies being made.

Reasoning   *Assuming that the administrators are right, which of the five predictions about the effect of the refit is most strongly supported by the information provided?* Suppose that only one card were sold and only 45 copies were made with that card. Then the amount that the user paid per copy would be 10 cents. Whatever the number of cards sold, provided the number of copies made per card averages less than 45, then the average revenue per copy would be more than 10 cents. This would produce an increase in total revenue if the total number of photocopy uses were no less than in previous years. The greater the number of cards sold, the greater the increase in total revenues, provided that the usage per card averages less than 45 copies. The lower the average usage per card, the greater the increase in photocopy revenue. The information provided suggests that the number of cards sold will be considerable, given that *most of the machines* are being refitted with card readers (and may be usable only with card readers).

A   The information provides no reason to suppose that library patrons would buy cards only for use on the same day they buy them. Furthermore, the claim that the number of copies made will not change suggests that this might be false; if, after the refit, patrons almost never make small numbers of copies and almost never make copies on impulse, one might expect a decrease in the number of copies made.

B   This is not supported by the information provided. For example, some library patrons could increase their usage while others make a compensating reduction in their usage.

C   If 51 percent of the cards sold *are used to their full capacity*, it could still be the case that average utilization per card would be substantially less than 50 copies. So it is possible that the total number of photocopy users would increase or remain constant over a given period even if there is no change in the number of copies made and most cards are used to their full capacity.

D   The given information suggests otherwise. If some but not most library patrons choose to use the card-operated machines, revenues will increase if utilization per card averages less than 45 copies.

E   **Correct.** Each card has a capacity of 50 copies, so 90 percent of that is 45 copies. If the total number of copies made in the library remains at least as great as before and utilization of each card averages less than 45, revenues will increase; the lower the average utilization, the greater the increase in revenue.

The correct answer is E.

242. Harvester-ant colonies live for fifteen to twenty years, though individual worker ants live only a year. The way a colony behaves changes steadily in a predictable pattern as the colony grows older and larger. For the first few years, the foragers behave quite aggressively, searching out and vigorously defending new food sources, but once a colony has reached a certain size, its foragers become considerably less aggressive.

If the statements above are true, which of the following can most properly be concluded on the basis of them?

(A) As a result of pressure from neighbors, some colonies do not grow larger as they become older.
(B) Unpredictable changes in a colony's environment can cause changes in the tasks that the colony must perform if it is to continue to survive.
(C) The reason a mature colony goes out of existence is that younger, more aggressive colonies successfully outcompete it for food.
(D) The pattern of changing behavior that a colony displays does not arise from a change in the behavior of any individual worker ant or group of worker ants.
(E) A new colony comes into existence when a group of young, aggressive workers leaves a mature colony and sets up on its own.

Argument Construction

Situation   The given information contrasts the lifespan of harvester-ant colonies (twenty years) with that of individual foragers in the colonies (one year). When the colony is young and relatively small, its foragers aggressively seek and defend food resources. But when the colony grows older and reaches a certain size, its foragers become less aggressive.

Reasoning   *Which answer choice is most strongly supported by the given information?* Obviously, the survival of a colony can be jeopardized by encountering unusual environmental challenges. But the given information suggests that, provided no unusual threats to the colony's survival are encountered, a colony's life cycle is biologically determined by constraints of colony size and age. The behavior of the individual foragers is correlated with the age and size of the colony; how a forager behaves in a colony near its maximum limits of size and age is quite different from an individual forager's behavior in the colony's early years. The behaviors of individual foragers are highly coordinated; the patterns of behavior of the colony are not caused by individual behaviors of the worker ants.

A   Although this might be true, the given information suggests that the limits on colony size do not depend on competition from neighbors but are, rather, general constraints that are based in harvester-ant biology.

B   Although this is likely true, the given information does not address the issue of how colony dynamics might be affected by drastic and unusual environmental changes.

C   Obviously, the survival of a colony that fails over a period to secure the food resources it needs would be threatened. But the given information does not state or imply that such failures are generally due to more aggressive competition by ants in another colony. It suggests that, in general, a colony's demise is primarily dictated by the biological constraints on colony size and age.

D   Correct. As explained, the given information suggests that, provided no unusual threats to a colony's survival are encountered, its life cycle is biologically determined by constraints of colony size and age, not by the behavior of individual forager ants or groups of such ants. The given information suggests that the biological constraints on a colony's size and longevity also determine behaviors of individual worker ants, who live about one year.

E   Nothing in the given information suggests that worker ants are the founders of a harvester-ant colony.

The correct answer is D.

243. Trucking company owner: Theft of trucks containing valuable cargo is a serious problem. A new device produces radio signals that allow police to track stolen vehicles, and the recovery rate for stolen cargo in trucks equipped with the device is impressive. The device is too expensive to install in every truck, so we plan to install it in half of our trucks. Using those trucks for the most valuable cargo should largely eliminate losses from theft.

Which of the following, if true, most strongly supports the trucking company owner's expectation about the results of implementing the plan?

(A) For thieves, a cargo is valuable only if it is easy for them to dispose of profitably.

(B) Some insurance companies charge less to insure cargoes transported in trucks protected by the device.

(C) Most stolen trucks are eventually found, but unless a stolen truck is found very soon after it is taken, the likelihood that the trucking company will recover any of its cargo is very low.

(D) Thieves generally avoid trucks belonging to trucking companies that are known to have installed the device in a large proportion of their trucks.

(E) The manufacturer of the device offers a five-year warranty on each unit sold, a longer warranty than any that is offered on any competing antitheft device.

Evaluation of a Plan

Situation A new device that can be placed in trucks allows police to track stolen vehicles and quickly recover stolen cargo. A trucking company owner proposes to install the device in half of the company's trucks and use those trucks to haul the most valuable cargo. The owner suggests that doing this will largely eliminate losses from theft.

Reasoning *What claim would most strongly suggest that trucking company owner's plan will meet the owner's expectations?* If thieves avoid stealing any trucks belonging to companies known to have installed the device in a large proportion of its vehicles, the company owner's expectations are likely to be met.

A If thieves believe they can dispose of some of the company's cargo very quickly, before police can recover the cargo, thieves may find the cargo to be valuable enough for them to risk stealing from the company. Therefore, this does not strongly suggest that the owner's plan will meet expectations.

B This suggests that insurance for the company will be less costly if the owner's plan is carried out. Most likely this is because insurance companies have found that thefts decline for trucks that have the device installed. It is nonetheless possible that even for trucks that have the device installed, there are still thefts, even if there are fewer of them. It is also possible that there will be no reduction in losses from thefts of cargo from the trucks that do not have the device installed.

C This answer choice actually gives us some reason to think the truck owner's expectations about the results of the plan will not be met. Half of the trucks will not have the device installed. If the trucks are not found quickly after they are stolen, the likelihood that these trucks' cargo will be recovered is low, and there may be significant losses from theft.

D **Correct.** If thieves find out that half of the company's trucks have the device installed, this answer choice suggests that the thieves may well avoid stealing any of the company's trucks.

E This answer choice suggests that for five years the company will not have to pay to replace any of the devices installed in its trucks. But that tells us nothing about the likelihood that the owner's expectations will be met.

The correct answer is D.

244. To improve customer relations, several big retailers have recently launched "smile initiatives," requiring their employees to smile whenever they have contact with customers. These retailers generally have low employee morale, which is why they have to enforce smiling. However, studies show that customers can tell fake smiles from genuine smiles and that fake smiles prompt negative feelings in customers. So the smile initiatives are unlikely to achieve their goal.

The argument relies on which of the following as an assumption?

(A) The smile initiatives have achieved nearly complete success in getting employees to smile while they are around customers.

(B) Customers' feelings about fake smiles are no better than their feelings about the other facial expressions employees with low morale are likely to have.

(C) The feelings that employees generate in retail customers are a principal determinant of the amount of money customers will spend at a retailer.

(D) At the retailers who have launched the smile initiatives, none of the employees gave genuine smiles to customers before the initiatives were launched.

(E) Customers rarely, if ever, have a negative reaction to a genuine smile from a retail employee.

Argument Construction

Situation Several large retailers where employee morale is low are requiring their employees to smile when they interact with customers; these requirements are known as "smile initiatives." The author of the argument concludes that because fake smiles create negative feelings in customers, these initiatives are unlikely to achieve their goal of improving customer relations.

Reasoning *What assumption is required by the argument?* Even if customers can tell fake smiles from real ones and have negative feelings about them, the fake smiles could nonetheless improve customer relations. How? Suppose customers' attitudes are less negative about the fake smiles than about other facial expressions that result from low morale. Therefore, the argument requires the assumption that customer feelings about fake smiles are no better than their feelings about other facial expressions resulting from low morale.

A The argument does not require this assumption. The initiative could fail to achieve its goal simply by failing to get employees to smile.

B **Correct.** As explained above, if customers' feelings about fake smiles are not as negative as their feelings about other facial expressions that result from low morale, the smile initiative might nonetheless help improve customer relations. As a result, the argument needs to assume that customers' feelings about fake smiles are no better than their feelings about these other facial expressions.

C The argument does not need to assume that the feelings employees generate in customers are a principal determinant of the amount customers will spend. Such feelings merely must have some effect on customer relations.

D The argument needs to assume that not all employees at these retailers will give customers genuine smiles as a result of the smile initiatives. The argument does not, however, need to make any assumption about how many employees gave customers genuine smiles before the initiatives (though, presumably, many did not).

E If this claim were false, then the argument would be even stronger. Therefore, the argument does not need to assume this claim.

The correct answer is B.

245. Many economists hold that keeping taxes low helps to spur economic growth, and that low taxes thus lead to greater national prosperity. But Country X, which has unusually high taxes, has greater per-capita income than the neighboring Country Y, which has much lower taxes. Some politicians have concluded from this that high taxes do not hinder national prosperity.

The politicians' reasoning is most vulnerable to criticism on which of the following grounds?

(A) It overlooks the possibility that even if Country X reduced its taxes, it would not experience greater national prosperity in the long term.

(B) It confuses a claim that a factor does not hinder a given development with the claim that the same factor promotes that development.

(C) It fails to adequately address the possibility that Country X and Country Y differ in relevant respects other than taxation.

(D) It fails to take into account that the per-capita income of a country does not determine its rate of economic growth.

(E) It assumes that the economists' thesis must be correct despite a clear counterexample to that thesis.

Argument Evaluation

Situation Many economists hold that keeping taxes low helps increase economic growth and national prosperity. But a high-tax country, Country X, has greater per-capita income than Country Y, which has lower taxes. Some politicians have concluded from this that high taxes do not hinder national prosperity.

Reasoning *What is a significant weakness in the politicians' reasoning?* Many factors besides level of taxation are likely to affect economic growth and national prosperity—factors such as having a highly skilled labor force, being rich in a valuable natural resource, and having effective and efficient government. So it is likely that more than one such factor is needed to sufficiently explain any country's level of economic growth or prosperity. A combination of such factors may be sufficient to outweigh any negative impact of high taxes on economic growth or national prosperity.

A This possibility is quite consistent with the politicians' reasoning that higher taxes do not necessarily impede economic growth.

B Nothing in the politicians' reasoning indicates that they believe that higher taxes contribute to economic growth or prosperity. They claim that higher taxes do not preclude economic growth and prosperity. Nothing suggests that the politicians conflate these two views in their reasoning.

C **Correct.** Even though Country X, with unusually high taxes, has greater per-capita income than Country Y, which has much lower taxes, Country X's high-tax regime may contribute to making the country's per-capita income and national prosperity less than it would be with a low-tax regime. As explained earlier, many different factors can affect a country's national prosperity; some non-tax factors, absent in Country Y, may be boosting Country X's prosperity and compensating for some negative effects of its high-tax regime.

D The politicians' reasoning suggests that high per-capita income may indicate, or result from, a high level of national prosperity or a favorable rate of economic growth. It need not—and does not—address the question of whether a country's per-capita income could decisively affect the country's rate of economic growth.

E The politicians' reasoning indicates their disagreement with the economists' thesis; it cites as a counterexample to that thesis the fact that a high-tax country, Country X, has a higher per-capita income than a low-tax country, Country Y.

The correct answer is C.

246. Urban rail systems have been proposed to alleviate traffic congestion, but results in many cities have been cited as evidence that this approach to traffic management is ineffective. For example, a U.S. city that opened three urban rail branches experienced a net decline of 3,100 urban rail commuters during a period when employment increased by 96,000. Officials who favor urban rail systems as a solution to traffic congestion have attempted to counter this argument by noting that commuting trips in that city represent just 20 percent of urban travel.

The response of the officials to the claim that urban rail systems are ineffective is most vulnerable to criticism on the grounds that it

(A) presents no evidence to show that the statistics are incorrect
(B) relies solely on general data about U.S. cities rather than data about the city in question
(C) fails to consider that commuting trips may cause significantly more than 20 percent of the traffic congestion
(D) fails to show that the decline in the number of urban rail commuters in one U.S. city is typical of U.S. cities generally
(E) provides no statistics on the use of urban rail systems by passengers other than commuters

Argument Evaluation

Situation   Urban rail systems have been proposed to help solve traffic congestion in cities. But critics have cited data from many cities to argue that this approach is ineffective. In one U.S. city that increased its urban rail service, over 3,000 fewer commuters used rail when employment expanded by almost 100,000. But officials who favor urban rail have countered this example by claiming that commuters account for only 20 percent of urban travel in that city.

Reasoning   *Which answer choice most undermines the officials' response to the claim that urban rail would be ineffective in relieving urban traffic congestion?* Theoretically, urban rail service should help reduce traffic congestion by encouraging people to travel by train instead of by car. However, there is purported evidence that this approach is ineffective: In at least one city, an increase in the availability of rail service correlated with a decrease in the number of commuters traveling by rail, even though the total number of commuters apparently increased. Some officials object that in that city, commuters account for only 20 percent of urban travel. The officials' point is presumably that even if there was a net decline in commuters using the rail system, there may have been an overall increase in the number of people who used rail instead of driving. However, the stated goal of building more rail systems is to reduce traffic congestion, not just to reduce the overall amount of urban car traffic. Even if commuting makes up only 20 percent of urban travel in the city in question, it might contribute disproportionately to traffic congestion, and if noncommuters typically use the rail system, commuting might even constitute most of the car traffic in the city. So a net movement of commuters from rail travel to car travel could be detrimental to the goal of alleviating traffic congestion even if a minority of urban travel is in the form of commuting.

A   The point the officials make is not based on any assumption concerning the correctness of the statistics, nor do the officials appear to believe that the statistics are incorrect.

B   In their response, the officials do not cite any general data about U.S. cities; their objection only addresses the use of data about a specific city.

C   **Correct.** As explained above, the stated goal of building more rail systems is to reduce traffic congestion, not just to reduce the overall amount of urban car traffic. Even if commuting makes up only 20 percent of urban travel in the city in question, it might contribute disproportionately to traffic congestion, and if noncommuters typically use the rail system, commuting might even constitute most of the car traffic in the city. So a net movement of commuters from rail travel to car travel could be detrimental to the goal of alleviating traffic congestion even if a minority of urban travel is in the form of commuting.

D   The officials' opponents appear to rely on the assumption that the decline in urban rail commuting in one U.S. city provides relevant evidence regarding the situation in other cities. However, the point that the officials make in response to that reasoning does not require that they show that the decline in urban rail commuting in one U.S. city is typical of U.S. cities.

E   Providing such statistics would at best be peripheral to the point that the officials make, which directly concerns urban rail utilization by urban commuters rather than by any other group of travelers.

The correct answer is C.

247. Mayor: The financial livelihood of our downtown businesses is in jeopardy. There are few available parking spaces close to the downtown shopping area, so if we are to spur economic growth in our city, we must build a large parking ramp no more than two blocks from downtown.

Which of the following, if true, most seriously weakens the mayor's reasoning?

(A) The city budget is not currently large enough to finance the construction of a new parking ramp.
(B) There are other more significant reasons for the financial woes of downtown businesses in addition to a lack of nearby parking spaces.
(C) Building a parking ramp as much as four blocks from downtown would be sufficient to greatly increase the number of shoppers to downtown businesses.
(D) Explosive growth is most often associated with large suburban shopping malls, not small businesses.
(E) Some additional parking spaces could be added to the downtown area without the construction of a parking ramp.

Evaluation of a Plan

Situation A mayor argues that to help spur economic growth in the city and sustain business in the city's downtown, a large parking ramp should be constructed no more than two blocks from downtown to alleviate a parking shortage for business customers.

Reasoning *Which answer choice provides the information that most seriously weakens the mayor's reasoning?* It is reasonable to assume that constructing a large parking ramp within two blocks of downtown will involve a large capital investment, made even larger by the high cost of land so near to downtown. If a ramp slightly farther from downtown could equally well serve downtown shoppers, and given that people are also likely to need nonresidential parking in another location, building a ramp in the specific location mentioned by the mayor would not be necessary. Note also that even if providing significantly more parking for business customers were necessary for the survival of downtown businesses, it might not be sufficient.

A This information addresses a problem that would need to be overcome in order to have a parking ramp constructed. For example, taxes may need to be raised or a bond issued to fund the construction. It does not directly address the question whether the parking ramp would be necessary. If it were necessary but could not be financed, the result would be that the goal would not be met.

B This information indicates that the construction of the parking ramp would likely not be sufficient to ensure the survival of downtown businesses and that other measures would also be needed. This does not weaken the mayor's argument that the ramp would be necessary.

C **Correct.** If this were true, a parking ramp four blocks from downtown would suffice to solve the downtown parking shortage. Therefore, the construction of a ramp exactly two blocks from downtown would not be necessary.

D This provides a superficial reason for wondering whether economic growth in the mayor's city could be spurred without the measure that the mayor advocates. However, the information provides no reason to suppose that this city has not already achieved all the growth that it can achieve from large suburban shopping malls. Furthermore, the contrast between large malls and small businesses is not clearly relevant; the downtown businesses whose livelihood the mayor wants to save may be large ones.

E This information does not significantly weaken the mayor's proposal, since it does not tell us whether the additional parking spaces would suffice for meeting the mayor's goal to spur economic growth in the city.

The correct answer is C.

248. Compact fluorescent light (CFL) bulbs are growing in market share as a replacement for the standard incandescent light bulb. However, an even newer technology is emerging: the light-emitting diode (LED) bulb. Like CFL bulbs, LED bulbs are energy efficient, and they can last around fifty thousand hours, about five times as long as most CFL bulbs. Yet, a single LED bulb costs much more than five CFL bulbs.

The information in the passage above most supports which of the following conclusions?

(A) LED bulbs are most likely to be used in locations where light bulbs would be difficult or costly to replace.
(B) CFL bulbs will need to come down further in price in order to compete with LED bulbs.
(C) LED bulbs are most likely to be used in locations where there is frequent accidental breakage of bulbs.
(D) CFL bulb designs are likely to advance to the point where they can last as long as LED bulbs.
(E) LED bulbs are likely to drop in price, to the point of being competitive with CFL bulbs.

Argument Construction

Situation   Both compact fluorescent light (CFL) bulbs and light-emitting diode (LED) bulbs are energy-efficient bulbs. LED bulbs can last around 50,000 hours, about five times as long as CFL bulbs, though (at the time the passage was written) they cost more than five times as much as CFL bulbs.

Reasoning   *What claim is most strongly supported by the given information?* The information in the passage gives only one reason not to prefer LED bulbs over CFL bulbs—which last five times as long as CFL bulbs—namely, that LED bulbs are more than five times costlier. Because of the greater cost of LED bulbs, it might make economic sense simply to change CFL bulbs numerous times rather than to use the longer-lasting LED bulbs. If, however, there were any practical reason that outweighed that particular economic reason—perhaps the repeated replacement of CFL bulbs would be particularly problematic—then it might be wise to choose LED bulbs over CFL bulbs.

A   **Correct.** In locations where replacing bulbs is particularly difficult and even costly, it would probably make sense to use LED bulbs rather than CFL bulbs. Assuming, then, that both types of bulbs are otherwise acceptable and that their users are rational, LED bulbs would be most likely to be used in such locations.

B   The given information indicates that LED bulbs at the time the passage was written cost more than five times as much as CFL bulbs, but LED bulbs last only about five times as long as CFL bulbs. That suggests that CFL bulbs were competitive at that price.

C   If there is frequent accidental breakage of bulbs in a certain location, then it is likely that the advantage of LED bulbs mentioned in the passage would not hold in such locations.

D   Nothing in the passage suggests that CFL bulbs can be made to be longer lasting.

E   Nothing in the passage indicates whether there was any evidence, at the time the passage was written, that manufacturers of LED bulbs would be able to bring down the cost of producing such bulbs.

The correct answer is A.

249. Tanco, a leather manufacturer, uses large quantities of common salt to preserve animal hides. New environmental regulations have significantly increased the cost of disposing of salt water that results from this use, and, in consequence, Tanco is considering a plan to use potassium chloride in place of common salt. Research has shown that Tanco could reprocess the by-product of potassium chloride use to yield a crop fertilizer, leaving a relatively small volume of waste for disposal.

In determining the impact on company profits of using potassium chloride in place of common salt, it would be important for Tanco to research all of the following EXCEPT:

(A) What difference, if any, is there between the cost of the common salt needed to preserve a given quantity of animal hides and the cost of the potassium chloride needed to preserve the same quantity of hides?

(B) To what extent is the equipment involved in preserving animal hides using common salt suitable for preserving animal hides using potassium chloride?

(C) What environmental regulations, if any, constrain the disposal of the waste generated in reprocessing the by-product of potassium chloride?

(D) How closely does leather that results when common salt is used to preserve hides resemble that which results when potassium chloride is used?

(E) Are the chemical properties that make potassium chloride an effective means for preserving animal hides the same as those that make common salt an effective means for doing so?

Evaluation of a Plan

Situation   New environmental regulations will increase the costs of disposing of the salt water that results from the use of large amounts of common salt in leather manufacturing. The manufacturer is considering switching from common salt to potassium chloride, because the by-product of the latter could be reprocessed to yield a crop fertilizer, with little waste left over to be disposed.

Reasoning   *In order to determine whether it would be profitable to switch from using common salt to using potassium chloride, which answer choice does the manufacturer NOT need to answer?* The chemical properties making potassium chloride an effective means of preserving animal hides might be quite different from those that make common salt effective, but there is no particular reason for thinking that this would impact the profitability of switching to potassium chloride. The relevant effects on the preserved hides might be the same even if the properties that brought about those effects were quite different. Thus, without more information than is provided in the passage, this question is irrelevant.

A   The savings in waste disposal costs that would be gained by switching to potassium chloride could be cancelled out if the cost of potassium chloride needed far exceeded that for common salt.

B   If switching to potassium chloride would force the manufacturer to replace the equipment it uses for preserving hides, then it might be less profitable to switch.

C   Even though there is said to be relatively little waste associated with using potassium chloride in the process, if the costs of this disposal are very high due to environmental regulations, it might be less profitable to switch.

D   If the leather that results from the use of potassium chloride looks substantially different from that which results when common salt has been used, then the leather might be less attractive to consumers, which would adversely affect the economics of switching to potassium chloride.

E   **Correct.** Note that the question as stated here presupposes that potassium chloride and salt are both effective means for preserving animal hides—so it does not raise any issue as to whether potassium chloride is adequately effective or as effective as salt (clearly, an issue of effectiveness *would* be relevant to profitability).

The correct answer is E.

250. Colorless diamonds can command high prices as gemstones. A type of less valuable diamonds can be treated to remove all color. Only sophisticated tests can distinguish such treated diamonds from naturally colorless ones. However, only 2 percent of diamonds mined are of the colored type that can be successfully treated, and many of those are of insufficient quality to make the treatment worthwhile. Surely, therefore, the vast majority of colorless diamonds sold by jewelers are naturally colorless.

A serious flaw in the reasoning of the argument is that

(A) comparisons between the price diamonds command as gemstones and their value for other uses are omitted

(B) information about the rarity of treated diamonds is not combined with information about the rarity of naturally colorless, gemstone diamonds

(C) the possibility that colored diamonds might be used as gemstones, even without having been treated, is ignored

(D) the currently available method for making colorless diamonds from colored ones is treated as though it were the only possible method for doing so

(E) the difficulty that a customer of a jeweler would have in distinguishing a naturally colorless diamond from a treated one is not taken into account

Argument Evaluation

Situation Colored diamonds of a type that comprises 2 percent of all mined diamonds can be treated so that they are not easily distinguishable from more valuable, naturally colorless diamonds, but many are too low in quality for the treatment to be worthwhile.

Reasoning *Why do the argument's premises not justify the conclusion that the vast majority of colorless diamonds sold by jewelers are naturally colorless?* Since the type of colored diamonds that can be treated make up only 2 percent of all mined diamonds, and many diamonds of that type are too low in quality for treatment to be worthwhile, the vast majority of mined diamonds must not be treated to have their color removed. However, we are not told what proportion of all mined diamonds are naturally colorless. Naturally colorless diamonds may be far rarer even than the uncommon diamonds that have been treated to have their color removed. Thus, for all we can tell from the passage, it could well be that most colorless diamonds sold by jewelers have been treated to remove all color.

A Even if some types of diamonds command higher prices for uses other than as gemstones, the types discussed in the passage evidently command high enough prices as gemstones to be sold as such by jewelers.

B Correct. The argument does not work if naturally colorless diamonds are rarer than treated diamonds, as they may be for all we can tell from the information provided.

C The argument's conclusion is only that jewelers sell more naturally colorless diamonds than diamonds treated to be colorless. Whether jewelers sell any colored diamonds or other gemstones is irrelevant.

D The argument only concerns the types of colorless diamonds sold now, not the types that may be sold in the future if other treatment methods are discovered.

E The argument does suggest this difficulty but implies that even so there are too few treated diamonds available for jewelers to sell in place of naturally colorless ones.

The correct answer is B.

251. The Sumpton town council recently voted to pay a prominent artist to create an abstract sculpture for the town square. Critics of this decision protested that town residents tend to dislike most abstract art, and any art in the town square should reflect their tastes. But a town council spokesperson dismissed this criticism, pointing out that other public abstract sculptures that the same sculptor has installed in other cities have been extremely popular with those cities' local residents.

The statements above most strongly suggest that the main point of disagreement between the critics and the spokesperson is whether

(A) it would have been reasonable to consult town residents on the decision
(B) most Sumpton residents will find the new sculpture to their taste
(C) abstract sculptures by the same sculptor have truly been popular in other cities
(D) a more traditional sculpture in the town square would be popular among local residents
(E) public art that the residents of Sumpton would find desirable would probably be found desirable by the residents of other cities

Argument Construction

Situation After the Sumpton town council voted to pay a prominent sculptor to create an abstract sculpture for the town square, critics protested the decision. A town council spokesperson responded to the critics.

Reasoning *What do the critics and the spokesperson mainly disagree about?* The critics argue that Sumpton residents dislike most abstract art and that art in the town square should reflect their taste. Since the critics are protesting the town council's decision, they are clearly inferring from the residents' general attitude toward abstract art that the residents will dislike the specific sculpture the prominent sculptor will create. The spokesperson replies by arguing that in other cities, sculptures by the same sculptor have been very popular with local residents. The spokesperson implicitly infers from this that the sculpture the prominent sculptor will create for Sumpton will be popular with Sumpton residents—and therefore that the critics are mistaken.

A   Neither the critics nor the spokesperson mentions consultation with the town residents on the decision.

B   Correct. As explained above, the critics raise points implicitly suggesting that the residents will dislike the sculpture, whereas the spokesperson responds with a point implicitly supporting the opposite conclusion.

C   The critics could concede that the sculptor's work has been popular in other cities, but nonetheless hold that Sumpton residents have different tastes from those of the other cities' residents.

D   The spokesperson gives no indication regarding the attitudes of Sumpton residents regarding traditional sculpture.

E   It may be that neither the critics nor the spokesperson holds this view. The spokesperson may hold that Sumpton residents are easier to please than residents of most other cities, whereas the critics may hold that Sumpton residents are far more traditional in their tastes than other cities' residents.

The correct answer is B.

252. Jay: Of course there are many good reasons to support the expansion of preventive medical care, but arguments claiming that it will lead to greater societal economic gains are misguided. Some of the greatest societal expenses arise from frequent urgent-care needs for people who have attained a long life due to preventive care.

Sunil: Your argument fails because you neglect economic gains outside the health care system: society suffers an economic loss when any of its productive members suffer preventable illnesses.

Sunil's response to Jay makes which of the following assumptions?

(A) Those who receive preventive care are not more likely to need urgent care than are those who do not receive preventive care.
(B) Jay intends the phrase "economic gains" to refer only to gains accruing to institutions within the health care system.
(C) Productive members of society are more likely than others to suffer preventable illnesses.
(D) The economic contributions of those who receive preventive medical care may outweigh the economic losses caused by preventive care.
(E) Jay is incorrect in stating that patients who receive preventive medical care are long-lived.

Argument Construction

Situation   Some of the greatest societal expenses arise from frequent urgent-care needs for people who have reached old age thanks to preventive medical care. But society also suffers economic loss when any of its productive members suffer preventable illnesses.

Reasoning   *What is Sunil assuming in his argument that Jay's argument fails?* Jay implies that by helping people live longer, expanding preventive medical care may actually increase the amount of urgent medical care people need over the course of their lives, and that societal expenses for this additional urgent care may equal or exceed any societal economic benefits from expanding preventive care. Sunil responds by implying that expanding preventive care would allow society to avoid economic losses from lost productivity caused by preventable illnesses. In order for Sunil's argument to establish that Jay's argument fails, the potential economic benefits that Sunil implies would arise from expanded preventive care must be greater than the economic losses from the increased need for urgent care that Jay points out.

A   This is not an assumption that underpins Sunil's suggestion that the societal economic benefits from expanded preventive care may exceed any resulting economic losses from urgent care.

B   If Jay intends the phrase "economic gains" to refer only to gains within the health care system, then Sunil's point about economic gains outside the health care system is not even relevant to Jay's argument about economic gains within it.

C   Even if productive members of society are not more likely than others to suffer preventable illnesses, it still may be true, as Sunil suggests, that the economic benefits of preventing productive members of society from suffering those illnesses may outweigh the economic losses of doing so. In that case, Jay's argument could still fail in the way Sunil indicates.

D   **Correct.** Sunil must assume this in order to rebut Jay's argument. As explained above, if the economic contributions of those receiving preventive care definitely do not outweigh the economic losses caused by preventive care, then Sunil's implicit point that expanding preventive care would help to prevent the loss of such contributions is insufficient to rebut Jay's argument.

E   Whether Jay is correct or incorrect in this respect, Sunil may be correct that Jay's argument fails because Jay has neglected to consider how preventive care produces larger economic gains outside the health care system.

The correct answer is D.

253. Boreal owls range over a much larger area than do other owls of similar size. The reason for this behavior is probably that the small mammals on which owls feed are especially scarce in the forests where boreal owls live, and the relative scarcity of prey requires the owls to range more extensively to find sufficient food.

Which of the following, if true, most helps to confirm the explanation above?

(A) Some boreal owls range over an area eight times larger than the area over which any other owl of similar size ranges.
(B) Boreal owls range over larger areas in regions where food of the sort eaten by small mammals is sparse than they do in regions where such food is abundant.
(C) After their young hatch, boreal owls must hunt more often than before in order to feed both themselves and their newly hatched young.
(D) Sometimes individual boreal owls hunt near a single location for many weeks at a time and do not range farther than a few hundred yards.
(E) The boreal owl requires less food, relative to its weight, than is required by members of other owl species.

Argument Evaluation

Situation The small mammals on which owls prey are relatively scarce in the forests where boreal owls live. That is why boreal owls range more extensively than do other, similarly sized owls in search of food.

Reasoning *Which answer choice, if true, would most help confirm the proposed explanation?* One way to confirm an explanation is by finding further information that one would expect to be true *if* the explanation is valid. If the explanation in the passage is valid, then one would expect that variations in the population density of available small-animal prey for boreal owls would be accompanied by variations in the ranges of the boreal owls. Naturally the population density of available small-animal prey is likely to be affected by how plentiful food is for those small animals.

A The comparison between different groups of boreal owls is not relevant to the comparison between boreal owls and other owls.

B **Correct.** This indicates that abundance of food for the boreal owls' small-animal prey in an area (and therefore abundance of small animals in that area) correlates with a smaller range for the boreal owls there. This strengthens the proposed explanation.

C This answer choice concerns a correlation between owls' need for food and the frequency with which owls hunt, whereas the phenomenon described in the passage and the proposed explanation have to do with the range over which owls hunt.

D If one were to assume that boreal owls never hunt near a single location for weeks, that would in no way undermine the proposed explanation.

E If anything, this answer choice tends to undermine the proposed explanation, because it suggests the possibility that boreal owls need not make up for the relative scarcity of prey in their habitats by ranging over larger areas.

The correct answer is B.

254. Microbiologist: A lethal strain of salmonella recently showed up in a European country, causing an outbreak of illness that killed two people and infected twenty-seven others. Investigators blame the severity of the outbreak on the overuse of antibiotics, since the salmonella bacteria tested were shown to be drug-resistant. But this is unlikely because patients in the country where the outbreak occurred cannot obtain antibiotics to treat illness without a prescription, and the country's doctors prescribe antibiotics less readily than do doctors in any other European country.

Which of the following, if true, would most weaken the microbiologist's reasoning?

(A) Physicians in the country where the outbreak occurred have become hesitant to prescribe antibiotics since they are frequently in short supply.

(B) People in the country where the outbreak occurred often consume foods produced from animals that eat antibiotics-laden livestock feed.

(C) Use of antibiotics in two countries that neighbor the country where the outbreak occurred has risen over the past decade.

(D) Drug-resistant strains of salmonella have not been found in countries in which antibiotics are not generally available.

(E) Salmonella has been shown to spread easily along the distribution chains of certain vegetables, such as raw tomatoes.

Argument Evaluation

Situation Antibiotic-resistant salmonella caused an outbreak of illness in a European country where patients need prescriptions to obtain antibiotics and where doctors dispense such prescriptions less readily than in other European countries.

Reasoning *What evidence would most strongly suggest that overuse of antibiotics was likely responsible for the outbreak, despite the cited facts?* The microbiologist reasons that because patients need prescriptions to obtain antibiotics in the country where the outbreak occurred, and the country's doctors dispense such prescriptions less readily than doctors in other European countries do, antibiotics are probably not being overused in the country—so antibiotic overuse was probably not responsible for the outbreak. Implicit in the microbiologist's reasoning is the assumption that overuse of antibiotics, if it had occurred, could probably have resulted only from overprescribing of antibiotics by physicians to treat illness in people in the country in question. Any evidence casting doubt on this complex assumption would suggest a weakness in the microbiologist's reasoning.

A This strengthens the argument by providing additional evidence that antibiotics are not being overprescribed in the country.

B **Correct.** This weakens the microbiologist's argument by indicating that an assumption implicit in the argument may be false: the salmonella outbreak could easily by explained by overuse of antibiotics in livestock feed (perhaps imported from other countries).

C Even if antibiotic use has risen in the two neighboring countries, antibiotics still might be underused in both countries.

D This suggests that antibiotic-resistant salmonella arises only in countries where antibiotics are used; even if this were true it would be quite compatible with the microbiologist's argument and does not weaken that argument.

E This describes one mechanism by which salmonella can spread in a population; it says nothing about whether an outbreak of antibiotic-resistant strains of salmonella might have been caused by antibiotic overuse.

The correct answer is B.

255. Economist: Construction moves faster in good weather than in bad, so mild winters in areas that usually experience harsh conditions can appear to create construction booms as builders complete projects that would otherwise have to wait. But forecasting one mild winter or even two for such areas generally does not lead to overall increases in construction during these periods, because construction loans are often obtained more than a year in advance, and because _____.

Which of the following, if true, most logically completes the economist's argument?

(A) construction workers often travel to warmer climates in the wintertime in search of work
(B) construction materials are often in short supply during construction booms
(C) many builders in these areas are likely to apply for construction loans at the same time
(D) it is frequently the case that forecasted weather trends do not actually occur
(E) mild winters are generally followed by spring and summer weather that promotes more rapid construction

Argument Construction

Situation According to an economist, construction booms can seem to occur when mild winters allow construction to proceed in places where harsh winters usually prevent it. But the economist suggests that the greater construction in mild winters than in harsh winters is not due to contractors prescheduling more construction during winters that are predicted to be mild. The economist says there are two reasons for this. One is that construction loans often need to be approved more than a year in advance.

Reasoning *Which answer choice is logically most suited to be the second of the two reasons referred to by the economist?* The economist seeks to explain why a forecast of an unusually mild winter does not result in an overall increase in construction scheduled to take place in upcoming winters. One reason suggested is that loan approval—and presumably financial planning—for a construction project might often need to take place at least one year in advance. However, forecasts a year in advance that a mild winter will occur are quite likely to turn out to be wrong. The unreliability of such forecasts would make it unwise to intentionally schedule greater amounts of construction for winters that may or may not turn out to be mild.

A If an adequate labor force were lacking for a project in a given area, that project might not proceed. However, as part of the planning of a project, construction firms would likely have an assurance that an adequate labor force would be available.

B This suggests a slightly plausible hypothesis for why greater amounts of construction would not be scheduled for mild winters: if the construction firms have reason to believe that other companies will also have a motivation to schedule more construction at those times, they might all tacitly agree to distribute the projects more evenly across time to avoid shortages. However, it is also reasonable to suppose that shortages are a result of unforeseen boom conditions, not planned ones, and if the companies plan well in advance, they should be able to arrange for adequate supplies of materials.

C A surge in loan applications might mean longer waits for loan approvals. Contrary to what the economist claims, the fact that *many builders* are planning projects tends to suggest that there could be a construction boom scheduled for winter. The economist aims to explain why forecasts of one or more mild winters in places where winters are usually harsh do not result in *overall increases in construction*.

D **Correct.** The high likelihood that a forecast of a mild winter might turn out to be wrong is one reason for construction firms not to plan winter projects for areas where winters are usually harsh. This reason converges with the other reason provided: the forecast of a mild winter would have to occur up to one year in advance in order to obtain a loan approval in sufficient time to start construction.

E This information does not contribute to explaining why prescheduled construction booms are unlikely during exceptionally mild winters where winters are usually harsh. If long-term winter-weather forecasts were reliable, this could be a reason why such construction booms might be planned for mild winters.

The correct answer is D.

256. Historian: Newton developed mathematical concepts and techniques that are fundamental to modern calculus. Leibniz developed closely analogous concepts and techniques. It has traditionally been thought that these discoveries were independent. Researchers have, however, recently discovered notes of Leibniz's that discuss one of Newton's books on mathematics. Several scholars have argued that since **the book includes a presentation of Newton's calculus concepts and techniques,** and since the notes were written before Leibniz's own development of calculus concepts and techniques, it is virtually certain **that the traditional view is false.** A more cautious conclusion than this is called for, however. Leibniz's notes are limited to early sections of Newton's book, sections that precede the ones in which Newton's calculus concepts and techniques are presented.

In the historian's reasoning, the two portions in **boldface** play which of the following roles?

(A) The first is a claim that the historian rejects; the second is a position that that claim has been used to support.
(B) The first is evidence that has been used to support a conclusion about which the historian expresses reservations; the second is that conclusion.
(C) The first provides evidence in support of a position that the historian defends; the second is that position.
(D) The first and the second each provide evidence in support of a position that the historian defends.
(E) The first has been used in support of a position that the historian rejects; the second is a conclusion that the historian draws from that position.

Argument Construction

Situation A historian discusses a controversy about whether or not Leibniz developed calculus concepts and techniques independently of Newton.

Reasoning *What argumentative roles do the two portions in **boldface** play in the passage?* The first four sentences of the passage simply provide background information. Both **boldfaced** sections are within the fifth sentence, which reports an argument by *several scholars*. The key word *since* indicates that the first **boldfaced** section is a premise in the scholars' argument. A second premise preceded by another *since* follows in the next clause. The final clause of the fifth sentence reveals that the second **boldfaced** section is the conclusion of the scholars' argument. In the sixth sentence, the historian expresses misgivings about the scholars' conclusion, for reasons presented in the seventh and final sentence.

A The historian does not reject the claim that Newton's book includes a presentation of Newton's calculus concepts and techniques. Instead, the historian merely points out that Leibniz's notes do not cover those sections of Newton's book.

B **Correct.** The first **boldfaced** section is one of two premises in the scholars' argument, and the second **boldfaced** section is that argument's conclusion. In the following sentence the historian expresses reservations about that conclusion.

C The historian does not defend the scholars' conclusion but rather expresses misgivings about it.

D The second **boldfaced** section is the scholars' conclusion and does not present any evidence. Nor does it support the historian's position that a more cautious conclusion is called for.

E The second **boldfaced** section presents not the historian's conclusion but rather the scholars' conclusion, about which the historian expresses misgivings.

The correct answer is B.

257. For over two centuries, no one had been able to make Damascus blades—blades with a distinctive serpentine surface pattern—but a contemporary sword maker may just have rediscovered how. Using iron with trace impurities that precisely matched those present in the iron used in historic Damascus blades, this contemporary sword maker seems to have finally hit on an intricate process by which he can produce a blade indistinguishable from a true Damascus blade.

Which of the following, if true, provides the strongest support for the hypothesis that trace impurities in the iron are essential for the production of Damascus blades?

(A) There are surface features of every Damascus blade—including the blades produced by the contemporary sword maker—that are unique to that blade.

(B) The iron with which the contemporary sword maker made Damascus blades came from a source of iron that was unknown two centuries ago.

(C) Almost all the tools used by the contemporary sword maker were updated versions of tools that were used by sword makers over two centuries ago.

(D) Production of Damascus blades by sword makers of the past ceased abruptly after those sword makers' original source of iron became exhausted.

(E) Although Damascus blades were renowned for maintaining a sharp edge, the blade made by the contemporary sword maker suggests that they may have maintained their edge less well than blades made using what is now the standard process for making blades.

Argument Evaluation

Situation   A sword maker may have recently rediscovered how to make Damascus blades using iron with trace impurities matching those in the iron from which historic Damascus blades were wrought.

Reasoning   *What evidence would suggest that the trace impurities are essential for producing Damascus blades? The passage says the sword maker seems to have created blades indistinguishable from historic Damascus blades by using iron with the same trace impurities found in those blades. But that does not prove the trace impurities are essential to the process. Evidence suggesting that Damascus blades have never been made from iron without the trace impurities would support the hypothesis that the trace impurities are essential to their manufacture.*

A   Damascus blades could vary in their surface features whether or not trace impurities are essential for their manufacture.

B   Whatever the source of the iron the contemporary sword maker used, it contains the same trace impurities as the iron historically used to make Damascus blades, which is what the hypothesis is about.

C   If anything, this might cast doubt on the hypothesis by suggesting that the special tools rather than the trace impurities could account for the distinctive features of Damascus blades.

D   **Correct.** This suggests that when the historic sword makers lost access to the special iron with its trace impurities, they could no longer make Damascus blades. Thus, it supports the hypothesis that the trace impurities are necessary for manufacturing Damascus blades.

E   Even if Damascus blades maintained their edges less well than most contemporary blades do, the trace impurities may not have been essential for manufacturing them.

The correct answer is D.

258. Images from ground-based telescopes are invariably distorted by the Earth's atmosphere. Orbiting space telescopes, however, operating above Earth's atmosphere, should provide superbly detailed images. Therefore, ground-based telescopes will soon become obsolete for advanced astronomical research purposes.

Which of the following statements, if true, would cast the most doubt on the conclusion drawn above?

(A) An orbiting space telescope due to be launched this year is far behind schedule and over budget, whereas the largest ground-based telescope was both within budget and on schedule.

(B) Ground-based telescopes located on mountain summits are not subject to the kinds of atmospheric distortion which, at low altitudes, make stars appear to twinkle.

(C) By careful choice of observatory location, it is possible for large-aperture telescopes to avoid most of the kind of wind turbulence that can distort image quality.

(D) When large-aperture telescopes are located at high altitudes near the equator, they permit the best Earth-based observations of the center of the Milky Way Galaxy, a prime target of astronomical research.

(E) Detailed spectral analyses, upon which astronomers rely for determining the chemical composition and evolutionary history of stars, require telescopes with more light-gathering capacity than space telescopes can provide.

Argument Evaluation

Situation   Earth's atmosphere distorts images from ground-based telescopes, whereas space telescopes orbiting above the atmosphere should provide superbly detailed images.

Reasoning   *What evidence would undermine the claim that ground-based telescopes will soon become obsolete for advanced astronomical research?* The argument implicitly assumes that advanced astronomical research can be accomplished more effectively with the more detailed, less distorted images produced by space telescopes and that therefore almost all advanced astronomical research will soon be conducted with space telescopes. This reasoning would be undermined by evidence that ground-based telescopes have substantial advantages for advanced astronomical research despite their distorted images or by evidence that space telescopes will not soon become common or affordable enough to support most advanced astronomical research.

A   Even if this is true, there may be several orbiting space telescopes that will be, or have been, launched on schedule and within budget, so this answer choice does not cast doubt on the conclusion of the argument.

B   Ground-based telescopes on mountain summits are still subject to more atmospheric distortion than are space telescopes orbiting above the atmosphere.

C   Atmospheric distortion of telescopic images may result mainly from factors other than wind turbulence.

D   Even the best Earth-based observations of the center of the Milky Way Galaxy may be vastly inferior to space-based observations.

E   **Correct.** This indicates an inherent limitation of space-based telescopes: unlike Earth-based telescopes, they lack the light-gathering capacity that astronomers need to perform one of their primary tasks, i.e., detailed spectral analyses. So Earth-based telescopes are unlikely to soon become obsolete.

The correct answer is E.

259. Generally scientists enter their field with the goal of doing important new research and accept as their colleagues those with similar motivation. Therefore, when any scientist wins renown as an expounder of science to general audiences, most other scientists conclude that this popularizer should no longer be regarded as a true colleague.

    The explanation offered above for the low esteem in which scientific popularizers are held by research scientists assumes that

    (A) serious scientific research is not a solitary activity, but relies on active cooperation among a group of colleagues
    (B) research scientists tend not to regard as colleagues those scientists whose renown they envy
    (C) a scientist can become a famous popularizer without having completed any important research
    (D) research scientists believe that those who are well known as popularizers of science are not motivated to do important new research
    (E) no important new research can be accessible to or accurately assessed by those who are not themselves scientists

    Argument Construction

    Situation   Research scientists desire to do important new research and treat as colleagues just those who have a similar desire. When a scientist becomes popular among a general audience for explaining principles of science, other scientists have less esteem for this popularizer, no longer regarding such a scientist as a serious colleague.

    Reasoning   *What assumption do research scientists make about scientists who become popularizers?* The community of scientists shares a common goal: to do important new research. What would cause this community to disapprove of a popularizer and to cease to regard the popularizer as a colleague? It must be because many scientists believe that becoming a popularizer is incompatible with desiring to do important new research.

    A   Many scientists make this assumption, of course—but it is not an assumption on which the explanation specifically depends. The explanation concerns the scientists' motivation, not their style of doing research.

    B   This statement gives another reason that scientists may reject a popularizer, but because it is not the reason implied in the passage, it is not assumed.

    C   Even if this is true, it does not address the core issue of the argument: what scientists believe about the *motivation* of popularizers.

    D   **Correct.** This statement properly identifies an assumption on which the explanation for scientists' rejection of popularizers depends.

    E   The passage is not concerned with whether nonscientists can understand new research, but rather with the beliefs and motivations of scientists who reject popularizers as colleagues.

    The correct answer is D.

260. Urban planner: When a city loses population due to migration, property taxes in that city tend to rise. This is because there are then fewer residents paying to maintain an infrastructure that was designed to support more people. Rising property taxes, in turn, drive more residents away, compounding the problem. Since the city of Stonebridge is starting to lose population, the city government should therefore refrain from raising property taxes.

Which of the following, if true, would most weaken the urban planner's argument?

(A) If Stonebridge does not raise taxes on its residents to maintain its infrastructure, the city will become much less attractive to live in as that infrastructure decays.

(B) Stonebridge at present benefits from grants provided by the national government to help maintain certain parts of its infrastructure.

(C) If there is a small increase in property taxes in Stonebridge and a slightly larger proportion of total revenue than at present is allocated to infrastructure maintenance, the funding will be adequate for that purpose.

(D) Demographers project that the population of a region that includes Stonebridge will start to increase substantially within the next several years.

(E) The property taxes in Stonebridge are significantly lower than those in many larger cities.

Argument Evaluation

Situation   When a city loses population due to migration, fewer residents remain to pay to maintain the city's infrastructure, so property taxes tend to rise. These rising property taxes then drive even more residents away. The city of Stonebridge is starting to lose population, so Stonebridge's government should not raise property taxes.

Reasoning   *What would weaken the urban planner's justification for concluding that Stonebridge's government should refrain from raising property taxes?* The urban planner implicitly reasons that raising property taxes in Stonebridge in order to maintain the city's infrastructure would make the city lose even more residents, leaving even fewer paying to maintain the infrastructure, and that this would worsen the funding problem the tax increase would have been intended to solve. The urban planner's argument would be weakened by any evidence that raising property taxes in Stonebridge would not drive residents away or that refraining from raising property taxes would cause the same problems as raising them would cause, or worse.

A   **Correct.** This suggests that refraining from raising property taxes could drive more residents out of Stonebridge than raising them would, and thus would not help the city avoid the problem the urban planner describes.

B   This does slightly weaken the argument because the grants may still be provided to maintain certain parts of the infrastructure, even if increased property taxes drive more residents away. But losing more residents could still make it harder to raise enough funds to maintain the rest of the city's infrastructure, as the urban planner argues.

C   Even if this approach would address the immediate maintenance funding problem, the small increase in property taxes could still drive more residents away, forcing additional future tax increases on those who remain, just as the urban planner suggests.

D   This does slightly weaken the argument, but the residents who will move to the region might still avoid moving to Stonebridge if the property taxes there are too high, and those who live in Stonebridge might still move to other cities in the region.

E   Residents fleeing Stonebridge because of high property taxes would likely avoid moving to the many larger cities with even higher property taxes, but they might be happy to move to many other places with low property taxes.

The correct answer is A.

261. Which of the following most logically completes the argument?

Utrania was formerly a major petroleum exporter, but in recent decades economic stagnation and restrictive regulations inhibited investment in new oil fields. In consequence, Utranian oil exports dropped steadily as old fields became depleted. Utrania's currently improving economic situation, together with less-restrictive regulations, will undoubtedly result in the rapid development of new fields. However, it would be premature to conclude that the rapid development of new fields will result in higher oil exports, because _____.

(A) the price of oil is expected to remain relatively stable over the next several years
(B) the improvement in the economic situation in Utrania is expected to result in a dramatic increase in the proportion of Utranians who own automobiles
(C) most of the investment in new oil fields in Utrania is expected to come from foreign sources
(D) new technology is available to recover oil from old oil fields formerly regarded as depleted
(E) many of the new oil fields in Utrania are likely to be as productive as those that were developed during the period when Utrania was a major oil exporter

Argument Construction

Situation A country that had been a major oil exporter has seen its exports decline in recent decades due to economic stagnation, a failure to invest in new fields, and the steady depletion of its old fields. But looser regulations and an improving economy will bring rapid development of new oil fields in the country.

Reasoning *Which answer choice would most logically complete the argument?* The passage describes the conditions that led to Utrania's no longer being a major oil exporter: a lack of investment in new oil fields due to a stagnant economy and restrictive regulations. The passage then says that due to changed regulatory and economic conditions, there will now be rapid development of new oil fields. Nonetheless, this might not bring about an increase in Utrania's oil exports. To logically complete the argument, one must explain how oil exports might not increase even when the condition that led to decreased oil exports has been removed. Suppose there were an increase in domestic oil consumption. A dramatic increase in the rate of car ownership in Utrania could reasonably be expected to significantly increase domestic oil consumption, which could eat up the added oil production from the new fields.

A   This answer choice is incorrect. There is no reason why stable oil prices should prevent Utrania's oil exports from increasing.

B   **Correct.** An increase in car ownership would increase Utrania's oil consumption—and this supports the claim that oil exports might not increase.

C   If anything, this suggests that oil exports should increase. So it would not be a good choice for completion of the argument.

D   The advent of new technology allowing oil to be extracted from fields previously thought to be depleted would mean that there is even more reason to think that Utrania's oil exports will increase.

E   This does not help to explain why exports would not increase. On the contrary, it suggests that the new fields will lead to increased exports.

The correct answer is B.

262. The use of growth-promoting antibiotics in hog farming can weaken their effectiveness in treating humans because such use can spread resistance to those antibiotics among microorganisms. But now the Smee Company, one of the largest pork marketers, may stop buying pork raised on feed containing these antibiotics. Smee has 60 percent of the pork market, and farmers who sell to Smee would certainly stop using antibiotics in order to avoid jeopardizing their sales. So if Smee makes this change, it will probably significantly slow the decline in antibiotics' effectiveness for humans.

Which of the following, if true, would most strengthen the argument above?

(A) Other major pork marketers will probably stop buying pork raised on feed containing growth-promoting antibiotics if Smee no longer buys such pork.

(B) The decline in hog growth due to discontinuation of antibiotics can be offset by improved hygiene.

(C) Authorities are promoting the use of antibiotics to which microorganisms have not yet developed resistance.

(D) A phaseout of use of antibiotics for hogs in one country reduced usage by over 50 percent over five years.

(E) If Smee stops buying pork raised with antibiotics, the firm's costs will probably increase.

Argument Evaluation

Situation   Using growth-promoting antibiotics in hog farming can produce widespread resistance to antibiotics among microorganisms, thereby making the antibiotics less effective in treating humans. The Smee Company, a pork marketer with 60 percent of the pork market, may stop buying pork raised on feed containing these antibiotics.

Reasoning   *What additional evidence would most help to support the conclusion that if Smee makes the change, it will significantly slow the decline in antibiotics' effectiveness for humans?* We are already informed that if Smee makes the change, it will eliminate the use of antibiotics in hog feed by farmers supplying at least 60 percent of the pork market. The argument would be strengthened by evidence that Smee's decision would indirectly cause use of the antibiotics to stop more broadly, for example in hog farms supplying significantly more than 60 percent of the total amount of pork marketed.

A   **Correct.** This suggests that if Smee makes the change, hog farmers supplying other major pork marketers will also have to stop using antibiotics in hog feed, making the change more widespread and thus probably more effective.

B   Even if the decline in hog growth from discontinuing the antibiotics cannot be offset, many hog farmers will still have to stop using the antibiotics as a result of Smee's decision. On the other hand, even if the decline can be offset with improved hygiene, that change might be too expensive or difficult to be worth its benefits for most hog farmers.

C   Whatever new antibiotics authorities are promoting, microorganisms may soon develop resistance to them as well. Smee may or may not refuse to buy pork raised on feed containing these new antibiotics.

D   This is evidence that Smee's decision may significantly reduce antibiotic use in hogs, but it provides no evidence of how this reduction may affect antibiotics' effectiveness for humans.

E   If anything, this provides reason to suspect that Smee will not stick with the change for long after the costs increase, so it weakens rather than strengthens the argument that the change will significantly slow the decline in antibiotics' effectiveness.

The correct answer is A.

263. In an experiment, volunteers walked individually through a dark, abandoned theater. Half of the volunteers had been told that the theater was haunted and the other half that it was under renovation. The first half reported significantly more unusual experiences than the second did. The researchers concluded that reports of encounters with ghosts and other supernatural entities generally result from prior expectations of such experiences.

    Which of the following, if true, would most seriously weaken the researchers' reasoning?

    (A) None of the volunteers in the second half believed that the unusual experiences they reported were supernatural.
    (B) All of the volunteers in the first half believed that the researchers' statement that the theater was haunted was a lie.
    (C) Before being told about the theater, the volunteers within each group varied considerably in their prior beliefs about supernatural experiences.
    (D) Each unusual experience reported by the volunteers had a cause that did not involve the supernatural.
    (E) The researchers did not believe that the theater was haunted.

    Argument Evaluation

    Situation   Volunteers in an experiment walked through a dark, abandoned theater. Those who had been told the theater was haunted reported more unusual experiences than those who had been told it was under renovation.

    Reasoning   *What evidence would most strongly suggest that the experimental results do not indicate that reports of supernatural encounters result from prior expectations of such experiences?* The researcher assumes that the half of the volunteers who had been told the theater was haunted were more inclined to expect supernatural experiences in the theater than were the other half of the volunteers. Based on this assumption and the greater incidence of reports of unusual experiences among the first half of the volunteers, the researcher concludes that prior expectation of supernatural experiences makes people more likely to report such experiences. The researchers' reasoning would be weakened by evidence that the volunteers did not actually have the expectations the researchers assumed them to have, or by evidence that any such expectations did not influence their reports.

    A   This strengthens the argument by indicating that the volunteers whom the researchers did not lead to expect supernatural experiences reported no such experiences.

    B   **Correct.** If none of the volunteers believed the researchers' claim that the theater was haunted, then the implicit assumption that several of those volunteers expected supernatural experiences in the theater is flawed, and so the inference that their prior expectations probably account for their reports of supernatural experiences is flawed.

    C   This is compatible with the researchers' inference and does not undermine it. Even if the volunteers' initial beliefs about supernatural experiences varied, the researchers' claims about the theater might have strongly influenced how many volunteers in each group expected to have such experiences in the theater specifically.

    D   The researchers argue that the volunteers' prior expectations account for all the reports of unusual experiences, and this is compatible with there being no genuine supernatural occurrences in the theater.

    E   Whatever the researchers personally believed about the theater, they might still have successfully influenced the volunteers' beliefs about it.

    The correct answer is B.

264. In order to reduce dependence on imported oil, the government of Jalica has imposed minimum fuel-efficiency requirements on all new cars, beginning this year. The more fuel-efficient a car, the less pollution it produces per mile driven. As Jalicans replace their old cars with cars that meet the new requirements, annual pollution from car traffic is likely to decrease in Jalica.

Which of the following, if true, most seriously weakens the argument?

(A) In Jalica, domestically produced oil is more expensive than imported oil.
(B) The Jalican government did not intend the new fuel-efficiency requirement to be a pollution-reduction measure.
(C) Some pollution-control devices mandated in Jalica make cars less fuel-efficient than they would be without those devices.
(D) The new regulation requires no change in the chemical formulation of fuel for cars in Jalica.
(E) Jalicans who get cars that are more fuel-efficient tend to do more driving than before.

Argument Evaluation

Situation   The Jalican government is requiring all new cars to meet minimum fuel-efficiency requirements starting this year. Cars that are more fuel efficient produce less pollution per mile driven.

Reasoning   *What evidence would suggest that annual pollution from car traffic will not decrease in Jalica, despite the new policy?* Air pollution from car traffic is unlikely to decrease if the new standards will result in more cars on the road or more miles driven per car; or if air pollution from car traffic in Jalica is increasing because of unrelated factors such as growing numbers of Jalicans who can afford cars, construction of more roads, etc. Evidence that any of these factors is present would cast doubt on the argument's conclusion and thus weaken the argument.

A   The question at issue is not whether the new policy will reduce dependence on imported oil as the government intends, but rather whether it will reduce air pollution from car traffic.

B   A government policy may have consequences that the government did not intend it to have.

C   Even if these pollution-control devices make cars less fuel efficient, the new fuel-efficiency standards may still improve cars' average fuel efficiency and thereby reduce air pollution.

D   Even if the fuel is unchanged, the new fuel-efficiency standards may still result in cars using less fuel and may thereby reduce air pollution.

E   **Correct.** If the new fuel-efficient cars are driven more miles per year than older cars are, they may produce as much or more pollution per year than older cars do even though they produce less pollution per mile driven.

The correct answer is E.

265. Plantings of cotton bioengineered to produce its own insecticide against bollworms, a major cause of crop failure, sustained little bollworm damage until this year. This year the plantings are being seriously damaged by bollworms. Bollworms, however, are not necessarily developing resistance to the cotton's insecticide. Bollworms breed on corn, and last year more corn than usual was planted throughout cotton-growing regions. So it is likely that the cotton is simply being overwhelmed by corn-bred bollworms.

In evaluating the argument, which of the following would it be most useful to establish?

(A) Whether corn could be bioengineered to produce the insecticide
(B) Whether plantings of cotton that does not produce the insecticide are suffering unusually extensive damage from bollworms this year
(C) Whether other crops that have been bioengineered to produce their own insecticide successfully resist the pests against which the insecticide was to protect them
(D) Whether plantings of bioengineered cotton are frequently damaged by insect pests other than bollworms
(E) Whether there are insecticides that can be used against bollworms that have developed resistance to the insecticide produced by the bioengineered cotton

Argument Evaluation

Situation   Although plantings of cotton bioengineered to produce an insecticide to combat bollworms were little damaged by the pests in previous years, they are being severely damaged this year. Since the bollworms breed on corn, and there has been more corn planted this year in cotton-growing areas, the cotton is probably being overwhelmed by the corn-bred bollworms.

Reasoning   *In evaluating the argument, which question would it be most useful to have answered?* The argument states that the bioengineered cotton crop failures this year (1) have likely been due to the increased corn plantings and (2) not due to the pests having developed a resistance to the insecticide. This also implies (3) that the failures are not due to some third factor.

It would be useful to know how the bioengineered cotton is faring in comparison to the rest of this year's cotton crop. If the bioengineered cotton is faring better against the bollworms, that fact would support the argument because it would suggest that the insecticide is still combating bollworms. If, on the other hand, the bioengineered cotton is being more severely ravaged by bollworms than is other cotton, that suggests that there is some third cause that is primarily at fault.

A   This would probably be useful information to those trying to alleviate the bollworm problem in bioengineered cotton. But whether such corn could be developed has no bearing on what is causing the bioengineered cotton to be damaged by bollworms this year.

B   **Correct.** If bollworm damage on non-bioengineered cotton is worse than usual this year, then bollworm infestation in general is simply worse than usual, so pesticide resistance does not need to be invoked to explain the bollworm attacks on the bioengineered cotton.

C   Even if other crops that have been bioengineered to resist pests have not successfully resisted them, that fact would not mean that the same is true of this cotton. Furthermore, the facts already suggest that the bioengineered cotton has resisted bollworms.

D   Whether other types of pests often damage bioengineered cotton has no bearing on why bollworms are damaging this type of cotton more this year than in the past.

E   This, too, might be useful information to those trying to alleviate the bollworm problem in bioengineered cotton, but it is not particularly useful in evaluating the argument. Even if there are pesticides that could be used against bollworms that have developed resistance to the insecticide of the bioengineered cotton, that does not mean that such pesticides are being used this year.

The correct answer is B.

266. Typically during thunderstorms most lightning strikes carry a negative electric charge; only a few carry a positive charge. Thunderstorms with unusually high proportions of positive-charge strikes tend to occur in smoky areas near forest fires. The fact that smoke carries positively charged smoke particles into the air above a fire suggests the hypothesis that the extra positive strikes occur because of the presence of such particles in the storm clouds.

Which of the following, if discovered to be true, most seriously undermines the hypothesis?

(A) Other kinds of rare lightning also occur with unusually high frequency in the vicinity of forest fires.

(B) The positive-charge strikes that occur near forest fires tend to be no more powerful than positive strikes normally are.

(C) A positive-charge strike is as likely to start a forest fire as a negative-charge strike is.

(D) Thunderstorms that occur in drifting clouds of smoke have extra positive-charge strikes weeks after the charge of the smoke particles has dissipated.

(E) The total number of lightning strikes during a thunderstorm is usually within the normal range in the vicinity of a forest fire.

Argument Evaluation

Situation Thunderstorms with unusually high proportions of positive-charge lightning strikes tend to occur in smoky areas near forest fires. Smoke carries positively charged particles into the air above fires, suggesting that smoke particles in storm clouds are responsible for the higher proportion of positive strikes.

Reasoning *What would cast doubt on the hypothesis that the extra positive-charge lightning strikes in thunderstorms near forest fires result from positively charged smoke particles carried into the storm clouds?* The hypothesis would be weakened by evidence that the positively charged smoke particles do not enter the storm clouds in the first place, or that they do not retain their charge in the clouds long enough to produce an effect, or that their positive charge cannot affect the charges of the storm's lightning strikes in any case, or that some other factor tends to make the lightning strikes above these storms positively charged.

A It could be that positively charged smoke particles cause these other kinds of rare lightning, too, so this does not seriously undermine the hypothesis.

B The hypothesis is not about the power of the positive-charge lightning strikes, only about why a high proportion of them occur in thunderstorms near forest fires.

C The hypothesis is about why positive-charge strikes tend to occur in smoky areas near forest fires that have already started before the strikes occur. Furthermore, an equal likelihood of positive-charge and negative-charge strikes starting fires cannot explain a correlation between fires and positive-charge strikes specifically.

D **Correct.** This means that even when drifting clouds of smoke persist for weeks after a fire, when the charge of their particles has already dissipated, the smoke somehow still makes the strikes positively charged in any thunderstorms arising within it. If so, some factor other than positively charged smoke particles must affect the strikes' charge.

E This information does not undermine the hypothesis. The hypothesis does not concern the possibility that there might be more lightning strikes in the vicinity of forest fires; rather it concerns the proportion of all such lightning strikes that are positively charged.

The correct answer is D.

267. Since 1990 the percentage of bacterial sinus infections in Aqadestan that are resistant to the antibiotic perxicillin has increased substantially. Bacteria can quickly develop resistance to an antibiotic when it is prescribed indiscriminately or when patients fail to take it as prescribed. Since perxicillin has not been indiscriminately prescribed, health officials hypothesize that the increase in perxicillin-resistant sinus infections is largely due to patients' failure to take this medication as prescribed.

Which of the following, if true of Aqadestan, provides most support for the health officials' hypothesis?

(A) Resistance to several other commonly prescribed antibiotics has not increased since 1990 in Aqadestan.
(B) A large number of Aqadestanis never seek medical help when they have a sinus infection.
(C) When it first became available, perxicillin was much more effective in treating bacterial sinus infections than any other antibiotic used for such infections at the time.
(D) Many patients who take perxicillin experience severe side effects within the first few days of their prescribed regimen.
(E) Aqadestani health clinics provide antibiotics to their patients at cost.

Argument Construction

Situation   In Aqadestan the percentage of bacterial sinus infections resistant to the antibiotic perxicillin has been increasing even though perxicillin has not been indiscriminately prescribed.

Reasoning   *What evidence most strongly suggests that the main reason perxicillin-resistant sinus infections are becoming more common is that patients are failing to take perxicillin as prescribed?* Any evidence suggesting that patients have in fact been failing to take perxicillin as prescribed would support the hypothesis, as would any evidence casting doubt on other possible explanations for the increasing proportion of perxicillin-resistant sinus infections.

A   This suggests that some factor specific to perxicillin is increasing bacterial resistance to it, but that could be true whether or not the factor is patients' failure to take perxicillin as prescribed.

B   If anything, this weakens the argument by suggesting that most people with sinus infections are never prescribed perxicillin, and that therefore relatively few people are getting prescriptions and then failing to follow them.

C   The relative effectiveness of perxicillin when it first became available does not suggest that the reason it is now becoming less effective is that many patients are failing to take it as prescribed.

D   **Correct.** These side effects would discourage patients from taking perxicillin as prescribed, so their existence provides evidence that many patients are not taking it as prescribed.

E   If the clinics do not charge extra for perxicillin, that would make it more affordable and hence easier for many patients to take as prescribed.

The correct answer is D.

268. Psychologist: In a study, researchers gave 100 volunteers a psychological questionnaire designed to measure their self-esteem. The researchers then asked each volunteer to rate the strength of his or her own social skills. The volunteers with the highest levels of self-esteem consistently rated themselves as having much better social skills than did the volunteers with moderate levels. This suggests that attaining an exceptionally high level of self-esteem greatly improves one's social skills.

The psychologist's argument is most vulnerable to criticism on which of the following grounds?

(A) It fails to adequately address the possibility that many of the volunteers may not have understood what the psychological questionnaire was designed to measure.

(B) It takes for granted that the volunteers with the highest levels of self-esteem had better social skills than did the other volunteers, even before the former volunteers had attained their high levels of self-esteem.

(C) It overlooks the possibility that people with very high levels of self-esteem may tend to have a less accurate perception of the strength of their own social skills than do people with moderate levels of self-esteem.

(D) It relies on evidence from a group of volunteers that is too small to provide any support for any inferences regarding people in general.

(E) It overlooks the possibility that factors other than level of self-esteem may be of much greater importance in determining the strength of one's social skills.

Argument Evaluation

Situation   In a psychological study of 100 volunteers, those found to have the highest self-esteem consistently rated themselves as having much better social skills than did those found to have moderate self-esteem.

Reasoning   *What is wrong with the psychologist citing the study's results to justify the conclusion that exceptionally high self-esteem greatly improves social skills?* The psychologist reasons that the study shows a correlation between very high self-esteem and how highly one rates one's social skills, and that this correlation in turn suggests that very high self-esteem improves social skills. This argument is vulnerable to at least two criticisms: First, the argument assumes that the volunteers' ratings of their own social skills are generally accurate. But very high self-esteem might in many cases result from a tendency to overestimate oneself and one's skills, including one's social skills. Second, the argument fails to address the possibility that good social skills promote high self-esteem rather than vice versa, as well as the possibility that some third factor (such as a sunny disposition or fortunate circumstances) promotes both high self-esteem and good social skills.

A   An experiment's subjects do not have to understand the experiment's design in order for the experimental results to be accurate.

B   To the contrary, the argument concludes that the volunteers with the highest self-esteem attained their enhanced social skills as a result of attaining such high self-esteem.

C   **Correct.** As explained above, very high self-esteem may often result from a tendency to overestimate oneself in general, and thus to overestimate one's social skills.

D   A group of 100 volunteers is large enough for an experiment to provide at least a little support for at least some inferences regarding people in general.

E   As explained above, the argument overlooks the possibility that some third factor may play a significant role in determining the strength of one's social skills. But even if some factor other than self-esteem is more important in determining the strength of social skills, that would still be compatible with very high self-esteem being of some importance in improving one's social skills.

The correct answer is C.

269. Political advertisement: Mayor Delmont's critics complain about the jobs that were lost in the city under Delmont's leadership. Yet the fact is that not only were more jobs created than were eliminated, but each year since Delmont took office the average pay for the new jobs created has been higher than that year's average pay for jobs citywide. So it stands to reason that throughout Delmont's tenure the average paycheck in this city has been getting steadily bigger.

Which of the following, if true, most seriously weakens the argument in the advertisement?

(A) The unemployment rate in the city is higher today than it was when Mayor Delmont took office.//
(B) The average pay for jobs in the city was at a ten-year low when Mayor Delmont took office.//
(C) Each year during Mayor Delmont's tenure, the average pay for jobs that were eliminated has been higher than the average pay for jobs citywide.//
(D) Most of the jobs eliminated during Mayor Delmont's tenure were in declining industries.//
(E) The average pay for jobs in the city is currently lower than it is for jobs in the suburbs surrounding the city.

Argument Evaluation

Situation Every year since Mayor Delmont took office, average pay for new jobs has exceeded average pay for jobs citywide. So, the average paycheck in the city has been increasing since Delmont took office.

Reasoning *Which answer choice, if true, would most seriously weaken the argument?* If average pay for new jobs continually exceeds that for jobs generally, new jobs pay better (on average) than old jobs that still exist. But suppose the following occurred. Every year all of the highest paying jobs are eliminated and replaced with somewhat lower-paying jobs that still pay more than the average job. The result would be that every year the average pay for a new job would be greater than that for existing jobs, but the average pay for all jobs would nonetheless decrease. Thus, if every year during the mayor's tenure the jobs that were eliminated paid better on average than jobs citywide, that would seriously weaken the argument: the conclusion could be false even if the information on which it is based is true.

A The percentage of people in the city who have a job has no direct bearing on whether the average pay for jobs citywide is increasing or decreasing.

B Whether the average pay was low when the mayor took office in comparison to the ten preceding years is immaterial to the comparison addressed in the argument's conclusion.

C **Correct.** This information weakens the argument because it opens up the possibility that the jobs eliminated had higher average pay than the jobs created during Mayor Delmont's tenure. This in turn would mean that the average pay was not increasing during Mayor Delmont's tenure.

D This, too, has no bearing on the argument, because we have no information about the average pay for jobs in those declining industries.

E This is also irrelevant. No comparison is made (or implied) in the argument between jobs in the city and jobs in the suburbs.

The correct answer is C.

270. To prevent a newly built dam on the Chiff River from blocking the route of fish migrating to breeding grounds upstream, the dam includes a fish pass, a mechanism designed to allow fish through the dam. Before the construction of the dam and fish pass, several thousand fish a day swam upriver during spawning season. But in the first season after the project's completion, only 300 per day made the journey. Clearly, the fish pass is defective.

Which of the following, if true, most seriously weakens the argument?

(A) Fish that have migrated to the upstream breeding grounds do not return down the Chiff River again.
(B) On other rivers in the region, the construction of dams with fish passes has led to only small decreases in the number of fish migrating upstream.
(C) The construction of the dam stirred up potentially toxic river sediments that were carried downstream.
(D) Populations of migratory fish in the Chiff River have been declining slightly over the last 20 years.
(E) During spawning season, the dam releases sufficient water for migratory fish below the dam to swim upstream.

Argument Evaluation

Situation   A new dam includes a mechanism called a fish pass designed to allow fish to migrate upstream past the dam to their breeding grounds. The number of migrating fish fell from several thousand per day before the dam was built to three hundred per day in the first season after it was built, indicating—according to the argument—that the fish pass is defective.

Reasoning   *What evidence would suggest that the fish pass is not defective?* The argument implicitly reasons that a defective fish pass would make it difficult for the fish to migrate, which would explain why the number of migrating fish fell when the dam was completed. Any evidence suggesting an alternative explanation for the reduced number of migrating fish, such as an environmental change that occurred when the dam was built, would cast doubt on the argument's reasoning.

A   A defective fish pass could prevent most of the fish from migrating upstream regardless of whether those that succeed ever return downstream.

B   This would suggest that dams with properly functioning fish passes do not greatly reduce the number of migrating fish, so it would provide further evidence that the fish pass in this particular dam is defective.

C   Correct. This suggests that the toxic sediments may have poisoned the fish and reduced their population. A smaller fish population could be sufficient to explain the reduced number of fish migrating, which casts doubt on the argument's assumption that the explanation for their declining numbers involves the fish pass.

D   A slight and gradual ongoing decline in migratory fish populations would not explain an abrupt and extreme decline right after the dam was built.

E   This supports the argument's proposed explanation for the declining fish population by ruling out the alternative explanation that the dam does not release enough water for the fish to migrate.

The correct answer is C.

271. Music critic: Fewer and fewer musicians are studying classical music, decreasing the likelihood that those with real aptitude for such music will be performing it. Audiences who hear these performances will not appreciate classical music's greatness and will thus decamp to other genres. So to maintain classical music's current meager popularity, we must encourage more young musicians to enter the field.

    Which of the following, if true, most weakens the music critic's reasoning?

    (A) Musicians who choose to study classical music do so because they believe they have an aptitude for the music.
    (B) Classical music's current meager popularity is attributable to the profusion of other genres of music available to listeners.
    (C) Most people who appreciate classical music come to do so through old recordings rather than live performances.
    (D) It is possible to enjoy the music in a particular genre even when it is performed by musicians who are not ideally suited for that genre.
    (E) The continued popularity of a given genre of music depends in part on the audience's being able to understand why that genre attained its original popularity.

    Argument Evaluation

    Situation Fewer musicians are studying classical music. This reduces the likelihood that those performing the music will have real aptitude for it, which in turn reduces audience's appreciation of classical music performances.

    Reasoning *What evidence would cast the most doubt on the support provided for the conclusion that encouraging more young musicians to study classical music is necessary in order to maintain the genre's meager popularity?* The music critic's argument is that because fewer talented classical musicians are performing, audiences hearing their performances will fail to appreciate the genre, and thus will abandon it. The critic reasons that to solve this problem, it will be necessary to encourage more young musicians to study classical music so that audiences will eventually be exposed to more talented classical performers and decide the genre is worthwhile after all. The argument would be weakened, for example, by evidence that hearing unremarkable live performances does not really drive many people away from classical music, or that the number of audience members hearing great performances does not depend much on the number of talented performers, or that encouraging young musicians to study classical music is either ineffective or not the only effective way to increase the number of talented classical performers.

    A   This does not weaken the critic's reasoning. However much confidence musicians studying classical music have in their own talent, a decline in the total number of classical musicians will probably result in a decline in the number of truly talented classical musicians, just as the critic assumes.

    B   The critic is only proposing a way to at least maintain classical music's current meager popularity, which might be accomplished even if the profusion of other genres prevents classical music's popularity from increasing.

    C   **Correct.** This suggests that classical music's meager popularity could at least be maintained by encouraging people to listen to great old recordings of classical music rather than by increasing the supply of great live performances.

    D   This does weaken the argument slightly. But even if a few audience members manage to enjoy mediocre classical music performances, they might still be more strongly drawn to other genres with more talented performers.

    E   Listeners exposed to more impressive live performances of classical music by talented performers would probably better understand why classical music was once popular than would listeners exposed only to mediocre classical performances.

The correct answer is C.

272. People with a college degree are more likely than others to search for a new job while they are employed. There are proportionately more people with college degrees among managers and other professionals than among service and clerical workers. Surprisingly, however, 2009 figures indicate that people employed as managers and other professionals were no more likely than people employed as service and clerical workers to have searched for a new job.

Which of the following, if true, most helps to resolve the apparent paradox?

(A) People generally do not take a new job that is offered to them while they are employed unless the new job pays better.

(B) Some service and clerical jobs pay more than some managerial and professional jobs.

(C) People who felt they were overqualified for their current positions were more likely than others to search for a new job.

(D) The percentage of employed people who were engaged in job searches declined from 2005 to 2009.

(E) In 2009 employees with no college degree who retired were more likely to be replaced by people with a college degree if they retired from a managerial or professional job than from a service or clerical job.

Argument Construction

Situation College graduates are more likely than others to search for another job while they are employed. A greater percentage of managers and other professionals are college graduates than of service and clerical workers. In 2009, however, managers and other professionals were no more likely than service and clerical workers to have searched for another job while employed.

Reasoning *What additional piece of information would most help resolve the apparent paradox described?* The apparent paradox concerns a 2009 phenomenon that initially seems at odds with a general pattern in job-search behavior. However, the phenomenon seems less puzzling when one considers the following. Depending on the current state of the employment market, some college graduates may choose to take a job as a service or clerical worker, seeing it as a way of paying their expenses while aiming to transition to a job more suited to their medium- and long-term career aspirations.

A This information provides one answer to the question, why do people choose to accept or decline a particular job? However, this has no clear relevance to the apparent paradox we are asked to resolve; the paradox concerns the proportions of people in different kinds of jobs who search for a new job even while employed.

B This information is too vague to contribute to resolving the apparent paradox. It is little more than a truism that, given certain labor supply and demand conditions, pay rates for different jobs vary.

C **Correct.** College graduates in clerical jobs might feel that they had more advanced skills than their jobs demanded. College graduates in managerial or professional jobs would be less likely to have a similar feeling.

D This information regarding a decline in job searches from 2005 to 2009 has no clear relevance to the apparent paradox we are asked to resolve. For example, we are not told that this decline occurred predominantly among managerial or professional workers.

E This information suggests that the supply of college graduates was larger in 2009 than it had been some decades before. If the supply were large enough in 2009, it could be the case that some college graduates accepted service or clerical jobs that, decades previously, would not have been filled by college graduates. But we lack enough specific information for this answer choice to help resolve the apparent paradox.

The correct answer is C.

273. To reduce traffic congestion, City X's transportation bureau plans to encourage people who work downtown to sign a form pledging to carpool or use public transportation for the next year. Everyone who signs the form will get a coupon for a free meal at any downtown restaurant.

For the transportation bureau's plan to succeed in reducing traffic congestion, which of the following must be true?

(A) Everyone who signs the pledge form will fully abide by the pledge for the next year.
(B) At least some people who work downtown prefer the restaurants downtown to those elsewhere.
(C) Most downtown traffic congestion in City X results from people who work downtown.
(D) The most effective way to reduce traffic congestion downtown would be to persuade more people who work there to carpool or use public transportation.
(E) At least some people who receive the coupon for a free meal will sometimes carpool or use public transportation during the next year.

Evaluation of a Plan

Situation In City X, the transportation bureau's plan to reduce traffic congestion involves giving every downtown worker who signs a form pledging to carpool or use public transportation next year a coupon for a free meal at any downtown restaurant.

Reasoning *What claim must be true for the transportation bureau's plan to reduce traffic congestion to succeed?* Obviously, if people sign the pledge just so they can get a coupon for a free meal, and if no one who signs the pledge actually carpools or uses public transportation, then the plan will not succeed. Therefore, for the plan to be successful, at least some of the people who receive the coupon must at least occasionally carpool or use public transportation during the next year.

A If this were true, it would certainly help the plan succeed. But the question asks what *must* be true for the plan to succeed, and it is not necessary that anyone fully abide by the plan. The plan could well succeed, for instance, if no one fully abided by the pledge but a large number of people only partially abided by the pledge.

B This is not necessary. Even if everyone prefers restaurants outside the downtown area, they may still want a free meal at a downtown restaurant.

C It could be that a majority of the downtown traffic congestion in City X results not from people who work downtown, but from people who shop downtown or live downtown but work elsewhere. The plan could still work as long as there was a sufficient reduction in the congestion caused by the downtown workers.

D The plan could work even if it is not the most effective way to reduce traffic congestion. If there is a more effective way to reduce traffic congestion, then it might be advisable to implement that plan instead of, or in addition to, this one. But second-best plans, for instance, can be successful.

E **Correct.** Certainly, this is not sufficient for the plan to succeed; compliance would probably need to be well above the minimal level. But, as explained above, this is necessary for the plan to succeed. Suppose someone objected to the idea that this must be true for the plan to succeed by saying that, even if no one who received the coupon carpooled or used public transportation, congestion could still be reduced if enough *other* people carpooled or used public transportation. That is true, but in that case, it would not be the *plan* that succeeded. The goal would be accomplished, but it would have been accomplished without the plan itself being successful at accomplishing it.

The correct answer is E.

274. Commemorative plaques cast from brass are a characteristic art form of the Benin culture of West Africa. Some scholars, noting that the oldest surviving plaques date to the 1400s, hypothesize that brass-casting techniques were introduced by the Portuguese, who came to Benin in 1485 A.D. But Portuguese records of that expedition mention cast-brass jewelry sent to Benin's king from neighboring Ife. So it is unlikely that Benin's knowledge of brass casting derived from the Portuguese.

Which of the following, if true, most strengthens the argument?

(A) The Portuguese records do not indicate whether their expedition of 1485 included metalworkers.
(B) The Portuguese had no contact with Ife until the 1500s.
(C) In the 1400s the Portuguese did not use cast brass for commemorative plaques.
(D) As early as 1500 A.D., Benin artists were making brass plaques incorporating depictions of Europeans.
(E) Copper, which is required for making brass, can be found throughout Benin territory.

Argument Construction

Situation   The oldest surviving cast-brass plaques from the Benin culture date to the 1400s. Records of a Portuguese expedition to Benin in 1485 mention cast-brass jewelry sent to Benin's king from neighboring Ife.

Reasoning   *What additional evidence, when combined with the argument's premises, would most help support the conclusion that Benin's knowledge of brass casting did not derive from the Portuguese?* The argument is that since the expedition records indicate that cast-brass jewelry from Ife was already known in Benin when the Portuguese first came there, Benin's knowledge of brass casting probably did not derive from the Portuguese. This argument assumes that receiving the brass-cast jewelry from Ife could have transmitted knowledge of brass casting to Benin, and also that knowledge of brass casting in Ife did not itself derive from the Portuguese. Any evidence supporting either of these assumptions would strengthen the argument.

A   This is compatible with a Portuguese origin for brass-casting in Benin. The expedition might well have included metalworkers even if the records do not mention whether it did. Furthermore, other Portuguese expeditions with metalworkers might have quickly followed the initial expedition.

B   **Correct.** If the Portuguese had no contact with Ife before 1500, then Ife's earlier knowledge of brass casting did not derive directly from the Portuguese. This increases the likelihood that knowledge of brass-casting in Benin did not derive from the Portuguese, even if it derived from Ife.

C   This is compatible with a Portuguese origin for brass-casting in Benin. Even if the Portuguese did not use cast brass for commemorative plaques, they could have used it for jewelry or other items they brought to Benin or manufactured there, and thus they could have transmitted the knowledge to the Benin culture.

D   This leaves open the possibility that the Benin culture learned about brass casting from the Portuguese in 1485 and started using it to produce plaques of this type by 1500.

E   Even if copper has always been common in the Benin territory, brass-casting techniques could have been introduced by the Portuguese.

The correct answer is B.

275. When new laws imposing strict penalties for misleading corporate disclosures were passed, they were hailed as initiating an era of corporate openness. As an additional benefit, given the increased amount and accuracy of information disclosed under the new laws, it was assumed that analysts' predictions of corporate performance would become more accurate. Since the passage of the laws, however, the number of inaccurate analysts' predictions has not in fact decreased.

Which of the following would, if true, best explain the discrepancy outlined above?

(A) The new laws' definition of "misleading information" can be interpreted in more than one way.
(B) The new laws require corporations in all industries to release information at specific times of the year.
(C) Even before the new laws were passed, the information most corporations released was true.
(D) Analysts base their predictions on information they gather from many sources, not just corporate disclosures.
(E) The more pieces of information corporations release, the more difficult it becomes for anyone to organize them in a manageable way.

Evaluation of a Plan

Situation It was assumed that new laws, implemented to increase the amount and accuracy of information released by corporations, would increase the accuracy of analysts' predictions about corporate performance. This outcome has not occurred, however.

Reasoning *What claim would best explain the new laws' failure to reduce the number of inaccurate analysts' predictions?* The new laws were intended to increase both the accuracy and the amount of information. If the amount of information increased to such a level that analysts became overwhelmed by it, this could help explain the laws' failure to reduce the number of inaccurate predictions.

A Even if the new laws' definition of "misleading information" can be interpreted in multiple ways, it could be that the accuracy of corporate information has increased. This fact alone does little if anything to explain the discrepancy.

B The fact that all industries are required to release information at specific times of the year is not helpful in explaining why the number of inaccurate analysts' predictions has not declined. Presumably analysts would wait for the information to be released to make predictions.

C This might help somewhat in explaining the failure to bring about the desired outcome. It would do so by ruling out one scenario that would make the outcome more likely to occur: If past predictions had been inaccurate because they were based on false information, it would seem likely that the law would reduce the number of inaccurate predictions. But even if most of the information corporations released in the past was true, one would still expect some improvement in the accuracy of predictions if the information became universally accurate, and there was more of it available.

D The fact that analysts base their predictions about corporate performance on information gathered from many sources in addition to corporate disclosures does not explain why, if corporate disclosures improved, there would not be at least some improvement in the accuracy of predictions about corporate performance.

E **Correct.** If the amount of information corporations release becomes so great that organizing it in a manageable way becomes difficult or impossible, then it could become more difficult to interpret and understand. This could interfere with analysts' ability to make accurate predictions about performance, even if the information provided is 100 percent accurate.

The correct answer is E.

276. Economist: Even with energy conservation efforts, current technologies cannot support both a reduction in carbon dioxide emissions and an expanding global economy. Attempts to restrain emissions without new technology will stifle economic growth. Therefore, increases in governmental spending on research into energy technology will be necessary if we wish to reduce carbon dioxide emissions without stifling economic growth.

Which of the following is an assumption the economist's argument requires?

(A) If research into energy technology does not lead to a reduction in carbon dioxide emissions, then economic growth will be stifled.

(B) Increased governmental spending on research into energy technology will be more likely to reduce carbon dioxide emissions without stifling growth than will nongovernmental spending.

(C) An expanding global economy may require at least some governmental spending on research into energy technology.

(D) Attempts to restrain carbon dioxide emissions without new technology could ultimately cost more than the failure to reduce those emissions would cost.

(E) Restraining carbon dioxide emissions without stifling economic growth would require both new energy technology and energy conservation efforts.

Evaluation of a Plan

Situation   An economist argues that without new technology, attempts to restrain carbon dioxide emissions will stifle economic growth. The economist concludes from this that if such emissions are to be reduced without stifling economic growth, there must be increases in governmental spending on research into energy technology.

Reasoning   *What assumption is required by the economist's argument?* An obvious question to the economist's argument is why an increase in *governmental* spending is required. Could nongovernmental spending alone not be at least as effective? If it could be, then the economist's conclusion would not follow. Therefore, for the economist's argument to be a good one, it would need to be true that nongovernmental spending alone would not be as effective for the intended purpose as increased governmental spending would be.

A   Nothing in the argument requires the assumption that only a reduction in carbon dioxide emissions can stifle economic growth. The argument is perfectly compatible, for instance, with the assumption that economic growth would be stifled if there were significant climate change—perhaps leading to severe crop shortages—as a result of increased carbon dioxide emissions.

B   **Correct.** As explained above, a natural response to the economist's argument is to ask, "Why can we not just use nongovernmental spending to come up with new technologies that will allow us to restrain carbon dioxide emissions without stifling economic growth?" Without an answer to that question, the economist's argument cannot be a good one. If answer choice B were true, it would bridge the logical gap by providing a reason that increased governmental spending—and not just nongovernmental spending—would be needed.

C   This does not have to be assumed. True, the argument assumes that *if* we try to reduce carbon dioxide emissions without increased governmental spending on research into energy technology, then the economy will be stifled. But the argument is compatible with the occurrence of economic growth despite a lack of governmental spending on research into energy technology, as long as carbon dioxide emissions are not reduced.

D   The argument does not require this assumption. As explained in answer choice A, the argument is compatible with the idea that the economy could be stifled by climate change that results from a failure to reduce carbon emissions. This could result in great economic cost.

E   The argument does not indicate that new energy technology alone cannot be sufficient for restraining carbon dioxide emissions without stifling economic growth.

The correct answer is B.

277. Researchers have developed a technology that uses sound as a means of converting heat into electrical energy. Converters based on this technology can be manufactured small enough to be integrated into consumer electronics, where they will absorb significant quantities of heat. A group of engineers is now designing converters to be sold to laptop computer manufacturers, who are expected to use the electrical output of the converters to conserve battery power in their computers.

Which of the following would, if true, provide the strongest evidence that the engineers' plan will be commercially successful for their group?

(A) The sound that is used by the converters is generated by the converters themselves.
(B) Most laptop computer manufacturers today receive fewer complaints than in previous years regarding shortness of operating time on a single battery charge.
(C) The overheating of microprocessors in laptop computers presents a major technological challenge that manufacturers are prepared to meet at significant expense.
(D) Although battery technology has improved significantly, the average capacity of laptop computer batteries has not.
(E) Electrical power generated by the converters can be used to power the fans installed to cool computers' components.

Evaluation of a Plan

Situation A group of engineers is designing converters that absorb heat and then use sound to convert it into electrical energy. The engineers hope to sell the converters to laptop manufacturers for the purpose of using the electrical output of the converters to conserve battery power.

Reasoning *Which claim provides the strongest evidence that the engineers' plan will be commercially successful?* A claim that reveals that there would be demand among laptop manufacturers for the converters would provide such evidence. If these manufacturers currently face a major challenge that they would be willing to meet at significant expense, they would provide a demand for this product if it could be shown to work well.

A   Whether the sound is generated by the converters or by something else would be irrelevant to whether the plan would be commercially successful, unless the sound production required a significant amount of electrical energy. If it did require a significant amount of electrical energy, this would tend to weaken the hypothesis that the plan would succeed.

B   This suggests that laptop manufacturers may not feel a great need to use these converters to conserve battery power.

C   **Correct.** If laptop manufacturers are prepared to meet the challenge of the overheating of microprocessors at significant expense, in a way that provides an additional benefit such as conserving battery power, they could very well be a receptive market for these converters.

D   This would not provide strong evidence that the plan will be commercially successful unless we had further evidence that laptop manufacturers see it as a challenge that they would be willing to meet at significant expense.

E   Presumably, the electricity generated by the converter should be able to contribute toward satisfying any of the energy needs of the computer. The passage provides no reason to think that the cooling fans are special in this regard. The converters generate electrical energy by absorbing heat so, in principle, there might even be circumstances in which the use described in this answer choice could undermine the converters' functionality.

The correct answer is C.

278. According to a widely held economic hypothesis, imposing strict environmental regulations reduces economic growth. This hypothesis is undermined by the fact that the states with the strictest environmental regulations also have the highest economic growth. This fact does not show that environmental regulations promote growth, however, since _____.

Which of the following, if true, provides evidence that most logically completes the argument above?

(A) those states with the strictest environmental regulations invest the most in education and job training

(B) even those states that have only moderately strict environmental regulations have higher growth than those with the least-strict regulations

(C) many states that are experiencing reduced economic growth are considering weakening their environmental regulations

(D) after introducing stricter environmental regulations, many states experienced increased economic growth

(E) even those states with very weak environmental regulations have experienced at least some growth

Argument Construction

Situation   Claims that strict environmental regulations inhibit economic growth are undermined by higher economic growth in states with such regulations. However, the passage infers (for a reason the argument omits) that the presence of higher growth in states with strong regulations does not prove that these regulations are the *cause* of the greater economic growth observed there.

Reasoning   *What would make it less likely that environmental regulations cause economic growth?* The argument notes that stricter environmental regulations correlate with higher economic growth, which undermines the hypothesis that such strict regulations reduce growth. The argument suggests, however, that environmental regulations may not actually cause growth. In that case, there should be other factors that contribute to the higher economic growth in states with strict environmental regulations.

A **Correct.** If higher investment in education and job training promotes the higher economic growth observed in states with strict environmental regulations, then those regulations may not cause that growth.

B Higher economic growth in states with moderately strict environmental regulations merely shows another correlation and implies nothing about the causes of that growth.

C States with poor economic growth might consider reducing regulations, but no evidence has been provided that such a policy would cause economic growth.

D Increased regulation directly preceding increased growth would tend to undermine the argument, not support it, especially if all other factors remained constant.

E The presence of some economic growth in states with low environmental regulations implies nothing about the causes of higher growth.

The correct answer is A.

279. The prairie vole, a small North American grassland rodent, breeds year-round, and a group of voles living together consists primarily of an extended family, often including two or more litters. Voles commonly live in large groups from late autumn through winter; from spring through early autumn, however, most voles live in far smaller groups. The seasonal variation in group size can probably be explained by a seasonal variation in mortality among young voles.

Which of the following, if true, provides the strongest support for the explanation offered?

(A) It is in the spring and early summer that prairie vole communities generally contain the highest proportion of young voles.
(B) Prairie vole populations vary dramatically in size from year to year.
(C) The prairie vole subsists primarily on broad-leaved plants that are abundant only in spring.
(D) Winters in the prairie voles' habitat are often harsh, with temperatures that drop well below freezing.
(E) Snakes, a major predator of young prairie voles, are active only from spring through early autumn.

Argument Evaluation

Situation   Prairie voles live in groups made up of relatives. Because they breed year-round, there are generally young voles in each group. These groups are larger in late fall and winter, while group size decreases in spring, summer, and early fall, probably because of a seasonal difference in the mortality rate of young voles.

Reasoning   *What provides support for the claim that increased mortality among young voles causes the annual reduction in vole group size observed in spring?* If vole groups are large in late autumn and winter and much smaller during the rest of the year, then something must be causing the reduction in group size that occurs each spring through early autumn. The explanation states that increased mortality in young voles probably accounts for the decline in group size. Therefore, identifying a likely cause of such increased seasonal mortality would support the explanation.

A   A higher proportion of young voles in spring would undermine the suggestion that their increased mortality causes a decline in group size at the same time.

B   There is no evidence that annual variations in overall prairie vole populations are related to the seasonal reduction in vole group size each spring.

C   An abundance of food in spring would not contribute to increased mortality among young voles at the same time.

D   Harsh winters would not account for increased mortality among young voles in spring, given the information in the passage that vole familial groups are large through winter.

E   **Correct.** If snakes that eat young voles are active in spring through early autumn, then that would support the explanation that increased mortality among young voles during the same period causes the seasonal decline in vole group size.

The correct answer is E.

280. From 1980 to 1989, total consumption of fish in the country of Jurania increased by 4.5 percent, and total consumption of poultry products there increased by 9.0 percent. During the same period, the population of Jurania increased by 6 percent, in part due to immigration to Jurania from other countries in the region.

If the statements above are true, which of the following must also be true on the basis of them?

(A) During the 1980s in Jurania, profits of wholesale distributors of poultry products increased at a greater rate than did profits of wholesale distributors of fish.
(B) For people who immigrated to Jurania during the 1980s, fish was less likely to be a major part of their diet than was poultry.
(C) In 1989, Juranians consumed twice as much poultry as fish.
(D) For a significant proportion of Jurania's population, both fish and poultry products were a regular part of their diet during the 1980s.
(E) Per capita consumption of fish in Jurania was lower in 1989 than in 1980.

Argument Construction

Situation   During a specific period—1980 to 1989—the population of Jurania increased by 6 percent, fish sales increased by 4.5 percent, and poultry sales increased by 9 percent. Some of Jurania's population growth was the result of immigration from nearby countries.

Reasoning   *What would necessarily follow from increased sales rates of fish and poultry products in Jurania relative to increased population over the same period?* If the population of Jurania increased by 6 percent, sales of fish increased by 4.5 percent, and sales of poultry products increased by 9 percent, all during the same period from 1980 to 1989, then changes in the relationship between population size and sales of those food products necessarily follow.

A   Many factors can affect profits, so a greater increase in poultry sales relative to fish sales would not necessarily cause wholesale distributors of poultry to experience a faster growth in profits than wholesale distributors of fish do.

B   The diets of Jurania's new immigrants are a possible contributing factor to the relative changes in sales of fish and poultry, but other factors could account for the same changes.

C   The increase in poultry sales is twice the increase in fish sales, but that relationship implies nothing about the overall consumption of fish versus poultry.

D   The consumers of fish and the consumers of poultry might be separate groups, and both fish and poultry might be consumed occasionally rather than regularly.

E   **Correct.** Fish consumption grew at a lower rate than the population did from 1980 to 1989, so per capita consumption of fish must be lower at the end of that period than it was at the beginning.

The correct answer is E.

281. Junior biomedical researchers have long assumed that their hirings and promotions depend significantly on the amount of their published work. People responsible for making hiring and promotion decisions in the biomedical research field, however, are influenced much more by the overall impact that a candidate's scientific publications have on his or her field than by the number of those publications.

The information above, if accurate, argues most strongly AGAINST which of the following claims?

(A) Even biomedical researchers who are just beginning their careers are expected to already have published articles of major significance to the field.
(B) Contributions to the field of biomedical research are generally considered to be significant only if the work is published.
(C) The potential scientific importance of not-yet-published work is sometimes taken into account in decisions regarding the hiring or promotion of biomedical researchers.
(D) People responsible for hiring or promoting biomedical researchers can reasonably be expected to make a fair assessment of the overall impact of a candidate's publications on his or her field.
(E) Biomedical researchers can substantially increase their chances of promotion by fragmenting their research findings so that they are published in several journals instead of one.

Argument Construction

Situation   Junior biomedical researchers believe that the volume of their publications is a major determinant of their career success. However, the people in charge of hiring and promotions are more interested in the significance of a candidate's publications than in the number of those publications.

Reasoning   *What is likely to be untrue if the people responsible for hiring and promotions in the biomedical research field are significantly more impressed by the impact, rather than the quantity, of candidates' publications? If junior biomedical researchers are mistaken in their belief that the sheer quantity of their publications is a major determinant of their success, it would follow that focusing on quantity is not their best strategy.*

A   The claim that impact matters more than quantity of publications does not imply that early-career researchers would not be expected to have published significant articles.

B   The information presented has no bearing on whether or not contributions in the field have to be published to be considered significant.

C   The information presented has no bearing on the question of whether or not the value of unpublished work would be taken into account.

D   The information suggests that the people responsible for hiring and promotions assess the impact of a candidate's publications, but it implies nothing about whether or not such assessments are fair.

E   **Correct.** If the people responsible for hiring and promotion are favorably impressed by the impact more than by the quantity of publications, then fragmenting research findings in order to increase the sheer quantity of publications is unlikely to help researchers attain promotion.

The correct answer is E.

282. Rabbits were introduced to Tambor Island in the nineteenth century. Overgrazing by the enormous rabbit population now menaces the island's agriculture. The government proposes to reduce the population by using a virus that has caused devastating epidemics in rabbit populations elsewhere. There is, however, a small chance that the virus will infect the bilby, an endangered native herbivore. The government's plan, therefore, may serve the interests of agriculture but will clearly increase the threat to native wildlife.

The argument above assumes which of the following?

(A) There is less chance that the virus will infect domestic animals on Tambor than that it will infect wild animals of species native to the island.
(B) Overgrazing by rabbits does not pose the most significant current threat to the bilby.
(C) There is at least one alternative means of reducing the rabbit population that would not involve any threat to the bilby.
(D) There are no species of animals on the island that prey on the rabbits.
(E) The virus that the government proposes to use has been successfully used elsewhere to control populations of rabbits.

Argument Construction

Situation Invasive rabbits are a problem for Tambor Island's agriculture. The government wants to kill the rabbits by introducing a virus, but that virus may also attack the native bilby. The virus's introduction will increase the threat to native animals.

Reasoning *Since the argument claims that introducing the virus clearly increases the risk to native wildlife, in this case the bilby, on Tambor Island, what does it assume about other factors that might affect that claim?* The claim that risk to the bilby would be clearly increased by the virus ignores other effects that could result from the virus. If the virus reduced other risks to the bilby, that might cause an overall reduction in risk to the bilby, even if the virus presents some risk.

A The claim that the virus will clearly increase risk to wild species is not based on any assumption about its effect on domestic species.

B **Correct.** The argument assumes that the rabbits' overgrazing does not present a major risk that herbivorous bilby populations will starve, because that danger would suggest that a declining number of rabbits might reduce overall risk to the bilby, even once the direct risk posed by the virus is taken into account.

C Concern for the risk the virus poses to the bilby is not based on an assumption that the rabbit population could be sufficiently reduced by a safer method.

D The argument is not based on an assumption about whether or not Tambor Island has species that prey on the rabbits but only describes a possible risk from attempting to reduce rabbit populations by means of a virus.

E The argument states that the virus has caused epidemics among rabbits elsewhere but does not assume that those epidemics were started by governments rather than occurring naturally.

The correct answer is B.

283. Telomerase is an enzyme that is produced only in cells that are actively dividing. Thus, as a rule, it is not present in adult tissue. Bone marrow is an exception to this rule, however, since even in adults bone marrow cells continually divide to replace old blood cells. Cancers are another exception, because their cells are rapidly dividing.

The information provided most strongly supports which of the following?

(A) Telomerase is the only enzyme that is present in cancerous cells but absent from cells that are not actively dividing.
(B) Embryonic tissue is less likely to become cancerous than tissue that has ceased to actively divide.
(C) The presence of telomerase in bone marrow is no indication of bone marrow cancer.
(D) Cancer of the bone marrow develops more rapidly than cancer growing in any other kind of adult tissue.
(E) The level of telomerase production is always higher in cancerous tissue than in noncancerous tissue.

Argument Construction

Situation   The enzyme telomerase is produced by dividing cells. Therefore, it is not typically present in adult tissues, but there are two types of tissue that continue to show cell division in adults and thus are exceptions to this rule: bone marrow and cancer.

Reasoning   *What is likely to be true if both bone marrow and cancer are exceptions to the general rule that telomerase is absent in adult tissues?* The information suggests that telomerase is present in rapidly dividing cancer cells and also in healthy bone marrow cells, which divide continually because of their function of replacing blood cells. Since telomerase is expected in healthy bone marrow, it would not indicate that the bone marrow is cancerous.

A   Telomerase's presence in cancer cells and not in nondividing cells does not support the claim that other enzymes do not occur in the same distribution.

B   The information might suggest that telomerase occurs in embryonic cells, not that such cells are less susceptible to cancer.

C   **Correct.** Since telomerase occurs normally in healthy bone marrow, its presence in bone marrow would not indicate cancer.

D   The information does not support the suggestion that the telomerase in bone marrow would promote faster growth of bone marrow cancers compared to other cancers.

E   The information does not suggest that telomerase production is always higher in cancers than it is in other tissues, such as bone marrow, that also produce telomerase.

The correct answer is C.

284. Which of the following provides the most logical completion of the argument?

Many of Vebrol Corporation's department heads will retire this year. The number of junior employees with the qualifications Vebrol will require for promotion to department head is equal to only half the expected vacancies. Vebrol is not going to hire department heads from outside the company, have current department heads take over more than one department, or reduce the number of its departments. So some departments will be without department heads next year, since Vebrol will not _____.

(A) promote more than one employee from any department to serve as heads of departments

(B) promote any current department heads to higher-level managerial positions

(C) have any managers who are currently senior to department heads serve as department heads

(D) reduce the responsibilities of each department

(E) reduce the average number of employees per department

Argument Construction

Situation   Vebrol's department heads are retiring in significant numbers. There are only about half as many qualified junior employees to fill the resulting vacancies. Vebrol will not hire department heads externally, have department heads lead multiple departments, or eliminate departments. For an unstated additional reason, some departments will lack department heads.

Reasoning   *If the total number of qualified junior employees is only half of Vebrol's projected need for department heads, and if Vebrol will not address that shortfall through external hiring, doubling department heads' responsibilities, or eliminating departments, what additional factor would guarantee that some departments will be without department heads?* If Vebrol will necessarily have departments without department heads, it follows that they are probably not using any means, including recruiting senior staff as department heads, to amend that projected shortfall.

A   The number of employees promoted per department would not affect the fact that the number of junior employees eligible for promotion is half the projected need.

B   Not promoting current department heads would be expected to limit the shortfall, not ensure it.

C   **Correct.** If Vebrol is ruling out an additional way to address the shortage of department heads—in this case, by not having senior employees serve as department heads—then that decision would logically ensure that some departments will not have heads.

D   Reducing the departments' responsibilities would not affect the availability of department heads.

E   Reducing the total number of employees per department would not affect the question of whether or not those departments have heads.

The correct answer is C.

285. Ecologist: The Scottish Highlands were once the site of extensive forests, but these forests have mostly disappeared and been replaced by peat bogs. The common view is that the Highlands' deforestation was caused by human activity, especially agriculture. However, **agriculture began in the Highlands less than 2,000 years ago.** Peat bogs, which consist of compressed decayed vegetable matter, build up by only about one foot per 1,000 years and, **throughout the Highlands, remains of trees in peat bogs are almost all at depths greater than four feet.** Since climate changes that occurred between 7,000 and 4,000 years ago favored the development of peat bogs rather than the survival of forests, the deforestation was more likely the result of natural processes than of human activity.

In the ecologist's argument, the two portions in **boldface** play which of the following roles?

(A) The first is evidence that has been used in support of a position that the ecologist rejects; the second is a finding that the ecologist uses to counter that evidence.

(B) The first is evidence that, in light of the evidence provided in the second, serves as grounds for the ecologist's rejection of a certain position.

(C) The first is a position that the ecologist rejects; the second is evidence that has been used in support of that position.

(D) The first is a position that the ecologist rejects; the second provides evidence in support of that rejection.

(E) The first is a position for which the ecologist argues; the second provides evidence to support that position.

Argument Construction

Situation　　An ecologist points out that the common position is that human activity—primarily agriculture—led to the replacement of the formerly extensive forests of the Scottish Highlands by peat bogs. The ecologist points out several factors that cast doubt on this explanation and instead point to natural processes as the cause. The ecologist points out that agriculture began in the Highlands less than 2,000 years ago, that peat bogs build up at only about a foot per 1,000 years, and that the peat bogs throughout the Highlands are at depths greater than four feet. Finally, in support of the alternative explanation, the ecologist points out that climate changes that occurred 7,000 to 4,000 years ago would have favored peat bog development over forest survival.

Reasoning　　*What role do the two portions in **boldface** play in the ecologist's argument?* The ecologist rejects the common position that agriculture primarily accounts for the replacement of forests by peat bogs in the Scottish Highlands. The ecologist puts forward three main pieces of evidence as grounds for that rejection: that agriculture began in the Highlands 2,000 years ago (the first **boldfaced** portion), that peat bogs build up at one foot per 1,000 years, and that tree remnants in peat bogs throughout the Highlands occur at depths greater than four feet (the second **boldfaced** portion).

A　　The first **boldfaced** portion is used in support of the ecologist's rejection of the common explanation; it has not been used to support that common explanation. The second **boldfaced** portion is compatible with the first and is not used to counter it.

B　　**Correct.** The first **boldfaced** portion—which states that agriculture began in the Highlands less than 2,000 years ago—is used in the passage as grounds to reject the common explanation for the Highlands' deforestation. That **boldfaced** portion serves as grounds for such a rejection in light of two claims, one stating that peat bogs build up at only one foot per 1,000 years, and the other—the claim made in the second **boldfaced** portion—that the remains of trees almost all occur at a depth greater than four feet, which would indicate that the deforestation occurred well before agriculture.

C　　The ecologist accepts, not rejects, what is expressed by the first **boldfaced** portion, and the second **boldfaced** portion has not been used to support what is expressed by the first **boldfaced** portion.

D　　The ecologist accepts, not rejects, what is expressed by the first **boldfaced** portion, and the second **boldfaced** portion is compatible with what is expressed by the first **boldfaced** portion and so is not used to reject it.

E　　The first **boldfaced** portion is simply asserted but not argued for; the second is compatible with the first but is not used to support the first.

The correct answer is B.

286. Background information: This year, each film submitted to the Barbizon Film Festival was submitted in one of ten categories. For each category, there was a panel that decided which submitted films to accept.

Fact 1: Within each category, the rate of acceptance for domestic films was the same as that for foreign films.

Fact 2: The overall rate of acceptance of domestic films was significantly higher than that of foreign films.

In light of the background information, which of the following, if true, can account for fact 1 and fact 2 both being true of the submissions to this year's Barbizon Film Festival?

(A) In each category, the selection panel was composed of filmmakers, and some selection panels included no foreign filmmakers.

(B) Significantly more domestic films than foreign films were submitted to the festival.

(C) In each of the past three years, the overall acceptance rate was higher for foreign than for domestic films, an outcome that had upset some domestic filmmakers.

(D) The number of films to be selected in each category was predetermined, but in no category was it required that the acceptance rate of foreign films should equal that of domestic films.

(E) Most foreign films, unlike most domestic films, were submitted in categories with high prestige, but with correspondingly low rates of acceptance.

Argument Evaluation

Situation   Both foreign and domestic films were submitted to the ten categories that comprise the Barbizon Film Festival. Foreign and domestic films were accepted at the same rate by each individual category. Nonetheless, a higher percentage of domestic submissions were accepted by the festival than the percentage of foreign submissions that were accepted.

Reasoning   *What factor would account for a lower overall rate of foreign films accepted, if foreign films were accepted at the same rate within each category?* The information states that foreign films have an overall lower rate of acceptance, despite having equal rates of acceptance within each category. These two facts can be reconciled if there are unequal rates of acceptance among the categories themselves, and if foreign films were disproportionately submitted to categories that accept a smaller percentage of total submissions.

A   A lack of foreign filmmakers on some panels could conceivably prejudice those panels against foreign films; however, the information states that acceptance rates within each category were equal.

B   The total number of domestic vs. foreign films submitted to the festival would not account for the discrepancy between acceptance rates of foreign films and domestic films.

C   If domestic filmmakers were annoyed by the better performance of foreign submissions in previous years, that might lead the festival to accept more domestic submissions; however, it would not reconcile the two facts that acceptance rates were equal within each separate category, but unequal overall.

D   The fact that equal rates of acceptance in each category were not required is not relevant to the question of why foreign films were accepted at equal rates within each category but at an overall lower rate relative to all submissions for the festival.

E   **Correct.** If foreign films were disproportionately submitted to categories that accepted a lower percentage of total submissions, then that would explain why their overall acceptance rate was lower than that of domestic films, even though acceptance rates within each category were the same for foreign and domestic films

The correct answer is E.

287. Beets and carrots are higher in sugar than many other vegetables. They are also high on the glycemic index, a scale that measures the rate at which a food increases blood sugar levels. But while nutritionists usually advise people to avoid high-sugar and high-glycemic-index foods, despite any nutritional benefits they may confer, they are not very concerned about the consumption of beets and carrots.

Which of the following, if true, would best explain the nutritionists' lack of concern?

(A) Foods with added sugar are much higher in sugar, and have a larger effect on blood sugar levels, than do beets and carrots.
(B) Most consumption of beets and carrots occurs in combination with higher-protein foods, which reduce blood sugar fluctuations.
(C) Beets and carrots contain many nutrients, such as folate, beta-carotene, and vitamin C, of which many people fail to consume optimal quantities.
(D) The glycemic index measures the extent to which a food increases blood sugar levels as compared to white bread, a food that is much less healthy than beets and carrots.
(E) Nutritionists have only recently come to understand that a food's effect on blood sugar levels is an important determinant of that food's impact on a person's health.

Argument Construction

Situation Beets and carrots have high levels of sugar compared to most other vegetables, and also score high on the glycemic index, which measures the elevation of blood sugar produced by eating a particular food. Such sugary, high-glycemic foods are not recommended by nutritionists, even when the foods in question have other important nutrients. Despite their sugar content and glycemic effects, however, nutritionists do not tend to warn against beets and carrots.

Reasoning *What factor would make nutritionists less concerned about the consumption of beets and carrots?* The information specifies that nutritionists warn against high-glycemic foods, even when those foods have significant nutritional value. If, however, some other factor moderated the blood-sugar effects of eating beets and carrots, that would help explain why nutritionists tend to be unconcerned about consumption of these two vegetables.

A The fact that other foods have worse effects on blood sugar than do beets and carrots does not explain why nutritionists would not warn against the lesser, but still harmful, effects of these vegetables.

B **Correct.** If beets and carrots are generally eaten in conjunction with higher-protein foods that moderate their impact on blood sugar levels, that would explain why nutritionists do not regard their high glycemic index as cause for concern.

C The information specifies that nutritionists warn against high-glycemic foods even when those foods have other important nutrients, so the presence of such nutrients in beets and carrots would not explain nutritionists' lack of concern about their effect on blood sugar.

D The fact that the glycemic index uses the effect of white bread as a baseline would not explain why nutritionists are unconcerned about the high glycemic index of beets and carrots.

E Even if nutritionists only became concerned about the effect foods have on blood sugar recently, that would not explain why they are currently unconcerned about the effects of beets and carrots.

The correct answer is B.

288. Biologist: Species with broad geographic ranges probably tend to endure longer than species with narrow ranges. The broader a species' range, the more likely that species is to survive the extinction of populations in a few areas. Therefore, it is likely that the proportion of species with broad ranges tends to gradually increase with time.

The biologist's conclusion follows logically from the above if which of the following is assumed?

(A) There are now more species with broad geographic ranges than with narrow geographic ranges.
(B) Most species can survive extinctions of populations in a few areas as long as the species' geographic range is not very narrow.
(C) If a population of a species in a particular area dies out, that species generally does not repopulate that area.
(D) If a characteristic tends to help species endure longer, then the proportion of species with that characteristic tends to gradually increase with time.
(E) Any characteristic that makes a species tend to endure longer will make it easier for that species to survive the extinction of populations in a few areas.

Argument Construction

Situation   A biologist states that species spread across a large area are likely to outlast species confined to narrow areas, because their broad distribution gives them greater resilience when faced with localized extinctions. The biologist concludes that species with broad distributions will tend to make up an increasing percentage of total species over time.

Reasoning   *What additional assumption is necessary for the conclusion to follow logically?* The biologist's conclusion that the total of broadly ranged species will tend to increase in number relative to narrow-range species implies an assumption that greater endurance of species leads to a greater overall proportion of those species. This might not be the case if, for example, new species with narrow ranges tended to appear much more often than new species with broad ranges. Therefore, the biologist's argument holds only if the implied supposition—that characteristics which prolong a species' survival also promote a greater proportion of species with those characteristics overall—is true.

A   The current proportion of species with broad ranges compared to species with narrow ranges does not support the assumption that the proportion of broadly ranged species tends to increase over time.

B   The biologist's argument suggests that broad distribution helps many, though not necessarily most, species survive localized extinctions, but the argument does not assume that fact.

C   Whether or not species can repopulate areas after localized extinctions is not relevant to the biologist's argument that the total number of broadly distributed species will increase proportionally over time.

D   **Correct.** The biologist's argument relies on the assumption that a characteristic which promotes a species' longevity will also tend to promote the overall proportion of species with that characteristic; if additional factors prevented such an increasing overall proportion, the argument would not hold.

E   The statement that factors which promote greater longevity of a species will help that species survive is most often true, not an underlying assumption of the biologist's argument.

The correct answer is D.

289. Mashika: We already know from polling data that some segments of the electorate provide significant support to Ms. Puerta. If those segments also provide significant support to Mr. Quintana, then no segment of the electorate that provides significant support to Mr. Quintana provides significant support to Mr. Ramirez.

Salim: But actually, as the latest polling data conclusively shows, at least one segment of the electorate does provide significant support to both Mr. Quintana and Mr. Ramirez.

Assuming Mashika and Salim's statements are all true, which of the following can be most reasonably inferred from them?

(A) At least one segment of the electorate provides significant support to neither Mr. Quintana nor to Mr. Ramirez.
(B) At least one segment of the electorate provides significant support to Ms. Puerta but not to Mr. Quintana.
(C) Each segment of the electorate provides significant support to Ms. Puerta.
(D) Each segment of the electorate provides significant support to Mr. Quintana.
(E) Each segment of the electorate provides significant support to Mr. Ramirez.

Argument Evaluation

Situation   Mashika and Salim are discussing voter support for three candidates. Mashika says that some voters support Ms. Puerta, and further states that if Ms. Puerta's supporters all also support Mr. Quintana, then no voters support both Mr. Quintana and Mr. Ramirez. Salim states that polling proves that some voters support both Mr. Quintana and Mr. Ramirez.

Reasoning   *What follows from the facts provided?* Mashika claims that if Ms. Puerta's supporters all also support Mr. Quintana, then no voters support both Mr. Quintana and Mr. Ramirez. This means conversely that if any voters do support both Mr. Quintana and Mr. Ramirez, then at least some of Ms. Puerta's supporters do not support Mr. Quintana. From Salim's claim that some voters do support both Mr. Quintana and Mr. Ramirez, we can then conclude that at least some voters who support Ms. Puerta do not support Mr. Quintana.

A   Even if Mashika's and Salim's statements are all true, it's possible that all the voters support Mr. Ramirez.

B   **Correct.** As explained in the reasoning section above, we can infer from Mashika's and Salim's statements that at least some voters support Ms. Puerta but not Mr. Quintana.

C   Given Mashika's and Salim's statements, it's possible that some voters support none of the three candidates. It's also possible that some voters who support Mr. Quintana or Mr. Ramirez don't support Ms. Puerta.

D   As explained in the reasoning section above, we can infer from Mashika's and Salim's statements that at least some voters support Ms. Puerta but not Mr. Quintana. And that means that not all voters support Mr. Quintana.

E   Given Mashika's and Salim's statements, it's possible that some voters support none of the three candidates. And although we're told that some voters support both Mr. Quintana and Mr. Ramirez, it's still possible that some other voters who support Ms. Puerta or Mr. Quintana don't support Mr. Ramirez.

The correct answer is B.

290. In a certain rural area, people normally dispose of household garbage by burning it. Burning household garbage releases toxic chemicals known as dioxins. New conservation regulations will require a major reduction in packaging—specifically, paper and cardboard packaging—for products sold in the area. Since such packaging materials contain dioxins, one result of the implementation of the new regulations will surely be a reduction in dioxin pollution in the area.

Which of the following, if true, most seriously weakens the argument?

(A) Garbage containing large quantities of paper and cardboard can easily burn hot enough for some portion of the dioxins that it contains to be destroyed.

(B) Packaging materials typically make up only a small proportion of the weight of household garbage, but a relatively large proportion of its volume.

(C) Per-capita sales of products sold in paper and cardboard packaging are lower in rural areas than in urban areas.

(D) The new conservation regulations were motivated by a need to cut down on the consumption of paper products in order to bring the harvesting of timber into a healthier balance with its regrowth.

(E) It is not known whether the dioxins released by the burning of household garbage have been the cause of any serious health problems.

Argument Evaluation

Situation   People in a specific region burn household garbage, a practice which releases toxic dioxins. New regulations mandate a reduction in paper and cardboard packaging for products sold in that region. Because dioxins are found in paper and cardboard packaging, the argument concludes that these new regulations will necessarily lead to lower levels of dioxins in the region.

Reasoning   *What factor might prevent the regulations from reducing dioxins?* The argument anticipates that reduced burning of paper and cardboard packaging—as one component of burning household garbage—will *surely* reduce dioxin pollution. The argument would therefore be weakened if some additional consequence of burning garbage with a significant percentage of paper and cardboard offset the expected reduction in dioxin pollution.

A   **Correct.** If garbage containing a large percentage of paper and cardboard burns hot enough to destroy some dioxins, then reducing paper and cardboard as a percentage of garbage burned might have the unintended consequence of lowering the temperature of garbage fires and thereby releasing more of the total dioxins, rather than destroying them. There is not enough information to determine whether overall dioxin emissions would be lower, higher, or the same, but this fact does weaken the argument that such emissions would *surely* be lower.

B   The proportion of packaging materials in household garbage does not affect the question of whether burning less paper and cardboard will necessarily reduce dioxins.

C   The relative use of paper packaging in urban vs. rural areas has no bearing on the question of whether the regulations will reduce dioxins.

D   The motive for the new regulations has no bearing on any argument about their effects.

E   The argument concerns a reduction in dioxins, not in the health effects from dioxins, so this fact would not affect the argument.

The correct answer is A.

To register for the GMAT™ exam, go to www.mba.com/register

5.0 GMAT™ Official Guide Verbal Review Question Index

5.0 GMAT™ Official Guide Verbal Review Question Index

The Verbal Review Question Index is organized by the section, difficulty level, and then by verbal concept. The question number, page number, and answer explanation page number are listed so that questions within the book can be quickly located.

Reading Comprehension Practice Questions—Chapter 4 Verbal Reasoning—Page 52

Difficulty	Concept	Question #	Question ID #	Page	Answer Explanation Page
Easy	Application	2	500175	52	110
Easy	Application	6	500502	54	113
Easy	Application	31	500509	64	127
Easy	Evaluation	5	500501	54	112
Easy	Evaluation	21	500206	61	121
Easy	Evaluation	26	500193	62	124
Easy	Evaluation	28	500195	63	125
Easy	Evaluation	33	500138	65	129
Easy	Evaluation	35	500140	66	130
Easy	Evaluation	43	500360	68	135
Easy	Evaluation	47	500364	70	137
Easy	Inference	10	500506	57	115
Easy	Inference	13	500158	58	117
Easy	Inference	15	500160	59	118
Easy	Inference	17	500202	60	119
Easy	Inference	19	500204	61	120
Easy	Inference	20	500205	61	121
Easy	Inference	22	500207	61	122
Easy	Inference	23	500208	61	123
Easy	Inference	24	500191	62	123
Easy	Inference	34	500139	65	129
Easy	Inference	36	500141	66	131
Easy	Inference	38	500143	66	132
Easy	Inference	40	500357	67	133

(Continued)

Difficulty	Concept	Question #	Question ID #	Page	Answer Explanation Page
Easy	Main Idea	4	500177	53	111
Easy	Main Idea	7	500503	55	113
Easy	Main Idea	8	500504	56	114
Easy	Main Idea	11	500156	58	116
Easy	Main Idea	32	500137	65	128
Easy	Supporting Idea	1	500174	52	110
Easy	Supporting Idea	3	500176	53	111
Easy	Supporting Idea	9	500505	56	114
Easy	Supporting Idea	12	500157	58	116
Easy	Supporting Idea	14	500159	59	117
Easy	Supporting Idea	16	500161	59	118
Easy	Supporting Idea	18	500203	60	120
Easy	Supporting Idea	25	500192	62	124
Easy	Supporting Idea	27	500194	63	125
Easy	Supporting Idea	29	500507	64	126
Easy	Supporting Idea	30	500508	64	127
Easy	Supporting Idea	37	500142	66	131
Easy	Supporting Idea	39	500144	66	133
Easy	Supporting Idea	41	500358	67	134
Easy	Supporting Idea	42	500359	68	134
Easy	Supporting Idea	44	500361	69	136
Easy	Supporting Idea	45	500362	69	136
Easy	Supporting Idea	46	500363	70	137
Medium	Application	53	500164	73	141
Medium	Application	55	500166	73	142
Medium	Application	71	500200	79	152
Medium	Application	72	500201	79	152
Medium	Application	76	500346	81	154
Medium	Application	91	500149	85	163

5.0 GMAT™ Verbal Review Question Index

Difficulty	Concept	Question #	Question ID #	Page	Answer Explanation Page
Medium	Application	104	500510	91	171
Medium	Application	109	500515	93	174
Medium	Evaluation	50	500198	71	139
Medium	Evaluation	54	500165	73	142
Medium	Evaluation	59	500184	75	145
Medium	Evaluation	60	500185	75	145
Medium	Evaluation	67	500179	77	149
Medium	Evaluation	69	500181	78	151
Medium	Evaluation	74	500344	80	153
Medium	Evaluation	80	500350	82	157
Medium	Evaluation	82	500352	83	158
Medium	Evaluation	84	500354	83	159
Medium	Evaluation	88	500146	84	161
Medium	Evaluation	89	500147	85	162
Medium	Evaluation	94	500367	86	165
Medium	Evaluation	97	500370	87	167
Medium	Evaluation	100	500373	89	168
Medium	Evaluation	103	500376	90	170
Medium	Evaluation	105	500511	91	171
Medium	Inference	49	500197	71	138
Medium	Inference	56	500167	73	143
Medium	Inference	58	500183	74	144
Medium	Inference	61	500186	75	146
Medium	Inference	62	500187	75	147
Medium	Inference	63	500188	75	147
Medium	Inference	64	500189	76	148
Medium	Inference	65	500190	76	148
Medium	Inference	68	500180	78	150
Medium	Inference	77	500347	81	155
Medium	Inference	78	500348	81	156

(*Continued*)

Difficulty	Concept	Question #	Question ID #	Page	Answer Explanation Page
Medium	Inference	81	500351	82	157
Medium	Inference	85	500355	83	159
Medium	Inference	90	500148	85	162
Medium	Inference	99	500372	88	168
Medium	Inference	108	500514	92	173
Medium	Main Idea	48	500196	71	138
Medium	Main Idea	51	500162	72	139
Medium	Main Idea	66	500178	77	149
Medium	Main Idea	70	500199	79	151
Medium	Main Idea	79	500349	81	156
Medium	Main Idea	83	500353	83	158
Medium	Main Idea	92	500365	86	163
Medium	Main Idea	106	500512	91	172
Medium	Main Idea	107	500513	92	173
Medium	Supporting Idea	52	500163	72	140
Medium	Supporting Idea	57	500182	74	144
Medium	Supporting Idea	73	500343	80	153
Medium	Supporting Idea	75	500345	80	154
Medium	Supporting Idea	86	500356	83	160
Medium	Supporting Idea	87	500145	84	161
Medium	Supporting Idea	93	500366	86	164
Medium	Supporting Idea	95	500368	87	165
Medium	Supporting Idea	96	500369	87	166
Medium	Supporting Idea	98	500371	88	167
Medium	Supporting Idea	101	500374	90	169
Medium	Supporting Idea	102	500375	90	170
Hard	Application	119	500218	97	180
Hard	Evaluation	114	500134	95	177
Hard	Evaluation	120	500219	97	180
Hard	Evaluation	131	500227	102	187

5.0 GMAT™ Verbal Review Question Index

Difficulty	Concept	Question #	Question ID #	Page	Answer Explanation Page
Hard	Evaluation	134	500211	104	189
Hard	Inference	111	500131	94	175
Hard	Inference	112	500132	94	176
Hard	Inference	113	500133	95	176
Hard	Inference	115	500135	95	177
Hard	Inference	121	500213	98	181
Hard	Inference	123	500215	99	182
Hard	Inference	125	500221	100	183
Hard	Inference	126	500222	101	184
Hard	Inference	127	500223	101	184
Hard	Inference	128	500224	101	185
Hard	Inference	129	500225	101	186
Hard	Inference	133	500210	103	188
Hard	Inference	135	500212	104	189
Hard	Inference	137	500378	105	191
Hard	Inference	138	500379	106	191
Hard	Inference	139	500380	106	192
Hard	Inference	142	500383	108	194
Hard	Main Idea	116	500136	95	178
Hard	Main Idea	117	500216	96	179
Hard	Main Idea	130	500226	102	186
Hard	Main Idea	132	500209	103	188
Hard	Main Idea	143	500384	108	194
Hard	Supporting Idea	110	500338	94	175
Hard	Supporting Idea	118	500217	96	179
Hard	Supporting Idea	122	500214	98	181
Hard	Supporting Idea	124	500220	100	183
Hard	Supporting Idea	136	500377	105	190
Hard	Supporting Idea	140	500381	107	192
Hard	Supporting Idea	141	500382	107	193

(Continued)

Critical Reasoning Practice Questions—Chapter 4 Verbal Reasoning—Page 196

Difficulty	Concept	Question #	Question ID #	Page	Answer Explanation Page
Easy	Argument Construction	149	500518	197	269
Easy	Argument Construction	150	500270	198	270
Easy	Argument Construction	156	500256	200	276
Easy	Argument Construction	159	500294	202	279
Easy	Argument Construction	162	500306	203	283
Easy	Argument Construction	163	500311	204	284
Easy	Argument Construction	166	500266	205	287
Easy	Argument Construction	169	500252	206	291
Easy	Argument Construction	170	500263	207	292
Easy	Argument Construction	172	500321	208	294
Easy	Argument Construction	174	500120	208	296
Easy	Argument Construction	180	500387	210	302
Easy	Argument Construction	182	500389	211	304
Easy	Argument Construction	183	500390	212	305
Easy	Argument Construction	184	500391	212	306
Easy	Argument Evaluation	144	500106	196	263
Easy	Argument Evaluation	145	500516	196	265
Easy	Argument Evaluation	146	500110	197	266
Easy	Argument Evaluation	148	500517	197	268
Easy	Argument Evaluation	151	500258	198	271
Easy	Argument Evaluation	152	500329	199	272
Easy	Argument Evaluation	155	500519	200	275
Easy	Argument Evaluation	157	500113	201	277
Easy	Argument Evaluation	161	500112	203	281
Easy	Argument Evaluation	164	500317	204	285
Easy	Argument Evaluation	168	500283	206	290
Easy	Argument Evaluation	171	500250	207	293
Easy	Argument Evaluation	173	500119	208	295

Difficulty	Concept	Question #	Question ID #	Page	Answer Explanation Page
Easy	Argument Evaluation	175	500122	209	297
Easy	Argument Evaluation	176	500123	209	298
Easy	Argument Evaluation	177	500126	209	299
Easy	Argument Evaluation	178	500385	210	300
Easy	Argument Evaluation	181	500388	211	303
Easy	Argument Evaluation	185	500392	213	307
Easy	Argument Evaluation	187	500394	214	309
Easy	Evaluation of a Plan	147	500314	197	267
Easy	Evaluation of a Plan	153	500114	199	273
Easy	Evaluation of a Plan	154	500235	199	274
Easy	Evaluation of a Plan	158	500268	201	278
Easy	Evaluation of a Plan	160	500115	202	280
Easy	Evaluation of a Plan	165	500262	204	286
Easy	Evaluation of a Plan	167	500269	205	289
Easy	Evaluation of a Plan	179	500386	210	301
Easy	Evaluation of a Plan	186	500393	213	308
Medium	Argument Construction	194	500300	217	316
Medium	Argument Construction	195	500253	217	317
Medium	Argument Construction	196	500230	218	318
Medium	Argument Construction	197	500304	218	319
Medium	Argument Construction	198	500102	219	320
Medium	Argument Construction	202	500107	221	324
Medium	Argument Construction	203	500326	221	325
Medium	Argument Construction	205	500271	222	327
Medium	Argument Construction	207	500303	223	329
Medium	Argument Construction	208	500265	224	330
Medium	Argument Construction	209	500286	224	331
Medium	Argument Construction	210	500228	225	332
Medium	Argument Construction	213	500285	226	335

(Continued)

Difficulty	Concept	Question #	Question ID #	Page	Answer Explanation Page
Medium	Argument Construction	215	500237	227	337
Medium	Argument Construction	217	500243	228	339
Medium	Argument Construction	220	500295	229	342
Medium	Argument Construction	222	500520	230	344
Medium	Argument Construction	223	500521	231	345
Medium	Argument Construction	224	500522	231	346
Medium	Argument Construction	225	500523	231	347
Medium	Argument Construction	227	500395	232	349
Medium	Argument Construction	228	500396	233	350
Medium	Argument Evaluation	200	500234	220	322
Medium	Argument Evaluation	201	500288	220	323
Medium	Argument Evaluation	204	500281	222	326
Medium	Argument Evaluation	206	500242	223	328
Medium	Argument Evaluation	211	500229	225	333
Medium	Argument Evaluation	212	500232	226	334
Medium	Argument Evaluation	214	500292	226	336
Medium	Argument Evaluation	216	500111	227	338
Medium	Argument Evaluation	219	500282	229	341
Medium	Argument Evaluation	221	500322	230	343
Medium	Argument Evaluation	226	500524	232	348
Medium	Argument Evaluation	233	500401	235	355
Medium	Argument Evaluation	234	500402	235	356
Medium	Evaluation of a Plan	188	500121	214	310
Medium	Evaluation of a Plan	189	500124	214	311
Medium	Evaluation of a Plan	190	500125	215	312
Medium	Evaluation of a Plan	191	500127	215	313
Medium	Evaluation of a Plan	192	500128	216	314
Medium	Evaluation of a Plan	193	500129	216	315
Medium	Evaluation of a Plan	199	500244	219	321

Difficulty	Concept	Question #	Question ID #	Page	Answer Explanation Page
Medium	Evaluation of a Plan	218	500284	228	340
Medium	Evaluation of a Plan	229	500397	233	351
Medium	Evaluation of a Plan	230	500398	234	352
Medium	Evaluation of a Plan	231	500399	234	353
Medium	Evaluation of a Plan	232	500400	234	354
Medium	Evaluation of a Plan	235	500403	236	357
Hard	Argument Construction	236	500236	236	358
Hard	Argument Construction	237	500254	237	360
Hard	Argument Construction	240	500272	238	363
Hard	Argument Construction	242	500275	239	365
Hard	Argument Construction	244	500280	240	367
Hard	Argument Construction	248	500100	242	372
Hard	Argument Construction	251	500118	243	375
Hard	Argument Construction	252	500324	244	376
Hard	Argument Construction	255	500323	245	379
Hard	Argument Construction	256	500261	246	380
Hard	Argument Construction	259	500309	247	383
Hard	Argument Construction	261	500241	248	385
Hard	Argument Construction	267	500297	251	391
Hard	Argument Construction	272	500293	253	396
Hard	Argument Construction	274	500290	254	398
Hard	Argument Construction	278	500404	256	402
Hard	Argument Construction	280	500406	256	404
Hard	Argument Construction	281	500407	257	405
Hard	Argument Construction	282	500408	257	406
Hard	Argument Construction	283	500410	258	407
Hard	Argument Construction	284	500411	258	408
Hard	Argument Construction	285	500412	259	409
Hard	Argument Construction	287	500527	260	411

(*Continued*)

Difficulty	Concept	Question #	Question ID #	Page	Answer Explanation Page
Hard	Argument Construction	288	500528	260	412
Hard	Argument Evaluation	239	500257	238	362
Hard	Argument Evaluation	245	500327	241	368
Hard	Argument Evaluation	246	500319	241	369
Hard	Argument Evaluation	250	500279	243	374
Hard	Argument Evaluation	253	500246	244	377
Hard	Argument Evaluation	254	500109	245	378
Hard	Argument Evaluation	257	500267	246	381
Hard	Argument Evaluation	258	500248	247	382
Hard	Argument Evaluation	260	500316	248	384
Hard	Argument Evaluation	262	500328	249	386
Hard	Argument Evaluation	263	500105	249	387
Hard	Argument Evaluation	264	500291	249	388
Hard	Argument Evaluation	265	500239	250	389
Hard	Argument Evaluation	266	500260	250	390
Hard	Argument Evaluation	268	500318	251	392
Hard	Argument Evaluation	269	500289	252	393
Hard	Argument Evaluation	270	500276	252	394
Hard	Argument Evaluation	271	500330	253	395
Hard	Argument Evaluation	279	500405	256	403
Hard	Argument Evaluation	286	500526	259	410
Hard	Argument Evaluation	289	500529	261	413
Hard	Argument Evaluation	290	500530	261	414
Hard	Evaluation of a Plan	238	500255	237	361
Hard	Evaluation of a Plan	241	500273	239	364
Hard	Evaluation of a Plan	243	500278	240	366
Hard	Evaluation of a Plan	247	500320	242	371
Hard	Evaluation of a Plan	249	500247	242	373
Hard	Evaluation of a Plan	273	500325	254	397

Difficulty	Concept	Question #	Question ID #	Page	Answer Explanation Page
Hard	Evaluation of a Plan	275	500104	254	399
Hard	Evaluation of a Plan	276	500108	255	400
Hard	Evaluation of a Plan	277	500101	255	401

To register for the GMAT™ exam, go to www.mba.com/register

Appendix A Answer Sheets

Reading Comprehension Answer Sheet

1.	30.	59.	88.	117.
2.	31.	60.	89.	118.
3.	32.	61.	90.	119.
4.	33.	62.	91.	120.
5.	34.	63.	92.	121.
6.	35.	64.	93.	122.
7.	36.	65.	94.	123.
8.	37.	66.	95.	124.
9.	38.	67.	96.	125.
10.	39.	68.	97.	126.
11.	40.	69.	98.	127.
12.	41.	70.	99.	128.
13.	42.	71.	100.	129.
14.	43.	72.	101.	130.
15.	44.	73.	102.	131.
16.	45.	74.	103.	132.
17.	46.	75.	104.	133.
18.	47.	76.	105.	134.
19.	48.	77.	106.	135.
20.	49.	78.	107.	136.
21.	50.	79.	108.	137.
22.	51.	80.	109.	138.
23.	52.	81.	110.	139.
24.	53.	82.	111.	140.
25.	54.	83.	112.	141.
26.	55.	84.	113.	142.
27.	56.	85.	114.	143.
28.	57.	86.	115.	
29.	58.	87.	116.	

Critical Reasoning Answer Sheet

144.	174.	204.	234.	264.
145.	175.	205.	235.	265.
146.	176.	206.	236.	266.
147.	177.	207.	237.	267.
148.	178.	208.	238.	268.
149.	179.	209.	239.	269.
150.	180.	210.	240.	270.
151.	181.	211.	241.	271.
152.	182.	212.	242.	272.
153.	183.	213.	243.	273.
154.	184.	214.	244.	274.
155.	185.	215.	245.	275.
156.	186.	216.	246.	276.
157.	187.	217.	247.	277.
158.	188.	218.	248.	278.
159.	189.	219.	249.	279.
160.	190.	220.	250.	280.
161.	191.	221.	251.	281.
162.	192.	222.	252.	282.
163.	193.	223.	253.	283.
164.	194.	224.	254.	284.
165.	195.	225.	255.	285.
166.	196.	226.	256.	286.
167.	197.	227.	257.	287.
168.	198.	228.	258.	288.
169.	199.	229.	259.	289.
170.	200.	230.	260.	290.
171.	201.	231.	261.	
172.	202.	232.	262.	
173.	203.	233.	263.	

Notes

Notes

Notes

Notes

Notes

GMAT™

Elevate your prep with our free resources!

1 **GMAT Official Starter Kit**

Sample 70+ real GMAT questions, a guided review, and Official Practice Exams 1 & 2, which simulate the real exam format and test-taking experience.